OXFORD JUNIOR
ENCYCLOPAEDIA

VOLUME V
GREAT LIVES

OXFORD JUNIOR ENCYCLOPAEDIA

GENERAL EDITORS
LAURA E. SALT AND ROBERT SINCLAIR
ILLUSTRATIONS EDITOR: HELEN MARY PETTER

VOLUME V

GREAT LIVES

OXFORD UNIVERSITY PRESS

Oxford University Press, Amen House, London E.C.4

GLASGOW NEW YORK TORONTO MELBOURNE WELLINGTON
BOMBAY CALCUTTA MADRAS KARACHI KUALA LUMPUR
CAPE TOWN IBADAN NAIROBI ACCRA

FIRST PUBLISHED 1953
REPRINTED WITH CORRECTIONS 1955, 1956
1960 (REVISED AND RESET)

PRINTED IN GREAT BRITAIN
AT THE UNIVERSITY PRESS, OXFORD
BY VIVIAN RIDLER
PRINTER TO THE UNIVERSITY

PREFACE

IN authorizing the preparation of this work the Delegates of the Oxford University Press had foremost in mind the need to provide a basic book of reference for school libraries. In form it was to be a genuine encyclopaedia, in treatment and vocabulary suitable for the young reader. To many children (and indeed to many adults) reading is not a natural activity: they do not turn to books for their own sake. But they can be trained to go to books for information which they want for some particular purpose—and thus, very often, to form a habit which will be of lifelong value. Their capacity to read continuously for any length of time being limited, they can absorb knowledge better if they get it in small quantities: therefore they will often read reference books when they may reject the reading of more extended matter. Again, it is probably true to say of such readers that their approach is from the particular to the general, and from the application to the principle, rather than the reverse, that their main interest is in the modern world around them, and that since they are not very good at conceiving things outside their own experience, their capacity for grasping abstract ideas is limited. On the other hand, once their interest is aroused, they will often pursue a subject to remarkable lengths, so long as its development is logical and the treatment avoids dullness.

But such generalizations can easily be overdone: many children using the books will not be of this type. Moreover, it was evident from the first that a project involving so great an amount of work, however exactly it might meet its principal mark, would be fully justified only if it could be of service to a far wider circle of readers. Even for the age-group first in mind, anything like 'writing-down to children' must plainly be taboo—but clear exposition and simple language are no bad qualities in writing for any audience. Here, then, it seemed, was the opportunity to provide a work of reference suitable for many readers to whom the large, standard encyclopaedias are too heavy and technical, and the popular alternatives for the most part neither sufficiently complete nor authoritative. The fact that the plan allowed for an exceptionally large proportion of illustrations to text (between one-quarter and one-third of the total space) is an advantage to any reader, since pictures may, in many instances, save whole paragraphs of involved explanation. With these secondary aims well in mind, therefore, the General

Editors have ventured to hope that the Encyclopaedia may find usefulness not only among certain younger children, but also among older students in clubs, libraries, and Young People's Colleges, and even to no small extent among their parents and other adults who may wish for a simple approach to some unfamiliar or forgotten subject.

SCOPE AND EMPHASIS. Within certain limits the OXFORD JUNIOR ENCYCLOPAEDIA purports to be reasonably comprehensive, though (in common with all general encyclopaedias) not exhaustive. Chief among these limits is that matter already easily available in school textbooks is included only so far as its presence is necessary for the proper understanding of the subject under discussion. Thus, although an immense field of history is surveyed, it will be found mainly under headings dealing with its effects, or in the biographies of those who lived to make it. Purely technical or scientific subjects, also, are omitted except when they have some general interest. In natural history and kindred studies the immense variety of forms necessarily led at times either to their treatment by groups or to their omission on purely arbitrary decisions as to which species would, in all probability, never be looked for, or because there was nothing particularly interesting to say of them. In point of general balance the stress is laid rather on the modern world, though due space is given to the factors which have shaped it, no less than to those which are changing it.

ARRANGEMENT. The Encyclopaedia is planned to consist of twelve volumes and an index. Each of the twelve main volumes is arranged alphabetically, and each deals with a particular range of related subjects (*see* PLAN OF VOLUMES, p. xii). Within its terms of reference, then, each volume is self-contained, and, owing to the great number of single-line cross-references, can well be used alone. The Index covers all entries in the Encyclopaedia. This arrangement, which has the incidental advantage of making the Encyclopaedia easier to revise, arose mainly from one consideration. If articles were to be kept really short—and, in fact, few approach and very few exceed 2,000 words—many subjects could be dealt with comprehensively only by referring the reader to other relevant articles—itself a desirable thing to do. It was clearly preferable for these to be under his hand, rather than be dispersed through any of the twelve volumes at the caprice of the alphabet. This the present arrangement achieves to a great extent. If it has led to a small amount of overlapping, that again is not without its advantages.

Cross-references, then, play an indispensable part in the make-up of the Encyclopaedia. They are of two kinds: references in the text to further articles amplifying a particular passage, and references at the end of the article to others which either take the whole subject farther or which fill in the significant background. The present volume is exceptional in one particular: its contents, being biographical, are arranged under the names of persons and not under the names of things or ideas. The biographies, however, observe the general principle of referring the reader to appropriate articles either in this volume or in others. The arrangement of the Encyclopaedia is such that the reader of any volume (other than this one), on looking up an article covering any wide subject, such as EDUCATION in Volume X, or SHIP in Volume IV, and following the cross-references from that article, is directed to the other principal articles dealing with the subject. These, again, will refer him to any subsidiary articles, as also, in many cases, to those of a complementary nature. Thus he may be guided either from the general to the particular or vice versa. It is believed that the titles of the twelve volumes (see p. xii), in conjunction with their sub-titles, will usually lead the reader straight to the volume containing the information he wants. In selecting headwords, the rules generally followed have been to prefer the familiar, or even the colloquial, reserving the technical alternative for a single-line entry, and to group narrow subjects under a headword of wider scope. Thus, for HORTICULTURE, *see* GARDENING; for GRAPHOLOGY, *see* HANDWRITING; for BRASSICA, *see* CABBAGE CROPS; for CHEQUE, *see* BANKING; for KU KLUX KLAN, *see* SECRET SOCIETIES.

L. E. S., R. S.

Oxford, 1953

LIST OF CONTRIBUTORS

VOLUME EDITOR

SHEILA SHANNON

CONTRIBUTORS

RICHARD I. AARON, Professor of Philosophy in the University of Wales, Aberystwyth

GERALD E. AYLMER

JOHN BAKER, M.A., D.Phil., D.Sc. (Oxon.), Lecturer in Zoology in the University of Oxford

P. J. BARLOW, Department of Art, National Museum of Wales, Cardiff

K. M. BAXTER

MAX BELOFF, Nuffield Reader in the Comparative Study of Institutions in the University of Oxford, and Professorial Fellow of Nuffield College

J. A. W. BENNETT, M.A., D.Phil. (Oxon.), Fellow of Magdalen College, Oxford, and Lecturer in English Language and Literature in the University of Oxford

C. H. C. BLOUNT, M.A., Senior History Master, King Edward's School, Birmingham

REV. A. C. BOUQUET, D.D., Hon.C.F., Lecturer in History and Comparative Study of Religion in the University of Cambridge

D. S. BREWER, M.A., Lecturer in English in the University of Birmingham

J. BRONOWSKI, M.A., Ph.D.

JOHN M. BUNTING

REV. G. W. BUTTERWORTH, Litt.D.

MEYRICK H. CARRÉ, M.A., Reader in Philosophy in the University of Bristol

JOHN CARSWELL, M.A.

LORD DAVID CECIL, C.H., Goldsmith Professor of English Literature in the University of Oxford

M. A. CLARKE

V. C. CLINTON-BADDELEY

MAURICE COLLIS

MARTIN COOPER

W. E. COSSONS, Publications Editor, Cadbury Brothers, Ltd.

D. P. COSTELLO

LEONARD COTTRELL

JOHN CULLEN

J. A. DAVISON, T.D., M.A. (Oxon.), Professor of Greek Language and Literature in the University of Leeds

PATRIC DICKINSON

CLIFFORD DYMENT, F.R.S.L.

JOAN EVANS, D.Litt.

THOMAS EVANS

ERICH EYCK, D.Phil., F.R.H.S.

DOROTHY ELWYN FORRESTER

KATHLEEN FREEMAN, D.Litt. (Wales), formerly Lecturer in Greek in the University College of South Wales and Monmouthshire

H. V. R. GEARY, M.C.

J. C. GHOSH

L. H. GIPSON, Research Professor of History Emeritus, Lehigh University, U.S.A.; sometime Harmsworth Professor of American History in the University of Oxford

ROBERT GITTINGS, M.A., sometime Fellow of Jesus College, Cambridge

CECIL GOULD, Assistant Keeper, the National Gallery

CECIL GRAYSON, M.A.

SIR HAROLD HARTLEY, F.R.S.

ARNOLD L. HASKELL, M.A., Director, Sadler's Wells School

AVERIL HASSALL

G. CRAIG HOUSTON, M.A. (Lond.)

ROSEMARY HUGHES

LUCY HUTCHINSON

LAURENCE IRVING

ADMIRAL SIR WILLIAM JAMES, G.C.B.

W. F. JACKSON KNIGHT, M.A. (Oxon.), F.R.S.L., Reader in Classical Literature in the University of the South-West, Exeter

BASIL LAM

R. C. LATHAM, M.A. (Cantab.), Reader in History in the University of London

G. H. L. LE MAY

G. L. Lewis, M.A., D.Phil., Lecturer in Turkish in the University of Oxford

Naomi Lewis

S. Lilley, M.Sc., Ph.D., Resident Tutor, Department of Extra-Mural Studies, University of Birmingham

C. C. Lloyd, F.R.Hist.S., of the Royal Naval College, Greenwich

Colin Mackenzie

J. D. Mackie, C.B.E., M.C., LL.D., Professor of Scottish History and Literature in the University of Glasgow

Neil Maclaren, Deputy Keeper, the National Gallery

Frederick Madden, B.Litt., M.A., D.Phil., Lecturer in the History of the British Commonwealth in the University of Oxford

William Somervell Mann, B.A., Mus.B., of the Music Editorial Staff of *The Times*

J. G. Manton, M.A. (Cantab.)

A. J. Marshall, B.Sc. (Sydney), D.Phil. (Oxon.), Reader in Zoology and Comparative Anatomy in the University of London

John Massingham

Harold Mattingly, M.A., F.B.A., formerly Assistant Keeper in the Department of Coins and Medals, British Museum

A. H. McDonald, M.A. (N.Z.), M.A., Ph.D. (Cantab.), Fellow and Tutor of Clare College, Cambridge, and Lecturer in Ancient History in the University of Cambridge

M. McKisack, Fellow and Tutor of Somerville College, Oxford

J. McManners, M.A.

E. G. Midgley, B.Litt., M.A.

Admiral Lord Mountevans, K.C.B., D.S.O.

Peter Murray, of the Courtauld Institute of Art, University of London

Norman Nicholson, F.R.S.L.

Harry T. Norris

Kate O'Brien

Luke Parsons

Robert Payne, formerly Professor of English Poetry in the University of the South-West, Kungming, China

T. Jones Pierce, M.A., F.S.A., Research Professor of Medieval Welsh History in the University of Wales, Aberystwyth

Phoebe Pool

Stephen Potter

F. N. L. Poynter, B.A., F.L.A., F.R.S.L., of the Wellcome Historical Medical Library

Keith R. Prowse

Abdul Qaiyum, M.A.

D. B. Quinn, Professor of History, University College, Swansea

W. L. Randell

D. A. Rees, M.A., Lecturer in Philosophy, University College of North Wales, Bangor

John M. Roberts, Fellow of Magdalen College, Oxford

Richard Robinson, B.Litt., M.A., Fellow and Lecturer in Philosophy, Oriel College, Oxford

Stella M. Rodway

A. S. Russell, M.A., D.Sc., Student of Christ Church, Oxford

A. P. Ryan

R. H. F. Scott

Harold Watkins Shaw

Janet Adam Smith

J. I. M. Stewart, M.A., Student and Tutor of Christ Church, Oxford

W. F. Stirling

A. J. P. Taylor, Fellow of Magdalen College, Oxford

Eric Taylor, M.A., B.Mus. (Oxon.), Director of Music, Stonyhurst College

Merlin Thomas

E. W. F. Tomlin, B.A. (Oxon.), Fellow of the Royal Asiatic Society

William Townsend, Teacher of Drawing and Painting in the Slade School of Fine Art

J. C. Trewin

Favell M. Van Oss, B.A. (Cantab.)

Phyllis Wallbank, Principal, The Gatehouse Montessori School, St. Bartholomew the Great, London

R. A. F. Wallis

Oliver Warner

Rex Warner

J. Steven Watson, Student and Tutor of Christ Church, Oxford

William Wells, M.A., A.M.A., Deputy Director, Manchester City Art Galleries

Margaret Whinney, D.Lit., F.S.A., Reader in the History of Art in the University of London

L. P. Wilkinson, M.A., Fellow and Senior Tutor of King's College, Cambridge

P. H. WILLIAMS, B.A. (Oxon.), Assistant Lecturer in History in the University of Manchester

CYRIL WINN, M.A., Fellow and Professor, Trinity College of Music, London

MARY WINSER

ELIZABETH WISKEMANN, M.A., M.Litt. (Cantab.), Associate of Newnham College, Cambridge

J. F. WOLFENDEN, Vice-Chancellor of Reading University

JOHN WOODWARD

Assistant General Editors—A. T. G. POCOCK, HESTER BURTON

Assistant Editors—GILLIAN AVERY, JENNIFER PETTY (*Illustrations*), BARBARA WITT

ACKNOWLEDGEMENTS

THE EDITORS wish to thank all those who have helped with the compilation of the text and illustrations. They are particularly indebted to John Johnson, C.B.E., M.A., Hon. D.Litt., for his help in the selection of material from the Constance Meade Memorial collection of ephemeral printing at the University Press, Oxford; to T. K. Derry, M.A., D.Phil. (Oxon.), for reading the proofs; the Ashmolean Museum, Oxford; the Wellcome Historical Medical Library and Museum; and the Parker Gallery.

The Editors also wish to thank G. T. Hollis, Hon. M.A. (Oxon.), and T. K. Derry, M.A., D.Phil. (Oxon.), for their advice in the revision of this volume.

COLOUR PLATES

1. THE EMPEROR AKBAR ENTERTAINED BY HIS FOSTER-BROTHER
AT DIPALPUR, PUNJAB, IN 1571. Illustration to the *Akbarnama* (Annals
of Akbar), *c.* 1600   *facing page* 64
By courtesy of the Victoria and Albert Museum

2. JAMES COOK, F.R.S. Portrait by Nathaniel Dance   ,,   128
By courtesy of the Trustees of the National Maritime Museum

3. MRS. SIDDONS. Portrait by Thomas Gainsborough   ,,   176
By courtesy of the National Gallery

4. LOUIS XIV AND HIS HEIRS. Portrait by Nicolas de Largillière   ,,   224
By courtesy of the Trustees of the Wallace Collection

5. THE DUKE OF MARLBOROUGH AT THE BATTLE OF DONAU-
WÖRTH, 1704. Tapestry designed by Josse de Vos, *c.* 1720   ,,   256
By courtesy of the Duke of Marlborough

6. LORENZO DE MEDICI. Detail from the fresco of the Adoration of the
Magi by Benozzo Gozzoli   ,,   336
Alinari Photograph

7. PAGE FROM PETRARCH'S SONNETS AND TRIONFI. Written in
Ferrara, *c.* 1470–80   ,,   400
By courtesy of the Bodleian Library

8. QUEEN VICTORIA OPENING THE GREAT EXHIBITION, 1 MAY, 1851.
Detail from the painting by H. C. Selous   ,,   432
By courtesy of the Victoria and Albert Museum

PLAN OF VOLUMES

I. MANKIND
EVOLUTION
ANCIENT WORLD
RACES AND NATIONS
RELIGIONS
MYTHOLOGY
FOLK-LORE

II. NATURAL HISTORY
BEASTS
BIRDS
FISHES
REPTILES
INSECTS
PLANTS

III. THE UNIVERSE
PHYSICAL LAWS
ASTRONOMY
GEOLOGY
WEATHER
GEOGRAPHY
COUNTRIES AND TOWNS

IV. COMMUNICATIONS
LANGUAGE
WRITING
PRINTING
BROADCASTING
LAND TRAVEL
AIRCRAFT
SHIPS

V. GREAT LIVES
PHILOSOPHERS
ARTISTS
WRITERS
SCIENTISTS
REFORMERS
LAWGIVERS
EXPLORERS

VI. FARMING AND FISHERIES
HOME CROPS
TROPICAL CROPS
DOMESTIC ANIMALS
FORESTRY
HUNTING AND TRAPPING
FISHING
GARDENING

VII. INDUSTRY AND COMMERCE
MINING
MANUFACTURE
MARKETING
MONEY
BUSINESS
TRADES

VIII. ENGINEERING
POWER
MACHINERY
FUELS
MATERIALS
TOOLS
INSTRUMENTS
STRUCTURES

IX. RECREATIONS
THEATRE
CONCERT
DANCE
CLUBS AND SOCIETIES
SPORTS
GAMES
PETS

X. LAW AND ORDER
WORLD AFFAIRS
GOVERNMENT
JUSTICE
ARMED FORCES
PUBLIC SERVICES
LOCAL GOVERNMENT

XI. THE HOME
HOUSES AND FURNITURE
HOUSEKEEPING
THE KITCHEN
THE NURSERY
CLOTHES
HEALTH

XII. THE ARTS
LITERATURE
DRAMA
MUSIC
PAINTING
SCULPTURE
ARCHITECTURE

INDEX AND READY REFERENCE VOLUME
Covering entries in all 12 volumes

HOW TO USE THIS BOOK

THIS VOLUME is one of twelve, each on a separate group of subjects, the whole set forming what is called an encyclopaedia, or work from which you can find out almost anything you want to know. (The word comes originally from the Greek *enkuklios*, circular or complete, and *paideia*, education.) Each of the twelve volumes is arranged alphabetically within itself, as twelve dictionaries would be.

The difference between a dictionary and an encyclopaedia is that, while the first gives you no more than the meanings and derivations of words, the second tells you a very great deal more about their subjects. For instance, from a dictionary you would find that PARLIAMENT, with the Sovereign, is the supreme legislature in Britain and is composed of the House of Lords and the House of Commons, and you would learn little more; but an encyclopaedia will tell you that Parliament had its origins in the King's Council and that it developed its control over the King by its ability to grant or withhold taxes; it will tell you about the conflicts between King and Parliament in the 17th century, and how the House of Commons became the most important element in Parliament. Then a dictionary contains nearly every word in the language; but an encyclopaedia deals only with words and subjects about which there is something interesting to be said, beyond their bare meanings. So you should not expect to find every word in an encyclopaedia—every subject is there, but not every word.

There are two ways in which you can find a subject in the OXFORD JUNIOR ENCYCLOPAEDIA. The first way is to study the Plan of Volumes on the opposite page, and then to decide in which volume the subject comes. The second way is to make use of the Index. Very often you will be able to tell from the title alone which volume contains the information you need; but if not, the list of sub-headings on the plan opposite will help to direct you. For example, if you want to read about people, the way they have lived at different times and places, and the things they have believed and worshipped, you would turn to Volume I. If, however, you want to find out about an animal or plant, you would look it up in Volume II, Natural History; but if you wanted to know how that animal or plant is used in something like farming, fishing, or trapping, you would find it in Volume VI. If your subject were something in nature that does not have life—such as the sun, or a particular country or river, or a kind of stone—you would find it in Volume III, with tides, earthquakes, the weather, and many other things. Matters connected with communication of any kind—of people, or goods, or even of ideas—are in Volume IV. So you would look there for languages and printing and broadcasting, as well as for ships and trains and roads. But if it is the engineering side of any of these things that interests you, Volume VIII, Engineering, is the place to try. Business and trade are in Volume VII. Recreations are in Volume IX, which includes games and sports, entertainment, clubs, animal pets, and sporting animals. How people are governed and protected by the State, the law, and the armed forces, and how they are served by other public organizations, is told in Volume X. Volume XI deals with almost everything connected with our homes, from the building and furnishing of the house to the clothes and health of those who live in it. Volume XII, The Arts, deals with music, literature, and the graphic arts. A rather fuller account of the volume you are now reading, on Great Lives, is given on page xv opposite. If you cannot find your subject readily by this means, then you must make use of the Index. An article on page xv of the Index Volume will tell you how to do this.

This volume deals with people, not subjects. As you read any article, you will probably come across the titles of other articles in some way connected with what you are reading. You will know that they are titles of other articles because they will be printed in capital letters. Either they will be followed by (q.v.) in brackets (this is short for the Latin *quod vide*, and means 'which see'), or else they themselves will be in brackets, with the word *see* in front of them. You can look up these other articles at once if you want to know more about the particular person dealt with, or you can save them up until you have finished the article you are reading. At the end of any article you may find the words 'See also', followed by one or more titles in small capital letters. If you look these titles up, they will tell you still more about the people that interest you.

WHAT YOU WILL FIND IN THIS VOLUME

THIS VOLUME IS ABOUT GREAT PEOPLE—PEOPLE OF ALL TIMES AND ALL COUN-
TRIES WHO IN ONE WAY OR ANOTHER HAVE MADE THEIR MARK ON HISTORY

The number of great men and women to be included has had to be confined to about 550 in order that the biographies should avoid being disappointingly bare entries. Even then, many great people have been given only very short entries. This means that many well-known people do not appear at all. The choice of whom to include is, therefore, bound to be to some extent a personal one: any group of editors would make a rather different selection.

Certain principles have guided the editors' choice. Apart from one or two outstanding people whose influence on their time or contribution to humanity has already been universally recognized, living people have not been included. People whose claim to fame depends on some achievement described in another volume, and whose lives are not otherwise particularly interesting, are included only with a cross-reference to the relevant volume. Some distinguished figures have been excluded because their contribution is too remote from the interests and imagination of the readers with whom this Encyclopaedia is principally concerned. The works of the French writer Montesquieu might well be considered as great as those of the poet BYRON, but Byron's are much more easily enjoyed by a young English-speaking reader. A few people have been included mainly because theirs are familiar names about which the reader may be curious—names such as W. G. GRACE, Judge JEFFREYS, or the Emperor NERO.

Most of the people whose lives are described in this book have in some way forwarded the progress of humanity—by the works of art they have created, the discoveries or inventions they have made, or because they were great statesmen and rulers, great soldiers or sailors, or, above all, great thinkers. Occasionally, however, a man is included because, like Adolf HITLER, his evil character and ill-doing have convulsed the world and changed history.

The editors and authors of this volume have been concerned (within limits of space) to present something of the personal life and character of famous people. Thus the articles on BACH and MOZART seek to describe the people who wrote great music rather than their contributions to musical history;

similarly, for the purposes of this volume the patient and courageous struggle of Pierre and Marie CURIE is as important as their eventual scientific discoveries.

BIBLE CHARACTERS. In a volume of biographies these present a special problem, chiefly for the reason that almost all we know of them is to be found in the Bible, which is accessible to everyone. The characters fall, however, into three divisions.

Firstly, those, such as Abraham, Jacob, and Moses, whose stories originated before the period of written history. These stories were handed down in popular tradition and have accumulated on the way so much legendary matter that it is impossible for us to be certain whether, or to what extent, we are reading about actual historical persons. The reader who wishes for some elucidation of the Bible stories concerning such characters is asked to turn to HEBREW CIVILIZATION and HEBREW MYTHS, Vol. I.

Secondly, those, chiefly kings, prophets, or priests, whose lives and work are described or referred to in the Bible but of whom we know little or nothing more and who are not of great importance. A short article on such characters could hardly go beyond what is recorded in the Bible. If you wish to find these references in the Bible quickly, turn to page 123 in the Index, where you will find A GUIDE TO THE PRINCIPAL PEOPLE AND PLACES IN THE OLD AND NEW TESTAMENT.

Thirdly, a few outstanding men whose life and work is important and has permanent value. The Bible narratives as they stand are not sufficient to give the ordinary reader a true idea of the characters of these men and their contribution to human progress. The resources of modern Biblical scholarship are needed to select, arrange, and illuminate the narratives. Accordingly in the present volume are included articles on DAVID and SOLOMON, who were responsible for the founding of the Hebrew monarchy and the establishment of its religious centre at Jerusalem; on ISAIAH and JEREMIAH, whose religious insight was never surpassed till the coming of Jesus Christ; and on ST. PETER and ST. PAUL, the leaders in the movement which issued in the Christian Church.

For the life and work of Jesus Christ the reader is referred to the article JESUS OF NAZARETH, Vol. I.

A

ABÉLARD, Peter (1079–1142). Abélard, a religious philosopher, was a native of Brittany in France. He lived in an age of intense religious energy—the time of the founding of many new monasteries (*see* MONK, Vol. I), the first CRUSADES (q.v. Vol. I), and the development of UNIVERSITIES (q.v. Vol. X) in which the doctrines of the Christian faith were taught and discussed. Abélard turned to a life of prayer and study rather than of active adventure: he said of himself, 'I preferred the strife of disputations to the trophies of war.' After a wandering studenthood, in which he made a reputation for his brilliance in argument, he came to Paris, where he won renown as a teacher. Wherever he lectured, crowds of young listeners, including some of the greatest minds of the age, gathered round him. He made Paris University famous throughout Europe as a centre of learning.

Abélard is best known to most people for his love of Héloïse, for his love-poems to her, and for the letters they wrote to each other. While teaching at the School of Notre Dame in Paris, he became tutor to Héloïse, the beautiful niece of Canon Fulbert. She was 17, he 38. They were happy until their love was discovered by her uncle; they fled from his anger to Brittany where they were secretly married and where Héloïse bore Abélard a son. But Héloïse, realizing that Abélard would be unable to rise to the position in the Church which his abilities merited if his marriage was known (since marriage was forbidden to priests), decided she must not stand in his way. So she returned to her uncle's house, publicly denied her marriage, and then fled to the convent of Argenteuil, where later she became a nun. Her uncle, in furious rage, sent ruffians who attacked Abélard and so brutally mutilated him that his preferment in the Church was after all made impossible. Abélard became a monk, and retired to the hermitage called Paraclete, where pupils and disciples soon gathered round him. He became abbot of a monastery in Brittany, but after 10 years retired to devote himself to a revision of his works.

His work and teaching were opposed by the great St. BERNARD (q.v.), who represented the orthodox way of thinking of this time, and to whom Abélard seemed a sower of doubts. Abélard, though no disbeliever, had an inquiring mind, ready to probe any question as far as reason would take him; and his motto 'Understand that thou mayest believe' expresses this principle. He wrote, for example, a book entitled *Sic et Non (Yes and No)* in which he placed side by side quotations from the Church Fathers which appeared to contradict each other, so calling attention to differences of opinion among the

A LECTURE AT PARIS UNIVERSITY IN THE 13TH CENTURY
Relief from the south porch of the cathedral of Notre Dame, Paris

National Buildings Record

CENTRE OF THE SOUTH FRONT OF KEDLESTON, DERBYSHIRE, DESIGNED BY ROBERT ADAM AFTER 1761, BUT NEVER COMPLETED
The design is based on a Roman triumphal arch, which is given variety by the dome and stairs, and movement by the contrast between their opposing curves and the upright columns

Fathers. The authorities of the Church feared that such teaching might weaken the ordinary man's faith in Church teaching as being beyond question; for in the 12th century it was not possible to discuss theological questions calmly, admitting that there might be truth on both sides.

Abélard was twice called before Councils of the Church to answer for his opinions. His teaching was condemned, and he was compelled to burn some of his work. He died on his way to Rome to defend himself against such attacks. His remains were sent to Héloïse who was in charge of a Sisterhood in Brittany. Héloïse herself lived for another 20 years; and now they are both buried in one grave in Paris.

ABRAHAM, *see* PREFACE, p. xvi. *See also* INDEX, p. 123.

ADAM BROTHERS. This family of four architect brothers, of whom Robert (1728–92) was the most important, were sons of the architect William Adam, Master Mason to the King in Scotland. Robert, the second son, was soon recognized as the genius of the family, and with the help of his brothers he became the greatest architect of his time. John, the eldest, did not take much part, but James and William looked after the business side of the work, so that Robert should be free to plan and design. They were a devoted family; only the elder brother married; the others lived together with their sister.

Robert's education, begun at Edinburgh University where he became friendly with David HUME (q.v.), was completed by a long stay in France, Italy, and Dalmatia (now in Yugoslavia). It was a custom of young architects to study and publish drawings of the ruins of temples and public buildings in Rome, and on these the design of many 18th-century country houses was based. Robert was anxious to make his name with an original work, so he drew, and later published, the ruins of Diocletian's palace at Spalato (Split) in Dalmatia, one of the few antique palaces in existence (*see* picture p. 138).

When he came to design houses in England, he felt that he had a free hand to invent his own decoration and detail, since so few examples of Roman private dwellings were known. Adam thought that contemporary domestic architecture was dull and heavy, so he tried to seize 'the beautiful spirit of antiquity, and to transpose it with novelty and variety', claiming that he and his brothers had brought about 'a greater movement and variety in the outside composition, and in the decoration of the interior an almost total change'. He varied the fine proportion of his rooms with curved walls and alcoves, and he decorated them with flat plaster ornamentation painted in delicate, pale colours and gilding. Often the graceful decoration of the ceilings was enriched with small, circular pictures.

About this time the old Roman cities of POMPEII (q.v. Vol. XII) and Herculaneum were excavated in an excellent state of preservation from under the ash and lava of Mount Vesuvius, and architects could see for the first time what Roman houses looked like. Motifs borrowed from Herculaneum and Pompeii inspired the coloured designs in brick-red and black which were often used in Adam's houses as inlay in white marble fireplaces or as decorations on walls and furniture. This style Adam called 'Etruscan'.

The Adam brothers were soon in great demand for designing both town and country houses. Both the plan and decoration of their houses, which were skilfully planned to be easy to run and convenient to live in, were original and suited to the taste of their patrons. In the town houses great ingenuity was shown in

Country Life

THE BALLROOM AT 20 PORTMAN SQUARE, LONDON, BUILT IN 1775
This is one of Robert Adam's finest town houses. The fireplace is in the 'Etruscan' style

making the most of a small site. Rober Adam not only designed the houses and decorated the rooms; he also designed the furniture and carpets for some of them, so that every detail of the rooms should be in keeping.

At this time London was growing fast, and the squares and residential streets of the West End were being built. In his London architecture Adam made simple designs for his exteriors in order to unify the design of a street or square (for example, Portland Place and Fitzroy Square) and kept his elaborate decoration for the interiors. In his country houses, such as Kedleston in Derbyshire and Ken Wood near London, he had more opportunity of giving the exterior 'variety of movement'.

In 1768 the Adam brothers built the Adelphi (Greek for 'brothers') in London. This consisted of terraces of small houses for middle-class tenants. The actor GARRICK lived there for a time and Josiah WEDGWOOD (qq.v.) had a showroom there. Built on the muddy riverside south of the Strand, the terraces were raised on huge arches at immense cost. This scheme proved a financial disaster and nearly ruined the Adams. Most of the houses were pulled down in the 1930's.

At the end of his life Robert Adam helped to design the New Town of EDINBURGH (q.v. Vol. III). He built the Register House, and the University and Charlotte Square are based on his designs. He always regretted that he was never commissioned to design a public building in London.

See also Vol. XII: GEORGIAN ARCHITECTURE.

ADDISON, Joseph (1672–1719). The name of Addison, as an essayist, is inseparably linked with that of the Irishman, Sir Richard Steele (1672–1729), for their co-operation in the daily journal, the *Spectator*. This non-political magazine was founded in 1711 to take the place of Steele's own *Tatler*. It was designed for the new English middle-class—Londoners above all—gentlemen who foregathered at the fashionable coffee-houses to discuss art, politics, and literature. Steele and Addison invented an imaginary Spectator Club and through its activities, especially those of its leading member, Sir Roger de Coverley, once a rake and later a country gentleman, all the chief topics of the day were described. Addison wrote 274 numbers of the original *Spectator*, besides further essays for

THE SPECTATORS' CLUB

Frontispiece to the *Spectator*, 1753. Drawing by Francis Hayman

Steele's *Guardian* and a final volume of the *Spectator* published in 1714. In addition, he was in his own day a successful poet and playwright.

Addison eventually quarrelled with Steele over politics, and, as was almost inevitable in the literary London of his time, he also quarrelled with Pope (q.v.), who satirized him cruelly in the character of 'Atticus'. It is, however, as an essayist that Addison achieved fame, and his easy, urbane style has rarely been surpassed.

Addison was a staunch Whig and held various minor political offices. In 1717 he became Secretary of State, but his political success was shortlived for he died in 1719 and was buried in Westminster Abbey.

See also Vol. XII: Periodicals.

AENEAS, hero of the *Aeneid, see* Virgil.

AESCHYLUS (*c.* 525–456 B.C.). This great Athenian writer of tragedy was born at Eleusis, the centre of worship of the goddess Demeter. As a young man he saw the rapid rise of the new democratic government in Athens (*see* Pericles), and took part in the great battles of the time, fighting against the Persians at Marathon in 490 B.C. and, probably, at Salamis 10 years later. Then, after the collapse of the Persian invasions, he watched the extraordinarily quick growth of Athenian power throughout the Mediterranean.

Aristophanes (q.v) in his comedy the *Frogs* contrasts Aeschylus with Euripides (q.v.), making Aeschylus into a representation of the good old times, 'the man of Marathon', with a grand style and a hatred for 'modern' cleverness and hair-splitting arguments which, according to Aristophanes, are the characteristics of Euripides. There is some truth in this picture, but it would be quite wrong to imagine that Aeschylus was not a great innovator himself. He was, in fact, the most daring thinker of all the great Athenian tragic writers, and it was he who set the pattern of Greek drama which others followed. He was remarkable, too, for elaborate effects of staging, such as huge choruses in strange masks, and flying monsters.

He wrote more than seventy plays, only seven of which survive, and we know that he was successful more than a dozen times at the annual dramatic festivals. An early play called the *Suppliants* has survived; also the *Persians*, the *Seven Against Thebes*, and the *Oresteia* consisting of three plays the *Agamemnon*, the *Choephoroe*, and the *Eumenides* which form a connected story. The other surviving play, the *Prometheus Bound*, was probably written late in the poet's life.

Aeschylus, like Milton (q.v.), wrote about 'great events'—the destruction of great armies, the effects of sin and pride from one generation to another, and defiance of the gods. The characters have a heroic strength, and behind the characters can always be felt the presence and the power of fate and of the gods. Aeschylus, whose writing has great lyrical qualities, has had a considerable influence on English poets— particularly on Milton and on Shelley (q.v.).

See also Vol. XII: Greek Drama; Tragedy.

AKBAR (1542–1605). This great Mogul Emperor, a descendant of Tamburlaine (q.v.), inherited his dominions in northern India when he was only 13. One of his father's generals acted as regent for the first 4 years of his reign, and then the young prince took the reins of government into his own hands. The Mogul Emperors were Moslems, ruling a largely Hindu population. Almost from the beginning of his reign, Akbar showed remarkable toleration, doing everything to surmount the barrier of religion and to win the affections of his non-Moslem subjects. For example, he married a Hindu princess, and later he lightened the burden of taxation on the Hindus. This far-sighted policy displeased some of his Moslem officers, and in 1567 he had to deal with a rebellion of which his own brother was ringleader.

Akbar carried on a series of wars to establish his authority over his neighbours, often riding and fighting at the head of his troops, and on one occasion wreaking such vengeance on the town of Chitor that it has been regarded as accursed ever since. By 1569 he controlled the greater part of northern India from his capital at Agra. He then proceeded to reorganize the finances of his country, reform the taxation, and protect his people from dishonest officials. He established a uniform system of weights and measures, built roads and promoted commerce, and instituted a police system to keep order. He also set up many schools and was a great patron of the arts.

Akbar, though naturally religious-minded, gradually grew more and more dissatisfied with his own ancestral religion, ISLAM (q.v. Vol I). Therefore he invited men of all faiths, including Christians, to debate their beliefs before him in his 'House of Worship'. Although Akbar could not himself read, he was able to follow the most complicated discussions. At last, being satisfied by none of the creeds which he heard expounded, Akbar announced that he intended to unite his people in a new faith, incorporating the best features of all religions. This religion, of which sun-worship formed a part, forbade all the practices of Islam, and introduced a new form of greeting: *Allah akbar*, an Arabic formula meaning 'God is Most Great', but which may also mean 'God is Akbar'. Very few people adopted the Emperor's new religion.

Although Akbar's religious experiment was a failure, he was nevertheless a great ruler, the first ruler of India who sought to unite the myriad different peoples and religions rather than to be the leading representative of one dominant race.

See also Colour Plate opp. p. 64.
See also Vol. I: INDIAN CIVILIZATIONS, section 4.

AKHNATEN (*c.* 1391–1350 B.C.). Amenophis IV of Egypt (who later took the name Akhnaten) ruled for about 17 years. He is remembered for the religious revolution he effected, with its profound effect upon EGYPTIAN ART (q.v. Vol. XII).

In ancient Egypt the authority of the priests of Amen-Re, the SUN GOD (q.v. Vol. I), the chief god of the Egyptians, had grown so great that it rivalled that of the Pharaohs themselves. The King, who was regarded as the son of Amen-Re, was bound all his life by a strict religious ritual. There were hundreds of lesser gods, and each district had its local god; and to bring order into this confusion, the priests of Amen-Re had, throughout many centuries, worked out a theological system of bewildering complication—in which lay much of their power. This wealth and influence of the priesthood was beginning seriously to perturb Akhnaten's father, Amenophis III, and his advisers.

In the meantime a small religious cult was developing, setting up as god the Aten, originally a manifestation of the old sun god Re of Memphis. Remains of a temple to the Aten have been discovered, in which for the first time in Egyptian history the King is represented as the god himself. This new cult might have come to

Griffith Institute

AKHNATEN

A model bust in the Louvre

nothing had it not appealed to the young prince who, after he succeeded his father, changed his name to Akhnaten ('it is well with the Aten') and moved his capital from the ancient city of Thebes to an entirely new city, Akhetaten, identified with the modern Tell-el-Amarna, though little trace of the ancient city now remains. There he lived with his beautiful wife Nefrotete, devoting himself to the new cult.

Most of what we know of this cult comes from a long and beautiful religious hymn, very likely written by Akhnaten himself, which glorifies the Aten as the creator and preserver of life:

Creator of germ in woman, who makest seed in men,
Who givest life to a son in his mother's womb,
Who givest life to vivify all that he has made. . . .

This hymn also contains these significant lines:

How manifold are thy works!
They are hidden from the face of men, O sole god,
Like unto whom there is none other.

This idea of a 'sole god' was a very new one in Egypt—indeed in the world; and many scholars have held that Akhnaten was the first real monotheist (believer in one god). It has been suggested that the prophet Moses may have lived at Akhnaten's Court and there imbibed the idea of an all-powerful, all-wise creator. Other scholars suggest that Akhnaten's cult was primarily a political move to counter the power of the priests, and to present a simpler religion with the unifying symbol of the sun, which all the peoples of the wide Egyptian Empire could understand and worship. Even if Akhnaten had some political aim, portraits of him suggest that he was more of a poet and a dreamer than a politician. There is no evidence that the new religion made much appeal to the mass of the people, and while the King was busy with it his empire fell into chaos.

These new religious ideas were expressed in sculptured reliefs and statues, which show a remarkable change. For thousands of years a strict convention had governed the portrayal of the Pharaoh, who, being the son of a god, might not be presented with any attempt at realism. The Queen rarely appeared at all. Akhnaten abolished these conventions, and his artists represented him as he was, with Queen Nefrotete, riding in his chariot, bestowing gifts on his followers, even kissing. These sculptured representations of the royal family are charming and human.

When Akhnaten died at 41 years of age, his half-brother Tutankhaten, a mere child, succeeded him. The Court returned to Thebes; the priests of Amen returned to power; the King changed his name to Tutankhamen; and everything possible was done to obliterate all traces of Akhnaten's 'heretical' religion.

See also RAMESES.
See also Vol. I: EGYPTIAN CIVILIZATION; GOD.
See also Vol. XII: EGYPTIAN ART.

ALARIC (died c. 410), see Vol. I: GOTHS.

ALBERT, Prince Consort (1819–61). Francis Charles Augustus Albert Emmanuel of Saxe-Coburg-Gotha married his cousin Queen VICTORIA (q.v.) in 1840. His position in England was difficult. He was distrusted as a foreigner, and was not made a peer for fear that a seat in the House of Lords might encourage him to meddle in politics. Parliament did not allow him a generous grant of money. At first, the Queen admitted him only to her private life, but, later encouraged by Sir Robert PEEL (q.v.), she began to take his advice on matters of State, and soon fell deeply under his influence. Yet he had no official standing until he was created Prince Consort in 1857.

Albert played an important part in building up the idea of a constitutional monarchy to meet the needs of a modern world, in which it was no longer possible for a Sovereign to treat Ministers as political servants to be appointed or dismissed at will. Albert believed that a Sovereign should be impartial, not to policies but to the Ministers who were appointed by the Crown because they had the confidence of the HOUSE OF COMMONS (q.v. Vol. X). A constitutional Sovereign, he wrote, 'should give himself no trouble about details, but exercise a broad general supervision, and see to the settlement of the principles on which action is to be based'. A Minister who departed from those agreed principles might, in his opinion, be dismissed—a view which the Cabinet accepted in a prolonged quarrel between the Crown and Lord PALMERSTON (q.v.), when Foreign Secretary. It was partly due to Albert's influence that Victoria was able to adapt herself, without undue friction, from aristocratic to democratic government.

Albert was not a happy man. He was neither generally liked nor appreciated in his lifetime. He was savagely attacked in the Press before the CRIMEAN WAR (q.v. Vol. X), for he was believed,

By gracious permission of H.M. the Queen

QUEEN VICTORIA, ALBERT PRINCE CONSORT, AND THEIR CHILDREN IN 1846
The children, from left to right, are Prince Alfred, Edward Prince of Wales, Princess Alice, Princess Helena, and the Princess Royal. Painting by Winterhalter

quite unjustifiably, to be pro-Russian. He was humourless, something of a pedant, and his stiff attention to duty could be mistaken for a smug righteousness. All these things often obscured his real talents as an administrator. He reformed the working of the royal palaces; his qualities as a military adviser caused the Duke of Wellington to suggest that he should be Commander-in-Chief of the British Army; his enthusiasm and determination were mainly responsible for the success of the Great Exhibition of 1851 (*see* EXHIBITIONS, Vol. VII), the profits of which were used to establish the Victoria and Albert Museum. Under his influence the Court ceased to be the extravagant, gorgeous, and even licentious centre of fashion that it had been under Victoria's Hanoverian predecessors. It became frugal, pious, businesslike, hard-working, and a model of domestic virtue, more likely to appeal

to the respectable, hard-working middle classes of Victorian England than to the aristocracy. Albert was an autocratic father to his nine children, especially to the Prince of Wales (Edward VII); but Victoria was devoted to him and went into retirement for many years after his death. He died, worn out by his labours, of typhoid fever in December 1861.

See also VICTORIA: see also Colour Plate opp. p. 432.

ALBERTI, Leon Battista (*c.* 1404–72). This Italian artist and writer was one of the great figures of the Italian RENAISSANCE (q.v. Vol. I). Like others who lived at this time of great cultural activity, he was something of a universal genius—a painter, sculptor, architect, and musician, and learned in classical studies, philosophy, religion, and various branches of natural science. His importance now rests on a few buildings which he designed, and on three learned books, one each on painting, sculpture, and architecture.

Alberti was probably born in Genoa, to which his father, a rich Florentine merchant, had been exiled. Alberti, however, was allowed to go to Florence as a young man, and he spent the rest of his life either there or at the Papal Court in Rome, in which he held a secretarial post for some 30 years.

Five buildings survive which were certainly designed by Alberti, each for a different reason a landmark in the history of architecture. The Rucellai palace in Florence was the first in which the walls are decorated with pilasters (flat columns), based on antique examples, alternating with the windows. On the west front of the church Santa Maria Novella in Florence, Alberti invented the system of linking the two storeys by means of large, S-shaped scrolls, a method which from the middle of the 17th century was used in almost all Roman Catholic churches (for example, the Brompton Oratory in London). In the two churches, San Andrea and San Sebastiano, at Mantua he devised two perfect plans for a church, the first long but spacious, the other centralized and symmetrical. At Rimini he converted the old church of San Francesco into a kind of temple of fame for the

Anderson

WEST FRONT OF SANTA MARIA NOVELLA, FLORENCE
This is one of the few buildings designed by Alberti that survive

ruling tyrant, Sigismondo Malatesta. The front of the church is based on a Roman triumphal arch.

Alberti was a most scholarly architect, basing his designs on a serious study of Roman buildings. Both in his buildings and in his books he approached his problems in so lucid and logical a way that one wonders that no one had done so before him. He believed, as the Romans had done, that fine buildings do honour to a city. He was in favour of a regular plan for a town, both for convenience and for beauty, and he made countless other very reasonable suggestions, many of which were put into practice by Italian painters and architects after his time.

See also Vol. XII: ITALIAN ART.

ALCIBIADES (*c.* 450–404 B.C.). This Athenian statesman and soldier, whose treachery and abuse of the power of leadership did much to bring ruin to the Athenian Empire, was for a time the idol of Athens. Being an orphan, he was brought up by his cousin, PERICLES (q.v.). He was an unmanageable boy, and grew into a vain, dissipated, and unscrupulous man, though with great charm. Even SOCRATES (q.v.), who recognized his talents, could not reform his character.

In 415 B.C., when about to sail on a naval expedition against Sicily, he was suspected of responsibility for an outrage on the sacred statues of Athens. His enemies made the most of this accusation, and later, when success seemed possible in Sicily, he was ordered home to stand trial. Alcibiades, in fury, escaped to Sparta, the enemy of Athens, and there directed Spartan policy with brilliant success for 2 years, causing Athens crippling losses to her fleet and her Empire. The Spartans, however, distrusted Alcibiades, who fled to Persia, where he became indispensable to the ruler. To win back Athenian favour, he persuaded Persia to help her against Sparta. As general of the Athenian army he defeated Sparta, and within 4 years restored to Athens the Empire he had previously caused her to lose. In 407 B.C. he was welcomed home as a hero; but his triumph was shortlived, for his next expeditions were failures, and his enemies again drove him into exile. On his way to seek Persian help once more, he was murdered by assassins in Spartan pay.

ALEXANDER II (1818–81). This Tsar of Russia, who is remembered particularly because of his work in emancipating the Russian serfs, came to the throne towards the end of the CRIMEAN WAR (q.v. Vol. X), in which Russia was defeated. This defeat discredited the brutal military despotism of his father, Nicholas I, and the time seemed ripe for a more liberal régime. Alexander, though an idealist, was incapable of designing and sticking to any long-term consistent policy; but for a time he managed to steer a successful middle course between those conservatives who wished to preserve the old tyrannies and the too hasty reformers whose demands were both impractical and rash.

In 1861 some 45 million serfs, about three-quarters of the population of European Russia, were emancipated. The problem was to provide the emancipated serfs with land. A system was adopted whereby the peasants bought from their former owners the land on which they had been living and paid for it gradually over a period of 49 years; but this system bore heavily on the peasants, especially those living on the poorer land, and in many cases they were worse off than before.

Alexander also introduced limited self-government in local affairs, and carried out much-needed reform in the judicial system. He organized the building of railways in European Russia, and encouraged the first steps towards industrial growth. His liberal and reforming policy was not, however, sufficiently progressive for the extreme element in the country, and a group of unpractical agitators known as Nihilists began to cause disturbances. Alexander grew alarmed and allowed his government to repress them severely. The Nihilists, denied all reasonable methods of protest and publicity, resorted to violence and even murder, and finally, after several unsuccessful attempts, they succeeded in assassinating Alexander by throwing a bomb at him near his palace (see ASSASSINATION, Vol. X).

See also Vol. I: RUSSIANS.
See also Vol. X: RUSSIAN REVOLUTION.

ALEXANDER THE GREAT (356–323 B.C.).

The son of Philip II of Macedon, Alexander inherited from his father a passion for conquest and a keen interest in military strategy. He excelled in hunting and riding, especially on his horse Bucephalus, which no one else could ride. He received an excellent education, ARISTOTLE

ALEXANDER THE GREAT
An idealized head in the Acropolis Museum, Athens

(q.v.), who greatly influenced him, being one of his tutors. He learnt to love poetry and is said to have carried a copy of Homer's *Iliad* on all his campaigns.

His father, Philip, having visions of world conquest, had re-formed the Macedonian army, inventing the *phalanx*, a new battle formation (see LAND WARFARE, Vol. X). Philip had subdued the city-states of Greece, partly by force, partly by bribery, the chief resistance coming from Athens, led by DEMOSTHENES (q.v.). Philip planned to lead the Greeks against their old enemy Persia, but he was murdered; and Alexander at 20 became King of Macedonia. Had he not acted with characteristic promptitude, his enemies would have dethroned him and his subjects everywhere would have revolted. Marching south, he made the Greeks acknowledge him as their overlord, and then marching north as far as the Danube he subdued the various barbarian tribes, so that within a year all was under his control. He then destroyed the city-state of Thebes in Greece which attempted a fresh revolt.

In the spring of 334 B.C. he started his great

expedition against Persia. With an army of about 30,000 infantry and 5,000 cavalry, he crossed the Hellespont and completely defeated the Persian army on the river Granicus, leading the attack himself and exposing himself to every danger. He proceeded south through Asia Minor, freeing the Greek cities there from Persian rule and crushing resistance. Then he again met and defeated the vastly superior forces of the Persian King Darius III. Darius fled, leaving his family behind, whom Alexander treated with every courtesy. He then turned south into Phoenicia and captured Tyre after a difficult 8 months' siege. In the winter of 332 B.C. he visited Egypt. By now Alexander had begun to think of himself as divine, and this idea was confirmed when an oracle in the desert claimed him as the son of the god Zeus. The Egyptians, grateful for their release from the hated Persians, gladly accepted Alexander. Whilst in Egypt he founded Alexandria, which later succeeded Athens as the centre of Greek culture.

Returning to Asia Minor, Alexander again defeated Darius and a huge Persian army, and this time Darius, trying to escape, was murdered. The assassins, however, who hoped for a reward from Alexander, were executed. Alexander spent the next 3 years campaigning in the wild country between Mesopotamia and the Indian frontier, and there he fell in love with and married Roxane, a chieftain's daughter. He invaded the Punjab in 327 B.C., defeated an Indian army mounted on elephants, and marched far into the Punjab, until his army would go no farther. When he reluctantly gave the order for retreat, his men blessed him because he had allowed himself to be conquered by them alone. He had hoped to reach the limits of the earth, which the Greeks thought was bounded by a river called Ocean. He followed the river Indus to its mouth, and then led a contingent of 30,000 men across the terrible desert of Baluchistan. Here, in the intense heat, tortured with hunger and thirst, half their number perished. In 323 B.C. Alexander reached Babylon, and there died of a fever before he was quite 33. His body, embalmed and encased in thin gold plates to preserve the beauty of its form, was taken to Alexandria and buried there in a magnificent sepulchre which became an object of pilgrimage.

Alexander had a brilliant grasp not only of generalship but of the principles of government;

he was courageous to the point of folly and extremely generous to the defeated, though capable of cruelty to those who resisted. He was affectionate, showing great devotion to his mother. He was violent, especially when he had drunk too much wine; he never forgave himself for killing his best friend Cleitus by hurling a javelin at him at a banquet. He regarded himself as leader of his non-Greek as well as his Greek subjects, and encouraged inter-marriage between Greeks and Asiatics. He had grandiose ideas regarding his own character and destiny, and a thirst for glory, saying 'It is sweet to live with courage and after death to leave behind immortal fame.' He inspired love in his followers because he shared their perils and hardships. After his death, his name became a legend throughout the countries he had conquered, and many stories are told of him.

See also map, INDEX, p. 52.

ALFRED (849–*c*. 99). This youngest son of Ethelwulf, King of the West Saxons, was born at Wantage, Berkshire, and succeeded his brother Ethelred when he was 22, at a time of grave national peril. For more than a generation England had been subject to increasingly violent attacks by heathen pirates from Scandinavia, and in 870 the 'Great Army' of the Danes had entered Wessex. Though Ethelred and Alfred defeated them at Ashdown (Berkshire), they only checked the Danes, who soon recovered the initiative. A great part of Alfred's active life was devoted to driving them from Wessex and the neighbouring territories. For a time he retreated to the marshes of Somerset to recover his forces, and then at Edington (Wiltshire) he won a decisive victory in 878. The Danish King Guthrum, having accepted Christianity, withdrew from Wessex and turned his attention to conquering East Anglia. Some 8 years later Alfred, having occupied London, concluded a treaty which confined the Danish kingdom to East Anglia, Essex, and part of the south midlands—an area later to be known as the 'Danelaw'. At this time, in the words of the *Anglo-Saxon Chronicle*, 'all the English people turned to Alfred, except those who were under the power of the Danes'. Alfred and Guthrum's Peace ended the worst period of the Danish wars. Although Alfred himself did not completely expel the invaders from England, he had made it possible for his son and grandson to do so.

THE ALFRED JEWEL, *c*. 880

The jewel, made of cloisonné enamel and gold, is inscribed in Anglo-Saxon 'Alfred had me made'. The figure probably represents a saint

Alfred, in order to achieve his victories, re-organized the army in such a way that half the men in each village were left at home to till the fields while the other half were on active service. This meant that the soldiers did not have to leave their wives and children unprotected while they were fighting at a distance. At points of strategic importance he erected earthworks, known as *burhs*, which were garrisoned and kept in repair by the men of the neighbouring villages. To ward off future invasions he built a small fleet of large ships, an original experiment which gives him a claim to being the creator of the English Navy. His victories won him fame on the Continent, and the German kings in their struggle with barbarian hordes adopted some of his methods of defence.

Towards the end of his reign Alfred issued a code of laws, based partly on earlier collections, which aimed at protecting the weak against oppression and strengthening the bond of loyalty between his subjects and the King and between the peasants and their lords. The code applied to all the kingdoms of southern England not under Danish control, and it affords important evidence of the new sense of national unity which Alfred's rule had inspired.

It is not only as warrior and lawgiver that Alfred is memorable. He was a man of deep religious principles, and he held it to be part of the duty of a king to educate his people, as well as to defend and govern them. For this purpose he summoned to his Court scholars such as the Frankish monk Grimbald, the Mercian Plegmund, and the Welshman Bishop Asser, who wrote his life. Attached to the Court was a school where the younger boys were taught to read and write English, and those who were to 'continue in learning' received instruction in Latin. Many of the monasteries which were the homes of Latin learning had been destroyed in the wars; and so Alfred himself translated into English certain books, such as the works of Pope GREGORY THE GREAT (q.v.) and the philosopher Boëthius, which might enlarge his people's knowledge of the world and of life. These translations and his own prefaces to them give him a place among the pioneers of English prose literature. He valued the inheritance of the past, and at his direction the first history of England in the English language—the *Anglo-Saxon Chronicle*—was begun at Winchester, the royal capital (*see* HISTORIES, Vol. XII).

Alfred the Great was a ruler of originality, deep insight, and active power, one of the first founders of the English monarchy. Some of the many legends about him, though not vouched for by any writer of his own day, illustrate his lasting renown among his fellow countrymen. When he died he was buried at Winchester.

ALVA, Duke of (1508–82), Spanish general, *see* PHILIP II, WILLIAM THE SILENT.

AMUNDSEN, Roald (1872–1928). This Norwegian explorer was the most successful of modern explorers because he attained the two objectives which had defeated scores of his predecessors—the North-West Passage (north of Canada) to the Pacific, and the South Pole.

An account of the tragic attempt of Sir John FRANKLIN (q.v.) in 1845 to discover the North-West Passage stirred Amundsen's enthusiasm as a boy. In 1903 he and six others sailed the 47-ton fishing smack *Gjöa* to complete Franklin's quest. They spent two winters at King William's Island, where skeletons of the Franklin expe-

AMUNDSEN AT THE SOUTH POLE

dition were found and the northern Magnetic Pole was located. Then, with only an inch of water under their keel, they pushed west through the strait previously discovered by McClintock and McClure in their search for Franklin, but which had been at that date frozen over. They were held up for another winter off the mouth of the Mackenzie River, but reached San Francisco in 1906. (The only other man to complete this passage is the Canadian H. A. Larsen, who sailed from the Pacific to the Atlantic in 1940–2 and back again in 1944.)

Amundsen had intended next to attack the North Pole, but on hearing of the success of the American PEARY (q.v.), he sailed south in the *Fram*, warning his English rival, R. F. SCOTT (q.v.), that he intended to beat him in the race for the South Pole. Both explorers started from the Ross Sea, but Amundsen began his sledge journey overland at a point 60 miles nearer the Pole, and used dogs where Scott used ponies. He got to the Pole and back—1,860 miles of the worst going in the world—in 99 days, having planted the Norwegian flag at the South Pole on 14 December 1911. Scott found it there a month later, shortly before he and his companions perished in a blizzard.

In 1918 Amundsen took the *Maud*, a boat about the same size as the *Gjöa* but with a hull shaped like an egg split in half, through the North-East Passage (north of Russia), a journey which N. A. Nordenskiöld had achieved in 1878–9 after three centuries of vain attempts by other explorers.

Amundsen next turned to the air, though flying was still in its infancy. Lincoln Ellsworth, a rich American, joined him in fitting out two seaplanes to fly over the Pole from the Norwegian island of Spitzbergen; but they were forced down into the ice-strewn sea 90 miles from their goal, and nearly lost their lives. The next year they joined the Italian General Nobile in a flight in the airship *Norge* from Spitzbergen to Alaska, 3 days after an American, Byrd, had first flown over the Pole.

Two years later, Nobile tried again to fly an airship over the Pole but got into difficulties, and, although the two had quarrelled, Amundsen immediately set off to the rescue. His seaplane crashed in the Polar Sea, and he was never heard of again.

Amundsen was a man of great patriotism and resolution, with a body and mind trained for feats of endurance and devoted solely to the single purpose of Polar exploration. He planned his expeditions carefully, and consequently was able to achieve the high speeds which were the secret of his success.

See also Vol. III: POLAR REGIONS (EXPLORATION).
See also Vol. IV: EXPLORATION.

ANDERSEN, Hans Christian (1805–75). This Danish story-teller was the only child of a poor shoemaker who died when Hans was 11. Hans gave up going to school and stayed at home playing with his toy theatre and reading plays. At 14 he walked to Copenhagen determined to make his fortune as an opera singer. Instead, he nearly starved; but friends took pity on him, and he was eventually educated at King Frederick VI's expense.

He wrote poetry, novels, and plays, but it was in writing fairy-tales that his real genius lay. Folk-lore provided the raw material for many of the tales, but Andersen's stories are not folk-tales. They are stories for children told by a poet, with humour, pathos, and a sense of wonder. The fairy-tales soon became popular

ST. ANDREW
Sculpture from the west front of Bath Abbey, *c.* 1500

all over Europe, and Andersen lived to see his native town of Odense illuminated in his honour. But he never forgot what it felt like to be humble and penniless: some of his most famous stories— *The Tin Soldier, Thumbelina, The Ugly Duckling*— are those that tell of the plight of innocent, helpless creatures in a harsh and dangerous world.

See also Vol. I: FAIRY TALES.
See also Vol. XII: CHILDREN'S BOOKS.

ANDREW, St. The patron saint of Scotland was a fisherman in Galilee, and he and his brother, Simon Peter, were the first disciples to follow Christ. He is mentioned several times in the Gospels, but our knowledge of his life after Christ's death is based only on tradition. It is said that he preached in Asia Minor and Greece, and that he was crucified at Patras in Achaea. In 357 what were thought to be his bones were taken to Constantinople; in 1204, they were removed again by Crusaders to Amalfi in Italy. According to a Scottish legend, however, a monk, St. Regulus, brought some relics of St. Andrew from Constantinople to Scotland in the 8th century, being guided there by an angel. Angus, the King of the Picts, gave Regulus land on which to build a church to shelter the relics, and this was the supposed origin of the Cathedral at St. Andrew. St. Andrew is also patron saint of Greece and of Russia, though the tradition that he preached in Russia is unlikely to be true. His feast is celebrated on 30 November.

See also Vol. I: SAINT; SCOTS.

ANGELICO, Fra (*c.* 1386–1455). The Italian painter Guido di Petro took the name of Fra Giovanni (Brother John) when he became a Dominican friar at a monastery outside Florence, and soon after his death became known as Fra Angelico—a name which may refer to the saintliness of his life or to the sweetness and purity of his painting, or perhaps to both.

We know nothing of his early life or who taught him to paint. He lived at the beginning of the RENAISSANCE (q.v. Vol. I) when exciting discoveries in art and learning were being made in his home town of Florence. BRUNELLESCHI had discovered the laws of perspective and MASACCIO (qq.v.) was using this knowledge in his paintings to make them appear truer to life than any which had been painted before. Classical architecture was being rediscovered by the

Alinari

THE ANNUNCIATION. PAINTING BY FRA ANGELICO
In the monastery of San Marco, Florence

study of Roman buildings. Fra Angelico, in the quiet of the monastery outside the city, was not ignorant of these developments but seems to have been content merely to absorb from time to time as much of the new science as he required for his purpose. This was to paint sacred scenes, particularly from the Gospels or lives of Saints, with such intense religious feeling that they would inspire people with a love of God.

No reproduction gives any idea of the purity and intensity of the colours in his pictures, though we can see with what gentleness and almost childlike simplicity he depicted the sacred characters. His most famous pictures are those which he painted in every cell of the monastery of San Marco at Florence, which was a daughter-house of his own friary at Fiesole. But in some ways his best work is the series of frescoes which he painted in his old age in the Vatican in Rome. In these the careful arrangement of the figures and their simple grouping are reminiscent of GIOTTO (q.v.), from whom Fra Angelico had learned much; and the sweetness of their expression and the beautiful arrangement of the folds of their drapery are typical of all his work. But to all this is added a feeling for space and solidity which he had learnt from Masaccio.

See also Vol. XII: FLORENTINE PAINTING.

ANSELM, St. (1033–1109). Anselm, Archbishop of Canterbury under William Rufus and Henry I, came of a noble Italian family from Aosta. He became a monk, and spent 33 years in the monastery of Bec in Normandy, of which he was abbot from 1078. In 1093 he succeeded Lanfranc as Archbishop of Canterbury. Under Anselm's leadership the dispute over the authority of the Pope came to a head. Anselm believed that the Pope held indisputable authority in the Church in all countries, even above that of the King; but the strong Norman kings resented anything which threatened their supreme authority. The quarrels were so violent that Anselm spent many years in exile. In 1107, however, a compromise was reached, and Anselm passed his last years peacefully at Canterbury. The conflict was renewed between HENRY II and Archbishop BECKET, and was not finally resolved until HENRY VIII (qq.v.) threw off Papal authority altogether.

In spite of his tenacity and single-mindedness in this struggle with the King, Anselm was not a fighter by nature, but a quiet, saintly man, the 'father and comforter of his monks', who loved above all things the peaceful routine of monastic life. He was a considerable scholar: as a theologian he taught unquestioning belief in the doctrines of the Church, and yet in his philosophic writings he set out to reconcile belief with reason. He was canonized in 1494.

ANSON, George (Baron) (1697–1762). Anson has been called 'the father of the Navy' because of the reforms he introduced. He entered the service at 15, and won fame by his voyage round the world in his ship the CENTURION (q.v. Vol. IV). He served with distinction against the French as a fleet commander, and was a member of the Board of Admiralty for nearly 20 years. He was partly responsible for the adoption of the blue and white uniform for naval officers. He brought the MARINES (q.v. Vol. X) under the control of the Admiralty. He revised the Navy's disciplinary code and the fighting instructions for the fleet. He classified ships into six 'rates' according to the number of guns they carried— a 'first rate' (or 3 decker) being a ship with over 100 guns; a 'second rate' having 90; and so on. Anson's great contribution to the victories of the Seven Years War (1756–63) was his ability, as First Lord, to maintain at fighting strength the strong and vigilant navy upon which Pitt's

LORD ANSON, ABOUT 1761
Mezzotint after the portrait by Joshua Reynolds (1723–92)

successful war strategy depended (*see* CHATHAM), and to select for high command brilliant officers such as HAWKE (q.v.). Anson was modest and retiring in manner; and it was said that he 'had been round the world, but was never in it'.

See also Vol. X: ROYAL NAVY; SEA WARFARE, HISTORY OF.

AQUINAS, St. Thomas (*c.* 1225–74). Aquinas was a great Italian religious teacher and philosopher. Towards the end of the 11th century, a marked revival of religious and intellectual life began in western Europe. Cathedrals were built, monasteries were established, and schools developed into universities. There arose great teachers, who tried to bring Christian doctrine into one clear, rational system. Some began to study natural science, but the interest of the age was mainly religious. The name given to this movement is Scholasticism, the teaching of the Schools. Thomas Aquinas became the greatest of the Schoolmen.

His name comes from an Italian town Aquino, near Cassino, north of Naples. His father was a nobleman, and his brothers army officers of high rank. But Thomas, a quiet boy of exceptional ability, was drawn to the orders of preaching FRIARS (q.v. Vol. I), Dominicans and Franciscans, who were at the height of their fame. After considerable opposition from his home, he persuaded his mother to let him join the Dominicans. In 1244 he was sent to Cologne to study under the philosopher Albert the Great, of whom it was said that God had never revealed so many of His secrets to one of His creatures. Albert recognized his pupil's genius; and when Aquinas was called 'the dumb ox of Sicily' in mockery of his reserved manner, Albert replied: 'That dumb ox will fill the world with his bellowing.' Thomas went to Paris and, having received his degrees, formed a school in which he taught with great success, until he was recalled by the Pope to teach in Rome, Pisa, and Bologna. The original aim of the orders of friars was not scholarship, but to preach the faith to the common people, and Aquinas's claim to be a university teacher was at first opposed. He was later recognized as the greatest theologian of his age; as such he was sent to attend the Council of Lyons in 1274. But he was already ill, and on the way he died as he was dictating an exposition of the *Song of Solomon*. He had reached the words, 'Daughters of Jerusalem, tell my beloved that I die for love', when his strength failed.

Aquinas was a prodigious worker, and his writings are enormous in extent. The chief are the *Summa Philosophica* and the *Summa Theologiae* —comprehensive accounts of the Christian faith treated, in the first philosophically (for the learned non-Christian world of the time), and in the second theologically. Hitherto Christian thinkers had treated philosophy and theology as one, because they assumed that reason could formulate and examine all doctrines. Aquinas introduced a distinction. Using the philosophy of Aristotle he proved, by natural reason, the existence of God. But the doctrines of the Trinity and the Incarnation could not, he felt, be thus proved: they are revealed in Scripture and must be accepted by faith, since apart from revelation they could never be known. They are not, he declared, contrary to reason but above it, and reason can show the falsity of objections made to them. Aquinas's writings are often marvels of clear thinking which reveal the greatest intellectual power.

Many modern thinkers diverge from Aquinas when he teaches that certain doctrines are revealed in the Scriptures and must be accepted by faith, whereas others must be tested by reason. They say that faith, which means trust in God, is necessary to all religion but that a particular doctrine also needs reason to justify it. They also say that since the Scriptures were imperfectly understood in the time of Aquinas, those doctrines which he accepted as revealed

British Museum

ST. THOMAS AQUINAS TELLING DANTE AND BEATRICE THE STORY OF ST. FRANCIS

Illumination by Giovanni di Paolo from a 15th-century manuscript of Dante's *Divine Comedy*. The saint, dressed as a Dominican, hovers above St. Dominic and St. Francis (*Yates Thompson MS. 36*)

in the Scriptures must be re-examined today—and if so, by what but reason?

Aquinas was known as the 'Angelic Doctor' to his pupils, because they thought he was above earthly things. His arguments are passionless—the works of pure intellect. But the author of the hymn 'Now, my tongue, the mystery telling', who never wrote or taught except after meditation and prayer, could not have been without feeling. He was canonized in 1323. His teaching is today accepted as a standard by the ROMAN CATHOLIC CHURCH (q.v. Vol. I).

See also Vol. I: PHILOSOPHY; RATIONALISM.

ARCHIMEDES (*c.* 287–212 B.C.). This famous Greek mathematician and scientist, whose achievements are mixed with legend, lived all his life in Syracuse in Sicily, except for a period of study in Alexandria. First and foremost come Archimedes' remarkable contributions to mathematics; he extended the method of EUCLID (q.v.) and made many original discoveries of his own.

His ingenious mechanical inventions, though less important, first made him generally famous. When a ship of the King of Syracuse was water-logged, Archimedes devised the Archimedean screw (or spiral pump) to pump the water out of the hold—an invention which the Egyptians may already have contrived. During the siege of Syracuse by the Romans he won a great reputation for inventing defensive weapons; and is reputed to have set the Roman ships on fire with a burning-glass or lens. He was killed during the sack of the city—but against the orders of the Roman general, who gave him an honourable burial. According to another story, the King, suspecting his crown to be made of impure gold, asked Archimedes to provide proof of its composition. But although he could tell its weight, he could not tell its volume and so could not judge how much inferior metal was mixed with the gold. Then, when in the public baths, he suddenly thought of ascertain-

ing the volume of a solid object by placing it in water and measuring the overflow. He was so excited that he ran home naked crying, *Eureka!* ('I have found it!'). This method is still used for finding the DENSITY of materials (q.v. Vol. III).

Archimedes also experimented with the LEVER (q.v. Vol. VIII) and is supposed to have claimed that if he had a lever long enough he could move the world.

ARISTOPHANES (*c.* 450–*c.* 385 B.C.). Almost nothing is known of the life of this great Athenian writer of comedies, who lived and wrote in the greatest period of ancient GREEK CIVILIZATION (q.v. Vol. I), the age of PERICLES (q.v.).

Aristophanes' comedies were produced by the State at the national dramatic festivals. Only eleven of his plays survive but all are remarkable for an extraordinary freedom of speech. Leading politicians, thinkers, and writers, all sorts of contemporary characters, come in for the most devastating ridicule and abuse. Anything of the same kind published or performed in our own day would most certainly involve the author in legal prosecution for libel. It is all the more extraordinary when we remember that nearly all Aristophanes' plays were written and produced during the Peloponnesian war—the life and death struggle between Athens and Sparta. Aristophanes himself was in favour of making peace with Sparta, and in his plays he vigorously attacks the democratic war party, and particularly its popular leader, Cleon. It is doubtful whether there is any other instance in history of the State actually encouraging such violent attacks on a leading statesman in the middle of a war.

Aristophanes also attacked the representatives of the new scientific thought, particularly SOCRATES (q.v.), who is mocked in the *Clouds*. In fact, we know that Aristophanes was on terms of personal friendship with Socrates. Both AESCHYLUS and EURIPIDES (qq.v.) are also portrayed in his plays. In the *Frogs*

British Museum
GREEK COMIC ACTOR
Terracotta figure, probably 2nd century B.C.

there is an imaginary literary contest between the two, in which Euripides is defeated. This play is not only full of fun, but shows the extraordinarily high level of critical appreciation in an Athenian audience. There is no doubt that the play was popular, since it received a first prize.

But there is more in Aristophanes than political invective and attacks on 'advanced' ideas and styles. The lyrical passages are of extreme beauty and there is a delightful feeling of fantasy in many of the plays, particularly in the *Birds*. The combination of high spirits, gaiety, violent personal abuse, quick brilliant thought, fantastic beauty is not to be found anywhere else in literature.

The *Frogs* was produced in 405 B.C. In the same year the last Athenian fleet was lost, and in the following year Athens was forced to surrender. The particular exuberance of her spirit, expressed so vividly in Aristophanes' earlier plays, seems to be lacking. Some 6 years later Socrates, instead of being made fun of on the stage, was condemned to death for his unconventional ideas, and Aristophanes may well have come to regret the false picture he had given of his friend in the *Clouds*.

In Aristophanes' later plays politics, general ideas, and individual characters of the day are of less importance; the fantasy and the unbridled freedom begin to disappear; plots are more regular, characters more ordinary, themes more conventional; whether because of war-weariness or of the beginnings of political censorship, the great age of confidence was over. Aristophanes, writing in that short and privileged time, made his unique contribution to literature, and is still regarded by many as the greatest comic writer that the world has known.

See also Vol. XII: GREEK DRAMA; COMEDY.

ARISTOTLE (*c.* 384–322 B.C.). This great Greek philosopher was born at Stagirus in Thrace, where his father was physician to Amyntas II of Macedon. At the age of 18 he went to Athens, and soon joined Plato's Academy (*see* PLATO), where he studied science and philosophy for 20 years, and wrote a number of works now lost. After Plato's death, Aristotle left Athens, and when about 40 he was invited by Philip to be tutor to his son, later ALEXANDER THE GREAT (q.v.). When Alexander succeeded to the throne, Aristotle returned to Athens and founded a school of his own, the Lyceum, a rival institution

to the Academy. Much of the teaching was given in the *peripatos* or covered walk of the building, and consequently Aristotle's school of thought came to be known as the Peripatetic School. The scientific work of the Lyceum was largely devoted to biology, while the Academy concentrated on mathematics and astronomy. Aristotle directed the Lyceum for 12 years, devoting himself to a vast range of inquiries, and teaching and working with enormous industry. In 323 B.C., on Alexander's death, the anti-Macedonian party in Athens accused Aristotle of impiety, and remembering the fate of SOCRATES (q.v.), he left Athens with some of his disciples. He died in the following year at the age of 62.

Aristotle's doctrines have survived only in a dry and formal shape, composed into books by Greek editors from a quantity of notes for lectures, covering an immense range of subjects. These include a long book named *Metaphysics*, dealing with such fundamental topics as the nature of matter, form, and causation; a series of works describing the physical universe and the theory of moving bodies; treatises inquiring into the nature of mind, how men come to think and know—an inquiry which we now call psychology; four books on animals, full of acute observation; the *Ethics* treating of moral conduct, and the *Politics* treating of the government of the CITY STATE (q.v. Vol. X) and the education of its citizens. Aristotle thought that it was the duty of the government to teach citizens to respect law and to see that justice is done. He accepted inequality as natural, since only a few men are capable of achieving the highest good; therefore he was satisfied with a civilization based on slavery.

Aristotle also wrote several books on logic in which he made a lasting contribution to the rules of correct reasoning. He defines, for example, the type of argument known as the syllogism (from a Greek word meaning 'putting together'). Many pieces of everyday reasoning can be shown to fall into a certain form when they are set out in full. If I say, 'The wind is cold, it is in the east', the reasoning, set out in full, becomes

> All east winds are cold
> This is an east wind
> Therefore it is cold.

This is a syllogism, a form of reasoning which, when fully expressed, is seen to consist of two statements, or 'premises', linked by a word or 'term' that is common to both (in our example the common term is 'east'), and a consequence or 'conclusion'. Aristotle worked out in detail the various types of possible syllogisms that can occur in reasoning, and gave the rules which they must obey in order to be correct.

Aristotle's unparalleled industry was directed largely to the world of nature and practical experience. He was fond of saying, 'This is plain not only in theory, but in fact.' He laid the foundations of the various sciences, but was at his best in the fields of biology and zoology, where he recorded for the first time careful observations of plants and animals. In his general principles he differed in some ways from the doctrines of Plato. For example, he thought mental activity to be more closely bound up with the body and the senses than Plato did. He also criticized Plato's theory of 'Forms'—ideal principles that exist beyond the world we see— considering them rather as inner tendencies towards the full development of its special nature to be found in every type of thing. In order to understand a thing—a piece of metal, a tree, or a man—Aristotle thought that we must consider not only its simpler origin, but also its mature state, that which, as it were, it is striving to become. Aristotle applied this idea of indwelling activity, shaping every material thing, to all kinds of change and movement in the world. This way of interpreting things is opposed to the outlook of modern science, which prefers to explain things in terms of the combination of simpler elements, such as atoms or cells. In a famous passage Aristotle shows that there is a supreme source of all movement upon which the whole of nature depends, a Being that causes motion without itself being moved by anything beyond it. This Being, the ultimate object of all desire, the life of perfect goodness and happiness, is God. Aristotle, who did not believe, as Plato did, in individual survival after death, held that the divine, and therefore immortal, element in man was the mind, especially reason.

In the Middle Ages, Aristotle, known through Arabic and Latin translations, was the supreme authority in science and philosophy. In the 12th and 13th centuries religious thinkers, in particular Thomas AQUINAS (q.v.), applied themselves to the task of combining his teaching with Christian theology and with the doctrines of Plato. Until the 17th century, Aristotle's logic and physical theories prevailed in the universities of Europe; but with the birth of modern science there was a violent recoil from his philosophy of nature. His logical doctrine, however, set forth in countless textbooks, still endures, and the terms that he invented have formed the basis of the common language of thought—terms such as quantity, quality, essential, premiss and conclusion, theory and practice. It is difficult to discuss abstract questions without using ideas that we owe to Aristotle; and it has been truly said that every thinker is his pupil, even when he does not know it.

See also Vol. I: GREEK CIVILIZATION; LOGIC; PHILOSOPHY.

ARKWRIGHT, Sir Richard (1732–92). This Lancashire manufacturer and pioneer of the British cotton industry started work as a barber and wigmaker at Bolton, but later turned to cotton-spinning. In 1765 he perfected a process of roller-spinning; and in 1769 he invented the famous 'water-frame' to work the roller-spinning process mechanically by WATER-POWER (q.v. Vol. VIII). The revolutionary advantage of his new method was that the thread spun by his machine was strong enough to be used as 'warp' (see COTTON MANUFACTURE, Vol. VII), and so for the first time fabric could be woven entirely of cotton, the more expensive linen thread no longer being needed for the warp. In 1771 Arkwright began to use his new process at Cromford in Derbyshire and soon at other mills in that county and in Nottinghamshire. In 1790 he applied steam-power to his Nottingham mill.

Arkwright was knighted in 1786 and the next year became high sheriff of Derbyshire; he had by that time become very wealthy. His water-frame has been neither superseded nor substantially modified in principle since he invented it, although it has had minor improvements and, of course, no longer depends on water-power. He was not, however, an inventive genius, but rather a thoroughly practical man who adapted other men's inventions and made them commercially practicable and profitable. He was lucky to meet and influence people with money who financed his schemes. He also had a talent for factory management and was the pioneer of modern continuous production by machines arranged in series.

See also Vol. VII: COTTON INDUSTRY.

ARNOLD, Matthew (1822–88). Matthew Arnold, son of the famous Rugby headmaster Dr. Thomas ARNOLD (q.v.), was a poet and one of the few great English literary critics.

As an undergraduate at Oxford he was a leader of fashion, gay, witty, and, as some of his friends thought, far from serious minded. These friends included A. H. Clough, upon whose death he wrote one of his finest poems, *Thyrsis*. Arnold won a Fellowship at Oriel, but he left the University to become secretary to Lord Lansdowne and for a while lived in the thick of politics. His first book of poems (1849) surprised his friends by its depth of feeling, and his 1853 volume, containing *Sohrab and Rustum* and *The Scholar Gypsy*, ensured his reputation as a poet.

By this time he had married and been appointed an inspector of schools—one of the most brilliant men to hold such a post. Later he was also for some years Professor of Poetry at Oxford. In middle and later life he turned to literary criticism, and in this field he is an acknowledged master, as his *Essays in Criticism* show. He believed firmly in the moral purpose of all art and in the classical tradition. His most famous dictum is that poetry should be a criticism of life.

ARNOLD, Thomas (1795–1842). This famous headmaster, often regarded as the creator of the modern PUBLIC SCHOOL system (q.v. Vol. X), was himself educated at Winchester and Corpus Christi College, Oxford. After taking his degree with first-class honours, he taught at Oxford privately until, at the age of 33, he was appointed headmaster of Rugby School. He had a clear idea of the changes and reforms he wished to introduce, and during the 14 years of his headmastership he had a great influence, not only on Rugby School itself but on the English public schools as a whole.

At that time practically nothing was studied in public schools except Greek and Latin; and the general habits of conduct and behaviour were often rough and harsh (as may be seen from *Tom Brown's Schooldays*). Arnold added modern history, modern languages, and mathematics to the curriculum; but his other reforms

Meade Collection

CRICKET AT RUGBY IN THE MID-19TH CENTURY

had more far-reaching results. He was determined that the boys of his school should be brought up as Christian gentlemen. Without undervaluing hard work and scholastic success, he stressed as the most important thing of all the training of character, especially in truthfulness, honesty, and kindliness, and the understanding of religion as the foundation of life and conduct. He made the school chapel the centre of the life of the school, and preached there a series of most impressive sermons. But for him religion was not something confined to the chapel; he made it the daily guide of all his actions.

It is often said that he invented the prefectorial system, by which authority and responsibility are given to senior boys. He did not invent it; it had existed in many schools for centuries. But he developed it, and deliberately gave the sixth form power and influence, so that his own high ideals were passed on by the senior boys to their juniors. He also laid great emphasis on the work of the form-master, whom he expected to teach a great many subjects, so that he might get to know his form as individuals and exercise a strong influence on them.

Arnold was an impressive man, of great personal dignity and force of character; but he did not find it easy to take part in the ordinary daily life and thoughts of boys, for he was by nature rather shy and aloof. The strength of his personality was almost overwhelming. Throughout his life he took a wide interest in public affairs, especially in Church matters. He was a deep student of history, and wrote several historical books. In 1841 he was appointed Professor of Modern History at Oxford University, but he died suddenly soon afterwards.

In Victorian times the sons of most of the families prominent in the political and social life of England passed through the public schools; so the new ideas which Dr. Arnold introduced had a considerable effect on the whole life of the nation. They were soon copied by the head-masters of other public schools, and are now accepted as part of the English educational system.

Thomas Arnold had nine children, the eldest of whom was Matthew ARNOLD (q.v.), the poet, critic, and educationalist.

See also Vol. X: PUBLIC SCHOOLS.

ARTHUR, King (5th–6th century), *see* Vol. I: ARTHURIAN LEGEND.

ASOKA (died 232 B.C.). Soon after the death of ALEXANDER THE GREAT (q.v.) in 323 B.C., a great Hindu warrior, Chandragupta, made himself master of northern India and established the Mauryan dynasty. Asoka was his grandson and when he came to the throne, in about 274 B.C., he inherited a well-organized empire which covered most of the Indian sub-continent from Afghanistan to Madras. Hardly anything is known of his early life: indeed, those dates which historians have decided on are only approximate. There are many stories about him—we may safely accept the tradition that he had proved himself a capable provincial governor during his father's reign, but we may safely reject the story that he murdered his ninety-nine brothers to guard his throne from possible rivals.

In 261 B.C. he undertook a war against his south-eastern neighbours. The devastation and misery which this war entailed, and for which he knew himself to be responsible, made so deep an impression on him that he decided to renounce war and to do his utmost to spread the law of right living. He had previously been influenced to some extent by the teachings of BUDDHA (q.v.), and now he became a devout Buddhist. Possibly his support of the new faith was influenced by a desire to undermine the power of the Brahmins, the ancient priestly CASTE (q.v. Vol. I). Whether this be true or not, Asoka threw himself wholeheartedly into the task of teaching his people the doctrines of Buddha.

From 257 B.C. onwards, rocks and pillars in various portions of his realm were inscribed with instructions (known as the Edicts of Asoka) on principles to be followed to attain right living. Among these principles were respect towards all religions, obedience to parents, and the abstention from the needless killing of animals. Asoka not only preached the virtues, but he showed his humanity in such practical ways as instituting medical services, digging wells, building rest-houses for travellers, and planting banyan trees along the roads to give shade from the fierce Indian sun.

Asoka was one of the few rulers of ancient times who tried to show their people how to live a good and gentle life; but it is hard to assess the effects of his teaching on his subjects. For all his pacific ideals and aversion to violence, Asoka governed his Empire firmly and efficiently. Yet perhaps because of the seeds of pacifism which he sowed, the Mauryan dynasty came to an end

THE TOP OF AN ASOKA PILLAR AT SARNATH, NEAR BENARES
IN NORTHERN INDIA

some 50 years after his death. Under his protection, Buddhism flourished, and Asoka took steps to root out certain abuses which had crept into it since the time of its founder. But Asoka's generous patronage of a creed which stressed the virtues of plain living unfortunately led to great numbers of self-seeking men being attracted to it. This ultimately weakened the faith and caused a decline of Buddhism in India.

See also Vol. I: Indian Civilizations; Buddhism.

ATATÜRK (1881–1938). This was the name (meaning 'Father Turk') assumed in 1934 by Mustafa Kemal, founder of modern Turkey. Its adoption marked the climax to the remarkable political and social changes which transformed Turkey from a backward Oriental country, ruled by a despotic Sultan, into a modern westernized State.

At the Turkish army cadet school in Salonica Mustafa Kemal was an intelligent pupil, though extremely reserved; 'a boy with whom it is impossible to be intimate' was the report made on him. Later, as a young army officer, he became associated with progressive reformers called the 'Young Turks' (*see* SECRET SOCIETIES, Section 4, Vol. X). These men, mostly army officers like himself, were angered by the Sultan's corrupt rule, and objected to the influence of foreigners—Greeks, Armenians, and Arabs—who held high office throughout the Ottoman Empire. But Kemal did not agree with all the aims of the leaders of the movement, which had come to power before the FIRST WORLD WAR broke out (q.v. Vol. X). In that war Turkey took the side of Germany, and Mustafa Kemal was given command in the Dardanelles. His tenacious leadership was largely responsible for the Allied disaster on that front, and he was soon promoted General.

After the war his revolutionary zeal had not slackened, and he regarded it as his sacred duty to save his country from disintegration. When entrusted by the Sultan with the task of disbanding the Turkish forces in Anatolia (Asia Minor), he instead began secretly building up a new national Turkish army. He chose a small town, Angora, in the centre of Anatolia as a meeting-place for members of the Turkish Parliament who supported him, and openly defied the government in Constantinople. A revolutionary national assembly was then formed, with Kemal as President; Angora, now known as Ankara, became the new capital. The break with the Sultan was complete.

The victorious Western Powers intended to divide Anatolia into a number of protectorates, and a Greek army landed at Smyrna for this purpose. Mustafa Kemal himself led his new Turkish army against the Greeks, and, after a fierce battle, forced them to retreat. A great wave of patriotism swept the country, and by the end of 1922 not a single foreign soldier was left on Turkish soil. There then followed a series of remarkable social changes. Kemal's first task was to abolish the chief symbols of the old régime. The Sultan, already thoroughly discredited as a mere pawn of the Allies, was soon removed. Turkey became a Republic, with Mustafa Kemal as President. At first, realizing the strong hold of the Moslem faith on the country, Kemal allowed the ex-Sultan's cousin to assume the title of Caliph (Moslem traditional leader); but before long he formally 'disestablished' the faith of ISLAM (q.v. Vol. I). Turkey became a secular State in which all religions were tolerated on condition that none interfered with politics.

Mustafa Kemal was a ruthless man who did not hesitate to arrest and often to execute his opponents. But unlike other dictators his activities were confined to changes within his own country; and these, however drastic, were on the whole progressive and beneficial. He introduced the Swiss civil code instead of the old Ottoman law. He discouraged the 'veil' (all Moslem women had been supposed to cover their faces in public), and also abolished polygamy (the right for a man to have more than one wife)— both steps towards the complete emancipation of women. He did away with the 'fez', ordering men instead to wear Western hats. A reform of much greater complication was the change from Arabic to Latin written characters, for this involved the reprinting of all Turkish books and the re-education of most of the people in the new script. Finally all Turks were ordered to adopt surnames. It was then that Mustafa Kemal took the name of Kemal Atatürk: Mustafa, being an Arab name, was dropped.

By the time he died Atatürk had already become a legend as the saviour of his people. Each year the anniversary of his death is observed by a period of silence throughout the country. He had made Turkey a strong, independent State on the Western pattern, respected and feared by foreign countries. It was his sincere hope that the results of his dictatorship would later make possible some form of democratic government in Turkey: indeed, in imitation of Western democracies he had even experimented in his lifetime with an official 'opposition'. This hope has been largely realized, for today Turkey already enjoys party government and her people greater liberties.

See also Vol. I: TURKS.

ATHANASIUS (*c.* A.D. 296–373). The so-called Athanasian Creed was not written by Athanasius, but was written later and named in his honour. He is best remembered because of his struggle against the heresy of Arius, a priest of Alexandria, who preached that Christ was not God but a created Being, standing as it were between God and man. The idea of demi-gods was familiar in those days, and the view of Arius became popular. Therefore CONSTANTINE THE GREAT (q.v.) called a Council of Bishops to meet at Nicaea in 325 to settle the true doctrine. Athanasius, who accompanied his bishop to Nicaea, so impressed the Council that Arius' teaching was rejected and the Creed of Nicaea, with its statement that Christ was 'of one substance' with the Father, was adopted. Athanasius became Bishop of Alexandria, and fought long and hard against heresy. He had many enemies and was exiled from his diocese four times—16 years in all.

See also Vol. I: CHRISTIAN CHURCH.

ATTILA (*c.* A.D. 406–53). Under this shrewd and ferocious leader the wandering tribes of HUNS (q.v. Vol. I) became united, and in the 5th century made large-scale invasions into the Roman Empire, carrying death and destruction from Constantinople in the East to Orleans in the West. Attila's reputation was such that he earned the name of 'Scourge of God'.

When young, Attila was sent to Rome as a hostage for the good behaviour of his tribe, but he was not deceived by the city's display of luxury and wealth. His observations of the fundamental weakness of the Empire were of great value to him when he became King of the Huns and the relentless enemy of Rome. His strength as a leader lay in the ruthlessness of his ambition. He was a daring horseman and warrior and a clever bargainer.

An eye-witness describes him as 'short but very stalwart', with a sallow complexion and deep-set eyes. He dressed very simply, and his wooden palaces, set in the midst of the Hunnish encampments of tents and chariots, were austerely furnished. He is reputed to have had 300 wives and at least 60 sons.

See also Vol. I: HUNS; ROMAN CIVILIZATION.

AUGUSTINE, St. (A.D. 354–430). Aurelius Augustinus, the greatest Latin religious teacher, not to be confused with St. Augustine, the first Archbishop of Canterbury (*see* GREGORY THE GREAT), was born of a wealthy Roman family in Numidia, a Roman province in North Africa. The Church was then firmly established, and Christianity was slowly replacing, at least outwardly, the ancient paganism. Augustine's mother Monica was a devout and pious Christian, but his father Patricius accepted the faith only shortly before his death. Much of Augustine's early life is told in his *Confessions*, writings which give a vivid record of his spiritual development. At the age of 16 he went to the University at Carthage, the second city of the Roman Empire, to study to be a lawyer. There, according to his *Confessions*, he lived a worldly and thoughtless life. He had a mistress who bore him a son, Adeodatus, a boy who grew up to be his close companion.

Augustine was recalled from his wild ways by

Bibliothèque Nationale, Paris

PAGE FROM ST. AUGUSTINE'S 'THE CITY OF GOD'

As a result of the Fall, Adam and Eve encounter Death outside the Garden of Eden. Below them the human race plunges into the mouth of Hell while *Gracia Dei* (the Grace of God) tries to save them. 15th-century French manuscript (*MS. Fr. 19*)

reading a passage from the Roman orator Cicero on the value of philosophy, which started him on the search for truth. He tried for a time to find truth in the teaching of an Eastern sect, the Manichees; but in 383 he went to Rome and on to Milan, where he obtained a post as Professor of Rhetoric. Here he met St. Ambrose, the bishop, whose eloquent sermons and saintliness deeply influenced him. He also read Plato with enthusiasm. Augustine went through a period of struggle between his longing for Christianity and his moral weakness. One day, when he was 32 and had retired to his garden in agony of soul, he thought he heard a child's voice singing: 'Take and read.' Rushing back into the house, he opened the New Testament at Romans xiii. 13–14 and read the passage: 'Let us walk honestly, as in the day; not in rioting and drunkenness . . . . not in strife and envying . . .'. This decided him. He and his son became Christians and were baptized by Bishop Ambrose.

Augustine resolved to return to North Africa, and before sailing he had a moving conversation with his saintly mother Monica, now on her death-bed. They talked to one another of eternal life, as Augustine records in his *Confessions* (Chap. IX). In Africa he was ordained priest, and in 395 he became Bishop of Hippo, an office he held until his death during a siege of Hippo by the VANDALS (q.v. Vol. I).

Augustine wrote many books, and has always been regarded as one of the four great Fathers of the Western Church, the others being Pope Gregory the Great, St. Ambrose, and St. Jerome. Much of his writing grew out of the controversies in which he became involved. One of these was with the followers of Pelagius, who asserted that any man could live a life without sin if he wished to—a statement which seemed to deny the need for God's grace. Augustine's sense of God's greatness was so profound that he ascribed all man's good works to Divine Grace—a statement which seemed to deny human free will. Pelagius's doctrine was condemned by the Church, but Augustine's doctrine also was later modified so as to allow man some responsibility for his own actions.

In 410 the GOTHS (q.v. Vol. I) captured Rome and sacked it. Europe was severely shocked by this catastrophe, for Rome was the centre to which all the civilized world looked for leadership. Augustine thereupon began to write *The City of God* in order to restore confidence to the Christian world. In this book he distinguishes two kingdoms, one belonging to earth, the other to heaven. These, he says, have existed from the beginning of the world; but the heavenly city is now represented on earth by the Church, whereas the earthly city might be said to be represented by the State. Augustine taught that the Christian Church had brought a new order into the world to take the place of the Roman Empire which was crumbling away. This book strongly influenced the theory of medieval Catholicism, that the Church is above the State and has the right to make or depose kings. Augustine was followed by LUTHER and CALVIN (qq.v.) in his teaching on grace and predestination. Protestantism therefore, as well as Roman Catholicism, owes much to Saint Augustine.

See also Vol. I: CHRISTIAN CHURCH.

AUGUSTINE, St. (died 604), Archbishop of Canterbury, *see* GREGORY THE GREAT.

AUGUSTUS CAESAR (63 B.C.–A.D. 14). Octavian, later the Emperor Augustus, the founder of the great Roman Empire, was a delicate child, and all his long and successful life he had to watch his health. Yet Octavian had advantages. JULIUS CAESAR (q.v.), his great-uncle, had adopted him and made him his heir, and when he came to Rome to avenge Caesar's murder, he could call on the loyalty of Caesar's old soldiers and supporters. Further, he knew how to use their support; for he was ambitious and mature in judgement.

Octavian joined with the Senate to check MARK ANTONY (q.v.), and then with Antony to defeat the republican leaders, Brutus and Cassius, at the Battle of Philippi. In 43 B.C. Octavian divided the Roman world with Antony. He took the West, which gave him the military strength in 31 B.C. to defeat Antony and Cleopatra at the naval battle of Actium. Having united the West against the threat of attack from Egypt, he then ruled as a national leader and saviour. Though Octavian had power and popular support, he knew from Julius Caesar's experience that Romans hated dictatorship. His exceptional political shrewdness and his understanding of his people led him to disguise his supremacy, and to keep up a show of republican government.

By the constitutional settlements of 27 B.C. and 23 B.C. Octavian, who now had the title

Anderson

AUGUSTUS CAESAR
Statue in the Vatican Museum, Rome

'Augustus', kept control of the military forces and of foreign affairs, together with general supervisory powers over the machinery of government, while the administration of Rome was in the hands of the Senate. A weak Senate, however, tended to depend more and more on Augustus, who was soon Emperor in everything but name. Augustus increased the efficiency of the armies and of provincial government by drawing on the best young men in Rome, and encouraging in them an ideal of service. He tried to restore the ancient standards of Roman morality and to restrain luxury by legislation. He encouraged great writers such as VIRGIL, HORACE, and LIVY (qq.v.). He did much to beautify ROME (q.v. Vol. III): it is said that he 'found the city built of brick and left it built of marble'. He built many other cities throughout the Empire. Augustus aimed at consolidating his Empire in the West rather than expanding eastwards. His armies were undefeated, with one exception: towards the end of his life, his general, Varus, was crushed by the famous German chief, Arminius.

Augustus had the personal pride of his family, and wished to pass on to one of his descendants the great position he had won. He had no sons, and his daughter Julia's two sons died young.

Augustus, therefore, was disappointed in his personal hopes, though his stepson Tiberius carried on his work.

When Augustus died, he left the Roman Empire established and strong. His extraordinary capacity for practical politics had brought enduring order out of chaos. Through his work, the Roman world entered on a period of peace and prosperity—a period we call the Augustan Peace. The Romans honoured him by calling the 8th month of the year after him.

See also JULIUS CAESAR; MARK ANTONY.
See also Vol. I: ROMAN CIVILIZATION.
See also Vol. III: ROME.

AUSTEN, Jane (1775–1817). The novelist, Jane Austen, was the last child but one of the Rector of Steventon in Hampshire. She had one sister, Cassandra, and six brothers. Jane was attractive to look at and had a very sweet, cheerful disposition, and was always a great favourite with children because of her gift for story-telling. Taught by her father, she got rather more education than most girls of her generation. She passed 34 years of her uneventful life in the two small Hampshire parishes of Steventon and Chawton, and the remaining 8 in Bath and Southampton. All her great novels were written from her country home: *Pride and Prejudice, Sense and Sensibility,* and *Northanger Abbey* were written as first drafts in the family drawing-room at Steventon when she was very young and revised at Chawton where she wrote *Emma, Mansfield Park,* and her last book *Persuasion.* The first manuscript of *Pride and Prejudice* was rejected by a publisher and did not appear till 1813. An even earlier work, *Love and Freindship,* dated 1790, shows almost all the characteristics of her mature work—her genius, wit, and taste. The parish, the country house, and the parsonage supplied all the nourishment her genius needed; for though her worldly experience was limited, her knowledge of people was considerable. Bath and London do figure in her novels, but though the scenes that take place in them are described with delightful wit, her heroines often do not feel at perfect ease in these surroundings. She did not include by any means the whole of the parish in her character-drawing; there are few villagers and servants; her men and women are, with very few exceptions (Harriet, in *Emma,* for instance) of the upper middle class. We never see the men

Radio Times Hulton Lib.

JANE AUSTEN AS A YOUNG WOMAN
Engraving after the water-colour by her sister

apart from the women, and except for parsons, sailors, and soldiers, few people in her novels are associated with work. Of these, Squire Knightley, Mr. Martin the farmer, 'poor Miss Taylor' once a governess, and Jane Fairfax who threatened to become one, all come in the same novel, *Emma*. Within her chosen orbit Jane Austen was supreme. The people of her novels belong to one period and one particular way of life, for she wrote of what she knew; she wrote with enjoyment and she was entirely unpretentious.

Jane Austen's novels are comedies. When her most famous heroine, Elizabeth Bennet, says, 'Follies and nonsense, whims and inconsistencies do divert me, I own, and I laugh at them whenever I can', she might have been speaking her creator's own mind. She describes with a perfect nicety of touch the absurdities of Sir Walter Elliot's snobbishness, the garrulous, good-natured, boring Miss Bates, the kind, hearty, but uncultured Sir John Middleton, the ridiculously self-important and yet obsequious Mr. Collins. But although her portraits could be merciless, she was never ill-natured. And again Elizabeth seems to speak for her when she says, 'I hope I never ridicule what is wise or good.' Delight in

the ridiculous is united to a finely tempered sense of moral justice, which is shown towards all her characters, except perhaps towards the Crawfords in *Mansfield Park*: she unfairly tips the scales against them; probably because they represented the urban values she disliked.

Jane Austen's view of life was realistic and unromantic, or rather anti-picturesque. In *Sense and Sensibility* especially, she mocks the over-romantic. Both her style and form express her serene sense of order, her intuitive feeling for good breeding and true good manners. Her other outstanding characteristic is her sanity, her clarity of perception that distinguishes between true and false, the illusion and substance. Her genius is peculiarly English: *Persuasion* is as English as Tolstoy's *War and Peace* is Russian. Nothing is overstressed; the inner spirit is shown through the presentation of outward manners. The events are undramatic: Louisa's fall off the harbour wall at Lyme Regis is perhaps the most spectacular happening in all the novels, yet everything is tremendously important—each disappointment, triumph, hope, regret, and mortification is felt. Her world, if limited in scope, is a world of daylight we can trust; a world of clear values and moral certainties, of proprieties which must be observed; a world that today seems wonderfully unperplexed.

See also Vol. XII: NOVEL.

AVERROËS (1126–98). This name, a corruption of Ibn Rushd, belonged to a famous Arabic philosopher of Cordova in Spain. In the 8th century the ARABS (q.v. Vol. I), inspired by MOHAMMED's teaching (q.v.), had spread as far as Persia in the East and Spain in the West, carrying with them a civilization conspicuous for art, science, and philosophy. Averroës was skilled in medicine and law, but he is most important as an interpreter of ARISTOTLE (q.v.), whose writings became known in the West through Averroës' Arabic texts, which were re-translated into Latin. Averroës' philosophic ideas based on Aristotle aroused opposition among Mohammedan and Christian theologians alike. He appears to have taught that the universe was eternal, that is, not created; that God was not concerned with individuals, but only with the general laws of the universe; and that individuals emerged from the Infinite and at death were absorbed into it again.

See also Vol. I: ARABS; ISLAM.

B

BACH, Johann Sebastian (1685–1750). Bach, one of the greatest composers the world has ever known, was born at Eisenach, a town in mid-Germany. For over 200 years before his birth the Bach family had been noted for musical skill, and later Sebastian's own sons, Friedemann, Carl Philipp Emanuel, and Christian, carried on the tradition.

At 9, Sebastian became an orphan and went to live with an elder brother who helped him in his musical studies. By the time he was 15 his brother, whose family was growing, no longer had room for him; but Bach, who had been a first-rate choirboy at school, found a position in a church choir; after his voice broke he played the violin there. Determined to learn all he could from famous musicians, he walked several times to Hamburg, over 150 miles away, to hear the great organist Reinken, then a very old man. After a period as a church organist, Bach married his cousin Maria Barbara, and finally settled at Köthen, the capital of one of the many small States that made up 18th-century Germany. Here Bach seems to have lived happily until, in 1720, his wife died, leaving four children, the eldest a girl of 12. Bach soon married again, his second wife, Anna Magdalena, being a good musician who sang and played the harpsichord; we still have the book in which her husband wrote pieces for her. He settled at Leipzig, where he remained as organist and choirmaster at St. Thomas's Church until his death.

Bach's duties included composing music as well as training and directing the choir and orchestra. Church music in Germany at this time was very elaborate and serious in style, with an orchestra and solo singers as well as choir and organ; nearly every Sunday a different cantata had to be performed, according to the season of the Church year. Bach would compose a CANTATA (q.v. Vol. XII), and then his family would write out the parts for the voices and instruments. He wrote nearly 300 in all.

Bach set the story of Christ's Passion to music several times. It had long been the custom as a set part of the Good Friday service to perform a musical version of the Passion story, with a narrator to sing the tale, and soloists to sing the words of Jesus, Peter, and the others. Bach's setting of the Passion story as told in St. John's Gospel (usually called the St. John Passion) is noble and exciting, with splendid dramatic choruses. But the St. Matthew Passion, which he composed later, is even more grandly yet movingly told in music; Bach uses two choirs, each with its own orchestra, as well as solo singers. Another of his great works, the Mass in B minor (see CHURCH MUSIC, Vol. XII), is too long for complete performance in church, though sections of it were probably given separately at different times. The Lutheran Church, to which Bach belonged, still used the Latin words of the Mass at some parts of the service. In the Mass Bach also uses vast choruses, airs for solo voices, special accompaniments for wind instruments, and others for solo violin. The St. Matthew Passion and the Mass in B minor are among the greatest pieces of sacred music in the world.

In spite of the immense amount of work involved in writing and performing his church cantatas, Bach found time to write instrumental music of every kind. For the clavichord, the quiet and expressive forerunner of the piano and Bach's own favourite instrument (see KEYBOARD INSTRUMENTS, Vol. IX), he wrote many pieces. These include some of the Preludes and Fugues in all the keys, which in England are known as 'The Forty-eight', or *The Well-tempered Clavier*, and have been loved and admired by musicians from Mozart onwards. Beethoven learnt them as a boy and they were favourites with Mendelssohn, Schumann, Chopin, and Brahms. For the more powerful and brilliant harpsichord Bach wrote many suites, the Chromatic Fantasia and Fugue and, towards the end of his life, the 'Goldberg' Variations. For the violin and 'cello he composed music of a kind scarcely attempted since, for these sonatas and suites are written for the one instrument without accompaniment. The most famous piece among them, the Chaconne (a type of variation movement) for violin, enables a single player to range through all the grandeur and tenderness of music. Other composers needed a large number of players and singers, or the full power of a huge organ, to express their feelings; Bach was content here with a single, unaccompanied violin.

During his lifetime Bach was chiefly known as the greatest organist in the world. He also knew a great deal about the design and construction of the ORGAN (q.v. Vol. IX) and was often consulted when a new instrument was proposed for a church. His own compositions for the organ are undoubtedly the greatest in existence. In many of them, such as the Chorale Preludes, based on the hymn-tunes of the Lutheran Church, Bach finds musical expression for the innermost meaning of the words. Others, such as the well-known Toccata and Fugue in D minor, an early work, show the extent of his own immense skill as an organist.

Bach was the greatest of all harmonists and his four-part chorales, arrangements for chorus of the Lutheran hymns, are wonderful examples of his genius. He was also unequalled in the art of counterpoint (see HARMONY, Vol. XII), the style then used by nearly all musicians, in which

C. Beitz, Arnstadt

THE KEYBOARD OF BACH'S ORGAN AT ARNSTADT

Now in the Bach Museum, Arnstadt. Bach was organist at the New Church at Arnstadt from 1703 to 1707

instead of a melody with harmonic accompaniment every part or voice is essentially important. He used ingenious devices with such mastery that the listener is often unaware of the amazing skill and almost mathematical calculation hidden in a fugue or concerto movement.

Of CONCERTOS (q.v. Vol. XII) Bach wrote a considerable number for the violin, which he also arranged for the harpsichord, and others for two, three, and four harpsichords, all with string orchestra. The most famous of his concertos are, however, of a different kind. The six 'Brandenburg' Concertos, written in 1720–1, are designed for different groups of solo instruments with strings—the second, for example, using as solos the flute (recorder), oboe, violin, and trumpet; the fourth, two recorders and violin. Though long neglected, they are now among the most popular of Bach's works.

As he grew older, Bach became more and more deeply interested in the basic problems of music, especially in the difficult questions of fugue (see MUSICAL FORM, Vol. XII) considered as a kind of mathematics. To show how these problems of combining themes could be solved he wrote a series of pieces, all on one theme, which he called *The Art of Fugue*. While he was busy on this profound study, as much science as music, his sight failed and he was unable to complete the last fugue. Two attempts were made to restore his sight, but shortly after he had a stroke and died.

Bach was soon forgotten by the world. He had published very little of his work and cared nothing for fame. Musical fashion was changing and popular appreciation turned away from his deep and learned art towards much simpler and more prettily tuneful music. Gradually, however, his fame revived. During the 19th century a society was formed to print all his music, and as the volumes appeared with hitherto unknown masterpieces, Bach began to take his true place in the history of music. In England the Bach Choir was founded, and performed the Mass in B minor (nearly a century and a half after it was written) and the St. Matthew Passion.

Bach's achievement, in extent and quality, has not been surpassed in the history of music. He belongs to the small group of supreme artists who have moulded the mind of Europe, and his equals are men like Dante and Shakespeare.

See also Vol. XII: MUSIC, HISTORY OF; CONCERTO; PASSION MUSIC.

BACON, Sir Francis (1561–1626). Bacon, who became Lord Chancellor of England, is chiefly famous not for his legal and political achievements but as a philosopher and writer. He was the younger son of Sir Nicholas Bacon, Lord Keeper of the Great Seal, and was born in London. He went to Trinity College, Cambridge, when he was 12, and at 15 was entered at Gray's Inn to start his legal training. For the next 3 years he was in attendance on the English Ambassador in Paris. When he was 18 his father died, leaving him poorly provided for.

While at Cambridge he had come to reject the accepted philosophy of ARISTOTLE (q.v.), and had determined to evolve a new system of his own, through scientific research. But, needing money to follow his ambition, he completed his legal studies, entered Parliament, and became the confidential adviser to the Earl of Essex, Queen Elizabeth's favourite, who rewarded him generously. When, however, Essex fell into disgrace, and was arrested for plotting against the Queen, Bacon, as one of Her Majesty's counsel, took part in the prosecution which led to the execution of his patron. Bacon's excuse must be that he was only disloyal to Essex when Essex himself was disloyal to the Queen.

When James I became King in 1603, Bacon, whom Elizabeth had neither trusted nor liked, hoped for advancement. In due course his assiduous services to the King were rewarded, and by 1621 he was Lord Chancellor and had been created Baron Verulam and Viscount St. Albans. At the height of his success he was accused by his enemies of accepting bribes; he admitted the charges but affirmed that the presents received had never influenced his decisions. Although, in fact, he did on several occasions deliver judgement against the givers, the evidence is against him on other occasions, and he was certainly not always scrupulous in his public conduct. The Lords finally passed sentence on him, fining him £40,000, condemning him to the Tower, and banning him from the Court and from holding public office. Though most of this sentence was remitted, Bacon retired from public life to live at Gorhambury, his estate at St. Albans, Hertfordshire. He died as the result of a chill contracted while stuffing a chicken full of snow to see if this would help to keep it fresh longer—an experimenter to the last.

Bacon had a direct, sparkling prose style. His *Essays*, the most celebrated of his writings, are on

National Portrait Gallery
SIR FRANCIS BACON
Painting by a follower of Paul Van Somer

various subjects—political and personal—and are concerned with what men do, rather than with what they ought to do. *The New Atlantis* is an account of a visit to an imaginary island and a description of the social and political conditions there. His account, in this book, of scientific academies, is thought to have led later on to the founding of the Royal Society. He followed up his early ambition to devise a new practical philosophy by which mankind might regain control of the forces of nature through a scientific appreciation of what those forces were. He believed, unlike most previous thinkers, that philosophy should be kept separate from theology; but he himself, wisely for the times he lived in, accepted orthodox religion. He intended to set forth his theories in a book in six parts, to be called the *Instauratio Magna* (Renewal of the Sciences), and to be written in Latin, since Bacon believed, as did many writers of his time, that only works in Latin could be sure of survival.

Bacon completed only two parts of his great philosophical work: the *Advancement of Learning* (first published in 1605), which explained the advantages of knowledge and how it may be increased, and the *Novum Organum*, his greatest and most original work, which sets out a method by which knowledge may become universal and man regain his power over nature. Bacon was the founder of the modern inductive method of reasoning, by which general principles are inferred from particular instances. The originality of his scientific method lies in the accumulation of evidence from accurate observation and experiment and in basing conclusions on actual fact: the Aristotelian method had been to elaborate theories without ever testing them against reality. Bacon worked by reason and expressed himself with the greatest clarity, and he applied inductive LOGIC (q.v. Vol. I) to scientific matters. While he appears not to have recognized the greatness of the men of science of his day and their new discoveries, he realized that science was to play an ever-increasing part in men's lives. The modern study of the natural sciences is based on his work.

See also Vol. XII: ESSAYS.

BACON, Roger (*c.* 1214–94). In the universities and schools of the Middle Ages the chief study was theology, that is, discussion about the nature of God. Yet hidden away in monasteries there were probably many men whose bent was towards mathematics and natural science. One of these monks, Roger Bacon, has become famous as a pioneer in science and philosophy.

Bacon was born at Ilchester, Somerset. He went to Oxford, and later spent some years in Paris, then the most important seat of learning in Europe. His commanding intellect soon made him widely known, but he despised the popular study of theology and scathingly attacked those who followed it. Instead he studied languages, including Greek, Hebrew, and Arabic, and also the natural sciences, chiefly astronomy, optics, mechanics, and chemistry. Knowledge of these sciences was then small, and there were few instruments for observation and experiment.

Bacon looked centuries ahead, for he asserted that one day carriages would move without horses and that men would be able to mount up into the air. His study of optics led him to the invention of the magnifying glass (*see* LENS, Vol. VIII), and from his chemical experiments he gained a considerable knowledge of EXPLOSIVES (q.v. Vol. VIII). All this seemed to the people of his day to be very dangerous. They feared and hated one who had such ideas, for they supposed that he must be in league with the Devil.

It was hard for a scholar in those days to work independently, and the influence of the religious orders in the universities was great. Bacon therefore joined the order of the Franciscan friars. They, however, were evidently afraid of his studies, and for 10 years kept him in close confinement without books or instruments. At last a leading Franciscan, who had known Bacon in England, was elected Pope and wrote to him asking to see his writings. Bacon joyfully dedicated one of his works to the Pope and sent it to him. After this, apparently, Bacon was allowed to work in comparative freedom for 10 or 12 years. In 1278, however, at a trial held by the Franciscans in Paris, he was condemned and imprisoned again for a time.

Bacon's mind was scientific—that is, he sought to discover truth by examining facts, especially

Bodleian Library

ROGER BACON WITH A PUPIL
From a 15th-century manuscript of Bacon's *De Retardatione Senectutis*

the facts of the natural world. Most religious men of his day felt that all the truth men needed to know had been revealed by God, and that this might be discussed, and minor points of difference debated, but that the substance of the faith must not be questioned. Bacon's rejection of this rule of authority was the cause of his being condemned by the Church. His chief book, the *Opus Maius* (Greater Work), has the freshness of a direct study of nature; in it he shows that there is no real opposition between the scientific and the religious approach, for both are necessary. In some ways he reminds us of his more celebrated namesake of the 17th century, Francis BACON (q.v.), who had so powerful an effect on the advance of scientific knowledge in his time.

See also Vol. I: PHILOSOPHY.

BADEN-POWELL, Lord (1857–1941). Robert S. Baden-Powell, the founder of the BOY SCOUT and GIRL GUIDE movements (qq.v. Vol. IX), was a soldier. He joined the 13th Hussars, and served in India and Afghanistan, and then in South Africa. He fought in the SOUTH AFRICAN WAR (q.v. Vol. X), and as lieutenant-colonel of the 5th Dragoon Guards he defended the garrison town of Mafeking during the famous siege of 7 months by a large Boer army. During this siege he organized the boys of Mafeking as guides, messengers, and first-aid corps, thereby releasing men for fighting. When the town was relieved on 17 May 1900, there was great excitement in England, and Baden-Powell was publicly honoured. As major-general he later organized the South African Constabulary.

Baden-Powell had always been interested in the training of boys and had written a military handbook called *Aids to Scouting*. In 1907 he laid the foundation of the Scout movement, a movement which has now spread all over the world; in 1910 he retired from the army and with the help of his sister, Agnes Baden-Powell, founded the Girl Guides on similar lines. In 1929, when widely known as Chief Scout, he was made a baron.

See also Vol. IX: BOY SCOUTS; GIRL GUIDES.

BAKEWELL, Robert (1725–95). Bakewell was one of the pioneers of the general improvement in British farming in the 18th century which we call the Agrarian Revolution (*see* AGRICULTURAL IMPROVERS, Vol. VI). He was born on his father's farm at Dishley in Leicestershire, and took over the farm when he was 30. He was greatly interested in Stock Breeding and travelled all over Britain studying it. He believed that by careful selective breeding any desirable characteristic of an animal could be improved and increased: for example, that in a few generations flesh could be bred on to an animal's body exactly where the butcher most wanted it. He turned his ideas to practical use, breeding predigree stock for other farmers to use, and charging stud fees for their services.

Bakewell had some financial setbacks, but later his fees for hiring out his rams alone exceeded £3,000 a year. He originated the new Leicester breed of sheep, which weighed 2 lb. for every 1 lb. weight of its predecessor; and he was equally successful in breeding cattle and horses. He treated his animals well, and even his bulls were docile. He also experimented in agricultural husbandry so skilfully that from his irrigated GRASSLAND (q.v. Vol. VI) he managed to get four cuts of grass a year.

See also YOUNG, Arthur.
See also Vol. VI: CATTLE BREEDS; SHEEP; STOCK-BREEDING.

BALL, John (died 1381). One of the leaders of the Peasants' Revolt, *see* TYLER.

BALZAC, Honoré de (1799–1850). This French novelist was born in Tours, the eldest son of an oldish and taciturn father, and a mother 30 years younger, who reserved her affection for her second son. After a rather unhappy childhood, much of it spent away at a boarding school, he left home and went to Paris where he spent most of the rest of his life. In 1826 a publishing firm with which he was associated went bankrupt, saddling him with heavy debts.

In 20 years Balzac published more than ninety works, a strain which undermined even his robust constitution, and he died when only 51. His enormous output was partly due to his energetic restless temperament, and partly to the desire to pay off debts and be able to live more extravagantly. He was greatly helped and encouraged throughout his life by a series of friends, above all by a Polish lady, Madame Hanska, whom he first met in 1833 and whom he married in 1850, shortly before his death. With her he maintained for 17 years a regular correspondence of the greatest literary and

Maison de Balzac, Paris

HONORÉ DE BALZAC, AGED 43
From a daguerrotype

autobiographic interest, published long after his death as *Lettres à l'Etrangère*.

Balzac conceived the idea of presenting a complete picture of modern civilization through a series of novels under the general title *La Comédie Humaine*. He grouped his novels in various categories, such as 'Scènes de la Vie Privée', 'Scènes de la Vie Militaire', 'Scènes de la Vie Parisienne'. Perhaps Balzac's most remarkable quality is his prodigious imagination. *La Comédie Humaine* covers almost the whole range of French society in the first half of the 19th century, from the aristocratic salons, through all levels of the powerful middle classes, down to the poor in both town and country-side, and includes members of nearly all the professions—doctors, priests, lawyers, bankers, journalists, and civil servants. The same characters, appearing in more novels than one, are seen in action in various environments and give a wholly convincing impression of contemporary society in all its ramifications.

Certain devices and ideas constantly recur. For example, there are minute and lively descriptions of the environment in which the characters are set, since Balzac believed in the influence of physical surroundings on character and behaviour. There are detailed descriptions of physical appearance, because he maintained that the passions and desires we experience leave their trace upon our faces, and so not only character but also the nature of a man's past life can often be deduced from his physical appearance. Even more important, there are detailed studies of human feelings, for Balzac believed that jealousy, avarice, vanity, or any other obsession is sometimes intensified by circumstances to such an extent that it dominates the whole personality.

It is difficult for the reader to know where to start with Balzac's novels. They overlap in time and subject-matter so that there is no obvious chronological order in which to read them. Well-known books, such as *Eugénie Grandet* and *Le Père Goriot*, can be read as isolated works, but they are neither the best nor the most representative. Balzac's tremendous power is better understood from *Illusions Perdues* and its sequel, or from *La Cousine Bette*. His deep understanding of a wide range of human experience, his immense creative imagination, his acute visual sense and dramatic instinct combine to make him, in the opinion of many, the greatest of all French novelists.

See also Vol. XII: NOVEL; FRENCH LITERATURE.

BANTING, Sir Frederick G. (1891–1941). Discoverer of Insulin, *see* Vol. XI: DIABETES.

BARNARDO, Thomas John (1845–1905). Dr. Barnardo, the founder of the Barnardo homes for destitute children, was born in Dublin of partly Jewish and partly English Quaker stock. When he was 17 he became a fervent evangelist, and determined to go to China as a missionary. To that end he began to train as a doctor, and worked in the East End of London through an outbreak of cholera in 1865. During this time he used to spend any spare time teaching in a 'ragged school' in the East End and preaching in the streets. One winter evening, he caught a ragged boy trying to hide all night in the schoolroom, and was horrified to learn that the child, Jim Jarvis, had no home at all. That night the boy Jim conducted Barnardo through the slums showing him large numbers of his fellow waifs homeless and sleeping in the open. Barnardo was so moved that he gave up his plans for China and devoted his life to saving destitute children in Britain.

His scheme grew rapidly from small beginnings. In 1870 he opened his first real 'Home' at Stepney, in which children rescued from the streets were fed, clothed, educated, and brought up as Christians, and finally equipped with a trade or craft. The children were often boarded out in suitable private homes where they could have a family life. In 1873 he founded a village home for girls at Barkingside, Essex. The girls were divided into 'families' of about fifteen or twenty and lived in cottages superintended by a 'mother'. For boys he provided a garden-city home, a technical school, and training schools for the Royal and Merchant Navies. Many of his children were sent on emigration schemes to Canada and Australia.

Barnardo, relying entirely on charitable donations, was at first very short of funds. But eminent reformers and philanthropists such as Lord SHAFTESBURY (q.v.) supported him, and the public soon responded to appeals. In 1868, Barnardo received £214. 15s. in response to his first appeal, but by 1878 the annual income had risen to over £30,000. Before he died he had collected £3,500,000.

Barnardo was a man with one purpose in life. Though at times autocratic and dictatorial, he excelled as an administrator, and when he died at the age of 60 his homes had rescued 60,000 children from destitution.

See also Vol. X: CHILDREN'S HOMES: CHILD WELFARE.

BARTÓK, Béla (1881–1945).

The Hungarian composer Bartók heard the peasants singing folk-songs when he was a boy and, remembering later what he had heard, he recalled many of the tunes in his music. At the Budapest school of music, where Bartók studied piano and composition, he made friends with Zoltan Kodály. Both being fascinated by Hungarian folk music, they went into the country and wrote down the tunes they discovered, making gramophone records of many. They found that every district had its own distinct types of folk-music. This music influenced them both in their own compositions, just as similar discoveries influenced VAUGHAN WILLIAMS (q.v.) in England.

The fierce, often complicated rhythms of these tunes and the unusual scales showed Bartók the way to a new music. At first his experiments sounded harsh and bewildering, but as he became more sure of himself, the exciting and noble thoughts that inspired his music became more clearly expressed and more easily understood. The six string quartets, which he produced at intervals all through his life, contain some of his most important and beautiful work. But it is easiest to get to know his music through the works he wrote after he went to live in America in 1940; the Third Piano Concerto and the wonderful Concerto for Orchestra are immediately attractive. Bartók also wrote six books of short piano pieces for beginners, called *Mikrokosmos* ('Little World'). He died in America very suddenly, a great Hungarian and a great musician who has changed the course of music in our time.

See also Vol. XII: MODERN MUSIC.

BAUDELAIRE, Charles Pierre (1821–67).

The French poet, Baudelaire, had an unhappy life and died in Paris when he was only 46, after much physical and spiritual suffering. As a boy he quarrelled with his step-father and fought his family's attempts to turn him from a literary career.

Though the author of some excellent criticism and some fine prose-poems, Baudelaire is best known for his collection of poems *Les Fleurs du Mal* (1857). He was a startlingly original poet, whose bitter violence shocked readers accustomed to Romantic poetry, and whose forthright

Musée Fabre, Montpelier

BAUDELAIRE IN 1853
Portrait by Gustave Courbet

sexual imagery caused him to be tried for obscenity, fined, and forced to cut out six poems. His originality lies chiefly in his subject-matter. Almost always present are the contrasting themes of *Spleen* or *Ennui*, and *Idéal*; the former concerned with the real world, its ugliness, sin, and suffering; the latter with the poet's imagined world of harmony and perfection. Baudelaire was preoccupied with the problem of sin, and in his conception of beauty there is a note of melancholy and corruption. He handles these themes with great musical sensitivity, his lines ranging from a smooth, haunting nostalgia to the most strident, forceful intensity. Baudeliare has had immense influence upon both French and English poetry.

See also Vol. XII: FRENCH LITERATURE.

BECKET, St. Thomas (1118–70). The son of a London merchant whose family originated in France, Becket is often known by the French version of his name, à Becket. This handsome, accomplished young man entered the Church and was taken into the service and favour of Theobald, Archbishop of Canterbury. In 1155 Theobald, who was growing old, recommended Becket to the new king, HENRY II (q.v.), as a suitable man for the post of Chancellor, the chief position in the State, hoping in this way to keep the King friendly to the Church. Henry appointed Becket, and the King and Chancellor became such close friends that people said they were entirely of one mind. Becket, though a minister of the Church, had practically no ecclesiastical duties, and he followed the pursuits and pleasures of a layman, even leading a company of knights in battle. As Chancellor, he had immense authority, and he became extremely wealthy, living in a luxury and magnificence equal to that of the King himself. In 1162, on the death of Theobald, Henry thought that by making his friend Becket Archbishop as well as Chancellor, he would be able to have his own way in matters both of Church and State. Becket was unwilling, knowing that as Archbishop he would have to forfeit either the King's favour or God's; but the King insisted, and he agreed. Becket, however, did not behave as the King expected. He resigned the Chancellorship, gave up his luxurious life, and directed all his energies towards maintaining what he held to be the rights and privileges of the Church.

Since the time of William the Conqueror,

bishops and priests and all clerks in minor orders (which included most educated people) were tried before Church courts for any offence, and were not subject to the King's courts, the ordinary law courts of the land (see CANON LAW, Vol. X). The most severe punishment which a Church court could give was to degrade an offender so that he became a layman—and consequently subject to the King's courts. This Church privilege was, in fact, often abused, priests and monks sometimes receiving very light punishment for serious crimes, even murder. Henry wished to bring all secular offences (that is, offences against the ordinary law of the land) under the King's courts, so that all should receive the same justice. Becket would probably have agreed to this had not the King claimed the further right of deciding which were secular and which spiritual offences. To this Becket resolutely refused to agree.

This brought to a head in England the struggle which had started in the time of ANSELM (q.v.) and William II, and which was going on all over Europe, the struggle between the authority of the Church and of the State. This struggle was not resolved in England until Henry VIII broke away from the Church of Rome altogether and the King became officially the head of the Church in England (see REFORMATION, Vol. I).

Henry II presented to a council of barons and bishops the famous Constitutions of Clarendon, which stated the degree of authority the State had over the Church. The Constitutions declared that the Church should not protect from the law men guilty of crimes; that, though the Church should make its own appointments, bishops and abbots should be chosen in the King's court, and therefore under his influence; that, when bishoprics and other sees fell vacant, the King should take the revenues till the successors were appointed; and that no appeals should be made to the Pope without the King's consent. The bishops were ready to agree to the Constitutions of Clarendon, and the Pope counselled Becket to act with moderation. Becket, therefore, agreed; but immediately he regretted this decision and refused to set his seal to the document. This defiance of the King put him in such danger that he fled to France, and appealed to the Pope.

It was several years before a reconciliation was brought about, during which time Henry took the revenues of the see of Canterbury. In

British Museum

THE MURDER OF THOMAS BECKET
12th–13th-century English Psalter (*Harley MS. 5102*)

1170, however, Becket returned to Canterbury; but fresh quarrels soon broke out, and the King is said to have exclaimed 'Is there none will rid me of this turbulent priest?' Four of his knights set off at once to Canterbury and murdered the Archbishop in his cathedral.

This deed shocked the Christian world, and Henry, at the orders of the Pope, made a spectacular public penance at the altar of Canterbury Cathedral. The Pope declared Becket to be a saint, and Canterbury became the most important place of pilgrimage for English people. Two centuries later Chaucer described in *The Canterbury Tales* how a band of pilgrims of many different types travelled to Canterbury to pray at the martyr's tomb. These pilgrimages ceased when Henry VIII had the tomb destroyed at the time of the Reformation.

See also Vol. X: CANON LAW.

BEDE (*c.* 673–735). The Venerable Bede, the title by which he was known from early times out of respect for his character and learning, is often called 'the Father of English History'. He was born in Northumbria, and when at 7 he became an orphan, was put into the care of Benedict Biscop, founder of the monastery at Jarrow. Here Bede spent his whole life. Benedict had travelled widely and had brought home from Gaul skilled masons and glaziers, costly metal work, embroidered silks for church services, and a noble collection of books. For Bede, a studious and religious boy, life in such a monastery was ideal, and in due time he also became a monk. Widely known and honoured throughout the Church, he remained essentially a scholar, loving the daily monastic round, the meditations on the Scriptures, and the singing in the choir. 'It has ever been my delight' he says, 'to learn, or teach, or write.' He wrote Latin commentaries on the Bible and other learned books for scholars, and translated parts of the Bible into English for the use of ordinary people.

We know little about his life, but learn from his books that he was gentle and tolerant, amazingly industrious, wise and truth-loving, and a vivid story-teller—all excellent qualities for a historian. Bede is best known as the author of *The Ecclesiastical History of the English Nation*, the only reliable account of this early period of our history. He tells briefly the history of Britain before the coming of the Saxons, and describes in detail the arrival of the monk Augustine at Canterbury, the conversion of the English, and the gradual re-establishment of Christianity throughout Britain during the next 150 years (*see* CHURCH OF ENGLAND, Vol. I).

See also Vol. I: MONK.
See also Vol. XII: HISTORIES.

BEETHOVEN, Ludwig van (1770–1827). Beethoven was one of the first professional composers who wrote music, not because it had been commissioned by an employer, but for its own sake, without caring whether it earned money or not. He was not only one of the greatest of composers, but he was also one of the most striking of men: there was nothing ordinary in his music or his character. He himself, struggling doggedly in the face of great affliction, had many of the heroic qualities he so much admired in others—in Leonora, the heroine of his opera *Fidelio*, for example, or in Egmont, the real-life hero of Goethe's poem for which he composed a famous Overture.

Beethoven was born at Bonn, in the Rhineland. His father was a professional musician at

E. O. Hoppé

LUDWIG VAN BEETHOVEN IN 1818
Painting by Klober

the Court of the Elector of Cologne; he was often drunk, and he was a hard task-master to his son, whose gifts he exploited. Ludwig began learning the violin and piano when he was only 5, and by the time he was 8 he began giving public concerts. He received very little education apart from music, but he was fortunate in having as a music teacher the Court organist, who recognized his abilities and taught him well. When he was 14 Ludwig was appointed second court organist, a post which gave him some opportunity to travel. He visited Vienna, where MOZART (q.v.) heard him play and said, 'Watch that young fellow; he is going to cause a stir in the world.' When he was 16 his mother died; and 3 years later his father was dismissed from his post at Court. Ludwig, with characteristic loyalty and devotion to his family, accepted responsibility both for his father and his two younger brothers.

After his father's death in 1792, Ludwig took his brothers to Vienna. There he had lessons in composition from HAYDN (q.v.), then aged 61, from whom, however, he did not feel that he learnt a great deal. Beethoven was undoubtedly a difficult pupil for he had a strongly indepen-

dent mind, and was impatient of accepted rules and conventions. In spite of this he rapidly became both a good violinist and a successful player and teacher of the piano. He published his first compositions (Trios, op. 1) at this period, dedicating them to one of the many aristocratic patrons who not only gave him financial help but even personal friendship—remarkable in an age when musicians were rated the equals of servants.

Yet Beethoven cannot have been an easy person to help, for he was quick to show resentment of patronage and social distinction, and easily grew suspicious. His behaviour was often rude and his manners uncouth—indeed, a friend said that he gave the impression of 'a very able man reared on a desert island and suddenly brought fresh into the world'. But if he was ever happy it was in these first 10 years in Vienna, when he was gradually establishing himself as a composer. He won recognition with piano sonatas such as the famous 'Pathétique' (1799) and the so-called 'Moonlight' (1801), with his first two piano concertos, and with the 1st Symphony. Though by no means rich, he was better off than at any other period in his life.

But a terrible disaster was to befall him. As early as 1798, when he was only 28 and his 2nd Symphony was not yet finished, he began to lose his hearing. At first he could not bear anyone, even his best friends, to know of his tragedy. We can hear his misery in a letter he wrote to his brother about his affliction in 1802: 'What humiliation when any one standing beside me could hear a distant flute that I could not hear, or a shepherd singing, and I could not distinguish a sound! Such circumstances brought me to the brink of despair and well-nigh made me put an end to my life: nothing but my art held my hand.' The disease worsened, and for the last years of his life he was completely deaf. But he went on working with all his strength, though much of his finest music he was never himself able to hear. He could converse with others only by writing: these scraps of paper, many of which have been kept, give a close picture of his daily life. He also kept sketch-books all his life in which he noted down every unusual idea; they show what an immense amount of thought and revision went into all his music. He never married, and his last years were made wretched by anxiety over a ne'er-do-well nephew who was his ward, by poverty, and by increasing ill health. In 1827 he died during a thunder-storm, his last action being to shake his fist in defiance at the storm outside.

Beethoven was a classical composer: the patterns of his tunes, the range of his harmonies, the shape his music takes, are all controlled in a way that musicians call 'classical' as opposed to 'romantic'. But in a certain sense he was the first musical romantic, for his ideas were expressed with a forcefulness and disregard for elegance which we do not associate with classical music. In his earlier music, the first few Piano Sonatas, the first two Piano Concertos, and the first two Symphonies, we still feel the spirit of Haydn, of the polite 18th century; but after these his music grew more and more original—that is, more and more typical of the Beethoven we know and love today. He ceased to follow others, becoming instead the exponent in music of the revolutionary ideas of the early 19th century (*see* MUSIC, HISTORY OF, Vol. XII).

First and foremost, Beethoven is a composer of extended music, that is, long works in several movements. He wrote nine Symphonies. The 3rd, the 'Eroica' (Heroic) Symphony, was originally dedicated to Napoleon, who had seemed to Beethoven the incarnation of the ideals of the French Revolution; later, when Napoleon proclaimed himself Emperor, Beethoven angrily tore out the dedication. The 5th is an example of how Beethoven could build a big musical structure from a very simple theme—in this case the rat-tat-tat-tat rhythm with which the symphony opens and on which practically the whole first movement is based. The 'Pastoral' Symphony (no. 6) tells of country life. The glorious 7th Symphony in A was composed at a comparatively cheerful period in Beethoven's life and is perhaps the happiest. The 8th was Beethoven's own favourite. In the mighty 9th (the 'Choral' Symphony written for the London Philharmonic Society) he introduces a chorus for the first time in a symphony and chooses words by Schiller to express supreme confidence in ultimate joy and happiness. No composer has put more of himself into his music: everything he felt, from titanic anger to the gentlest tenderness and from the depths of misery to the crest of hope, is to be found there.

Beethoven wrote five Piano Concertos (no. 5 is the 'Emperor'); a Violin Concerto and a Concerto for violin, cello, and piano; twelve Violin Sonatas (including the 'Spring' and the 'Kreutzer'); nine Trios, sixteen String Quartets, and more than thirty Piano Sonatas, including the 'Pathétique', the 'Moonlight', the 'Appassionata', and the 'Hammerklavier' (which is exceptionally difficult to play). He also wrote a number of Overtures (including the three *Leonora* Overtures originally written for his opera *Fidelio*) and the Masses in C and D (the *Missa Solennis*). In his last works, especially the last five of the Quartets, Beethoven moved farther away from traditional forms as he struggled to express his musical vision. His audience did not find these works easy to understand, though today we find them more comprehensible. They remain the loftiest and most personal compositions of one of the world's greatest musical thinkers.

See also Vol. XII: SYMPHONY; SONATA; CONCERTO; OVERTURE.

BELLINI, Giovanni (*c.* 1430–1516). This Italian painter was the earliest of the great Venetian masters. The year of his birth is not known, but he was grown up by 1459. He came of a family of Venetian painters, his father, Jacopo, and his elder brother, Gentile, being also painters of repute. Very little of Jacopo's work remains, but in Venice there are a number of large pictures showing scenes from Venetian life painted by Gentile, and from 1479 to 1481 he was in Constantinople working for the Sultan Mohammed II. During their own lifetime Gentile was the more famous of the two brothers and secured the better commissions, though we now think of Giovanni as by far the greater. Another family connexion was the great Paduan painter, MANTEGNA (q.v.), who married the sister of Gentile and Giovanni Bellini in 1453.

Giovanni Bellini seems to have developed slowly and to have produced some of his best work only towards the end of his life. In his youth the works of DONATELLO (q.v.) at Padua, near Venice, probably influenced him. His early painting of the Dead Christ clearly owes much to a relief made by Donatello at Padua; but Bellini's painting is more moving than Donatello's relief, and the sorrow he has expressed in the face and attitude of the Virgin is almost unbearable. The background of this picture, with its glimpse of hills, and more particularly with the luminous sky overhead, shows us another of Bellini's interests. He loved to give his figure subjects landscape backgrounds with vivid and

National Gallery

MADONNA OF THE POMEGRANATE: PAINTING BY GIOVANNI BELLINI

luminous colours. For this reason he soon abandoned the older method of painting in tempera and took to oils, in which it is easier to make the colours glow (*see* PAINTING, Vol. XII). He may have been led to this by the arrival at Venice in 1475 of the painter Antonello da Messina, who had learnt the Flemish method of painting in oils.

Giovanni Bellini was an intensely religious man, and his painting, most of which is of religious subjects, expresses his piety with great feeling. But he also painted some magnificent portraits (of which the one of the Doge, Leonardo Loredan, in the National Gallery, is the most famous). At the very end of his life, when he was probably at least 80, he showed that he was able to keep abreast of much younger artists, such as GIORGIONE or TITIAN (qq.v.), by painting one of their type of subjects ('the Feast of the Gods', now at Washington) for the first time, and making a masterpiece of it.

See also Vol. XII: VENETIAN PAINTING.

BENEDICT, St. (*c.* 480–*c.* 540). Benedict, the founder of the Benedictine order of monks, was born of wealthy parents at Nursia in central Italy. He went to Rome to be educated, but was so shocked by the behaviour of his companions that, as a mere boy, he ran away. He took refuge in a remote cave where, under the care of a kindly monk, he lived as a hermit for several years. He became famous for his holiness and, when still very young, agreed to the request of some neighbouring monks that he should preside over them. But his discipline proved too severe, and he left the monastery accompanied by two of the monks. With these and others who soon followed them, Benedict established twelve small monasteries, each containing twelve brothers with a 'father' at their head. After many difficulties, he finally retired to Monte Cassino where, on a rocky and almost inaccessible height, he built a monastery on the site of an ancient temple to Apollo. This became the headquarters of the great Benedictine order, and the place where the famous Benedictine Rule was thought out and put into practice.

Before Benedict's time, the monasteries in the West were loosely organized, with no fixed code of discipline or 'rule'. In the Eastern Church there were a number of 'rules' in existence, of which the most famous was the Rule of St. Basil, established in A.D. 370. The Rule of St. Benedict, established in 527, though strict, was less severe than these, and an earnest-minded man could keep its regulations without undue strain. It had the characteristic Roman qualities of order and discipline. So well did Benedict's rule answer the needs of the time that in two centuries it became the pattern for monastic rules in the West (*see* MONK, Vol. I).

A Benedictine monastery was organized as a self-contained community with farm, mill, gardens, and workshops. Opportunities for study were also provided, and by the copying of manuscripts much valuable ancient literature was preserved.

When Benedict founded Cassino, the Roman Empire in the West had collapsed, and Italy was being overrun by tribes of GOTHS (q.v. Vol. I). In such days a compact and well-organized monastery offered the best prospect of a quiet and useful life to men of religious and studious disposition.

Little is known of Benedict's private life except that, once a year, he used to visit his sister, Scholastica, of whom he was very fond, and whose zeal for the monastic life was as great

Alinari

THE MONASTERY OF MONTE CASSINO, FOUNDED BY ST. BENEDICT IN 529

This monastery is the mother-house of the Benedictine Order. It stands on a hill near Cassino, midway between Rome and Naples. It has been destroyed five times since its foundation, mostly by war (the last time was in the Second World War), and once by earthquake, and is now again restored

as his own. Even the date of his death is not known for certain. He must have been a man of great personal courage, for he is said to have gone out to meet the fierce Gothic chieftain Totila (*see* GOTHS, Vol. I), and by the force of his calm courage to have at least temporarily restrained him.

See also Vol. I: MONK.

BENTHAM, Jeremy (1748–1832). This extremely influential English writer on law and ethics was the first of the 19th-century 'philosophical radicals', thinkers who challenged and questioned the purpose and value of all traditions and practices. Their outlook was a common sense one and was called 'Utilitarian'— a term which Bentham invented in 1802. He also invented the word 'international'—there being previously no word for this idea.

Bentham, educated at Westminster and Oxford, the son of a prosperous London lawyer, became himself a lawyer to please his father; but he never practised as he did not like court work. He lived by his writings, and later, on his private income. He early made his name by his *Fragment on Government*, a brilliant critical attack on some aspects of the English constitution and laws. This great work contains the foundations of all his subsequent thoughts and writings on the subject of the law. As Mill said: 'He found

the Philosophy of law a chaos, he left it a science.'

Bentham's interests were many, and his ideas generally very practical. He praised the FRENCH REVOLUTION (q.v. Vol. X), and was made a citizen of France in recognition. He urged that English prisons should be built on a circular plan, so that they could be supervised from a central point, with the prisoners isolated in cells rather than herded together; his ideas later bore fruit (*see* PRISONS, Vol. X). As a result of his labours the harshness of the POOR LAW and of the system of criminal PUNISHMENT (qq.v. Vol. X) was considerably modified. He proposed cutting canals at SUEZ and PANAMA (qq.v. Vol. IV) some generations before these were both achieved. He was the first to propose a register of births, marriages, and deaths, a regular census of the population, and the cheapening of the postal rates. He was also associated with Robert OWEN in social welfare among factory workers, and with WILBERFORCE (qq.v.) in the anti-slavery movement.

Bentham is best known for his work in developing the Utilitarian philosophy in association with the Scotsman, James Mill, the father of John Stuart MILL (q.v.). The Utilitarians believed that man's objective in life was happiness—that is, the acquisition of pleasure and the avoidance of pain. They made no distinction between the quality of one pleasure and another: the happiest individual was he who obtained the greatest quantity of pleasure. The aim of statesmen should therefore be the greatest happiness of the greatest number, with 'every man counting as one and nobody as more than one'. Bentham did not originate these ideas; he owed much to Locke and others. But he first marshalled them logically, put them forward forcefully, and applied them practically.

Bentham taught that an individual's pleasure was diminished if his liberty to seek it was obstructed, and that therefore laws were evil because they obstructed this liberty. The only justification for a law was that the evil it prevented was greater than the evil of the law itself. The adoption of this doctrine by successive governments in the 19th century led to that general removal of economic restrictions on trade and industry which is known as free trade or the policy of *laissez-faire*. As a young man Bentham was a Tory; but in 1808 he became a convinced radical, and many of the political reforms that he advocated, with his usual practical good sense and attention to detail, were later adopted.

The Queen's College, Oxford
JEREMY BENTHAM
Drawing by G. F. Watts (1817–1904)

Bentham in his personal life was a kind and gentle man. One of the practical disadvantages of his doctrine is that it depends for its success on the law being framed and administered by men as benevolent as himself. He was an indefatigable worker and a great letter-writer. All his life he had worked at the codification of the law—especially international law—and shortly before his death he wrote, 'I am alive; though turned of eighty, still in good health and spirits, codifying like any dragon.' In his will he directed that his body should be dissected, and that his skeleton, clothed in his normal garments, should be preserved in University College, London, where it still remains.

See also MILL, John Stuart.

BERKELEY, George (1685–1753). Bishop Berkeley, the religious philosopher, was born of an aristocratic Irish family and educated at Trinity College, Dublin, where he remained as fellow and tutor. He became a great friend of SWIFT (q.v.). All his best work was written very early, and by the age of 27 he had made a reputation as a writer on philosophy. In 1712 Berkeley came to London and associated with the literary men of the day, among whom he was warmly welcomed. Pope speaks of him as having 'every virtue under heaven'. 'So much understanding,' wrote another contemporary, 'so much knowledge, so much innocence, and such humility, I did not think had been the fashion of any but angels, till I saw this gentleman.'

Berkeley travelled widely in Italy and France, and then spent a few years in the English colonies of North America and the West Indies, where he had hoped to found a missionary college. When this hope failed, he returned to Ireland, and in 1734 was appointed Bishop of Cloyne, in the county of Cork. He spent 18 years administering his diocese, living a happy family life with his wife and children, and writing books on both philosophical and practical subjects. In 1752 he retired to Oxford, where he died the next year.

Berkeley's claim to fame rests on his philosophic writing. His system is chiefly explained in his *Treatise concerning the Principles of Human Knowledge* and in the *Three Dialogues between Hylas and Philonous*, in which Hylas stands for educated scientific common sense, and Philonous for Berkeley himself. He wrote these books in reply to the views of John LOCKE (q.v.), whose

Essay concerning Human Understanding had been issued in 1690, and whose teaching made it seem as though the fundamental essence of the world was matter, and that mind was no more than a passive instrument. Berkeley placed mind first, instead of matter. He asserted that things can be said to exist only when they are perceived by a mind. Berkeley admitted that many things exist which man has not yet perceived, but he said that such things have their existence in the mind of God. Thus Berkeley is called an Idealist, one who believes that mind comes before matter, rather than a Materialist who makes everything depend upon matter.

Beyond his strictly philosophical works, Berkeley was interested in natural science and mathematics. He wrote an *Essay towards a New Theory of Vision*, in which he attempted to explain how we are able to judge the distance of objects from us. Though science has made great advances since Berkeley's day, his essay is still of value.

See also Vol. I: PHILOSOPHY.

BERLIOZ, Hector (1803–69). This French composer was born in the mountainous southeast of France, and his earliest and deepest impressions were of the romantic beauty of that countryside. There was no musical tradition in the family, and his first musical impressions were quite unconventional—the flageolet and the guitar rather than the usual piano, local amateur music-making instead of symphony concerts or opera. In 1821 he was sent to Paris to study medicine, which he hated, and despite his family's strenuous opposition he entered the Paris Conservatoire (School of Music) in 1826. After several attempts he won in 1830 the much sought annual Rome Prize, which enabled him to study in Italy. His first works were inspired by Goethe's *Faust* and by Shakespeare, who shared with Virgil the first place among his favourite writers. BEETHOVEN, GLUCK (qq.v.), and Weber were his favourites among musicians. His love of Shakespeare led to his meeting in Paris and falling in love with Harriet Smithson, an Irish actress. Their love-affair, which led to an unsuccessful marriage, served him as a subject for his first masterpiece, the *Symphonie Fantastique*.

In Italy he stored his imagination with vivid scenes of peasant life, on which he drew later for some of his best works—the *Roman Carnival*, *Benvenuto Cellini*, and *Corsair* overtures, and the symphonies *Harold in Italy* and *Romeo and Juliet*. He returned to Paris in 1832 and set about earning his living by musical journalism and occasional concerts of his own. In addition, he was helped by the generosity of the great violinist Paganini. Berlioz won fame as a conductor, and received many invitations to visit Germany, Russia, and England, where he introduced his own works and set a new standard of orchestral playing. After *The Damnation of Faust* (1846) the works of his later years included the huge two-part opera, *The Trojans*, based on Virgil's *Aeneid*.

Berlioz united in his music the brilliant colour, vivid emotional suggestion, and loose structure typical of the ROMANTIC MOVEMENT (q.v. Vol. XII) with the nobility, the clear vision, and controlled design of the 18th century. He revolutionized the art of ORCHESTRATION (q.v. Vol. XII) and, as the first orchestral conductor in our modern sense, the technique of performance. He could conceive works on the grandest scale, with hundreds of performers, as well as songs whose lyrical essence is distilled in a few pages. Almost alone of his contemporaries, he had no interest in the piano and wrote exclusively for the orchestra. He is still a disputed figure, regarded by some as the only legitimate successor to Beethoven among 19th-century composers, and by others as an artistic genius but a musician whose imaginings are always greater than his actual productions.

See also Vol. XII: SYMPHONY.

BERNARD, St. (*c.* 1090–1153). Bernard of Clairvaux was one of the most important characters in medieval church life. He was a member of an aristocratic French family, and his mother was a deeply religious woman. It was as a result of her teaching that Bernard decided to become a MONK (q.v. Vol. I), in those days considered the highest calling that a man could follow.

So strong was Bernard's capacity for leadership that when, at the age of 22, he left home, he persuaded thirty young noblemen, including his five brothers, to accompany him. They joined the strictest monastery in Europe, that of the Cistercian order at Cîteaux, then ruled by its English founder, Stephen Harding of Sherborne. The addition of so many members caused Cîteaux to grow too large, and in 1115 Bernard was chosen to lead twelve of its brothers in search of a new home. They came to a desolate valley in Champagne, which they renamed Clairvaux, the Bright Valley. Here they built a rough wooden building for a monastery.

At Clairvaux Bernard lived a life of great hardship. His wonderful energy led him to take a considerable part in the affairs of both Church and State, and to write many letters on worldly as well as religious matters. It was a new thing for the abbot of a monastery to take part in so many worldly disputes; but Bernard's advice was eagerly sought, and his reputation grew so great that the gifts of prophecy and even of working miracles were attributed to him.

When Bernard was 40 a dispute arose at Rome over the election of a new Pope, two candidates, Innocent II and Anacletus II, having been appointed by rival parties. There was danger of serious trouble; but so great was Bernard's prestige in Europe that he was called upon to settle the dispute. He decided in favour of Innocent II who, after some delay, was universally recognized. When on Innocent II's death, Eugenius III, a pupil of Bernard, was chosen Pope, Bernard's power in the Church was supreme.

Eugenius appealed to the kings and nobles of western Europe to lead a fresh Crusade to rid the Holy Land of infidels. The first Crusade in 1096 had been partially successful, for Jerusalem had been taken and a kingdom established there. But by this time the Mohammedans were again threatening the Holy City. Bernard was untiring in his efforts to stir up enthusiasm for this enterprise, preaching vigorous and eloquent sermons in churches, market-places, and highways throughout Europe. Finally, largely owing to his efforts, the Second Crusade set out. It proved, however, a disastrous failure and cast a deep gloom over Europe (*see* CRUSADES, Vol. I).

Bernard, whose teaching was strictly orthodox, helped to secure the condemnation of ABÉLARD (q.v.) for heresy; he also condemned one of his own pupils, Gilbert, Bishop of Poitiers. Both attacks were efforts to forbid the practice of reasoned examination of religious doctrine: for Bernard, as a contemporary historian says, 'held in abhorrence those who trusted in the wisdom of this world and were too much attached to human reasonings'. This attitude of Bernard does not seem to us very enlightened; but in the 12th century it was not unusual. On the other hand, when, at the beginning of the Crusade, a fanatical priest incited the people in many cities

of Germany to terrible massacres of the Jews, it was Bernard who used the whole weight of his authority to stop so un-Christian an act. In this he was ahead of the moral standard of his day.

Many monasteries of the Cistercian order took their rise from Cîteaux, and these included several well-known English ones—Waverley in Surrey, Tintern in the Wye Valley, and Fountains in Yorkshire. Though Bernard was not the actual founder of the Cistercian order, it owed most to his vigour and inspiration. He was a preacher of the first rank and must have possessed a magnetic personality; it was the human qualities of love and mercy in Christ which roused his devotion.

See also Vol. I: MONK.

BERNHARDT, Sarah (1844–1923). The 'Divine Sarah', one of the greatest actresses of all time, was born in Paris, the eleventh child of her parents; her mother was of Jewish descent. She studied at the Conservatoire, the Paris school of dramatic art, and later played for a short time with the Comédie Française—the French national theatre. Wayward, independent, and undisciplined, Bernhardt had to fight her way to the top in spite of her obvious qualities.

Her first real success was as Zanetto in François Coppée's verse play, *Le Passant*, at the Odéon Theatre in 1869; her finest part is

SARAH BERNHARDT
Coloured wood engraving by Sir William Nicholson

generally agreed to have been Phèdre in RACINE's verse tragedy (q.v.), a part which moved her so much that she never acted it twice running. Her other famous parts included the heroine of Victor HUGO's *Hernani*, and of DUMAS' *La Dame aux Camélias* (qq.v.); the hero in Rostand's play about Napoleon's son, *L'Aiglon*; and Hamlet (in a rather flat French prose translation), in which she appeared for a single performance at the Memorial Theatre, Stratford on Avon.

She had great poise and remarkable beauty of movement, a true command of the stage, and an exquisitely governed voice. Her energy was unceasing, and her acting career lasted for more than 60 years. Today she is already a legend.

See also Vol. IX: ACTING.

BERNINI, Giovanni Lorenzo (1598–1680). This Italian sculptor, architect, and painter was the most influential artist of the 17th century and the creator of the BAROQUE style of art (q.v. Vol. XII). Bernini was born in Naples, the son of a sculptor, but he spent most of his life in Rome, often enjoying the personal favour of the Pope. None of his paintings (other than a few small portraits) has survived, but his sculpture and architecture can be seen—mostly in Rome.

Bernini's first important work was the vast bronze canopy above the high altar in St. Peter's, Rome, a work of sculpture large enough to count as architecture. In this way it is typical of the Baroque style, in which the old barriers between painting, sculpture, and architecture were broken down and all were used to give a unified effect. Most of Bernini's buildings were executed late in his life; the most famous being the colonnades in front of St. Peter's in Rome. The plan of these is an ellipse which, by an optical illusion, makes the cathedral appear narrower than it really is. Bernini loved optical tricks of this kind, and much of his work has this theatrical quality. As a sculptor he was immensely skilful, especially with marble, which he could carve to look like leaves, or clouds, or draperies freely floating in the wind.

Bernini visited Paris in 1665 at the invitation of King LOUIS XIV (q.v.) to redesign the Louvre Palace. There he met, for a few moments, the young Christopher WREN (q.v.). Bernini's work was not well received in France at the time, and his designs for the rebuilding of the Louvre were not used; but later his Roman buildings and his

Anderson

THE HIGH ALTAR IN ST. PETER'S, ROME
The bronze baldachino canopy over the altar was designed by Bernini

sculpture had considerable influence there as in most other European countries.

See also Vol. XII: BAROQUE ART.

BESSEMER, Sir Henry (1813–98), *see* CARNEGIE; *see also* Vol. VIII: STEEL-MAKING.

BISMARCK, Prince Otto von (1815–98). Bismarck, the Iron Chancellor of Prussia, created from a medley of kingdoms and petty States a single powerful nation—a unified Germany His methods of bringing this about were harsh and often unscrupulous; he himself said that methods of 'blood and iron' were needed rather than rule by Parliament. He went directly after what he wanted, worrying little about the morality of the means he employed.

Bismarck came of a good Prussian family and in the normal course entered the service of the kingdom of Prussia, but he showed distaste for its discipline and soon retired to manage his family estates. He soon abandoned the liberal opinions which were fashionable among young Germans in the years following Napoleon's fall, and when he re-entered public life in 1847, at the age of 32, it was as a staunch believer in the Prussian monarchy, the Prussian army, and the Protestant Church, and an opponent of democracy—'I look for Prussian honour in Prussian abstinence . . . from every shameful union with democracy.'

During the revolutionary years 1848–9 he opposed the new Prussian constitution which was intended to give the people more control. He also opposed the attempt to create German unity by setting up a Parliament of all the German States at Frankfort, of which the Prussian King might have become the head. Bismarck was more concerned at this time to preserve unchanged the old Prussian monarchy, with its army and civil service, than to further the unity of the German States. During the period of Bismarck's ascendancy a tremendous industrial development took place in Germany. It was largely because the new railways and industries were making Germany into a single economic whole that the demand for political unity was growing stronger. Bismarck, after the revolutions of 1848 had been suppressed, went to represent Prussia in the German Diet, which was not a real Parliament but a meeting-place of German Governments to handle their common concerns, held under Austrian presidency. Here Bismarck steadily opposed the policies of Austria, Prussia's great rival for leadership in Germany. Austria was not, like Prussia, a truly German State, since the dominions of the Austrian Emperor contained people of many other races. Bismarck decided that Austria must be excluded altogether from a united Germany.

After an interlude as Ambassador in Russia and France, Bismarck became Chancellor (Prime Minister) of Prussia in 1862. He set to work to enlarge and reorganize the Prussian army despite the opposition of the Prussian Parliament, which Bismarck alternately bullied and ignored.

During the next 9 years he achieved those objects for which he is best known to history. In 1863 he supported Russia in the cruel repression of the Poles, who had risen against Russian rule, fearing that a Polish success might encourage the Poles under Prussian rule to rebel. A more far-

BISMARCK
Engraving from von Sybel, *The Founding of the German Empire*, 1880

reaching motive was his wish to keep on good terms with Russia because in the series of carefully planned wars which he intended Prussia to launch, leading towards the final isolation of France, he wished to be sure of Russian support, or at least neutrality. Above all he wished to guard against the risk of a war on two fronts. In 1864 Prussia, in partnership with Austria, took the lead in a war of the German States against Denmark over the disputed control of two small duchies on the borders between Denmark and Germany. The defeat of Denmark incidentally made it possible for the Germans later on to build the KIEL CANAL (q.v. Vol. IV), which greatly helped German naval warfare against Britain in the 20th century.

Two years later Bismarck provoked a war with Austria, and completely defeated her in what was called 'the seven weeks' war'. Bismarck now had a free hand in Germany. He directly annexed some of the smaller German States that had taken Austria's side, including Hanover. Most of the remaining States were united with Prussia in what was called the North German Confederation. One step remained, a German war against the old enemy, France.

Bismarck made a pretext out of France's opposition to a Prussian prince as candidate to the vacant throne of Spain. Cunning diplomacy was needed, however, to provoke Napoleon III, the French Emperor, into declaring war. The Prussian King himself thought that peace could be preserved, not realizing that his Chancellor was determined to unite all the German States against France so as to further his plan of a permanent unity under Prussia.

Bismarck's calculations were again wholly successful. The French were soundly beaten, their Emperor captured, and Paris subjected to a long and terrible siege. In January 1871 the somewhat reluctant King of Prussia, William I, was proclaimed German Emperor in the French palace of Versailles. The new German Empire had the form of a Parliamentary constitution, but it was really only an expansion of the old Prussian State which controlled every part of national life.

Bismarck had now got what he wanted; his next concern was to preserve the existing state of things against his internal and external enemies. At home, this meant a series of political battles against the Liberals, the Roman Catholic Church, and the new forces of trade-unionism and Socialism. He realized that it would be wise to do something to lessen the hardships of the workers under the increasing industrialization; so he introduced an insurance scheme to protect them against the effects of sickness and old age. It was the first scheme of its kind, and did much to diminish the danger of revolution.

Bismarck's greatest fear was that the other nations of Europe might unite to force Germany to give up some of her recent gains. He built up, therefore, a friendship with Austria and Russia, and kept a careful eye on France, from whom he had seized two rich provinces, Alsace and Lorraine, and whom he suspected of a desire for revenge; at one moment he nearly decided to attack her again.

The death of William I showed the real weakness in Bismarck's position, for he still depended on the royal will and not on popular support. William's successor, Frederick, was a dying man at his accession, and his reign was brief. He was succeeded by William's young grandson, William II (the Kaiser of the First World War), who found his dependence on his grandfather's Minister irksome. After some stormy scenes, Bismarck resigned and spent the remaining 8 years of his life in grumbling retirement, watching the fumblings of his successors, and writing his celebrated memoirs.

See also Vol. I: GERMANS.

BIZET, Georges (1838–75). The Frenchman Bizet, composer of the opera *Carmen*, began his serious musical training when he was 9, and finished it at 19 by winning the Rome Prize, coveted by every French composer. Almost immediately he began to write operas, none of which was especially successful. The only one of lasting importance is *The Pearl Fishers*, with its famous friendship duet and its two lovely tenor songs. Like many of Bizet's operas it is set outside France—actually in Ceylon. Some of the others, however, contain some striking and original music. Much more popular is his incidental music for Daudet's play *l'Arlésienne*.

During his lifetime Bizet was laughed at as a hot-headed revolutionary, with no sense of tune. His last opera, the immortal *Carmen*, set in Spain, was considered indecent and noisy; but in spite of this criticism, which greatly depressed Bizet, *Carmen* was performed twenty-three times in the last 3 months of the composer's life, and since his death has been sung all over the world. There can hardly be a Frenchman who does not know the tune 'Habanera' and the Toreador's Song. Bizet's fame rests on his work for the stage; but he also wrote some orchestral works, including the jolly suite *Jeux d'Enfants* (to which a delightful ballet has been composed), some piano music, and songs.

See also Vol. XII: OPERA, HISTORY OF.

BLACK PRINCE (1330–76), *see* GAUNT, John of. *See also* Vol. X: HUNDRED YEARS WAR.

BLAKE, Robert (1599–1657). This great admiral, although a landsman until nearly 50, commanded CROMWELL's fleet (q.v.) in the first Dutch War (1652–4). His exploits against Holland and later in the Mediterranean against Spain restored Britain to her place as a leading maritime power.

Blake was the eldest of twelve sons of a Bridgwater merchant. On leaving Oxford he took up his father's trade and settled to a quiet country life. In 1640 he was elected a member of Parliament, and on the outbreak of the CIVIL WAR (q.v. Vol. X) he joined the Parliament forces. He quickly won Cromwell's respect and con-

THE BATTLE OF THE GABBARD BANK, FOUGHT ON 4 JUNE 1653 AT THE MOUTH OF THE THAMES
The Dutch Admiral Tromp's flagship, the *Brederode*, in the left foreground, is seen engaging the British flagship, the *Resolution*. The British fleet was victorious. Painting by H. Witmont

fidence. He held Lyme Regis, in Dorset, with a scratch force against ten times the number of Royalists, and his defence of Taunton for 12 months, when much of the town was reduced to ruins, won him personal renown and proved a turning-point in the war. After the Parliamentarians had defeated the Royalists on land, Blake, with two others, was put in command of the fleet, then in a weak condition. Within 2 years he had defeated Prince RUPERT's squadron (q.v.) and driven the remaining Royalist ships from British waters.

In 1652-3 four bitter engagements were fought against the Dutch in the struggle for command of the seas. In May, Blake forced back the Dutch Admiral Tromp with over twice the number of ships. In September he defeated DE RUYTER (q.v.) at the mouth of the Thames. In November he was outnumbered and defeated by Tromp in a 2-day fight off Dungeness. (The story runs that Tromp lashed a broom to his masthead to show that the English had been swept from the Channel.) But in the following February, with a force of eighty ships, Blake once again encountered Tromp, and there followed a furious running battle from Portland to Calais. Blake, himself seriously wounded, having sunk five Dutch fighting ships and captured four, as well as thirty or more merchant ships, won a complete victory. Blake was too unwell to take much part in the further battles some months later, when the Dutch fleet was finally shattered.

In 1654 Blake sailed for North Africa, and his sweep along the North African coast, where he destroyed a Tunisian pirate fleet, and round Italy laid the earliest foundations of British SEA POWER (q.v. Vol. X) in the Mediterranean. Three years later, after a declaration of war with Spain, Blake performed his last and most spectacular service. Hearing that the Spanish West India fleet had arrived at the port of Santa Cruz in the Canary Islands, he took advantage of a following breeze and with great daring entered the port and destroyed the entire enemy fleet of sixteen ships as well as the town. A change of wind enabled him to withdraw with few casualties. On the voyage home he died of fever in his flagship, the *George*, within sight of Plymouth.

Blunt, determined, and a sea-officer by instinct, Blake's spectacular career recovered for the British fleet a respect that had waned since the days of Elizabeth. The Royalist historian

Clarendon generously wrote of him that he 'was the first that infused ... courage into the seamen, by making them see what mighty things they could do, if they were resolved'.

See also RUPERT; DE RUYTER; CROMWELL.
See also Vol. X: SEA POWER; SEA WARFARE, HISTORY OF; CIVIL WAR.

BLAKE, William (1757–1827). Only a fraction of the poetry and painting with which William Blake filled the 70 years of his life has come down to us, for in his lifetime few people valued his work and he remained almost unknown to his contemporaries. Most of the poetry which has survived Blake etched himself on copper plates, and then printed and coloured the pages with his wife's help. These small, beautiful books, the design interwoven with the words in a unique way, are now worth hundreds of pounds, yet when he was alive few people bought them. He made his living as an engraver and, being poor, did any work that was offered him, from engraving pictures of teapots for Wedgwood's pottery catalogue to illustrating Young's poem *Night Thoughts*, which he did with some of his most beautiful illustrations.

Born in Soho, London, towards the end of George II's reign, Blake grew up when the fashion in poetry and painting was for a smooth and artificial finish which often disguised an emptiness of thought. Even as a boy Blake disliked the manner, and the emptiness of thought behind it enraged him. To Blake poetry and art were not trivial things but profound prophecy; and to this biblical vision of his task he held all his life, without compromise. He always put this vision into the kind of words in which he had first learned it as a boy, reading the Bible and the chapel hymn-books. As a young man, when studying drawing at the Royal Academy Schools, he conceived a contempt for academic drawing and a lifelong hatred for Sir Joshua REYNOLDS (q.v.). Blake found it more natural to draw what he saw in his visions than what he saw in the material world.

While Blake was an engraver's apprentice, the American colonies revolted against British rule. He was much affected by this fight for independence, and remained all his life a supporter of young and forceful ideas against established authority. As a boy he had written some charming poems which were later published; but during the 10 years that followed his apprentice-ship, between 1779 and 1789, he wrote almost nothing. He opened a print-shop with his much loved younger brother Robert; and when Robert died soon after, Blake believed that he talked with him in his dreams, and that it was Robert who first revealed to him his original method of engraving his books.

The outbreak of the FRENCH REVOLUTION (q.v. Vol. X) in 1789 moved Blake deeply. He was so excited that he wore the red cap of liberty in the streets of London. He began to write poems again, some of them mystical, some with plain titles like *The French Revolution* and *A Song of Liberty*; above all, this hopeful mood produced the happy lyrical poems *Songs of Innocence*. These poems, the finest that Blake wrote, are free from anger and protest, and their language is as direct and untroubled as their thought. But the French Revolution did not bring the new world which Blake had hoped for. The Reign of Terror followed, England declared war on France, and soon Napoleon was turning the new Republic into an Empire. Blake, sadly disillusioned, wrote the *Songs of Experience*, in which the bright dreams of the *Songs of Innocence* have already faded. Influenced by SWEDENBORG's philosophy (q.v.), Blake had all his life a very strong sense of the 'two contrary states of the human soul', the balance of good and evil. Where once, in the *Songs of Innocence*, he had said

> Mercy has a Human Heart,
> Pity a Human Face,
> And Love, the human form divine,
> And Peace, the human dress.

he now answered himself in *Songs of Experience*:

> Cruelty has a Human Heart,
> And Jealousy a Human Face. . . .

Yet Blake remained a friend to the French Revolution even when it was most hated in England. It was he who warned Tom PAINE (q.v.) to fly to France in 1792, twenty minutes ahead of the warrant for his arrest; and he was himself tried for sedition in 1804. But his heart was no longer in such matters; he was already writing those long mystical poems, usually called the *Prophetic Books*, which, though vague and difficult to understand, contain many magnificent passages. The theme is still the revolt of free man against authority, but now Blake writes of it in the form of mystical symbolism. At the invitation of a well-meaning patron he went to

'THE ANCIENT OF DAYS': COLOUR PRINT BY WILLIAM BLAKE

Frontispiece to Blake's poem *Europe*, 1794

live in the country at Felpham in Sussex; but he felt the loss of independence so much that he came back to London in 1803, and worked in great poverty. He wrote less and less; but in 1809 he exhibited his pictures, issuing a Descriptive Catalogue which explained them and contained many excellent comments on art in his unmistakably direct, forcible, and epigrammatic prose. Southey, who went to the exhibition, was confirmed in his opinion of Blake's madness; Lamb, on the other hand, appreciated his genius. About 1818 a group of other young artists, such as John Linnell and Samuel Palmer, became his friends and disciples, and Linnell, though poor himself, paid Blake to make designs for the *Book of Job* and Dante's *Divine Comedy*. Blake, now 60, was free for the first time from the sense of want and of opposition; and these designs are the most beautiful he made (*see* Vol. XII, opposite p. 288). At 70, Blake died, singing, and entirely serene.

BOADICEA (1st century A.D.). This fierce warrior-queen—more correctly called Boudicca

—led half Britain in a dangerous revolt against the Roman occupation. Prasutagus, King of the Celtic tribe of Iceni in eastern Britain, was allowed to retain his kingship under Roman rule; but directly he died in A.D. 61 the Romans broke faith by seizing his territory and grossly ill-treating his wife Boadicea, his daughters, and tribesmen.

The Iceni rose in wrath under Boadicea, and were joined by other tribes who resented Roman taxation and conscription. The time was auspicious, for the Governor-General, Suetonius Paulinus, and his troops were far away in Wales. Led by Boadicea, the Britons fell upon the Roman colony of Colchester, massacred all its inhabitants, and burnt it to the ground. They then annihilated the Roman 9th Legion which marched against them from Lincoln. London and Verulam (St. Albans) were also overrun, for Paulinus, hurrying eastwards with a small cavalry force, realized that he could not defend them without his main army. When, however, he had assembled his whole army he utterly defeated the Britons somewhere between London and Colchester. Realizing that all was lost, Boadicea took poison and died.

BOCCACCIO, Giovanni (1313–75). This Italian novelist and poet, the author of the *Decameron*, was the illegitimate son of a Florentine merchant. He spent a rather unhappy childhood in the care of his stepmother at Certaldo, his father's house, among the vines and cypress trees which surround Florence. His father apprenticed him to a merchant, with whom he did, he says, 'nothing for 6 years but waste irrecoverable time'. Sent to Naples to study law, he spent his time hunting, dancing in the open air, and banqueting with gay young people from the Court. When he was 23 he saw in church a young married woman whom he called Fiammetta. 'The shining eyes of the lovely lady looked sparkling into mine', he wrote, 'with a piercing light, along which, so it seemed, came a fiery arrow of gold.' He remained in love with Fiammetta for 12 years, until the Black Death came to Italy, and the beautiful Fiammetta died.

To please her, he had already written long novels and epic poems, but his greatest work, the *Decameron*, was written when the plague had left him poor and alone in the world. After 1350 he lived mostly in Florence, studying Greek and Latin, reading DANTE, and enjoying the

The Earl of Leicester

THE SCENE IN THE CHURCH OF SANTA MARIA NOVELLA, FLORENCE, AT THE BEGINNING OF THE 'DECAMERON'
Seven young women, meeting in the church, decide to go into the country to avoid the plague. They are joined by three young men. From a manuscript illuminated by Taddeo Crivelli between 1467 and 1471

friendship of the poet PETRARCH (qq.v.). He spent more than he could afford on books and was too proud to borrow, and in the winter of 1373 he was found at Certaldo, alone except for an old housekeeper, cold, ill, and terrified by the approach of death. He recovered enough to lecture on Dante in the University of Florence with his old vigour and clarity; but heartbroken at the news of Petrarch's death, he died shortly afterwards at Certaldo.

In spite of a life of poverty, disappointment, and loneliness, Boccaccio left a store-house full of good humour and wisdom in the *Decameron* (Greek for 'ten days'), a collection of 100 short stories related during 10 days by an imaginary party of young people who have left Florence during the plague for a villa in the hills. The stories are woven together by an exquisite sense of this setting, the fountains, the terraced gardens, the smiling men and girls. Boccaccio wrote about men and women as he knew them, and everyday life in the 14th century was often brutal and crude—as some of the stories are. But Boccaccio was a devout Christian and tells his tales with a large charity towards the faults of his characters. In England alone, Chaucer, Shakespeare, Dryden, Keats, and Tennyson have thought well enough of Boccaccio to borrow from his tales.

See also Vol. XII: ITALIAN LITERATURE.

BOLÍVAR, Simon (1783–1830). The best-known figure of the 19th-century revolutionary movements in the oppressed Spanish colonies in America is Bolívar, the 'Liberator', after whom BOLIVIA (q.v. Vol. III) has been named. He was born in Carácas, Venezuela, and came of a noble Spanish family long settled there.

He went to Madrid to study law, and travelled to France towards the end of the FRENCH REVOLUTION (q.v. Vol. X). His mind was formed by the writers of the 'Age of Reason', such as VOLTAIRE, Montesquieu, ROUSSEAU, and LOCKE (qq.v.), and this liberal education laid the foundation for much of his later actions and political thought. He cherished two ideas for many years, projects which caused him much trouble at the peak of his career. One was for a constitution in the English form for Greater Colombia (a federation of the modern Venezuela, Colombia, and Ecuador); the other for an international congress of the new Latin American States to meet at Panama and discuss both internal questions and matters concerning relations with the rest of the world. He achieved neither of these ideals.

The impression he left on Latin America was due as much to his character as to his education. He had much of the poetic imagination of BYRON (q.v.), who greatly admired him and named a boat after him; but he had also a

INDIAN CAVALRY ATTACKING SPANISH TROOPS IN COLOMBIA

Bolívar used native cavalry with great success in the liberation of Colombia. Engraving from J. P. Hamilton, *Travels through the Interior Provinces of Colombia*, 1827

relentless inflexibility of purpose and a capacity for clear, reasoned thought and rapid and decisive action. He was eloquent, speaking with a creative power which fired his listeners. He grew easily impatient with other people, and found it hard to bear the difference between his ideals and actual conditions.

Bolívar's dislike for the arrogant Spanish Government and the dictatorship of Napoleon, together with his admiration for the democratic institutions he saw in the U.S.A., combined to arouse in him a desire to fight for independence. He offered his services to the first movement of independence started in Carácas in 1810, and was later sent to Britain to win British support for the short-lived first Venezuelan Republic (*see* MIRANDA). When the Republic fell, he obtained command of the revolutionary troops, and in 1813 he triumphantly entered Carácas, saluted for the first time as Liberator. He was soon expelled by the Spaniards, however, and fled to the West Indies, from where he made repeated attacks. By 1817 he had secured the independence of Colombia, and in 1821 he beat the Spaniards conclusively at Carabobo, and re-entered Carácas.

Venezuela and Colombia being freed, the revolutionaries next decided to free Ecuador. Bolívar led an army under immense difficulties across desert and mountain, where only troops inspired with personal devotion to a great leader would have gone. He entered Quito in 1822,

and incorporated Ecuador into the Colombian-Venezuelan Union. In Ecuador he met SAN MARTÍN (q.v.), the liberator of Argentina and Peru. No agreement was reached between the two leaders, and San Martín, realizing that there was not room for two leaders, and that Bolívar's help for Peru was essential, generously retired from the field, leaving Bolívar as sole commander.

Bolívar defeated the Spaniards at the Battle of Junin which was fought in the high Andes between horsemen, scarcely a shot being fired; and his second in command, General Sucre, destroyed the remaining Spanish forces at Ayacucho. By 1824, Spanish power in South America had been brought to an end.

In 1826 a general assembly of Southern American Republics met at Panama, with the idea of forming a Supra-National Court of Reference for settlement of disputes among Latin American States. But some of the new Republics were afraid of Bolívar's dictatorial power; support from Europe and the U.S.A. was not forthcoming, and consequently the assembly failed. Bolívar was bitterly disillusioned. He tried for the next few years to enforce his idea of government for the Republics of Latin America; but the Constitution which he had drafted for the new Republic of Bolivia proved unworkable, and the Union of Greater Colombia began to fall apart. In 1830, disillusioned and in failing health, he retired, and died in the same year at the early age of 47.

Though Bolívar's life appeared to end in failure, his ideas remained sound throughout the years that followed, and still have a powerful influence on the political life of Latin America.

See also MIRANDA; SAN MARTÍN.
See also Vol. I: VENEZUELANS; COLOMBIA, PEOPLES OF.

BOOTH, William (1829–1912). The founder and first 'General' of the Salvation Army was brought up in Nottingham in extreme poverty. From an early age he was inspired with religious fervour, saying 'I like my tea as I like my religion—hot!' He became a METHODIST (q.v. Vol. I) and spent his few leisure hours as a wandering preacher. In 1855 he married Catherine Mumford who, in spite of suffering from perpetual ill health, assisted him in all his work and bore him eight children.

In 1865 Booth, having left the Methodists, began to establish his own mission in the East End of London. Regarding his work as a war against sin and the Devil, he founded an 'army' and called his followers not ministers but 'soldiers'. Convinced that the best way to save the poor from damnation was to provide alternatives to the gin-palace, Booth made his mission as attractive as possible with rousing hymn-tunes, drums, trumpets, and banners. Men and women, mostly poor and illiterate, flocked to join his 'army', and within a few years it was leading 'campaigns' all over the world. In places it met with persecution. In England the attacks upon it sometimes caused uproars in very poor districts, and its officers were imprisoned for disturbing the peace. But the 'Army' grew and flourished and its work won respect and admiration. It founded hospitals, homes, and every kind of social institution, and its 'soldiers' penetrated the worst slums where nobody else went.

Booth's wife died in 1890 and he himself went blind; but his energy and organizing ability remained to the end of his life, by which time his work had spread into fifty-nine countries. The leadership passed to members of his family; but, later, means were devised for electing a General and appointing other officers.

See also Vol. X: SLUMS.

BORGIA FAMILY. This family achieved great prominence and power in 15th-century Italy, and Pope Alexander VI and his illegitimate children, Caesar and Lucrezia, are notorious characters in history.

The Borgias were originally a Spanish noble family, who first came to Italy in 1443 in the train of a Spanish conqueror. One Borgia became Pope as Callixtus III, and gave cardinal's rank to his nephew, Rodrigo, who later became Pope as Alexander VI. Alexander was an able man, but dissolute and corrupt, anxious to amass wealth, to extend his power, and to further his children's interests. He fostered political ambition in his son Giovanni, Duke of Gandia,

made his other son Caesar a cardinal, and married his daughter Lucrezia to a member of the powerful Sforza family. He annulled this marriage later to marry her for political reasons to the son of the Spanish King of Naples. He pursued a double policy between the two rivals for Italian possessions, France and Spain, though not very successfully, and in fact Charles VIII of France entered Rome as conqueror in 1494.

Alexander's son Giovanni was murdered in 1497, probably by his brother Caesar, who renounced his cardinalcy and aspired to political power. Caesar Borgia, a clever and unscrupulous opportunist, roused MACHIAVELLI's admiration (q.v.), and was Machiavelli's model of the ideal Prince. With French aid, he seized the chief cities of the Romagna in central Italy and became Duke of the Romagna, his father

Alinari

CAESAR AND LUCREZIA BORGIA: DETAIL FROM A FRESCO BY PINTURICCHIO

The fresco, in the Borgia apartment of the Vatican, represents the disputation of St. Catherine. Caesar is portrayed as the Pope and Lucrezia as St. Catherine

having eliminated his chief rivals by treachery. Caesar then caused Lucrezia's husband to be murdered, which brought to an end any alliance with Spain, and Lucrezia was married to Alfonso d'Este, heir to the Duke of Ferrara.

In 1503, when Caesar was at the height of his power, his father, the Pope, died and he himself fell ill, possibly from poison. This marked a change in his fortunes. He had made his peace with many of his foes, for he was not strong enough to fight them; and a declared enemy, Giuliano della Rovere, was elected Pope as Julius II, and determined to reclaim the Romagna for the Church. Julius arrested Caesar and compelled him to give up most of his gains. Caesar escaped to Naples, but was again captured and sent to prison in Spain. From there he escaped to Navarre, where he was killed fighting at the age of 32.

Caesar and Lucrezia shared their father's indulgence in sensual pleasure, and stories of their extravagances in the Papal Court have become legend. The Borgia apartment in the Vatican, with frescoes by Pinturicchio, remains witness to their ideas of luxury. Yet Lucrezia, the passive instrument of her father's and brother's politics, became on her marriage to Alfonso d'Este a lady of distinction in society, winning affection by her beauty and charm. Nobles loved her and poets sang her virtues. She died when she was 39, lamented by innumerable friends and admirers.

Here the story of the Borgias virtually ends. One of Caesar's daughters married a French nobleman and carried the line into France. In Spain the Dukes of Gandia retained the name and some of the former splendour of the family down to 1748.

See also MACHIAVELLI.

BORROW, George Henry (1803–81). Borrow, an original writer and a strange character, was the son of a recruiting-officer. Consequently the family was constantly on the move. All his life Borrow remained a restless man, contemptuous of security. As a boy he had a passion for languages and could speak a dozen by the time he was 18, including Romany, the gypsy language. Having failed to make his way as a writer in London he took to the roads, and for 7 years wandered through Europe, Russia, and the Far East, sometimes alone, and sometimes in company with the gypsies. While in Spain, he worked for the British and Foreign Bible Society, and one of his first books, *The Bible in Spain*, is a magnificent account of his adventures in that wild country. His most famous books, *Lavengro* and its sequel *The Romany Rye*, are unique in quality; both are traveller's tales rather than novels, and the robust, rambling narrative is full of curious conversations with wayfarers and gypsies. Many of the experiences related are romanticized accounts of Borrow's own adventures, and many of the characters reflect the solitary dignity of his own nature.

In 1840 Borrow married; as he grew older, he travelled less and spent more of his time on his wife's estate near Lowestoft. He died there on 26 July 1881.

See also Vol. I: GYPSIES.

BOSWELL, James (1740–95), Biographer of Johnson, *see* JOHNSON.

See also Vol. XII: BIOGRAPHY; DIARIES.

BOTTICELLI, Sandro (*c.* 1445–1510). The Italian painter Alessandro Filipepi is always

Anderson

PALLAS ATHENE RESTRAINING A CENTAUR
Painting by Botticelli. Pitti Palace, Florence

known as 'Botticelli' ('little tub'), which was a nickname given to his elder brother, with whom he lived.

Botticelli spent all his life in Florence, except for a visit to Rome in 1481–2 as one of the artists called in to paint the walls of the Sistine Chapel in the VATICAN (q.v. Vol. XII). He is said to have been a pupil of Fra Filippo Lippi, whose style has much in common with Botticelli's, though the latter is perhaps the greater artist.

In the 15th century Lorenzo de MEDICI (q.v.) gathered at his Court in Florence many of the great scholars and artists of the RENAISSANCE (q.v. Vol. I). Botticelli worked for Lorenzo, painting some portraits and many religious pictures and frescoes, including the 'Adoration of the Magi' (*see* p. 305). But his most interesting paintings are the scenes illustrating Greek and Roman legends and contemporary poems with a classical setting.

Among his best-known pictures are the 'Primavera' or 'Spring' and the 'Birth of Venus'. His 'Pallas Athene restraining a Centaur' is smaller but equally characteristic in the effect of charm and lightness, which he achieved by drawing graceful outlines to the figures and their draperies, by the rhythm of their movements, and by the delicacy of his details. The subject, too, is typical; it is an allegory showing the goddess Pallas Athene (symbolizing Wisdom) restraining a centaur (symbolizing Violence). Both the characters, which are taken from classical legends, and the idea, which is a moral one, would have been popular at the court of Lorenzo, for which the picture was painted.

In his later years Botticelli fell under the influence of the monk SAVONAROLA (q.v.), who preached against the irreligious life of the Medici Court. When Savonarola called on the Florentines to burn their 'vanities' Botticelli allowed some of his paintings to be burnt. During the last 10 years of his life he hardly painted at all.

See also Vol. XII: FLORENTINE PAINTING.

BOYLE, Robert (1627–91). The Hon. Robert Boyle, a pioneer of British science and founder of modern chemistry, lived in a brilliant period of scientific history, during which the Royal Society was founded and Isaac NEWTON (q.v.) was at the height of his powers.

Boyle, whose father, the Earl of Cork, was a remarkable man, left school at the age of 11 to

Ashmolean Museum

ROBERT BOYLE, WITH A MODEL OF HIS AIR-PUMP
Boyle devised this air-pump for his experiments with low pressures. From a contemporary engraving

go with a tutor on the grand tour of Europe. He lived in Switzerland and Italy till he was 17, and then settled, first in Devonshire, later in Oxford, till he was 40. After that he lived in London. He was tall and slender, and never enjoyed very good health. He never married, was deeply religious, had great charm of manner, and was a brilliant talker who was welcomed everywhere.

Before Boyle's day almost nothing was known of the modern theory of chemistry (*see* CHEMISTRY, HISTORY OF, Vol. VII). There was a vague idea that by trial and error one metal might eventually be made into another, and there were theories that MATTER (q.v. Vol. III) could be resolved into simple units or elements. Newton, the greatest genius of physics, did many experiments in chemistry but with little result. Boyle first studied chemistry for its own sake and not as an aid to something else; he realized that progress could come only from honest experimental work. He greatly improved much of the apparatus in use in his time. He was the first man to distinguish between a mixture and a compound (*see* CHEMISTRY, Vol. III), and to give a clear definition of an element as something which could not be changed by chemical means into anything simpler. Although his list of elements was small compared with that known within 100 years' time, it destroyed the old belief that such things as earth, air, fire, and water were basic elements. He prepared phosphorus and came near to concluding that its glow was due to its combining with something in the air. He prepared hydrogen gas but confused it with air. He knew about ACIDS and ALKALIS (qq.v. Vol. VII) and their effects upon such colouring matters as litmus.

In physics he proved by experiment that a gas confined in a vessel becomes proportionately smaller in volume as the PRESSURE (q.v. Vol. III) upon it is increased. This is now known as Boyle's Law. He investigated the expansive nature of water when it froze. He was the first in Britain to make a sealed-in mercury thermometer, and with its help to note that blood in human beings was unexpectedly warm and, except in illness, always of the same degree of temperature.

See also Vol. III: CHEMISTRY; MATTER; PRESSURE.
See also Vol. VII: CHEMISTRY, HISTORY OF.

BRAHMS, Johannes (1833–97). The German composer Brahms was born in Hamburg, the son of a double-bass player, who gave him his first music lessons. As a youth, while he was studying music, he used to play the piano in a sailors' tavern and dancing saloon. A meeting with the violinist Joachim in 1853 led to introductions to LISZT and SCHUMANN (qq.v), and to a close friendship with Schumann and his wife, Clara. After several concert-tours he settled permanently in Vienna in 1864. Hitherto he had composed chiefly piano music (including the D minor Concerto), songs, and chamber-music. In 1866, after the death of his mother, he wrote the 'German Requiem', but the first of his four famous symphonies was not heard until 1876. Apart from summer holidays in the Austrian countryside or in Italy, Brahms rarely left Vienna, where he was half-unwillingly regarded as the champion of musical tradition against the innovators of the 'New German' school—such as Liszt and WAGNER (q.v.). He never married, and won the reputation of being a difficult, somewhat bearish bachelor, though his life-long devotion to Clara Schumann and his many inimitable love-songs show his tender heart. His outwardly uneventful life was wholly devoted to music, which he never ceased composing until a few months before his death at the age of 64.

As a musician, Brahms was conscious, at times overwhelmingly, of the great tradition of which he was the last representative. It was the shadow of Beethoven, the symphonist, which kept him for so long from attempting a symphony of his own, and throughout his songs and chamber music—the most perfect examples of his art—there are many echoes of the past. Some of his most beautiful songs are re-creations of German folk-songs, and his greatest piano music consists of variations on themes by HANDEL (q.v.) and Paganini, while his piano style was deeply influenced by that of Schumann. It is not true to say that Brahms was unoriginal; his mature style in every sort of music is profoundly personal, and the tender, tuneful moments of his symphonies, when he forgets the past and allows his music to sing, and the quiet, lyrical, short piano-pieces called Intermezzos, are like no other music. Though not an enemy of novelty he lacked sympathy for the many new ideas which flooded the music of his day, an unhappy condition which finds an echo in the wistful, autumnal atmosphere of much of his work. His lack of religious faith, other than a somewhat half-hearted stoicism, gives his 'German Requiem' and *Song of Destiny* a certain mood of unchanging

CARICATURE OF BRAHMS
In the original silhouette the hedgehog was red, in allusion to Brahms's favourite restaurant, 'The Red Hedgehog'. It is also, perhaps, a reference to Brahms's rather prickly character. From Karl Geiringer, *Brahms* (George Allen & Unwin, Ltd.)

gloom, but his lyrical inspiration and the perfection of his craftsmanship assure him a high place among composers.

See also Vol. XII: Song, History of; Chamber Music.

BRAMANTE, Donato (*c.* 1444–1514). This Italian architect was one of the great artists of the 15th century, who brought Renaissance Art (q.v. Vol. XII) to its highest and most logical expression. He came from Urbino but moved to Milan, where he came in contact with Leonardo da Vinci (q.v.). Amongst Bramante's work in Milan is the bulk of the church of S. Maria delle Grazie, in which Leonardo painted his 'Last Supper'.

The last 15 years of his life, the most important in his career, Bramante spent in Rome. Pope Julius II commissioned him to rebuild St. Peter's and the Vatican (qq.v. Vol. XII), but he did not finish either. St. Peter's, indeed, was hardly more than begun; at the time of his death only the four great arches designed to support the dome were finished. Hardly any further progress was made until Michelangelo (q.v.) some 30 years later took over and continued the cathedral on a rather different plan of his own. A much smaller building—the Tempietto in the courtyard of a church in Rome—gives a better idea of Bramante's work. The symmetrical plan and the forms inspired by ancient Roman temples (though not exactly like any of them) express the Renaissance striving for the ideal of classical perfection.

Bramante's character seems to have been extremely forceful and unscrupulous, and he was probably largely responsible for setting up his kinsman Raphael (q.v.) in Rome in opposition to Michelangelo.

See also Vol. XII: Italian Art.

BRIDGES, Robert Seymour (1844–1930). The English poet, Bridges, was born at Walmer near Deal. His family had lived in Thanet for generations and were rich landowners. As a boy at Eton he was good at games, extremely intelligent, enjoyed music and poetry, and was deeply interested in religion. At Oxford, he rowed for his college and read Classics; he made many friends, including Gerard Manley Hopkins, and his interests turned more and more towards the arts. It was probably the sudden death of a beloved younger brother that caused him to take up medicine, not as a career, but rather as a

Anderson

THE TEMPIETTO: DESIGNED BY BRAMANTE

This stands in the courtyard of San Pietro Montorio, Rome

useful means of studying human nature. He entered St. Bartholomew's Hospital, London, and took his M.B. in 1874. During this time he felt increasingly drawn towards poetry, and in 1873 he published a small book of poems. 'I went to the seaside for 2 weeks and wrote it there', he said. Bridges's best lyrics are full of the sea and the wind—his childhood at Walmer had influenced him profoundly.

In 1882, after a serious illness, Bridges retired from his medical work. He married soon after, and for the next 20 years lived at Yattendon in Berkshire, where much of his work was written. Finally he removed to Boars Hill, near Oxford, where he lived till his death.

Bridges was greatly interested in the study of language and metre. His work was brilliant in technique, a kind of poetry that appealed to an intelligent, select audience, and when in 1913 he was made Poet Laureate, in spite of public clamour for Kipling (q.v.), few people had read his work. As he grew older his work seemed always to improve both in its crystal clarity of utterance and its rhythmical subtlety, and in the year before his death his masterpiece, a philosophic poem called the *Testament of Beauty*, was published—on his 85th birthday. This poem, together with many of his perfectly wrought lyrics, assured Bridges's place in literature. But he has another curious claim to fame, for after G. M. Hopkins's death in 1889, Bridges took charge of Hopkins's manuscripts. Believing that his friend's poetry was too revolutionary in technique to gain acceptance at that time he withheld the poems from publication (with the exception of single poems occasionally inserted in anthologies) until 1918. There is much difference of opinion as to whether he did right or not; but that Hopkins had a profound influence on future poets is indisputable.

BRIGHT, John (1811–89), *see* COBDEN.

BRONTË, Charlotte (1816–55) and **Emily** (1818–48). The Brontë family is famous because two of its members, Charlotte and Emily, were very great writers. But all the Brontës were extraordinary. There were six of them, five girls and one boy, Branwell, the children of the Reverend Patrick Brontë, and they spent their lives in his parish at Haworth in the wild moorland country of Yorkshire. Their childhood was grim. They were poor, they were delicate with a tendency to consumption, and their mother died when they were small. The elder girls were first sent to a harsh school at Cowan Bridge which Charlotte afterwards described in her first book, *Jane Eyre*. Shortly afterwards the two eldest died. Branwell and the three girls, Charlotte, Emily, and Anne, were brought up by an aunt, an old servant, and their alarming and eccentric father. They were intellectually very precocious children, and occupied themselves in writing long chronicles about two imaginary countries called Gondal and Angria. For want of enough paper they learned to do this in an extraordinarily minute handwriting. Later Charlotte went to a better and happier school at Roe Head.

When they grew up, the girls, in order to make a living, took up teaching, sometimes in schools and sometimes in private families as governesses. Anne was fairly successful; but Charlotte and Emily were both very unhappy. Indeed, Emily, who made herself ill with homesickness whenever she went away, soon gave it

ANNE, EMILY, AND CHARLOTTE BRONTË

Painting by their brother Branwell, *c.* 1835. Originally there was a head, probably Branwell's, between Emily and Charlotte.

up and came home. In 1842 they thought they would start a school of their own, and Charlotte and Emily, in order to be fully qualified for this, went to Brussels to study French in a school run by M. and Mme Héger. As usual Emily was too homesick to stay, but Charlotte remained on and off for over a year. She was devoted to Héger, but she found teaching his pupils English a depressing task. Feeling sad and lonely, she also returned home.

The sisters gave up the idea of the school and took to writing instead. Their first book, *Poems by Currer, Ellis, and Acton Bell* (they kept their real initials though not their own names) was scarcely noticed, though it contained some magnificent lyrics by Emily. But Charlotte's first novel, *Jane Eyre*, which appeared in 1847, had a tremendous success. In it memories of her own life and the outpourings of her passionate nature were combined with a thrilling and dramatic story. *Agnes Grey* by Anne and *Wuthering Heights* by Emily were published in 1848; but though *Wuthering Heights* is one of the greatest of English novels, neither attracted any attention at first.

Meanwhile one dreadful thing after another began to happen to the Brontë family. Branwell, though clever, was a boy of weak character. He could not keep a job, was always in trouble, and ultimately took to drugs and drink, to the great distress of his sisters, who loved him and hoped much of him. All the family's spare money went to pay his debts. He died in 1848 from consumption, to be followed shortly afterwards by Emily, and by Anne in the next year. Charlotte was left alone to look after her father at Haworth. Her next book, *Shirley*, a tale of the Industrial Revolution and the troubles and riots it brought about among the working people of the North, appeared in 1849. She visited London, where she received much appreciation and encouragement, and her last novel, *Villette*, which is founded on her experiences in Brussels, came out in 1853. In 1854 she married her father's curate, the Reverend A. B. Nicholls, but died a year later. An early story, *The Professor*, was published after her death.

Even if they had not been famous writers the Brontës would have been remarkable as people. Their genius and their strange upbringing in such a remote place made them unlike other people—wild, fiery, their heads full of strange poetic dreams, but with stern ideas of right and wrong and acutely aware of how tragic human life can be. The two greatest, Charlotte and Emily, alike in these characteristics, were otherwise different from each other. Charlotte was more normal and understandable. Small and plain, she had a pathetic love of the fuller life from which she was cut off; she was interested in other human beings whom she liked or disliked violently; and she longed passionately, at first to see more of the world, and later to live an ordinary, peaceful, homely existence. Almost the last thing she said before she died was, 'Must I die just when I was beginning to be happy!' Emily's was a stronger and stranger personality. Tall and striking-looking, she was happiest alone with her dog, roaming over the moorland. She had from time to time an intense mystical sense of the presence of some divine spirit. She fought against her last illness, would not see a doctor, and got up and came downstairs on the very day she died. Anne was more like Charlotte, but quieter, gentler, and without the same genius.

Their books are like them and very unlike the books of other authors. Contemporary with Dickens, Thackeray, and the other great Victorian novelists, they yet have little in common with them. Not that they are difficult to read. On the contrary, both Charlotte and Emily were born story-tellers whose novels, full of odd, strangely marked characters and surprising dramatic incidents steeped in their own atmosphere, can be read for the plots alone. But they are much more than thrilling tales: they express intenser feelings and suggest deeper meanings. Charlotte's tell the story of her heart. Her heroines are always in love; and she portrays this love with intense reality, showing it in conflict with the heroine's idea of right and wrong and with the disasters brought upon her by chance and circumstance. Sometimes the plot is unlikely, but Charlotte tells it so vividly and with such conviction that generally she persuades us it is true. Emily's was a much grander, more mysterious genius. It appears most concentrated in the best of her poems, such as *Remembrance* or *Last Lines*. She displays her powers at their fullest in her single novel, *Wuthering Heights*—one of the most extraordinary books ever written. It is a wild, savage chronicle of vengeance and passion and ghosts in a remote farm in the Yorkshire Dales; but the spirit in which Emily Brontë describes it makes the result beautiful, with a haunted, storm-swept beauty. The farmhouse of *Wuthering Heights* becomes a symbol for the universe where spiritual forces—good and bad, glorious and terrible—clash together, only to be reconciled in the end in a serene harmony. *Wuthering Heights* has more in common with one of the great tragedies of Shakespeare than with the ordinary novel.

See also Vol. XII: NOVEL.

BROWN, John (1800–59). Brown was a fanatical supporter of the movement to abolish SLAVERY (q.v. Vol. X) in America. There was a strain of madness in his family, and Brown himself, who had tried his hand unsuccessfully at surveying, sheep-farming, and other jobs, was convinced that he had a divine mission to free the Negroes who were employed as slaves in the Southern States of America. With a few followers, including several of his twenty children, he murdered slave-owners in Kansas and Missouri, and helped the slaves to escape into Canada. Brown then devised a wild plan for invading all the slave States, and for setting up a new State in the mountains of Virginia, where the freed Negroes could find refuge. In 1859, he picked on Harper's Ferry, in west Virginia, as his base of operations, and led about twenty armed men in a raid on the town. He captured the arsenal, but was soon overwhelmed and sentenced to death.

Brown's frantic career made the Southern States even more anxious to break away from the Union, for they feared that Brown was supported by powerful abolitionists in the North who might soon take office. When the AMERICAN CIVIL WAR (q.v. Vol. X) broke out, Brown had become a popular hero in the North, and one of the best-known marching songs of the Northern armies was 'John Brown's body lies a mould'ring in the grave, but his soul goes marching on'.

BROWN, Lancelot (1716–83). This English landscape gardener designed the grounds of many great houses throughout the country, the most famous being those of the Duke of Marlborough at Blenheim Palace in Oxfordshire. He was better known as 'Capability' Brown because of his habit of referring to the capabilities he saw in the grounds he had to redesign. He was celebrated as a 'natural' gardener because his landscape layouts looked as if they had grown up naturally, with their winding paths, lakes, and clumps of trees, all of which were, in fact, carefully arranged and planted.

His gardens and parks were designed to give a picturesque view from the house as far as the eye could reach, and at the same time, by the use of sunk fences or 'ha-has', to make it appear as though the natural landscape came right up to the house. Later, when the trees were fully grown, people forgot that the landscape had been once artificially planned by Brown.

Brown was appointed Royal Gardener in 1764, and some of his work may still be seen in Kew Gardens, on the side nearest the river.

See also Vol. VI: GARDENING, HISTORY OF.
See also Vol. XII: LANDSCAPE ART.

BROWNING, Robert (1812–89) and **Elizabeth Barrett** (1806–61). Almost everybody today knows of the romantic courtship and marriage of Robert Browning and Elizabeth Barrett, but (apart from poems such as *The Pied Piper of Hamelin*, *How They Brought the Good News from Ghent to Aix*, and *The Last Ride Together*) few people are familiar with their poetry.

Robert Browning was born in Camberwell, then a suburb of London. His father was an official in the Bank of England and his mother was the daughter of a German ship-owner who had settled in England. Robert had little orthodox schooling, his real education coming from his parents and from his own reading. His mother encouraged in him a love of music, and his father, who loved literature and painting and had a gift for ingenious versifying, passed on these enthusiasms to his son. In his father's library Robert discovered a delight in books and out-of-the-way learning. He became an ardent admirer of the Elizabethan dramatists and of the works of BYRON, SHELLEY, and KEATS (qq.v.). He was one of Shelley's earliest disciples and was much influenced by him.

When he was 20, Browning published anonymously a long poem, *Pauline*. Then he travelled mostly in Russia and Italy for a year or two, and in 1835 published *Paracelsus*, a dramatic poem based on the life of the medieval astrologer and alchemist. This was a highly significant event in his career: whereas *Pauline*, in its command of language and skilful examination of a young poet's feelings, was a work of great promise, *Paracelsus* was a definite achievement which gained him the notice of such literary men as Wordsworth, Dickens, and Carlyle. After this dramatic poem, Browning, urged by his friend William Macready the actor, tried drama proper: *Strafford* was produced at Drury Lane Theatre in 1837, though not with great success. *Sordello*, one of Browning's most difficult poems, appeared in 1840, but left most readers mystified. While gathering material for *Sordello* in Italy, Browning also got the idea for *Pippa Passes*, a dramatic poem in which Pippa, a young working girl on her annual holiday, goes through the town singing; her songs as she passes are heard by various people at a critical moment in their lives, and awaken their better feelings, altering their actions.

When Browning first met Elizabeth Barrett, in 1846, she was already a poet and scholar of established reputation, and he was still almost unknown. He, however, had a private income and was not dependent on earning money by writing. Elizabeth was the eldest child of a family of eleven, a brilliant and precocious girl. The family was living near the Malvern Hills when Elizabeth, aged 15, injured her spine while saddling her pony. She had never been strong and after this accident she was treated by her father—quite wrongly as later events

National Portrait Gallery
ROBERT BROWNING IN 1858
Painting by Michele Gordigiani

proved—as an incurable invalid. When she was 22, her mother died and the family settled in London. Lying most of the time on her back in her room, she studied and wrote, at first mostly translations and imitations, but in 1838 she published her first truly individual work, *The Seraphim and other Poems*, and a few years later her two volumes of *Poems*.

She was living with her family at 50 Wimpole Street, London, when she got to know Robert Browning, at first through correspondence. Her father, whose love for his children was very possessive, forbade them to marry, and Robert's courtship of Elizabeth in the summer of 1846 and their marriage in the following autumn had to be kept secret. After their elopement Elizabeth never again returned home, and was never reconciled to her father. The marriage was a very happy one. Elizabeth's feelings for her husband are passionately expressed in *Sonnets from the Portuguese* (1850)—original poems describing her own love-story. Accompanied by Elizabeth's maid and her dog Flush, the couple went to Italy, Elizabeth's real home for the rest of her life. In Italy she continued writing poetry, and *Aurora Leigh*, a modern novel in verse, was published in 1856.

After her death in Florence, Robert returned to England and became a renowned figure in society and in literary circles. During this period he wrote some of the finest poems of his career, including *Dramatis Personae* and the mighty narrative called *The Ring and the Book*. Towards the end of his life he began to travel again, and at the age of 77 died in Venice.

Robert Browning rebelled against the excessively graceful and melodious poetic manner of his time, which he felt was incapable of expressing what he had to say. He evolved a style which is tough, lively, and close to the rhythms of the spoken word. But Browning's poetry is sometimes very difficult: in his intellectual excitement he leaps from one island of thought to another without providing the bridges that would enable the reader to follow him. His intense interest in the oddities of human nature finds expression in his dramatic lyrics and monologues—poems energetically and vividly conceived, in which unusual characters in unusual situations speak their thoughts. Thus in *My Last Duchess* a husband explains why he has murdered his wife, and in *Fra Lippo Lippi* a monk excuses his human frailties and his delight in art.

Elizabeth's poems are now less interesting than her husband's because they are more conventional in style. In choice of subject, however, she showed great courage: her *Cry of the Children* is a brave protest against the inhuman conditions in which little children were employed (*see* CHILD WELFARE, Vol. X); she also criticized Negro slavery and was always sympathetic to the cause of people unjustly treated.

BRUCE, Robert (1274–1329). Robert I of Scotland, the hero of the Scottish war of liberation from the English, belonged to an illustrious Scottish family descended from Robert de Bruis, a Norman knight who had come to England with William the Conqueror. Robert Bruce was inspired in his struggle against the English by the example of the great leader, William WALLACE (q.v.), with whom he fought until Wallace's capture and death in 1305.

At this period Scottish fortunes seemed to be at their lowest; not only did the English under Edward I completely dominate the country, but Scotland was divided into two parties, the followers of Bruce and those of Baliol (led by John Comyn). In a quarrel between these two rivals, John Comyn was killed, and Bruce then

Kunsthistorisches Museum, Vienna

A PEASANT WEDDING FEAST. PAINTING BY BRUEGHEL

claimed the Scottish throne and was crowned in 1306 at Scone. For a time he met with nothing but disaster, fighting both the English and his fellow countrymen, and he was driven farther into the Highlands and even out of Scotland. It is to this period in his career that the well-known story of the spider belongs, and, indeed, Bruce's valiant and persistent struggle against failure can be well compared to the spider's struggle to climb to her web. At last this brilliant leader succeeded in rallying the Scots and driving the English slowly farther south and almost out of Scotland, until only Berwick and four castles, among them Stirling, remained in English hands. In 1314 Edward II brought a mighty army of some 10,000 men to relieve Stirling, and Bruce with his much smaller army of some 3,000 routed the English at the Battle of Bannockburn.

The war continued for another 14 years, the Scots invading northern England and inflicting further defeats on the English armies. At last Edward III signed the Treaty of Northampton, renouncing finally any claim whatsoever to Scotland. The war had lasted altogether 32 years, the Scots fighting losing battles most of the time against overwhelming odds. They fought, however, under two great leaders, Wallace and Bruce, and, as their Parliament declared in 1320, 'not for glory, not for wealth, nor honours, but for freedom only, which no good man surrenders but with his life'.

See also Vol. I: Scots.

BRUEGHEL, Peter (*c.* 1525–69). This Flemish painter, usually known as 'Peasant' Brueghel, was probably born in a village of that name near Antwerp. He is said to have studied under a painter called Pieter Koecks van Alost, whose daughter he later married. He was enrolled a member of the Antwerp guild of painters, and travelled in France and Italy, visiting Rome and Naples.

On Breughel's return he worked for an Antwerp publisher, one of his tasks being to redraw for engraving the compositions of the Dutch painter Bosch (*c.* 1460–1518), whose strange pictures, often with a moral or satirical meaning, combining symbolism and nightmare fancy, had a considerable influence on Brueghel.

Almost all Brueghel's paintings were made during the last 10 years of his short life. In the earlier ones, such as the 'Proverbs' and 'Children's Games', he drew his themes from folklore. These pictures teem with an inexhaustible variety of little figures; there seemed no end to the artist's powers of invention. Later, from the time that Brueghel moved from Antwerp to Brussels, the pictures became more monumental in composition, with larger and fewer figures. Brueghel's humorous and yet matter-of-fact vision of reality is most fully expressed in his pictures of peasant weddings and merrymakings.

As a landscape painter Brueghel made important innovations. The landscapes of other Flemish painters of the time are idyllic rather than realistic, but Brueghel evoked the actual mood of a place at a particular time of day and season of the year.

His two sons, Pieter and Jan, were also painters: Pieter imitated the style of his father, but in a more gruesome manner (hence his nickname 'Hell'); while Jan, known as 'Velvet', painted fantastic landscapes with animals and flowers, in which he developed a more individual style.

See also Vol. XII: FLEMISH PAINTING.

BRUNEL, Isambard (1806–59), Engineer, *see* Vol. IV: STEAMSHIPS, HISTORY OF; BRIDGES, RAILWAY.

BRUNELLESCHI, Filippo (1377–1446). This Italian architect, in association with his friend the sculptor DONATELLO (q.v.), was the most important pioneer of RENAISSANCE ART. He is said to have been the inventor of linear PERSPECTIVE (qq.v. Vol. XII), by which artists could give an appearance of reality and depth.

Brunelleschi had first been trained in Florence as a sculptor but afterwards turned to architecture. He thought that Gothic buildings lacked the correct proportions to be seen in the buildings of ancient Rome. He therefore went to Rome and made many careful measurements and drawings of buildings there. On his return to Florence he designed churches, such as San Lorenzo and Santo Spirito, with columns and other details based on classic examples. The effect of Brunelleschi's buildings, though inspired by his Roman studies, was entirely his own, for he was applying Roman principles to purposes which did not exist in the ancient world.

Brunelleschi's most famous work was the

Anderson

INTERIOR OF SAN LORENZO, FLORENCE, DESIGNED BY BRUNELLESCHI

building of the gigantic dome of Florence Cathedral. This had been designed a century before, but the scale was so great that no one had dared to undertake it. Brunelleschi's task in this case was therefore that of engineer rather than of designer.

The new style was developed by other artists of the Renaissance, and formed the basis of European architecture until modern times.

See also Vol. XII: ITALIAN ART.

BRUTUS (85–42 B.C.), *see* JULIUS CAESAR.

BUDDHA (*c.* 6th century B.C.), *see* GAUTAMA.

BUNYAN, John (1628–88). The author of the *Pilgrim's Progress* was born at Elstow in Bedfordshire, the son of a poor tinker. He lived during the troubled times which covered most of the reign of Charles I, the Civil War, the Commonwealth, the reign of Charles II, and most of James II's reign. Bunyan had very little education; at 16 he was drafted into the Parliamentary army and served under the Puritan knight whom

Samuel Butler ridiculed as Sir Hudibras. Bunyan always delighted to describe military scenes in his books, and such characters as Greatheart are drawn from memory. One incident impressed him profoundly: a companion who took his place for him in a fight was killed, and Bunyan ever afterwards felt that he had been specially preserved by Providence. At 19 he was released from military service, and shortly after married a poor but very pious girl. Even as a child Bunyan had been haunted by religious terrors, and now he was oppressed by a terrible sense of sin. So far as we know, his worst vices were a love of dancing on the village green, bell-ringing, and an almost irresistible desire to blaspheme on holy occasions. But he believed himself damned, and suffered great agony of spirit which he described in a book called *Grace Abounding to the Chief of Sinners*. He finally found comparative peace by joining a strict Nonconformist congregation in Bedford. The pastor of this congregation, John Gifford, is thought to be the original for Evangelist in *Pilgrim's Progress*, the man who showed Christian the way to the wicket-gate.

In 1655 Bunyan's wife died, leaving him with four young children, to one of whom, a blind little girl, he was particularly devoted. About 3 years later he married again. As Bunyan's gift for preaching became recognized, he was sent to minister to various congregations in the villages around Bedford, until, after the Restoration in 1660, Nonconformists such as Bunyan were forbidden to preach. Bunyan refused to obey and was put in prison, where he remained for 12 years. His imprisonment, though severe at times, was not always what we should understand by imprisonment; for he was allowed to conduct services in prison, where there were others guilty of no other offence than their religious opinions, and sometimes he was even allowed to go out and minister to congregations in chapels and in the woods. He taught himself to make laces and sold them at the prison door in order to help support his family. In 1672, when he was 44, a general pardon for such offenders as Bunyan brought about his release. He soon became famous both as a preacher and a writer, but 3 years later he was again arrested and this time imprisoned for 6 months. It was during this second imprisonment that he wrote the first part of *Pilgrim's Progress*.

The *Pilgrim's Progress* 'from this world to that which is to come' is one of the best-known books in the world, and has been translated into 108 languages and dialects. It is an allegory which takes the form of a dream experienced by the author. Its language is the vigorous simple English of everyday speech, enriched by the language of the Bible, which Bunyan continually quotes and alludes to with astonishing skill. It presents us with a gallery of human portraits. *Pilgrim's Progress* was an immediate success, 100,000 copies being sold during Bunyan's lifetime, and it had a great influence in other countries as well as in England.

In 1680 Bunyan wrote the *Life and Death of Mr. Badman*, picturing a progress from bad to worse, and in 1682 *The Holy War*. He writes as an evangelical with an acute consciousness of sin together with the serenity which comes from the sense of sin forgiven. But he is free from the harshness and narrowness of view which sometimes accompany these feelings, and everywhere displays a loving sympathy and concern for his fellow men.

See also Vol. XII: Pilgrim's Progress.

BURGHLEY, Lord (William Cecil) (1520–98), *see* Cecil Family.

BURKE, Edmund (1729–97). Burke was not only a statesman and orator but also the author of notable writings on political philosophy, such as *Thoughts on the Cause of the Present Discontents* and *Reflections on the Revolution in France*. He played an important part in establishing the idea that the British Commonwealth (q.v. Vol. X) should act as trustee for the development of its backward peoples. He stoutly defended the British system of party government (*see* Political Parties, Vol. X), defining a political party as 'a body of men united for promoting by their joint endeavours the national interest upon some particular principle in which they are all agreed'.

The son of an Irish solicitor, he was educated at Trinity College, Dublin. He came to London to study law at the Middle Temple, but soon turned to writing, especially on political philosophy, and was the originator of the famous record of events, the *Annual Register*. He also joined the literary circle of Samuel Johnson, Goldsmith, and others (qq.v.).

He entered politics at the age of 36 and became private secretary to the Whig Prime Minister, Lord Rockingham. When Rockingham's Ministry fell, Burke remained active in party affairs, his eloquence and political knowledge being of great value to his party. He defended the right of the Middlesex electors to return John WILKES to Parliament, and drafted pamphlets against GEORGE III's attempts (qq.v.) to gain control of Parliament by ruling through a powerful group of friends at Court. From the beginning Burke supported the American colonists in their quarrel with Britain (*see* AMERICAN WAR OF INDEPENDENCE, Vol. X); he made great speeches on American taxation and on conciliation with the colonies, urging the British Government to adopt a more liberal policy towards them. 'The question with me is not whether you have a right to render your people miserable but whether it is not your interest to make them happy.' Had the government listened to Burke, the war might have been averted.

In 1774 Burke, as member for Bristol, went against the wishes of his electors in supporting Free Trade with Ireland and a more tolerant attitude towards Catholics, and consequently lost his seat. He opposed the movements for parliamentary reform, urging instead certain economies such as the abolition of unnecessary government offices. When the Whigs were returned to power in 1782, Burke was made Paymaster of the Forces; but the government fell a year later, and Burke never again held office.

In 1788 Burke opened the trial of Warren HASTINGS (q.v.), the Governor-General of India, with a passionate speech about the shame of treating a great country like India only as a source of income. Two years later his most famous work, *Reflections on the Revolution in France*, appeared. This anticipated with horror the bloodshed of the FRENCH REVOLUTION (q.v. Vol. X) and pleaded for the preservation of the old social order, an attitude which caused him to break with the Whigs, who at first welcomed the Revolution, and to join the Tory party under PITT (q.v.). His speeches and writings on the Revolution won him his greatest reputation; but he later became so frenzied in his denunciation of France that he spoke and acted in an exaggerated way, on one occasion throwing a dagger on the floor of the House in an attempt to awaken Britain to her danger.

Burke's desertion to the Tories weakened the Whig party for many years, just as he had earlier

EDMUND BURKE
Caricature published in 1782

strengthened it by giving it a philosophy. He was intensely patriotic and, unlike most 18th-century statesmen, religious and imaginative in his approach to politics. His speeches were magnificently eloquent but too long and not well delivered: his contemporaries called him 'the dinner-gong'. His greatest achievement was to present an idea of the State as a stable, divinely ordered institution which is yet capable of growth and change; and to awaken the conscience of the English about their colonies.

See also PITT; FOX, CHARLES JAMES.
See also Vol. X: BRITISH COMMONWEALTH.

BURNS, Robert (1759–96). Burns, the national poet of Scotland, was born at Alloway, in Ayrshire, on 25 January—a date still celebrated by Scotsmen His family were small tenant farmers from the north-eastern county of Kincardine, and Burns spent his early life in the Ayrshire countryside and, as he grew up, in the lively tavern company of Ayrshire's little market towns: Maybole, Ayr, Irvine, and Tarbolton. Brought up on the sound Scottish system of village education, he read widely—both in contemporary English authors of the sentimental school and in the Scottish poets, Allan Ramsay and Robert Fergusson, whose verses preserved the tradition of poetry in broad Scots, the vernacular which was still alive in the mouths of the people among whom Burns spent his boyhood.

Burns's strong passions, his retentive musical memory and gift for words, and his vigorous, unforced gaiety made him a leading spirit among the young people. His early poems, which were circulated through Ayrshire in manuscript long before they were printed, reflect a round of gaiety, love-affairs, and conflict with Calvinist authority. Many of them are satires at the expense of the respectably conventional—'the unco guid'—like 'Holy Willy' (a church elder) and 'Dr. Hornbrook' (the village grocer-druggist). Others, also in the Ayrshire dialect, reflect Burns's love of his native countryside.

In 1784 Burns's father died, and he became a tenant farmer in his own right at Mossgiel, near Mauchline. But his farming did not prosper, and 2 years later he was considering emigration. It was partly to raise the passage money that he arranged for the publication of his first book,

Scottish National Portrait Gallery
ROBERT BURNS
Painting by Alexander Nasmyth, *c.* 1827

Poems chiefly in the Scottish dialect, which appeared in Kilmarnock in 1786. Its success encouraged him to give up the idea of leaving Scotland and to go instead to Edinburgh, then at the height of its glory as an intellectual centre.

Burns was now committed to poetry, especially to the lyric poetry in which he has never been excelled. But he did not expect to live by it. After 2 years in Edinburgh, during which he gained some footing in upper-class society, he again took up farming, this time at Dumfries, combining it with a post he had been given in the Excise. He had married one of his early loves, Jean Armour, whose father had earlier forbidden their marriage because of Burns's reputation. A growing family, with a higher standard of living, drew him into debt. His openly expressed admiration for the FRENCH REVOLUTION (q.v. Vol. X) in its early phase did not go well with the holding of a government post, and he had to retract to save himself from dismissal. But although troubled by shortage of money, and also by bouts of depression and illness, these last 8 years of his life were the most fruitful of all. During these years he contributed much to two collections of Scottish poems from which come the most famous of his more than 300 songs, many of which are now known throughout the English-speaking world. Among the best-loved are *Scots Wha Hae, Auld Lang Syne, My Luve's like a red, red rose,* and *Ye Banks and Braes o' Bonnie Doon. Tam o' Shanter*, his most successful long poem (except *The Jolly Beggars* which belongs to his Ayrshire youth), was also written at this time. When only 37, his health already undermined by hard living, he died of rheumatic fever at Dumfries, and was buried there.

Burns did naturally what Wordsworth and the romantic poets later did deliberately (*see* ROMANTIC MOVEMENT, Vol. XII). He could write in educated English when he chose, but his genius found its true expression in the words and rhythms of the broad Scots which was his native speech. Writing for the most part in a dialect which only a few million people can read without a glossary, he became the Scottish national poet, and on him, deliberately or not, other national poets modelled themselves. His aim, like that of the German song-writers who followed him, was to fix in writing the sung and spoken tradition of the people in whom it still lived, and return it to them, when they had lost

THE EMPEROR AKBAR ENTERTAINED BY HIS FOSTER-BROTHER AT
DIPALPUR, PUNJAB, IN 1571

Illustration to the *Akbarnama* (Annals of Akbar)

that tradition, as living literature. This required not mere zest for collection, but the genius for fusing words with music, and the profound sympathy for the simple, which enabled Burns to transmute humble human experience into great poetry.

See also Vol. XII: LYRIC POETRY.

BURTON, **Sir Richard** (1821–90). Burton and his companion J. H. Speke, both officers in the Indian Army, are famous for their exploration in search of the source of the river NILE (q.v. Vol. III) in Central Africa.

Burton was a handsome, reckless adventurer with an extraordinary gift for languages: by the end of his life he had mastered thirty-five. His passion for adventure led him when he was 32 to go on a Moslem pilgrimage disguised as an Indian Pathan, an exploit which he describes in his book *Pilgrimage to El Medinah and Mecca*. In 1854 he and Speke were sent to explore the unknown and wild regions of Somaliland, which they did with such success that they were commissioned by the Royal Geographical Society to explore the equatorial lakes of Africa and the headwaters of the Nile. After discovering Lake Tanganyika, Burton fell ill, and Speke alone discovered Lake Victoria and convinced himself that here was the source of the Nile. He made a further expedition in 1860 to prove his discovery, and was about to defend his case against Burton's doubts at a British Association meeting when he was killed in a shooting accident.

Burton spent the rest of his life as British Consul in Brazil, Syria, West Africa, and elsewhere, travelling and exploring as the opportunity arose. He was knighted in 1886 and died 4 years later at Trieste. He published a great many books, the best known being his translation of the ARABIAN NIGHTS (q.v. Vol. XII).

See also Vol. III: NILE.

BUTLER, **Samuel** (1835–1902). This writer and scholar, the son of a clergyman and the grandson of a bishop (who was also headmaster of Shrewsbury), was educated at Shrewsbury and Cambridge. He angered his father, with whom he was never on good terms, by refusing to become a clergyman, and so he emigrated to New Zealand in 1859. There he settled in Canterbury. His letters and articles written there were published in 1863 as *A First Year in the Canterbury Settlement*. In 5 years he had made enough money raising sheep to enable him to return to London. He published *Erehwon* in 1872, a satire on the society of his time disguised as the story of an imaginary country (Erehwon is 'nowhere' spelt backwards) in which disease is a crime and crime a disease.

Butler wrote a number of other books including some original scientific works. His most famous book is *The Way of All Flesh*, an ironic story based on Butler's own unhappy experience of the tyranny and hypocrisy of Victorian family life at its worst. His ideas were advanced in their own time, and his original but perverse genius—seen perhaps at its best in *The Notebooks of Samuel Butler*—has influenced many writers, including Bernard SHAW (q.v.).

BYRD, **William** (1543–1623), English Composer, *see* Vol. XII: SONGS (Section 2).

BYRON, **George Gordon** (**Baron**). (1788–1824). More than any other poet Lord Byron has been identified with his own heroes—with Childe Harold, the romantic traveller; with Manfred, the outcast from society; with Don Juan, the cynical, heartless lover. Although Byron used his own life as the material for much of his poetry, it is by no means purely autobiographical. It is, however, in his long poems that Byron's genius most truly resides rather than in the lyrics which usually represent him in selections.

Byron was born into an aristocratic family of doubtful reputation. His father died of drink and debauchery when Byron was 3, and when he was 10 his great-uncle—the 'wicked' Lord Byron—also died. Byron inherited the title, a vast house called Newstead Abbey, and estates already mortgaged or in decay.

Byron's father, by his first marriage, had a daughter, Augusta, Byron's half-sister. His father's second wife, Byron's own mother, was a proud, irascible, Calvinistic Scotswoman named Catherine Gordon of Gight. He was born with a malformed foot—a disability which tortured him with self-consciousness in his youth. He went to Harrow and to Trinity College, Cambridge, where, amongst other eccentricities, he kept a bear. While an undergraduate he published his first book of poems, *Hours of Idleness*. The adverse criticism it deservedly got stung Byron not to despair but to revenge, and he replied with a satire in the manner of POPE

National Portrait Gallery
BYRON IN GREEK DRESS
Painting by Thomas Phillips (1770–1845)

(q.v.) called *English Bards and Scotch Reviewers*. After Cambridge, Byron went on the grand tour of Europe, traditional for men of his education; but owing to the Napoleonic Wars, his route took him, not overland, as was usual, by way of Paris to Rome, but by sea to Lisbon, Spain, and the Mediterranean. For nearly 2 years he wandered about Greece and the Aegean Islands. This was the shaping time of his imagination.

When he was 23 his mother died, and he came home, an extremely handsome young man, to install himself boisterously at Newstead Abbey. He entered London society and spoke in the House of Lords. It was now that he showed his friend, R. C. Dallas, a new satire, *Hints from Horace*. Dallas, secretly not much impressed, asked if he had anything else; Byron quite casually said that he had 'a lot of Spenserian stanzas'. Dallas read them with astonishment and delight, showed them to Murray the

publisher, and on 20 February 1812 the first two cantos of *Childe Harold* were published. They took the town by storm. Byron became famous overnight. He could not now write fast enough, and in the next 4 years appeared a series of romantic poems, the best among them being *The Corsair* and *The Bride of Abydos*. It is said that 14,000 copies of *The Corsair* were sold in a day.

Byron had always been susceptible to women and attractive to them; now that he was successful they threw themselves at his head. For 3 years he lived in the limelight, and then, quite unaccountably, married Ann Milbanke, a frigid, correct, intellectual woman, entirely unsuited to him, but very wealthy. She bore him a daughter and left him within a year, hinting that he had an immoral relationship with his half-sister Augusta. Society turned against him, as lavish now with calumny and spite as it had been with praise and flattery. Byron would not stay to be insulted; he left England for good.

The next few years were spent mostly in Venice, where Byron established himself with a menagerie of strange animals and conducted various love-affairs. It was in Italy that his masterpiece *Don Juan* was written. This brilliant, caustic, rambling satire is written in a colloquial style which is the result of a mastery of technique. Byron, always a fluent writer, was not over-critical of his own work; but *Beppo*, *A Vision of Judgement*, and *Don Juan* more than justify his reputation as a great poet. His influence on European literature—both by what he wrote and by the general idea of the romantic figure of Childe Harold—the typical Byronic hero—was very great.

Like many poets, Byron was at heart a man of action. He loved the idea of freedom, and threw himself with intense energy into the Greek struggle for independence from Turkey. In 1823 he left Italy for Greece, but the next year, worn out with the ardours of the campaign, he caught rheumatic fever and died at Missolonghi, mourned as a national hero by the Greeks.

See also Vol. XII: ROMANTIC MOVEMENT.

C

CABOT, John (died 1498) and **Sebastian** (*c.* 1483–1557). The Genoese John Cabot and his son Sebastian were the first explorers known to have sailed from England, but we know little about them because all their logs and letters have been lost. John became a spice merchant at Venice, where he learned the difficulties of bringing the spice caravans overland from the east without their being intercepted by the Turks. So he, like Columbus (q.v.), was stirred with the desire to find a western route to Cathay (China) and the Spice Islands in the East Indies.

Cabot tried in vain to persuade the King of Spain to support his exploration as he had supported Columbus. He then settled at Bristol and managed to persuade Henry VII to allow him to sail from that port in 1497 in the ship *Matthew*. Cabot wanted to discover any territory not yet appropriated by the Spanish and Portuguese, who were trying to divide the world between them. He sailed westwards and discovered Newfoundland and Nova Scotia, which he believed to be 'the country of the Grand Khan' (the Chinese Empire); and for this Henry gave him £10 on his return. Indeed, it is probable that Cabot actually reached the mainland of America before Columbus did. In 1498 Cabot sailed again, but nothing definite is known of this voyage beyond the discovery of the Newfoundland Banks where, Cabot said, 'the sea is swarming with fish which can be taken not only with the net, but in buckets let down with a stone'.

It is not known if his son Sebastian went on these voyages; but after his father's death he certainly commanded an expedition in 1509 in search of a North-West Passage to Asia, after it had been realized that America was a new continent. He sailed north-west as far as the entrance of Hudson Bay about 100 years before Hudson (q.v.) did, then returned south along the American coast as far as what is now called Chesapeake Bay. Later explorers took up the search for the North-West Passage (*see* Exploration, Vol. IV), but the British claim to North America is founded on the voyages of the Cabots. As Henry VIII took no interest in exploration, Sebastian served under the King of Spain for a period, but returned to England in 1548 after having been imprisoned for failing to find a South-West Passage through the river Plate. In England, Sebastian Cabot was venerated as 'a good old man', famous for his skill as a map-maker and navigator. He became Governor of the 'Company of Merchant Adventurers for the Discovery of Regions unknown' (*see* Chartered Companies, Vol. VII); and inspired the attempt of Willoughby and Chancellor in 1553 to find a North-East Passage, which resulted in the foundation of the Muscovy Company and trade with Russia.

See also Columbus; Cartier; Hudson.
See also Vol. IV: Exploration.

CADBURY, George (1839–1922). Cadbury was an outstanding example of the best type of 19th-century business man, who concerned himself not only with successful business but also with the social welfare of his employees. Cadbury came of a Devonshire Quaker family, and he inherited the family characteristics of enterprise and integrity in business, and simplicity in personal life.

When he was only 21, George and his elder brother Richard took over the cocoa and chocolate manufacturing business which their father had founded in Birmingham 20 years earlier, and which after a prosperous beginning was in difficulties. They set to work to put it on its feet again, and by working long hours and denying themselves any relaxation, and by introducing improvements in methods of working and in the quality of their goods, they made the business show a profit in about 5 years.

In 1879 they set up a new factory about 4½ miles outside Birmingham at a place they called Bournville. This move enabled George Cadbury to carry out some social experiments which he had long had in mind. He had for some time been teaching nearly every Sunday in a Men's Early Morning School, a practice he continued for 50 years. These schools, before the days of

AERIAL VIEW OF THE FACTORY AND HOUSES AT BOURNVILLE

The houses in the foreground, built by George Cadbury about 1900, form a contrast to the straight rows in the background which were built about the same time by speculative builders

compulsory free education, set out to teach men to read and write, to give them some simple religious ideas, and to stress the advantages of thrift and other good social habits. In this way Cadbury got to know hundreds of working men, and to understand the difficulty of living a decent life in the cramped and squalid dwellings of Birmingham's slums, amidst drunkenness, dirt, and cruelty. Cadbury felt the absurdity of preaching the advantages of soberness, cleanliness, and other Christian virtues in such conditions; it would be better to give people the chance to live decent lives.

In the country at Bournville, therefore, Cadbury started to build good, cheap houses, with plenty of space for light and air, and gardens to occupy men's time and interest. Instead of providing houses for his workpeople only, he sought to attract people of differing incomes, social habits, and experience, so that a balanced community might grow up. He saw that if his experiment was to be an example to others, he must show that it paid its way. He sought no

profit, but used the money that was made by letting and selling houses to enlarge and improve the property and to help people elsewhere who wished to start similar schemes.

The Bournville Village Trust, which owns the estate, now controls over 1,100 acres of land at Bournville itself, on which there are some 3,000 houses, and also much other property, including land for public open spaces and farm-land which helps to make a 'green belt' round the city and stops houses and factories spreading out into the country-side. The Bournville experiment has had a great influence on the development of TOWN AND COUNTRY PLANNING (q.v. Vol. X).

Cadbury and his sons and grandsons also concerned themselves with developing schemes for improving conditions of work in the factory— conditions which are taken for granted now, but which 70 years ago were remarkable innovations. The Cadburys introduced the system of payment in proportion to work done (piece-work); they gave weekly half-holidays and occasional days off long before these became a regular thing in industry; they allowed the younger workers time off to go to night school.

From these small beginnings grew a network of schemes, many of which have been adopted by industry generally and some of which are now enforced by law. These included methods for training apprentices, and for general education for young people; old-age pensions and children's allowances; medical services; encouragement of sports, games, and physical training; and the cultivation of arts and crafts.

Perhaps the most important feature of the Bournville factories is that all those employed—whether ordinary labourers or highly skilled craftsmen, newly joined juniors or the heads of large departments—take a share in organizing and administering these schemes and contributing to the cost. This helps to give the sense of responsibility for the common welfare which is a mark of the good citizen.

See also Vol. X: GARDEN CITIES AND NEW TOWNS.

CALVIN, John (1509–64). This important leader of the REFORMATION (q.v. Vol. I) was born at Noyon in France, and educated at Paris. His early interests were not religious, for he studied law and moved among scholarly men who thought freely and critically on all subjects. About 1533, however, he experienced what he describes as a 'sudden conversion', and from that time he dedicated his life to religion. In Germany LUTHER (q.v.) was preaching reform. In France Francis I was taking repressive measures against the French Protestants or HUGUENOTS (q.v. Vol. I), and this roused Calvin, when only 26 years old, to write his *Institutes*, a reasoned statement and defence of Protestant teaching, with a preface addressed to Francis I. This remarkable book already contained in outline all the essentials of Calvinism. In 1536 Calvin went to Geneva, where he was invited to carry into effect his ecclesiastical ideas, and to make Geneva an example of an ideal Christian city. At first the city rebelled against the severity of his discipline, and he was expelled; but he was recalled later, and although he met with some opposition, he became the virtual ruler of Geneva till his death. His plan was to give the Church such authority that it could regulate the morals and religion of all citizens.

He was a stern and unyielding disciplinarian, but never self-seeking. Simple in his habits, direct and truthful in speech, and a loyal friend, he was yet fanatical enough to instigate the trial and martyrdom of a religious opponent. His great contribution was to bring order into both the doctrine and organization of Protestantism. He taught Predestination—that men are chosen by God for salvation or damnation apart from their own efforts or merits. His influence, which

A 17TH-CENTURY VIEW OF GENEVA

The elephant of war is a symbol of the strength of Calvinism. Bédier et Hazard, *Littérature française* (Larousse)

was widespread, especially in the Netherlands, Scotland, and among the Puritans of England, is described in the article CALVINIST in Vol. I.

See also Vol. I: CALVINIST; REFORMATION.

CANNING, George (1770–1827). Canning began his political career as a disciple of the younger PITT (q.v.). When he was 37, at a critical period of the NAPOLEONIC WARS (q.v. Vol. X), he became Foreign Secretary. Pursuing a shrewd, vigorous policy, he unhesitatingly seized the neutral Danish fleet at Copenhagen to thwart Napoleon's ambitions in the Baltic, and when Spain flared into revolt against the French he promptly sent an army under WELLINGTON (q.v.) to her help. But after 2 years he quarrelled with the Secretary of State for War, Castlereagh, and retired from office.

Castlereagh later became Foreign Secretary and handled the critical peace negotiations at the end of the Napoleonic Wars. But in 1822, just as Canning was about to depart to India as Governor-General, Castlereagh committed suicide, and Canning again became Foreign Secretary. In this second period of office Canning brought to an end the European Congress system (*see* METTERNICH), thus freeing Britain from alliances: 'every nation for itself and God for us all', he declared. He also recognized the independence of the South American republics which had revolted from Spain (*see* BOLÍVAR).

In 1827 Canning became Prime Minister and set up a National government composed of moderate Tories and Whigs; but he died before he had time to achieve anything. He was a great wit and brilliant orator.

CARLYLE, Thomas (1795–1881). This great Scottish historian and essayist was born in Dumfriesshire, of working-class parents belonging to a strict CALVINIST sect (q.v. Vol. I). Calvinist severity and the grinding poverty of early industrial Scotland formed the background of his boyhood. He went to the village school, and then to Edinburgh University, which he entered (walking the 100 miles from his home) when he was 14. He gave up his original idea of going into the Church and tried teaching, studying in turn mathematics and law; but finding satisfaction in neither, turned, at 23, to a literary life, and for more than 12 years picked up a living by private teaching and journalism.

In 1826 he married Jane Welsh, a woman of great wit and charm, whose feelings for Carlyle were probably more those of admiration than love. They settled first at Edinburgh, then in Dumfriesshire, where Carlyle, though still obscure, entered into a friendly and admiring correspondence with Goethe, who was then an old man. Carlyle was deeply attracted by the ideas of both GOETHE and SCHILLER (qq.v.), and the fusion of German romanticism with his biblical upbringing had a lasting influence both on his character and on his literary style. In 1831 Carlyle finished his first, and in many ways his most readable book, *Sartor Resartus*, based on his own early life. It attracted little notice when published as a serial in England, but in America it made EMERSON (q.v.) Carlyle's admirer.

In 1834 the Carlyles, who had no children, moved to London and settled in Cheyne Walk, Chelsea, where they lived for the rest of their lives. Both were morbidly sensitive, and Carlyle, unable to bear noise, built a sound-proof room, with no windows but a skylight, to keep out household noise and the sound of 'demon fowls' next door. Soon Carlyle and his wife—one of the most notable letter-writers and conversationalists of her time—came to form part of the radical literary circle which included Leigh HUNT, MAZZINI, and John Stuart MILL (qq.v.). On one terrible occasion Mill's servant accidentally used the manuscript of the first part of Carlyle's *French Revolution* to light the fire—a disaster destroying 5 months' work which could be repeated only with the greatest difficulty. When it was published in 1837, the *French Revolution* made Carlyle famous; he became one of the literary 'giants', who counted in Victorian society as much for what they were as for what they wrote. He gave crowded lectures, including those later published as *On Heroes and Hero-Worship*, and among his admirers were DICKENS, RUSKIN, and Robert BROWNING (qq.v.), on the last of whom his influence is obvious.

After his excellent edition of Cromwell's *Letters and Speeches* (1845), Carlyle started on his final great work, the *Life of Frederick the Great*, which took him 13 years to write. He became an almost legendary figure for profundity and learning; but he suffered increasing ill health and personal unhappiness, caused by the strain between himself and his wife, and by her death which took place very soon after *Frederick* was finished. Soon after Carlyle's own death, J. A.

Glasgow Art Gallery and Museum
THOMAS CARLYLE
Portrait by J. A. McN. Whistler, 1874

Froude, the historian, a close friend of his old age, published Carlyle's papers and a biography of him. He described Carlyle as an embittered curmudgeon who treated the world, and in particular his brilliant wife, with churlish prejudice—a picture too near the truth ever to be completely effaced. Yet Carlyle, with his ruthless hatred of cant ('gigmanity' as he called it), his independence, and his extraordinary power over words, was well fitted to be the self-appointed conscience of Victorianism.

As an historian he tried to convey impressions rather than to give accounts. His *French Revolution* recreates for us the spectacle of a national convulsion. The style is too rhetorical and exaggerated to be a good model, but it did demolish the elegant and artificial prose style of his predecessors, and turned writers back on the search for personal expression in prose.

Carlyle has been seen as an intellectual forerunner of fascism (*see* TOTALITARIANISM, Vol. X). His contempt for middle-class materialism (which he shared with MARX), his sarcastic intolerance, and his admiration of force are strains which can be found in the theories of NIETZSCHE and others and in the practice of HITLER and MUSSOLINI (qq.v.). But we might

also say that his passion for individual utterance was the beginning of a movement towards greater individual freedom and a willingness to break away from conventions. Among his 'Heroes' he included not only NAPOLEON and CROMWELL, but DANTE, SHAKESPEARE, J. J. ROUSSEAU, and Robert BURNS (qq.v.).

See also Vol. XII: HISTORIES.

CARNEGIE, Andrew (1835–1919). This self-made multi-millionaire, an outstanding example of the initiative and enterprise of 19th-century industrialists, is now best remembered for the vast sums of money he gave to benefit the public, especially by founding libraries. He was the son of a poor weaver of Dunfermline, Scotland. During the depression of the 'hungry forties' his father, a CHARTIST (q.v. Vol. X), emigrated with his family to Pennsylvania, U.S.A., where Andrew started work at the age of 13 in a cotton factory, and worked for 12 hours a day for about 5*s.* a week. At 18 he became a railway clerk and telegraph operator.

Railways were then rapidly developing in North America, and anyone who could invest in business connected with railways was fairly sure to make money. Carnegie laid the foundations of his fortune by investing about £100 in a railway company with money borrowed by a mortgage on the family cottage. In the meantime he won promotion from his employers, and at 24 was head of an important department of the railway. The AMERICAN CIVIL WAR (q.v. Vol. X) broke out in 1861, and Carnegie, noticing that the price of iron rose steeply as the war went on, set up companies to make rails, locomotives, and iron bridges, with the financial assistance of friends who trusted him. All these ventures prospered, and Carnegie made enough money to take shares in the first oil-drilling companies in Pennsylvania and Ohio.

After the Civil War, Carnegie, on a visit to England, became convinced that the new steel-making process invented by Henry Bessemer would revolutionize the IRON AND STEEL INDUSTRY (q.v. Vol. VIII). Therefore, on his return to the U.S.A., he opened steelworks to operate on the Bessemer process. By the time he was 46 he was the foremost iron-master in the country and more than a millionaire in dollars, and by the end of the century he was one of the wealthiest men in the world. He had a genius for choosing the right people to work for him, and his considerate treatment of all his staff resulted in his getting the best work from them.

By that time Carnegie was tired of accumulating money, and had become more interested in plans for spending it. In 1900 he published a book called *The Gospel of Wealth*, the theme of which was that 'the man who dies rich dies disgraced'. Acting on his own advice, he sold the Carnegie Steel Company to the United States Steel Corporation, and received £60 million in cash and stock as his personal share. He then retired from business and devoted the rest of his life to using the money for the public good. He first set aside $4 million as an accident and pension fund for the workers who had helped to build up his fortune, and $1 million for libraries in and around Pittsburg, Pennsylvania, the great steel-making city which his activities had largely created.

Carnegie, remembering how much of his own education he owed to a library provided by a benevolent American, concentrated most of his interest on the establishment of LIBRARIES (q.v. Vol. IV). Few towns had public libraries in those days, and most of those that did exist were intended for the poorest and least-educated people and had been given, and were sometimes maintained, by charitable private persons or organizations. Carnegie, as far back as 1879, had offered his first library to his native town of Dunfermline, providing the building and the books on condition that the borough council provided the land and paid for maintenance— for Carnegie had more faith in schemes of self-help than in pure charity.

Between 1882 and his death he spent $60 million in establishing libraries, principally in the English-speaking countries. In the British Isles alone 660 libraries owe their original foundation to Carnegie's generosity. He also made large grants to the Scottish Universities Fund, to the Carnegie Institute in Washington, U.S.A., and to the 'Hero Funds' to provide pensions for people killed or injured in the service of others. He endowed his home town with baths and a technical college, as well as a library, and settled on it a trust fund of £750,000 'to bring into the lives of the toiling masses of Dunfermline more sweetness and light'. Many other charities and public works benefited from his gifts.

In his later life he spent much time on an estate he bought in Sutherlandshire. As an honour from his native country he was installed as Lord Rector of St. Andrews and Aberdeen Universities. When he died, he left only enough money to keep his wife and daughter in comfort. The rest, altogether some $300 million, he had given away.

See also Vol. IV: LIBRARIES, Section 2.

CARROLL, Lewis (1832–98). The author of *Alice's Adventures in Wonderland* was a distinguished university mathematician whose real name was Charles Lutwidge Dodgson. He was educated at Rugby and Christ Church, Oxford, and became Lecturer in Mathematics at that college.

Carroll was a shy, retiring man but fond of children. It was to amuse a little girl, Alice Liddell, daughter of the Dean of Christ Church, that he wrote *Alice's Adventures in Wonderland*, published in 1865, with pictures by Tenniel; *Through the Looking Glass and What Alice Found There* followed in 1872. They are among the first children's books to be written from a child's point of view: no moralizing spoils the ruthless energy of the story. Alice always remains a completely matter-of-fact human being, and, on its own fantastic level, the story makes sense. The strange humour, the brilliantly inconsequent happenings, the superb nonsense of the poems, are enjoyed by grown people as well as children.

Carroll was also the author of the weird nonsense poem called *The Hunting of the Snark*

British Museum

ALICE'S ADVENTURES IN WONDERLAND

Dance of the Mock Turtle and the Gryphon. Drawing by Lewis Carroll from the original manuscript, called *Alice's Adventures Under Ground*

and a charming children's story called *Sylvie and Bruno*.

See also Vol. XII: CHILDREN'S BOOKS; COMIC VERSE, Section 3.

CARTIER, Jacques (1491–1557) was the first notable French explorer and the discoverer of Canada. He was a citizen of St. Malo, a town in Brittany renowned for its daring pirates and for the deep-sea fishermen who went to the New-foundland Banks every summer after CABOT (q.v.) had discovered the cod-fisheries there.

In 1534 the French King, Francis I, commissioned Cartier to undertake a voyage of exploration to the New World, hoping to acquire for France a kingdom as fabulously rich as Mexico or Peru, which had fallen to his enemy, Spain. Cartier, already an experienced navigator, made a swift passage to the Gulf of the ST. LAWRENCE (q.v. Vol. III). Hoping, perhaps, to discover a North-West passage to Asia, he sailed all round the enormous Gulf from the icy Strait of Belle Isle to the warm and fertile Prince Edward Island, 300 miles to the south. At Cape Gaspé, among friendly Indians, he set up a huge cross inscribed *Vive le Roy de France*, and he then anchored north of Anticosti Island, where the strong current told him that he was at the mouth of a great river. But it was now late summer, and he turned back for France, taking two Indians with him. In the following year the King, encouraged by Cartier's reports, commissioned another expedition. Cartier had learned from the Indians that the country was divided into three 'kingdoms'—Saguenay, Canada, and Hochelaga. Cartier decided to sail up the St. Lawrence to the chief village of Canada, Stadacona (now QUEBEC). Then, against the advice of their chief, Donnacona, he set off for the kingdom of Saguenay, pushing on up-river to Hochelaga, a village on an island near a commanding height which he named Mount Royal, or MONTREAL (qq.v. Vol. III). Above Hochelaga, however, the Lachine rapids blocked his way, and he had to return to Stadacona. In the spring, after a hard winter, he took Donnacona with him and returned to France.

Donnacona told the King fantastic stories of the fabulous wealth of Saguenay, and so he commissioned in 1541 a third expedition, with Cartier as navigator, to establish a permanent French colony. Although Cartier was not re-

MAP OF NORTH AMERICA MADE IN 1553, SOON AFTER CARTIER'S DISCOVERY OF CANADA

The map is drawn with North at the bottom. Bédier et Hazard, *Littérature française* (Larousse)

sponsible for the colonists, he drew up a remarkably practical and far-seeing plan for colonization. After endless delays, Cartier was ordered to go ahead with five ships, not waiting for the colonists. It was late in the season, and after spending a fruitless time at Montreal, he left again for France, only to meet the colonists on their way out. In France, disillusion awaited him, for the gold and diamonds which he had brought back proved to be only iron pyrites and mica. By 1543 the whole colonial venture had collapsed, and it was not till 65 years later that Champlain founded Quebec and began to build New France in the country that Cartier had discovered.

After the failure of his last expedition, Cartier retired to St. Malo where he lived, honoured as a great explorer. Besides great physical vigour, Cartier had a remarkably clear mind and the rare faculty of accurate observation; his records and maps are outstanding for their exactitude.

See also Vol. I: CANADIANS.
See also Vol. IV: EXPLORATION.

CARUSO, Enrico (1873–1921). This great Italian tenor, to many people the greatest singer of the present century, was born in Naples, and first sang in opera there. He sprang to fame at the age of 29 after a season at Monte Carlo, and was soon engaged by Covent Garden, London, and the Metropolitan Opera House, New York, where he often appeared. He was only 48 when he died.

Caruso's voice was rich and mellow and powerful, with ringing loud and melting soft top notes and an unusually warm, baritone-like lower register. His only fault as a singer was a habit of breaking the vocal line with sobs, to represent emotion, an ugly trick which many singers have copied. He was a natural comedian, and eventually learned to be a convincing though never great serious actor. Off the stage he was a warm-hearted generous man, as popular with other singers as with his public. He sang French and Italian heroic and lyric operatic roles, but not German ones. He was one of the first great singers to record for the gramophone, and his records are models of fine singing, prized by collectors.

See also Vol. IX: SINGING.

By gracious permission of H.M. the Queen

CATHERINE THE GREAT
Painting by Michail Schibanoff

CATHERINE THE GREAT (1729–96). Catherine, the daughter of a Prussian general, became Empress Catherine II of Russia. As the result of successful diplomatic intrigue by Prussia, she married in 1745 the Grand Duke Peter, the heir to the Russian Empress Elizabeth, daughter of PETER THE GREAT (q.v.). Peter, a weak-witted booby, had also been brought up in Germany and was openly contemptuous of everything Russian. Catherine soon quarrelled with him and, being shrewd and far-sighted, saw how his attitude gave offence to the proud Russians; therefore she deliberately set out to ingratiate herself by becoming more Russian than the Russians. The Empress was suspicious of her and would let her take no part in public life, so Catherine established a group of intimate friends and spent her time reading the books of the most advanced French political philosophers of the day.

When the Empress Elizabeth died in 1762 and Peter became Tsar, he immediately began to Prussianize everything about the Court, including the uniforms and drill of the guard regiments. Even at the moment of victory in the Seven Years War he made Russia change from the Austrian to the Prussian side. The Russian nobility were furious, and as they never hesitated to dethrone a ruler who displeased them, and as Catherine had endeared herself to them, they mutinied and declared her Empress. Peter was murdered a few days later.

Catherine almost certainly would have liked to have carried out in Russia the political doctrines of the philosophers she had studied and to have improved the conditions of the great mass of Russian serfs, who were entirely at the mercy of their owners. But she could do nothing displeasing to the nobles to whom she owed her throne, and in fact her reign is notorious for the extension of serfdom throughout Russia.

In her foreign policy also Catherine followed the will of the ruling class and pursued an aggressive policy. With the help of the great General SUVAROV (q.v.), she added vast areas of Turkish and Polish land to Russia, carrying Russia's frontiers to the Black Sea and to the borders of Germany. It is for this extension of Russian territory that she carries the title 'Great'.

See also PETER THE GREAT; ALEXANDER II.
See also Vol. I: RUSSIANS.

CAVOUR, Count Camillo Benso de (1810–61). At the beginning of the 19th century Italy consisted of half-a-dozen weak States and several minor territories, divided by jealousy and dominated by their fear of Austria. Three famous names are associated with the liberation and uniting of Italy—those of Cavour, MAZZINI, and GARIBALDI (qq.v.). Their names became known throughout the world, although their methods differed and their policies were sometimes violently opposed. Mazzini was an idealist who preached a united nation without any compromise. Garibaldi was a soldier who tried to win his way by the sword. Cavour was the responsible practical statesman and diplomat, the secret bargainer, who seized opportunities as they occurred. As Prime Minister of the King of Sardinia, he brought almost all the peninsula under one rule—that of his master, as King of Italy.

Cavour was born of a noble family in Piedmont, in north-west Italy. He became an army officer, as young noblemen often did, but soon resigned because his political views were too advanced. For nearly 20 years he lived as a private gentleman, farming, studying, and travelling in England and France. In these countries he formed friendships with many distinguished liberal thinkers and economists, including John Stuart MILL and Richard COBDEN (qq.v.).

In the 1840's he turned again to politics. In many European countries there was a revolutionary ferment against oppressive government of various kinds. The echoes of the FRENCH REVOLUTION (q.v. Vol. X) being still in men's ears, and the example of the British Parliament before their eyes, they began to demand government by DEMOCRACY (q.v. Vol. X). In Italy this revolutionary spirit was mixed with a new national feeling. A few far-seeing men in the various States began to think of themselves as members of an Italian nation. Some of the divisions in Italy were long-standing; others had been made by the powerful governments which met at the Congress of Vienna in 1815 to ensure that Europe remained under strict control after the disorders of the NAPOLEONIC WARS (q.v. Vol. X). The position was that two Italian northern States, Lombardy and Venetia, were under the rule of the powerful Austrian Empire, and the rulers of some other small States were Austrian princes. Southern Italy and the Island of Sicily were ruled by the King of Naples, who was of Spanish descent. The central belt of Italy, including the city of Rome, was ruled by the Pope, who had his own army. The only ruling family of genuine Italian blood in all Italy was the King of Sardinia, who also ruled Cavour's homeland, Piedmont. Mazzini and his 'Young Italy' society were preaching national unity and liberty, and great changes were due.

In 1846 a new Pope granted some political reforms in the Papal States. Other rulers were bound to follow the Pope's example; amongst them was the King of Sardinia who removed the censorship on the Piedmontese Press. Cavour then started a newspaper *Il Risorgimento* ('The Resurrection'), a name which was for years the battle-cry of Italian freedom.

Then, in 1848, the revolutionary movements in Italy, as in other countries, came to a head. In Lombardy the people of Milan rose against their Austrian rulers, and the King of Sardinia marched across the border to help them. After a few Italian successes the Austrians recovered, beat off the Sardinian army, and stayed masters of Lombardy. The other rulers of Italy now felt that they could safely withdraw the reforms they had unwillingly granted, and proceeded to do so, led by the Pope. For the moment the revolutionaries were defeated, although for some months Rome held out under a republican government which had turned out the Pope.

After 1848 a new King of Sardinia, Victor Emmanuel II, made Cavour a Minister, and later Prime Minister, and he immediately began to carry out reforms. He caused Sardinia to join in the Crimean War, and so, at the peace conference, he was able to bring before the nations the question of Austrian rule in north Italy. He began bargaining with the French Emperor, Napoleon III, offering to give Savoy and Nice (then Sardinian) to France on condition that French armies would help Sardinia against Austria. Cavour then organized Sardinian armies in so provocative a way as to force the Austrians to attack in 1859. This gave the French an excuse to intervene; and the Austrians were driven out of Lombardy. The French Emperor refused to complete Cavour's aim by driving the Austrians from Venetia also, although he helped Cavour to bully some small Italian States to merge with Sardinia.

In the following year, with Cavour's secret knowledge, Garibaldi led a sudden and successful campaign against Sicily and Naples. Cavour then used his efficient Sardinian army to seize central Italy from the Pope, leaving him only the actual city of Rome. This left the King of Sardinia, Victor Emmanúel, in command of the whole of Italy except Venetia, and the kingdom of Italy was immediately proclaimed. Cavour's work was done, and he died soon after, worn out.

But Cavour's policy left one enduring division in Italy. Southerners could not forget that unity was brought about entirely from the north—by a Sardinian King, a Piedmontese Minister, and French armed support; in a sense, the south was conquered rather than united with Italy.

See also GARIBALDI; MAZZINI.
See also Vol. I: ITALIANS.

CAXTON, William (*c.* 1422–91). The first English printer was born in Kent, became apprenticed to a London silk merchant, and later went to Bruges. There he prospered and became governor of the English MERCHANT ADVENTURERS (q.v. Vol. VII) in the Low Countries. He also learnt something of the new craft of printing, which had recently been invented in Germany. About 1474, when attached to the household of Margaret, Duchess of Burgundy and sister of Edward IV of England, he com-

CAXTON'S TRADE MARK

Meade Collection

pleted his translation of a popular French romance, *The Recuyell of the Historyes of Troye*, and on a printing-press which he set up in Bruges he printed some copies. Next he printed a book on chess. Then, in 1476–7, he returned to England and set up a press at Westminster. Due to his own hard work and the patronage of wealthy men, his output both as printer and translator was enormous. His works included Chaucer's *Canterbury Tales*, Malory's *Morte d'Arthur*, and translations from the classics. The books were printed in Gothic lettering similar to that used on manuscripts; they had no title-pages and little punctuation. Copies still exist of about one-third of Caxton's works. When he died his pupil, Wynkyn de Worde, carried on the Press.

See also Vol. IV: PRINTING, HISTORY OF.

CECIL FAMILY. Many members of the Cecil family have played a prominent part in public affairs since the time of Henry VII, in whose reign David Cecil, of Stamford in Lincolnshire, became mayor of that town, and later received royal favours at Court.

David's grandson William was the first member of the family to become famous. William Cecil (1520–98) (known to history by his later title of Lord Burghley) went to Henry VIII's court as a rich young man, his father having been given Church estates at the Reformation. At 30, Cecil's abilities as an organizer were so great that he was made Secretary of State or chief Minister to Edward VI. When Queen Mary succeeded, Cecil conformed to Catholicism, and under Queen Elizabeth he became a Protestant. Elizabeth made him Secretary of State, and later created him Lord Burghley and appointed him Lord High Treasurer. For 40 years he was Queen ELIZABETH's (q.v.) principal adviser, the most powerful and ablest of her Ministers. His astute and cautious policies did more than anything else to make her reign glorious. His methods were sometimes questionable: he kept an army of spies and informers—his detective police whom he used without scruple, especially in his fight against Roman Catholic plots. But his purpose was for the glory of England. Elizabeth valued him truly and felt his death, some 5 years before her own, very deeply. She showed her displeasure to him only once—after the execution of MARY, QUEEN OF SCOTS (q.v.), when she wanted to avoid responsibility for an act which she had desired.

WILLIAM CECIL, LORD BURGHLEY, RIDING ON A MULE

Hanging on the tree is his coat of arms, surrounded by the Garter

Burghley married twice, and founded two distinct lines of Cecils. By his first wife he was father of Thomas, later first Earl of Exeter; and by his second wife he was father of Robert, later first Earl of Salisbury. In course of time both families were raised from the rank of Earl to that of Marquess, but the Exeter branch, though distinguished, has played a less prominent part in public affairs than the Salisbury branch. It was the first Lord Salisbury who built the famous

Hatfield House, which has been the seat of the Salisbury Cecils ever since, and which contains the historic State papers of Lord Burghley.

Nearly 3 centuries after Burghley, a Lord Salisbury became Prime Minister under Queen Victoria. He had a long career as a Conservative leader, holding various government posts, first in the House of Commons and later, on his father's death, in the House of Lords. When the Conservative leader, DISRAELI (q.v.), died, Salisbury took his place, and in 1885 he became Prime Minister. He held this post for 14 out of the next 17 years, including the period of the SOUTH AFRICAN WAR (q.v. Vol. X). He vainly sought at one time to reform the House of Lords by introducing non-hereditary peers.

One of his sons, Lord Robert Cecil, was distinguished after the First World War for his attempts to promote international peace, and for his support of the League of Nations (*see* INTERNATIONAL CO-OPERATION, Vol. X). He was awarded the Nobel Peace Prize, and was himself created a peer as Viscount Cecil of Chelwood.

CELLINI, Benvenuto (1500–71). This Italian goldsmith, sculptor, and adventurer came from Florence, where he was originally trained as a musician. His unruly behaviour often compelled him to wander from place to place, and for a time he worked in France for King Francis I.

Kunsthistorisches Museum, Vienna

GOLD SALT-CELLAR MADE BY BENVENUTO CELLINI FOR FRANCIS I

This ceremonial salt-cellar, 13 inches across, represents the union of Earth and Sea

Like many men of the RENAISSANCE (q.v. Vol. I), he had many accomplishments and immense vitality. He was a man of action (at times a ruffian) but also a great artist. He could fight bravely as a soldier, but was always getting into trouble by fighting duels. He was immensely conceited, and it is difficult to believe more than half of what he says about himself in his *Autobiography*; nevertheless, the book is of great interest for its vivid picture of life in 16th-century Italy, and for the descriptions of artistic techniques. Although his most famous work is the large bronze statue of Perseus in Florence (of the making of which he wrote a detailed description), it **is** perhaps in the smaller pieces, such as the golden salt-cellar made for Francis I (now at Vienna), that he was at his best. In these there is a delicacy of craftsmanship and an originality of invention which no one has surpassed.

See also Vol. XII: BRONZE SCULPTURE.

CERVANTES (1547–1616). Miguel de Cervantes Saavedra, author of *Don Quixote*, was born in Spain at the university town of Alcalá, not far from Madrid. He led a hard life, but despite many misfortunes, among them poverty and imprisonment, he won a great reputation, and when he died he was mourned throughout all Spain.

Cervantes was the son of a poor apothecary, who travelled from city to city selling medicines and prescribing cures for people who could not afford a doctor. So, although Cervantes had ample opportunity for getting to know not only his country but all sorts of people (of whom many found their way into *Don Quixote*), his education was very haphazard.

At this time, PHILIP II, King of Spain (q.v.), ruled over a great Empire, and was the most powerful Catholic monarch in Europe. Many distinguished people came to his Court, among them the special envoy of the Pope, Cardinal Acquaviva, to whom Cervantes, aged 21, had the good fortune to be presented. The Cardinal, impressed by his bearing and intelligence, offered Cervantes employment in his household, and shortly afterwards took him to Italy. Nothing could have been better for a young man who had always dreamed of being a poet than a visit to the country of PETRARCH and DANTE (qq.v.). He learned Italian and enthusiastically studied Italian literature, and many of his own works reflect this period of his life.

Cervantes was not only interested in books. When the Pope called a crusade to drive the heathen Turks off the Mediterranean Sea, Cervantes enlisted as a soldier. In September 1571 the Christian fleet, under the command of Philip II's half-brother, Don John of Austria, attacked the Turks and inflicted a crushing defeat on them at Lepanto. Cervantes fought well in the battle, and was congratulated by Don John himself. But he lost the use of his left hand through a wound, and was afterwards known throughout Spain as *el manco de Lepanto*, 'the maimed man of Lepanto'.

He continued to fight against the Turks until, a few years later, his ship was captured by Moorish pirates, who took the crew to Algiers. Fortunately for him, Cervantes had in his possession some important documents, and the Moors, thinking that he was a political prisoner of great value, decided to hold him for ransom, instead of selling him into slavery or killing him out of hand. He remained a prisoner for more than 4 years, an experience which he later described in the story of the Captive, one of the most vivid episodes in *Don Quixote*. Cervantes made several daring attempts to escape, but although he succeeded in getting some of the other prisoners away, he was always recaptured himself. Many of his fellow prisoners, in daily fear of torture and death, told afterwards how Cervantes's courage and gaiety had inspired them and kept up their spirits.

When he was finally ransomed, Cervantes found himself without work. His marriage was unhappy, and he soon left home and drifted to Madrid, where he tried to carry on a literary career. In 1585 he published his first important work, a pastoral romance called *Galatea*. He wrote many plays, none of them particularly successful, and finally had to accept small and uncongenial posts as government collector of grain and other foodstuffs to supply the SPANISH ARMADA (q.v. Vol. X), and as collector of revenues for the Kingdom of Granada. He was accused of having collected more than he actually had accounted for, and was thrown into prison, where he is said to have begun *Don Quixote*.

In 1605 the first part of *Don Quixote* was published. The book was at once enormously popular; its fame spread quickly, and translations into other languages soon appeared. Consequently, Cervantes, although never prosperous, suffered no more serious misfortunes. He died

DON QUIXOTE KEEPING VIGIL BY HIS ARMOUR IN THE INN YARD

Illustration by Gustav Doré in an English edition published by Cassell, 1864–6.

10 days before his great contemporary, Shakespeare.

Don Quixote is the story of a poor gentleman of La Mancha, a man of amiable character, who has read so many of the exaggerated chivalrous romances of his day that his wits have become disordered, and he imagines himself bound to set forth as a knight-errant in search of adventure.

Dressed in rusty, old-fashioned armour, he starts out on his old horse Rosinante, attended by his faithful squire Sancho Panza, a country fellow, both simple and shrewd. The poor knight converts the most commonplace happenings into fearful and romantic situations, and in his attempts to act with chivalry becomes involved in absurd adventures, in which he always gets the worst of it. Cervantes in *Don Quixote* was not only mocking the romantic literature of his day but also the behaviour of 16th-century Spanish society. Much of the fascination and freshness of the book comes from the leisurely, discursive style and the fact that Cervantes includes anything that may occur to him.

Cervantes took 10 years to complete the second

part of *Don Quixote*, constantly putting it aside while he wrote poems, plays, and stories, which seemed to him, then, far more important. Cervantes's greatest ambition was to be a poet and to found a national drama; but it is not as a poet or dramatist that he is remembered but as the creator of Don Quixote.

The word 'quixotic', meaning impracticably idealistic, and the phrase 'tilting at windmills', meaning to fight against an imaginary difficulty, have become part of our language as a result of *Don Quixote*.

See also Vol. XII: Spanish Literature.

CÉZANNE, Paul (1839–1906). This French painter is the key figure in the development of modern painting. Like other pioneers, he was misunderstood, ridiculed, and then ignored until almost the end of his life. Yet he stubbornly continued to paint in his own way, and today his pictures have a place of honour in the principal art galleries of the world.

Cézanne was born and lived practically the whole of his life in the south of France. His father, a prosperous business man in Aix-en-Provence, allowed him to break off his legal training to study art for a few years in Paris before returning to the south to settle down. Cézanne never needed to earn his living and could afford to ignore public taste in art, which he despised.

At first Cézanne was strongly influenced by the romantic and literary genius of Delacroix; but in Paris he was won over by the realism of Courbet and Manet (qq.v.). From Impressionist Painting (q.v. Vol. XII), he learnt the value of painting directly from nature on an easel out-of-doors (as against studio painting from outdoor notes). But soon he broke away from the Impressionists and began on many years of original experimental painting.

In all he painted—landscape, portrait, still life—Cézanne sought to reveal every aspect of his subject, its solidity, its colour, its relation to other objects in space. For Cézanne the accepted treatment of perspective and light and shade was not sufficiently true to reality, nor was the traditional method of building up an imaginary composition. The Impressionists had abandoned these methods in an effort to portray the movement and colour of light on objects. Cézanne wanted to combine the structure and solidity of the old masters with the brilliance of colour and

Tate Gallery

PAUL CÉZANNE: SELF-PORTRAIT, ABOUT 1882

light in contemporary paintings. The problem was immensely difficult and Cézanne, working very slowly, was often disheartened by his failures. His work was rejected by most art galleries in his lifetime, and he became increasingly touchy and self-centred. He died bitterly resenting the hostility of his critics. Yet his real achievement was so great that his work brought about revolutionary changes in the whole outlook of artists.

See also Vol. XII: Post-impressionist Painting; Modern Art.

CHALIAPIN, Feodor Ivanovich (1873–1938). This great Russian singer was born of a peasant family. At 17, with little training but with an obviously excellent bass voice, he joined an opera company, and by 1896 was appearing in Moscow and attracting attention by his powerful acting and heavy, rather sinister voice. He was soon playing in opera houses all over the world. His most famous role was that of Boris Godunov in Mussorgsky's opera, but he appeared also as Mephistopheles in Gounod's *Faust*, as Leporello in Mozart's *Don Giovanni*, as King Philip in Verdi's *Don Carlos*, and as Don Basilio in Rossini's *Barber of Seville*—all with an effect that made operatic history.

His strength as an interpreter was in the rich variety of colours and shades that he could produce from his voice. In his Russian roles such as Boris, there seemed to be almost as much speech-voice as singing, but this in itself could be moving, as we can tell from his gramophone records. This power, together with his noble presence—he was very tall—and his mastery of acting, made him an operatic artist of outstanding greatness.

See also Vol. XII: OPERA, HISTORY OF.

CHAMBERLAIN, Joseph (1836–1914). The son of a London business man, Chamberlain was sent to Birmingham when he was 18 to join his uncle's engineering firm. He was so successful in business that he was able to retire with a large income at the age of 38 and devote the rest of his life to politics. He was Mayor of Birmingham from 1873 to 1875.

His politics changed as he grew older, but he was at first a Radical. He was elected Liberal M.P. for Birmingham in 1876; he helped to reorganize the Liberal party and joined GLADSTONE'S Government (q.v.). But disagreeing with Gladstone's policy of granting Irish Home Rule, he left the Liberal party, and later allied himself with the Conservatives as a Liberal Unionist, favouring Ireland's continued union with England (*see* POLITICAL PARTIES, Vol. X). He became Colonial Secretary in Lord Salisbury's Government of 1895. As Colonial Secretary he set up commissions of inquiry into tropical diseases and established schools of tropical medicine in London and Liverpool, in an attempt to counter Africa's reputation as 'the white man's grave'. His chief work was in developing Dominion relations so that the Empire might become a partnership of self-governing equals (*see* BRITISH COMMONWEALTH, Vol. X). The Jameson Raid of 1895, which later led to the SOUTH AFRICAN WAR (q.v. Vol. X), had made Britain unpopular among the nations of Europe; and Chamberlain believed that the countries of the Empire should unite in self-defence against possible war in Europe. When war in South Africa became unavoidable, Chamberlain's friendly Dominion policy reaped its reward; troops were sent from Australia, New Zealand, and Canada to help the British armies. Chamberlain himself went to South Africa just after the end of the war and was largely concerned in the peace settlement.

Chamberlain believed that a closely knit British Commonwealth could be based only on common economic interests, and he wanted the Dominions and Colonies to have preference over foreign nations in exporting goods to Britain. But as the Dominions mostly produced food, they could be given preference only if Britain taxed food imported from foreign countries. This policy was against the free-trade traditions of the period. So Chamberlain resigned, and devoted the rest of his political life to a campaign to convert the country to his views. For this purpose he founded the Tariff Reform League (*see* INTERNATIONAL TRADE, Vol. VII).

Both his sons rose to high office. Austen, the elder, became Chancellor of the Exchequer and later Foreign Secretary. Neville succeeded Stanley Baldwin as Prime Minister in 1937, and conducted negotiations with Hitler and Mussolini in 1938 in an attempt to prevent the outbreak of the Second World War.

CHARLEMAGNE (742–814). Charles the Great, King of the Franks, was the first really great ruler to arise among the barbarian kingdoms which had grown up in Europe on the ruins of the Roman Empire (*see* DARK AGES, Vol. I). He is rightly regarded as one of the principal founders of Western civilization. His friend and biographer, Einhard, has left us a vivid picture of Charlemagne. He was tall, with a massive round head, a long nose, brilliant eyes, fine white hair, a thick neck, and prominent stomach. A man of rude health and great appetite, he despised doctors and chafed at the fasts imposed by the Church. Riding and hunting were his outdoor recreations, but he also enjoyed music and listening to tales of the great deeds of his people. Though proud and obstinate, he was also warm-hearted and generous, deeply devoted to his family and to the friends with whom he loved to feast and talk.

Charlemagne was first and foremost a soldier, the greatest conqueror of his time; but he was also a champion of the Christian religion and set himself to convert as well as to conquer the enemies of his kingdom. When he became king, Charlemagne determined to capture Saxony, the main stronghold of German heathenism. In a long series of cruel wars he overcame the Saxons and incorporated their country, up to the river Elbe, in his own realm. He divided Saxony into bishoprics, and arranged for missionary teaching. He then conquered the barbarian kingdom of the Lombards in north Italy and made one of his sons its ruler. Next he conquered the Asiatic robber-state of the Avars in the Danube provinces, and restored Christianity there. In the south of his own kingdom, he established a fortified border district, known as a 'march', against the Saracens in Spain. In the course of 30 years of almost ceaseless warfare he thus carried the frontiers of the Frankish monarchy to the Elbe, the lower Danube, and the Mediterranean, and united Western Christendom in one great imperial State.

Charlemagne's kingdom was highly organized and well governed in accordance with Frankish ideas, its backbone being the poor freemen,

descendants of the tribesmen who had conquered the Roman Empire, whose rights Charlemagne protected and whose agriculture and commerce he encouraged. The Empire was divided into counties, each under a local count who was responsible for raising troops and for presiding in the local courts. From time to time, royal envoys, known as *Missi Dominici*, were sent round the counties to supervise the counts, to do justice, and to see that the King's dues were being collected and that his edicts were being enforced. The King being also head of the Church, his envoys had to satisfy themselves that the services were properly conducted in the monasteries and cathedrals and that the buildings were kept in good repair.

Charlemagne, though not himself a cultivated man, greatly admired culture, and he threw himself wholeheartedly into the task of restoring learning and raising the standard of education. His palace at Aix-la-Chapelle (Aachen) became the centre of a great revival of learning and art, and his palace school became the model for many lesser schools under bishops and abbots. Foreign scholars were invited to the Court, the greatest among them being an Englishman, Alcuin of York, who had been a leading figure in the great revival of learning in Northumbria which we associate with the name of the Venerable BEDE (q.v.). It was by the Northumbrians that the Franks were inspired to illuminate manuscripts, to carve in stone, to study the authors of the ancient world, and themselves to write Latin in the beautiful script known as Carolingian (*see* HANDWRITING, Vol. IV).

It was Alcuin who taught Charlemagne to think of himself as the ruler of Christendom, divinely appointed to govern the Western world in temporal matters as the Pope governed it in spiritual matters. On Christmas Day, A.D. 800, after mass had been said at St. Peter's, Rome, the Pope placed a golden crown on the head of Charlemagne, and all the people hailed him as Emperor of the Romans. This great event marked the beginning of the HOLY ROMAN EMPIRE (q.v. Vol. I) which was to last, in one form and another, for a thousand years. Though Charlemagne left no worthy successor, and his conquests fell apart after his death, the idea of a single European State under an Emperor who was ruler and guide of the people of God survived as an inspiration to the Middle Ages; and in the CHANSON DE ROLAND (q.v. Vol. XII) the

Louvre

BRONZE STATUETTE OF CHARLEMAGNE

Though this is traditionally said to be a portrait of Charlemagne, probably only the head is contemporary

poets of those times pictured Charlemagne as the Christian paladin fighting the powers of darkness.

CHARLES I (1600–49). Charles is the only English King who was tried and executed by his subjects. His father, James VI of Scotland, had succeeded his cousin ELIZABETH I (q.v.) as James I of England, thus uniting the two kingdoms, and Charles himself came to the throne in 1625.

During the first years of his reign Charles was dominated by George Villiers, Duke of Buckingham, his father's favourite and his own close friend, whose advice led Charles into many difficulties. They waged war on both Spain and France, the expeditions against both countries being costly failures. Quarrels with Parliament soon started about Charles's choice of councillors and commanders (in particular Buckingham), about taxation and other means of raising money, and about religion. The King was suspected of being pro-Roman Catholic, and inside the Church of England he favoured the High Church party at the expense of the Low Churchmen (or Puritans). The fundamental constitutional issue —who has the last word, King or Parliament?— was beginning to emerge. In 1628 Buckingham was assassinated, and Charles never again gave his full confidence to any minister or favourite. In 1629 he dissolved Parliament, and for 11 years he and his Ministers ruled without Parliament, as if attempting to prove that the King was absolute Sovereign. They resorted to unconstitutional ways of getting money by forced loans, fines, the granting of monopolies, and so on.

Charles was remarkable among the kings of his time as being a good husband and father, faithful and devoted; he was dignified, upright, and well-meaning towards his subjects, but he was unable to compromise. He believed MONARCHY (q.v. Vol. X) to be the only true form of government—a trust to the King from God, and he considered himself to be above the law and the common rules of conduct which are binding to ordinary people. The King and his people, therefore, drifted apart. Charles patronized literature and the arts, but he suppressed political and religious opposition, and thousands emigrated to New England. Charles meant to rule in the interests of all classes and to protect the poor; but the more progressive business and farming people, with their interest in moneymaking, opposed him. Religious disputes between High Church and Puritan grew more

Louvre

CHARLES I
Portrait by Van Dyck, about 1635

frequent. Charles relied increasingly on the advice of Archbishop LAUD, and Thomas Wentworth, Earl of STRAFFORD (qq.v.). Strafford, though honest, efficient, and just, was ruthless and dictatorial, and Laud, also upright and sincere, was rigid and narrow-minded.

In 1640, when Charles had to summon Parliament again in order to get supplies for subduing a religious rebellion in Scotland, the Long Parliament, led by John Pym, determined to limit the power of the throne, attacked Charles's Government. In 1641 Laud was imprisoned and Strafford, despite Charles's promises that he would protect him, was executed. The next year the Civil War broke out, in which Charles had the support of about half the nation. The Parliamentary leaders had alienated a good deal of support because they went too far in attacking the Church and the Crown. Charles lost the war, but remained unrepentant to the last, refusing to plead at his trial because he declared the trial to be illegal: a man can be tried by his peers only, and a king's only peers are other kings. He died, as he had lived, with dignity, but in his death he excited an enthusiasm which he had never aroused in his life.

CHARLES II DANCING BEFORE THE DUTCH COURT DURING HIS EXILE
Painting by Cornelis Janssen (1593–1664)

Charles's tragedy was that his character did not fit with the circumstances of his time. He misunderstood and was misunderstood. He was neither a tyrant nor a saint, but simply the wrong man in the wrong place.

See also STRAFFORD; LAUD; CROMWELL; HAMPDEN.
See also Vol. X: CIVIL WAR; SHIP MONEY.

CHARLES II (1630–85). The son of CHARLES I (q.v.), executed in 1649, Charles II did not become king until the monarchy was restored in 1660. From the age of 16 he was in exile, except when, shortly after his father's execution, he came to terms with the Scots. He invaded England from Scotland, but was decisively defeated by Oliver CROMWELL (q.v.) at Worcester, and escaped back to France only after a series of adventures. After the death of Cromwell, when the country was near to anarchy, General Monk took control, and a new Parliament was elected. This at once voted for a return of the Monarchy, and Charles, already in communication with Monk, returned to England on 29 May 1660. He was welcomed with tremendous enthusiasm.

Charles's policy when he returned to the throne was in the first place to keep his throne—never, as he expressed it, to go on his travels again. Beyond that, he wanted toleration for Roman Catholics (his brother, later James II, was an open Catholic and Charles himself a secret one); to be independent of Parliament in money matters and foreign policy; and to enjoy himself without criticism or interference. Charles was very fond of hunting and enjoyed gay and rather coarse company.

Charles had no legitimate son, and the crisis of the reign arose over the question of the succession. In 1678 a so-called Popish plot was 'discovered' to kill the King and seize power, and this led to a fierce persecution of Catholics. One party in Parliament (the Whigs), who wanted to reduce the King's power, wished to secure the succession for Charles's illegitimate but Protestant son, the Duke of Monmouth. The other party (the Tories), who believed in the King's right to rule, wanted to secure the succession for the King's Catholic brother, James. Charles eventually secured the succession for his brother and, thanks to money grants from Louis XIV (whom it was his secret policy to support) and to the increased yield from Customs and Excise resulting from the growth of trade, he was able to dissolve Parliament and rule for the rest of his life without it.

Charles was genuinely interested in science, in the development of the Navy, in the expansion of trade, and in colonial development. During his reign, England acquired from the Dutch territories which later became New York, New Jersey, and Pennsylvania (*see* PENN). In this period of progress in learning and the sciences— the age of LOCKE and NEWTON (qq.v.)—the ROYAL SOCIETY (q.v. Vol. XII) was founded under the King's patronage. The arts also revived after their suppression under the Commonwealth, though, especially in the plays of the period, they reflected the cynicism of the gay, pleasure-loving Court (*see* RESTORATION DRAMA, Vol. XII). On the stage actresses, instead of boy actors, for the first time took the women's parts, and Nell Gwynn, Charles's favourite mistress, was the most famous actress of the day. Charles was also a patron of music and painting. The age is intimately recorded by the diarist PEPYS (q.v.), and it was he who gave Charles invaluable assistance when the King took personal charge of the attempts to control the GREAT FIRE OF LONDON (q.v. Vol. X).

Although Charles had not the heroic qualities of his father, he was able to succeed where his father, and later his brother James II, came to grief. He knew when to yield and how to use his charm and quick wits to out-manœuvre his opponents.

See also Vol. X: REVOLUTION OF 1688.

CHARLES V (1500–58). This Hapsburg Emperor ruled over one of the greatest accumulations of territories in history. As heir to the Hapsburgs, he inherited Austria and the Netherlands. In 1519 he was elected to succeed his grandfather, Maximilian I, as Emperor of the HOLY ROMAN EMPIRE (q.v. Vol. I). As heir to Ferdinand and Isabella through his mother, he succeeded to the Spanish Crown with its South American colonies and the kingdoms of Sicily and Naples (*see* Map, INDEX, p. 54). He was of medium stature, with little personal charm; his pale face was disfigured by the protruding Hapsburg underlip, but enlivened by bright and intelligent eyes.

The diversity of Charles's realms in race and religion involved him in so many problems that he was often forced to temporize in one place while he reached his goal elsewhere. As soon as he became Emperor, he was faced with the religious problem in Germany, where Martin LUTHER (q.v.) was beginning his Protestant activities. Charles summoned his first Diet (parliament) at Worms in Germany in 1521, before which Luther had to appear to defend himself. Charles outlawed Luther, but gave him a safe conduct. Charles's aim was to reunite the Germans in a Catholic Church, which he wanted to reform by means of a General Council—a policy unpopular, not only with the Lutherans, but also with the Catholics, who resented reform, and Charles dared not undertake it while other dangers threatened him.

Francis I of France, fearing encirclement by the great Hapsburg Empire, tried to conquer Milan and northern Italy. But Charles completely defeated him at the Battle of Pavia (1525), took him prisoner, and made him promise great concessions before he would release him, promises which Francis did not keep. Pope Clement VII, also afraid of the power of the Emperor, organized an anti-Hapsburg league. But

Anderson

CHARLES V
Portrait by Titian. Prado Museum, Madrid

Charles's army of Spanish and German soldiers stormed Rome and sacked the city with the utmost brutality. During these wars King Henry VIII of England took part sometimes on the one and sometimes on the other side. Finally, having signed the Peace of Cambrai in 1529, Charles returned to Germany, where the Reformation had progressed considerably.

Charles prepared to unite the churches, but could not do so because, while he was involved in wars against the Turks and then against Mediterranean pirates, the German Protestants organized a league to defend themselves, even by force, against the Emperor. When Charles returned in 1547, open war broke out. Charles was completely victorious, partly because one of the most powerful Protestant princes, Maurice Duke of Saxony, joined him against the Protestants. When, however, Charles tried again to enforce religious unity and to add to his own Imperial power, Maurice turned traitor and joined with the new king of France against the Emperor. Charles, ill with gout, had to flee across the snow-bound Alps, and in 1552 was compelled to sign a treaty with the German princes, both Catholic and Protestant, which gave religious freedom to the Protestants.

Charles was bitterly disappointed at this failure, and during the following years he resigned one crown after another. He installed his son PHILIP II (q.v.) as his successor in Spain and the Netherlands. He had earlier ceded Austria to his brother Ferdinand, who in 1555 succeeded him as Emperor. In 1557 Charles retired to a monastery in Spain, where he died the next year.

Charles followed the policy of binding Europe together by a vast network of family marriages, and consequently, by the time of his death, nearly every royal house in Europe was linked with the Hapsburg dynasty.

CHATHAM, Earl of (1708–78). William Pitt, called 'the Elder' to distinguish him from his equally famous son, also William PITT (q.v.), was one of the greatest statesmen of the 18th century. He was created Earl of Chatham at the age of 57. He was the grandson of 'Diamond' Pitt, a merchant who, having made a fortune in India, had established his family as country gentlemen.

Pitt entered Parliament when he was 27, and soon distinguished himself by a powerful attack on Robert WALPOLE's Ministry (q.v.), and on George II's preoccupation with European affairs. Pitt believed that Britain should free herself from entanglements in Europe and press forward with increasing her colonies overseas. He was a man of great abilities and imperious will, with a profound sense of mission, conscious of his own talents ('I know that I can save this country and that no one else can'), and prepared to use any means to bring himself to public attention. The outbreak of the Seven Years War (1756–63) with France gave him his opportunity, in particular to forward his colonial ambitions.

The war began so disastrously that most politicians sought to escape responsible positions, but Pitt welcomed the chance of taking control. He took office as Secretary of State, and dominated the Cabinet, led the House of Commons, and was virtually Prime Minister. He subordinated everything to a great war effort, giving money to Prussia so that she could tie down France in Europe while Britain sent armies to attack France's colonies. Pitt, who had more control over the armed forces than any previous politician, himself chose his military commanders and planned many of the operations. The basis of his strategy was a brilliant use of SEA POWER (q.v. Vol. X). With the French fleets blockaded in Brest and Toulon, Pitt was able to attack French trade in Canada and the West Indies. WOLFE (q.v.), in assaulting the Heights of Abraham to capture Quebec, threw open Canada to conquest, and the rich West Indian island of Guadeloupe was captured from the French. In the same glorious 'Year of Victories' (1759), the French fleet made a last desperate attempt to break the blockade and was shattered by HAWKE (q.v.) at Quiberon Bay. Pitt had led the country from disastrous defeat to overwhelming success, but only 2 years later, after the accession of GEORGE III (q.v.), who was determined to end the war, he was forced from office.

In 1766–8 Pitt was again head of the Government; but this time he failed, one reason being that he had been created Earl of Chatham and entered the House of Lords. There, he was no longer 'the tribune of the people', and never commanded the same great respect that he had won in the Commons.

Pitt, though a magnificent commander of men, was a poor colleague. He refused to consider the weaknesses of politicians or the dull routine of Cabinet government, and failed to work with his colleagues. This was partly due to

Parker Gallery

THE COLLAPSE OF LORD CHATHAM IN THE HOUSE OF LORDS
Engraving by Bartolozzi after J. S. Copley

the gout and to the melancholia which afflicted him as he grew old; but it is also true that he was at his best only in the crisis of a war, when great objectives and not careful calculation were the business of a statesman.

After 1768 Pitt's role was that of an elder statesman warning his country against the government's harsh policy towards the American colonists (*see* AMERICAN WAR OF INDEPENDENCE, Vol. X), and, later, attacking the Opposition's proposal to evacuate America altogether. His last speech was worthy of his dramatic best. Swathed in wrappings, half carried by friends, he made a passionate speech on the American War. In the midst of it he collapsed, was carried from a horrified House, and died soon afterwards.

See also PITT.

CHAUCER, Geoffrey (*c.* 1340–1400). Chaucer, author of the CANTERBURY TALES (q.v. Vol. XII), was the greatest English poet before Shakespeare. Because of his career as a courtier we know more about Chaucer than we do about most medieval English poets. His father was a well-to-do London merchant who found him a post as page to the Countess of Ulster when he was about 17 years old. Before this he must have learned to speak French, the language of the Court, and to read Latin. In 1359 he went on a campaign in France, was captured, but was soon ransomed. In 1366 he married Philippa, a lady-in-waiting, and the next year was appointed a 'yeoman' in King Edward III's household. His duties ranged from making the King's bed to going on diplomatic missions and entertaining the Court—then the most brilliant and best organized in Europe—with music, song, and tales of love and adventure. His first long poem, *The Book of the Duchess*, was written to commemorate the charming young wife of John of Gaunt, Duke of Lancaster, who died in 1369 during an epidemic of plague. He went on several missions abroad, two of which took him to Italy, where BOCCACCIO and PETRARCH were then writing and the works of DANTE (qq.v.) were already famous.

In 1374, on being appointed a Controller of Customs in London, he took a house on the city wall and later became a Justice of the Peace and a member of Parliament. His wife died in 1387, and from 1389 to 1391 he was Clerk of the King's Works, his duties being to hire workmen, buy materials, direct building, and so forth, at Windsor Castle, Westminster, and elsewhere. In 1394 he received a pension, but, although not poor, he was often in debt. He died at his house in Westminster, and was buried in the Abbey. The 15th-century poet, Lydgate, says that in old age he was courteous and kind, and a contemporary portrait shows him plump and bearded. He probably had two sons, for one of whom he wrote his treatise on astronomy (*The Astrolabe*).

Chaucer was the first Court poet to write in English and to use it as a literary language. This did not lessen his love for Latin, French, and Italian poetry, and as a young man he translated some of the great French love-poem, *The Romance of the Rose* (*see* MEDIEVAL ROMANCE, Vol. XII). *The Book of the Duchess* was his first original work. In another early poem, the *House of Fame*, he tells how he dreamt that a learned eagle carried him up through the heavens (giving him scientific lessons on the way) to where Fame and Rumour dwell. This poem contains a well-known passage describing how Chaucer studies accounts all day, and at night reads till he is dazed. *The Parliament of Fowles*, another dream poem, is a delightfully lively and humorous poem whose underlying theme is the nature of love.

Troilus and Criseyde, based on Boccaccio's *Il Filostrato*, tells the story of Troilus's love for Criseyde, their sorrow when she has to leave Troy, and his despair when she proves faithless. The magnificent handling of the seven-line

Britsh. Museum

GEOFFREY CHAUCER

Marginal drawing from Hoccleve's *The Regement of Princes* (Royal MS. 17 D VI)

stanza, the novel-like plot, the splendid descriptions, the skilful characterization and portrayal of varied emotions show Chaucer's real greatness as a poet for the first time Its conclusion, addressed to all 'yonge fresshe folkes', is that God must be loved first of all. The *Canterbury Tales*, Chaucer's last, longest, and most famous work, is unfinished. It begins with a vivid Prologue, a most delightful and accomplished piece of writing, in which Chaucer uses the heroic couplet (*see* VERSIFICATION, Vol. XII) This Prologue describes some thirty pilgrims (Chaucer among them) who agree to tell each other tales on their way from London to Canterbury. The tales vary from the Knight's noble romance of chivalry to the coarse domestic comedy of the Miller and Reeve, from the satire of the Pardoner's tale to the pathos of the Prioress's and the piety of the Parson's tale They combine all the qualities found in the earlier works— humour, philosophical seriousness, understanding of all kinds of people and of all kinds of love, great metrical skill, and dramatic artistry. Though Chaucer was writing well over 500 years ago, his mind and imagination were so clear and vigorous, and he used the English language so boldly and freshly that, once the few simple principles of pronunciation and accent are understood, his poetry can be enjoyed in the original with remarkably little difficulty today.

Chaucer lived at a time when plagues, rebellion, and misgovernment troubled England, but in his writings he concentrated mainly on stories of personal relationships. He combined practical experience with much reading, and deep piety with a humour which only Shakespeare equals. His work dominated English poetry up to the Elizabethan period.

CHEKHOV, Anton (1860–1904). This great Russian dramatist and short-story writer was the grandson of a Russian serf who, by hard work and the most careful saving, collected enough money to buy freedom for himself and his family. Chekhov's father became a shopkeeper, though not a successful one, and the family was very poor. When Anton was 16 his father's business failed, and he began to earn his living by teaching and writing. While still at school he had shown a great gift for writing funny stories, and now he managed to make enough by his writing to finish his schooling and to take a medical degree at Moscow University. At 24 he took a post in a hospital He continued to write with some success, and at 28 he won the Pushkin prize for literature. He was by now extremely interested in the theatre and his first play had already been produced.

All his life Chekhov was deeply concerned with the way people lived, and he now undertook one of those quixotic adventures which were typical of him. He made a journey right across Siberia in order to find out for himself just how the convicts lived at Sakhalin—and through his report certain reforms were actually made. Shortly after his return there was a serious famine in Russia and Chekhov helped to organize relief work and to fight an outbreak of cholera. The considerable strain of all this, added to early years of struggle, made him ill and the tuberculosis which had always threatened him grew rapidly worse. Fortunately, he had made enough money to buy a farm and to move himself and all his family from Moscow into the country; and there he concentrated on recovering his health, and on writing. Except for one play, *The Seagull*, which was a failure when it was first presented (though it was later very successful in Moscow), his plays and stories were immensely popular. When his father died he sold the farm and built a house at Yalta in the Crimea, where the warm climate suited him. He missed his friends—mostly authors, actors, and scientists in Moscow, but in 1901 he married the actress Olga Knipper, and she shared with him the great triumph of his last play, *The Cherry Orchard*, produced in the Moscow Art Theatre just before he died in 1904.

Chekhov was a great comic writer and a great humanist. He wanted to show his countrymen the way in which they wasted their lives, the futility, falsity, and squalor of so much of it. He believed that if they could only realize what they were really like they would live very differently. But the Russians, rather like the English, enjoyed seeing themselves so truly and so amusingly portrayed. They were delighted and not at all penitent. Some producers have tried to make his plays—even a great comedy like *Uncle Vanya* —into tragedies, plays of melancholy disillusion, but this (in part due to faulty translation perhaps) is entirely to miss their irony and humour, which is extremely delicate and subtle, especially in such a play as *The Three Sisters*.

Chekhov disliked writing about himself, but his plays and stories and letters show clearly enough his generous and sympathetic nature, his understanding of other people's problems, and his subtle and vivid humour.

See also Vol. XII: RUSSIAN LITERATURE.

CHOPIN, Frédéric (1810–49). The composer Chopin was born near Warsaw in Poland. His father, a Frenchman, had married a poor relation of the Polish family with whom he was the tutor. Chopin started playing the piano in public and composing when he was 6; at 15 he played before the Tsar and published his first work. After 3 years' study at the Warsaw School of Music he went abroad for the first time, to Germany and Austria, and finally to Paris, where he virtually spent the rest of his life. He

Archives Photographiques
FRÉDÉRIC CHOPIN
Portrait by Delacroix. Louvre

never forgot his family or his country, whose tragic fate in the unsuccessful revolution against the Russians made an indelible impression on his sensitive nature.

In Paris his friends soon included LISZT, BERLIOZ, and MENDELSSOHN (qq.v.), and many writers and painters. The extraordinary charm and originality of his playing and of his compositions quickly made his name. On a visit to Germany in 1835 he fell in love with Maria Wodzinska but her family objected to Chopin on the grounds of his health, for, as the result of not caring for himself properly in Paris, he was by now almost certainly consumptive.

The next year he met the French woman novelist, George Sand, fell in love with her, and spent the winter and spring of 1838–9 with her in Majorca and the south of France, and was her constant companion for several years, until they quarrelled and separated. Chopin's health fluctuated but gradually declined, and in 1848 his illness was aggravated by a concert tour in Britain. This, his first appearance in public as a pianist since 1843, was also his last; he returned to Paris in November 1848 and died there 11 months later.

Chopin was not only gifted with a supreme understanding of what the piano could do—it was still a new instrument in his day—but he was also a composer whose harmonic language was greatly in advance of his contemporaries. Nearly all his music was written for the piano (see KEYBOARD INSTRUMENTS, Vol. IX). He is probably best known for his smaller pieces, which are tuneful and picturesque but still graceful and elegant—the waltzes, preludes, and nocturnes which he raised from drawing-room prettiness to deeply felt and perfectly expressed art. The ballades, scherzos, and two sonatas, as well as the two piano concertos, show a grander side of his character, noble and tragic, and he was the first composer to give artistic value to pianoforte exercises or studies. The gaiety and tenderness of his music, coupled with its unfailing good taste, depth of feeling, and technical originality, more than justify its popularity.

CHRIST, *see* Vol. I: JESUS OF NAZARETH.

CHRISTINA OF SWEDEN (1626–89). The only child of the great GUSTAVUS ADOLPHUS (q.v.), Christina succeeded her father when she

Ashmolean Museum
CHRISTINA OF SWEDEN
Engraving of 1654

was not yet 6. Sweden was at that time at the height of her power—the leader of the Protestant States in the Thirty Years War. During her minority Gustavus's great Chancellor, Axel Oxenstierna, governed and continued to conduct Swedish operations in the war, as well as to instruct the young Queen in politics. Christina became jealous of his high reputation and, when she became of age in 1644, she brought to an end the War on which his reputation largely depended. Consequently Sweden gained less at the peace than she would otherwise have done.

Christina was enthusiastic, brilliant, and physically attractive, but her egotism and extravagance prevented her from becoming a great Queen. She ruled with energy, encouraging Swedish trade, manufacture, literature, and science. She filled her Court with foreign scholars, artists, and philosophers—including DESCARTES (q.v.). Indeed, her characteristic egotism in demanding that he should give her lessons at 5 a.m. in a Swedish winter was indirectly the cause of Descartes' death. The Riksdag (Parliament) urged her to marry her most unattractive cousin, Charles Gustavus, to ensure the succession, but she would do no more than appoint him her successor. After 10 years' reign, Christina finally decided to abdicate, and the Swedes, realizing that she could not be persuaded to marry and produce an heir and that her extravagance would cripple the finances of the country, were willing for her to go. She abdicated partly from weariness of the restraints of queenship, partly from a desire to become a Catholic, but mostly, perhaps, because she felt it would 'startle the world'. She became a Catholic and went to live in Rome; but when, in 1660, Charles Gustavus died, she hastened to Sweden in vain efforts to recover her throne. In Rome, where she lived largely on the charity of the Pope, she created one of the social centres of Europe, charming everybody, and liberally patronizing the arts—though without much discrimination.

Had Christina taken trouble to develop any one of her gifts, she might have achieved genuine greatness. As it is, she has become a study in brilliant but unrewarding eccentricity.

CHURCHILL, Sir Winston (born 1874). The most famous Englishman of his day, Winston Leonard Spencer Churchill has been Prime Minister, held many other high offices of State, seen active service in India, Africa, and France, and stands out among his contemporaries as a master of spoken and written English.

His finest hour came when he was called to lead the nation in 1940, with the armies of Nazi Germany triumphant across the Channel. 'I have nothing to offer', he told his countrymen at that grim and historic moment, 'but blood, toil, tears, and sweat.' This lion-hearted and realistic optimism inspired Britain and the whole free world and led, after years of fighting on land and sea and in the air, to victory at the end of the SECOND WORLD WAR (q.v. Vol. X).

Unlike LLOYD GEORGE (q.v.), the Prime Minister in the First World War, who was a Welsh son of the people, Churchill comes from a great English aristocratic family. He is the grandson of the seventh Duke of Marlborough and a descendant of Britain's most brilliant general, the victor of Blenheim. His father, Lord Randolph Churchill, had a meteoric career in Victorian politics. He married the daughter of a prominent American citizen, Leonard Jerome, and Winston Churchill owed much of his extraordinary vitality to his beautiful American mother.

From Harrow School, Churchill went to the Royal Military College, Sandhurst, and was commissioned in 1895 in the 4th Hussars. He first saw fighting, in Cuba, as an observer attached to the Spanish Army. He was sent out to India where, while other young officers were sleeping through the heat of the day, he read hard. He later saw active service on the frontier in the Malakand and Tirah campaigns. There was not enough work for professional soldiers in those peaceful days, and, when Churchill tried to join an expedition in the Sudan, KITCHENER (q.v.), the commander, said he had no room for him. Churchill, brooking no refusal, got into the field as a newspaper correspondent and, attached as an officer to the 21st Lancers, charged with the cavalry at the Battle of Omdurman. He was an eye-witness of the SOUTH AFRICAN WAR (q.v. Vol. X), again as a correspondent, and was taken prisoner and escaped.

In 1900 he became a Conservative member of Parliament, but soon crossed the House to join the Liberals because he was a Free Trader (see INTERNATIONAL TRADE, Vol. VII). When the Liberals came into power in 1905, he was given office as Under-Secretary of State for the Colonies. In a few years he became a power in the Cabinet. He was in turn President of the Board of Trade, Home Secretary, and First Lord of the Admiralty. In this latter post he threw himself furiously into the task of preparing the Navy to meet the German Grand Fleet, should war occur. When the FIRST WORLD WAR (q.v. Vol. X) broke out, Churchill strongly supported the campaign in the Dardanelles, a campaign which was a failure and brought Churchill unpopularity in high political and military circles. Losing his position at the Admiralty, he went to France on active service and commanded an infantry battalion. But he was brought back to take charge of the Ministry of Munitions, where he did great work in equipping the armies.

After the war Churchill held various government posts, among them Chancellor of the Exchequer, in both Coalition and Conservative Governments. From 1929 to 1939, he held no government office, but spoke in Parliament as a private member, often criticizing British policy.

When the SECOND WORLD WAR (q.v. Vol. X) broke out Churchill became head of the Admiralty under Neville Chamberlain; but in the crisis of May 1940 both Parliament and the nation called upon Churchill to lead the country. He accepted responsibility for tremendous decisions, and dominated his fellow countrymen of all ranks, in public and behind the scenes, infecting them with his energy and with his faith.

Realizing that victory depended on American aid, he quickly established and maintained close friendly relations with President ROOSEVELT (q.v.). Although already nearly 70, he never spared himself exhausting and dangerous journeys. He flew to America, Africa, and Russia, and he sought hard, but in vain, to win the confidence of the Russian leader, STALIN (q.v.)

After the war he fought three General Elections as leader of the Conservative Party, and in 1951 again became Prime Minister. He retired from office in 1955, acknowledged by all parties to be one of the most brilliant orators the House of Commons has ever listened to—inspiring in his great speeches and brilliantly quick in repartee.

Churchill's short, plump, sturdy figure, cigar in mouth, and fingers raised in the gesture of the V sign for 'Victory', was a memorable sight during the war. His voice, from the front bench and over the air, compelled attention as great as that accorded to any orator in British history. Some of his sayings deserve always to be remembered. When Hitler, at the height of his success, threatened to invade Britain, Churchill told the House of Commons: 'We shall defend our island, whatever the cost may be; we shall fight on the beaches, we shall fight on the landing grounds, we shall fight in the fields and in the streets, we shall fight in the hills; we shall never surrender'. Speaking of the Royal Air Force and its victory over the German air fleets in the Battle of Britain in 1940, he said, 'Never in the field of human conflict was so much owed by so many to so few'.

He wrote long books about each World War, and *A History of the English-Speaking People,* as well as vivid works describing his earlier days, and biographies of his father and of his distinguished ancestor, the first Duke of MARLBOROUGH (q.v.). Had he no other claim to fame, he would be remembered as a writer.

See also Vol. X: FIRST WORLD WAR; SECOND WORLD WAR.

CICERO, Marcus Tullius (106–43 B.C.). This Roman orator, writer, and statesman won his fame and high office by his oratorical genius. In 70 B.C. he made one of his most famous speeches when he impeached the magistrate Verres for infamous extortions in Sicily. In 63 B.C., in another great speech in the Senate, he exposed the plots of the conspirator Catiline, and for a time became the great man of his day. Cicero, who always tended to waver between one policy and another, fluctuated between supporting POMPEY and JULIUS CAESAR (qq.v.). For a time he was in exile, but when civil war broke out he joined Pompey. After Pompey's defeat and death, he returned to Rome as a private citizen, though he soon began to resent Caesar's dictatorship. He did not join the conspirators who brought about Caesar's death, but he rejoiced in the event. He tried, however, to rally the Senate to control MARK ANTONY (q.v.), making another great speech, and was consequently outlawed, pursued, and finally murdered.

His importance lies in his contributions to Latin language and literature. He perfected Roman RHETORIC (q.v. Vol. XII), and about half his 106 known speeches survive. During his periods of enforced retirement he composed philosophical dialogues and treatises of no great originality but valuable because of his development of the scope of the Latin language. These writings profoundly influenced some of the early Christian Fathers; and the 14th-century Renais-

The Times

THANKSGIVING FOR VICTORY, MAY 1945

Mr. and Mrs. Churchill leaving St. Paul's Cathedral after the service to commemorate the end of the fighting in Europe in the Second World War

sance was primarily a rediscovery of Cicero, whose elegant style and humane approach attracted writers such as Petrarch. Cicero wrote a great many letters, mostly not meant for publication, which are frank, witty, racy, self-revealing, and have served to bring alive the exciting years of the Roman Revolution.

Cicero was a self-centred and vain man, but he was genuinely warm-hearted, and generally tried to live up to his sincerely held principles. But his imagination foresaw difficulties vividly, and this made him apprehensive and vacillating.

See also JULIUS CAESAR; POMPEY.

See also Vol. XII; LATIN LITERATURE.

CID, The (c. 1043–99). This was the title (from the Moorish *Sidi*, 'Lord') given to the Spaniard Rodrigo Diaz, one of the greatest of all soldiers of fortune. He lived at a time when Spain was a patchwork of Christian and Moslem States (*see* SPANIARDS, Vol. I). It was an age of disorder; religious and racial warfare alternated with bitter family feuds, and military heroism was the most prized of all virtues.

Rodrigo was a Christian nobleman of Castile. In his early 20's he is known to have commanded the army of the King of Castile, and by defeating in single combat a champion put forward by the ruler of Navarre he earned the title of *campeador* ('conqueror'). Rodrigo remained high in royal favour until, some years later, he was driven into exile by a new king. With a faithful band of knights he set out to make for himself a brilliant career, first as a general in the service of the Moorish King of Saragossa, and then for 5 years as ruler in his own right of the rich territory of Valencia. He twice defended his lands successfully against large armies of Moors, who were in possession of south and central Spain; but he is said to have died of grief in 1099 when his forces suffered defeat by the Moors. He was no mere freebooter, and more than once offered to fight for Alphonso, his former overlord, when his help was needed.

It is difficult to disentangle the truth from the legends which have gathered round him. Contemporary Moorish writers called him this 'dog of a Galician'; though they were forced to admire his exploits, they suggest that he was nothing more than a cruel and faithless adventurer. But an epic poem written in Spanish about 40 years after his death probably gives a fairer estimate of his character—brave and

Graften & Co.

THE CID ON HIS HORSE BABIECA

According to legend Babieca lived to be 60 years old. Woodcut from the title-page of *Chronica del Famoso Cavallero Cid Ruy Diez Campeador*, 1593

loyal and, neither quixotic nor reckless, a splendid warrior, who sought not fame alone, but also money and great lands as his reward.

In the 12th century the Cid became the hero of the troubadours, who credited him with fantastic adventures such as a fabulous invasion of France. In the 17th century the French dramatist CORNEILLE (q.v.) made the Cid the hero of a great play.

See also Vol. XII: SPANISH LITERATURE.

CLARENDON, Earl of (1608–74), *see* Vol. XII: HISTORIES.

CLAUDE (1600–82). Claude Gellée, generally known by his Christian name or by the name of the province of his birth, 'Lorraine', was a great French landscape painter. When a boy, he walked over the Alps to Rome and worked for a while as cook in the house of a painter, Tassi. Before long he was helping Tassi with landscapes. Then he returned to France and assisted a court

ASCANIUS SHOOTING THE STAG OF SYLVIA

Painting by Claude, 1682

painter in Nancy. When he was 27 he returned permanently to Rome and settled in a colony of French painters.

Claude had little education—it is said that he signed his name with difficulty. His pictures do not attempt historical accuracy, but he had a strong sense of the poetry of antiquity, of romantic ruins, and of the effects of light and atmosphere, which he studied in the country around Rome. He soon had a great number of commissions, and his paintings were so much imitated that he was forced to keep a record of them. At that time landscape was not considered the highest form of art, so Claude (or perhaps another painter) added figures to give his paintings a biblical or classical significance. Though he made sketches from nature, his landscapes were not realistic but 'ideal', for he believed that as nature was always striving towards perfection, it was the duty of the painter to correct her when she was not successful. His work greatly influenced 18th-century taste, especially in England.

CLEOPATRA (69–30 B.C.), Queen of Egypt, *see* MARK ANTONY; PTOLEMIES.

CLIVE, Robert (Baron) (1725–74). Clive, the founder of the British Empire in India, was brought up in the Shropshire town of Market Drayton. As a schoolboy he thought nothing of taking 'protection money' from the shopkeepers who were anxious to be spared the window-breaking of the gang of boys he led, and once he terrified the townspeople by climbing and sitting astride the church steeple. He was reckless and ill-mannered; unscrupulous, quarrelsome, and resentful of command; and so, indeed, he remained throughout his life.

At the age of 18 Clive was sent to Madras as a clerk in the EAST INDIA COMPANY (q.v. Vol. VII). At that time the Company possessed not only extensive trading rights but some powers of government, and was engaged in fierce rivalry with the French East India Company. Both were anxious to extend their commercial interests, and to increase their political power by winning the support of the Indian rulers. In 1742 the War of the Austrian Succession broke out in Europe (*see* MARIA THERESA); and with Britain and France engaged on opposite sides it was not long before the fighting spread to India. Clive, who hated the monotony of office routine and had twice attempted suicide because of it, was given an opportunity for action.

Madras was captured by the French in 1746, but Clive escaped in disguise to join the British garrison at Fort St. David. Soon afterwards he obtained approval for a plan to relieve the British garrison, besieged in Trichinopoli, by a diversionary assault on the city of Arcot. His small force of 500 forced their way through the monsoon to find that the enemy had fled. They occupied the town and held it against counter-attacks for 53 days, inflicting heavy losses on the many thousands of native and French troops brought there from Trichinopoli. The valiant defence of Arcot and Clive's further victories won respect for British arms, and led to a settlement in south India in Britain's favour in 1752.

Clive returned to England with a great fortune amassed from prize money and 'presents'. But within 3 years he had spent almost the whole of it. He returned to India as Governor of Fort St. David at a critical time for the British. In Bengal the Nawab, the Indian ruler, had pounced upon the Company's settlement at Calcutta and imprisoned for one hot Indian night 146 British men and women in a room less than 20 feet square (known afterwards as 'the black hole of Calcutta'): the next morning only twenty-three were still alive. Clive was at once sent north to restore British influence. He recaptured Calcutta, took the French settlement at Chandernagore, and defeated the Nawab's forces.

Clive then became involved in a complicated plot to replace the Nawab as ruler with Mir Jaffir, the Nawab's own military commander. When Clive's go-between threatened to divulge the plot, Clive offered him a huge sum of money, which in fact he had no intention of paying, and forged his own commander's signature to a false document confirming the terms. Mir Jaffir was won over to the British side, and with little more than 3,000 men Clive defeated the Nawab's immense army of 50,000 Indians, backed by French gunners, at the Battle of Plassey (June, 1757). Mir Jaffir rewarded Clive with a sum of over £230,000 and a considerable amount of land. But despite the immensity of this gift Clive, when 16 years later he was cross-examined by a Parliamentary Committee, expressed himself 'surprised at his own moderation' in not demanding more.

When Clive returned home, he was fabulously rich. He entered Parliament, and was later raised to the peerage. But 5 years later, after widespread reports of corruption by East India Company servants, and of military unrest, he returned to Bengal as Governor. During the brief 2 years of his administration Clive made up for many of his previous mistakes. He did all he could by raising the salaries of the Company's servants to prevent their engaging in private trading and taking bribes, and he himself refrained from amassing any great wealth. He introduced a 'dual system' whereby the Nawab executed justice in the State, and the Company collected the taxes and paid the Nawab a pension. He further tried to establish a central government in Bengal to control the other English presidencies of Bombay and Madras.

The corrupt practices continued, however, and finally Clive was recalled to England and cross-examined by a strongly critical Parliamentary Committee. But though he was found guilty of fraud and of greed in his dealings with Mir Jaffir, the committee's resolution that he had rendered 'great and meritorious services to this country' was unanimous. But the strain of the proceedings and the vote of censure caused Clive to take to opium, and he soon afterwards committed suicide.

Clive's achievement was remarkable. In little more than 10 years he had laid the foundations of a British Empire in India and had secured a reasonably honest form of British rule for the future. But many of his methods were by modern standards inadmissible, and Lord Macaulay's estimate is perhaps the most generous: 'Like most men born with strong passions and tried by strong temptations', he committed 'great faults', but was nevertheless 'truly great in arms and in council'.

See also HASTINGS.
See also Vol. I: INDIAN CIVILIZATIONS; INDIAN PEOPLES.
See also Vol. VII: EAST INDIA COMPANY.
See also Vol. X: COLONIES, HISTORY OF.

National Portrait Gallery
ROBERT CLIVE
Portrait by Nathaniel Dance

COBBETT, William (1762–1835). This writer, politician, and agriculturist was born at Farn-

There is but one man in the Country who can extricate it from difficulties why dont you send Him to Parliament

Meade Collection

COBBETT MAKING AN ELECTION SPEECH

Cobbett stood unsuccessfully for Parliament in 1821 and 1826 before he was finally elected in 1832. Caricature by John Doyle (1797–1868)

ham, Surrey, the son of a small independent farmer and innkeeper and the grandson of a farm labourer. Cobbett was proud of his rural descent and of the fact that he had been born in a small agricultural market-town. Although his career was varied, and he several times left England, he always championed English rural life and considered the English yeoman and farm labourer the backbone of the nation.

He joined the army and served in Nova Scotia for some years. Then for a short time he was a teacher of English in France. Later, for 8 years, he was a bookseller and hot-headed journalist in America, writing under the name of 'Peter Porcupine', and getting into great trouble for his violent statements. In 1800 he returned to England and joined the Tory party, but very soon after became editor of a Radical paper. Then for 13 years he farmed at Botley, in Hampshire. In 1809 he raised an agitation about the flogging of soldiers, which landed him in Newgate prison. As a leading Radical he fled to America to avoid arrest during the labour troubles in 1819. In 1832 he became member of Parliament for Oldham. He wrote a great number of tracts and educational books, a history of the Reformation, and his two most famous books, *Rural Rides* and *Cottage Economy*.

Cobbett represented the point of view of the countryman. He was the champion of the craftsmen and the cultivators, especially the cottagers, whose little properties gave them the independence, the self-respect, and the happy, self-supporting life he prized above all things. He went back to the Middle Ages for support of his ideas, because medieval England was based on the peasant-cultivator, the small market-town, and the self-supporting monastery. The fundamental thing he cared about was the worth and dignity of the human person and the wholeness of his life. He wished to see England a self-supporting country depending for its prosperity on the self-supporting farmer rather than on the industrial towns. But he had the whole age against him, and his cause was overwhelmed by the irresistible impulse of the 19th century towards the development of industry and the growth of large cities filled with organized workers.

He was a tremendous agitator for the Reform Bill of 1832 (*see* ELECTION, PARLIAMENTARY, Vol. X). But his hopes were disappointed; the Bill not only failed to give votes to his own people, the farmers and labourers, but placed in power the 'cotton lords', the new rich, and the industrial magnates who represented all that Cobbett had strenuously resisted. He saw the old England he loved displaced and shattered by the new England of the slum-towns and factories; the 'workshop of the world', with the financiers enthroned. This failure of his hopes broke his heart, and he died in 1835.

Cobbett was his own worst enemy. He engaged in public disputes in the wildest manner. As a crusader he was a total failure. He became one of the best-hated men in England. His attacks were often so violent and even misdirected that he failed to get recognition for the wisdom and truth of his teaching.

See also Vol. VI: AGRICULTURAL HISTORY.
See also Vol. VII: INDUSTRIAL REVOLUTION.

COBDEN, Richard (1804–65). This political leader, son of a Sussex farmer, whose name is usually associated with John Bright (1811–89), headed the agitation for the abolition of taxes on food imported into Britain, in particular the tax on corn. The purpose of the Corn Laws had been to protect the British farmer from the competition of cheap foreign grain; but by the 19th century the growing population of industrial workers living on low wages complained that the Corn Laws made bread dear and filled the farmers' pockets at their expense.

Cobden and his friend Bright were both successful manufacturers, typical products of the Industrial Revolution, their friendship being based on a similarity of ideas. In 1838 Cobden, who had for some time been writing free trade pamphlets, assisted in the foundation of the Anti-Corn Law League in Manchester; and Bright shortly afterwards became his chief supporter. Both men entered Parliament and continued to work for free trade in the House of Commons. In 1846 the Tory Prime Minister, Sir Robert PEEL (q.v.), although elected to support the Corn Laws, persuaded Parliament to abolish them, admitting that he took this step largely as the result of Cobden's agitation.

Cobden and Bright were spokesmen for what was often called the 'Manchester School' of thought—the belief of Lancashire manufacturers and many workmen that prosperity and democracy depended on unrestricted free trade, that taxes, customs duties, and government control smacked of tyranny and led to oppression at home and wars abroad, and that colonization should aim at the eventual freedom of the native peoples. The 'Manchester School', therefore, opposed the warlike foreign policy of Lord PALMERSTON (q.v.). Cobden led this hostility, and so criticized the CRIMEAN WAR (q.v. Vol. X) and the British war on China in the mid-19th century that he and other members of the 'Manchester School' lost their seats in Parliament in 1857. This was the year of the Indian Mutiny, and Bright made what then seemed the revolutionary suggestion that Indians should be freely admitted to senior administrative posts in India —a step which was not taken for many years. In 1860 Cobden negotiated the famous Cobden commercial treaty with France, which helped to restore friendly relations between the two countries. He also fervently supported the removal of legal disabilities on Jews, who at that

Radio Times Hulton Lib.

JOHN BRIGHT (*left*) AND RICHARD COBDEN

time were excluded from membership of Parliament and certain other privileges.

Bright, who after Cobden's death accepted office in the Liberal government, used his great gifts of oratory with less bitterness than Cobden, and without Cobden's intolerance towards the aristocracy and the armed forces. He endeared himself to all through his human sympathy and his transparent honesty and sincerity.

See also Vol. VII: INTERNATIONAL TRADE, Section 4.

COKE, Thomas William (1752–1842). Thomas Coke of Norfolk, created Earl of Leicester when he was 85, was a great agriculturist, one of those enlightened 18th-century squires, who, though he lived like a prince on his vast estates, in Parliament was a friend of reform. It was largely owing to the personal influence of such men that England was able to bring about social improvements by gradual reform instead of by revolution, as happened in France.

When he was 24, Coke inherited a big estate in Norfolk with its great palace-like house, Holkham Hall, designed in the Georgian style for his great-uncle. Here Coke began the scientific and experimental farming on which his fame rests, transforming land which had 'but one blade of grass, and two rabbits fighting for it' into an estate of great prosperity. He increased his annual rent-roll from £2,000 to some £20,000. Every year at Holkham Hall, at the time of the sheep-shearing, a congress was held, where those methods of scientific agriculture and stock-breeding which form the basis of modern farming were propounded and discussed.

Coke represented Norfolk in Parliament for nearly 50 years, and became known as the 'Father of the House of Commons'. He was frequently offered a government post, but always refused. A man of vigorous health and sturdy individualism, he was popular wherever he went.

See also BAKEWELL, Robert.
See also Vol. VI: AGRICULTURAL IMPROVERS.

COLERIDGE, Samuel Taylor (1772–1834). The outstanding thing about Coleridge—poet, philosopher, essayist, critic, and conversationalist —is the extraordinary range of his genius. The thirteenth child and youngest son of a Devonshire clergyman, he was born at Ottery St. Mary. After the death of his father he was sent when he was 9 to Christ's Hospital, London, where he made friends with Charles LAMB (q.v.). Books became his chief delight and he won a reputation as a brilliant classical and English scholar. But at Cambridge University he never

SAMUEL TAYLOR COLERIDGE IN 1795
Portrait by Peter Vandyke

National Portrait Gallery

took his degree, and he there began that characteristic dissipation of his energies in innumerable interests which, so often throughout his life, prevented his finishing what he had begun with enthusiasm. During this period he made friends with Southey; with other young revolutionaries he planned to found an ideal settlement on the banks of the Susquehannah in America. Nothing came of it; but as a result Coleridge met his wife, Sarah Fricker, one of seven sisters, two others being married to Southey and Lovell, another revolutionary. At this time Cottle, a Bristol publisher, took Coleridge's first book of poems. Cottle proved a loyal and generous friend: indeed, all his life Coleridge was provided for largely by the generosity of friends and admirers. When he was 24, Coleridge went to live at Nether Stowey. William and Dorothy WORDSWORTH (q.v.) came to live at Alfoxden nearby, and all Coleridge's greatest poems were written during the subsequent period of contact with the Wordsworths. Together they planned the *Lyrical Ballads*, to which Coleridge, who had undertaken to supply the supernatural element, contributed the *Ancient Mariner*. The element of mystery and wonder, so remarkable in the *Ancient Mariner*, is Coleridge's unique contribution to poetry. *Kubla Khan* and the first part of *Christabel*, written in the following year, have the same magical quality; but though Coleridge remained a poet all his life he seldom recaptured the music and the vision of these early works. *Fears in Solitude* was written in 1798, and his last great poem, *Dejection: an Ode*, in 1802.

Coleridge had seriously thought of becoming a Unitarian minister, but the WEDGWOOD brothers (q.v.) gave him sufficient resources on condition that he devoted himself to literature. He went with the Wordsworths to Germany, and stayed there some time studying the German philosophers, in particular KANT. He also made an extremely fine translation of SCHILLER's *Wallenstein* (qq.v.).

When he returned to London in 1799, he worked fitfully at journalism and lectured on politics and literature. (His later lectures on Shakespeare, of which we only have fragments, were, according to contemporary opinion, incomparably fine.) Above all Coleridge talked, for his brilliant talk fascinated people of all kinds. In 1800 he took his family to Keswick, where he shared a house with Southey. Gradually Coleridge drifted away, leaving his wife and children in Southey's care. Both his son Hartley (for whom as a baby Coleridge had written the moving and tender lyric *Frost at Midnight*) and his daughter Sara were gifted children, but they rarely saw their father.

Coleridge's natural irresolution was aggravated by taking the drug laudanum, a habit formed as a young man to relieve acute headaches. In 1816, he made a determined effort to cure himself of drug-taking. He went to stay with James Gillman, an apothecary at Highgate, and there, in fact, he remained for the last 18 years of his life, treated with the utmost kindness by his hosts. There he wrote his famous book of criticism, *Biographia Literaria*, another fragment, but containing his fine analysis and defence of Wordsworth's poetic genius (written at a time when Wordsworth was still unpopular and misunderstood), and much general literary criticism besides. At Highgate many people visited him for the sake of his conversation and doctrine: his *Table Talk*, with its melodious prose, gives some idea of what his visitors heard. But Coleridge talked also to himself, pen in hand, in a long series of notebooks ('Flycatchers' was his word for them), a selection from which was later published in *Anima Poetae*. There was nothing in the range of human knowledge which Coleridge ignored; he read and reflected on everything for himself, his humorous spirit often alternating with a profound and startling seriousness.

See also WORDSWORTH; HAZLITT.

See also Vol. XII: ROMANTIC MOVEMENT; LITERARY CRITICISM.

COLET, John (*c.* 1467–1519), *see* ERASMUS.

COLUMBUS, Christopher (1451–1506). This famous explorer of the New World, later known as America, was an Italian in the service of Spain. Columbus was born at Genoa, the son of a weaver. As a young man he made several trading voyages in the Mediterranean, and then settled in Lisbon as a maker of charts. He visited the Guinea coast of Africa, recently opened to Portuguese trade by the exploration directed by Prince HENRY THE NAVIGATOR (q.v.). Columbus became much interested in the Portuguese attempt to find a way round Africa to India, an interest which increased when he married the daughter of one of Prince Henry's captains and inherited records of the exploration of the west coast of Africa and of the discovery and settlement of the Atlantic islands.

According to the best geographical ideas of the time, the earth was thought to be a sphere with a circumference about one-third less than we now know it to have. Asia was thought to extend much farther east than it really does. The combined effect of these two mistakes was that 15th-century geographers placed Japan in roughly the position occupied, in fact, by the West Indies (*see* PTOLEMY). At that time no European, not even the 13th-century traveller, MARCO POLO (q.v.), had ever visited Japan, though Marco Polo knew of its existence. No European dreamed of the existence of the huge American continent (although the Viking ERICSSON (q.v.) had probably landed there nearly 500 years earlier).

Explorers believed, therefore, that a comparatively short voyage westward from the Atlantic islands (the Portuguese Azores or the Spanish Canaries) would bring a ship to the East Indian islands, the source of the fabulously lucrative spice trade. Columbus became a fanatical pleader for an expedition based on this theory—no new theory, but Columbus was the first man who had sufficient confidence in the ships and methods of navigation available to him to undertake so long a voyage out of sight of land.

Columbus first proposed his scheme in 1483 to King John II of Portugal; but all Portugal's interests and shipping resources were devoted to the search for a route to India round Africa. So in 1484 Columbus went to Spain, which was being left far behind Portugal in the search for overseas trade and possessions. But all Spain's resources were devoted to the conquest of the last Moorish stronghold in Spain, Granada, and there was no money to spare for exploration. In 1492, however, the Moors being finally conquered, Columbus managed to fire Queen Isabella and her advisers with the prospect of rich trade and of converting heathen peoples to Christianity. The Queen signed an agreement granting Columbus the hereditary position of viceroy of all the lands he discovered, together with one-tenth of the value of their trade. In August 1492 Columbus sailed from Spain in command of three small ships, the SANTA MARIA (q.v. Vol. IV), the *Nina*, and the *Pinta*, and 120 men. Just over a month later he left the Canary Islands and sailed west. The expedition

COLUMBUS LANDING ON WATLING ISLAND IN 1492
He is welcomed by natives who bring him gifts. Engraving from de Bry,
Americae, 1593

spices, and hardly any gold. Further exploration failed to reveal Japan or any part of Asia. In October 1495 a royal official arrived from Spain to seek the reasons for the almost complete failure of Columbus's great promises, and Columbus had to return with him to defend himself.

Columbus's reputation never recovered from this failure, and he had great difficulty in raising the money and men for his third and fourth voyages. On his third voyage (1498–1500) he discovered Trinidad and the mainland of South America; but as governor of the lands he had discovered he proved a failure, and officials had to be sent from Spain to restore order. In the end Columbus was sent home under arrest. Although he was later restored to royal favour, his right to govern the lands he discovered was withdrawn. On his fourth voyage (1502–4) he explored a long stretch of the coast of Central America, looking for gold and a strait which would lead to Asia; but he found neither.

Columbus spent the rest of his life in Spain living in luxury on his 10 per cent. share of the value of the trade from his newly discovered lands; but never forgiving the government for depriving him of his promised hereditary vice-royalty. He was a dreamer and a visionary rather than a practical man. His confidence in his dreams made him the unintentional discoverer of the New World, but his lack of practical ability prevented his understanding the true geographical significance of his discoveries.

See also MAGELLAN; CORTÉS; PIZARRO.
See also Vol. IV: EXPLORATION; SANTA MARIA.

sailed before a favourable wind for 33 days without sighting land. Navigation was hazardous. Columbus could discover the latitude of his ship (its distance from the North Pole) by measuring the angle of the sun or stars (*see* NAVIGATION, HISTORY OF, Vol. IV); but longitude (the distance east or west) was a matter of guesswork. Then Columbus sighted what is now called Watling Island, one of the outer islands of the Bahamas, and explored the eastern coasts of Cuba and Hispaniola before sailing for home in January 1493. He arrived back in Spain early in March, convinced that he had found islands hitherto unknown to Europeans in the neighbourhood of Japan, and that further exploration would quickly reveal the mainland of Asia with India lying beyond. So he called the islands the West Indies, and they have borne the name ever since.

Columbus's glowing description of the newly discovered islands and his certainty that the Spice Islands of the East Indies were now within easy reach, led to the dispatch of a much larger fleet under his command, comprising seventeen ships and about 1,500 men. But when he got to the islands Columbus found no spices except pepper, the most plentiful and cheapest of the

CONFUCIUS (*c.* 550–479 B.C.). The Chinese sage's real name was Kung Fu Tzu (Master Kung), which was latinized by the Jesuit missionaries into Confucius. He was born in a small Chinese State, Lu, now part of the North China province of Shantung. His father, who was probably a soldier, died when he was 3 years old, leaving the family in poverty. Kung himself married at the age of 19 and lived to be over 70. He seems to have held various appointments in local government, but eventually gave these up and became a wandering teacher and reformer. After 12 years he returned to Lu, where until his death he belonged to a class of Chinese known as Ju. These, rather like the Sophists of ancient Greece, acted as tutors to young nobles, and were not unlike domestic chaplains in great houses.

Confucius was not himself the founder of a new religion (see CHINESE RELIGION, Vol. I), and hardly perhaps a philosopher, but rather a social reformer. He was a deeply religious man: 'Heaven', he said, 'has entrusted me with a mission.' But that mission was not so much to invent something new as to recall his countrymen to their true and traditional way of living, and especially to teach them the importance of right relationships with one another, and the sacredness of family life. He said: 'I am one who regards antiquity with trust and affection.' The word *li* used by Confucius, which is often translated by the English word 'religion', really means something more like ceremonial or ritual, the correct observance of which is needed for maintaining friendly relations with the Power or Powers of the unseen world (see RITUAL, Vol. I). Confucius accepted this as something not to be neglected by any well-bred Chinese. But he was chiefly interested in conduct: and, as shown by the written record which his disciples made of his sayings, he seems to have had a gift for putting wisdom into short pithy sentences. It is possible that he wrote nothing himself, but he carefully collected and set in order what he believed to be various ancient records of China: *The Book of History, The Book of Odes, Notes on Behaviour, The Book of Changes,* and *The Spring and Autumn Annals.* Much of these have been greatly altered since his time, for under the dictator Huang-Ti many of his works were destroyed and had to be written out again from fragments and from memory; but the *Odes* and the *Annals* are probably genuinely his collections. These works are known as the Confucian Classics, and to these must be added the *Lun Yu* or 'selected sayings', known in English as the *Analects.* The majority of these are Confucius' own comments on life, committed to memory by his followers, and recorded at a much later date.

It is difficult, however, to arrive at their true meaning, for Chinese words, being pictures, cannot be translated literally; they lend themselves to a variety of translations (see CHINESE LANGUAGE, Vol. IV). For example, one saying of Confucius has been translated in these two different ways: 'To learn the Way in the morning; to die at night; there's nothing wrong about that'; or 'If truth has been revealed to you in the morning, you may die in the evening without repining'.

Many of the Analects have become well-known sayings, such as:

Men of true breeding have dignity, but they are not arrogant.
Men of no breeding are arrogant, but have no dignity.
The man who sins against heaven has no one to whom he can pray.
If a man learns but does not think, he is nothing. If he thinks but does not learn, then he is in a dangerous state.
Among the truly educated, there is no distinction of classes.

Chinese wisdom, though it owes much to Confucius, is far bigger than his teaching alone. As fully developed it includes the doctrines of many teachers, some of whom admired Confucius' teaching, while others differed considerably from the Master. Most believed in the natural goodness of human nature (though Confucius himself does not explicitly say he does). The supreme virtue, according to Confucius, is *jen*, which has been translated as 'loving-kindness'. Confucius' followers have not always regarded this as something to be impartially exercised, but as a 'graded love', with a preference for your own relatives and friends. Marxists regard the teaching of Confucius as patriarchal and aristocratic, and therefore tend to reject it. The part that Confucius' teaching played in making what came to be known in later days as 'State Confucianism' is described in Volume I in the article CHINESE RELIGION.

See also Vol. I: CHINESE CIVILIZATION.

CONGREVE, William (1670–1729), *see* Vol. XII: RESTORATION DRAMA.

CONRAD, Joseph (1857–1924). The novelist and master mariner, Josef Konrad Korzeniowski, was a Pole, born in Russian-occupied Podolia; but he wrote his great tales of the sea in English. As a boy he was exiled with his parents to

Lady Bone

JOSEPH CONRAD
Bronze bust by Jacob Epstein, 1924

northern Russia, where he read the works of Victor Hugo and Walter Scott; the sea writers Marryat and W. W. Jacobs later influenced him. His first sight of ships was at Marseilles when he was 17, and thereafter his life was spent mostly at sea, visiting the ports and strange sea-boards, especially in Malaya, that he later wrote about.

Conrad obtained his master's ticket in the British Merchant Navy, which inspired him by its courage and devotion to duty. Not all his best books, however, are about the sea—*The Secret Agent* and *Under Western Eyes* tell of revolutionary intrigue in England and Russia, and *Heart of Darkness* is based on his voyage up the Congo during which he contracted fevers that made him give up sailoring. Of his other books, *Typhoon* and *Tales of Unrest* are as stirring as their titles, and *The Mirror of the Sea* is an imaginative record of 20 years at sea, mostly in sail. *Lord Jim* which, with *Chance*, is his best-known book, tells of a brave man who redeems himself after once giving way to fear. In his prose Conrad brilliantly conveys his heroic view of life together with his own direct personal experience. Sentimentalists have accused him of pessimism, but in fact his books reflect the robust philosophy of a man of action who knows that life, if lived to the full, is more often like fighting a tempest than sailing in fair weather. There is no better introduction to Conrad than his en-

thralling and typical long short-story *Youth*, in which a young second mate tells the story of 'an English barque burnt at sea'.

CONSTABLE, John (1776–1837). Constable was one of the greatest landscape painters and one of the very few English artists who have had an important influence on European painting. He was born at East Bergholt, in Suffolk, in 1776, the son of a well-to-do miller. The valley of the river Stour and its water-meadows, clumps of great trees, square towers of village churches, and mills with their water-wheels, sluices, and wooden bridges, were familiar to and loved by Constable in all their detail and in all moods of weather. His art springs from this familiarity. 'Painting', he wrote, 'is with me but another word for feeling, and I associate my careless boyhood with all that lies on the banks of the Stour; these scenes made me a painter.'

His father did not favour art as a profession, and Constable as a boy worked almost secretly, painting in the cottage of the local plumber, John Dunthorne, an amateur painter himself. For a year he did try his hand at milling. Strong and well-built, he was called 'the handsome miller'. But his love of painting was so irrepressible that a friend persuaded his father to send him to London to study. After some 2 years in London he returned to his father's business for a year, and then in 1799 he entered the Royal Academy School in London, and embarked on his career. Henceforward he lived in London, making long visits to Suffolk. He never went abroad. His progress was slow—towards worldly success very slow. Yet he was industrious, moderate in his needs, and a man of attractive and sociable character who might have been expected to succeed. He tried to make his living by painting portraits, but his heart was never in this and he achieved no popularity.

Constable studied and admired the works of CLAUDE (q.v.) and other masters, but he scorned the conventions of landscape painting of his day, whereby pictures were composed according to rules derived from other pictures and not from the study of nature. He despised the fashion for painting in golden brown colours in imitation of the look of old masters. Constable felt there 'was room enough for a natural way of painting' by which to re-create landscapes as he felt and knew them, with the changing weather and cloud formations that millers knew, but which fashionable painters thought unsuitable for art. He put into his landscapes the cattle, horses, and people who would be working there, and the dew, the moisture, the bloom and freshness of the countryside. 'His landscapes made me call for my umbrella', said another artist, and his pictures seemed to his contemporaries rustic, crude, and rough in finish. So little was he appreciated that the purchaser of the first picture to be sold got another artist to paint out Constable's sky.

When he was about 35 Constable at last found a friend, the Rev. John Fisher, afterwards Archdeacon of Salisbury, who appreciated and understood his genius, and who was able occasionally to buy the large landscapes on which Constable had set his heart. This friendship of over 20 years was the greatest encouragement Constable ever received, and visits to Salisbury inspired a series of magnificent paintings of the cathedral.

In 1816 Constable married Maria Bicknell, with whom he lived very happily and by whom he had seven children. His friend and biographer, the painter Leslie, says 'his fondness for children exceeded that of any man I ever knew'. In 1828 Mrs. Constable inherited a fortune from her father, and this, together with Constable's own legacy from his father, made Constable secure from financial need.

In 1824 several of his important pictures, including 'The Hay Wain', were exhibited in Paris where they made an immediate impression. They considerably influenced the work of DELACROIX (q.v.), the French landscape painter, and later of the IMPRESSIONISTS (q.v. Vol. XII). In England Constable never received the recognition that he felt was his due, though he was elected A.R.A. in 1819 and R.A. in 1829.

Outwardly Constable's later life was placidly and industriously spent, surrounded by his children, though he was continuously concerned over his health, his family's prospects, and his lack of fame. He held his opinions firmly and never hesitated to defend them; he attacked his critics sharply, and disdained to curry favour,

Victoria & Albert Museum

STUDY FOR 'THE HAY WAIN': PAINTING BY JOHN CONSTABLE

Constable made full-size studies for a number of his large pictures which show more vividly than the finished works his brilliant rendering of sunlight and clouds

flatter, or please the fashionable world. Consequently he made enemies. Most of his paintings and studies were in his possession, unsold, when he died, though 50 years later they were recognized as great national treasures.

See also Vol. XII: British Art; Landscape Painting; Colour Plate opp. p. 448.

CONSTANTINE THE GREAT (A.D. 274–337).

The two most memorable facts about Constantine are that he was the first Roman Emperor to accept Christianity and to give it official status, and that he founded Constantinople, now Istanbul (q.v. Vol. III), and shifted the centre of the Roman Empire from the west to the east (see Byzantine Empire, Vol. I).

When Diocletian (q.v.) became Emperor in A.D. 284, he took over an empire threatened on all sides by barbarian attacks, and internally disunited and in financial chaos. He proceeded completely to reorganize it, but he found that to do this effectively he must subdivide the authority. He divided his territories, making a separate ruler of the west, and he appointed 'Caesars' to rule subdivisions of the Empire. One of these Caesars was Constantine's father, Constantius, who ruled Britain, Gaul, and Spain. When Diocletian abdicated in 305, Constantius succeeded him as Emperor in the west.

Constantine was the eldest son of Constantius

ARCH OF CONSTANTINE, ROME
By tradition this commemorates his victory in A.D 312

and St. Helena, who, according to tradition, later visited Jerusalem and discovered the Holy Sepulchre and the Cross, and whom her son always honoured and loved. Constantine was brought up at Diocletian's Court where, being handsome, strong, and ambitious, he was a favourite. He was serving in Britain when his father died in 306. Constantine was proclaimed Emperor by the troops. For the next few years he fought against many rivals in a struggle to win the whole Empire. In 312, before a decisive battle outside Rome, Constantine is said to have seen a vision of a cross of light in the evening sky and beneath it the words 'In this sign conquer'. A further vision told him to set the sign of Christ on his own helmet and on the shields of his men. Constantine did this; and there followed a great victory. Like his father, he had always allowed a measure of toleration to Christians, in opposition to the persecutions of Diocletian and others, but now he gave the Church both support and wealth. His successful conquests continued, and by 323 he had become sole Emperor of both east and west (see Map, Index, p. 52).

The Christian Church (q.v. Vol. I) by the 3rd century had become a firmly organized society, growing in numbers and authority. Constantine realized that, since it could not be crushed, it must be built as a corner-stone into his Empire. It must, therefore, be united, without heresies. So, at his instigation, the leaders of the Church met at the Council of Nicaea and drew up the Nicene Creed (see Athanasius). How far Constantine's own Christianity was a spiritual conviction and how far a mere political move it is impossible to tell; but it seems most likely that he had a real conviction of the glory, majesty, and might of God. He was a wise diplomat, but also a warm-hearted and passionate man to whom a cold and calculating attitude would not have been natural. He was not actually baptized, however, until shortly before his death.

Constantine was a successful military leader; he was also a wise ruler who legislated for his great Empire with courage, energy, and purpose. His chief creation was the rebuilding of the old city of Byzantium on the Bosphorus into his new capital, Constantinople. He was often wastefully extravagant, and indulgent to unworthy seekers of his favour. His family life was blotted by the sudden arrest and execution of his son

Crispus and, shortly after, the murder of his wife, Fausta, possibly because Constantine discovered too late that she had brought false charges against her stepson to advance her own sons.

Constantine's contribution to the Christian Church, and consequently to Western civilization, is enormous. By the early Church he was thought of as a thirteenth Apostle.

See also Vol. I: ROMAN CIVILIZATION; CHRISTIAN CHURCH.

See also Vol. III: ISTANBUL.

COOK, James (1728–79). Cook is perhaps the greatest English explorer (*see* EXPLORATION, Vol. IV), not only because he discovered Australia and New Zealand, but because he set new standards in the accuracy of CHARTS (q.v. Vol. IV) and in the preservation of the health of seamen (*see* SEA TRAVEL, Vol. IV).

Cook was the son of a farm labourer at Marton, in the North Riding of Yorkshire, and himself worked on a farm as a young boy, receiving little education. He served for a short time in a haberdasher's shop and then ran away to sea, and was apprenticed at the age of 17 to a Whitby firm of coal-shippers, in which hard school he learned the art of NAVIGATION (q.v. Vol. IV). It was in small ships of the collier type that he made all his voyages of discovery.

At the outbreak of the Seven Years War he volunteered for the Royal Navy. The captain of his ship soon realized that this tall, silent, modest north countryman was not only strong and handsome but also a dependable and efficient seaman who would make an excellent master or navigating officer. As such he served in a number of line-of-battle ships, in one of which he helped to pilot the fleet which took General WOLFE (q.v.) to Quebec.

The charts he made in Canada won him a high reputation as a surveyor, and this led to his appointment in 1768 to command the ENDEAVOUR (q.v. Vol. IV), the ship chosen by the Admiralty and the Royal Society to go on a scientific expedition to the newly discovered island of Tahiti. The avowed purpose of the expedition was to observe the astronomical transit of the planet Venus; its real purpose was to anticipate the French in the discovery of a continent called Terra Australis Incognita, which was supposed to exist in the South Pacific.

Finding no land to the south of Tahiti, Cook turned west to discover and chart the east coast of New Zealand, the west having been discovered by TASMAN (q.v.) in 1642. In 6 months Cook charted 2,400 miles of coastline with extraordinary accuracy. He then continued west, and reached the eastern coast of Australia (which he called New South Wales), the north-western parts having been discovered, but not settled, even before Tasman's time, and named New Holland. On 29 April 1770, Cook landed at Botany Bay, the place to which the first fleet of convicts was sent a few years after his death. On her way north to Java the *Endeavour* ran aground on the Barrier Reef. So excellent was Cook's leadership that Joseph Banks, who sailed with him, recorded with admiration 'the cool and steady conduct of the officers, who never gave an order which did not show them to be perfectly composed and unmoved by the circumstances'.

One of Cook's great contributions to seamanship was his strict attention to health and cleanliness on board and his discovery of how to keep down scurvy and dysentery among the crew by a proper diet and an absence of dirt. In his second voyage in 1772, with the *Resolution* and the *Adventure*, he did not lose a single man from disease, an unprecedented achievement. On this voyage he introduced a new method of ascertaining the longitude by proving the efficiency of Harrison's CHRONOMETER (q.v. Vol. IV) which was only 7 minutes 45 seconds slow after over 3 years at sea. He was also able finally to disprove the legend of a southern continent by crossing the Antarctic circle for the first time in history. His long stay in the Polynesian islands and New Zealand enabled him to add much to our knowledge of primitive life and customs (*see* PACIFIC ISLANDERS, Vol. I).

On his return home he was promoted captain, received the Royal Society's highest award for the preservation of life at sea, and, when the results of his discoveries were published, enjoyed a brief taste of fame. His *Voyages* has always been a very popular travel book.

In 1776 he set out with the *Resolution* and *Discovery* on his third voyage, this time to search for a North-West Passage near Vancouver Island (named after an explorer who sailed with him). Sailing by way of the Cape and New Zealand, he again visited Tahiti and then discovered the Hawaiian islands on his way to the American coast. He missed the strait leading to the modern town of Vancouver, but refreshed his men on the

CAPTAIN COOK LANDING AT TANNA IN THE NEW HEBRIDES
He is holding a green branch as a symbol of peace. From Cook, *A Voyage towards the South Pole and round the World*

island. He followed the coast north, searching in vain for a passage, until he sailed through the Bering Strait (discovered by the Russians in 1741) as far as latitude 70° N., where he was stopped by a wall of ice.

On his return to Hawaii he was killed in a sudden quarrel with the natives on 14 February 1779—a tragic end since one of his qualities was his ability to make friends with natives of all sorts by treating them with kindness and justice. His crew made another attempt to penetrate the icepack that summer, but, on failing to do so, the ships returned home by way of China the next year.

The secret of Cook's success was his capacity for taking pains. He showed his quality in the way he faithfully obeyed his instructions on his first voyage and then carried out his own ideas with the greatest courage and perseverance on his second and third. The accuracy of his charts and the health record of the men under his command were remarkable achievements. He was entirely fearless, sailing his small ships over a wider area of unknown seas than any other explorer, and he could endure hardship better than most men. His temper was stern and his discipline strict, but he could be 'exceedingly affable to the crew' and he never had to contend with mutinies such as occurred in the ship BOUNTY (q.v. Vol. IV) under Bligh (one of Cook's officers) a few years later. When Cook

died, one of his men said, 'We all felt that we had lost a father'.

See also colour plate opposite p. 128.
See also Vol. I: AUSTRALIANS.
See also Vol. IV: ENDEAVOUR, H.M.S.; EXPLORATION.

COPERNICUS, Nicholas (1473–1543). The modern belief that the sun is a star, that the planets revolve around it, and that the earth is just one of these planets, derived from the work of the astronomer Copernicus. Before his time it was generally believed that the earth was stationary in the centre of the UNIVERSE (q.v. Vol. III), and that the sun, moon, planets, and stars all circled round it. This change of view has had a revolutionary effect on all man's thought. The old, or Ptolemaic, theory led men to think of the universe as created for the benefit of humanity, whereas the new, or Copernican, view gave man a much more modest place in the universe and forced subsequent generations to think out anew all the problems about man's place in the scheme of things.

Copernicus, son of a leading merchant, and nephew of a bishop, was a Pole. His university studies at Cracow were mainly in law and medicine, but he gave much time privately to mathematics and astronomy. He studied in Italy until his early 30's, then returned to Poland and took up an administrative appointment at Frauenburg Cathedral. There he lived quietly for the rest of his days, dividing his time between his official duties and his astronomical research, besides giving free medical services to the poor.

The existing astronomical theory, called the Ptolemaic system after its founder PTOLEMY (q.v.), was very involved (*see* ASTRONOMY, HISTORY of, Vol. III). To make the theory fit the observed motions of the planets complicated geometrical tricks had to be used: one of these was to make the planet move in the curve called an 'epicycloid'—the sort of curve that is followed by a point on the edge of a sixpence, when it is made to roll round the edge of a half-crown.

Copernicus had begun to think of these things while a university student. When he was about 39 he circulated among his friends a manuscript setting out his new ideas, showing that the whole theory of the heavenly bodies could be immensely simplified by abandoning the belief that the earth is stationary and by assuming instead that it has two motions of its own: (1) rotating on its own axis every 24 hours, and (2) circling round the sun once a year. His great book, *Concerning the Revolutions of the Heavenly Spheres*, which set out his theory in detail, was published in 1543, the year of his death.

Copernicus did not succeed in completely eliminating epicycles and other complications from the theory; that could not be done until

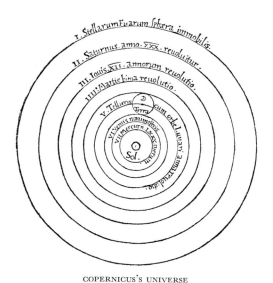

COPERNICUS'S UNIVERSE

From *De Revolutionibus Orbium Coelestium*, 1565. This gives an extremely simplified version of the universe as conceived by Copernicus, with the sun in the centre surrounded by the planets and stars

KEPLER (q.v.), more than half a century later, had shown that the true paths of the planets were not circles but ellipses. Nevertheless the Copernican theory was much simpler than Ptolemy's.

Copernicus's theory, scorned by such men as LUTHER and CALVIN (qq.v.), was not generally accepted until well into the 17th century, partly because of religious and other prejudices, and partly because Copernicus had failed to solve many of the scientific problems involved, so that his theory seemed to be inconsistent with the known behaviour of moving bodies. General acceptance of his views had to await the work of KEPLER and GALILEO, through whom it led eventually to the great gravitational theory of NEWTON, which was not superseded till the time of EINSTEIN (qq.v.).

See also Vol. III: ASTRONOMY, HISTORY OF.

CORNEILLE, Pierre (1606–84). Corneille, the first major French dramatist, wrote thirty-four plays, a number of works on dramatic theory, and some poetry. He began by writing comedies, showing considerable skill in handling the stock themes of comedy of intrigue. But it was not until 1636, with *Le Cid*, a tragi-comedy, that he obtained his first great literary success. This play, which established the pattern of French poetic drama for the next 200 years, is typical of Corneille's tragedies. At the outset his principal characters are placed in a dilemma in which their reason and their sense of what is right urge them along one path, while their emotions incline them towards another. This mental conflict forms the theme of the play, which usually ends with the triumph of reason over the emotions, of duty over love. In *Le Cid*, Rodrigue is forced to kill the father of his beloved Chimène or be forever dishonoured. When after much anguish he does so, Chimène must fight against her love for him, her father's murderer, and seek his death. Using this kind of situation, Corneille wins from his audience pity for the victims in their plight, and admiration for the courage they show.

Le Cid had great immediate success in the theatre—the phrase '*beau comme Le Cid*' became proverbial; but the play was attacked by certain critics for transgressing what were the generally accepted rules for writing tragedy. Chief among these was the classical rule of the three unities of action, time, and place, which demanded that there should be only one main theme to a play, and that all the events of the play should take place within 24 hours, and in the same place. Corneille, who had an irascible temper, resented the censure of Cardinal Richelieu's newly formed Académie Française—although, in fact, he accepted the principle of the unities. He often found it difficult to keep the unity of time, because in this type of tragic plot there had to be a series of obstacles for the hero to vanquish. In *Le Cid*, for example, Rodrigue fights two duels and wins a battle all in the course of 24 hours. This rule of the three unities did not necessarily hamper the producer, for they suited very well with the conditions in which plays were then performed; stages were often small, the lighting and effects of the simplest, and attention was concentrated on the words rather than on ingenious production. Corneille wrote in rhymed couplets, and the rhythm and sound of the words was a very important element in the plays.

Le Cid was followed by three fine tragedies: *Horace*, on the theme of patriotism against love; *Cinna*, where pardon overcomes vengeance; and *Polyeucte*, where religious belief is in conflict with earthly love. In 1643 he produced his best comedy, *Le Menteur*, and in 1647 he was at last elected to the Académie Française. But his popularity was declining, and on the complete failure of his play *Pertharite* in 1652, he abandoned the theatre for 7 years. During this time Corneille wrote religious poetry and works on dramatic theory, and then in 1659 produced *Oedipe*, his last play to be well received. He felt bitterly his gradual loss of popularity, and this was emphasized by Racine's rise in favour.

Corneille's private life was unremarkable. He came of a prosperous middle-class family in Rouen, was educated at a Jesuit College, and became a lawyer. He and a younger brother Thomas, to whom he was devoted, married two sisters, Pierre having seven children. He moved to Paris where he lived for the last 20 years of his life, and he died, comparatively poor and neglected, at the age of 78.

Corneille's tragedies are still read and acted not only because they are tense and moving, but also because of the breadth and nobility of their

THE RESCUE OF ANDROMEDA, FROM CORNEILLE'S 'ANDROMÈDE'
Perseus appears on his horse Pegasus to rescue Andromeda (right) and overcome the monster. Engraving from the edition of 1651

poetry, which can still inspire the actor and grip the spectator.

See also RACINE; CID, THE.
See also Vol. XII: FRENCH LITERATURE; DRAMA.

COROT, Jean (1796–1875), *see* Vol. XII: LANDSCAPE PAINTING.

CORREGGIO, Antonio da (1494–1534), *see* Vol. XII: VENETIAN PAINTING.

CORTÉS, Hernando (1485–1547). Cortés, the conqueror of Mexico, was the son of an impoverished Spanish noble, and early decided to win fame and fortune with his sword. When he was 19 he went out to the West Indian islands, 12 years after their discovery by COLUMBUS (q.v.), and told the governor's secretary: 'I come to get gold, not to till the soil like a peasant.'

He became a civil official of the Spanish colony of Cuba and earned a reputation for efficiency in this newly settled island. When, in 1518, the Spaniards decided to try to conquer the ancient and wealthy AZTEC Empire in Mexico (q.v. Vol. I), Cortés was given command of the expedition. In 1519 he landed in Mexico, and to inspire his men with his own spirit of determination, he burned the ships which provided their only means of escape if they were defeated. The story of Cortés's conquest of Mexico, as told by W. H. Prescott, the historian, is more exciting and more improbable than the wildest story of imaginary adventure. Cortés's force consisted of about 400 Spaniards, 15 horses, 13 muskets, and 7 small cannon, and with this tiny army he set out to conquer a populous, extensive, and old-established empire with an apparently impregnable capital, built on an island in the middle of a great lake. The basic reason for Cortés's success was undoubtedly his own remarkable character as a leader of men. He was utterly fearless, no matter what the odds against him; never without a stratagem, no matter how apparently hopeless the situation; pitilessly cruel when he considered it necessary to terrorize the enemy. Cortés and his soldiers also believed that it was their duty to convert the natives to Christianity and to put an end to their hideous human sacrifices and cannibalism. The vivid accounts of eye-witnesses suggest that had Cortés been killed on any of the many occasions when he was near death, his little party

would have been butchered to a man. But, since the Aztecs ruled their subject peoples with brutal oppression, many of these enthusiastically supported Cortés's attack on their overlords, and he was further helped by the tendency of the natives, even the Emperor Montezuma himself, to accept as gods these strange men with their magic firearms and horses.

Cortés and his companions reached the capital, which they seized by guile. They were admitted as honoured guests because the Emperor Montezuma thought they were sent by heaven. When belief in their divinity began to wear thin, the tiny band of Spaniards took the Emperor prisoner in his own capital, and ruled his Empire by forcing him to issue their orders as his own. At last the people, led by Montezuma's brother, rose against the oppressiveness and rapacity of the Spaniards' rule, and Montezuma was killed in the fighting. Cortés and his men had to fight their way out of the capital by night against hordes of infuriated natives who attacked them as they made their way along the narrow causeways which connected the city with the land. A large part of the Spanish force was lost. Cortés, however, gathered a new army of the subject peoples of the Aztec Empire, and recaptured the capital after a long struggle in which the beautiful city was totally destroyed.

After conquering the whole empire, Cortés quarrelled with the Spanish Government, who feared his power and determined to thwart it. He went home to Spain and died there in disgrace.

See also PIZARRO.
See also Vol. I: AZTEC CIVILIZATION; MEXICANS.

COTMAN, John (1782–1842), *see* Vol. XII: WATER-COLOUR.

COURBET, Gustave (1819–77). This French painter came of robust country stock long settled around Ornans in eastern France. Most of his life was spent in Paris, but Courbet remained a countryman, revisiting Ornans almost every year to paint its landscape and people. He became a painter against his family's wishes and without regular art training. Handsome, energetic, conceited, generous, sure of his purpose and his power as a painter, he soon made his way in Paris. His pictures, shown each year in the official exhibition, roused furious controversy. His everyday scenes and humble people, painted as they were with no attempt to beautify them

or give them literary interest, flouted alike the doctrines of the classical and the romantic schools of painting. Such 'realism', as he called it, inspired the younger painters (*see* IMPRESSIONISTS, Vol. XII). The choice of humble subjects led some to claim his work as championing the poor, but Courbet, who declared himself a socialist after the 1848 revolution in Paris, only later took to active politics. In 1871 he was a member of the revolutionary Commune and, on its defeat, was judged responsible for the destruction of the Vendôme Column (a memorial to Napoleon). He was imprisoned, released, and ordered to pay an impossible fine. He died in exile in Switzerland.

See Illustration, p. 33.
See also Vol. XII: FRENCH ART.

CRANMER, Thomas (1489–1556). The Archbishop, martyr, and maker of the Book of Common Prayer, was the son of a Nottinghamshire country gentleman. He became a Fellow of Jesus College, Cambridge, and did not take holy orders until nearly 40. When HENRY VIII (q.v.) sought to divorce his wife Catherine of

National Portrait Gallery

ARCHBISHOP CRANMER, 1546
Portrait by Gerlach Flicke

Aragon and the Pope would not grant the necessary licence, Cranmer suggested that the case should be examined in an English court and not at Rome. The King, on hearing this suggestion, exclaimed: 'This man has got the right sow by the ear', and from that time he made Cranmer his friend and adviser. Cranmer did what the King wanted, rarely questioning his judgements.

When the Archbishop of Canterbury died in 1532, the King nominated Cranmer to succeed him. Cranmer approached the Convocations of the Clergy about the King's marriage, and they gave their opinion that the King's first marriage (to Catherine) was null and void, and that the Pope had exceeded his lawful powers in giving a licence for it. Then, at an ecclesiastical court held at Dunstable, Cranmer pronounced the King's marriage with Anne Boleyn lawful, and the week after crowned her queen. Later, he stood godfather to her daughter Elizabeth. Yet he annulled the marriage in 1536, making only a mild protest. He also divorced Henry from Anne of Cleves and was persuaded of Catherine Howard's guilt.

Cranmer supported the REFORMATION (q.v. Vol. I) and opposed Papal supremacy; but he held no extreme views and took little part in the political acts by which the change was accomplished. He was suited for a scholarly life and lacked the independence of mind and courage needful for a man of affairs. He condoned many acts of harsh persecution, although he tried to prevent some of the more severe measures. He did not see the same urgent need for reforming the Church, especially the monasteries, that Bishop Latimer saw. He was easily influenced: Ridley, for example, when his chaplain, moved him towards Protestant doctrine, and he gave Continental Protestants not only a refuge but important teaching positions. He found it genuinely difficult to make up his own mind amidst conflicting views, and this often led him to act like a time-server and a coward.

Cranmer's supreme gift to his Church and country is the Book of Common Prayer. The First Prayer Book of 1549 probably expresses his real faith; but in 1552 he agreed to many changes to meet Protestant criticisms, and the Second Prayer Book was issued. The inspiration and the magnificent language of this book, especially of the Collects, shows Cranmer at his best.

THE BURNING OF LATIMER AND RIDLEY AT OXFORD, 16 OCTOBER 1555
Cranmer watches from his prison on the right. He was burnt at the same spot a few months later. Woodcut from Foxe, *History of the Actes and Monuments of the Church*, 1563

In Edward VI's reign Cranmer had little political influence. He could not play the part that Latimer, a rougher and more outspoken man, never ceased to play in condemning the greed of the new rulers who were plundering England to enrich themselves. Then, when the young King was dying, Cranmer was induced to sign the King's will barring his sister Mary from the succession because she was a Roman Catholic. This attempt to exclude Mary failed, however, and soon after her accession Cranmer was imprisoned in the Tower of London. He was later transferred to Oxford prison where Ridley and Latimer were held, and from his high prison window he witnessed the burning of these two martyrs. Latimer kept his outspoken courage to the end, and spoke his last immortal words: 'We shall this day light such a candle by God's grace in England, as I trust shall never be put out.' Cranmer was not of the hard stuff of which most martyrs are made, and 'for fear of death, and to save my life if it might be' he made one

recantation after another. But at the last hearing, in St. Mary's, Oxford, courage and a sure confidence came to him. He repudiated all his former recantations, declaring 'And forasmuch as my hand offended in writing contrary to my heart, it shall be first burned'. He went boldly to his death, putting his right hand into the flame with the words, 'This hand hath offended', and holding it there to the end. Today a monument called the Martyrs' Memorial stands in Oxford in honour of these three.

See also Vol. I: CHURCH OF ENGLAND.

CROESUS (6th century B.C.). This last King of Lydia, part of what is now Turkey, ruled from about 560 to 546 B.C. He has become an almost legendary figure because of his fabulous wealth and the luxury and extravagance of his court at Sardis. He was greatly attracted by Greek culture and sent lavish gifts to the sanctuaries in Greece, especially to Delphi (*see* TEMPLE, Vol. I).

When the Persian King, CYRUS (q.v.), defeated the King of Media, Lydia's eastern neighbour, Croesus in alarm consulted the Delphic Oracle; the answer came that 'if he warred with the Persians he would overthrow a mighty empire'. Assuming that the 'mighty empire' meant Persia, not Lydia, Croesus boldly attacked the Persians, who defeated him utterly, and captured his capital, Sardis. What happened to Croesus in the end is uncertain; he may have been slain at Sardis, but, according to one story, he was taken to the Persian Court and treated with great liberality—which was quite in accord with the character of Cyrus.

CROME, John (1768–1821), see Vol. XII: LANDSCAPE PAINTING.

CROMWELL, Oliver (1599–1658). Cromwell was the most powerful person, and for a time the absolute ruler, in Britain during the only period in British history when the monarchy has been abandoned. Cromwell achieved his remarkable eminence partly as a result of the CIVIL WAR (q.v. Vol. X) in which his genius as a military leader brought him to the front, and partly because of his great strength of character and his passionate religious convictions.

Cromwell's father was a gentleman farmer in Huntingdon, in East Anglia, where they lived 'neither in any great height nor yet in obscurity'. Cromwell went to Huntingdon Grammar School, and then to Cambridge. In 1617 he inherited a small estate. As a boy he was not particularly religious, but enjoyed riding and other outdoor sports, and also music. In early manhood he underwent a conversion and became a strict Puritan, believing that he had been chosen by God for salvation, which imposed a tremendous obligation on him to do God's will. Though he sat as member for Huntingdon in the Parliaments of 1628 and 1640, and was related to John HAMPDEN and other leaders of the opposition to CHARLES I (qq.v), he was at first little known outside East Anglia.

When the Civil War broke out, Cromwell, then 43 and with no previous military experience, raised and led a troop of cavalry for Parliament. Two years later he was a Lieutenant-General, and largely responsible for the defeat of Prince RUPERT (q.v.) at Marston Moor. A year later, as second-in-command under Fairfax of all Parliament's forces, he defeated King Charles's army at Naseby. These successes were due to his brilliance as a tactician and leader of cavalry. His columns of horsemen were determined, well-trained, and well-disciplined (see CAVALRY, Vol. X). Cromwell helped to choose the men for the 'New Model Army', as it was called. He believed that virtuous living and sound religion made the best soldiers: 'If you choose Godly, honest men to be Captains of Horse, honest men will follow them. I had rather have a plain russet-coated captain that knows what he fights for and loves what he knows, than what you call a gentleman and nothing else.' He was against religious tyranny of any sort, Presbyterian as much as Anglican: 'The State', he said, 'in choosing men to serve it takes no notice of their opinions; if they be willing faithfully to serve it, that satisfies.'

By 1649 Cromwell and the senior army officers supported by the Independents (the extremists in Parliament) had control of the country. The King was executed, the Presbyterians or moderate Parliamentarians subdued, and the Levellers (the democratic radicals) and the Agitators (the spokesmen of the common soldiers) crushed. For the next 4 years England was ruled as a Commonwealth—a republic in which power was divided between the army, under Cromwell, and some surviving members of Charles's Parliament. As most members of the House of Commons had been expelled or had ceased to attend, the surviving members were known as the Rump.

Cromwell was at once faced with troubles in Ireland and Scotland. In Ireland civil war was raging, and Cromwell, who believed that the Catholic Irish were fit only to be the servants of English and Scottish colonists, treated them with extreme severity. His terrible massacre of the garrisons at Drogheda and Wexford, after they had already surrendered, is the worst stain on his record. In the meantime, Charles I's son, later CHARLES II (q.v.), was winning support in Scotland. On his return from Ireland Cromwell at once invaded Scotland and won a decisive victory at Dunbar. But in the following year Charles gathered another army, which met Cromwell's army at Worcester and was completely defeated. Cromwell called this victory his 'crowning mercy'. Charles escaped to France, and the Civil War came to an end.

The problem of how Britain was to be governed had to be resolved. Cromwell and the army officers wanted a new constitution and

OLIVER CROMWELL
Portrait by Robert Walker

a more representative Parliament; but the Rumpers, who had become increasingly dilatory and corrupt, wished to continue in power. Cromwell, firmly believing that he had a 'dispensation' from God to break the deadlock, at last became convinced that he must expel the Rump, which he did in April 1653. This removed the last vestige of constitutional or legal authority in England: even the Judges were appointed by Cromwell. Cromwell, however, had no wish to rule by force alone, and almost at once called a new Parliament. But the element of extreme Puritans in this 'Little Parliament' or 'Barebones Parliament' made it as obstructive as the Rump, and it, too, was dissolved. The army then made Cromwell Lord Protector, and for the next 6 years (1653–9) the government was known as the Protectorate. Cromwell lived in the old royal palaces, held Court on a modest scale, and assumed more and more the functions and airs of a king. He did not abandon his idea of governing constitutionally, and during the Protectorate two more Parliaments were called. But Cromwell quarrelled with both of them, and neither lasted much more than a year.

Cromwell's failure as a constitutional ruler was due partly to a deep sense of insecurity in the country: many people believed that sooner or later the King and the old order would return, and attempts were even made on Cromwell's life. His fatal weakness was his dependence on the army, for the maintaining of an army takes money. If Cromwell depended on Parliament to raise the money, the landowners and merchants in Parliament who most disliked military rule would insist on a larger share in the government. If it was raised without the consent of Parliament, all pretence of constitutional government would vanish and the system would appear in its true colours as a military dictatorship. Compromise was hardly possible. But during Cromwell's life the issue was put off, although in 1655, partly in order to put down Royalist plots, he unhesitatingly divided the country into military districts, each under a Major-General.

Cromwell pursued an active foreign policy, and his armies won great respect for Britain. The British fleet, brilliantly led by Robert BLAKE (q.v.), swept first the Dutch and then the Spanish navy from the seas, and again made Britain mistress of the seas. British troops supported France against Spain in the Netherlands, and in the Spanish West Indies Jamaica was added to Britain's overseas possessions. This alliance with France against Spain, however, inadvertently helped forward the real rival to English overseas trade and conquest: Spain was in decline, whereas France under LOUIS XIV (q.v.) was becoming the strongest power in Europe.

When Cromwell died in September 1658, worn out with illness and care, the Republic very quickly collapsed. The government was heavily in debt, none of its problems had been settled, and Cromwell's son, Richard, was totally unfitted to succeed him. Richard was forced to abdicate in the following year, and after a year of extreme confusion, General Monk, Cromwell's Commander-in-Chief in Scotland, recalled Parliament, and Charles II was invited to return. Cromwell's body was removed from Westminster Abbey, hung up in public like that of a common criminal, and afterwards buried beneath the scaffold at Tyburn.

Though neither the Commonwealth nor the Protectorate was a totalitarian dictatorship in the modern sense, in both cases a minority enforced its will on the rest of the country. Cromwell was a reluctant dictator, though when convinced that he was the instrument of God's purpose, he could act with extreme ruthlessness. He was undoubtedly a great soldier and a man of tremendous determination. But despite the victories of British fleets and armies, Cromwell's experiment in government was a failure. This failure was due partly to his own sincere desire to govern constitutionally when circumstances made constitutional government difficult, and partly because there was no one to succeed him.

See also CHARLES I.
See also Vol. X: CIVIL WAR; TOTALITARIANISM.

CROMWELL, Thomas (*c.* 1485–1540), *see* HENRY VIII.

CURIE, Pierre (1859–1906) and **Marie** (1867–1934). Pierre and his wife Marie worked together in Paris on magnetism and the new science of radioactivity, and isolated the element radium (*see* MATTER, Vol. III).

Pierre Curie, a Frenchman born and brought up in Paris, was a physicist, especially interested in MAGNETISM and ELECTRICITY. His wife, Marie (Manya) Sklodowska, a Pole born and brought up in Warsaw, was a chemist interested in MINERALS and METALS (qq.v. Vol. III). She belonged to a clever family, not at all well off, and had been encouraged by her father, a schoolmaster, to love learning for its own sake and to take life seriously. Had she remained in Poland she might never have done her great work in science, but the oppression of the Polish people by the Russian government of the Tsars drove her to seek freedom in western Europe. By the time she was 24 she had saved up enough money from her salary as a teacher to go to Paris, where she worked desperately hard in the greatest poverty. She and Pierre made friends over their work, and in 1895 they were married. Pierre Curie at that time was teaching physics in a technical college at a small salary and devoting all his spare time to his experimental work in physics. Marie decided to take a degree at Paris by doing original work in the science of metals. Late in 1895, however, came the discovery of X-rays by Röntgen in Germany (see RADIATION, Vol. III), and this important event led to the discovery of the radioactivity of uranium by Becquerel in Paris in 1896 (see ATOM, Vol. III).

The Curies, friends of Becquerel, decided to work together on this new and exciting subject. The new science needed both chemists and physicists; therefore Marie being the chemist and Pierre the physicist, they made one of the greatest scientific partnerships ever known. One of their many difficulties was to find a laboratory in which to carry out their experiments. Marie used an old store-room in the University, cold and damp, and lacking in proper apparatus or adequate space.

At first all that was known about radioactivity was that the element uranium gave off energy continuously and that this energy could electrify the air. Pierre, the expert in physics, found exact ways of measuring this electrification. Marie, as a chemist, experimented to discover if substances other than uranium could also be radioactive. In 1898 they found that thorium, an element similar to uranium, was even more radioactive than uranium. No other element then known had this property. It had become clear that radioactivity was something which concerned atoms (whose nature was then little known) and that it was confined to the very heaviest elements. Were uranium and thorium the only radioactive elements? The Curies decided to find out. They noted that a mineral called pitchblende, containing uranium but no thorium,

L. E. A.
MADAME CURIE IN HER LABORATORY

was about five times as radioactive as it ought to have been. Madame Curie therefore analysed some, isolating every substance in it and handing it over to Pierre Curie for testing. Traces of what appeared to be bismuth and barium in the mineral were found to be strongly radioactive. The Curies supposed from this, correctly, that they had discovered small amounts of the two new elements, which resembled bismuth and barium chemically, but which could not be bismuth and barium themselves, for these were known not to be radioactive. The Curies then laboriously and patiently worked up the bismuth and barium residues from many tons of the mineral pitchblende, and eventually Madame Curie separated from the bismuth in a pure state a radioactive element which she called polonium (in honour of Poland) and from the barium a radioactive element to which she gave the name of radium.

All this was done when the Curies were poor, hardly known, and the parents of a 1-year-old child. They had to work against the greatest difficulties. A bigger laboratory than Marie's store-room was essential, and after long search and pleading, all they could obtain was an old wooden shed with no floor and a leaking roof, stifling in summer and freezing in winter. In this for 4 devoted years they worked, smelting their pitchblende which had to be secured from Austria, and treating the ore with chemicals, failing again and again until, in 1902, Marie at last obtained a tiny piece of pure radium. Most of this time Marie was also teaching science in a girls' school near Paris to augment their income.

These discoveries brought them fame. The scientific world is always excited when a new element is found, and radium proved to be the most important discovery of this kind in the past 60 years. Its remarkable radioactive properties, far outshining those of uranium and thorium, attracted many research workers to this subject. Very soon after, the scientists Ernest RUTHERFORD (q.v.) and Frederick Soddy made further important discoveries about radioactivity.

The Curies continued with their work, and in 1904, along with Becquerel, they were given the NOBEL Prize (q.v.) in physics for their pioneer work, and Pierre Curie was promoted to be professor at the University of Paris. In 1906, however, he was killed in a street accident. Madame Curie succeeded him as professor, the first woman professor at the University of Paris. Later an institute was founded in which she and those who assisted her could work entirely on radium and its problems. By 1911 her work in radioactivity had been so remarkable that she was again awarded the Nobel Prize, this time unshared. Honours came to her from many countries. When she visited England, the United States, or Poland towards the end of her life she was received like royalty.

Marie Curie, who was of middle height, with a pale face and very intelligent eyes, was the first woman to do outstanding work in science and to win world fame from it. She remained unspoiled by her great success. She was fortunate in being married to Pierre Curie, and in being in Paris in 1896, a time when the study of radioactivity was beginning. But she had the wisdom to seize the great opportunity and the courage and energy to persist regardless of failure, until magnificent success crowned her efforts.

See also RUTHERFORD.
See also Vol. III: ATOM; RADIATION.

Oriental Institute, Chicago

TOMB OF CYRUS AT PASARGADAE, PERSIA

Cyrus established his capital and royal palace at Pasargadae. Nearly 200 years after his death his body was discovered in this tomb by Alexander the Great

CYRUS THE GREAT (died 529 B.C.). In 25 years Cyrus created a Persian Empire that stretched from the Mediterranean to the borders of India. When he became King of Persia, the Medes and Persians, though descended from the same Iranian race, formed separate kingdoms. Cyrus in 550 B.C. mastered Media, and then conquered Lydia and the Greek cities of Asia Minor. In 539 B.C. he attacked Babylonia, which stretched from Mesopotamia to Palestine. Balshazzar, prince of Babylon, according to the story in the Book of Daniel (ch. v.), was warned of the invasion in the middle of his feasting and revelries by a mysterious handwriting on the wall.

Cyrus was a great soldier, but also a wise, just king, and merciful to his enemies. He released the subject peoples of the lands he conquered, restoring to them their native lands and local religions—the Hebrews, for example, who had been captive in Babylon, were restored to Jerusalem to rebuild their temple (*see* JEREMIAH)—and this enlightened treatment of his subject peoples greatly strengthened Cyrus's Empire. The circumstances of his death are uncertain, but he probably died while campaigning in the East. His son, Cambyses II, succeeded him.

See also DARIUS; XERXES; CROESUS.
See also Vol. I: PERSIAN ANCIENT CIVILIZATION.

D

DA GAMA, **Vasco** (*c.* 1460–1524). This Portuguese navigator and explorer was the first man to travel from Europe to India by sea, sailing down the coast of Africa and round the Cape of Good Hope. Previously all travellers had gone overland (*see* TRADE ROUTES, Vol. IV). Little is known of his life apart from his famous sailing exploits. He was born about 1460, the son of an official, and served as a soldier before making an outstanding reputation as a sea-captain.

After the death of Prince HENRY THE NAVIGATOR (q.v.) in 1460, little exploration of the West African coast was undertaken until 1481,

when all the resources of Portugal were thrown once more into the effort to find a way round Africa to India in the interests of trade. Then in 1487–8 Bartholomew Diaz's ship was carried south of the African continent by a northerly gale, and seeking to regain the west coast he reached instead the east coast, having accidentally rounded the southern tip of Africa out of sight of land. But Diaz, instead of continuing on, sailed back, this time seeing the capes which form the southern extremity of Africa, Cape Agulhas and the Cape of Good Hope.

The way to India now lay open to the Portuguese, the reward of 67 years of persistent and skilful exploration. They fitted out an expedition of four ships, filled with goods to exchange in India for the precious spices which they sought. Vasco da Gama was chosen to command the expedition.

He left Lisbon in July 1497 and, instead of following the African coast, sailed to the Cape Verde Islands and from there to South Africa out of sight of land for 3 months. This was the longest voyage out of sight of land yet made by a European, considerably longer than Columbus's more famous voyage from the Canaries to the West Indies in 1492 in which they were out

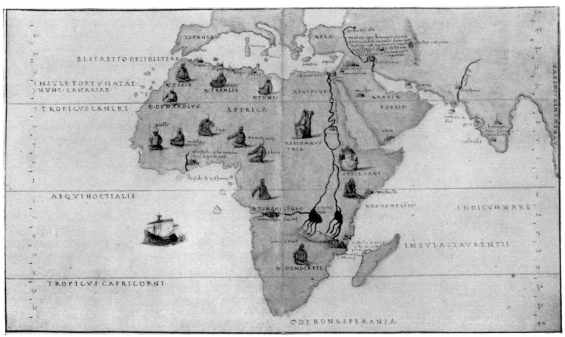

National Maritime Museum

AFRICA AS KNOWN TO THE EXPLORERS OF THE MID-16TH CENTURY
Map from an Italian portolan atlas, 1554

of sight of land for only 33 days. Da Gama, like
COLUMBUS (q.v.), could measure by the sun and
stars his distance from the Poles or Equator, but
had to guess his distance east or west. He
followed the unexplored coast of East Africa to
Malindi, where he was lucky enough to pick up
an experienced Moslem pilot, who steered the
expedition straight across the Indian Ocean to
the important Indian port of Calicut—a journey
of about 4 months. Here because of opposition
from the local Moslem merchants, and because
the trading goods they had brought were unsuitable, da Gama had much difficulty in ex-
changing his cargo for pepper and cinnamon.
Finally he reached Lisbon in September 1499
with the first seaborne cargo of spices from India.
He was rewarded with a title, land, and money.
The fabulous profits of the spice trade, hitherto
in the hands of the Italians and earned by overland caravans only, were now open to the
Portuguese by sea, and they soon established a
trading settlement in India.

In January 1502 da Gama, with the title of
Admiral of India, sailed in command of ten
heavily armed ships to restore the Portuguese
settlement in India which Moslem merchants
had destroyed. He bombarded Calicut and
forced trade agreements favourable to Portugal
on the ports of the Malabar coast, and then returned to Lisbon with his ships laden with spices.
The rewards he received made him one of the
richest men in Portugal and he retired to enjoy
his wealth, though continuing to advise the King
on the expansion of Portuguese power in the
Far East.

The Portuguese proceeded to develop their
trade in India, and to establish naval bases from
which they could protect their own trade and
cut off that of rivals. In this way a scattered
empire grew up. By 1524 the administration of
this empire had become so difficult that Vasco
da Gama was called from retirement and
appointed viceroy again in order to improve
matters. But da Gama died soon after reaching
India.

See also HENRY THE NAVIGATOR.
See also Vol. IV: EXPLORATION; TRADE ROUTES.

DALTON, John (1766–1844). This great
English scientist was the son of a Quaker weaver,
who, after some years' teaching in Kendal, left
his native Cumberland and settled in Manchester. His great achievement there was the

Science Museum
DALTON'S SYMBOLS OF THE ELEMENTS
Photograph from the original lecture diagram owned by
the Manchester Literary and Philosophical Society

discovery of the atomic theory in chemistry (*see*
MATTER, Vol. III). The idea of an indivisible
atom started with the Greeks, and shortly before
Dalton's day it had been suggested as the basis
of chemistry. Dalton's great service was that he
convinced the world that it was true by very
careful experiments.

He earned a living as a schoolmaster until
funds were found to enable him to devote
himself wholly to science. He observed and
theorized extensively on the behaviour of gases
and on the new science of the study of the
weather. Perhaps his most useful work outside
chemistry was the discovery in 1794, through
his own and his brother's experience, that men
could be colour-blind. He was a Quaker and a
man of high character, with a calm and gentle
demeanour and a slow and cautious way of
reasoning.

See also Vol. VII: CHEMISTRY, HISTORY OF.

DAMIEN, Father (1840–89). This Belgian
monk volunteered to look after a settlement of
abandoned and uncared-for lepers in Honolulu,

and finally himself died of the disease. Robert Louis Stevenson, who visited the settlement in 1889, describes him thus: 'It was a European peasant: dirty, bigoted, untruthful, unwise, tricky; but superb with generosity, residual candour, and fundamental good-humour . . . a man, with all the grime and paltriness of mankind, but a saint and a hero all the more for that.'

Damien's real name was Joseph de Veuster. His family was a religious one, and his elder brother had become a monk and his sister a nun. Joseph was being trained for a business career, but he developed so strong a desire also to enter the monastic life that his father, after some opposition, gave way. Joseph chose Damien as his name in his new life—the name of a 4th-century physician who had become a martyr.

Damien of his own eager desire went as a missionary to the South Seas. He reached Honolulu in 1864, and was sent to a lonely outpost where he was the only white man. The work was pioneer work, which he loved. He himself had to cut down wood and build churches, and then to train his own helpers, who were native islanders.

Soon Damien heard that the dreaded disease of LEPROSY (q.v. Vol. XI) was prevalent in the island, and was spreading widely. No hospital treatment was available: the authorities merely shut off the lepers in a settlement at Molokai, another Hawaiian island, and left them to fend for themselves. Owing to the danger of infection, no leper was allowed to leave the settlement. The condition into which this helpless community soon fell may be imagined.

When the Bishop spoke to his clergy of the lepers' needs, Damien at once offered to go to Molokai to live there and to serve the lepers. This meant perpetual exile from his friends and a life spent among people whose sufferings often made them repulsive to look at. In those days too, when there was no known treatment for leprosy, it meant almost the certainty of dying himself of the disease. To a man in the full vigour of life, it was the most complete self-sacrifice imaginable.

When Damien arrived at the settlement, he found it a place of horror. Deformed and distorted creatures were everywhere, with no medical attention or nursing. Having nothing but death to expect, many had become morally degraded. One of Damien's first tasks was to make the graveyard decent, acting himself both

Balliol College, Oxford
FATHER DAMIEN
Drawing by Edward Clifford

as grave-digger and undertaker. He had, of course, to build his own dwelling. He cleaned and decorated a rough chapel which a priest before him had built, and in which he could provide opportunities for worship with all the colour and beauty that was possible.

Damien made repeated requests to the government for food, building materials, and medical supplies. He was, with some justification, accused of being rude and overbearing; but his excuse lay in the difficulty of making people realize his needs. He grew bitter with disappointment, and when a brother priest was sent to help in the work, the priest was so offended by Damien's autocratic manner that he left. Having been forced for so long to do everything himself, Damien found it hard to cooperate with others. But with his parishioners, the lepers, he was always gentle.

In 1885, when he was 45 years old, Damien found himself suffering from leprosy. Attempts were made to treat him, but he was so restless in hospital that he was finally allowed to return to Molokai, where, to his great joy, he was joined by an English lay brother, John Dutton, who found his vocation in this kind of religious work. Damien had also the great happiness of learning that his work had become known to the outside world. Religious sisters, too, came to serve at Molokai, and Damien knew that the lepers would not be abandoned when he had gone. He died on Easter Monday in 1889.

After his death, English people of all shades of belief provided a memorial to be erected in Molokai and established a Damien Institute for the study of leprosy.

See also Vol. I: MISSIONARY.
See also Vol. XI: TROPICAL DISEASES.

DAMPIER, William (1652–1715). This English pirate, navigator, explorer, and writer, the son of a Somerset farmer, was sent to sea when he became an orphan at the age of 16. After voyages to Newfoundland and the East Indies and service in the Navy in the Dutch War of 1672–4, he spent 4 years with pirates in the Gulf of Mexico. Through these years of danger and hardship he kept a diary in which he doggedly noted details of weather, geography, and pilotage. From this diary he later drew the materials for books which established him as an expert navigator and a popular writer.

Dampier continued his career of piracy for some years, with intervals, until in 1688 he was marooned with three others on Nicobar Island in the Indian Ocean. They escaped in a native boat and survived a terrible storm, during which Dampier finally resolved to give up piracy and earn his living honestly. He returned to England in 1691. In 1697 he published his *New Voyage round the World*, followed by *Voyages and Descriptions*, which contains his 'Discourse of Winds', a valuable scientific treatise on weather.

Dampier was given command of a ship to explore the west coast of Australia, but in 1701 he was court-martialled for his conduct as a commander. On a later occasion, the crew of a ship under his command marooned the ship's master, Alexander Selkirk, on Juan Fernandez Island in the South Pacific, an incident which gave Daniel DEFOE (q.v.) the idea for his story *Robinson Crusoe*. Five years later, on his last voyage, Dampier rescued Selkirk from his solitary confinement.

See also Vol. IV: PIRATES.

DANTE (1265–1321). The Italian poet, Dante Alighieri, is not only one of the greatest writers who has ever lived, but was also one of the most striking personalities of the Middle Ages. Of Dante's loves, hopes, and sufferings in the turbulent years of Italian politics at the close of the 13th century, his great poem, the DIVINE COMEDY (q.v. Vol. XII), is the impassioned expression. Few lives and their literary production are so closely interwoven.

Born in Florence of a middle-class family, Dante passed his early years in study and the cultivation of poetry. His early poems were inspired by his love for a young girl called Beatrice whom he had known in childhood and who later married Simoni de Bardi. Dante idealized his love until it came to mean something mystical and symbolic, and, when in 1290 Beatrice died of plague, he celebrated her memory in the *Vita Nuova*, a collection of lyrics woven into a prose account of his love. In this work she appears as a divine messenger, sent to enlighten Dante and all mankind.

At about 28, Dante married Gemma Donati, who bore him two sons and a daughter called Beatrice. Italy at this time was the great battle-ground for the struggle between Church and State; in Florence, the clash between their respective supporters, the Guelfs and Ghibellines, was particularly violent. Dante took an active part, fighting in the Battle of Campaldino in 1289, in which the Guelfs, the Church party to which he belonged by family tradition, were triumphant. Against this troubled background Dante held office in the councils of the Commune, ultimately being nominated as one of the six Priors of the city in 1300 when he was 35. Though a Guelf, he was of the moderate party and rigorously opposed the designs of Pope Boniface VIII to gain control over the Tuscan cities; it was this among other things which eventually led to his exile. Events came to a crisis in 1301, when the Pope sent Charles of Valois to secure the subservience of Florence. The Commune in an attempt to forestall this visit sent three representatives to Rome, among them Dante. He never again set foot in Florence, for his party was overthrown in his absence, and he learned of his banishment while returning by Siena in January 1302. A first sentence of temporary exile and a heavy fine on apparently unfounded charges of political corruption was soon followed by a decree of perpetual banishment and the threat of being burnt alive if he returned.

For a time Dante tried with other exiles to obtain readmission, but he soon broke with these compatriots, and turned to a wandering existence which took him to various cities in Tuscany and the Romagna. A sense of injustice, pride, and love of his native city burned within him, and he sought partly to restore his reputation in two works, both left unfinished. One, the *De Vulgari Eloquentia*, written in Latin, is a treatise on language and poetry, remarkable for its understanding of the development of languages and of the Italian language in particular. The other, the *Convivio*, written in the mother tongue he loved and passionately championed, is a philosophical commentary on certain allegorical poems he had written, and an exaltation of human wisdom. Both works reveal that characteristic pride which came from a sure realization of his own greatness as a poet.

We do not know why he did not complete these works, but it seems likely he put them aside

to attend to the composition of the *Divine Comedy*, the conception of which probably formed in his mind at this time. He had experienced the disruption of his own city, seen corruption in the Church, observed in his travels the immorality and lawlessness of other Italian States. The need not only for a supreme ruler who should restore law and order but for a spiritual reawakening to the divine order governing all things impressed itself upon him, and took shape in his poem—the great epic of medieval Catholicism—on which he spent the rest of his life. When, in 1310, the Holy Roman Emperor descended on Italy to assert his authority, Dante welcomed him enthusiastically and called on him to rid Italy of her dissensions. But the expedition was ill-fated and the Emperor died in 1313 without having achieved anything. It

Alinari

DANTE AND THE 'DIVINE COMEDY'
Painting by Michelino (1417–91) in Florence Cathedral. Dante stands between Paradise outside Florence, on his right are souls descending into Hell. Behind him repentant sinners climb up the terraces of Purgatory

was probably at this period that Dante wrote his Latin treatise, *De Monarchia*, setting forth ideally the separate powers of Church and Emperor (*see* HOLY ROMAN EMPIRE, Vol. I). After this Dante took no further active part in practical politics. He rejected offers in 1315 to return to Florence under ignominious conditions, but, joined by his sons, continued to live in various cities of northern Italy, until his death in Ravenna in 1321.

In the *Divine Comedy*, one of the greatest poems in the world, Dante describes a vision in which he travelled to Hell, Purgatory, and Paradise. At first, Virgil, the poet he revered above all others, is his guide; but when he reaches Paradise Beatrice comes to guide him and to explain the heavenly mysteries. As he moves down the ever-decreasing circles of Hell to the centre of the earth, up the terraces of Mount Purgatory, and through the luminous spheres of Paradise, Dante encounters figures of his own past, of history and of legend, and speaks with them of those very human, artistic, political, and spiritual problems which had formed the substance of his own life. In this vast journey his own personality emerges against the background of the actual events of his times—proud, disdainful, tender, and vehement, a visionary filled with a sense of a divine mission as an interpreter of eternal truth. The *Divine Comedy* represents the pilgrimage not only of one man in a particular age from youth to maturity, but of all men at all times from sinfulness to purification. It does indeed appear to be, as Dante himself said, a poem to whose composition both heaven and earth had set their hand.

See also Vol. XII: ITALIAN LITERATURE; DIVINE COMEDY.

DANTON, Georges Jacques (1759–94). Danton was probably the most able and sincere of the leaders of the FRENCH REVOLUTION (q.v. Vol. X). He came from a family of farmers, but went to Paris as a young man to train as a lawyer. In one of the most revolutionary parts of Paris, now called St. Germain-des-Prés, with a large working-class population, Danton's violent and inspiring speeches together with his humble background made him immensely popular. He was a huge, brawny man, with striking, pock-marked features, and a voice of tremendous power.

In 1791 he became public prosecutor for the

J. E. Bulloz

GEORGES JACQUES DANTON

Portrait by an unknown painter of the 18th century. Musée Carnavalet, Paris

Commune (the body which governed Paris). At this time the Revolution was growing steadily more violent, and the extreme revolutionary party could rely on the Paris mob to force through any constitutional changes they considered necessary by threats of violence. Danton played an important part in the rising that led to the deposition of the King and was rewarded by being appointed Minister of Justice.

France had already declared war on Austria and now Danton threw himself into the work of organizing the country's defence. Besides raising troops, visiting the armies at the front, and speeding up the supply of arms, his great speeches inspired the National Assembly and the crowds which packed its public gallery. '*Il nous faut de l'audace, et encore de l'audace, et toujours de l'audace, et la France est sauvée . . .*' he cried in his most famous speech, when rallying the country to meet the threat of invasion.

In 1793 Danton led the extreme revolutionary party called 'the Mountain' (*see* ROBESPIERRE) against the moderate 'Girondins', and when the Girondins were expelled from office, Danton and

Robespierre became the leaders of the Assembly. Danton was one of the original members of the dictatorial Committee of Public Safety, which was set up to govern France, but Robespierre soon suspected him of being too moderate in his views. Indeed, Danton had done his utmost to curb the ruthless severity of the Committee ('I prefer being guillotined to guillotining', he once said).

During the Reign of Terror, the most violent phase of the Revolution, Robespierre turned Danton off the Committee and accused him of corruption and of excessive moderation towards the enemies of the Republic. Danton, though warned of his danger by his friends, was unwilling to divide the Revolution against itself by attacking Robespierre. Robespierre moved quickly, and when Danton returned from some weeks of rest with his newly married wife in the country, he was arrested. At his trial his brilliant defence so embarrassed the prosecutor, who feared that popular sympathy might save Danton, that his evidence was illegally cut short, and he was condemned and guillotined. On the scaffold Danton said to the executioner: 'You should show my head to the people; it's worth showing.'

Oriental Institute, Chicago

THE TOMB OF DARIUS

The tomb is cut in the cliff behind Darius's palace at Persepolis. Above the colonnade is a sculptured relief showing the king worshipping before a fire altar

DARIUS I (548–485 B.C.). This great King of ancient Persia succeeded Cambyses II, son of the famous empire-builder CYRUS (q.v.), in 521 B.C. At first he had to put down revolts all through his Empire. On his expedition against the Scythians in the Caucasus he led a large army across the Bosphorus on a bridge of boats. He invaded India and waged several wars to strengthen his frontiers. Then he concentrated on his real work, that of consolidating Cyrus's vast Empire. He divided it into provinces and appointed governors or 'satraps' to administer them. Officials, known as the 'King's Eyes' or 'Ears', travelled round the Empire reporting any signs of local insubordination, or of abuse of power among the governors. Darius encouraged road-building and improvements in farming, and introduced for the first time a gold and silver coinage, copied from the Greeks.

Darius belonged to the ZOROASTRIAN faith (q.v. Vol. I) which became recognized as the State religion of Persia, though all local religions were still tolerated. This humane and able administration gave Darius's subjects security and prosperity, and did much to make from very diverse elements a single Empire which, despite a succession of weak kings, lasted until conquered by ALEXANDER THE GREAT (q.v.) about 150 years later.

In 492 Darius led an expedition against Greece, which had been instigating rebellion among the Greek cities in his Empire. His invasion fleet, however, was wrecked in a storm. A second attempt was decisively beaten at the famous Battle of Marathon; and before a third expedition was ready, the King died. He was succeeded by his son XERXES (q.v.).

See also Vol. I: PERSIAN ANCIENT CIVILIZATION.

DARWIN, Charles (1809–82). The scientist Darwin's theory of EVOLUTION (q.v. Vol. II) by means of Natural Selection was as revolutionary in its effect on human thought as were the achievements of the 16th- and 17th-century physicists—COPERNICUS, KEPLER, GALILEO (qq.v.)—who discredited the idea that the earth was the centre of the universe. Darwin worked out a convincingly true story of Man's creation and his place in the animal kingdom. His researches made it clear that the first chapter

Meade Collection

CHARLES DARWIN

father's profession. When he was 16 his father told him: 'You care for nothing but shooting, dogs, and rat-catching, and you will be a disgrace to yourself and your family.'

Darwin went to Edinburgh to study medicine. There he read a paper to the local Natural History Society on the subject of marine animals that he had dredged up while trawling with fishermen; but his distaste for both lectures and operating-rooms made it evident that he was wasting his time, and he returned home. His father suggested the Church as a profession, and Charles, who at this period did not in the least 'doubt the strict and literal truth of every word of the Bible', went to Cambridge in 1828 intending to take holy orders.

Again he showed little enthusiasm for formal studies, but he had the good fortune to become associated with the famous botanist, Henslow, whose deep piety and learning made so great an impression on him that he tried to mould his behaviour on his hero's example. Henslow was probably the first person to realize Darwin's own great potentiality. Darwin also met the botanist, Robert Brown, and the geologist, Sedgwick. At about this time he began to 'work like a tiger at geology'. He took a 'pass' B.A. degree in 1831—scarcely a brilliant beginning.

At this period most people accepted Bishop Ussher's calculation that the world had been created at a single stroke in 4004 B.C. Fossils were generally considered to be the remains of animals destroyed in the Deluge—those that were not taken into the Ark. While Darwin was at Cambridge he read the first volume of Lyell's revolutionary *Principles of Geology*, which cast grave doubt on accepted beliefs concerning the age of the earth. At this stage Darwin was familiar with Lamarck's theory of evolution but viewed it as blasphemous nonsense. Then an opportunity came his way which changed his whole life.

The naval survey ship *Beagle*, a clumsy barque-rigged brigantine of 242 tons, was about to set off on a voyage around the world, and her Captain wanted an official naturalist to sail with him without pay. There were many naturalists better qualified than Darwin, but Henslow recommended him for the job. His father opposed the venture, saying: 'No man of sense would advise such a trip'; but his uncle Josiah Wedgwood, son of the famous potter, helped him persuade his father to consent. The Captain,

of the Book of Genesis in the Bible should not be taken as literal truth. Darwin himself was a most courteous, tolerant, and truly sincere man, but his work drew upon him the enmity and even abuse of many worthy people who feared that it would permanently undermine the Christian religion.

Darwin did not 'discover evolution'. Various people had put forward theories of evolution since before the birth of Christ; in fact, Darwin's own grandfather, Erasmus Darwin, had done so. The French natural scientists, Buffon and Lamarck, preceded Charles Darwin with theories of evolution based on the inheritance of acquired characteristics, but their theories were not accepted. Darwinism, however, aided by modern studies in genetics and other fields, became firmly established.

Darwin was born at Shrewsbury, the son of a successful physician of talkative and domineering character. His mother died when he was so small that he scarcely remembered her. He was not particularly interested in school lessons, but got much more pleasure from making 'all the gases' in the tool-shed at home; his friends, in fact, called him 'Gas'. He grew to love the countryside, and showed little interest in following his

too, was persuaded, and on 27 December 1831 Darwin set sail on the great adventure. 'The voyage of the *Beagle*', he said later, 'has been by far the most important event in my life, and has determined my whole career.'

During the voyage around South America, among the volcanic Galapagos Islands, and across the Pacific to Australia, Darwin made a series of observations that, for the first time, led him seriously to question the literal truth of the Book of Genesis. In South America he compared the living animals with the fossils that he found ashore. In the Galapagos Isles he saw that though each island was very similar, each was inhabited by a rather different set of animals from the others, and different again from the mainland close by. What did this geographical variation mean? Did it mean that a distinctive set of animals had been created for each small island—a most unlikely solution to the problem? Was it possible that all the animals had once belonged to a common mainland stock, and that isolation had allowed the creatures of each island to evolve into separate species? In Australia he thought much about the curious pouch-bearing animals (*see* MARSUPIALS, Vol. II) and their development into animal forms that appeared similar to, though they were actually very different from, familiar European animals. After an absence of almost 5 years Darwin reached home, and immediately set to work to classify the geological and animal material that he had collected. He had returned a convinced believer in evolution.

In 1838 Darwin read T. R. Malthus's book *On Population*, in which he suggested that the people of England might easily outstrip their country's capacity to provide food for them. Malthus said that already the 'struggle for subsistence' was harsh and constant. Quickly Darwin saw that a 'struggle for subsistence' was taking place in Nature. He saw how, for example, out of the myriad young fishes in a single shoal in tropical seas, or the thousands of seedlings sprouting up towards the life-giving sunlight in dank equatorial forests, only the 'fittest' organisms would survive and reproduce their kind. Darwin also saw that all living things varied—no two individual cats, or even peas in a pod, are completely alike, some being stronger or faster or otherwise better adapted than others for the struggle for existence. The naturally weak would be beaten in competition with those

more fitted for survival, and the latter would mature and breed. Gradually—and Lyell's *Geology* had convinced him that Nature had millions of years in which to work—there would emerge species that were best adapted to live in the ever-changing world about them. Darwin set out patiently to accumulate facts and to write out a draft of his ideas; but as yet he did not publish them, for he was almost afraid of his own discoveries. 'It is like confessing a murder', he wrote to a friend.

Meanwhile he married his cousin Emma Wedgwood, and living on an allowance made by his uncle Josiah, they settled at Down, in Kent, a house that is now a Darwinian Museum. Darwin was now free from financial worry, but he suffered from sleeplessness and intermittent ill health for the rest of his life.

In 1856, some 20 years after his trip, Darwin felt that he had accumulated enough evidence to write his great book *On the Origin of Species by Means of Natural Selection*. He had finished the first ten chapters when he received a letter from the zoological collector, Alfred Russell WALLACE (q.v.), who, working in the Dutch East Indies, had reached substantially the same conclusions as himself. On 1 July 1858, Darwin's and Wallace's views were read jointly before the Linnean Society of London. After the papers were delivered, members stood in hushed and agitated groups discussing this wicked new theory. When Darwin's book was published, the storm heightened. Copies were burned by indignant men who believed Darwin to have asserted that man was descended from apes. Darwin said nothing of the sort: he merely believed that some time in the dim past man and ape had a common ancestor, just as had, for example, horses and cattle (*see* CHART opp. p. 1, Vol. II). In 1860, at the British Association meeting at Oxford, there took place one of the most exciting debates in the annals of science between Bishop Wilberforce and Darwin's self-appointed spokesman, Thomas Henry HUXLEY (q.v.), in which Huxley routed the Bishop.

Besides the work for which he became universally famous, Darwin also produced treatises on his travels, on coral reefs, barnacles, orchids and their fertilization by insects, variations of animals and plants domesticated by man, the origin of man, sexual selection, the emotions in man and animals, insectivorous plants, and many other topics.

Darwin continued to be attacked by persons who misunderstood what he wrote; but as people came to understand that his work was in no way an attack on religion in its best and truest sense, his views became accepted. When he died on 18 April 1882, he was buried in Westminster Abbey.

See also Huxley; Jenner; Wallace, A. R.
See also Vol. I: Evolution of Man.
See also Vol. II: Evolution; Heredity.

DAVID I (*c*. 1080–1153). Scotland's great 'King of Peace' was the youngest son of Malcolm III and the famous Queen, St. Margaret, who did much to revive Christianity and civilization in Scotland. In 1124 he succeeded his wise brother Alexander I as King of the Scots.

David supported the claim of his niece Matilda, Henry I's daughter, to the English throne and invaded England; but after his defeat at the Battle of the Standard, peace was made, and David spent the rest of his life in building up the unity and welfare of Scotland. The Welsh-speaking kingdom of Strathclyde in south-west Scotland and the English-speaking districts of the south-east had only recently come under the Scottish Crown. David brought them into a real union with the old Gaelic-speaking kingdom north of the Forth, not by a forced unity, but by making all his various peoples feel that each was a part of the kingdom of Scotland, with its own rights and duties. This wise and liberal attitude attracted Flemish and English merchants to his prosperous kingdom; Norman

The Duke of Roxburghe

DAVID I AND HIS GRANDSON MALCOLM IV
Initial letter of the charter granted by Malcolm IV to the Abbey of Kelso

knights were glad to take service with him and settled in Scotland—indeed several great Scottish families are descended from these new-comers.

David lived at a time when the barbarous confusion of the Dark Ages (q.v. Vol. I) was beginning to give way to an outburst of new life in religion, in learning, in the arts, and in government. Most of these great new movements began in France, but spread through all Christian Europe. David encouraged the establishment of the new orders of monks, who brought with them their love of learning and skill in farming; he also encouraged the erection of new buildings, and the foundation of new towns to help trade. He continued his brother's work of organizing the legal system under sheriffs in each county, and he brought in the French custom of trial by jury (*see* Scottish Law, Vol. X). He introduced the system of land-holding by service in war, called the Feudal System (q.v. Vol. X). He was too wise to adopt new ideas merely because they were new, but he adapted those that were good to the special needs of Scotland. Thus he built the feudal system into the older clan system, retaining the personal man-to-man relationship between lord and tenant, which formed the great strength of Scottish feudalism. He did not force these reforms upon his people, but because they loved and trusted him, they followed willingly where he led. When he died they honoured him as St. David.

DAVID, Jacques (1748–1825), *see* Vol. XII: French Art.

DAVID, King of Israel (1038–970 b.c.). David's chief claim to greatness is that he gave unity, and with it permanence, to the scattered and disunited Israelite tribes that had entered Canaan. Though this unity was later broken after Solomon's death, enough was preserved to form a home for the moral and religious treasure which the Hebrew Civilization (q.v. Vol. I) gave the world. From David there sprang a line of kings continuing without break till the destruction of Jerusalem by the Babylonians in 586 b.c. The Jews regarded David as the ideal king, and cherished the hope that another David would arise to restore the glories of their first kingdom.

The son of Jesse, a prominent Bethlehemite, we first hear of David when he was called to

Bibliothèque Royale de Belgique

DAVID AND GOLIATH
Miniature from the Peterborough Psalter.
Early 14th century

Saul's Court to assuage with his music the King's fits of despondency. He was then described as handsome, a brave and practised warrior, a skilful harpist, and an able man of business. There is a tradition that as a boy he watched his father's sheep and performed deeds of bravery and strength. The story of his encounter with Goliath is only legend. In the 2nd Book of Samuel the killer of this giant is said to have been Elhanan, one of David's heroes, and perhaps Elhanan's feat was later attributed to his leader.

The youthful David had unusual personal charm. At first sight Saul loved him greatly, as did Jonathan, Saul's son; the association of David and Jonathan is one of the famous friendships of history. We read, too, that Michal, Saul's younger daughter, married David not only because her father commanded, but because she loved him. The Israelite women sang of his warlike exploits with such exaggerated praise that Saul became jealous and determined to kill him.

So David went into exile in the wild mountain country of Judah, where with 600 followers he became an outlaw chief. Saul pursued him relentlessly but, though David had opportunities of killing him, he would not. Although David improved his position by marrying Abigail, widow of a rich chieftain, he was finally in such despair of his life that he had to take refuge with the PHILISTINES (q.v. Vol. I), who were about to attack Saul. The Philistines defeated Saul and Jonathan and killed them both on Mount Gilboa.

Though Saul left another son, Eshbaal, the men of Judah preferred their kinsman David, whom they made king. Seven years of sporadic warfare followed, during which David captured the city of Jerusalem, which was thought to be impregnable. Finally, after Abner, the most powerful warrior of Israel, had been killed, and the Prince Eshbaal murdered, David, the only possible candidate for kingship over the united tribes, became king.

David, now 38 years old, defeated the Philistines, who apparently gave him no further trouble, and subdued the other surrounding peoples. His conquests may have been exaggerated, but he certainly gained security for the last 30 years of his reign. His desert followers developed into a permanent bodyguard of trained and trusty men, among whom non-Israelites predominated. The sacred ark (see TEMPLE, Vol. I), recovered from the Philistines, was lodged in Jerusalem where David also built himself a palace. He took several wives, as was the custom of oriental rulers. He was held in high respect; justice was well administered by officers of State, and there was a right of appeal to the King as supreme judge.

David's standards of morality, being naturally those of his own age, are difficult to compare with ours. Jonathan had left a lame son, whom David sought out and treated with honour; this, since he was protecting a possible rival for the throne, was unusual conduct in those days. On the other hand he ordered Uriah the Hittite to be killed because he wanted to marry Uriah's wife, Bath-sheba. (Bath-sheba gained such authority that when David died she was able to secure the succession of her son, Solomon.) David's later years were troubled by family quarrels and rivalries. He was a weak, indulgent father to his children, and Absalom in particular rebelled against him, a rebellion which was crushed by the firmness of David's loyal general

Joab. David's lament for Absalom shows his great love for his son.

David worshipped the Hebrew God, Yahweh or JEHOVAH (q.v. Vol. I). But he was still far from thinking of Jehovah as the one and only God; he thought of Him rather as the Hebrew national God. His foundation of Jerusalem, however, as a centre alike for religion and government, strengthened the worship of Jehovah. David was called 'the sweet psalmist of Israel'; but in fact most of the Psalms must have been written centuries after David's time. Many Psalms speak of or allude to the Temple, which did not exist during David's life; and all the Psalms declare or assume Jehovah to be the only God, whereas David allowed images in his house, and still believed that if he was driven outside the borders of Israel he would have to worship other gods. Yet it is likely that a minstrel, such as David was, would compose his own songs. The majestic lament over Saul and Jonathan suits the conditions of its time and is probably David's own work. If so, it bears witness to his essential nobility of heart. 'Saul and Jonathan', he wrote, 'were lovely and pleasant in their lives, and in their death they were not divided.' And of Jonathan, the friend of his youth, he said 'Thy love to me was wonderful, passing the love of women' (2 Samuel i).

See also Vol. I: HEBREW CIVILIZATION; JUDAISM.

DAVID, St. (*c*. 6th century). The patron saint of Wales, whose festival falls on 1 March, was the son of a Welsh prince. Facts about him are few, legends many. He became a monk of a very austere order, and is supposed to have founded many churches and monasteries in Wales. It is undoubtedly true that there was a monastic revival at that time. His own monastery was at Menevia in south-west Wales, on the site of which the cathedral of St. Davids was built. About 560 he was said to have been elected primate of the Welsh Church, and to have accepted only on condition that the episcopal seat should be moved from Caerleon to Menevia (St. Davids)—where it has remained since.

After his death at a great age his shrine became a popular place of pilgrimage. In the early 12th century the Pope canonized him at the request of Henry I, and also pronounced that two pilgrimages to St. Davids would earn equal spiritual merit to one pilgrimage to Rome.

See also Vol. I: SAINT; WELSH.

DAVIS, John (*c*. 1550–1605). This Dartmouth sailor explored very many parts of the world and contributed largely to the science of navigation. He was born in the same parish as Sir Humphrey GILBERT (q.v.), but in a humbler station of life. He became a deep-sea fisherman until Gilbert introduced him to merchants who wished to follow up FROBISHER'S search (q.v.) for a North-West Passage to Asia. In the summers of 1585-7 Davis pushed farther north through the strait which bears his name until he reached 73° North, where, though still convinced that a passage existed, he was forced back by ice. The SPANISH ARMADA campaign (q.v. Vol. X), in which he served as a pilot, interrupted further Arctic exploration.

In 1591 he joined Sir Thomas Cavendish's second expedition in an attempt to sail round the world—his first voyage in 1586-8 having been a great success, resulting in the capture of the Spanish Manila galleon, the richest vessel afloat. This second attempt, however, was disastrous. Cavendish was separated from Davis in the Magellan Straits by 'an outrageous storm in a hell-dark night', and he died in mid-Atlantic, falsely accusing Davis of deserting him. Davis, having searched three times for his ship, made for home. Though he discovered the Falkland Islands on the way, this voyage was one of the worst on record, only 15 of the original 76 men returning alive. No one but a remarkably fine navigator and a tough leader of men could have brought that little ship back at all.

Davis spent the next few years on shore writing the first manual of navigation, *The Seaman's Secrets*, and inventing navigating instruments known as the backstaff and double quadrant, which were still being used to ascertain latitude 200 years after his death. Davis answered the call of the sea again when he became pilot of the first Dutch expedition to the East Indies, where they loaded 140 tons of pepper. Two more voyages to the East followed, one in the service of the new English EAST INDIA COMPANY (q.v. Vol. VII). On 30 December 1605, however, when his ship was off the coast of Malay, the old seaman was murdered in a skirmish with Japanese pirates.

Davis was a real 'ancient mariner', a professional sailor, and no enthusiastic amateur as were many of his contemporaries.

See also Vol. IV: EXPLORATION; NAVIGATION, HISTORY OF.

JAMES COOK, F.R.S.
Portrait by Nathaniel Dance

DAVY'S SAFETY LAMPS FOR MINERS

The first four lamps are early experimental models, and the lamp on the right was the first to prove practical. Davy
began his experiments in safety lamps in 1815, and had completed his invention by the end of the year

DAVY, Sir Humphry (1778–1829). This Cornish chemist, the inventor of the miners' safety lamp, rose to be the leading scientist of early 19th-century England. As a child Davy showed little interest in science but was a great reader; he loved Bunyan's *Pilgrim's Progress*, read a great deal of poetry, and wrote some verse. He first acquired a taste for experimental science from a Cornish saddler near his home, who was a Quaker and a thoughtful man of an original turn of mind. With home-made electrical and mechanical apparatus he instructed Davy in the rudiments of natural and experimental science.

When Davy's father died, the boy was apprenticed to a local surgeon to be trained as a doctor. He became acquainted with a distinguished chemist of St. Bartholomew's Hospital, London, who allowed him to use his laboratory, and encouraged his work. In this way, and by the careful study of works of science, Davy educated himself. When he was 20 he went to Bristol to work for the Pneumatic Institution, which had been set up to examine the medical properties of gases. Davy found the work so interesting that he soon decided to give up medicine in favour of experimental science.

His new work had its dangers: he was the first person to investigate fully the properties of nitrous oxide or 'laughing gas', now much used

by dentists and surgeons as an ANAESTHETIC (q.v. Vol. XI). When investigating carburetted hydrogen he tried the gas on himself, and was only brought round from unconsciousness with difficulty. His writings on the subject soon attracted attention, and in 1801 he was appointed assistant lecturer in chemistry at the Royal Institution in London. A year later he was appointed professor, and when he was 27 he became director of the laboratory. Here he repeated many of the ingenious experiments he had learned as a boy from his old tutor, the Cornish saddler.

His work at the Royal Institution led to spectacular success. His lecture-room was so crowded that his public lectures had to be given in large public halls, to which audiences of 1,000 or more would often come. The result of these lectures and of his articles in the scientific journals was that science became both popular and fashionable. In 1807 Davy gave a notable lecture on *Some Chemical Agencies of Electricity* before the Royal Society, in consequence of which his reputation spread to the Continent. He was awarded several important prizes, among them the Napoleon Prize of the Institut de France, and he began to grow rich. In the next few years he made a series of important discoveries about the nature of metals, discovering for the first time the existence of metals such as sodium and magnesium. In 1812 Davy was given a knighthood, and was later made a baronet.

It was Davy who first recognized the talents of FARADAY (q.v.), who later became a renowned physicist and chemist. In Davy's later years his main researches were in electro-magnetism, with Faraday's assistance, and in the problem of galvanic action in the presence of sea-water, which had interested him as a young man in Cornwall. He was the first inventor of a practical and safe MINERS' LAMP (q.v. Vol. VIII) for use in coal-mines filled with explosive gas, an important invention in the history of coal-mining. A few years before his death he was elected President of the Royal Society, the highest scientific office in the kingdom.

See also Vol. VII: CHEMISTRY, HISTORY OF.

DEBUSSY, Claude Achille (1862–1918).
Debussy, the son of a small shop-keeper near Paris, began to study music seriously when he was 15. He studied at the Paris Conservatoire and won the valuable Prix de Rome, which enabled him to go to Rome to study and compose. But he had to send his compositions back to Paris for the approval of the Prize Committee, who did not think much of his work, and Debussy left Rome in despair.

Back in Paris, he continued to compose, but found great difficulty in inducing anyone to publish his music. Although his orchestral piece, the *Prélude à l'après-midi d'un faune*, had been successfully played at concerts, he was still so wretchedly poor that when he married in 1899, he had to give piano lessons on his wedding day to pay for the wedding breakfast.

In 1901 he became music critic for a magazine, and later he collected his brilliant writings on music into a book. His only complete opera, *Pelléas et Mélisande*, first performed in 1902, won him fame at last. During the last 10 years of his life he performed with increasing success both as pianist and conductor, in most of the great cities of Europe. He died in Paris in March 1918.

Debussy brought new and subtle effects to music, and expressed strange and exciting musical thoughts. He was greeted in France as one who had rescued his country's music from the influence of German romantic ideas (chiefly those of WAGNER (q.v.)) which, the French thought, were out of keeping with the clear, graceful, cultured spirit of French art. Debussy's new effects were produced through 'colour' (what is called 'timbre' in music) and through harmonic effects (*see* HARMONY, Vol. XII). Some of his loveliest pieces are made up of chords connected by a mere suggestion of melody, and by the atmosphere that, between them, they suggest. In fact, the appeal of his music is to a large extent due to its powers of suggestion. Many of his pieces have titles like those of pictures—'The submerged cathedral', 'The girl with flaxen hair', 'Dialogue between the wind and the sea'. And Debussy has been named as the musical counterpart of the French Impressionist painters, such as Monet, who set out to suggest effects of light and movement. NIJINSKY's ballet *L'Après-midi d'un faune* (q.v.) affirms this power to evoke scene and atmosphere.

He wrote many pieces for piano in which these strangely beautiful effects occur, and some fine orchestral pieces, particularly 'The Sea', 'Iberia' (which is about Spain), and three nocturnes. In his songs the voice seems to do little more than speak the poetry on fixed notes, yet they are

Bibliothèque Nationale

'L'APRÈS-MIDI D'UN FAUNE'

Woodcut by Manet illustrating the poem by Mallarmé which inspired Debussy's tone poem most moving and satisfying. Debussy's experiments laid the foundations of modern music.

See also Vol. XII: MODERN MUSIC.

DEFOE, Daniel (c. 1660–1731). The author of *Robinson Crusoe* was nearly 60 when he wrote his first great novel: indeed, he was nearly 40 before he started to write at all. Defoe's father, John Foe, was a successful butcher; his son, more ambitious, added a 'De' to the family name. He tried various trades without success and at last turned to writing, but retained all his life his interest in trade and the good tradesman's practical sense and attention to detail.

Defoe was a moderate man in politics and religion and a true lover of liberty, and the comparatively progressive policy of William III's Government suited him. He decided to try his hand at writing pamphlets and poems in its service. One poem, *The True-born Englishman* (1701), which mocked those who insisted on the 'purity' of the British race and on the exclusion of 'refugees', pleased the King, who was himself a Dutchman. But the King died in the following year, and Queen Anne's new Tory Government liked neither Defoe nor his writing. For satirizing the Tories in a pamphlet called *The Shortest Way with the Dissenters* Defoe was imprisoned and sentenced to stand 3 days in the pillory. But this ordeal ended triumphantly, for the citizens of London, recognizing him as a writer who had pleased them, covered the pillory with flowers instead of throwing stones at him.

About 50 years earlier, NEWSPAPERS (q.v. Vol. IV) had first begun to appear, and the demand for up-to-date information was so great that Defoe, a born journalist, decided to found a paper himself. While still in prison he began *The Review*, which ran from 1703 to 1714. When real news was scarce, Defoe made it up, having an uncanny knack for inventing wholly convincing detail. His curious and observant nature and his extraordinary energy and industry enabled him to write the whole paper himself, contributing articles on a vast number of subjects. Stories of adventure at sea were particularly popular, and inspired by the story of Alexander Selkirk (*see* DAMPIER), marooned alone on a desert island for more than 4 years, Defoe produced *The Life and Strange Surprising Adventures of Robinson Crusoe*, which pretended to be the true story of a man shipwrecked on a desert island for 28 years. Defoe, having actually met Selkirk

ROBINSON CRUSOE
Frontispiece from the edition of 1719

and having read many travel books, made his story so realistic that everyone, with Selkirk fresh in their minds, believed it. The booksellers could not print copies fast enough; hawkers sold what they claimed to be bits of wood from Crusoe's boat, or pieces of skin from Crusoe's boots. The book was not originally intended for children at all—but today every child knows Robinson Crusoe; how he learned to catch goats and to make pots, how he invented an umbrella and found Man Friday's footprints.

Robinson Crusoe, the first great English novel, was followed by more, as good if less famous. In quick succession came *Captain Singleton* and *Duncan Campbell, Moll Flanders* and *Colonel Jack, Memoirs of a Cavalier* and *A Journal of the Plague Year*. Defoe wrote more than 100 books in all, including a great guide-book, *A Tour through the whole Island of Great Britain*. His famous account of the Great Plague of 1665 was written vividly from the point of view of an eye-witness, though Defoe, in fact, was only 6 at the time and could have remembered very little. In all these books he uses his extraordinary faculty for selecting commonplace and trivial detail to create an irresistible sense of reality. He shows, too, his warm-hearted compassion for human suffering and his admiration of human courage, endurance, and vitality.

See also Vol. XII: NOVEL.

DELACROIX, Eugène (1798–1863).

This French painter was the leader of the ROMANTIC MOVEMENT (q.v. Vol. XII) in painting. His family were prosperous civil servants, and he was brought up in the cultured society of Paris amongst artists, writers, and musicians.

Delacroix worked quickly and produced a great number of paintings. He believed that painting should depict the reality and violent emotions of life. His subjects are romantic and far from everyday life, for he chose his subjects from books, from history, and from foreign countries, but his figures are more alive than those of the previous generation of painters, and he uses light and colour to suggest dramatic effects. The most striking innovation in his painting is his use of rich colours. A few days before his painting 'The Massacre of Scio' was to be shown in an exhibition, Delacroix saw a painting by CONSTABLE (q.v.), the vivid colouring of which so impressed him that he is said to have repainted parts of his picture in purer, more brilliant colours.

The violence of many of his pictures shocked the public, but he finally gained a certain amount of official recognition. For many years he kept a *Journal* in which he described his many friendships, his views on life and art, and his methods of painting.

DE LA MARE, Walter (1873–1956).

There is no mistaking the genius of this great writer. Like William BLAKE (q.v.), he does not belong to the main stream of English literature. Both in his prose and poetry he is simply and uniquely himself.

Henry Newbolt was the first to recognize de la Mare's great gifts and to print his early poems in a magazine which he edited. Newbolt used his political influence to secure de la Mare a grant from the King's Bounty, a fund available for helping young artists, and he persuaded him

Archives Photographiques

THE MASSACRE OF SCIO

Painting by Eugène Delacroix of an incident in the Greek War of Independence. Louvre

to risk giving up his job in the city in order to devote his whole time to writing. His early poems are already hall-marked with the peculiarly beautiful and subtle rhythms and cadences of his style, and as he grew older his style did not so much develop as become more perfect. The mood of questioning which pervades all his poetry never became repetitive: for de la Mare, every day was new; his sense of wonder and his curiosity about all kinds of life and experience were never satisfied. Conversation with him was like a game of leap-frog—question leaping over question in an ever more fascinating and seemingly endless chain.

In particular, he brooded over the mysteries of childhood and those states of mind where 'dream' and 'reality' intermingle. He was always exploring human personality and always with compassion and sympathy for the oddity, the misfit, and the helpless. He is unique, also, in that his prose is of a stature equal to his poetry. His *Memoirs of a Midget* is one of the strangest and most original novels of the 20th century; but it is in his long short stories—such as *Allhallows* or *Seaton's Aunt*—that he is at his best. Most of these stories have a hint of the supernatural; but they are far from being mere ghost-stories. His own love of poetry and immensely wide knowledge make his anthology, *Come Hither*, one of the best ever compiled.

DEMOSTHENES (*c.* 383–322 B.C.). This great Athenian orator and statesman made his first public speeches before he was 20—against his guardians, who had cheated him of his property. These speeches were spoilt by faults of delivery, and for some years he confined himself to speech-writing, while he studied law.

Philip of Macedon, father of ALEXANDER THE GREAT (q.v.), was at this time, by a mixture of force and diplomacy, making Macedonian influence felt throughout Greece. Demosthenes saw that, although Philip treated Athens considerately, the military autocracy of Macedon was a threat to Athenian democracy. In his *Philippics* and many other speeches he roused the people to defend themselves against the Macedonians. For some 15 years he campaigned against Philip, both in Athens and in other Greek States; but when open warfare at last broke out, the Athenians and their allies were utterly defeated at the Battle of Chaeronea in 338 B.C., and Philip was able to impose his terms on the Greek States.

Demosthenes' influence at Athens was not diminished, and during the reign of Alexander he worked patiently to rebuild the city's strength. In 324, however, he was banished (nobody knows whether rightly or not) for accepting bribes. The next year, when Alexander died, Athens revolted, and Demosthenes was brought back in triumph. But Athens and her allies were soon defeated, and Demosthenes only escaped the Macedonians by taking poison which was hidden in his pen.

See also Vol. XII: RHETORIC.

DE QUINCEY, Thomas (1785–1859). De Quincey, author of *The Confessions of an English Opium Eater*, a book containing some of the most fascinating personal reminiscences in the English language, was a remarkable character. He might have been a fine classical scholar, but he was by nature a wanderer. As a pupil at Manchester Grammar School, he ran away to Wales and later to London, where he nearly starved. After this interlude, vividly and movingly recounted in the *Confessions*, his guardians persuaded him to continue his studies at Oxford. It was while he was an undergraduate that he first took drugs to relieve toothache, and so formed the habit which he never entirely overcame. After leaving Oxford, De Quincey, a great admirer of WORDSWORTH and COLERIDGE (qq.v.), settled near them in the Lake District, and later wrote fascinating but not always accurate accounts of them and other literary men. The last part of his life he spent in Edinburgh, writing a great deal for literary periodicals—often at far too great length, but sometimes with brilliant imaginative effect—on such topics as 'Murder Considered as One of the Fine Arts'.

DE RUYTER, Michael Adrianzoon (1607–76). This great Dutch admiral, the son of a potboy in a waterfront tavern, rose to command the Dutch Navy when Holland was the chief maritime power in the world. He fought gallantly in the three Dutch Wars against the English, and his cruises in the Mediterranean, the Baltic, and across the Atlantic were a constant threat to the commercial interests of other European powers.

De Ruyter was sent to sea as a cabin boy at the age of 11, and for many years served as a merchant

National Maritime Museum

MICHAEL ADRIANZOON DE RUYTER
Engraving by H. Bary after F. Bol

seaman. He later became a naval officer and, with Martin Tromp as his commander-in-chief, took part in the bitter and prolonged struggles with BLAKE's fleet (q.v.) during the First Dutch War (1652–4). On Tromp's death he was made Admiral of the United Provinces. In the Second Dutch War (1664–7), at the age of 60, he scored his greatest success when, after blockading the Thames, he sailed up the Medway to Chatham where he set fire to the English fleet at anchor there, and towed home the English flagship the *Royal Charles*. This brilliant feat caused the greatest consternation in London and added immensely to the glory of his country's navy.

When commanding a combined Dutch-Spanish fleet against the French in the Mediterranean De Ruyter received his first serious wound in a life of battles, and died in Sicily. He was a man of unflinching courage, simple and unaffected in manner, and popular with all his seamen.

DESCARTES, René (1596–1650).

This French philosopher, born in Touraine in north-west France, was educated at a Jesuit college. On leaving the college he travelled, and also served for some years in the army. When he was about 25 he decided to devote his life to the study of scientific and philosophic subjects. He spent some years in further travel, including periods of study in Paris, and then settled in Holland, where he thought he would be more free to write as he wished than he would be in Catholic France. Descartes never married; but he had a daughter, whose death at the age of 5 was his greatest sorrow. He had a long correspondence on philosophic questions with the young Princess Elizabeth, daughter of the Elector Palatine and grand-daughter of James I of England; and he became a friend of Queen CHRISTINA (q.v.) of Sweden. Christina, a serious and learned woman, persuaded Descartes to come to Sweden to teach her philosophy. But the cold climate combined with the duty of giving the Queen a lesson at 5 a.m. every morning undermined his health, and in less than 2 years he died at Stockholm of inflammation of the lungs.

Descartes lived in an age when great changes in thought were taking place. By the 17th century the theories of COPERNICUS, followed by the discoveries of GALILEO (qq.v.), were revealing that the earth, far from being the centre of the universe, was only a small planet revolving

Archives Photographiques

RENÉ DESCARTES
Portrait by Franz Hals, in Louvre Museum

round the sun. Careful observations and experiments were leading to a deeper understanding of nature and natural laws; and man was beginning once again to investigate his own nature. Among the more educated, truth was being sought by reasoning based on experience, instead of being accepted as revealed in the Bible and taught by the Church.

After some 6 years of secluded study in Holland, Descartes had published in 1637 his famous book, *Discours de la Méthode*—often simply called the *Method*. Everything, he said, should at first be doubted—not because doubt is in itself a satisfactory state of mind, but because we can only be convinced of the truth after satisfying our doubts. He argued that if he doubted the existence of everything—of earth, sea, sky, minds, or bodies—as though there was always someone trying to deceive him about the existence of these things, then, even if he were being deceived, at least he would know that he might be being deceived. This proved to him that he at least existed, since without existing he could not think, much less doubt. And so he framed the famous phrase: *Cogito, ergo sum* ('I think, therefore I am').

Descartes believed thought to be the foundation of all knowledge. The senses may deceive us and often do; but ideas which are clear and distinct to the mind must be true. Man, he argued, has an idea of perfection which his own limited and imperfect existence could not of itself have given him; so such an idea must come from something outside man: in fact, there must exist a Being, namely God, beyond humanity, who corresponds to man's idea of perfection. Thus Descartes, in spite of the severe RATIONALISM (q.v. Vol. I) of his thought, believed in the existence of God.

Descartes recognized also the existence of the external world; but he believed that this world could be truly known only by being thought about—not by being seen or touched. So he distrusted everything which depended solely on the evidence of the senses. The only existence he could confidently believe in, besides the mind, was that of matter extending in space and possessing the power of movement. This could be measured and calculated, and Descartes regarded the physical world as one great machine. In his last book, the *Passions of the Soul*, he described the human body as also a machine, moved by the mind. If the mind had always clear and distinct ideas, able always to see things in their true light, man would never do wrong. Descartes is justly criticized because he failed to show how the mind could act on the body if, according to his system, mind and matter were completely apart from one another.

Descartes had such confidence in his system—the Cartesian system as it is called—that he thought it would supersede all previous knowledge and lead to a new era of happiness for mankind. What it actually did was to encourage a change from the religious to the scientific view of the universe. Descartes made a number of advances in mathematics, a science which is a pure activity of the mind: in fact, it was his emphasis on the importance of mathematics in the study of PHILOSOPHY (q.v. Vol. I) that led him to be called the 'Father of Modern Philosophy'.

DIAGHILEFF, Serge (1872–1929). As a young man Diaghileff became the leading spirit of a brilliant group of young writers, painters, and musicians in St. Petersburg. They founded a remarkably successful magazine intended to free Russian art from its social and political ties and to bring it into direct contact with the rest of Europe, especially with Paris. In 1908 Diaghileff began his career as an impresario, presenting a season of opera in Paris which first established there the popularity of Russian music and, through the wonderful singing of CHALIAPIN (q.v.), of Russian opera in particular.

Russia had had for many years an outstanding ballet company, but the productions had become stilted and old-fashioned. Diaghileff, who saw in ballet a remarkable medium for uniting the arts, surrounded himself with a brilliant group of artists—among them Benois and Bakst, decorative artists, and Michael Fokine, choreographer, to arrange the ballets according to Diaghileff's new ideas, with PAVLOVA, Karsavina, and NIJINSKY (qq.v.) to lead the dancers. This company he took to Paris in 1909.

Diaghileff's unique genius enabled him to unite dancers, painters, and musicians to create such perfect ballets as 'Schéhérazade', 'Dances from Prince Igor', 'Les Sylphides', and 'Carnaval'. He became a major influence in European art, launching such composers as Stravinsky, Prokofiev, and Auric, and introducing to an enormous public painters such as PICASSO (q.v.) and Matisse. This man, who was neither dancer, painter, nor musician, played a commanding role in all three arts, and when he died he left behind him a world-wide love of ballet.

See also Vol. IX: BALLET; OPERA.

DICKENS, Charles John Huffam (1812–70). Charles, the second of eight children, was born at Portsmouth, where his father was a clerk in the Navy Pay Office. Both his parents were descended from old-established families which had come down in the world.

Before long the family moved, first to Chatham, then to London, where Dickens's father contrived to get himself seriously in debt; his mother, in an attempt to stave off disaster, took a house in Gower Street and boldly announced an 'Establishment' for the education of Anglo-Indian children. Dickens wrote later, 'I left at a great many other doors a great many circulars calling attention to the merits of the establishment. Yet nobody ever came to school, nor do I recollect that anybody ever proposed to come, or that the least preparation was made to receive anybody. But I know that we got on very badly with the butcher and the baker; that very often we had not too much for dinner; and that at last my father was arrested.' In 1824 the household possessions were sold, and in this strange

DICKENS READING HIS CHRISTMAS TALE, 'THE CHIMES', TO HIS FRIENDS ON THE 2ND OF DECEMBER, 1844
Drawing by Daniel Maclise

family it was the 12-year-old Charles who was considered the fittest person to negotiate with the pawnbroker.

Charles's father was sent to Marshalsea Prison for debt, and his mother and the younger children went with him, a normal procedure in those days. Charles lived alone in Camden Town and went to work in a blacking factory on a Thames-side wharf at a wage of 6*s.* a week. The misery and indignity of this affected him so deeply that when he grew up he could never bear to speak of it, though some character or scene from his early life can be found in every book he wrote. After 3 months' imprisonment a fortunate legacy enabled Mr. Dickens to pay his debts, and he was released. Charles was able to return to school; and then, at 15, to become a junior clerk in a lawyer's office. After 1½ years he was reporting in the law-courts, but, finding the work dull, he first thought of going on the stage, and then made his choice between acting and writing by becoming a reporter in the House of Commons and at political meetings all over the country, travelling by every sort of conveyance and meeting all sorts of people.

Before long he began writing for the literary papers. The *Monthly Magazine* published his first humorous sketch in 1833. Other sketches (over the signature 'Boz') followed in the *Evening Chronicle* and elsewhere. They attracted no great attention, but one publisher agreed to print the collected *Sketches by Boz*, and another commissioned a monthly serial to accompany a set of sporting prints. In 1836 the first number appeared of *The Posthumous Papers of the Pickwick Club*, and after the arrival (in the fifth number) of Sam Weller (even more popular than Mr. Pickwick himself), the new serial suddenly became the rage. Dickens had become a famous author. The next year, he accepted the editorship of another monthly magazine, the chief attraction of which was the new serial *Oliver Twist*. All Dickens's novels were written as serials, generally monthly, sometimes weekly—a fact which powerfully influenced the shape of his stories and in the early days caused many difficulties. *Pickwick* overlapped with *Oliver Twist*, *Oliver Twist* with *Nicholas Nickleby*, and 4 years of astonishing success were marred by publishers' disputes because Dickens failed to fulfil impossible undertakings. Only after 1840, with the publication of *Master Humphrey's Clock*, and its serial *The*

MRS. GUMMIDGE CASTS A DAMP ON OUR DEPARTURE

ILLUSTRATION BY PHIZ TO 'DAVID COPPERFIELD'
Peggotty and Mr. Barkis, accompanied by Little Em'ly and David, set off for their wedding

Old Curiosity Shop, did he find himself free from arguments and the demands of printers. But Dickens never took things easily: later on, in addition to all his other work, he burdened himself for 20 years with the editorship of his own weekly magazine (*Household Words* 1850–9, and afterwards *All the Year Round*). He married in 1836 Catherine Hogarth, daughter of the editor of the *Evening Chronicle*, but the marriage was not happy and ended in separation.

Charles Dickens had an impulsive nature, easily made happy, easily cast down, affectionate yet quick to resent criticism; he was a great fighter, and attached himself passionately to liberal causes. He was a humorist with a mission —to attack oppression wherever he found it, whether at home in the scandal of the WORK-HOUSE (q.v. Vol. X) or the factory system, or abroad in the scandal of the copyright laws—for his own books were published in America without permission or payment. Living when he did, he knew England before and after the Reform Act of 1832, before and after the decline of the stage-coach and the coming of the railways, before and after the reform of the theatre laws. He was a witness, assistant, and recorder of the social evolution of his country in the period of its greatest change (*see* INDUSTRIAL REVOLUTION, Vol. VII).

Dickens's novels always contain reliable social information: the state of the Yorkshire schools, for example, was in no way exaggerated in the entertaining but terrible account in *Nicholas Nickleby*. *The Times* of the period carried advertisements quite as absurd as Mr. Wackford Squeers'. The humour of Dotheboys Hall was all his own; the facts were true, even to the most grotesque details. Boys did sleep five in a bed in the worst boarding-schools of the 1830's. The other books are not less informative—*Pickwick* with its inns and election scenes, *Martin Chuzzlewit* with its funeral and its nurses, *David Copperfield* with its account of the factory, the pawnbroker's, the poor lodgings of Dickens's youth, and the dismal adventures of his own father, thinly disguised as Mr. Micawber. Life in a debtor's prison is recorded in *The Pickwick Papers*, *David Copperfield*, and *Little Dorrit*; the law courts form a principal background of *Bleak House*; and memories of his legal days illuminate all his books with brilliant portraits of solicitors, clerks, barristers, and judges. Travels in Europe influenced the writing of *Dombey and Son* and *Little Dorrit*, and travels in America provided the central part of *Martin Chuzzlewit*; but Dickens was never at his best outside his own country, or indeed, outside his own period. The historical novel, *Barnaby Rudge*, is less successful than the others, and *A Tale of Two Cities* is successful not because it is good history but because it is first-class romantic drama—and Dickens's sense of the dramatic was very strong. If he had chosen he might have been a fine actor; all his writing, even his punctuation, bears the mark of a dramatic method, and throughout his life he enjoyed getting up theatricals and entertainments.

In 1858 he began giving public readings from his works; but the strain of these performances, enormously successful as they were both in England and in America, was largely responsible for his death. He died suddenly at the height of his fame when only 58, and was buried in Westminster Abbey.

See also Vol. XII: NOVEL.

DIDEROT, Denis (1713–84). The editor of the great French *Encyclopédie* was a writer with a wide range: he wrote novels, plays, philosophical works, and articles on painting and the theatre which are both shrewd and original; he was also a brilliant letter-writer and conversationalist, the friend of VOLTAIRE and ROUSSEAU (qq.v.). Influential people, including the Empress Catherine II of Russia, gave him their friendship and patronage. He had a restless, inquiring mind, strong visual imagination, and much intellectual courage—qualities which, early in his career, brought him up against the authorities, who imprisoned him on account of one of his books.

In 1746 Diderot was invited by an eminent lawyer to undertake the prodigious task of compiling the *Encyclopédie*, and this occupied him almost exclusively for the next 20 years. His first-rate critical sense set and controlled the tone of eager yet dispassionate inquiry which characterizes the whole work. He persuaded most of the distinguished writers of the day to contribute articles on the new knowledge, particularly scientific knowledge, which was transforming men's ideas in the 18th century, and he wrote more than 1,000 articles himself—chiefly on art and industry. Diderot's spirit of free critical inquiry aroused fear and enmity from both Church and State, and the *Encyclopédie* was officially suppressed. Diderot, however, courageously continued the work, and the last volumes were published in 1766.

See also Vol. XII: ENCYCLOPEDIAS.

DIOCLETIAN (A.D. 245–313). This clear-sighted and ruthless Emperor restored the Roman Empire to order when 50 years of anarchy, barbarian invasions, economic disorder, and the resulting famine and plague had almost destroyed it.

Diocletian started by delegating authority, choosing Maximian as joint-emperor, or 'Augustus', and later two subordinates, or 'Caesars', so that the Empire was ruled in four sections, and was then again subdivided into twelve dioceses and many small provinces. He enlarged the army, setting up a mobile force easily

RUINS OF THE PALACE OF DIOCLETIAN AT SPLIT (YUGOSLAVIA)
Engraving from a drawing by Robert Adam, who visited the palace in 1754

rushed to any danger point. He financed his activities by imposing crushing taxes to be paid largely in goods, and when men began to abandon their trades to avoid paying, he forbade anybody to change his job or give up his farm. When his reform of the currency failed to check inflation, he fixed maximum prices for food and clothing. All this demanded complete discipline throughout the Empire. Diocletian considered the Christians a threat to discipline, for they refused to sacrifice to the Emperor; therefore he started the last great Christian persecution in 303.

Diocletian's reforms turned the Empire into a totalitarian State ruled by an autocrat; but they saved its existence. After a rule of 21 years Diocletian abdicated, and retired to a palace at Split on the Dalmatian coast; there, apart from a brief interlude, he remained, growing cabbages as he said, until his death.

See also CONSTANTINE THE GREAT.
See also Vol. I: ROMAN CIVILIZATION.

DIOGENES (*c.* 412–323 B.C.). This Greek philosopher belonged to the school of Cynics in Athens, the forerunners of the Stoics (*see* ZENO). Diogenes, believing that all the luxuries of civilization only hinder the 'good life', practised a strict ASCETICISM (q.v. Vol. I), living, as he said, like a dog, eating and wearing only the coarsest food and clothing, sleeping on the bare ground, and even adopting some sort of tub as a dwelling. He proclaimed his brotherhood not only with all men but with all animals, and lived by begging. The Athenians, though not wishing to imitate him, admired his contempt for comfort; but his high-handed behaviour often caused trouble. He is said on one occasion to have called for men to gather round and hear him, and when they came, to have hit them with his staff crying, 'It was men I called for, not scoundrels'. Another famous story tells how ALEXANDER THE GREAT (q.v.) came to see him and asked if there was any favour he desired. 'Only to stand out of my light', replied Diogenes.

During a voyage, he was captured by pirates and sold as a slave in Corinth, where he lived the rest of his life, becoming the much-respected tutor of his master's sons. The people of Corinth erected a pillar in his memory surmounted by a marble dog—'dog' being the half-derisive, half-affectionate nick-name for Diogenes, and the symbol adopted by the Cynics. The word 'cynic', originally meaning 'like a dog', has changed its meaning considerably. It now usually means 'one who disbelieves in good motives'.

DISRAELI, Benjamin (Earl of Beaconsfield) (1804–81). The career of this great Conservative statesman was a triumph of ability and ambition. Starting with few of the advantages then required for political office, Disraeli was twice Prime Minister, refashioned the Conservative party, and left a reputation as the most enigmatic and colourful of all 19th-century political leaders. He also wrote a dozen novels.

Born a Jew, Disraeli was baptized when he was 12—a fortunate event for his political ambitions, for until 1858 Jews were not allowed to sit in the House of Commons. He early made a reputation as a clever, undisguisedly ambitious young man, stating openly that he intended to be Prime Minister. He entered Parliament at the fifth attempt as a Conservative, when he was 33.

Disraeli had already developed a theory of politics. In his view, English government had been perverted in the interests of a single class: first by the 18th-century Whig magnates, and then by the middle-class manufacturers. Disraeli held that government should be based firmly on the three natural supports of society— the Crown, the Church of England, and the landed gentry. It should remain in the hands of a 'natural aristocracy', but should have a clear social policy, giving justice to the poor. He put forward these views in speeches and pamphlets, and also in his novels *Coningsby* and *Sybil*.

In 1845 Disraeli's support of the 'landed interest' brought him into conflict with the Conservative Prime Minister, Sir Robert PEEL (q.v.), who proposed to repeal the Corn Laws which protected English agriculture. Disraeli attacked him in a series of bitterly clever speeches. As one of the leaders of a rebel wing of the Conservative party, he later defeated Peel after the Corn Laws had been repealed.

This episode made Disraeli one of the most discussed men in the country. In the House of Commons he was unique—un-English in every way, dandified in appearance, and grotesque in dress. He sometimes wore bottle-green trousers, fancy waistcoats, and an elaborate assortment of rings and chains. His hair was black, and carefully arranged so that a forelock fell over his forehead. His speeches were carefully composed, full of epigram, and often barbed with malicious wit. He delivered them with impassive calm, appearing unmoved while the House rocked with laughter or applause. Though many of the most able Conservatives, such as GLADSTONE (q.v.), had broken with the party after the defeat of Peel, it was nevertheless Disraeli's greatest personal achievement that he gained the leadership of a party whose members prided themselves on being 'the gentlemen of England'.

From about 1865 English politics were dominated by the great political duel between Disraeli and his rival Gladstone. Gladstone, reverent and earnest, looked on politics almost as a religious duty; Disraeli was flippant and brilliant. Gladstone enclosed his principles in copious speech; Disraeli spoke often in epigrams and slogans. Gladstone accepted office almost with awe, feeling that providence had preserved him for a high purpose; Disraeli seized office with undisguised triumph: 'I have reached the top of the greasy pole at last', he remarked. The two men cordially disliked each other. Disraeli once stated that Gladstone was no gentleman;

National Portrait Gallery

BENJAMIN DISRAELI, EARL OF BEACONSFIELD
Portrait by J. E. Millais (1829–96)

Gladstone was convinced that there was something diabolical in Disraeli, that his policies were not only wrong but immoral, and that his relations with Queen VICTORIA (q.v.), whose influence he used for his party's advantage, were unconstitutional.

They differed equally in their political philosophies. Where Disraeli thought of communities, and 'balanced interests', Gladstone thought rather of the individual. Gladstone emphasized the importance of political rights, such as the vote; Disraeli thought rather of social rights, such as housing, health, and fair working conditions (which might need the intervention of the State to secure). In foreign affairs, Gladstone opposed unnecessary British interference with other nations, and disapproved of British overseas expansion. Disraeli on the other hand was the greatest Imperialist of his day. Yet it was Disraeli who, largely for party reasons, piloted the Second Reform Bill (1867) through Parliament (*see* ELECTION, PARLIAMENTARY, Vol. X).

Although the Conservatives had held office for three short periods since 1846, they never enjoyed a clear majority until 1874. Then, with real power in his hands at last, Disraeli was ill and ageing. He was bent and in pain; his hair was dyed black, and his forelock damped and fixed to his forehead. Nevertheless, this Ministry accomplished so much social legislation that it was said that 'the Conservatives have done more for the working-classes in five years than the Liberals have done in fifty'. Measures were introduced favouring trade unions and improving housing conditions; and an important public health Act was passed, which remained the backbone of English sanitary legislation for the next 60 years. Abroad, Disraeli annexed Cyprus and bought for the British Government a controlling interest in the Suez Canal (borrowing the money from his friend, ROTHSCHILD (q.v.), because there was no time to go to Parliament for it). By Act of Parliament Queen Victoria took the title of Empress of India which she had desired. Disraeli (who became Earl of Beaconsfield in 1876) himself represented Britain at the Congress of Berlin (a meeting of the European Powers to settle a quarrel between Russia and Turkey), and brought back 'Peace with Honour'.

This marked the peak of Disraeli's fame. Afterwards, the effect of a world-wide business depression and unpopular wars in Zululand and Afghanistan turned public opinion against the government. Gladstone, who had been in retirement, rallied the public against Disraeli's aggressive Imperialism. In the general election of 1880 Disraeli was defeated and he died the following year.

Disraeli built his policy on two planks: Imperialism abroad and social improvement at home. He gave to the idea of Empire a glamour and a romantic appeal which it had previously lacked. He re-created the Conservative party, transforming it from an assembly of country squires into a broad-based cross-section of the country, and giving it a policy which was later called 'Tory Democracy'. It was largely through his influence that the Conservatives, previously a body associated with special privileges, were able to remain a force in an age seeking social equality.

See also GLADSTONE; VICTORIA; PEEL.
See also Vol. X: POLITICAL PARTIES.

DOMINIC, St. (1170–1221). Dominic was a Spaniard, born in Castile. He lived at the same time as St. FRANCIS (q.v.); and the two men, though very different in character, both founded orders of Preaching FRIARS (q.v. Vol. I), who went into the world to teach the Christian faith.

Dominic studied theology at Palencia University for 10 years. Then he served as a canon at Osma Cathedral until, when he was 35, his bishop, Acevedo, chose him to accompany him on a mission to the land of the Albigenses, in south-west France, where the people were following a false religion. The churches there were almost deserted, and many of the clergy lived idle or evil lives. The Pope tried to deal with the heresy of the Albigenses by sending papal legates who came with pomp and luxury. But Dominic rebuked them. 'This was not the way', he said. 'Zeal must be met by zeal, false sanctity by real sanctity, humility by humility, preaching error by preaching truth.' The Pope then tried to crush the heresy by sending a crusading army against the Albigenses and slaughtering many of them, a cruel persecution which Dominic to his discredit supported.

When the mission returned to Spain, Dominic decided to stay behind, and he gathered a few like-minded men to help him to teach the heretics. In 1216 the Pope finally allowed Dominic to found an order of his supporters, and in 1220 its constitution was framed. The order was to be a mendicant one, that is, its members

National Gallery

ST. DOMINIC

Wing of an altar-piece painted by Duccio (1260–1339)

were to own nothing and to beg for their daily bread. There was a 'master-general', and various 'provinces' were formed, each under a 'provincial prior'. There were nunneries for women, who became of great service as teachers.

Dominic died the next year; but his order grew and spread over western Europe, including France, where they became known as 'Jacobins', and England, where they were called 'Black Friars'. As with the Franciscans, however, the rule of mendicancy in its strict sense was soon found to be impracticable. The Dominicans excelled in learning. Dominic had sent his men to the centres of education, Paris, Rome, and Bologna, because he wanted to influence the great teachers and leaders of thought. Soon they were occupying the chairs of theology in the Universities of Oxford, Paris, and Cologne; and two of the greatest medieval theologians, Albert the Great and St. Thomas AQUINAS (q.v.), were Dominicans.

DONATELLO (1386–1466). Donato di Niccolo, called Donatello, was the greatest Italian sculptor of the 15th century. He was born in Florence and lived there for most of his long life. He was probably brought up by a wealthy merchant who is said to have loved him for his goodness and cleverness, and he soon acquired fame for the life-like quality of his sculpture. He worked with his friend, the architect BRUNELLESCHI (q.v.), introducing many new ideas into their buildings and sculpture. Many Italian painters throughout the 15th century modelled their work on Donatello's statues and reliefs, sometimes even including his figures in their paintings.

Donatello observed nature much more closely than earlier Italian sculptors had done; he also set himself to solve his problems by studying ancient Roman sculpture. Little of this was to be seen in Florence, but a certain amount could be found in Rome, which he visited in 1431–3. Donatello never slavishly copied Roman models and in many cases invented variations of his own. His figures of saints have such strongly individual features that many were thought to be portraits of contemporaries.

Donatello adorned his native city of Florence with statues in bronze and marble, and also worked for a short time at Siena and at Prato, near Florence. He went to Padua in 1443, stayed there 10 years, and left two great works in bronze; the first a statue of the soldier Gatte-

Anderson
THE ANNUNCIATION, MARBLE TABERNACLE BY DONATELLO
This was carved after Donatello had visited Rome and seen antique buildings. Santa Croce, Florence

melata on horseback—the first equestrian statue of its kind which had been made in Italy since Roman times (*see* Vol. I, p. 400); the second an altar for the church of San Antonio, decorated with bronze statues of the Virgin and saints and with reliefs depicting scenes from the life of St. Anthony. The many figures are modelled with extraordinary skill so that, although the relief is low, there is an impression of space and depth.

During the last 13 years of his life Donatello, now back in Florence, made a number of sculptures, mostly in bronze, in which the violence of the figures is very different from the Roman art which had originally inspired him, or from his own earlier work, such as the delightful reliefs of singing and dancing children.

See also Vol. XII: ITALIAN ART.

DONNE, John (1573–1631). The poet Donne, the famous Dean of St. Paul's, preached magnificent sermons which not only moved his hearers to the utmost, for he was a superb orator, but have remained unequalled examples of English rhetorical prose. Yet Donne's immortality rests neither upon his piety nor his oratory but upon his poetry, and chiefly upon his love-poetry.

Donne is the earliest writer of METAPHYSICAL POETRY (q.v. Vol. XII). Love-poetry before Donne, the poetry of Wyatt or Surrey, Sidney or Spenser, had followed the artificial tradition of PETRARCH (q.v.), a tradition in which both lover and beloved behave ideally. The vocabulary of such poetry is as formal as the imaginary behaviour of the lover. Donne wrote of love and women in a direct, realistic way: 'For God's sake hold your tongue and let me love', he begins a poem. He used the language and rhythms of ordinary speech, and he used similes and metaphors drawn from the new and exciting world he lived in—from scientific discovery, mapmaking, chemistry, any subject that interested him—to illuminate his passion. This expression of passion in terms of the intellect, and the use of sometimes far-fetched imagery to do so, is what we mean by 'metaphysical'—a kind of poetry not always easy to understand.

Donne was brought up as a Catholic, but after much heart-searching became an Anglican. His secret marriage, though strongly opposed by his wife's relations, brought trouble but much personal happiness, and it was his wife's death in 1617, combined with his naturally religious and deeply passionate nature, that turned him finally towards the Church. As a young man he had lived fully and dangerously: he had, for example, accompanied Essex's triumphant expedition against the Spaniards at Cadiz and the Azores. His love-poetry, which owes little to any of his contemporaries,

By gracious permission of H.M. the Queen

JOHN DONNE
Miniature by Isaac Oliver

was written in his early 20's. Later, he brought to religion the same ardent temperament; and his divine poems are no less truly love-poems than his secular ones.

Only four of his poems were published in his lifetime, though they were freely circulated in manuscript. His greatness as a poet was little recognized in the intervening centuries, until our own time. Today, however, Donne is acknowledged as one of our finest poets and as a great innovator in the use of language.

DOSTOEVSKY, Fyodor Mikhailovich

(1821–81). The Russian novelist Dostoevsky was born in Moscow. Unlike earlier great Russian writers, he was a commoner, his father being a doctor of modest means, his mother of merchant stock. Dostoevsky went to St. Petersburg to study engineering, and then entered the army as an engineer officer. His experience of comparative poverty made him want to get rich quickly, so after a year he left the army and tried various unsuccessful schemes for making money.

His first novel, *Poor People*, published in 1846, was greeted enthusiastically by the critics, and won Dostoevsky a place among the leading writers of the day, a position of which he was extremely vain. He joined a socialist study-circle and, in the repression which followed the European revolutions of 1848, was arrested with the other members of the group. After several months in prison, they were subjected to a frightful practical joke by the authorities, who took them to the place of execution and read them the death sentence. They were awaiting the volley of the firing-squad when the real sentence was made known to them—penal

servitude in Siberia. One of the prisoners went mad under the strain; Dostoevsky himself never recovered from the effects of this incident, and the mild epilepsy he had suffered from was made worse. He was in Siberia for 9 years, where for much of the time the only reading permitted him was the Bible. This he read and re-read, and finally built up a creed of his own—a kind of nationalist Christianity, in which the suffering common people of Russia were identified with the figure of Christ.

While in Siberia he began a novel, *The Village of Stepanchikovo*, a study of cruelty practised not by bodily violence but by the mind. In 1860 he was permitted to return to St. Petersburg, where he wrote novels based directly on his Siberian experiences, and began to publish his own literary journal, which was, however, suppressed by the authorities. In 1862 he travelled in England, France, and Germany, and then made a second attempt to publish a periodical, which again failed. In order to pay off his debts he wrote with furious speed *Memoirs from the Underground* and his great work, *Crime and Punishment*. In 1867 he went abroad for 4 years, where he wrote *The Idiot*, *The Eternal Husband*, and *The Possessed*. When he returned home he was appointed editor of a conservative weekly paper, and in 1876 he began again to publish his own periodical. His last book, *The Brothers Karamazov*, appeared in 1880. Shortly before he died he made a famous speech on the occasion of the unveiling of the monument to the poet PUSHKIN (q.v.) in Moscow.

Dostoevsky's reputation as one of the great novelists of the world is chiefly founded upon the novels *Crime and Punishment. The Idiot, The Possessed*, and *The Brothers Karamazov.* The dominating theme of these novels is the battle by the hero—usually a man of little social consequence—to regain his sense of human dignity after suffering unjust injury and humiliation at the hands of society. A Russian critic writes, 'In order to feel himself a real, complete man, the Dostoevsky hero must have the courage himself to wrong someone else'. By committing a crime he shows his independence; by breaking the law, both moral and otherwise, he shows his superiority to it. Yet 'crime is inevitably followed by punishment', writes the critic, 'the tormentor must himself suffer; but this suffering is justified; it is lawful retribution, and does not offend against human dignity. It must not be evaded but endured with meekness.'

Dostoevsky's great novels, despite their complicated plots, carry the reader along by the force and intensity of the writing and by the violence of their feeling. The range of characters is vast—people completely convincing but strangely unlike those one meets in the real world. Most of them are unbalanced, obsessed, self-tortured, often evil, more rarely saintly, inhabiting a gloomy and tragic world, yet commanding our understanding and exciting our deepest sympathy.

See also Vol. XII: RUSSIAN LITERATURE; NOVEL.

DOUGHTY, Charles Montagu (1843–1926).

This traveller and poet was the son of a Suffolk squire and clergyman. An impediment in his speech prevented his carrying out his childhood's ambition of joining the Navy; instead, he went to Cambridge and read science. After graduating in 1865, he studied geology, archaeology, and the history of language on his own, and also read widely in 16th-century literature. He was a tall, fine-looking man with a reddish beard and aquiline features. Rather fierce and intolerant as a young man, he grew gentle and patient.

In 1870 he set out on his travels, first in Europe where he climbed Vesuvius during an eruption, and eventually in the Middle East. He rode through Sinai on a camel to the ancient rock city of Petra and to Maan, north-east of the Red Sea in Transjordan. Here he learnt that similar monuments, unknown to Westerners, existed at a place called Medain Saleh, in Arabia, on the pilgrim route to Medina and Mecca. Doughty spent a year in Damascus learning the Arabic language, and then joined a pilgrim caravan to the Holy City of Mecca. Arabia at that time was wild and dangerous and fanatically suspicious of any stranger, especially of someone like Doughty who despised disguise and travelled as a declared Christian and Englishman. As Doughty wrote later, Arabia offered nothing to the traveller save 'a wasteful wilderness full of fear where every man's hand is ready against another, a lean wild grit and dust stiffened with everlasting drought'. His health suffered from the burning heat of the desert and the continual diet of biscuits, dates, and bad water. At Medain Saleh he left the caravan to inspect the magnificent monuments, tombs, and inscriptions. He then attached himself to the wandering BEDOUIN (q.v. Vol. I) and travelled over much of Central Arabia collecting more information about the country and the people than had ever before been known to the West.

Doughty, who genuinely loved the Bedouin, described their faults as well as their virtues, and as he later said, 'If one live at any time with the Arab, he will have all his life after a feeling for the desert'.

In 1878 Doughty, half blind and broken in health, arrived at Jedda on the Red Sea, and eventually reached England. He settled down to write an account of his travels and scientific observations, writing in the Elizabethan English style because he thought its forcefulness and directness were best suited to describe his amazing experiences. The *Travels in Arabia Deserta*, published in 1888, at first appealed only to scholars, but the original work, first abridged and introduced by Edward Garnett and later reissued with an introduction by T. E. LAWRENCE (q.v.), who called it a 'Bible of its kind', has gradually established itself as a minor classic.

Doughty married and spent the rest of his life in seclusion in France and England writing poetry, mostly long poems and dramas in the same archaic style.

See also Vol. I: ARABS; BEDOUIN.

DOYLE, Sir Arthur Conan (1859–1930).

The creator of Sherlock Holmes, the first popular detective of fiction, was the originator of logical deduction and scientific analysis in crime detection. Doyle was a Scotsman of Irish descent who, having received a medical training at Edinburgh, where fees were low, came to England to start a medical career. Having no money to buy a practice from a retiring doctor, he took cheap rooms at Southsea, and, since etiquette forbade him to advertise, put a brass plate on his door, hoping that it would attract some patients. But patients were few, so Doyle began writing stories for magazines and book-publishers to earn money. For one series of stories he hit on the idea of an amateur detective whose clear brain penetrated mysteries that baffled the police. This detective, Sherlock Holmes, distrusted the obvious, saw through false trails, could find clues by a single glance round a room, and used scientific methods and instruments. The stories of Holmes's detections were related by an imaginary Dr. Watson, a slow-witted friend who asked simple questions which served to show up Holmes's brilliance.

These stories were immensely popular, and

The Times

AN EXHIBITION MODEL OF SHERLOCK HOLMES'S SITTING
ROOM

The room was supposed to be in No. 221 b Baker Street.
Holmes's deer-stalker cap and Inverness cape are hanging
on the door, beside Watson's top hat and stethoscope

brought Doyle much more money than his medical practice or his 'serious' historical novels, with which he would have much preferred to have made his name, and of which he wrote nearly twenty. Editors and publishers in Britain, America, and other countries, clamoured for Sherlock Holmes stories, and Doyle, having given up medicine, reluctantly continued to write them. He tried to bring them to an end by making Holmes fall over a cliff to his death; but 10 years later public insistence drove Doyle, now a rich man and a knight, to revive Holmes, ingeniously explaining that he had only pretended to die to mislead his enemies. The stories were translated into twenty-two languages, and their author received letters from all parts of the world from people who believed that Holmes was a real person. Today, his work is often revived on radio and in theatre and cinema.

Since Conan Doyle's time, detective fiction has become a substantial part of popular literature, and all his prophecies about scientific detection with microscopes and chemistry have come true (*see* C.I.D., Vol. X).

See also Vol. XII: DETECTIVE STORIES.

DRAKE, Sir Francis (*c.* 1540–96). Drake was the founder of British sea-power. In appearance he was a stocky west-countryman, with reddish hair and a sharp, pointed beard. At sea he maintained strict discipline, but was admired by his men for his daring and generosity. A Spaniard, who regarded him as a dangerous sea-rover, described him as 'sharp, restless, well-spoken, inclined to liberality, ambitious, boastful, not very cruel'.

He was born on a farm near Tavistock but was brought up at Chatham, where his father was employed to read prayers to the sailors, and where Francis learned sea-craft on board Thames coastal vessels. His first voyage abroad was in 1567, when he commanded the *Judith* in an expedition led by his kinsman John HAWKINS (q.v.). A treacherous attack made by the Spaniards during that expedition in the Gulf of Mexico left an indelible impression on his mind and confirmed his hatred of Spain. As he told a prisoner on his voyage round the world, 'I am not going to stop until I have collected the two millions that my cousin John Hawkins lost there.'

During the next 10 years he made many daring raids on the Spanish Main, notably in 1572 when he sacked the very wealthy town of Nombre de Dios in Panama, and returned with plunder worth £40,000. When his ships entered Plymouth on a Sunday morning, the people flocked out of the churches to welcome the most famous of the Devon sea-dogs.

From 1577 to 1580 Drake made a voyage round the world in the GOLDEN HIND (q.v. Vol. IV). The reasons for this journey are obscure, but Queen Elizabeth backed it in order to avenge herself for the attacks on English shipping made by the King of Spain. Drake himself prized the honour of being the first English circumnavigator, and realized the possibilities of loot in Spanish seas. Though his ship was blown south into what is now called Drake Strait after emerging from the Magellan Straits at the extreme tip of South America, he was not driven far enough east to discover Cape Horn, though he guessed there was a passage from the Atlantic.

The *Golden Hind*'s unexpected appearance in the South Sea caught the Spaniards unprepared, and financially the voyage was extremely successful, paying £47 for every £1 invested in it. Drake may or may not have been looking for the western exit of the North-West Passage (*see*

DRAKE'S ATTACK ON SAN DOMINGO IN 1585

Drake's fleet is shown at anchor before the town. A landing was made to the left, and the English troops are seen advancing on the town. One of a set of plates published in 1588

EXPLORATION, Vol. IV), but he certainly landed and took possession of 'New Albion' near San Francisco before crossing the Pacific. Soon after his return the Queen knighted him on board his ship at Deptford. In those days, says a contemporary, 'his name and fame was in all places, the people swarming daily in the streets to behold him'. He became mayor of Plymouth.

When open war broke out with Spain in 1585, Drake was the obvious choice to command the fleet sent to destroy Spanish power in the Caribbean Sea. As 'General of Her Majesty's Navy' this was Drake's first official command; before he had always acted as an independent privateer. He sacked San Domingo and Cartagena, and on his return took home the first Virginian colonists who had gone out the previous year to found the British Empire in America (see RALEIGH).

When in 1587, the SPANISH ARMADA (q.v. Vol. X) was nearly ready to invade Britain, Drake with a strong force entered Cadiz harbour and destroyed thirty-three store-ships, a bold attack which he called 'the singeing of the King of Spain's beard' and from which he escaped unscathed. Drake fully understood the strategic truth that the best defence is often attack; but this idea was not acceptable to the Queen in 1588, when Drake tried to persuade her that 'the advantage of time and place in all martial actions is half the victory'. She thought he was too rash and relegated him to the position of second-in-command. When the Lord Admiral, Howard of Effingham, arrived at Plymouth, the fleet was ordered to guard the entrance to the Channel. The ships were in harbour and Drake and the other commanders were playing bowls on the Hoe when the news arrived on 19 July that the Armada was in sight. It was only by extraordinarily skilful seamanship that the fleet managed to get to sea in time to take up a position astern of the Spanish ships as they moved in majestic formation up Channel. Soon afterwards Drake was able to cut off the *Rosario*, one of the largest galleons, and bring her in to Torbay. On 30 July, after the fireship attack at Calais had broken up the Spanish Armada, Drake led his squadron again and again in gun duels with the enemy in what was the first great English victory at sea. He chased the Spanish ships up the north-east coast as far as the Firth of Forth, after which a great many of the already damaged vessels were shipwrecked in their attempts to escape round Scotland and the west of Ireland.

The next year Drake led an expedition against Lisbon in an attempt to follow up the victory; but it was a complete failure, and the English lost a great many men from disease. Drake, consequently, fell into disgrace. After a few years on shore he was recalled from retirement to share the command with Hawkins in another descent on the West Indies. The Spaniards, however, by this time had built up an efficient defence system there, and Drake was unable to repeat his previous success. Hawkins died before operations began, and Drake died of dysentery on 28 January 1596 off Porto Bello, where he was buried at sea. His drum (used in those days on board ships for signalling orders to the crew) was brought back to his home at Buckland Abbey (now a Drake museum), where the legend grew up that it would sound every time England was in danger.

Drake shares with Nelson the honour of being England's greatest admiral. He founded the offensive spirit in tactics, and he embodied those qualities of courage, initiative, and good leadership which mark the British naval tradition. His success was chiefly due to his ability to seize opportunities and plan his attacks carefully, making use of the element of surprise.

See also ELIZABETH I.

DRYDEN, John (1631–1700). 'Glorious John Dryden', the unrivalled leader of English poetry and criticism in the latter part of the 17th century, was the eldest of the 14 children of a Northamptonshire Puritan gentleman. He was educated at Westminster School and at Cambridge; and at 26 he came to London, where he remained all his life.

In 1659 Dryden wrote his *Heroic Stanzas on the Death of Cromwell*; 2 years later, at the Restoration, he welcomed Charles II to the throne with his *Astraea Redux*. This quick change of sides is understandable when it is remembered that Dryden found the inspiration for his poems most easily in great contemporary events, and that, valuing peace and security above all things, he saw both Cromwell and Charles as symbols of order and firm government. His finest topical poem *Annus Mirabilis* commemorates the eventful year of 1666, marked by two big naval battles against the Dutch and the Great FIRE OF LONDON (q.v. Vol. X).

At the Restoration the theatres, closed by the Puritans, were reopened, and during the next 20 years Dryden wrote some twenty plays, of which the best is *All for Love* (1678), a version of the story of Antony and Cleopatra written in blank verse. As a rule, however, Dryden preferred the rhymed heroic couplet (*see* VERSIFICATION, Vol. XII) which he used with varying though never with complete success in his many heroic tragedies. Among the comedies, *Marriage à la Mode*, the most effective, is still sometimes acted. As well as poet and dramatist, Dryden was a master of English prose and a great critic. His critical writings include the excellent *Essay of Dramatic Poesy*, generous appreciations of Chaucer, Milton, and Ben Jonson, and his justly famous praise of Shakespeare.

National Portrait Gallery

JOHN DRYDEN
Portrait by Sir Godfrey Kneller

When Dryden was 50, already Poet Laureate and the most renowned poet of his day, he wrote what is now considered his first really great poem *Absalom and Achitophel*, a brilliant political satire against Shaftesbury, the opponent of Charles II. Dryden used the characters of the Bible story—King David, his son Absalom, and the tempter Achitophel—to represent Charles, his illegitimate son the Duke of Monmouth, and Shaftesbury. This satire was followed by others, including the mock-heroic poem *MacFlecknoe*, an attack on the poet Shadwell and the model for POPE's (q.v.) famous satire, *The Dunciad*.

In 1685 James II, a Catholic, became king, and Dryden, who had always longed for 'an omniscient Church'—that is, one Church of Supreme Authority—and whose poem *Religio Laici* had already shown his half doubts of Anglicanism, himself turned Catholic. Two years later he wrote *The Hind and the Panther*, defending his new faith and his own conversion: the 'milk-white hind' represents the Roman Catholic Church and the fierce panther the Church of England.

When, with the REVOLUTION OF 1688 (q.v Vol. X), James fled the country and the Protestant William and Mary succeeded, Dryden lost his laureateship, his other State posts, and his pension, and turned again at the age of 57 to earn his living. With amazing energy, he produced five more plays, his great translation of Virgil, and, barely a month before his death, *The Fables*, which are admirable verse translations from Ovid, Boccaccio, and Chaucer.

The new AUGUSTAN AGE (q.v. Vol. XII)—the age of Pope—looked back to Dryden as its master. 'What was said of Rome adorned by Augustus may be applied by an easy metaphor to English poetry embellished by Dryden,' wrote Dr. Johnson: *Lateritiam invenit, marmoream reliquit*—'He found it brick, and he left it marble.'

See also Vol. XII: RESTORATION DRAMA; SATIRE.

DUMAS, Alexandre (1802–70).

The French novelist, Dumas, was the son of a republican general born in the West Indies of mixed white and black parentage, who had married the daughter of a hotel-keeper near Paris. Dumas had no literary pretensions and next to no knowledge of history, but he had great imagination and unlimited energy. After an early struggle, he launched himself successfully into the writing of a series of romantic historical dramas, and later turned to novels with even greater success. *The Three Musketeers*, *The Count of Monte Cristo*, and *Twenty Years After* are all famous still. Dumas regarded history as a convenient peg on which to hang an exciting tale— *'L'histoire n'est qu'un clou où le tableau est accroché'*, are his own words. He had an exuberant gift for telling a story swiftly in a thrilling way; but his characterization is inferior, his historical local colour inaccurate, and his style rough and repetitive—defects which prevent his being considered a great artist. He wrote an enormous amount, undoubtedly using assistants to a considerable extent. Nevertheless he successfully launched romanticism in the theatre, and made the novel into a popular art-form.

His illegitimate son, Alexandre Dumas (1824–95), is most famous for his novel *The Lady with the Camellias*, which he himself adapted as a play.

DUNS SCOTUS, John (c. 1265–1308).

Duns the Scot, one of the best-known of the medieval religious thinkers known as Schoolmen, was a monk of the Franciscan order who taught at Oxford, Paris, and Cologne. His philosophy was opposed to that of Thomas AQUINAS (q.v.), the great teacher of the Dominican order. Aquinas maintained that by reason, the supreme human endowment, all religious truths could be proved, except the Trinity, the Creation of the world out of nothing, and the Incarnation. Duns Scotus regarded religion, and the theology which expressed religious belief, as beyond reason and resting on faith, which is an act of will. Beyond this, reason was free to speculate over a wide field. The two schools of 'Thomists' and 'Scotists' argued fiercely with one another, and our term 'dunce' is a relic of this long controversy.

See also Vol. I: PHILOSOPHY.

DÜRER, Albrecht (1471–1528).

This painter and engraver was the outstanding representative of the art of the Renaissance period in Germany. The son of a Hungarian goldsmith who had settled in Nuremberg, Dürer, after training in his father's workshop, was apprenticed to a leading Nuremberg painter and maker of woodcuts. He then travelled in Germany and in Switzerland, where he learned book illustration.

On his return to Nuremberg, Dürer married, then made a brief visit to Venice, and in 1498 published his first great series of woodcuts, the

A KNIGHT, DEATH, AND THE DEVIL
Engraving by Albrecht Dürer

'Apocalypse', illustrating the Book of Revelation. He began work on two more series and also painted portraits and altar-pieces. In 1505 he made a second visit to Venice, remaining there about 18 months. To his great delight, Giovanni BELLINI (q.v.), the foremost Venetian painter of that time and then a very old man, came to visit him and wanted one of his pictures.

The effect of the RENAISSANCE (q.v. Vol. I) had not at this time spread north from Italy, and the style in which Dürer had been trained was still medieval. But in Venice he met scholars, musicians, and connoisseurs, and he avidly learnt from them all he could concerning the principles of beauty. It was believed that these principles had been known to the artists of classical antiquity and depended on obedience to ideal standards of proportion when depicting the human body. Later Dürer wrote a treatise on this subject, exemplifying his ideas in his painting of Adam and Eve. Dürer's pictures show the influence of Bellini, but they are more restless in composition than those of the Italian artist, for at heart Dürer remained very much a northern artist and to some extent even a medieval one. He probably preferred making engravings—which were very popular—to paintings, and in 1512 he was employed as an engraver by the Emperor Maximilian and was given a pension. In 1520 Dürer went with his wife to Flanders; a record of his stay there is contained in a sketch book and travel diary which he kept.

Towards the end of his life Dürer wrote a great deal on artistic and scientific matters. He became a follower of LUTHER (q.v.), and his last painting, 'The Four Apostles', is inscribed with lines from Luther's translation of the New Testament.

See also Vol. XII: GERMAN ART.

DVOŘÁK, Antonin Leopold (1841–1904). The music of Dvořák derived much from the folksongs and dances of his native Bohemia (now part of Czechoslovakia) which he heard as a boy; in some of his later music, written when he was in America, the influence of NEGRO SPIRITUALS (q.v. Vol. XII) is clear. Dvořák's music is essentially melodious; it flows as easily as a stream. The lively tunes and buoyant lilt of peasant dance music flowed even into his symphonies and other major works.

Dvořák went to the village school for 2 years where he learnt the violin well enough to play in the village band. When he was sent to Zlonice to learn German his headmaster taught him the organ, piano, and viola. At 16 he attended the famous church organ school at Prague and later won his way as a viola player into the orchestra of the Czech National Theatre, of which the Czech composer Smetana was then conductor. Dvořák's first published work was his successful set of Slavonic Dances. Soon after came his *Stabat Mater*, which made him known in England, for he was invited to conduct it in London in 1884. When he was 50 he went to New York to become head of the National Conservatoire (music school). The music written during his 3 years in America includes most of his best-known works—the Humoresque, the symphony *From the New World*, the 'Nigger' Quartet, and the Cello Concerto.

On returning to Prague in 1895, Dvořák wished to write works reflecting the life of his own people: the results were his not very successful operas *The Jacobins* (an earlier work revised), *Russalka*, and, less Bohemian in character, *The Devil and Kate*. He died suddenly at the age of 62, and was deeply mourned by his country.

E

EDISON, Thomas Alva (1847–1931). This prolific inventor of the 19th century, with over 1,000 patents to his credit, shares with the Englishman, Sir J. W. Swan (1828–1914), the honour of inventing electric lighting as we know it. Edison, an American of mixed Dutch and Scottish ancestry born in Ohio, had only 3 months' regular schooling, and started work at the age of 12 as a railroad newsboy. Later he became a telegraph operator, and spent his spare time experimenting.

One of Edison's earliest inventions helped materially to bring the telephone into practical use, and so to make the Bell Telephone Company of America a commercial success. At about the same time he invented the 'phonograph' (or 'speaking machine'), as the earliest GRAMOPHONE (q.v. Vol. IX) was called. His phonograph used cylindrical records made of wax.

Edison had some part in creating the modern electric lamp. In 1860 Swan, the real pioneer, had constructed a lamp with a carbon filament which glowed, though not brightly. Nearly 20 years later both Edison, working on Swan's idea, and Swan himself devised greatly improved lamps. The work of these two men made possible the modern domestic lighting bulb.

See also Vol. IV: SPEECH, TRANSMISSION OF.
See also Vol. VIII: ILLUMINATION.

EDWARD I (1239–1307). Edward succeeded his father Henry III as King of England in 1272 at the end of a period of civil war in which the prestige of the monarchy had fallen low. Edward's aim was to restore order and to strengthen his own position. By a series of famous Statutes he cleared up many confusions in the existing law, provided for the policing of the countryside, and extended his control over the nobles. He is often called Edward the Lawgiver.

Edward was also the first king seriously to attempt the unification of Great Britain. The patriotic Welsh prince, Llewelyn, was conquered in two brilliant campaigns, and his Principality annexed to the English Crown and later bestowed upon the King's eldest son, the first English Prince of Wales. The Statute of Wales provided for the government of the country on English lines; the great stone castles, such as Harlech and Caernarvon, were garrisoned with English troops, and English merchants were encouraged to settle in Wales. In Scotland, Edward hoped to achieve a peaceful union by marrying his eldest son to the heiress of Scotland. But the princess died; whereupon the Scots appealed to Edward as their overlord to decide between the many claimants to the Scottish Crown. John Baliol, however, on whom his choice fell, was a weak character who proved unacceptable to the Scottish barons, and there was a national rising. In the course of the long series of campaigns which followed, England was neither rich enough nor strong enough to achieve a final conquest. Edward made many mistakes, choosing the wrong men to represent him in Scotland and underrating the spirit of the Scots. By his execution of William WALLACE (q.v.) he provided Scotland with a martyr to the

Reece Winstone

EDWARD I AND HIS QUEEN, ELEANOR OF CASTILE
Statues on a buttress of Lincoln Cathedral

cause of independence. In Robert BRUCE (q.v.), chosen king in 1306, the Scots found a fine leader; and when Edward died a year later Scotland was still unconquered.

The heavy taxation necessary to pay for these wars aroused opposition from barons and clergy, who in 1297 forced Edward to make formal confirmation of MAGNA CARTA (q.v. Vol. X) granted by his grandfather, John. It was chiefly in order to raise money that he several times summoned knights and burgesses from the shires and boroughs to join the parliament of barons. More than any other single individual, he is the creator of our representative PARLIAMENT (q.v. Vol. X).

Both physically and politically, Edward I was a strong king. Perhaps the 'Hammer of the Scots' may have been respected more than he was loved, but in the troubled centuries which followed men looked back to his reign as a time of national unity. His achievement as the conqueror of Wales, as lawgiver, and as one of the creators of Parliament ensures his permanent place among the great medieval kings.

See also Vol. X: LAW, ENGLISH; PARLIAMENT.

EINSTEIN, Albert (1879–1955). Einstein's is the greatest name in mathematical physics in the present century—he is the Newton of our age, the man with new ideas. His startling theory of RELATIVITY has altered people's ideas of the nature of the universe, and even of TIME and SPACE themselves (qq.v. Vol. III). His work has made the atomic-physicist take an interest in the universe as a whole; he has helped to make the astronomer realize that the infinitely little may be the key to some of his problems. He has made the philosopher take an interest in physics; he has awakened the physicist into an awareness of philosophical and moral problems.

Einstein led a simple and outwardly uneventful life. He was born of a Jewish family in south-west Germany, where his ancestors had lived for generations; he was brought up there and in Switzerland. As a young man he became devoted to mathematics, taking life seriously and liking to be by himself. His hatred of the German military ideas of the 1890's and the brutal barrack life enforced on young conscripts made him take Swiss citizenship at 21. But when he was 34 and beginning to be famous, he accepted a special professorship at the University of Berlin, and remained there for 18 years. In 1932, however, when the Nazi movement in Germany aimed at suppressing thought and began to persecute the Jews, Einstein left again. After a year spent as a Fellow of Christ Church, Oxford, he settled in America; at Princeton he received a university appointment, and every kindness and facility for his researches.

Einstein's theories are hard to understand; even his explanations are difficult. Yet few men have tried more seriously to interpret nature with simplicity. In the article on RELATIVITY in Volume III an attempt has been made to explain as simply as possible the outlines of his great discoveries, and to show how he has revolutionized the theories established by NEWTON (q.v.). Einstein tackled his problems as a very young man in Switzerland by means of mathematical calculation, and within a few years he was on the road to solving them. Building on the best work of the past, he did the hard and brilliant thinking which provided the answers. In 1905, when he was only 26, he published his first startling theory, which offered a partial solution to some of the scientific problems, and 10 years later he completed the full theory of relativity on which his fame rests.

Huddersfield Art Gallery

ALBERT EINSTEIN
Bronze bust by Jacob Epstein

His genius lay in mathematical inventiveness. Other men had measured space and time, as well as the atoms and the stars, by means of electricity, photography, laboratory experiments, and ingenious mathematics. Einstein, using only pencil and paper, showed that some of the apparent contradictions in nature disappeared if mathematics was used in a new way, and the old ideas about time and distance were discarded. Since Einstein first put forward his theory, it has stood the test of research by many scientists. His general view of the universe was that it is not infinite. It is very vast, but finite though unbounded. What is beyond the bounds does not concern the physicist because it is incapable of being observed by any real or potential means.

At the time of his death, Einstein was engaged in perfecting formulae for a 'unified field theory' which would embrace gravitation.

See also NEWTON; EUCLID.
See also Vol. III: RELATIVITY; SPACE; TIME; LIGHT; UNIVERSE.

ELGAR, Sir Edward (1857–1934). Elgar, the first English composer since PURCELL (q.v.) to be respected all over the Western world, was born in Worcester where his father kept a small music-shop. He was a good amateur organist and violinist, and he began to learn music at an early age, gaining all the knowledge and practical experience he could by playing in local orchestras and learning as many musical instruments as he was able to get hold of. In 1886 he married one of his pupils, Alice Roberts, who later wrote many of the poems which he set to music. The England Elgar grew up in was musically barren and provincial. It was Elgar's music—the music of 15 marvellously rich and productive years (1897–1913)—which brought England once more into the international world of music.

It was not until he was 36 that Elgar composed the first of his popular works, the Serenade for Strings, and not until 1897, when the 'Enigma' Variations were performed for the first time, that England discovered that he was an outstanding composer. In 1900 his *Dream of Gerontius* (an ORATORIO (q.v. Vol. XII) based on NEWMAN's poem (q.v.)) was given its first performance in Birmingham, and was followed by *The Apostles* and *The Kingdom*. By this time Elgar's genius had been recognized by the award of knighthood. Though he never gave up writing choral music, he now wrote more and more for orchestra—a form of music in which he showed great skill and knowledge of what would be effective (*see* ORCHESTRATION, Vol. XII). He matched this skill with romantic and melodious themes in his two symphonies, in the concertos for violin and for cello and, perhaps most magnificent of all, in the symphonic study *Falstaff*.

Elgar was a proud and loyal Englishman. *Falstaff* was not only a tribute to Shakespeare but also to England in the stirring days of Henry IV and V. Elgar also left a tribute to London in his overture *Cockaigne*. The musical language he used was often reminiscent of WAGNER and BRAHMS (qq.v.), but his work is essentially English and English people understand his thoughts—whether commonplace or original—because he appeals to what is English in them. During the First World War he wrote some patriotic pieces, but his most popular work of that kind was written in 1901—the 'Pomp and Circumstance' marches, the first of which contains the tune now sung as 'Land of Hope and Glory'.

After his wife died in 1920, Elgar composed nothing of much importance. In 1924 he was appointed Master of the King's Music.

See also Vol. XII: ORATORIO.

ELIOT, George (1819–80). This was the pen-name chosen by Mary Ann (or Marian) Evans, author of *Adam Bede*, *The Mill on the Floss*, *Silas Marner*, and *Middlemarch*—great novels of provincial life in the English midlands. She was born in Warwickshire, where her father, a farmer of unusual character, had risen from being a carpenter's son to managing a large estate. Marian, his youngest child, was a dark-haired, clever, but plain little girl, devoted to her brother Isaac, whom she later drew as Tom, in *The Mill on the Floss*— his sister Maggie Tulliver being a portrait of herself. At 17, soon after her mother's death, she took over the care of her father's house. But though she loved the country and its people, and in her brief leisure read and studied widely, it was a lonely, unsatisfying life for a girl of such ability. Many years later, in *Daniel Deronda*, she wrote: 'You may try, but you can never imagine what it is to have a man's force of genius in you, and to suffer the slavery of being a girl.'

When she was 21 her father handed over the farm to Isaac and retired with Marian to live in

GEORGE ELIOT, AGED 30

Engraving by G. J. Stodart from the painting by M. D'Albert-Durade

Coventry. Here she made friends with a ribbon manufacturer named Bray, and his wife, under whose influence she began to question (and eventually abandon) her own narrow and intense evangelical beliefs. After her father's death in 1849, she went abroad with the Brays, and on her return she began to write articles for *The Westminster Review*. These so impressed the editor that he invited her to come to London as his assistant. In this post she made many new and valuable friends, among them Herbert Spencer, the scientific philosopher, and the lively writer, George Henry Lewes, who had been an actor. In 1854 George Lewes and Marian Evans began to live as husband and wife, a legal marriage not being possible, for, although Lewes had been deserted by his wife, he could not obtain a divorce. Lewes and Marian Evans continued to live together very happily until Lewes's death, 25 years later. She brought up his three children, who were devoted to her.

Marian Evans was nearly 40 when she began to write stories. Some early sketches of country life provided the basis of her first and very successful work of fiction, the charming *Scenes of Clerical Life*. Three fine novels followed: *Adam Bede*, the story of Hetty Sorrel, a pretty but empty-minded village girl who is loved by the carpenter, Adam Bede, and of Dinah Morris, the Methodist; *The Mill on the Floss*, which reflects much of her own childhood and girlhood; and *Silas Marner*, the tale of a weaver who adopts a baby girl whom he finds mysteriously at his door. Of her later books, *Romola* is set in 15th-century Italy, and *Daniel Deronda* in 19th-century Europe, while *Middlemarch*, which many think her greatest work, gives a cross-section of middle-class life in an English provincial town. She also published a volume of essays and several narrative poems. She became famous and was much revered. In the last year of her life, after the death of Lewes, she married John Walter Cross, a young and devoted admirer.

George Eliot was a serious novelist much concerned with the deep problems of ordinary daily life. Her themes are sombre; she describes with great poignancy the overwhelming tragedy that can come to ordinary simple people. Yet her accounts of country men and women—the Garth family in *Middlemarch* or the Poysers of Hall Place Farm in *Adam Bede*, for example— have humour and a delightful freshness. She had particular skill in setting down conversations, and always wrote well about children.

See also Vol. XII: NOVEL.

ELIZABETH I (1533–1603). The daughter of HENRY VIII (q.v.), a strong-willed man, and Anne Boleyn, a flirtatious woman, Elizabeth inherited the characteristics of both. She inherited also both danger and opportunity. The Catholics, who had not accepted Henry's separation from Catherine of Aragon, regarded her as base-born; to the Protestants she was the child of the marriage which symbolized Henry's repudiation of the Pope. She was declared illegitimate in 1536 when Henry had her mother executed, but was later restored to her place in the succession, a matter of less importance after the birth of Henry's son, Edward. Elizabeth was well educated, but somewhat neglected during her father's life.

When it became plain that Edward VI would have no children, Elizabeth's importance increased; and during the reign of her Catholic sister, Mary, she was in grave peril. Mary's unpopularity because of her marriage with PHILIP II (q.v.) of Spain caused the Protestants to regard Elizabeth as their champion. She did everything she could to avert suspicion; but she was strongly suspected of complicity in a rising against Mary in 1554, was sent to the Tower, and narrowly escaped with her life. When released, she lived in retirement until her sister's death in 1558 made her Queen.

Elizabeth became Queen in a time of great difficulty. England had lost the strong position established by Henry VIII and appeared to be at the mercy of the rival Catholic powers, France and Spain. For the Catholics the true heir to the English Crown was Elizabeth's cousin MARY QUEEN OF SCOTS (q.v.), married to the Dauphin of France. It was generally supposed that Elizabeth, in order to keep her throne, would have to profess Catholicism and accept the protection of Spain. Elizabeth, perhaps with the advice of her wise minister, William CECIL (q.v.), found a bold way out of the difficulty. Assuming that Spain, rather than have a half-French Queen upon the English throne, would support her, she adopted a middle course, not unlike that followed by her father. In religion, in foreign policy, and in domestic policy, she acted with courage as well as with caution.

Her Act of Supremacy asserted her authority over the English Church, but she emphatically proclaimed that she was only 'governor', and claimed no spiritual function. Her Act of Uniformity the same year enforced the use of the English Prayer Book in all public services, but she altered the wording of the Communion Service in such a way that Catholics might accept it, and made at first no effort to interfere with the private exercise of religion. She gave no encouragement to the extreme Protestants (or Puritans) who wished to abolish ceremonies and vestments and to substitute Communion tables for altars. When in 1570 the Pope issued a Bull excommunicating and deposing her, she was compelled for a time to deal more hardly with the Catholics and to rely more upon the Puritans; but as soon as possible she returned to her middle way.

Her foreign policy showed the same mixture of boldness and caution. She defended the Protestant cause but declined to go to war. Confident that France could not and that Spain would not effectively intervene, she supported the Protestant revolution in Scotland, so that when Mary Queen of Scots returned as a widow to Scotland in 1561 she found her hands tied.

When Mary tried to assert her claim to be Elizabeth's successor, Elizabeth professed friendship but evaded the issue until in 1568 Mary, being forced to abdicate in Scotland, had to seek refuge in England. Elizabeth, saying she could not decide a quarrel between the Scottish Queen and her subjects, kept her in 'honourable detention' in England for nearly 19 years. Meanwhile she established English influence in Scotland and made an alliance with Mary's son, the young King James VI, who was brought up a Protestant and hoped to inherit the English Crown.

Elizabeth followed the same kind of policy in Europe. France for the greater part of her reign was weakened by the 'Wars of Religion'. Elizabeth, except for an unsuccessful expedition to Le Havre (1562–3), gave no official support to the Huguenots, the French Protestants: indeed, she signed a treaty of alliance with France against Spain in 1572. She knew that Spain was the greater danger, but even against Spain she hoped to avoid actual war. She would not side openly with the Netherlanders in their struggle for independence from Spain, but she lost no opportunity of weakening Spain by giving help to the Netherlanders. Her sailors intercepted in the Channel the money sent to pay Spanish troops; English volunteers went to fight in the Netherlands; English sea-captains plundered Spanish colonies in the West Indies and took a rich booty from the Pacific, hitherto completely in the hands of Spain. Yet an open breach was still avoided. Philip II, the champion of Catholicism, refrained from attacking England only because he wanted to settle the Netherlands first and because he did not wish to set Mary of Scotland with her French sympathies on the English throne.

Then two events happened which hastened the inevitable clash. The heroic Dutch leader, WILLIAM THE SILENT of Orange (q.v.), was murdered in 1584 as the result of Spanish plots, and every Englishman feared that they would next plan the assassination of Elizabeth. Elizabeth, consequently, allowed Lord Leicester to take a force to Holland. Secondly, after the discovery of a plot led by Anthony Babington to murder Elizabeth and to put Mary Queen of Scots on the throne, Mary was condemned and executed in 1587.

Philip immediately began to prepare for the conquest of England, and in July 1588 the

SPANISH ARMADA (q.v. Vol. X) was launched. The Queen, who for long had refused to believe in the danger, behaved with great courage when the crisis came. She rode to the camp at Tilbury and gave a spirited address to her troops, telling them, 'I know I have the body of a weak and feeble woman, but I have the heart and stomach of a king, and of a king of England too'. The troops were not needed. The Spanish fleet was soundly beaten by the English Navy and finally destroyed by storms. Philip prepared new armadas; but the crisis was passed. The Protestants of the Netherlands took fresh courage, and Elizabeth now actively supported HENRY OF NAVARRE (q.v.), who in 1589 became Henry IV of France. Later, she crushed a rebellion in Ireland, and forced a Spanish garrison there to capitulate

In her domestic policy Elizabeth showed herself her father's daughter, though she was less skilful than Henry in managing parliaments. She rebuked the Commons for discussing high questions of policy, especially her marriage and religion. When the crisis of her reign was past, she bluntly told them that their privilege of freedom of speech was to say 'Aye' or 'No'; and on one occasion she imprisoned five members who defied her. On the other hand she knew when she must give way to them, and in 1601, at the last Parliament which she attended, she made a noble speech to them which the members received on their knees 'This I count the glory of my Crown', she said, 'that I have reigned with your loves.'

Her reign was notable for the passing of social legislation, from the Statute of Apprentices in 1563, which aimed at regulating conditions of labour in industry, to the famous POOR LAW of 1601 (q.v. Vol. X). England grew wealthier as the result of the development of trade and the establishment of CHARTERED COMPANIES (q.v. Vol VII). Industry developed, and towns, especially London, grew in wealth and importance

While she thus governed strongly, Elizabeth liked to be regarded as an attractive woman. She was fond of clothes and jewellery, and had an immense wardrobe. She liked good-looking young men, and expected her courtiers to admire her in exaggerated terms and foreign princes to make proposals for her hand. Perhaps she never intended to marry. Early in her reign she used the uncertainty about her marriage to keep both France and Spain anxious. At one time it was thought that she would marry the Earl of Leicester, and as late as 1582 she carried on a flirtation with the Duke of Anjou, the younger brother of the King of France. She had great favourites, but she never allowed her personal favour to save them from the effects of their own shortcomings. The Earl of Essex, for example, a great favourite, was disgraced when he disobeyed her orders, and executed when he made a hot-headed rising. She depended most on her faithful friend, the wise and upright Lord Burghley (see CECIL FAMILY), and she never recovered from his death in 1598. It was his son who got into touch with James of Scotland to ensure the smooth succession of the Scottish King to the English throne on the death of the Queen. She herself had always refused to name her successor.

Elizabeth's popularity had declined with her declining years, but her reputation remained untarnished. She had not shrunk from double-dealing and meanness in her diplomacy; her treatment of Mary was unjust; she was intolerant of Puritans and impatient of parliaments; she was vain and often petty; but she had a high courage, a fine intellect, and a real devotion to her country. She brought England through a difficult crisis, established her national Church, and set her fairly upon the road to empire. Her captains did great things, her court was splendid, and in her 'spacious times' English literature rose to its supreme heights. She was well named Gloriana.

EMERSON, Ralph Waldo (1803–82). This American philosopher, essayist, and poet was descended from a long line of Protestant clergymen, and himself became a clergyman at the age of 26. His unorthodox religious views, however, caused his resignation 3 years later, and he left for Europe. In England he made friends, among other writers, with CARLYLE (q.v.), with whom he carried on a correspondence for some 38 years. When he returned to America he devoted his life to lecturing to popular audiences all over the country and to writing philosophical essays and verse. As a lecturer his serene, kindly manner and obvious sincerity made him widely popular.

As a philosopher he believed that conscience was the supreme judge in all spiritual matters, and maintained that intuition was a form of

Duke of Portland

ELIZABETH I
Painting by Marcus Gheeraedts

divine guidance and should be followed. He was opposed, therefore, to all dogmas, creeds, bibles, and Churches. These conclusions were the subject of many of his essays and addresses, and often the cause of violent controversy. He believed that poetry was a form of divine revelation. His own poetry, which he wrote throughout his life, is now little read.

Emerson died at the age of 79 at his home in Concord, Massachusetts, where he had lived for nearly 50 years. At the end of his life he helped and encouraged many young American writers, including Walt WHITMAN (q.v.).

See also Vol. XII: AMERICAN LITERATURE.

EPICURUS (c. 342–270 B.C.). About 306 B.C.

Epicurus set up in Athens a school of philosophy in which he taught a doctrine which he had developed from the teaching of Democritus, a philosopher who had lived some 100 years earlier. Epicurus is recorded as having written a great many books, but practically nothing survives, and his philosophy is best known to us through the Roman poet Lucretius (a contemporary of Julius Caesar) whose long poem *De Rerum Natura* (*Concerning the Nature of Things*) describes the Epicurean philosophy.

Epicurus was a materialist who held that everything—the world and man also, both body and soul—was formed of a combination of atoms, and could be understood only through the senses. Since our senses were our only guide to truth, the wise man would seek sensations of pleasure and avoid those of pain, especially of fear. The highest pleasures were those of tranquillity—not of excitement. Epicurus never advocated luxurious and sensual living, as he later gained a reputation for doing, for indulgence did not in the long run, according to him, bring pleasure, as a simple and abstemious life did. Epicurus did not deny the existence of gods, but thought that they dwelt in a state apart from men, since man's soul perished with his body. It seemed to him, therefore, that religion, which taught survival after death, brought nothing but unhappiness, because it made men suffer from the unnecessary fear of Hades (or Hell).

Epicurus established a community in Athens, where he had a house and garden in which he taught. Various friends with their families joined him, and they lived extremely simply— chiefly on bread and water, with cheese on feast days. Epicurus himself suffered much pain during his life, which he endured courageously. In private he was gentle and lovable; in public controversy a great fighter.

See also Vol. I: PHILOSOPHY.

ERASMUS, Desiderius (c. 1466–1536). Gerrit

Gerritszoon, who himself devised the name Desiderius Erasmus, was a great religious scholar. He was born at Rotterdam in Holland, the illegitimate son of a physician's daughter and a young priest, who were not married, since priests were forbidden to marry. Both parents died early, and Erasmus, on his guardian's advice, entered a monastery, in order to secure a livelihood and conditions in which he could develop his intellectual gifts. He was not suited for monastic life, and he passed 6 rather unhappy years before he was ordained priest and permitted to become secretary to the Bishop of Cambrai. He left the monastery, never to return. Some years later, in 1517, Pope Leo X freed him from his monastic vows, and also from the legal handicaps attaching to him because of his illegitimate birth. He was thenceforth a free man. Later he wrote the story of his parents, which Charles Reade made the subject of his novel, *The Cloister and the Hearth*.

When he was nearly 30 Erasmus went to Paris to study theology. But the scholastic theology, as then taught, involved much disputation about points which Erasmus felt to be either of no importance, or about matters which seemed to him beyond the reach of human reason. He was at this time more interested in the classics than in theology. Manuscripts of the ancient Greek writers had been brought to Italy in large numbers during the 15th century, and their study led to the RENAISSANCE (q.v. Vol. I), or Revival of Learning. Erasmus was a humanist, who felt that the great classical writers, especially the Greeks, could open men's minds and teach them how to live wisely and graciously. The recent invention of PRINTING (q.v. Vol. IV) was making it possible to issue books with a rapidity hitherto unimagined, and Erasmus, taking full advantage of this, was soon recognized as a competent classical scholar and, in addition, a witty essayist.

Erasmus did not stay long in Paris. Indeed, all his life he was a wanderer, with no settled home. He stayed in various European centres and made several visits to England, where he

Archives Photographiques
ERASMUS IN 1523
Portrait by Hans Holbein. Louvre

found happiness at Oxford in the society of Sir Thomas MORE (q.v.), Colet, later Dean of St. Paul's, and others. At one time he taught at Cambridge for a period of 3 years. Association with More and Colet fixed his attention more closely on religion. Colet, lecturing at Oxford, presented St. Paul's Epistles in a fresh way, interpreting the Greek text naturally and applying it to everyday life, while avoiding the fanciful meanings and far-fetched doctrines extracted by teachers of the established theological schools. This led Erasmus to the preparation of a New Testament in the original Greek to take the place of the Vulgate, a Latin New Testament itself translated from the Greek over a thousand years earlier. This new Greek Testament was issued in 1516. The teaching of Christ seemed to Erasmus a simple thing, capable of appealing to men and women everywhere. He wanted people to be able to read the Scriptures themselves instead of being dependent for their knowledge upon religious teachers. 'I wish', he wrote, 'that they might be translated into all tongues, so that not only the Scots and the Irish, but also the Turk and the Saracen might read and understand. I wish the countryman might sing them at his plough, the weaver chant them at his loom, the traveller beguile with them the weariness of his journey.'

When Erasmus visited Rome he was appalled at the luxury and corruption he saw, even among the chief rulers of the Church. The Pope rode as a warrior might into conquered cities; how different from Peter and Paul! In consequence he wrote his *In Praise of Folly*, a satire in which Folly, in the guise of a young woman, unsparingly attacks popes and cardinals, as well as monks, not only for their moral offences but also for some parts of their teaching.

In 1517 LUTHER (q.v.) began his reforming movement in Germany, a movement which Erasmus's writing had done much to provoke. But though he agreed with Luther on many points, Erasmus would not support him. He disliked Luther's violent manner, and the even greater violence of his followers. The calmly reasoning mind of Erasmus could not accept Luther's extreme teaching on faith and free will. He was much criticized for this, but, he said, he would not leave the Church until he had found a better.

During Erasmus's time, the idea of nationality was developing fast (*see* NATION AND STATE, Vol. X), raising fresh problems of government, and of the relations between one nation and another. Erasmus discussed these problems in works such as the *Education of a Christian Prince* and the *Complaint of Peace*. He was keenly conscious of the folly and brutality of war.

Erasmus wrote a vast amount. Besides many editions of the classical authors and Christian Fathers, he made a collection of wise sayings from the classics, with comments on them, called the *Adagia*. He also wrote the *Colloquies*, a series of witty, satirical essays, generally in dialogue form, on problems of the day, which were long used as a school book. In both he shows his love for freedom, justice, and truth. When he died at Basle most of the ideals for which he fought seemed to have temporarily come to grief; but his influence is not yet dead.

See also Vol. I: RENAISSANCE.

ERICSSON, Leif (11th century). This Viking explorer was probably the first European to reach America. He was the son of Eric the Red, a Scandinavian leader, who emigrated from Norway to a new colony in Iceland (where Leif was born), and from there went on to discover Greenland in 982. Leif 'the Lucky' was converted to Christianity on a visit to Norway and then, in 1002, after his return to Greenland, 'put to sea and was driven about for a long time and lighted on new lands where wild wheatfields and vines were growing'.

According to Icelandic tradition, he discovered three lands: Helluland, the land of flat stones, which some think was Labrador or Newfoundland; Markland, possibly Nova Scotia; and Vineland the Good, which may have been New England. He was followed by his brother, who was killed by Eskimos, and in 1024 by Karlsefni, who is said to have stayed 3 years there. No later voyages were made, and the 15th- and 16th-century explorers probably knew nothing about the discoveries of these hardy Vikings in their longships. The half-legendary deeds of Leif Ericsson lay forgotten in the Icelandic sagas until modern times.

See also Vol. I: Norwegians.
See also Vol. IV: Viking Ships.

EUCLID (4th century B.C.) Euclid was a Greek mathematician who lived about 300 B.C. at Alexandria, then one of the great centres of learning in the world. His *Elements* is the most important book in the whole of mathematics. It proves many elementary truths about triangles, rectangles, circles, proportions, numbers, and solid figures on which future mathematicians have based their work. He completed each proof with the letters 'Q.E.D.' (*quod erat demonstrandum*—'which was to be shown').

The *Elements* is also of vital importance in the study of Logic (q.v. Vol. I) because it shows how a number of truths can be proved by logical deduction from a very few 'postulates'—things assumed to be true and used as a basis of reasoning. Euclid, in fact, deduced all his geometrical conclusions from these 5 simple postulates:

1. A straight line can be drawn from any point to any point.
2. A finite straight line can be produced continuously in a straight line.
3. A circle can be drawn with any centre and distance.
4. All right angles are equal.
5. If a straight line cutting two straight lines makes the interior angles on one side less than two right angles, the two straight lines, if produced indefinitely, meet on that side.

Euclid's books reached western Europe, as did much Greek learning, through translations from Arabic into Latin, and then into English. For over 2,000 years the *Elements* was the standard work on Geometry (q.v. Vol. VIII), and until recently was believed to be perfectly accurate when applied also in astronomy. It is now known, however, that the 'space' envisaged by Euclid is not so close to reality as are the 'spaces' of Einstein (q.v.) and other modern scientists.

EUGENE, Prince (1663–1736), *see* Marlborough.

EURIPIDES (*c.* 480–406 B.C.). Plenty of gossip is known about this great Athenian playwright, but not many reliable facts. He was constantly being attacked by Aristophanes (q.v.), who represents him in his comedies as a morose highbrow with a miserable family life and a disrespectful attitude towards religion, a picture which is, as it was meant to be, absurdly exaggerated.

Euripides seems to have spent much of his life on the island of Salamis, near Athens, taking little part in politics, though he must have served in the army and have attended debates in the assembly. He first produced plays at the Athenian dramatic festival in 455 B.C., 13 years after the first appearance of Sophocles (q.v.). He composed ninety-two plays, nineteen of which still survive. He won the first prize only five times, but he certainly had an enthusiastic following and, after his death, his work grew even more popular both in Athens and elsewhere. He composed one of the last and greatest of his plays, the *Bacchae*, at the court of the King of Macedonia.

To his contemporaries and to many people since, Euripides seemed to be, first and foremost, the representative of the new scientific thought which criticized accepted beliefs in morals, politics, and religion. There is much truth in this view, and Euripides, like Socrates (q.v.), a great admirer of his plays, represented this new thought at its best. Euripides lacked piety in the sense that he puts on the stage gods and goddesses who behave thoroughly badly (the goddess Aphrodite, for instance, in his *Hippolytus*); he mocked at oracles and soothsayers, and seemed, so far as it was possible to do, to reject orthodox religion and to be searching for some different way of expressing the idea of god. He has been called 'Euripides the rationalist', but there is much more in his poetry than such a phrase suggests. ARISTOTLE (q.v.) called him 'the most tragic of poets', by which he may have meant that his plays are particularly remarkable for the pity shown for all kinds of human suffering and for the poignancy with which this suffering is presented. Far more than Sophocles, Euripides is aware of the horrors of war and of its effects. He is also far more concerned with the emotional problems of individuals; and in creating such characters as Medea or Phaedra (in the *Hippolytus*), women in the grip of violent passions, he offended the conservative opinion of his day, but laid the foundations for the more realistic literature of the future.

There is great variety in his work. Some of his plays (the *Helen*, for example) are more like romantic comedies than tragedies. His choruses take less part in the action than do the choruses of the other dramatists—indeed, sometimes they serve simply as a kind of musical interlude of supreme beauty between the acts.

Less profound than Aeschylus, less technically perfect than Sophocles, Euripides is, in the modern sense, the most 'human' of the three, and his plays (of which there are various translations) are the most often adapted to the modern stage.

See also AESCHYLUS; SOPHOCLES; ARISTOPHANES.
See also Vol. XII: GREEK DRAMA; TRAGEDY.

EVELYN, John (1620–1706), *see* Vol. XII: DIARIES.

EYCK, Jan van (*c.* 1390–1441). The name of this Flemish painter is often linked with that of his supposed elder brother, Hubert, as the first of the great school of Flemish painters. Of Hubert little is known other than that he was working in Ghent in 1425 and that he died the following year. No paintings can be ascribed to him with certainty, though the Latin inscription on the celebrated altar-piece now reassembled in the church of St. Bavon in Ghent, called 'The Adoration of the Lamb', states that the altar-piece was begun by him and finished by his brother. It may, however, have been carried out entirely by Jan at two different periods of his career.

About Jan van Eyck, a much less shadowy

Mansell

THE ADORATION OF THE LAMB, PAINTING BY JAN VAN EYCK
Lower part of the central panel of the altar-piece in the church of St. Bavon, Ghent. It may have been begun by Hubert van Eyck, but was completed by Jan in 1432

National Gallery

JAN ARNOLFINI AND HIS WIFE
Painting by Jan van Eyck, 1434

figure than Hubert, quite a number of facts are known. Several paintings exist bearing his signature, and there is a portrait of his wife Marguerite. At first he worked for John of Bavaria, Count of Holland, and later in life as painter and personal attendant to Philip the Good, Duke of Burgundy, who valued him both as an excellent painter and a discreet and trustworthy ambassador. His last years were spent in Bruges, where he is known to have bought a house in 1431.

His works include religious pictures, portraits, and some drawings. Of the religious pictures the largest is the famous Ghent altar-piece, which consists of about twenty panels, twelve of which are displayed when the altar-piece is open, the remainder being on the exterior of the folding wings. Above the central panel showing the Adoration of the Lamb, God the Father sits enthroned between the Virgin Mary and St. John the Baptist, flanked on either side by choirs of music-making angels and the figures of Adam and Eve. In the lower panels are landscapes of dreamlike beauty. Jan van Eyck's portraits are carefully accurate in detail, recording good and bad features with the same painstaking attention.

If not the inventor of oil painting, Jan van Eyck was the first to exploit all the possibilities of the medium (*see* PAINTING, Vol. XII). Deriving from a flourishing school of manuscript illumination, he combined a loving use of intimate detail and perfect finish with space and light and brilliant colour to create an astonishing illusion of reality.

See also Vol. XII: FLEMISH PAINTING.

F

FABRE, Jean Henri (1823–1915). This celebrated French entomologist and writer was called by his own countrymen 'the insects' Homer', and was acknowledged by DARWIN (q.v.) to be 'an incomparable observer'.

The son of a poor peasant in southern France, Fabre, with the help of scholarships, trained as a teacher and finally took a post in a secondary school in Avignon. But his lifelong interest was in natural history and this came to be concentrated on insects. When he was 46 he lost his teaching post because he dared to teach girls about the reproduction of plants and animals. He retired to a little country house and there wrote his books about insects. His ten books, all of which have been translated into English under various titles, were based on long and patient observation of insect behaviour. His accounts are interspersed with many intimate autobiographical details which make them delightful reading.

See also Vol. II: INSECTS; BIRDS.

FARADAY, Michael (1791–1867). Faraday was the discoverer of electrical induction, and therefore of man's power to generate electricity. He came of a simple Yorkshire family, his father being a blacksmith, and his brother Robert working as a gas fitter. The family had moved to Newington, then a Surrey village, and there Michael was born.

When he was 5 years old the Faradays moved to rooms over a coach-house near Manchester Square in London; here at the age of 10 Michael became errand-boy at a bookseller's shop in Blandford Street, close to his home. After a year of running errands, delivering newspapers, shop-sweeping, and window-cleaning, he was apprenticed as a bookbinder in the same shop. His mind was awakening, and he began to read many of the scientific books which passed through his hands for binding. Electricity and chemistry fascinated him; he copied into notebooks extracts from many sources. He built an electrical machine and an elementary battery or 'pile', and made as many experiments in chemistry as he could afford on his weekly pocket-money.

When Faraday was 21, a customer of the bookshop who was a member of the Royal Institution took him to a course of four lectures on chemistry delivered there by the great scientist, Sir Humphry DAVY (q.v.). From one who saw him we have a record of Faraday 'perched, pen in hand, his eyes starting out of his head'—so eager was he not to miss a word. Having taken full notes of these lectures, he copied them out in beautiful style, bound the sheets as a book, and sent the volume to Sir Humphry with a letter asking for help in finding more congenial work.

Davy agreed to meet Faraday, but at the first interview advised him to stick to his trade. Later on, however, when the Institution's laboratory assistant was dismissed for carelessness and rudeness, Davy remembered Faraday, wrote to him, and offered him the position. His salary was 25s. a week; he lived in two rooms at the top of the Royal Institution building in Albemarle Street, Piccadilly. Thus in 1813 began an association with that Institution which was to last for the rest of his life.

Almost at once Davy took Faraday on a continental tour as his secretary and, at first, as his manservant. Davy was then reaching the height of his fame, and he and Faraday met many of the most distinguished European scientists during the 18 months' tour.

The next few years of hard work at the Institution showed Faraday to be a good scientist. At the age of 31 he had the honour of reading his first paper, on a chemical theme, before the Royal Society; at 33 he was elected a Fellow of that Society. He now began to concentrate on the study of electrical phenomena. He was appointed Director of the Laboratory of the Royal Institution, and one of his first acts was to start evening meetings for discussion among its members. These became very popular, and formed the origin of the Institution's well-known Friday evening discourses. He also began the series of Christmas lectures to young people which are still an annual event.

Faraday had found his place in the world, but as yet he could hardly be called famous. It was in 1831, while carrying on his studies of electromagnetism, that he discovered that a momentary current of electricity flowed in a wire whenever a magnet approached or receded from it—a discovery which has formed the basis of the great electrical industry of today. Several eminent investigators must have been on the very edge of the same discovery. They knew that electricity could produce magnetism; it was reserved for Faraday to settle the question: 'If electricity can produce magnetism, cannot magnetism produce electricity?'

His success was the more striking because he knew little of mathematics. 'It is in the highest degree astonishing', wrote one scientist, 'to see what a large number of general theorems, the methodical deduction of which requires the finest powers of mathematical analysis, he found by a kind of intuition, with the security of instinct, without the help of a single mathematical formula.'

The far-reaching consequences of these fruitful years are described in the article ELECTRICAL ENGINEERING, HISTORY OF (q.v. Vol. VIII). They meant, to Faraday himself, immediate

recognition as one of the great pioneers. He received many honours. Oxford University conferred on him the degree of Doctor of Civil Law; the Royal Society awarded him its Copley Medal; he was appointed first Fullerian Professor of Chemistry at the Royal Institution; as the years passed and his fame spread, he was elected a Fellow of many learned societies abroad; yet he remained simple-hearted, modest, and perfectly indifferent to financial reward.

His investigations continued, and were by no means confined to electrical matters. He broke new ground in the domain of chemistry, and did original work on the structure of various steels. For 30 years he held the position of adviser to TRINITY HOUSE (q.v. Vol. IV), examining the processes of lighting in lighthouses and reporting upon different types of lamp. With the year 1845 a final period of brilliant research began; it occupied 10 years, and part of it was concerned with the relationship between MAGNETISM and LIGHT (qq.v. Vol. III).

In old age Faraday still undertook lighthouse inspection, and some of his journeys at the age of 70, in days when travel was mostly uncomfortable and slow, tried his reserves of strength severely—for example, a trip to Dungeness in winter, when he slept at the lighthouse, and went to sea at night in order to compare the visibility of oil lamps with that of electric light at a distance of several miles.

At intervals his health and his memory troubled him, and very unwillingly the Royal Institution accepted Faraday's resignation in 1865. Two years before, he had written to a friend: 'My words totter, my memory totters, and now my legs have taken to tottering'; yet so extraordinary was his energy that in 1864 he made twelve reports to Trinity House, some of them on complicated matters.

Faraday was happily married but had no children. He loved children

Royal Institution

FARADAY IN HIS LABORATORY
Water-colour by Harriet Moore, 1852

and used to hold jolly parties for his nephews and nieces in his rooms at the Royal Institution, when he would take the children to the lecture theatre, and delight them with experiments. He died in his study chair at Hampton Court, where, through the thoughtfulness of Albert, the Prince Consort, a house had been provided for him.

See also DAVY.
See also Vol. VIII: INDUCTION, ELECTRIC.

FAWKES, Guy (1570–1606). Fawkes was a Yorkshireman, converted to Catholicism before he was 21. He fought with the Spanish army against the Protestants in Flanders, and was then persuaded by some discontented English Catholics to join in a plot to blow up the Houses of Parliament when King James I was present. A room adjoining the House of Lords was rented, and Fawkes, acting as caretaker, kept watch there while the others dug down under Parliament House, intending to undermine it. They abandoned this scheme, however, and hired a cellar directly beneath the House of Lords. It was Fawkes's part to conceal thirty-six barrels of gunpowder in the cellar and to make preparations for exploding them.

One of the conspirators betrayed the plot by warning a peer not to attend Parliament. The Government ordered the cellars to be searched on November 4, the day before Parliament was to meet, and Fawkes was arrested. He showed great courage, disclosing the names of his fellow conspirators only when he was exhausted from torture. He and some of the conspirators who had not already been killed trying to escape were executed in January 1606.

FERDINAND (1452–1516) **and ISABELLA** (1451–1504). In 1479 Spain became united for the first time under Ferdinand of Aragon who had married Isabella of Castile. Ferdinand and Isabella inherited a disorganized and lawless country, which included the independent Moorish kingdom of Granada (*see* MOORS, Vol. I). They proceeded to centralize the government under the Crown, thus reducing the dangerous independence of the nobility, and they formed a militia-police to enforce the laws. Then, in order to unite all Spain under Catholic rule, they attacked and vanquished the Moorish kingdom. At first the Moors were allowed to practise their own religion, but the intolerant missionary zeal of Isabella and her adviser,

Cardinal Ximenes, soon forced them to choose between conversion and exile. The notorious monk Torquemada, Isabella's confessor, established the INQUISITION (q.v. Vol. I) in Spain to enforce Catholicism on both Moors and Jews, and as a result Spain lost many of her most cultured and industrious citizens.

In 1492, following the conquest of Granada, Ferdinand and Isabella supported the expedition of COLUMBUS (q.v.) to the Indies, the first step towards the founding of Spain's great American Empire. The wealth of the New World together with Ferdinand's astute diplomacy made Spain one of the great powers in Europe. He made marriage alliances with England, Germany, and Portugal; he won territories, including Naples and Milan, from France, his chief rival; and he strengthened his position in the Mediterranean by seizing various places along the North African coast.

Isabella, apart from her religious intolerance, was gentle and beautiful and won the devotion of her subjects. But Ferdinand was the cleverer ruler. He was a Prince after MACHIAVELLI's own heart (q.v.), willing to use any methods to secure his ends. They were succeeded by their grandson CHARLES V (q.v.).

See also Vol. I: SPANIARDS; MOORS.

FIELDING, Henry (1707–54). Fielding, author of *Tom Jones*, one of the first great English novels, was born of a distinguished and aristocratic family. His mother died when he was 14, and his father and his grandmother quarrelled over the administration of her money and the care and education of the children. Fielding spent 3 years at Eton, and then went to Holland to study at Leyden University. Back in London he took to writing. Before he was 21 he wrote a comedy which was produced at Drury Lane, and he was still under 30 when his twenty-third work was produced at the Haymarket Theatre. Although most of his plays are comedies, his dramatic importance depends on his burlesques (in which he mocks with great wit and gaiety the artificial literary fashions of the period) and on his political satires. In such works as *The Author's Farce* and *The Historical Register for the Year 1736* he makes blistering attacks on the Government, with unflattering portraits of WALPOLE (q.v.), the Prime Minister. Walpole answered these attacks by passing the Licensing Act of 1737, which prohibited the performance

ILLUSTRATION TO FIELDING'S 'JOSEPH ANDREWS'

The young Joseph, a footboy in Sir Thomas Booby's house, is catechized in the kitchen by the curate, Mr. Abraham Adams. Etching by T. Rowlandson

of any play without the Lord Chamberlain's licence, and confined the London drama to Covent Garden and Drury Lane. Fielding, who had his own theatrical company at the Haymarket Theatre, was put out of business.

His career as playwright and manager being over, Fielding began to study law—a career he had often considered before. But his urge to write soon led him to start a thrice-weekly periodical, *The Champion*. Then he published anonymously *An Apology for the Life of Mrs. Shamela Andrews*, a brilliant skit on Richardson's novel *Pamela*, which was soon followed by *Joseph Andrews*, the story of the alleged brother of Pamela. In this novel what was begun as a burlesque turns into a work of creative genius, for in laughing at the Richardson kind of novel —conventional, romantic, and sentimental— Fielding, with his great skill in drawing character, substituted for romance an ironic comedy in which the modern novel has its foundation.

Fielding became a barrister in 1740, and 8 years later, through the influence of a friend, was appointed principal magistrate for Westminster. At that time, when Londoners were being terrorized by highwaymen and murderers, Fielding brought wisdom, integrity, courage, and tireless devotion to work which had often been corruptly and incompetently discharged. His firmness suppressed the London riots of 1749, and his pamphlet containing advice on crime and drunkenness became the basis for several reforming Acts of Parliament. In 1753 he organized a kind of detective force which successfully reduced the numbers of murders and street robberies in London (*see* POLICE, HISTORY OF, Vol. X). Fielding performed a work of incalculable value to the development of English justice; but he made next to nothing out of it for himself, for he would not follow the practice of the times and take fees from the poor, and he often assisted people instead of sentencing them. Later his work was carried on by his half-brother, Sir John Fielding, the famous blind magistrate of Bow Street.

Fielding's greatest book, *The History of Tom Jones, a Foundling*, appeared in 1749, and soon after came the less successful *Amelia*, modelled on the virtues of his much-loved first wife, who had died. By 1752 Fielding was already very ill, and in 1754 he set sail, with his second wife and his daughter, for Portugal, a journey delightfully described in *A Voyage to Lisbon*. But in Lisbon he died, not yet 48.

See also Vol. XII: NOVEL.

FITZGERALD, Edward (1809–83), translator of Omar Khayyám, *see* KHAYYÁM.

FLAUBERT, Gustave (1821–80). This French novelist, the son of a surgeon, was born in Rouen. As a young man he travelled extensively in Europe and the Near East, and then settled in Croisset near Rouen, working unremittingly at his novels.

Flaubert was a deeply original novelist. He wrote realistically as BALZAC (q.v.) had done, but he thought that the way he wrote was more important than what he wrote about. In choosing the most exact words, he demanded also that their sounds should fit their meaning, and that the rhythm of each phrase should convey the mood of the passage. His books are of two kinds: he wrote stories of contemporary bourgeois society for which he had the deepest contempt, such as *Madame Bovary* and *The Sentimental Education*; and he wrote historical novels such as *Salammbô*, in which his hatred for modern mediocrity is implicit in his romantic admiration for the past. Both his 'bourgeois' and historical novels show the same scrupulous attention to accurate detail, acquired by the closest scrutiny of French provincial life or by intensive reading of history. They are remarkable for their vivid characterization, firmly constructed narratives, and brilliant suggestion of atmosphere, as well as for their remarkable style.

See also Vol. XII: NOVEL.

FOX, Charles James (1749–1806). This famous Whig politician was for 20 years the opponent of the younger PITT (q.v.). The son of a wealthy and unscrupulous politician, the first Lord Holland, Fox became a member of Parliament at the age of 19.

During the AMERICAN WAR OF INDEPENDENCE (q.v. Vol. X) he gave wholehearted support to the rebellious colonists, and his eloquence and influence did much to bring to an end the government of Lord North, GEORGE III's favourite Minister (q.v.). Soon afterwards, in 1783, Fox accepted the office of Secretary of State, in alliance with North, a change of face which brought him discredit; and his attacks on royal influence earned him the dislike of the King. When this Ministry collapsed, Fox spent the 20 years of Pitt's supremacy in fruitless opposition. Fox gave life-long support to unpopular causes: he supported the FRENCH REVOLUTION (q.v. Vol. X); he denounced injustice in Ireland and corruption in India (*see* HASTINGS); he championed the movement against the slave trade and the agitation for Catholic emancipation; he called for parliamentary reform. In 1806, on the death of Pitt, Fox at last returned to office (under Grenville), but only lived long enough to pass his motion for the abolition of the slave trade.

Fox had a passion for gambling and enjoyed the dissolute society gathered round the Prince of Wales, later GEORGE IV (q.v.). But after a night of dissipation Fox would appear in the House and speak with classical eloquence and reckless fervour. He threw away a fortune at cards and lost half his support in Parliament, but never lost a warmth of heart and power of mind which bound many friends to him. After his death his memory helped to shape the Whig party's attitude to the great reform movement of the 19th century.

See also PITT; BURKE.
See also Vol. X: POLITICAL PARTIES.

FOX, George (1624–91). The founder of the Society of Friends, or QUAKERS (q.v. Vol. I), was the son of a Leicestershire weaver. He left home at 19 to become a wandering preacher, and travelled all over England and Wales, as well as in Europe and America, teaching a simple faith based on the Bible and spiritual revelation. He believed in salvation for all who seek it, strongly opposing the prevalent CALVINIST belief in predestination (q.v. Vol. I). His objection to formalized religion led him to interrupt church services: he despised churches —'steeple-houses' as he called them—declaring that the Church was composed of its living members, not of wood and stone. His preaching and his numerous pamphlets made him enemies among both Churchmen and Puritans, and he was frequently arrested and imprisoned; but he continued to make thousands of converts. His

Meade Collection

CARICATURE OF CHARLES JAMES FOX, 1782

Fox is out of favour, accused of trying to wreck the government in order to gain power. He is locked out of the Treasury and notices of his debts are pinned to the wall

genius for organization succeeded in turning this great following of excited enthusiasts into an orderly society renowned for its piety and good works. In this he was much assisted by a Lancashire woman, Margaret Fell, whom eventually he married. In the course of his work he travelled to the West Indies, America, Holland, and Germany.

The best story of his life is in his *Journal*. Fox was a tall, heavily built man, with long, straight hair, who lived simply, treating all men as equals. Although he was often indiscreet, his honesty, courage, and kindliness won him the devotion of his followers.

See also PENN.
See also Vol. I: QUAKERS.

FRANCIS OF ASSISI, St. (1182–1226).

Francis Bernardone was born at Assisi in central Italy, the son of a prosperous cloth merchant. He learned to read, and knew French and some Latin; but he was not highly educated, and indeed always wrote with difficulty. His early life was wild and pleasure-loving. He had plenty of money and many gay companions. He intended to be a soldier, and when, as was frequently happening, Assisi was attacked by the neighbouring city of Perugia, Francis took part in the fighting and was taken prisoner. He remained a prisoner for a year until, when he was 22, the cities made peace.

On returning home Francis became very ill; and during his illness he thought seriously about the way he was spending his life. When he recovered, his irrepressible spirit of adventure led him to dream that he might win glory by joining a military expedition; but he was ill again and had to abandon his intention. During this second illness he began to think he might seek adventure in quite a different way—by serving his fellow men. He began to help the poor: for example, when a leper begged alms of him, he jumped from his horse and gave all the money he had, kissing the leper's hand. He took Christ's words, 'Follow me', as a personal call, and not only gave away his own money but also his father's goods. Finally his exasperated father brought him before the Bishop to disinherit him. Francis willingly agreed to give up everything, even the clothes he was wearing, with the words, 'Hitherto I have called Pietro Bernardone my father; but now I desire to serve God.'

Francis retreated to the half-ruined chapel of St. Damian on the outskirts of Assisi, where he had often gone to pray. He lived on the food people gave him, and spent his time restoring the chapel, gathering stones how and where he could. When this task was finished, he turned to another decaying sanctuary, St. Mary of the Angels, generally called the Portiuncula, and restored it also. This chapel afterwards became the cradle of the Franciscan movement.

One day, as Francis was listening to the words of the Gospel which tell of the orders Christ gave to his disciples when he sent them out to preach, it seemed to him that these orders were being given directly and literally to him. 'Provide neither gold, nor silver, nor brass in your purses, nor scrip for your journey, neither two coats, neither shoes, nor yet staves: for the workman is worthy of his meat' says the Gospel (St. Matt. x. 9–10). The next day Francis began to preach in simple, vivid words that found an immediate response among simple people, for they saw that he had indeed given up all out of love for God and men. Soon companions gathered round him, and formed a band who called themselves *Joculatores Domini*, which might be translated as 'God's merry men'. Francis declared that he was married to 'Lady Poverty', the most beautiful of all brides.

Francis's followers soon grew so many that it seemed advisable to obtain the sanction of the Church for the work they were doing. In 1210, therefore, a group of twelve made their way to Rome to interview Pope Innocent III. The Pope feared that they were adopting a way of life too severe to be the basis of a permanent rule, but he gave a provisional blessing to the brotherhood, stipulating that they should appoint a responsible superior; and Francis was chosen. Francis regretted that his work had to be so much organized, and would have much preferred to remain free. But it was inevitable that his movement should be caught up in the organized machinery of the Church.

In 1212 a nobly born girl of Assisi named Clare was, at her urgent request, allowed to start a sisterhood which should obey the same rule as the brothers, except in regard to preaching and missionary work. Clare and her followers took up their abode at St. Damian, the brothers having made the Portiuncula their headquarters. She kept in close touch with the Franciscan brothers even after their great

Anderson

ST. FRANCIS BLESSING THE BIRDS
Fresco said to be by Giotto in the church of St. Francis at
Assisi

he would not allow his brothers even to possess books; but this, and also the literal application of the rule of poverty, had to be modified. Indeed, in later times, the Franciscans came to own churches and friaries and communal wealth which was far from Francis's original intention. But the mass of his followers remained wandering preachers, travelling far and wide, and delivering their message in plain words that ordinary men could understand.

Francis's own life was short. Yet he managed to visit North Africa, Spain, Syria, and even Egypt. He is said to have obtained an audience of the Sultan of the Saracens against whom the Crusaders were fighting, and to have preached the Christian message to him. His last few years were spent in quiet retreats in Italy and, when only 44, worn out by suffering and sickness, he died.

So intense were his meditations on the sufferings of Christ that, according to the legend, his hands became marked with scars resembling the marks of the nails on Christ's hands. One day, when staying with St. Clare, he became rapt in thought, and in that ecstatic state he composed the *Canticle of the Sun*, a hymn of praise to God for the beauty and joy of created things, for sun and light, moon and stars, for water and fire, for good and merciful men, and finally for 'sister death'. The true spirit of Francis is better reflected in this poem of childlike simplicity than in the subsequent works of his order, useful and great though these are.

The little walled town of Assisi, with its beautiful church of St. Francis, and the magnificent series of frescoes by GIOTTO (q.v.) portraying the incidents of his life, remain as a vivid memorial to him.

See also Vol. I: FRIAR.

leader's death. The lives of these men and women had a freshness and pure simplicity which has rarely if ever been matched in Christian history. Francis had sympathy with the whole of creation. He loved flowers and animals; he preached to the birds, he called the donkey his little brother, and he tamed a savage wolf which came to him with an injured foot. The records speak of many visions and miracles, which are described in the *Fioretti*, or *Little Flowers*, a collection of tales describing the spiritual experiences not only of Francis, but of Brother Juniper and Brother Giles and many others, including also St. Clare.

The Franciscans were first known as the Penitents of Assisi, and later as the Minor or Lesser Brothers. They were also called Grey Friars from the colour of their dress. At the time of their foundation DOMINIC (q.v.) the Spaniard was also gathering his company of preaching friars. Hitherto monks had retired from the world to save their own souls; but Francis and Dominic sent their followers into the world to save others. So eager was Francis to appeal to men solely by the example of a Christian life that

FRANKLIN, Benjamin (1706–90). This American statesman, who also won fame as a journalist and scientist, was the fifteenth child of a poor Boston family. At the age of 12 he was apprenticed to his brother, a printer, and soon became an expert. But at 17 he decided to leave Boston, and arrived practically penniless in Philadelphia. He soon found work as a printer, and after a few months made the acquaintance of the British governor of the colony. The governor promised to lend him enough money to start a printing business of his own, and persuaded him to go to England to collect whatever

Parker Gallery

BENJAMIN FRANKLIN
Mezzotint after a portrait by M. Chamberlin

materials he needed. But when Franklin arrived in London no one would honour his letters-of-credit, and he had to work in a London printing-house for 18 months to make enough money to return home.

Eventually Franklin set up a successful printing-house of his own, and at 23 purchased a newspaper, the *Pennsylvania Gazette*. Under his editorship this became the most influential newspaper in America. He founded the College, later University, of Pennsylvania, and when he was 40 he experimented in the new field of electricity and in other sciences. He was, for example, the first to suggest that buildings might be protected by lightning conductors, and discovered the course and many important characteristics of the Gulf Stream. At 48 he became a member of the Royal Society.

But Franklin's scientific experiments were cut short by an active political career, begun when he was already over 50. For 20 years he had been a member of the Pennsylvania Assembly, and in 1757 he supported the Assembly's claim to be allowed to tax the Penn family in England, the hereditary proprietors of the province under a royal charter issued to the founder William PENN (q.v.). In order to reach an agreement

with the proprietors, the Assembly sent Franklin to England. Negotiations dragged on for 5 years, but eventually Franklin was successful and returned to America. But only 2 years later he was back in London to protest against the unjust taxes which the British Government had imposed on the colonies. He fought the Stamp Act of 1765, and was largely responsible for its repeal a year later. He returned to America in 1775 and was one of the signatories to the Declaration of Independence (*see* AMERICAN WAR OF INDEPENDENCE, Vol. X). Early in 1777 he was sent to France to enlist French help for the colonists.

Franklin was 71 when he arrived in Paris, but his great skill as a negotiator and his popularity won for America a treaty of alliance with France and much money and arms. When the war was over Franklin helped to draw up the peace terms with Britain. Back in America he attended the Convention which in 1787 drew up the present AMERICAN CONSTITUTION (q.v. Vol. X). When Franklin died after 30 years of unbroken public service he was mourned by the new American nation as its first citizen.

FRANKLIN Sir John (1786–1847). The long-sought North-West Passage (the sea route to Asia, north of the American continent), eventually mastered by AMUNDSEN (q.v.) in 1906, was probably first discovered by the English Admiral Franklin. But he and all who were with him perished on that expedition.

Franklin had served as a midshipman at Trafalgar, and later became governor of a colonial settlement at Tasmania. But his real interest lay in the Arctic. Franklin led two remarkable expeditions to chart the coastline of the Canadian North and to explore the Mackenzie Basin. He was away 3½ years on his first expedition, journeying by land and water over 5,000 miles, often under fearful conditions. He reached the Arctic Sea both on his first and second expeditions and charted thousands of miles of coastline.

More than 20 years later, in 1845, when nearly 60, he took H.M.S. *Erebus* and *Terror*, the first steamers in the Arctic, with 134 officers and men, to try to find a passage between Baffin Bay and the Beaufort Sea; but the ships were beset by ice west of King William's Land. It seems probable that some of his men discovered a passage between Victoria Island and the mainland, but Franklin himself died in June 1847 before anything further could be done. As another Arctic winter was approaching, Captain Crozier, now in command, and the hundred survivors abandoned the ships and tried to make their way overland. But the whole party perished before they could reach Hudson Bay.

Ten years later, Sir Leopold McClintock, who sailed at the request of Lady Franklin, found some of the skeletons of the party and pointed out the whereabouts of a North-West Passage. Franklin's expedition was not, therefore, without result; but the loss of life involved was the greatest that has ever occurred in Arctic exploration.

See also Vol. III: POLAR REGIONS (EXPLORATION).
See also Vol. IV: EXPLORATION.

FREDERICK BARBAROSSA (c. 1123–90).

The Emperor Frederick I, 'the red-bearded', possessed the heroic and colourful qualities most admired in his time and was more suited to rule the German people than any ruler since CHARLEMAGNE (q.v.). When he was elected German King in 1152 Germany was in decay as the result of a long-drawn-out struggle between the Hohenstaufen family to which Frederick belonged and the rival Welf (Guelph) family led by Duke Henry the Lion. Frederick, whose mother was a Welf, succeeded in making peace with Henry, and so uniting Germany. This enabled him to put all his strength into achieving his main objective, the freeing of the Empire from the domination of the Pope (see HOLY ROMAN EMPIRE, Vol. I).

Frederick led six campaigns altogether into Italy in his attempt to re-establish the power of the Empire. He was opposed not only by the Pope but also by the rich cities of northern Italy, which had so greatly progressed economically and politically that they meant to govern themselves without the interference of the Emperor. Frederick repeatedly broke their resistance by superior military power, and then in 1158 he assembled a Diet (Parliament) of the Empire in Italy, which decreed that as Emperor he was entitled to govern the Italian towns through an imperial official, instead of by elected representatives. This provoked passionate resistance, which Frederick broke with the utmost harshness, completely destroying Milan, the leading city.

The Emperor, however, was not so successful in his conflict with the Pope, Alexander III. He tried to support a rival to the Papacy, assembling a council of clerics under his domination to depose Alexander. Alexander replied by excommunicating the Emperor as a usurper, and, with the support of the Kings of England and France, who thought the Emperor was assuming too much power, he joined with the Italian cities to form a powerful league. In 1167 Frederick's army in Italy was almost annihilated by a plague, and this gave the Pope's forces time to gather strength. When Frederick returned some years later with a new army, he was routed at the Battle of Legnano in 1176. Realizing that he must come to terms with the Pope and the Italian towns, he acknowledged Alexander as the legitimate Pope and gave up his attempt to establish the Emperor's supremacy over the Papacy.

Frederick then returned to Germany to crush Henry the Lion, his old rival, who had refused to support the Italian expeditions. In so doing he restored the authority of the Emperor in Germany. In 1186 he succeeded in arranging the marriage of his eldest son to Constance, the heiress presumptive of the rich and powerful kingdom of Sicily. Three years later he undertook a crusade, but before reaching the Holy Land he was drowned while crossing a river in Asia (see CRUSADES, Vol. I).

Barbarossa's strong and majestic personality so much impressed the German people that there arose the myth that he never died but only slept in the mountain Kyffhäuser, and would one day arise again to restore the Empire's glory.

See also Vol. I: HOLY ROMAN EMPIRE.

FREDERICK THE GREAT (1712–86).

Frederick II of Prussia built a great kingdom from which BISMARCK (q.v.), some 100 years later, built the united German Empire.

Frederick had a bitter and frustrating youth, which hardened his character and steeled his will. His father, Frederick William I, though an excellent administrator who created a strong army and a full exchequer, was a narrow-minded, brutal man. He despised his son because he cared more for culture, especially French culture, than things military, and forced upon him so rigid a type of military education that Frederick, when he was 18, tried to escape to England. For this he narrowly escaped execution as a deserter. His father had him beaten and imprisoned, and his friend and confidant

FREDERICK THE GREAT REVIEWING TROOPS AT POTSDAM
Engraving by Daniel Chodowiecki

beheaded before his eyes. Frederick, recognizing that opposition was useless, submitted to his father's will and married according to his father's wish (though he later deserted his wife). When in 1740 he became king, he was ready to take unscrupulous advantage of the strong position which his father had built up. In one of his many political and historical writings he said, 'politics is the science of acting always by convenient means conformable to one's own interests'. He was a follower of the doctrine of MACHIAVELLI (q.v.).

His opportunity arose when a woman, MARIA THERESA (q.v.), succeeded to the Austrian throne. Although her succession to her father's empire had been guaranteed by the great powers, including Prussia, Frederick demanded the rich territory of Silesia, and enforced his demand with an army of 30,000 men. This started a European war, France and Bavaria supporting Frederick, and England and Hanover supporting Austria. Frederick's superior army forced Maria Theresa

to give up Silesia in 1742. When, 2 years later, Frederick attacked again in order to consolidate his hold on Silesia, he was defeated in Bohemia; but his military superiority was so great that Maria Theresa still had to abandon Silesia. Frederick, having got what he wanted, broke without scruple his alliance with France, who was continuing her struggle against England, and made a separate peace.

Frederick then applied his high intelligence and indefatigable energy to developing his State and army in the following 11 years of peace. His theory of government was liberal and progressive: he called himself 'the first servant of his State'—a new conception of MONARCHY (q.v. Vol. X). But in fact, he was a dictator, considering his country too immature for democratic rule. He encouraged, however, freedom of worship, and was inspired by the philosophy of 'enlightenment' expounded by VOLTAIRE (q.v.), who preached that tradition must be subjected to the criticism of reason. He induced

Voltaire to visit his court, but the visit ended with a violent and scandalous quarrel.

In 1756 Frederick unleashed another European war by a perhaps unjustifiable attack on Saxony, using the pretext that Saxony, a member of a great coalition, was about to attack him. This time, however, he had made an alliance with England, and was opposed by Austria, France, and Russia. Frederick, faced with a situation he had not foreseen, showed his great quality: by heroism, tenacity, and considerable adroitness he maintained his losing fight until he was saved by the death of the Russian Empress, Elizabeth, which took Russia out of the war. He was then able to conclude the Seven Years War without loss of territory. Towards the end of his reign he played his part in bringing about the first partition of Poland, whereby he gained the province of West Prussia.

Frederick, aged prematurely by the strain of the Seven Years War, now worked assiduously and with despotic severity to restore and develop his war-stricken kingdom. He was partially successful, but he became increasingly unpopular, and when he died at the age of 74, a solitary, bitter, and exhausted man, the people of Berlin rejoiced.

See also MARIA THERESA; VOLTAIRE.
See also Vol. I: GERMANS.

FREUD, Sigmund (1856–1939). As the originator of the science of psycho-analysis, Freud (pronounced Froyd) holds an important place in the history of PSYCHOLOGY (q.v. Vol. XI). The scientific study of human behaviour and the reasons for it present many difficult problems. Freud did pioneer work in this field by his researches into the subconscious processes of the human mind. His work has had a great effect on people's attitude to the mentally ill and to criminals. It has also made them kinder and more understanding to young children.

Freud was born at Freiburg, in Moravia, of a Jewish family, and lived most of his life in Vienna. As a young man he was fascinated by his research into the physiology of the nervous system, but, unable to afford to continue research work, he set up as a specialist in nervous diseases, which were then generally treated by drugs or by confining the patient.

He discovered that he could cure one patient of hysteria by allowing her to talk freely about her troubles while she was under HYPNO-TISM (q.v. Vol. XI). So he began to urge his other patients to talk freely without being hypnotized, but merely with the sympathetic encouragement of the doctor; during this talk one subject would lead to another until the patient's complete mental history was revealed. When the patient refused to talk, or memory failed, Freud was often able to track down the cause to some unhappy experience in the past, sometimes in very early childhood. By drawing these memories from the 'unconscious' (as he called the region of hidden memories and desires inside every person) into the conscious mind, he was able to free the patient from the symptoms arising from these 'repressions'.

This method, first called the 'talking cure' and later 'psycho-analysis' (the analysis of the *psyche* or soul)—originally applied to sick people—gave Freud such an insight into the workings of the human mind that he was able to tell us much about the reasons behind the behaviour of healthy people too. He found that childhood impressions associated with such basic emotions as love, hatred, fear, and jealousy have a very important influence on adult behaviour. This showed that much of the bad behaviour for which people are punished as criminals is a kind of illness which may be helped by psychological treatment.

Many of Freud's ideas, sometimes in a garbled form, have found their way into modern thought and literature. But although his views have become so widely known, they are not wholly accepted in medical circles. Freud has had a number of important followers. Two of the most important of these, Jung and Adler, disagreed with some of his theories and broke away from him to found systems of their own.

As a political refugee from Austria, Freud found a welcome in England in 1938. He died in London just after the outbreak of the Second World War.

See also Vol. XI: PSYCHOLOGY; PSYCHIATRY.

FROBISHER, Sir Martin (c. 1535–94). This typical Elizabethan seaman combined service in the Spanish War as an officer in the Queen's service with exploration on his own account, backed by one of those syndicates of merchants who financed these early voyagers. In 1576, on the publication of a discourse by Sir Humphrey GILBERT (q.v.) proving the existence of a North-West Passage to the East, he sailed in command of two 25-ton ships to begin a search which was completed only in the present century (*see* AMUNDSEN). He thought he had found the strait, 'having upon either hand a great main or continent'; but the land was Greenland, and not Asia, as he thought. Having named the strait after himself, he returned with some black stone which was believed to contain gold. Two further voyages were undertaken to collect this

SIR MARTIN FROBISHER AT THE AGE OF 39
Portrait by Cornelis Ketel

ore, but when it turned out to be iron pyrites, a common ore, Frobisher gave up Arctic exploration.

In 1585 he became vice-admiral to DRAKE (q.v.) in the raid on the West Indies, and distinguished himself in the fighting. In the SPANISH ARMADA campaign (q.v. Vol. X) he commanded the *Triumph* with great skill when his squadron was cut off near Portland, and was soon afterwards knighted. After Drake's disgrace, Frobisher and Sir John HAWKINS (q.v.) became the two leading sea commanders, and both cruised unsuccessfully off the Azores to intercept the Spanish treasure fleets. In 1594 Frobisher was mortally wounded when leading his men in an attack on a fort near Brest. He is described by a contemporary as 'very valiant, yet harsh and violent'. He was a fighter and a tough, selfish adventurer rather than a great commander and explorer.

See also Vol. IV: EXPLORATION.

FROEBEL, Friedrich (1782–1852). Froebel, the educationalist, was born in Thuringia, Germany, the fifth son of a village clergyman. His mother died soon after he was born, and he was a lonely child, an experience which, perhaps, helped him to understand the needs of children.

Froebel considered that play materials, practical occupations, and songs were needed to develop the child's real nature, which he believed to be fundamentally good. He spent 2 years as a young man with Pestalozzi, a famous Swiss educationalist, and though he admired much that he saw, he disagreed with certain things. For instance, he thought that Pestalozzi asked for too much learning by heart.

In 1816 he got a chance to develop his own ideas. His two brothers died, and he undertook the education of their children and opened a school. He became a 'gardener of children', calling his school a kindergarten, German for 'children's garden'. But most of the children did not come to him till they were 9 or 10 years of age, and Froebel soon realized that a gardener needs to exercise very early guidance over the plants within his care. In 1837 he was able to open a kindergarten for really young children at Blankenburg. From this school the kindergarten movement spread. His helpers and followers carried his methods—his 'gifts' of balls, blocks, and coloured tablets for education

AN EARLY KINDERGARTEN
Illustration to a manual on Froebel's methods published
in 1864. Froebel Educational Institute

through self-activity—all over Europe. Today many teachers are trained in Froebel's methods, and many modern methods have grown from the doctrines of this great teacher.

See also Vol. X: EDUCATION, MODERN.

FROISSART, Jean (*c.* 1337–1410), French Chronicler, *see* Vol. XII: HISTORIES.

FRY, Elizabeth (1780–1845). Elizabeth Fry, famous for her great work in reforming prison conditions, especially for women, was born in Norwich and brought up at Earlham near by. She was the third daughter of Catherine and John Gurney, a wealthy wool merchant and banker. The Gurneys and their twelve children were members of the Society of Friends (*see* QUAKERS, Vol. I), though they were not as strict as many Quakers, and the girls wore pretty clothes and had gay parties. They worshipped every Sunday, however, at the Friends' Meeting House in Norwich.

One evening, when Elizabeth was 17, she heard a sermon preached by an American Quaker, William Savery, which changed the whole course of her life; she determined then to dedicate herself to the service of God. Soon her family noticed that she had grown quieter and more serious. Instead of joining her brothers and sisters in their games and dancing, she began to visit the poor. A visit to London, where she went to plays and parties, confirmed her in her belief that she had no taste for worldly gaieties. She adopted the sober Quaker dress worn by 'Plain Friends', and began to teach the poor children in the village of Earlham. Soon her 'school', held in an attic of their house, grew till there were over sixty children. The family called them 'Betsy's Imps'.

It was about this time that an old Quaker woman whom she met prophesied that she would be 'a light to the blind, speech to the dumb, and feet to the lame'.

When she was 20 Elizabeth married Joseph Fry, also a banker and a Quaker, who was later to be a great help and support to her in her public work. The Frys lived at first in London, but later moved to Plashet in Essex (now in East Ham). Together they brought up eleven children, but in spite of the cares of her household Elizabeth always found time to help the poor. She nursed the sick, taught in the schools, and even helped to vaccinate the Plashet children against smallpox.

Gradually she overcame her natural diffidence about speaking in public, and began to testify at Quaker meetings. In spite of all her good work, Elizabeth often felt that she was falling short in the service of God: instead of a 'useful instrument in the Church Militant', she felt herself to be a 'careworn wife and mother merely devoted to the things of this life'.

In 1813, when she was 33, a friend described to Elizabeth the terrible condition of the women prisoners in Newgate, the principal London jail. Low wages and high prices, which were partly the result of the Napoleonic Wars, had helped to bring about a great increase in crime, and the prisons were badly overcrowded. The penal laws were very savage: more than twenty offences were awarded the death sentence, many convicts were transported to the colonies, and long terms of imprisonment were imposed for quite small crimes. The jails were dark, dirty, and unhealthy, and many prisoners died of diseases they caught in prison. Discipline was brutal and corrupt, the prisoners'

Country Life
WAX PORTRAIT OF ELIZABETH FRY

a better place for the children. They seemed deeply moved by what she said.

Before long Elizabeth began to visit Newgate regularly. She won the mothers' confidence by offering to start a school for the children in an empty cell. A committee of educated women was formed to help, and one of the prisoners was chosen as teacher. As she got to know the women better, Elizabeth talked to them, prayed with them, and read to them from the Scriptures. Her calm, gentle dignity impressed even the most hardened criminals, bringing to them a sense that God had not forgotten them. She once said, when questioned about her dealings with the prisoners, 'I never refer to their past; we have all sinned and come short'.

'What struck me most', wrote someone who had heard her speak to the prisoners, 'was that she always classed herself with them: she never said "you" but "us" when speaking to those who were lost: giving them to understand that in the sight of God we are all sinners'.

Elizabeth then began to provide useful work for the women to do in the prison, so that they could make and mend their children's clothes and make things for sale. Naturally their general behaviour greatly improved. The governors of Newgate, who had at first doubted whether Elizabeth's schemes could do any good, were much impressed, and her work aroused widespread interest. Members of Parliament examined the state of the jails, and praised her efforts highly. She began to visit prisons all over the country, and to establish committees in many places to carry on her work. The result of her work on the prisoners was so marked that those in authority were ready to listen when she pleaded for better conditions, or made practical suggestions about prison routine. She urged that solitary confinement should be abolished, and that women prisoners should be in the charge of women. She produced such evidence to show that criminals behaved better when they were treated humanely that the idea that prisons should be places of reform began to be accepted.

Elizabeth felt some anxiety at the fame her work had brought her, as her diary shows: 'I have thought whether my being made so much of, and also being so publicly brought forward, may not prove a temptation and lead to something of self-exaltation or worldly pride . . . Lord, be pleased to help and strengthen me in this that I may in no way be a cause of reproach.'

only comfort lying in bribing the jailers to bring them drink. Badly behaved criminals were kept in solitary confinement or chained up. First offenders were herded with hardened criminals, and lunatics with the sane. Many women prisoners had their children with them, and no provision was made for them. Nothing at all was done to encourage the prisoners to become good citizens again. Once a criminal, always a criminal, was the accepted theory.

Elizabeth Fry, moved by what she was told, went with a friend to visit the women prisoners in Newgate. Having obtained the governor's permit, she persuaded the unwilling jailers, or turnkeys, to let her go alone into the filthy room where some 300 women were fighting, swearing, and screaming. Many were so violent that even the turnkeys were afraid of them. The women were so astonished to see an unprotected woman come among them fearlessly that they crowded round in curiosity. Elizabeth picked up one of the children and, while allowing him to play with her gold watch and chain, she spoke to the women about their children. To the turnkeys' amazement, the tumult died down when she spoke. The women listened while she suggested that she might help them to make the prison

MRS. SIDDONS
Portrait by Thomas Gainsborough

In 1828 Joseph Fry suffered a great financial loss and became bankrupt, and the family had to leave Plashet for a house at Upton near Greenwich. But troubles could not shake Elizabeth's faith, or keep her from her work. In 1838 and 1839 she visited prisons in France, and later she made long tours through Germany, Denmark, and the Low Countries. Foreign statesmen and officials consulted her about prison reform, and on her advice many improvements were made. She was received by kings and queens. Catholics and Protestants alike flocked to hear her speak at meetings, listening reverently when she spoke of her work and of the duties of a Christian life, or when she read from the Bible in her beautiful expressive voice. Those of her family who were with her were touched by the reverence and love that she inspired. She pleaded in high places the cause of the prisoners as courageously as she had preached the Gospel to the desperate women of Newgate. She petitioned the Kings of Prussia and Denmark to grant their subjects greater religious freedom, and spoke to the Dutch King 'very boldly, though respectfully', about the state of the prisons in Holland.

These journeys so injured her health that on her return home from abroad in 1841 she was forced to rest, and after a last visit to France in 1843 she had to give up her foreign tours. But her interest in prison work continued until her death at Ramsgate in 1845.

In Elizabeth Fry the power of goodness was recognized by everyone she met, from criminals

By gracious permission of H.M. the Queen

ELIZABETH FRY READING TO THE WOMEN PRISONERS AT NEWGATE

Water-colour by Richard Dighton, 1820

to Cabinet Ministers. Those who saw her remembered all their lives her dignity and sweetness of expression. The Duke of Argyll wrote of her, 'She was the only really very great human being I have ever met in whom it was impossible to be disappointed. . . . The words that came into my mind when I saw her were "the peace of God which passeth all understanding".'

See also Vol. X: PRISONS, HISTORY OF.

G

GAINSBOROUGH, Thomas (1727–88). Gainsborough alone among English artists reached greatness both as landscape painter and as portraitist. He said, as CONSTABLE (q.v.) said later, that the Suffolk countryside made him a painter, and a landscape painter he remained all his life, though his landscapes brought him little beyond admiration. A warm-hearted, sociable temperament, love of gay company, ambition, and the tastes of his age urged him, rather against his will, to give most of his time to portraiture.

Gainsborough, born at Sudbury in 1727, was the youngest of the nine children of a cloth merchant. He went to a school in his native town and spent his spare hours roaming the woods and sketching. He is said to have got his school-friends to do his arithmetic for him while he made drawings in their books. When he was 15 he went to London to study art, and there he also learned engraving. He was really self-taught—learning landscape painting from the Dutch masters and figure painting through copying VAN DYCK (q.v.). Gainsborough married, settled in Ipswich, and began to make his way as a portrait painter. In 1759 he moved to Bath, which was then the centre of fashion.

Soon aristocrats and reigning beauties, soldiers, statesmen, and men of letters such as Samuel Richardson and Sheridan flocked to his painting-room. The company of actors and musicians was specially agreeable to him, for he was a passionate lover of the theatre and of music and a passable amateur performer on several instruments. His portraits of Garrick and of the actresses, Mrs. Siddons (*see* Colour Plate, p. 176) and 'Perdita' Robinson (*see* Vol. XII: opp. p. 352), are among his best known.

In 1761 he began to exhibit in London the great series of full-length portraits that made him famous. Many of these were informal and almost too natural for the taste of the time, but Gainsborough's brilliant and delicate brushwork and his fine sense of restrained colour defeated criticism. He had, too, the power of giving poetic charm to his figures and the scenes they moved in without unduly flattering either. In 1768 he became a founder member of the Royal Academy; but later he quarrelled about the hanging of his pictures and refused to exhibit with the Academy any more.

In 1774 he left Bath for London, where he took a fine house in Pall Mall. His success continued and in 1781 he painted the first of his portraits of George III and Queen Charlotte. To this period belongs his famous portrait of Master Buttall, known as the 'Blue Boy'. In 1788, at the trial of Warren Hastings, he caught a chill which brought to light a fatal disease. Though an impulsive, and even quarrelsome man, Gainsborough was generous and always ready to make up a quarrel. When he was dying

National Gallery

VISCOUNT KILMOREY
Portrait by Gainsborough

he asked Sir Joshua REYNOLDS (q.v.), his great rival and the President of the Royal Academy with whom he had previously quarrelled, to visit him.

See also Vol. XII: BRITISH ART; PORTRAITS.

GALILEO (1564–1642). Galileo was the first truly modern scientist—the first whose outlook and methods would not be out of place even today. He made important advances in both astronomy and mechanics, but his greatest achievement was the creation of the experimental-mathematical method that has lain at the basis of all progress in physical science since his time. The son of an Italian merchant of Pisa, he was a remarkably intelligent boy, very skilled at drawing and music, who spent his spare time making mechanical toys.

Shortly after he began studying medicine at Pisa University he made his first scientific discovery—that the swing of a pendulum takes the same time, whether it swings in a large arc or a small one. According to the story he watched a hanging lamp swinging in Pisa Cathedral, and timed it with his pulse. This led him to design an instrument for timing pulse-beats for medical purposes, and at the very end of his life he worked out designs for a pendulum clock.

Mathematics was not part of his university course; but on one occasion he happened to overhear an able mathematician giving a lesson. He was so interested that he used to hide himself in the mathematician's room to follow these lessons. Soon he was deeply engaged in this branch of study, and with such success that when he was 25 he was appointed Professor of Mathematics at Pisa. His studies led him seriously to question the teachings of ARISTOTLE (q.v.), which were still almost universally accepted. Aristotle held, for example, that a heavy body falls to earth much faster than a light one. But Galileo said that, apart from the effect of air resistance, the two fall at the same speed. He is said to have demonstrated this by dropping heavy and light weights from the leaning tower of Pisa (*see* GRAVITATION, Vol. III).

His rebellions against accepted opinions made him so unpopular at Pisa that he gladly accepted an appointment as mathematical lecturer in the University of Padua in 1592. There he lectured officially on mathematics and astronomy, and privately at home on mechanics and engineering. He invented a mathematical instrument for simplifying the calculations of gunners, military engineers, and others, and he manufactured this and other instruments in his own workshop. He also invented an air THERMOMETER (q.v. Vol. VIII).

In 1609 he heard a report that a Dutch spectacle-maker had accidentally succeeded in putting two lenses together in such a way as to make distant objects seem larger and nearer— in other words, he had invented what we now call a TELESCOPE (q.v. Vol. VIII). Galileo after some thought was able to use the theory of optics also to design a telescope, and with this he made a series of wonderful discoveries. He found many new stars, and discovered that the Milky Way was really made up of myriads of very faint stars, that the moon was not, as was then believed, a perfectly smooth sphere but had its mountains and hollows, and that the planet Jupiter had four moons or 'satellites' circling round it just as our moon moves round the earth (*see* UNIVERSE, Vol. III).

Although Galileo had long ago adopted the new astronomical theory of COPERNICUS (q.v.) concerning the motion of the earth round the sun, his telescope now gave him new evidence. Jupiter's moons showed that there could be moons circling round a planet which was itself moving, just as the Copernican theory said that the earth moved round the sun and the moon round the earth.

His telescopic discoveries gave Galileo such a high reputation that he was able to return to Pisa as First Mathematician of the University, and Philosopher and Mathematician to the Grand Duke of Florence. He carried on his telescopic observations, making further remarkable discoveries (*see* ASTRONOMY, HISTORY OF, Vol. III).

By now his discoveries and opinions were arousing the hatred of those who still claimed that the earth was the centre of the universe, and that everything else moved round it. The Court of the Holy INQUISITION (q.v. Vol. I) declared the Copernican theory to be heretical, and instructed Galileo to teach it no, more. In spite of this, however, in 1632 Galileo published his great book, which was a powerful argument for Copernicus' theory. He was once more brought before the Inquisition and, after examination under the threat of torture, he was brought to recant his opinions. He was treated, however, quite mildly for those intolerant days,

Alinari

GALILEO
Portrait by Sustermans. Uffizi, Florence

his sentence amounting to little more than a sort of 'open arrest' for the rest of his life.

In 1638, when he was 74, and almost blind, he published his greatest book, *Dialogues concerning two new Sciences*, the first half of which explains how the strength of a beam varies with its length, breadth, and thickness, and the second half with the behaviour of moving bodies. He showed that a body falling freely does so with constant acceleration, and that the path of a projectile is a curve called a parabola. He had also made a near approach in his book of 1632 to the concept of inertia—that a body moves in a straight line at constant speed, except in so far as forces are acting on it. These discoveries formed a great part of the basis on which NEWTON (q.v.) was to build his theories (*see* MOTION, Vol. III).

More important still, in this book Galileo gave the first complete example of what has since become the standard method of physical science. The scientist first makes a guess (hypothesis) about the phenomena under consideration; then he uses mathematics or logical deductions to see what consequences would follow if the hypothesis were true; finally, he uses experiments to discover if the deductions fit the facts or not, accepting or rejecting the

hypothesis accordingly. In one form or another, every great physical discovery from Galileo to our own time has been made by the use of this method.

See also Vol. III: UNIVERSE; ASTRONOMY, HISTORY OF; MOTION.

GANDHI, Mohandas Karamchand (1869–1948). This great Indian political leader played a major part in his country's struggle to win independence from Britain (*see* INDIA, GOVERNMENT OF, Vol. X). A man of saint-like humility, and of unshakeable courage and determination, Gandhi brought to millions in India, especially to the poor and oppressed, a new hope and comfort; he tried always to heal the angry rift between Hindus and Moslems (*see* JINNAH) that threatened to tear his country apart; and many people outside India found inspiration in his constant work for international brotherhood and the relief of suffering.

As a modern political leader, Gandhi was unique: he was able to influence millions simply by personal example or gesture. He was once described as 'a man who cares nothing for sensual pleasures, nothing for riches, nothing for comfort or praise or promotion, but is simply determined to do what he thinks is right'. He preached and practised tolerance, though he was not easily persuaded to accept another's point of view. He did not believe that the logical argument was always right. 'About some matters', he explained, 'we need no proof.' But when it came to finding practical solutions to many Indian political problems, his vagueness disappointed responsible people.

'The Mahatma' ('Great Soul'), as he came to be called by his followers, was born in a small State in western India. His father was an official who belonged to the third, or Vaisya, Hindu CASTE (q.v. Vol. I). At school Gandhi showed no particular brilliance, and was a shy, nervous boy who hated all games and physical exercise. When he was only 13 he was married. (Such marriages were very common at that time in India and are not unknown today.) He became later a life-long opponent of child marriage and did much to influence public opinion against it. As a boy he made friends with the boy whose job it was to clean out the lavatories in his home—an 'untouchable' according to the orthodox Hindu Caste system. Later, his defence of the 'untouchables' was one of his bravest and most successful campaigns. He renamed these poor outcasts *Harijan* ('Sons of God'), and used this name for a weekly paper which he published.

When he was 17 Gandhi went to London to study law, and for the first time became familiar with the teachings of Christianity. After he had passed his examinations, he accepted a legal post in South Africa where he remained for 21 eventful years. He organized Indian ambulance units for the British during the SOUTH AFRICAN WAR (q.v. Vol. X), and served with them under fire. He formed a friendship with a Christian missionary, C. F. Andrews, and corresponded with the Russian writer TOLSTOY (q.v.), being greatly influenced by the teachings of both men. But his main work was for his fellow countrymen. Indians in South Africa suffered many hardships and humiliations—for example, they were forbidden to move from one part of the country to another without formal permission. Gandhi never spared himself in his efforts to help them; his most dramatic move was to lead 3,000 Indians unlawfully across a State boundary, his object being to force the South African Government to arrest as many of his countrymen as it could, and thus draw attention to what he considered an unjust law. He called these tactics 'passive resistance', because he would instruct his followers to offer no resistance to arrest, and to behave well and lawfully, except in relation to the one regulation which they had elected to break. Later, in India, Gandhi's most successful 'civil disobedience' campaigns were carried out in a similar way.

At 45 Gandhi returned to India, and soon became the recognized leader of the Indian National Congress in its struggle to make Britain withdraw from India and to establish an independent Republic. Gandhi attacked the British Government on every possible occasion, though he always maintained that he greatly respected the British people, and was outspoken in his criticisms of those Indian customs and beliefs which he considered inferior to those of Britain. In support of Indian nationalism he published newspapers and pamphlets, and visited all parts of the country, often travelling on foot and wearing the simplest clothes. When he visited a city he often stayed in the poorest quarter. Before long he had millions of followers of all classes, who called him affectionately *bapu* ('daddy'). He sent chosen followers into remote villages, teaching hygiene, first-aid, and encouraging the villagers to set up local handicraft industries. Gandhi urged people always to work with their hands rather than use machines, for he disapproved of industrialization. He spun all his own clothing himself—indeed, he was seldom seen without his spinning wheel—and persuaded many other political leaders to do likewise.

To most Indians the advance towards the self-government which the British had promised seemed intolerably slow, and Gandhi began to agitate and harass the British authorities. Although he always tried to prevent violence, very serious disturbances broke out. The British often took what seemed harshly repressive measures, and Gandhi himself was always in and out of prison.

One of Britain's most difficult tasks in deciding her policy towards India was to find some basis of agreement between the Hindus and Moslems. Gandhi himself tried always to bring the two groups together, and often included Moslem (as

Radio Times Hulton Lib.

GANDHI OUTSIDE NO. 10 DOWNING STREET, LONDON, IN 1931

well as Sikh and Christian) scriptures in the prayer meetings which he conducted, and at which he made his most important pronouncements. Nevertheless many Moslems were not convinced of his sincerity, and others felt that when the British left India the Hindus, being in the majority, would be tempted to override his teachings.

When the SECOND WORLD WAR (q.v. Vol. X) broke out, Gandhi declared that the Allies could expect support only from a 'Free India', and in 1942 he led his most bitter campaign of civil disobedience. Once more he was arrested and imprisoned with other Congress leaders. After the war the British Government made a last attempt to reach agreement between the Congress party and the Moslem League. Gandhi again played a leading, though unofficial, part in the conferences, and 'in his inscrutable way', wrote *The Times*, 'he was sometimes helpful and sometimes the reverse'. At last, when failure faced the Conference, Gandhi agreed reluctantly that Congress must accept a separate Moslem State, PAKISTAN (q.v. Vol. III), as a condition of India's own independence, though amid the general rejoicing on Independence Day he could only say 'I feel little joy, only sorrow that my country should be "dismembered" '.

When savage riots between Hindus and Moslems with terrible atrocities occurred in some districts, Gandhi set out on foot to many of the affected areas, and announced that he would fast until normal conditions were restored. This was, in fact, the fourteenth time that Gandhi had fasted, either as penance for misconduct of his followers, or as a personal sacrifice to draw attention to something he held to be wrong. On this occasion it inspired the leaders of both parties to discipline their followers, and restored peace where the police and army had failed. But Hindu extremists began to attack Gandhi openly as a traitor to India and to Hinduism, and not long afterwards, when he was on his way to conduct a prayer meeting, he was assassinated by a member of one of these extremist organizations.

See also JINNAH.
See also Vol. I: INDIAN PEOPLES; HINDUISM; ISLAM.
See also Vol. X: INDIA, GOVERNMENT OF.

GARIBALDI, Giuseppe (1807–82). Garibaldi was a legendary figure in the 19th century, particularly in England, owing to the spectacular part he took in the liberation of Italian States and the creating of a united Italian nation. His power of inspiration was unexcelled, though his practical achievement was less than that of the other two great heroes of Italian nationalism, the statesman CAVOUR and the idealist MAZZINI (qq.v.). (The main events of the period are outlined in the article on CAVOUR.)

Garibaldi, the son of a poor fisherman of Nice (then an Italian town), ran away to sea, and later joined Mazzini's patriotic 'Young Italy' movement. He shared in an attempt at revolution in Genoa, for which he was sentenced to death, but he escaped to South America. There he fought in the civil wars of Brazil and Uruguay, was captured, escaped, and ran off with a pretty girl whom he married. He soon showed the talent for which he became famous, leadership of irregular troops, and organized a band of Italian volunteers—political exiles like himself—as an 'Italian Legion'. They were the first to wear the red shirts that later became part of the uniform of all his followers.

But Garibaldi's heart was in Italy. When, in the revolutions of 1848, the north Italians rose

Clive Holland

GARIBALDI

against their Austrian rulers, Garibaldi returned to Italy and, raising 3,000 volunteers, led them against the Austrian army. They were defeated, and Garibaldi escaped to Switzerland. He next came to Rome, the capital of the Papal State, in which patriots had proclaimed a Republic and had driven the Pope into exile. The tiny Republic, ruled by a 'triumvirate' of three dictators, the chief of whom was Mazzini, kept at bay the troops of the King of Naples and the French Emperor for 9 months. Garibaldi gallantly organized the defence. When the Republic collapsed, he and 4,000 volunteers beat an adventurous retreat through north Italy, harried by the troops of four armies. His wife who was with him died on the way. Eventually he escaped once more to America.

He spent a few years in New York, where he made some money as a candle-maker and shipowner, later acting as a merchant sea-captain; and then he retired to farm on an island near Italy. But in 1859, when the Sardinian and French armies were driving Austria out of north Italy (*see* CAVOUR), Garibaldi joined his countrymen and fought at the head of special mountain units which cleared the enemy from the Italian Alps.

Then came the most spectacular of all Garibaldi's achievements. While Italian nationalists, directed by Cavour, were unifying the various small States of northern Italy, Garibaldi set out, on his own initiative, at the head of over 1,000 volunteers, to capture the entire south, which was held by the King of Naples. 'The Thousand', as the red-shirted volunteers were called, conquered Sicily in 3 months, then crossed to the mainland, fought various battles, and entered Naples in triumph. Garibaldi handed over southern Italy to the King of Sardinia, newly proclaimed King of the whole of Italy, and went back to his farm.

Garibaldi believed that Italian independence was not complete so long as the city of Rome remained the Pope's territory, instead of being the capital of the kingdom. Twice, in 1862 and 1867, he raised supporters and tried to march on Rome to capture it, but each time he was stopped, not without bloodshed.

Garibaldi's last years were devoted to writing on behalf of oppressed nations throughout Europe, and against the Pope. He also wrote a few novels, was twice more married, and served as a member of the Italian Parliament. His last

fighting was done on behalf of the new French Republic which was set up after the collapse of the French Emperor in the war against Prussia of 1870. When he died he was mourned and respected by lovers of liberty everywhere.

See also CAVOUR; MAZZINI.
See also Vol. I: ITALIANS.

GARRICK, David (1717–79). When this great English actor died, his friend, Dr. JOHNSON (q.v.), said that his death 'eclipsed the gaiety of nations'. It was a tribute to a man who dominated the London stage, both as tragedian and comedian, during the middle of the 18th century, and who changed the style of English acting.

David Garrick was born at Hereford, the son of an impoverished army officer, and educated in the Staffordshire cathedral town of Lichfield, where Johnson, 7 years the elder, had Garrick for a time as a not very bright pupil. In the spring of 1737 the two young men set out together on horseback to seek their fortunes in London, Johnson by his pen and Garrick by studying law. Garrick, however, soon gave up law and joined an elder brother as a wine merchant not far from the two great theatres, Drury Lane and Covent Garden. But he was a born actor, and, after certain amateur attempts, he managed to get the part of Shakespeare's Richard III, playing at a small theatre in Stepney; and to Stepney during the next few months went many distinguished people to see him act. His triumph, at the age of 24, was startling. Alexander POPE (q.v.) was emphatic: 'That young man never had his equal and he will never have a rival.' Garrick played each part with absolute conviction; and his 'easy and familiar yet forcible style' made an exciting contrast with the harsh, melodramatic declamation which until then had been the accepted manner.

Garrick, unlike many tragedians, was only of moderate height, 5 ft. 4 in., but this never worried him. He was uncommonly graceful, and he made great play with his features. The stage in those days was candle-lit, and an actor had to be facially expressive. Garrick's dark eyes and mobile features were most effective; even the deaf, it was said, could understand him. He moved to Drury Lane Theatre, and gradually added King Lear, Hamlet, Macbeth, and other major parts to his repertoire. On one occasion, when he was acting the part of Macbeth, he said so intensely to the murderer in the banquet scene, 'There's blood upon thy face', that the actor, putting up his hand involuntarily, exclaimed: 'Is there, by God?' Garrick could glitter in comedy as well: he was a volatile Benedick in Shakespeare's *Much Ado About Nothing*, and he had one of the strangest successes of his career in the tiny part of a young tobacconist, Abel Drugger, in Ben Jonson's comedy, *The Alchemist*.

In 1747 Garrick became manager of Drury Lane, where he played no fewer than ninety parts with almost unfailing success. He failed, however, in the part of Othello because, having to black his face, he could not exploit his gift of facial play. He retired temporarily in 1763, at the zenith of his fame, and travelled in Europe with his affectionate Austrian wife, who had been a dancer. But inevitably he soon returned to the stage, and made his final appearance only 3 years before his death.

He aspired to be a dramatist as well as an actor, and had a hand in thirty-five plays, including many adaptations of Shakespeare; but it is as an actor that he is remembered—one of the most compelling, adaptable, and graceful in the history of the stage. Conceited though he was and snobbish though he could be, he had more friends than enemies and a devoted public. He died aged 62 and was buried in Westminster Abbey.

See also Vol. IX: ACTING, HISTORY OF.

GAUGUIN, Paul (1848–1903), French painter, *see* Vol. XII: POST-IMPRESSIONISTS.

GAUNT, John of (1340–1399). This fourth son of Edward III was the ancestor of the Royal House of Lancaster, and the richest man in England. He was patron of the poet CHAUCER (q.v.).

As a soldier in his early life Gaunt never won the fame nor the popularity of his eldest brother,

Garrick Club

DAVID GARRICK AS MACBETH

In the 18th century actors usually wore contemporary dress. Painting by Zoffany

the Black Prince. When, in 1377, his young nephew Richard II became King, Gaunt was the chief ruler during the King's minority. He was suspected of designs on his nephew's throne, though in fact his main object seems to have been to support and strengthen the monarchy. But as time went on Richard relied increasingly on a group of friends at Court, and Gaunt found his own influence diminishing. By the end of Richard's reign he had become, as Shakespeare depicts him, an isolated figure whose years had won him a certain reputation for wisdom.

When Gaunt died Richard foolishly seized his uncle's Lancastrian estates. This led to Richard's deposition by Henry Bolingbroke, Gaunt's son, who became King Henry IV.

GAUTAMA (*c.* 6th century B.C.). Siddhartha Gautama, the Buddha (or Awakened One), commonly believed to have been the founder of BUDDHISM (q.v. Vol. I), was the son of a local landed magnate in the State of Nepal, and was brought up as a Hindu. Very little is known for certain about his life, not even the exact date and place of his birth. Almost certainly nearly all the stories about his youth and early manhood are legend. Some may even have come from the Christian gospels; others, such as the walking on the water and the multiplying of food, may belong to the common folk-lore of the East regarding holy personages. Many of his sayings were not put into writing until long after his death, and almost certainly many of the comments on them made at various times by teachers have become incorporated as part of his original sayings.

Gautama, when a young man, travelled to various centres of education, and met the principal Hindu teachers of his day. Then he returned home, married, and had a son. But he could not settle down, and his deep concern to discover a way by which his fellow men, as he knew them, could make the most of a brief and uncertain bodily life drove him forth again, leaving his wife and child. He probably expected to do no more than bring back to his own hill-country some new knowledge from the cities of the plain. According to one story, he had a conversation with a King of Kosala, who had just ended a war, and was speaking of the enjoyment of leisure. Gautama replied: 'What would you do, Sire, if you were told that a mighty landslide was rolling inevitably upon you and your city, and that you could not escape?' The King answered: 'Live righteously, for there would be nothing else to do.' Then said Gautama: 'I tell you, Sire, old age and death are rolling in upon you. What is there that you can do?' Again the answer was of course: 'Live righteously.' Such positive teaching is very different from the teaching which some of Gautama's followers later attributed to him.

One day, after spending many years under various teachers, he made, in what circumstances we do not precisely know, a momentous spiritual discovery, and, declaring himself to be full of happiness, he began without delay to try to share his discovery with others. His first few disciples remained faithful to him as long as he lived. He began preaching and travelling—much as John WESLEY (q.v.) did—spreading as widely as he could his new religion, Buddhism.

Briefly Gautama's teaching was a scheme of mental and moral training, the object of which was to set free the individual from such selfish passions as lust, hatred, and false longings which cramp and fetter the soul, so that the soul might enter into the state called *Nirvana*, which is unspeakable happiness. Gautama taught that in this way the individual could escape from *Samsara*, the endless succession of rebirths into this world which is a general condition of mankind according to the doctrine of HINDUISM (q.v. Vol. I), and become absorbed as it were, into the 'Whole'—a state most to be desired. He always declined to give positive definitions of what we call 'God' and 'the soul'. But he was certainly not an atheist, or a disbeliever in individuality—rather, he found it hard to express himself on these matters without giving rise to misunderstanding, since he seems to have believed 'Reality' to be a higher state of being, in which such terms lose their ordinary meaning.

As Gautama grew old, many of his younger followers seem to have treated him as rather old-fashioned, revering and obeying him, but already engaged in changing his teaching—or, as they would have said, drawing out its true meaning. They made it, however, less human, less progressive, and more a teaching for monks than for ordinary people. In the end, when he was about 80, Gautama died in the open, on a couch spread by the wayside beneath two trees.

Some of the pictures and statues of the Buddha show him as seated cross-legged and motionless in what is known as the *yoga* or meditative attitude; others represent him either as standing erect with a hand raised to teach or bless, or as sitting down, with one leg bent, as though in the

THE FUTURE BUDDHA LEAVING HIS HOME TO BEGIN HIS MINISTRY

Deities support the horse's hoofs so that they make no noise, and the Prince's departure is undetected. The umbrella which a servant holds is a sign of princedom.
Relief from Amaravati, *c.* A.D. 200

act of moving. The latter represents more faithfully his real spirit; the former might seem like distortion of his teaching. As he gave it to the world of his day, his was a teaching of growth and progress and movement, not of negation.

See also Vol. I: BUDDHISM; SACRED BOOKS, Section 3.

GENGHIS KHAN (1162–1227).

This founder of the Mongol Empire and one of the greatest conquerors of history was born at Dulun-Boldaq, near what is now the northern frontier of Outer Mongolia. The MONGOLS (q.v. Vol. I) consisted of tribes of nomadic peoples who lived mainly by raiding their settled neighbours, especially in China, and who were united only when there arose a leader strong enough to hold them. Temujin (Genghis Khan's original name) was the son of one of these tribal leaders, who died when Temujin was about 12. The tribe, refusing to accept so young a chief, deserted him and all his family. They suffered great hardship for a while, even living on 'mountain-mice and field-mice'. But Temujin throve on hardship; he learned to endure the numbing winter cold and the heat of summer, and to match man and beast in speed and cunning. As he grew older his fame as a leader spread, and warriors attached themselves to him.

Then Temujin decided to join forces with a powerful Christian people of Eastern Mongolia, called the Keraits (tales of whom gave rise to the legend of the great Christian leader PRESTER JOHN (q.v.)). With the Keraits Temujin helped for some years to defend the Chinese borderland against the TARTARS (q.v. Vol. I), and won great renown. About 1196 his followers proclaimed him Khan (lord or ruler), and he took the title *Chinggis*, which Western writers spell 'Genghis' or 'Jenghis'. A few years later the Keraits, jealous of his growing power, plotted to destroy him; but he was forewarned, and shortly after he attacked and utterly defeated the Kerait army. This made him master of Eastern Mongolia.

By 1206 Western Mongolia had also fallen before him, and at a gathering of the tribes he was proclaimed *Qa'an*, 'Great Khan'. Next he attacked China and conquered Peking. Then he turned westward, and by 1218 had added Eastern Turkestan to his dominions. Before he died in 1227 his Empire stretched from the Pacific to the Black Sea and the Persian Gulf.

He won this Empire through brilliant generalship, iron discipline (embodied in a code of laws known as the *Yasa*), and unimaginable cruelty. Only his own people mattered, and settled, civilized folk were his natural prey. He made a practice when he had conquered a town of driving the inhabitants forward as living shields for his army in the next attack. He was a good administrator as well as a great conqueror, and he organized his Empire into States which lasted longer than most Asiatic Empires (*see* Map, INDEX, p. 53).

An eye-witness described him as taller than most Mongols, with eyes like those of a cat, a broad forehead, and in later life a long beard. An even more vivid picture of him comes from the legends recorded in the *Secret History of the Mongols* (1240): his ancestors were a grey wolf and a white deer, and he was born holding a clot of blood in his hand. His grandson, KUBLAI KHAN (q.v.), carried on his Empire and completed the conquest of China.

See also Vol. I: MONGOLS.

GEORGE III (1738–1820).

George III succeeded his grandfather, George II, in 1760 and reigned altogether for 60 years, though for the last 9 years the Prince Regent ruled for him. He was popular because in contrast to his German grandfather and great-grandfather he was born and brought up in England and was sincerely patriotic. As a boy he lacked self-confidence, being very dependent on his mother, and suffered from moods of melancholia. Although capable of screwing himself up to an obstinate and unreasonable determination, he always needed friends to lean on, who could bolster up his fundamental lack of confidence. George had the nature and lived the private life of a country squire, and this made him popular with many of his ordinary subjects, who called him 'Farmer George'. Although stiff rather than dignified on formal occasions, when informal he liked to chat commonplaces, ending his sentences with a fussy 'What, what?' He honestly confessed that he found much of Shakespeare 'sad stuff'; he much preferred giving advice on practical subjects such as agriculture and he wrote articles for agricultural papers under the pseudonym of Ralph Robinson. He was a good husband, but he was stiff with his children and made his home so dull that his sons reacted against it by leading dissipated lives. He quarrelled

GEORGE III
Portrait by Zoffany, 1771

particularly with the Prince of Wales, who supported his father's political opponents.

Eager to govern, as well as to reign, he believed it his duty, with the help of his friend Lord Bute, to purge political life of evil men, and to break the power of the political groups who had been supreme in Government for the previous 40 years (*see* POLITICAL PARTIES, Vol. X). The politicians he rejected accused him of unconstitutional acts. For some 10 years, until North came into power, there were constant changes of ministry in an attempt to find a combination which satisfied both the King and Parliament. George divided the world into white (those on his side) and black (those who opposed him); and the attacks of 'that devil Wilkes' upon the government he took as a personal quarrel (*see* WILKES). Although England as a whole was very short-sighted about the American colonies, George has to take special responsibility for the dogged obstinacy with which he refused to give way when things were going wrong (*see* AMERICAN WAR OF INDEPENDENCE, Vol. X), in spite of the grave dangers into which he was running his country. He insisted on keeping Lord North as Minister though public opinion had turned against him.

After the disaster of the loss of the American colonies the King found a strong and able

Minister whom he could trust in William PITT (q.v.) the Younger, who brought England safely through the French wars. George did not always understand Pitt's ideas, or realize the significance of the industrial changes which were taking place (*see* INDUSTRIAL REVOLUTION, Vol. VII). Although the King remained physically strong, the attacks of insanity which had come upon him at intervals all through his reign increased in intensity and finally overwhelmed him altogether. In the last years of his reign, after the death of his favourite daughter, the Princess Amelia, in 1810, he became deaf, blind, and hopelessly insane.

GEORGE IV (1762–1830). Although George was widely unpopular as Prince Regent and later as King, he is remembered as the leader of a brief but flamboyant period in English manners. In the social circle which gathered round him, the riotous display and wild living which had flared up at times in the 18th century had its last fling before expiring under the pressure of the public disapproval of a graver age.

George was already known as the 'first gentleman of Europe' when he became Prince Regent in 1811, owing to the madness of his father GEORGE III (q.v.). The Prince considered him-

PAPIER-MÂCHÉ PORTRAIT OF GEORGE IV

self a leader of taste, fashion, and the arts. He commissioned the architect John NASH (q.v.) to lay out Regent Street (now largely rebuilt) and Regent's Park in London. We now use the terms 'Regency' art and 'REGENCY' ARCHITECTURE (q.v. Vol. XII). Its most extravagant and delightful expression is in the Regent's own Pavilion in Brighton. The Prince had versatile talents, expecially as a young man; he was handsome, could be a witty conversationalist, and had some taste in music. But he

Victoria & Albert Museum

ST. GEORGE AND THE DRAGON

15th-century carved oak chest in York Minster. By permission of the Dean and Chapter

was a heartless libertine, a spendthrift, an untrustworthy friend, and a bad son, husband, and father. In 1785, in spite of a secret and illegal marriage with a Roman Catholic widow, Mrs. Fitzherbert (which he denied), George, under pressure from his father, married Caroline of Brunswick. He treated her extremely badly, separating himself from her immediately after the birth of their only child. When he became King in 1820, he refused to acknowledge the Queen, excluded her from the Coronation, and began divorce proceedings in the House of Lords. These, however, were abandoned because of intense public feeling against the King, and the Queen died a year later.

Nevertheless, for all his personal failings, George IV was a skilful politician, often handling his Ministers with adroitness. He never pushed his own views to extremities; and he gave way on several questions (such as Catholic Emancipation in 1829) on which his Ministers were insistent. He quarrelled with his old friends, the Whigs, at the beginning of his Regency: later, he quarrelled with the extreme Tories. This left him without a large personal following in Parliament; and indirectly strengthened the power of the Cabinet, who could insist on their point of view, knowing that it would be difficult for the King to replace them.

At the end of his reign, his years of dissipation showed in his shattered constitution and bloated appearance. He began to suffer from delusions, thinking that he had led a charge at Waterloo and ridden a winning horse at Goodwood.

GEORGE, St. (*c.* 3rd century). Almost nothing is known for certain about St. George, the patron saint of England, whose day, 23 April, is the English national day. According to some accounts he was born in Cappadocia (now part of Turkey) and was burnt to death under the Roman Emperor Diocletian because he tore down an edict against the Christians at Nicomedia (near Istambul) on 23 April 303. The historian Gibbon confuses him with another George of Cappadocia, Bishop of Alexandria, who was torn to pieces by the mob in a revolt. There is no reason to doubt that St. George was a real person, and that he suffered martyrdom in one of the later persecutions of the Church. As early as the 5th century, or even earlier, churches in Syria were dedicated to him. By the 6th century his fame had spread widely in Europe, and by the 7th had reached Britain.

The cross, as representing the irresistible power of goodness, overthrowing the dragon, the symbol for the evil of the world, was a common idea in the early Church: the Christian Emperor CONSTANTINE (q.v.) is said to have had such a representation painted over the doorway of his palace. Therefore it is easy to see how the story of St. George's fight with the dragon grew, the chivalrous knight bearing the cross and the princess representing suffering humanity in need of rescue from the powers of evil.

In the 11th and 12th centuries the crusaders brought back stories of how St. George had appeared from heaven and driven back the infidels with celestial darts, supporting first

William the Conqueror's son Robert, and later Richard Coeur-de-Lion. This led to his formal adoption as English patron saint by Edward III in the 13th century, and the founding of St. George's Chapel, Windsor, in his honour.

See also Vol. I: SAINT; CRUSADES; DRAGON.

GIBBON, Edward (1737–94), *see* Vol. XII: HISTORIES.

GIBBONS, Grinling (1648–1720). This carver and sculptor, born in Rotterdam of English parents, came to England and, in 1671, was discovered by the diarist John Evelyn, who showed his work to King Charles II and also to WREN (q.v.). Gibbons is chiefly notable for his carving of naturalistic trails and festoons of fruit and flowers, cut in soft wood in very high relief. His great skill brought him many commissions for decoration, his most important works being at Windsor Castle, Whitehall Palace, Trinity College, Cambridge, Hampton Court Palace, and the choir stalls in St. Paul's Cathedral. He is said to have had a pot of carved flowers in his window so delicate that the flowers shook with the passing of coaches. His style was imitated by other carvers, and much work is often wrongly attributed to him. In 1693 he was

Royal Commission on Historical Monuments
CARVED OVERMANTEL BY GRINLING GIBBONS IN HAMPTON COURT PALACE
By gracious permission of H.M. the Queen

appointed Master Sculptor and Master Carver to the Crown. His sculpture is less remarkable than his woodcarving, the best example being the bronze statue of James II (now outside the National Gallery in London). He also carved a number of marble tombs.

See also Vol. XII: WOODCARVING.

GILBERT, Sir Humphrey (c. 1539–83). This pioneer of Elizabethan exploration was born near Dartmouth, in Devon. Half-brother of RALEIGH (q.v.), Gilbert was imaginative, intelligent, brave, restless, and grasping. He was educated, like the sons of many country gentlemen, at Eton and Oxford, and then found his way to Court and saw service abroad as a soldier. He drew up a remarkable scheme for the liberal education of royal wards, called *Queene Elizabethes Academie*, in which both modern and ancient languages were to be taught and book learning was to be combined with instruction in riding and shooting and soldiering. But his real interests are seen in his *Discourse of a Discoverie for a New Passage to Cataia* (China), which was later printed to announce FROBISHER's quest (q.v.) for the North-West Passage.

After an unsuccessful first expedition in 1583, Gilbert sailed with five ships to colonize NEW-FOUNDLAND (q.v. Vol. III), which he annexed, but returned almost immediately with the colonists. On his way back his two ships were separated by a storm, and the last that was seen of him before the lights of the *Squirrel* disappeared was 'sitting abaft with a book in his hand, crying out to us in the *Hind*, "We are as near to heaven by sea as by land"'. Raleigh's colony in Virginia was a continuation of Gilbert's dream of founding a British Empire overseas.

See also Vol. IV: EXPLORATION.
See also Vol. X: COLONIES, HISTORY OF.

GILBERT, Sir William (1836–1911), *see* SULLIVAN.

GIORGIONE (c. 1478–1510). The real name of this Italian painter was Giorgio. His home city was Castelfranco, near Venice. Very little is known of his short life; we do not know when he was born nor who taught him to paint, though it is supposed to have been one of the BELLINIS (q.v.). He was in his own time and still is considered one of the greatest painters. His pictures were extremely original, and most Venetian painters of the time, including TITIAN (q.v.), imitated him to some extent. In consequence, very soon after his death there were differences of opinion about which pictures were by him and which by his followers. This uncertainty has lasted until the present day—indeed, there is only a handful of pictures which are indisputably his.

Before Giorgione, most artists painted religious or mythological subjects or portraits, and centred the interest in the figures; landscape was used merely as a background with little importance. Giorgione's originality is shown, for example, in his small painting, 'The Tempest'. Landscape and figures are equally important; indeed, the figures seem part of the landscape, while the strange light, the rich colour, and the stormy sky contribute as much to the air of mystery as do the figures themselves. We do not know who the figures represent nor what they are doing. The picture has the unreal effect of a dream. Many of the small pictures by Giorgione and his followers have this same quality. Most typical of all are the paintings of two or three people making music, in which the sweet and sad qualities of the song are most clearly expressed.

See also Vol. XII: VENETIAN PAINTING.

Anderson

THE TEMPEST
Painting by Giorgione. Accademia, Venice

GIOTTO (*c.* 1266–1337). Giotto was the earliest of the great Italian painters. He came from Florence, but became so famous that he painted for the Pope in Rome, for the King of Naples, and for other great patrons. We know extremely little for certain of his life, though there are a great number of legends. It is not even certain that it was he who painted the frescoes of the life of St. Francis in the Upper Church of St. Francis at Assisi, though these— among the most famous pictures in the world— are usually attributed to him.

The first authentic paintings by Giotto are the frescoes in the Arena Chapel in Padua, which were painted in 1305. There are thirty-seven scenes from the lives of the Virgin and Christ painted along the walls of the chapel, and a Last Judgement over the entrance. One of these scenes, that of the parents of the Virgin, St. Joachim and St. Anne, meeting at the Golden Gate in Jerusalem, may stand as typical of the treatment of them all. The picture seems so simple that the skill of its design is not at first obvious. Attention is concentrated on the two principal figures by their position on the little bridge, which not only emphasizes their importance but isolates them from the four women beneath the arch on the right, who are treated as a group rather than as individuals. The tender and touching embrace of the solemn, elderly couple rouses the lively interest of the four women, in contrast to the lack of interest of the woman with the dark hood, who may be a beggar.

Nearly all Giotto's frescoes show these two principles—a dramatic representation of the story, and a careful arrangement of the setting to accentuate the principal figures. To his contemporaries Giotto's art seemed marvellously lifelike, for he obviously studied nature more closely than any other painter had done since Roman times. His scenes are arranged so that the figures look solid and have space around them in which they are free to move. Yet he had no real knowledge of the principles of anatomy and perspective, sciences which were only discovered a hundred years later by the great Florentine painters of the Renaissance. But the drama in Giotto's pictures and the simple grandeur of his figures are something which went beyond the mere copying of nature, and it is for this that he is still considered one of the greatest Italian painters.

Anderson

THE MEETING OF ST. JOACHIM AND ST. ANNE
Painting by Giotto. Arena Chapel, Padua

The frescoes painted by Giotto at Naples have disappeared, but there are paintings by him in the church of Santa Croce, Florence, and several attributed panel pictures. He designed at least part of the belfry of Florence Cathedral which bears his name (*see* picture, Vol. III, p. 167).

See also Vol. XII: FLORENTINE PAINTING.

GLADSTONE, William Ewart (1809–98).

Gladstone, one of the foremost figures of the Victorian age, was leader of the Liberal party for nearly a quarter of a century, and four times Prime Minister. The son of a rich Liverpool merchant, Gladstone was educated at Eton and Oxford, where he soon made a reputation as a debater in the Union Society. Indeed, he showed as a young man those qualities which were characteristic throughout his life: religious zeal, a mastery of subtle language, prodigious powers of work, and a tendency to look on most problems as contests between good and evil.

Gladstone had first intended to enter the Church; instead he became a member of Parliament at 23, but he never quite divorced religion from politics. He was at first a Conservative and, in Macaulay's phrase, 'the rising hope of those stern and unbending Tories'. His rise was rapid: he held junior office under Sir Robert

PEEL (q.v.), and when Peel formed his second Tory Ministry in 1841, Gladstone went to the Board of Trade and soon entered the Cabinet. This was one of the great formative periods of his life. He mastered thoroughly the details of trade and finance and, as always, was prepared to change his earlier opinions to accord with facts as he saw them. ('I have been a learner all my life', he said half a century later.) He soon began to realize, as did Peel, that protection for agriculture (to which the Conservatives were pledged) was not in the best interests of the country since it raised the price of food and was bitterly unpopular with manufacturers. In 1846 he supported Peel's repeal of the Corn laws—a measure which antagonized many landlords and broke the Conservative party.

For some 13 years Gladstone was out of sympathy with both major political parties, and seemed to have no career ahead of him. But in 1859, united by a common sympathy with the movement for Italian independence (*see* CAVOUR), he joined PALMERSTON (q.v.) in what was the first real Liberal Ministry.

As Chancellor of the Exchequer under Palmerston, Gladstone made a great reputation as a financier and reformer. Britain was growing steadily more prosperous, and Gladstone believed that the proper task of the State was to remove any barriers in the way of individual advancement, to diminish taxation (he hoped to abolish income-tax altogether) by lessening State expenditure, to reduce armaments, and to promote peace abroad and administrative reform at home. This policy strengthened his hold over the sympathies of middle- and working-class voters in the towns. But he often disagreed with Palmerston; it was said that the chimneys of 10 Downing Street smoked with Gladstone's letters of resignation.

In 1868 he became Prime Minister—the year in which DISRAELI (q.v.) achieved the leadership of the Conservatives and had himself been Prime Minister. The fierce rivalry between these two political giants of diametrically opposed characters dominated public life for the next 12 years.

Gladstone's first Ministry (1868–74) was one

Radio Times Hulton Lib.

GLADSTONE FELLING TREES AT HAWARDEN

as the Midlothian Campaign, helped to win the general election of 1880 for the Liberals.

His second Ministry (1880–5) was a period of frustration. New conditions were developing in Britain and abroad, which the older Liberal doctrines of individualism and the limited role of the State could not control. Although Gladstone disapproved of Imperialism, he was forced to intervene in Egypt and the Sudan when British interests there were threatened; and the death of GORDON (q.v.) in Khartoum brought him bitter unpopularity. Although he wished to conciliate Ireland, he was driven to govern by force. Obstruction in Parliament, both by Conservatives and by Irishmen, hampered his legislation, and the House of Lords threatened to reject his measures. The Reform Act of 1884 (giving the vote to agricultural workers) was passed only after an angry struggle. All this took place against a background of unemployment and distress which shook the mid-Victorian belief in inevitable progress.

In 1885 Gladstone resigned; but after a general election had brought him back into power with a narrow majority, he made the bold decision, without consulting his most important followers, that Ireland must have a Parliament of her own. He felt that this was not only just, but the only way to attain Irish friendship. This seemed to many the first step towards breaking up the Empire, and his Irish Home Rule Bill was defeated, splitting the Liberal party in two. From then on Gladstone concentrated on Irish Home Rule. In his fourth Ministry (1892–4) the Bill passed the Commons but was rejected by the Lords. Gladstone, by now growing blind and deaf, resigned in 1894 and died 4 years later.

Gladstone's inexhaustible energy continued almost to the last. Hundreds came to watch him felling trees, one of his favourite exercises, at his home in Hawarden; thousands stood and heard him, sometimes in cold and rain, at public meetings. As he grew older, he came to resemble an eagle with his high forehead and his flashing eye, which could be terrible in scorn, inspiring in praise. His public speaking was complex and involved, appealing to the reason rather than the emotions; he coined few splendid phrases, but he could make even a budget speech into a triumph of oratory. Though superb in moving the minds of the masses, he was unhappy in dealing with individuals, to

of the greatest of the century. He intended to pacify Ireland, where wretched social conditions and a growing movement for independence (*see* PARNELL) had joined hands in organized and violent agitation. He disestablished the English Church in Ireland and altered the Irish land laws in favour of the tenants. In England, he reorganized the army, abolished the purchase of commissions, opened the CIVIL SERVICE to public competition, admitted Nonconformists to the universities, introduced the secret ballot in Parliamentary ELECTIONS, and laid the foundations of universal elementary EDUCATION (qq.v. Vol. X). Nearly all these measures, however, angered sections of his supporters, and the general election of 1874 brought Disraeli to power.

In 1875 Gladstone resigned the Liberal leadership; but a year later his disapproval of Disraeli's foreign policy brought him again into opposition. A series of pamphlets and speeches, culminating in the tremendous orations known

whom he seemed cold, remote, over-dignified. He never understood how to deal with Queen VICTORIA (q.v.), and never broke down her deep hostility to him. She herself was never comfortable in his presence, and disapproved of his policies, which she thought revolutionary.

Gladstone was a legend in his own lifetime. To his supporters he was 'the Grand Old Man'; to his enemies a wild Radical, disrupting the constitution. In fact he never abandoned a certain conservatism, believing that timely reform might be the best way to prevent violent change. His name will always be associated with certain great principles: a belief in the dignity and worth of the individual, and progress through individual effort; belief in freedom of thought, speech, and conscience; a conviction that persuasion is better than force; and a belief in a universal justice ('the combined opinion of civilized Europe') that should transcend national interests and boundaries.

See also Vol. X: POLITICAL PARTIES.

GLENDOWER, Owen (*c.* 1354–1416). This Welsh national hero, the leader of a rebellion against Henry IV, is amusingly portrayed by Shakespeare in his play *Henry IV, Part I.* His name, Glyndwr (Glendower is an anglicized form), comes from a beautiful glen in the upper reaches of the river Dee, where the family lived. Some 80 years before his birth, when Wales had come under English rule (*see* EDWARD I), a few members of the old royal families were allowed to keep some of the lands which their ancestors had once ruled as princes. Both Owen's father and mother held such estates, and Owen succeeded to both inheritances.

Glendower received a sound social and military education in England—an unusual experience for even an upper-class Welshman in that period. He also served for a time in the King's army. His happy and prosperous family life has been vividly described for us by the native minstrels who frequented his home; their songs make it clear that his schooling in England had not made him insensitive to the culture and traditions of his own people.

In 1400, when Glendower was already middle-aged, a personal grievance against a neighbouring lord—an Englishman—for which he could get no redress, caused him to take the law into his own hands and to attack his enemy's castle and lands. The Welsh people, already discontented under English rule, were stirred by this action to take up arms once more against their oppressors. Within a few months Glendower found himself—whether by design or not we may never know—at the head of the last and most serious Welsh rebellion.

The rebels at first met with much success and soon had the greater part of Wales completely within their control. Glendower was proclaimed Prince of Wales; he summoned a national Parliament, planned to set up a separate Welsh Church and University, and entered into treaties of alliance with France and Scotland, and even with the King's leading enemies in England. But after 1406 the English forces gradually regained the whole country. Glendower himself held out for several years in the mountains of central Wales; but after 1412 he is heard of no more, though he evidently lived some 4 years longer, probably at Monnington, a secluded spot in Herefordshire, the home of one of his daughters.

Though Glendower failed to re-establish the independence of his people, one of his cousins founded a family from which Henry VII, the first Tudor King, was descended;

Reece Winstone

THE GATEHOUSE OF HARLECH CASTLE, CAPTURED BY OWEN GLENDOWER FROM THE ENGLISH IN 1404 and thus the aristocracy of Wales have their place in the ancestry of the British royal family of today. Owen Glendower remains in popular imagination the outstanding figure in the history of Wales.

See also Vol. I: WELSH.

GLUCK, Christoph Willibald von (1714–87). Gluck's father, a Bohemian (or what we should now call a Czech), was a forester working in Bavaria. When Christoph was 3 the family returned to Bohemia, where the boy was educated, and at 18 he went to the University of Prague. Having decided on a musical career, Gluck worked in Vienna and Italy, producing his first opera in Milan. He travelled widely and met many interesting people, including Handel, Haydn, Mozart, Voltaire, Rousseau, and Marie-Antoinette, who was his pupil. Much of the later part of his life was spent in Vienna, where he died.

Gluck was almost exclusively an opera composer, though he wrote some ballet music, notably *Don Juan* (1761). His early operas were in the universally popular Italian style, a style which made almost no attempt to present the story of the opera dramatically, and was little

Kunsthistorisches Museum, Vienna
GLUCK AT THE PIANOFORTE
Portrait by J. S. Duplessis, 1775

more than a setting for singers. But in *Orpheus and Eurydice* (1762) Gluck began to express the story and the feelings of the characters sincerely and dramatically, and to make the music and the singers serve this end. That is what he meant when he said, 'when I sit down to write an opera I try to forget that I am a musician'. In the Preface to his opera *Alcestis* (1767) he said he was seeking 'a beautiful simplicity'. Such ideas, although they had been forgotten, were not new: they had been pursued by Monteverdi well over 100 years before in Italy.

These operas, and also *Paris and Helen* (1770), were first produced in Vienna. Later *Iphigenia in Aulis* (1774) and *Iphigenia in Tauris* (1779) were produced in Paris, where the new-style operas caused immense controversy between Gluck's supporters and those who preferred the Italian style.

See also WAGNER.
See also Vol. XII: OPERA, HISTORY OF.

GOETHE, Johann Wolfgang von (1749–1832). Germany's greatest poet, the author of *Faust*, was born at Frankfort-on-the-Main of well-to-do parents. He had a happy childhood, early showing that vivid response to experience which characterized him all his life. At 16 he went to study law at the University of Leipzig, then an intellectual and social centre with a rather artificial classical tradition. Here he attended an art academy, wrote light verse, and enjoyed student life to the full. At the end of his first year he fell seriously ill; a long convalescence gave him time to think much about religious and philosophical problems. Early in 1770 he went to Strasburg, studying medicine there as well as law. Here he had his first experience of love, with the pastor's daughter, Friederike Brion. He also met Herder, a writer who was opening up a new era in German intellectual life and from whom he absorbed the flood of new ideas then sweeping over Europe (*see* ROMANTIC MOVEMENT, Vol. XII).

During the summer of 1772, spent at Wetzlar, Goethe's love for Charlotte Buffe gave him the basis of his novel *The Sorrows of Werther* (1774), which consists mainly of letters written by the hero, embodying the despairs and exaltations of Goethe's own youth, and which ends with the hero's tragic suicide. He also published an historical prose tragedy *Götz von Berlichingen* which, with some of his early lyrics, made him famous throughout Europe. These years of youth were marked by an immense richness of inspiration— much more, including the *Faust* tragedy, being already alive in his imagination.

When he was 26, Goethe went to be the friend and counsellor of the young Duke of Weimar in central Germany. His physical beauty and his abounding vitality and genius rather alarmed the sedate court circle. A friendship with Frau von Stein, the wife of a court official, developed into a deep attachment, and his love-poetry of this period was inspired by her. For some 10 years he devoted himself to his State duties, for he held a number of important posts which demanded responsibility and hard work.

All this time he felt a passionate longing for Italy, and in 1786 he went to Rome and spent 2 years studying the principles of classic art. This great experience of his life turned the young romantic writer into the representative classical poet of Germany. The immediate results are the poetic dramas *Iphigenie auf Tauris* and *Torquato Tasso*. On his return to Weimar, Germany seemed to Goethe barbaric and intellectually uncouth; and he immersed himself in scientific studies, which all his life had deeply interested him. He produced a number of scientific works on optics, on anatomy, on colour, and on natural history. He again fell in love, this time with a girl called Christiane Vulpius, who bore him a son and whom he married in 1806. In 1794, he met Schiller (q.v.) at a scientific gathering, and so began a famous friendship which lasted until Schiller's death in 1805. It was Schiller who inspired Goethe to finish his *Faust*, the great drama of man's search for spiritual satisfaction, completed only in the last year of his life. Goethe died in Weimar at the age of 82.

Goethe was above all a great personality. Both emotionally and intellectually he lived an extremely full life. As a lyric poet, he expressed

Städelsches Kunstinstitut, Frankfurt

GOETHE AMONG RUINS NEAR ROME
Painting by J. H. W. Tischbein

the deepest feelings in verses which are superb in beauty of form and loveliness of sound. His art as a song-writer culminates in the poems written for the early version of his novel, *Wilhelm Meister*, and made familiar by the musical settings of his great contemporaries, Beethoven and Schubert (qq.v.). The completed *Wilhelm Meister*, which is the study of the forming of a young man's character through the experiences of life, established what was to become a national type—the novel of an education. Though less satisfactory in form than the earlier *Werther*, it embodied Goethe's most mature wisdom. Although *Faust*, Goethe's masterpiece, may be called a poetic-philosophical drama, Goethe was not a philosopher in the strict sense, but his view of man and the world he lived in was profound. He held that man's true purpose is not to know why the world is what it is, but to discover and obey the natural laws which govern its life— laws of ordered development and patient obedience. It was by such principles that he governed his own life, achieving in this way a balanced and harmonious personality.

See also Vol. XII: German Literature; Faust.

GOGH, Vincent Van (1853–90), Dutch painter, *see* Vol. XII: Post-Impressionist Painting.

National Portrait Gallery

OLIVER GOLDSMITH
Studio of Reynolds, *c.* 1770

GOLDSMITH, Oliver (1728–74). The author of *The Vicar of Wakefield* was an Irishman, the son of a clergyman. After taking his degree at Trinity College, Dublin, he led a wandering life, mostly on the Continent, earning his living by playing the flute. He arrived in London in 1756 without any money and, after some 3 years of extreme poverty, he tried his hand at journalism, writing among other things some excellent essays for the periodical magazines. In 1761 he met Dr. JOHNSON (q.v.) and was elected a member of the famous Literary Club. In 1764 he published a long poem, *The Traveller*, impressions of his wanderings through Europe written with the greatest charm and simplicity. In the same year, according to Boswell, Johnson, finding Goldsmith besieged by his landlady for the rent, discovered a manuscript of a novel, which he took to the booksellers and sold for £60, thus freeing Goldsmith from debt. This novel was *The Vicar of Wakefield*, the charming, sentimental story of Dr. Primrose and his family. Another fine poem, *The Deserted Village*, describes 18th-century rural England. An exuberant, farcical comedy, *She Stoops to Conquer*, very different from the sentimental comedy then in fashion, added to Goldsmith's reputation.

Goldsmith was unpractical, generous, and irresponsible, but a man of great charm, much loved by his many friends.

GORDON, Charles George (1833–85). This British soldier, colonial administrator, and philanthropist, died defending Khartoum against a rebel Sudanese army, and crowned a hero's life with a death which many people at the time regarded as a martyrdom.

Gordon was a Regular Army engineer who had served in the Crimean War, and had taken part in the capture of Peking in 1860, during the war between Britain and China. At the request of the Chinese Government he entered the Chinese service to put down outbreaks of rebellion; and he fashioned the small native army he was given into a brilliant hard-fighting unit. The rebellion was crushed, and Gordon, refusing the lavish gifts which the Chinese offered him, returned to England to take command of the engineers' garrison at Gravesend. There, in his leisure, he gave his time and money to helping the children of the poor, organizing 'ragged schools', and doing his best to give promising boys a start in life.

At 43 Gordon was appointed by the Khedive of Egypt to govern Sudan at a salary of £10,000, but he accepted only £2,000. He brought peace and order to much of this vast territory, which for years had been the hunting-ground of slave-traders. A few years later, after he had retired, the British Government pressed him to return to the Sudan as Governor-General to deal with an armed revolt under the leadership of the Mahdi. Gordon was ordered to evacuate, or at least to report on evacuating, the threatened Egyptian garrisons; Egypt had been told to abandon the Sudan.

When Gordon reached Khartoum the government at home thought that he was trying to exceed his orders. Gordon, instead of withdrawing, talked exaltedly of 'smashing the Mahdi'; but a few weeks later Khartoum was surrounded. After months of delay, the British Prime Minister, GLADSTONE (q.v.), decided to send an expedition to rescue Gordon. An advance guard, sailing up the Nile, arrived in sight of Khartoum only to find that the town had fallen 2 days before. Gordon had organized the defences for 317 days of siege with a dispirited garrison of mixed races, and with supplies running so low that bread was made from the bark of trees. Eventually the Mahdi's forces had broken through the defences and had killed Gordon on the steps of the Palace. His head was severed and carried to the Mahdi; his body was flung down a well and has never been found. Gordon's death sent a thrill of horror through England. He had long been a national hero, and, from the Queen downwards, the country held the British Government responsible for his death.

Gordon was an outstanding example of the strenuous Christianity of Victorian England. Deeply religious, he believed it his duty to surrender himself to God's will. He was never an easy subordinate; he had a quick temper, whose heat was matched by the remorse which followed its outbursts. His selflessness, his indifference to reward, and his almost mystical courage impressed all those who knew him. Years after his death, it was commonly said among the Sudanese that, had Gordon only been of the Moslem faith he would have been nearly a perfect man.

GOYA, Francisco de (1746–1828). The Spanish painter Francisco José de Goya y Lucientes was born near Saragossa. He studied painting in Spain and, for a short time, in Italy, and by the age of 30 had settled in Madrid. His first important commission was a series of designs for royal tapestries. He also began etching, and continued to turn out prints throughout his life. From 1785 onwards he undertook more and more portrait-painting; he was appointed one of the court painters in 1789, and later became the senior court painter.

When Goya was 46 a severe illness left him almost completely deaf. In the bitter loneliness

Anderson

PAINTING BY GOYA OF THE 3RD OF MAY, 1808
This depicts the execution by French soldiers of the defenders of Madrid during the Spanish Peninsular War.
Prado, Madrid

that he then felt, he produced the *Caprichos*, a series of satirical etchings mocking contemporary Spanish society. Goya held his position as senior court painter throughout Napoleon's occupation of Spain; but in spite of this he expressed his hatred of the French invaders and war in general in a series of etchings depicting violence and brutality, known as *Disasters of War*. Copies of this series spread Goya's fame in many countries. When the French were expelled, Goya again served the Spanish Court, but he found the new king a tyrant, so he emigrated to France, and died at Bordeaux 4 years later.

At first Goya followed the style of earlier Italian painters who had worked in Spain, but he himself, at a later date, said that his real masters had been 'Velazquez, Rembrandt, and Nature'. It is true that only when he had studied the work of VELAZQUEZ (q.v.) was he able to evolve a completely personal style which allowed him to express himself fully. The etchings of REMBRANDT (q.v.), too, certainly inspired much of his later work, above all the haunted fantasies of the *Caprichos* and the *Disasters of War*. Goya painted hundreds of portraits, many of them mere pot-boilers, although, when moved by the personality of his model, he was capable of delicate feeling and understanding. The most important part of his work, however, is the great series of paintings and etchings of 1794 onwards in which he satirized and denounced human stupidity and cruelty with a passionate sincerity that has rarely been equalled.

Goya had no following of any consequence in his own country, but his influence on French 19th-century painting has been great.

See also Vol. XII: SPANISH ART.

GRACE, William Gilbert (1848–1915). W. G. Grace, probably the greatest of all cricketers, transformed a game into a national institution. In an unparalleled career of 43 years of first-class cricket, he scored 54,896 runs, played 126 innings of 100 runs and over, and took 2,876 wickets.

'W.G.' (other nicknames included 'The Old Man' and 'The Champion') was a doctor by profession. He had first played for the Gentlemen of England when he was 17. In 1876, at the peak of his career, he made 400 not out, and in three successive innings scored 344, 177, and 318 not out. In the first Test Match to be played in England against Australia he made 152. He

Meade Collection

MENU OF THE DINNER GIVEN TO CELEBRATE W. G. GRACE'S HUNDREDTH CENTURY

played his last first-class match in 1908, when he was 60.

Grace's burly frame, his great black beard, and his characteristic stance at the wicket with the left toe cocked skywards, were familiar all over England. Notices outside grounds sometimes read: 'Admission 6d. If Dr. Grace plays, Admission 1s.' Though most remarkable as a batsman, Grace was also a cunning bowler and a master of the craft of captaincy. It was difficult to get the better of him at any point; he never broke the rules, it was said, but he could do remarkable things to his own advantage within them.

See also Vol. IX: CRICKET, HISTORY OF.

GRANT, Ulysses Simpson (1822–85). This American general commanded the victorious Northern forces in the AMERICAN CIVIL WAR (q.v. Vol. X), and was twice President of the United States. Grant, who was a superb horseman, first served with distinction in the Mexican War (1845–8). But he soon acquired the reputation of being an excessive drinker, and, when he

was 32, resigned his commission to avoid being tried by court-martial.

In civil life, as a farmer and salesman, Grant was a failure. When the American Civil War broke out in 1861 he at once answered President LINCOLN's call for volunteers (q.v.). His bad reputation clung to him, however, and he gained an appointment as colonel only after several rebuffs. But officers were badly needed for the huge, untrained Northern armies, and once enlisted, Grant was soon promoted to brigadier-general. In February 1862 he won a notable victory by capturing a Southern stronghold and over 14,000 prisoners. Again there were stories of his heavy drinking, and but for Lincoln's personal support he would probably not have kept his command.

Off the battlefield, Grant was undistinguished, even seedy in appearance; his dress was slovenly, and he was nearly always chewing or smoking a cigar. But behind these externals Lincoln recognized Grant's great physical and moral courage, and at a time when the Northern forces were discouraged and badly led, a commander of Grant's iron determination was highly valued.

The next year Grant repaid Lincoln's confidence by a brilliant campaign of manœuvre and hard fighting, ending in the capture of Vicksburg with 30,000 prisoners and over 170 cannon. Three months later he had driven the enemy from Tennessee, and in the following year was appointed general-in-chief of all the Northern forces. By then the North was clearly superior to the enemy in manpower and resources, and had plenty of reserves. Grant was determined, as he said, 'to hammer continuously against the armed force of the enemy until by mere attrition, if in no other way, there should be nothing left to him but . . . submission'.

For the grim campaigns which followed Grant concentrated his forces into several armies, all moving simultaneously against the South. Whilst Generals Sherman, Sheridan, and Thomas moved in wide, sweeping movements to strike round the flanks into the heart of the South, Grant, in the centre, gripped General LEE's main Southern army (q.v.) and hammered and ground it into exhaustion. Lee defended stubbornly, but Grant was prepared 'to fight it out on this line, if it takes all the summer'. His losses were heavy, but he knew that the South was, proportionately, suffering more heavily still. At length Grant drove Lee back into hastily pre-pared trenches near Richmond. Confined there, and blocked from all escape, Lee was left with the alternatives of annihilation or surrender. Grant's strategy was brilliantly developed, and his other widely scattered armies raced forward deep into Southern territory. Thirteen months after launching his offensive, Grant accepted Lee's surrender at Appomattox, and the war was virtually at an end.

In the North, Grant was now a symbol of victory. He found himself drawn into politics, first as Secretary of War and then as the successful Republican candidate for the Presidency. But as a statesman he was on unfamiliar ground, and his two terms as President were a failure. His friends were untrustworthy, and there were ugly scandals throughout his terms of office, some involving charges of corruption against his closest associates.

Eight years after his retirement Grant lost all his savings in a bank-failure, and was reduced to poverty. To save himself and his family he began to write his memoirs. Though in agony from cancer, he struggled on to complete them only 4 days before he died, and their publication in the following year provided a small fortune for his widow.

Grant's courage in this last battle did much to efface the unpleasant memories of his Presidency, and when he died his popularity was restored.

GRAY, Thomas (1716–71), Poet, *see* Vol. XII: ELEGY.

GRECO, El (*c.* 1546–1614). This Spanish painter, Domenikos Theotokopoulos, generally known by his Spanish nickname of 'El Greco' (the Greek), was born in Crete, which at that time belonged to the Venetian Republic. Nothing is known of his early years, but a few pictures have survived which show that he began by painting in the style of BYZANTINE ART (q.v. Vol. XII). He went to Italy, and seems to have studied in Venice as a pupil of TITIAN (q.v.), later going to Rome. He developed a style based partly on Titian and to a lesser extent on other Venetian painters, which was later modified by his study of MICHELANGELO (q.v.).

There is a story that El Greco left Italy for Spain to escape the resentment of the Roman artists after he had boasted that if Michelangelo's *Last Judgment* in the Sistine Chapel were destroyed he would paint another just as good. It

Mas, Barcelona

ASSUMPTION OF THE BLESSED VIRGIN
Painting by El Greco. San Vicente Museum, Toledo

Spanish poet, Luis de Góngora, who wrote a sonnet in his memory when he died.

It was in Spain that El Greco developed fully the highly individual and vivid style by which he is best known. There are several contemporary references to the extravagance of his paintings; for example, Francisco Pacheco, father-in-law of the painter VELAZQUEZ (q.v.), who visited his studio some years before his death, speaks of him as 'singular in everything, as he was in painting'. The distortion of natural forms and the violent contrasts of colour and light, which El Greco took from the Byzantine tradition and contemporary Italian painters, became in his hands the means of giving the greatest possible expressiveness and drama to his mystical imagination. Many writers criticized him, but as many others valued his work truly.

There are many repetitions and variants of most of his compositions. He himself often painted several of each, and still more were produced in his studio by his assistants.

See also Vol. XII: SPANISH ART.

GREGORY THE GREAT (*c.* A.D. 540–604). In the 6th century, when the centre of the old Roman Empire had become established at Constantinople, and Italy was subject to attacks by barbarians, the man who filled the office of Bishop of Rome, or Pope, had to be not only the head of the Church but also a wise leader in worldly affairs. Gregory was particularly well suited to carry out this double duty.

Gregory, born in Rome of wealthy and aristocratic parents, received a good education. His father was a government official, and Gregory himself, when little more than 30 years old, was made chief magistrate of Rome. But on his father's death he became a monk, devoting most of his fortune to pious uses, and living with extreme austerity. As soon as he had been ordained, he was sent as the Pope's representative to Constantinople, where one of his chief tasks was to try to obtain military help for Italy against barbarian invasions. But in spite of these duties his heart was with his few companions in the monastery; for he describes himself as 'bound, as by an anchor's chain, when tossing in the waves of secular affairs, to the quiet shore of prayer'.

When he was about 45, he left Constantinople to spend 5 happy years as abbot of his beloved monastery in Rome. But in 590, when the Pope

was quite in El Greco's character to have made such a boast, but, in fact, he probably went to Spain to seek work in decorating the palace-monastery of the Escorial, on which King Philip II was spending much money.

El Greco settled in Toledo, but he painted only two pictures for the King, for he failed to please him. He painted countless pictures, however, for churches and monasteries not only in Toledo, where he spent the rest of his life, but also throughout central Spain. He had many learned friends in Toledo, among them the great

died, all Rome, clergy and laity alike, persuaded Gregory, much against his will, to succeed him. A hard task lay before him. He himself compares Rome to an old and shattered ship, leaking on all sides, beaten by continual tempests, and in imminent danger of becoming a wreck. Yet in the $13\frac{1}{2}$ years of Gregory's papacy the ship weathered the storm.

It was probably during his early life as a monk that Gregory saw the Saxon boys from Britain in the slave market at Rome, and on being told that they were Angles (*Angli*), remarked that they looked like angels (*angeli*). This incident made him wish very much to bring Christianity to Britain, and although it was impossible for him to go himself, when he became Pope, he sent Augustine with a small band of monks to Kent in 597 to convert the Anglo-Saxons and to make contact with the Celtic Church in the west.

Although he was far from strong, Gregory

POPE GREGORY WITH THREE SCRIBES
Ivory relief, 9th century. The Holy Spirit, in the form of a dove, inspires the Saint

displayed immense energy. His daily activities are described in detail in his many letters, which are preserved. Men appealed to him for advice and accepted his judgements not only in Italy, but in Gaul and Spain, North Africa, and Britain. He kept a strict discipline in the Church, deposing offenders from their offices and correcting abuses in the monasteries. The four great Councils, of Nicaea, Constantinople, Ephesus, and Chalcedon, had formulated the main doctrines of the Christian faith, and Gregory, having no theological disputes to trouble him, was able to give his whole attention to pastoral and administrative work. Thus he paved the way for the claims to universal authority made by later Popes.

Gregory appointed officers to administer efficiently the landed estates that had been left as endowments to the Church. He wrote letters to these officers, which reveal his interest in all that was going on and his desire that nothing should be done in his name of which the Church need be ashamed.

Gregory left many writings, including a book on *Pastoral Care* for bishops and priests, which was very popular for centuries and which King Alfred translated into English. The Gregorian Sacramentary was a revision of the older Roman service of the Mass to which he had made certain changes and additions. He was also interested in Church music, and founded a school for choristers in Rome.

See also Vol. XII: PLAINSONG.

GRENVILLE, Sir Richard (*c.* 1541–91), *see* RALEIGH. *See also* Vol. IV: REVENGE, H.M.S.

GRIEG, Edvard Hagerup (*c.* 1843–1907). This Norwegian composer, grandson of a Scotsman, was born at Bergen into a musical household. His mother, a good pianist, began to teach her son when he was 6. When he was 15 he travelled to Leipzig in Germany for musical training, where he worked so hard that he became very ill with pleurisy. This left him with poor health for the rest of his life; but he completed his studies with honours, and returned to Norway determined to write music that could properly be called Norwegian. He did, in fact, find a musical style all his own, as the smallest of his songs or piano pieces shows. He also composed orchestral pieces and full-size chamberworks, and one Piano Concerto—probably his best-known work excepting the incidental music to IBSEN's *Peer Gynt* (q.v.). In 1867, when he was established as a composer, he married his cousin, the singer Nina Hagerup, and wrote for her many lovely songs, perhaps his most typical music. His gentle harmonies evoke the scene and atmosphere of the poems he set to music; but, above all, Grieg was a writer of tunes.

GRIMALDI, Joseph (1779–1837). 'Joey' was a great English clown during that curious period in the history of the theatre when acting was at its finest, contemporary drama at its lowest, and playgoers loved the tinsel of HARLEQUINADE AND PANTOMIME (q.v. Vol. IX). The 'picture-frame' stage, as we know it now, was introduced in the 1820's; gas-lighting was on the way; the theatre had begun to change. Grimaldi was to the comic stage of the time as Edmund KEAN (q.v.) was to the tragic theatre. No one could match him in his invention and delicate clowning. He was the theatre's Master of the Drolls, and the song that he made famous, 'Hot Codlins',

> A little old woman her living she got
> By selling codlins hot, hot, hot . . .

GRIMALDI AT HIS LAST BENEFIT PERFORMANCE
Illustration by George Cruikshank from *Memoirs of Joseph Grimaldi*, 1828

was remembered and revived for many years after his death. So, too, were 'Tippitywitchet' and 'An Oyster crossed in love'. The critic, Leigh HUNT (q.v.), wrote of Grimaldi's performance in pantomime, 'Though he scarcely ever utters a syllable, he is a more entertaining and even elegant performer than many who talk well enough.' Hunt went on to talk of Grimaldi's grins and shoulder-shakings, his short and deep snatches of laughter, 'all those perfections of the clown which before this time perhaps were confined to the Italian stage'.

Grimaldi, himself of Italian descent, the illegitimate son of a comedian who was ballet-master at Drury Lane, was not 3 years old when he first danced at Sadler's Wells. When his father died, he played at Sadler's Wells and Drury Lane on the same night, running between the two theatres, where he was, for a time, a silent actor in dramatic spectacles. But in 1806, in a *Mother Goose* pantomime at Drury Lane, he first showed his genius as a clown. He was all manner of other things: a superb acrobat, dancer, and comic singer, galvanic in his energy. As a clown he revelled in mischievous schoolboy tricks.

Grimaldi made his last appearance in 1828. His family life was unhappy, and towards the end of his life the great comedian became a lonely cripple. He died in his sleep during the summer of 1837, and was buried, near his last lodgings, on Pentonville Hill. But 'Joey's' fame lived on; and probably no comedian in any age has won so much public affection.

See also Vol. IX: CLOWNS.

GRIMM, Jacob (1785–1863) and **Wilhelm** (1786–1859). These two brothers, authors of the world-famous collection of German fairy-tales, were both learned students of German language and literature, and both became professors in Berlin. Wilhelm was the more sociable, Jacob the greater scholar. It was Jacob who established philology, or the study of languages, as a science by his researches into the origins of German and related languages.

The brothers were also serious mythologists. They made a great collection of folk-tales and ballads during their researches among ancient books, and learned many more from country people. These they published, and English translations of these *Popular Stories* soon appeared with spirited illustrations by George Cruikshank.

Some of their folk-tales are a good deal more savage than the average modern fairy-tale, but *Snow White, The Goose Girl, Rumpelstiltskin,* and *Hansel and Gretel* are among the most famous and popular children's stories in the world.

See also Vol. I: FAIRY TALES.

GROTIUS, Hugo (1583–1645). Grotius, the son of a distinguished Dutch burgomaster of Leyden, became an important religious philosopher and authority on law, especially international law. He was born at a time when Holland had practically thrown off the domination of Spain and had established a peaceful republic under the leadership of Maurice, son of WILLIAM THE SILENT (q.v.).

Holland had accepted the Protestant religion in the CALVINIST form (q.v. Vol. I), and bitter controversies were beginning to arise over the meaning of certain doctrines, especially predestination. Grotius took part in these controversies, which roused violent political as well as religious passions; and in 1618, when Prince Maurice, for the sake of peace, repressed the disputes, Grotius was sentenced to imprisonment for life. Grotius's wife, after 2 years' noble work on his behalf, effected his escape, and they took refuge in France, never to return to their native land. Grotius entered the Swedish diplomatic service and became ambassador to France, work in which he was neither very successful nor happy. He died at 63, on his way back from Stockholm.

Grotius is chiefly remembered now for his work on INTERNATIONAL LAW (q.v. Vol. X), and for his famous book the *Law of War and Peace*. By the 16th and 17th centuries the international authority of the Roman Catholic Church, which had united Europe in the Middle Ages, had disappeared, and strong national States were growing up (*see* NATION AND STATE, Vol. X). Grotius was the first to try to establish the existence of principles of right between nations, independent of religious beliefs, and to lay the foundations of a science of international law. He was, for instance, an early advocate of the principle of the freedom of the seas. So successful was his work that its influence lasted almost up to the present time.

The outstanding feature of Grotius's character was a strong desire for peace and concord. His work, therefore, on law was more in accord with his nature than his religious controversies.

Ashmolean Museum

HUGO GROTIUS
Contemporary engraving

Grotius saw no need for quarrels between the sects, and recognized no insuperable barrier to Protestant co-operation with the Church of Rome. But in this he was opposed to the spirit of his age.

See also Vol. I: CALVINIST; REFORMATION.
See also Vol. X: INTERNATIONAL LAW.

GUSTAVUS ADOLPHUS (1594–1632). This famous Swedish King, the 'Lion of the North', the most outstanding military leader of the Thirty Years War, had been educated to the idea that he should be the defender of Protestantism in the North. He was immensely talented. As a young child he spoke German almost as well as Swedish, and learnt Latin, Italian, and Dutch. Later, he also mastered enough Spanish, Russian, and Polish to be able to express himself. By the age of 13 he was able to take an intelligent part in public affairs, and by 15 he was given sole charge of his own Duchy of Vestmanland. He came to the throne when he was only 17. The first 6 years of his reign he spent making peace in the Baltic region and bringing the wars with Denmark and Russia to an end. Then war was renewed with Sweden's old rival, Poland, a long-drawn-out war in which Gustavus, though not completely successful, gained valuable experience.

GVSTAVO ADOLPHO D.G. SVECORVM REX

Ashmolean Museum

GUSTAVUS ADOLPHUS
Contemporary engraving

In 1629 Gustavus decided to come to the defence of the north German Protestants in their struggle against the Catholic League led by the fervently Catholic Emperor Ferdinand and his brilliant General WALLENSTEIN (q.v.). Gustavus not only wanted to support the German Protestants but also to gain control of Germany's Baltic ports, and forward his project of maintaining the Baltic Sea as a Swedish 'lake'. The German Protestants, though glad of his help against the Catholics, were opposed to his plans for the Baltic, and consequently they did not entirely welcome his intervention. They also disliked his scheme for a predominantly Protestant German Federation, with Gustavus as its head.

Gustavus landed in Germany in the summer of 1630. He cleared Pomerania, forced the Protestant Electors (rulers) of Brandenburg and Saxony rather unwillingly on to his side, and made a treaty with France, by which he received subsidies. In September 1631 he thoroughly defeated the Catholic general, Tilly, at Breitenfeld, north of Leipzig. He then moved over to the Rhine, and, sweeping south, occupied Frankfort and Mainz. By May 1632, he was in Munich, but then marched northwards, not trusting the loyalty of the Elector of Saxony. He met the Emperor's army under Wallenstein at Lützen on 6 November, and in the indecisive battle that followed Gustavus, getting separated from his main army in a thick mist, was killed.

As a general, his fame rests for the most part on his modernization of land warfare. He used his ARTILLERY (q.v. Vol. X) brilliantly, and his troops, besides being put into a distinctive uniform, also carried better muskets than their enemies. His German campaign may have been faulty at times in its strategy, but his energy, tactical brilliance, and actual achievements made the Swedes an important power in Europe for many years. He was a man of passionate sincerity and integrity, a wise statesman, and a great leader of men. He was succeeded by his only child, a daughter, Christina.

See also CHRISTINA OF SWEDEN.
See also Vol. I: SWEDES.

GWYNN, Nell (1651–87), Actress, *see* CHARLES II.

H

HADRIAN (A.D. 76–138). Succeeding the Emperor TRAJAN (q.v.), who had expanded the Roman Empire by conquest, Hadrian's task was to strengthen its frontiers and to establish an efficient administration. He travelled up and down his great Empire, tirelessly inspecting and reorganizing, interviewing officials, and having roads and temples built. Typical of his work was the great wall in Britain from Tyne to Solway which marked the north-western extremity of the Empire.

The Roman civil service had grown up at random; Hadrian turned it into an organized service offering a regular career to men of the middle classes. He codified the Roman law, making it a fixed law for the whole Empire. He was a benefactor wherever he went, a patron of learning and a founder of libraries.

This zealous administrator baffled and sometimes alienated his contemporaries by his artistic and unpredictable temperament. He painted and sang; wrote verse, and was a patron of literature; on his tours he made a point of visiting all the ancient monuments; he even climbed a mountain to watch the sun rise.

See also Vol. I: ROMAN CIVILIZATION.
See also Vol. X: LAW, HISTORY OF.

HAKLUYT, Richard (c. 1552–1616). This writer's *Principall Navigations, Traffiques and Discoveries of the English Nation* has been called the epic of the English because it describes in heroic language the Elizabethan seamen's 'high courage and singular activity in the search and discovery of the most unknown quarters of the world'. But Hakluyt was more than a chronicler: he was a geographer, an economist, and a patriot who, foreseeing the maritime destiny of England, played a practical part in the advancement of exploration, though he never went to sea himself.

As well as his vision of an empire beyond the seas, Hakluyt had the historian's regard for truth.

He came of an old Herefordshire family who pronounced the name 'Hacklit'. In the noble dedication of his book he tells how, as a scholar at Westminster, he first took a 'rare delight' in geography as a result of visiting a cousin on whose table he saw 'certain books of cosmography with a universal map'. He studied the subject at Oxford and became a lecturer there, at the same time learning from returning mariners all that he could about their voyages. When he published the first edition of his book in 1589 he allowed the mariners, where possible, to describe their voyages in their own words, though he rewrote some accounts himself. The second larger edition which appeared in 1600 included the first English world map on Mercator's projection (*see* MAP PROJECTIONS, Vol. IV). All his life he collected materials and advanced the arguments necessary to promote exploration, trade, and overseas settlement, particularly in Virginia and in the East Indies. A further collection of Hakluyt's manuscripts was printed by a disciple, Samuel Purchas, and the modern Hakluyt Society, founded in 1846, continues the same sort of work.

Hakluyt is buried in Westminster Abbey, where he was a prebendary for some years.

British Museum

INDIAN VILLAGE OF POMEIOC IN VIRGINIA

This village was reached by the colonists in 1585, and is described in the third volume of Hakluyt's *Principall Navigations*. Drawing by John White

HALS, Frans (*c.* 1580–1666), *see* Vol. XII: DUTCH ART.

HAMILTON, Alexander (1757–1804). This American statesman played a leading part in drawing up the present AMERICAN CONSTITUTION (q.v. Vol. X). He was also one of the founders of the American Republican party (then called the Federalist party).

When the AMERICAN WAR OF INDEPENDENCE (q.v. Vol. X) broke out Hamilton joined the rebel army, and at 20 became an important member of General WASHINGTON's staff (q.v.). After the war he turned his attention to politics, and was elected to Congress. The States were then nearly bankrupt, and Hamilton felt that the country needed a new constitution. Largely through the efforts of Hamilton and also James Madison a meeting was called in Philadelphia in 1787 for this purpose. Hamilton himself wanted to set up a republic with a strong central government, and was opposed to granting any great powers to the separate States. Though his plan was set aside, he supported the constitution in its final form by a series of essays, written in collaboration with Madison, which became famous as the *Federalist Papers*, and which remains one of the greatest political works in the English language. The following year Hamilton helped to start what is now known as the Republican party.

When the new government was formed in 1789, Hamilton, who was then only 32, was appointed Secretary of the Treasury. His financial policy did much for the welfare of the new nation, though his attempts to win greater authority for the central government led to several clashes with Thomas JEFFERSON (q.v.), then Secretary of State and the leader of the Democratic party. At the age of 47 Hamilton was killed in a duel by an embittered political rival.

See also Vol. X: AMERICAN CONSTITUTION.

HAMPDEN, John (1594–1643). Hampden, a cousin of CROMWELL, was one of the leaders in Parliament's quarrel with CHARLES I (qq.v.). In 1638 he won fame by his refusal to pay SHIP MONEY (q.v. Vol. X). The principle at stake was whether or not the King could levy taxes without the consent of Parliament. The judges finally decided for the King, but by a majority of only seven to five. This was looked upon as

Ashmolean Museum

JOHN HAMPDEN
Drawing by H. F. Gravelot (1699–1773)

a moral victory for Hampden, and other people began to default in payment. Hampden was closely associated with John Pym, especially in the IMPEACHMENT (q.v. Vol. X) of Charles's advisors Buckingham and later STRAFFORD (q.v.), Hampden doing the work behind the scenes and Pym taking the more prominent part.

When the CIVIL WAR (q.v. Vol. X) broke out, Hampden raised a regiment of infantry for Parliament, but was killed early in the war in a minor skirmish on Chalgrove Field, Oxon. He was a political leader in the background, a debater and committee man rather than an orator. But he was regarded as among the subtlest and most dangerous of the King's enemies, although among the most honourable and sincere.

See also CHARLES I.
See also Vol. X: CIVIL WAR.

HANDEL, George Frederick (1685–1759). The German composer, Handel, who later became a naturalized Englishman, was born in the same year as BACH (q.v.). His father, a doctor, though recognizing his son's talent for music, was determined he should be a lawyer. Handel, however, used to practise secretly at night, and when he was 8 the Duke of Saxony was so much impressed by his playing that he persuaded Handel's father to let him take up music. After studying in Berlin and Hamburg, where his first opera *Almira* was performed, Handel went to Italy. There he learnt to compose in the fashionable Italian manner, which meant chiefly composition of tuneful and florid airs for the voice. Much of Handel's undying popularity is due to his lovely melodies, the result of his tour of Italy. On returning to Germany he was appointed musical director to the Elector of Hanover.

In 1710 Handel obtained leave to visit England, and found himself so happy and successful in London that eventually he settled there—without asking the Elector of Hanover to release him. The event that decided him to live in England was a commission from Queen Anne to write a *Te Deum* in celebration of the Peace of Utrecht (1713), and for this Handel was granted a comfortable pension for life. In 1714, however, Queen Anne died, and her successor was none other than the Elector of Hanover (George I) whose service Handel had so tactlessly left. The King, however, took Handel back into favour and gave him his full support for the rest of his life. (The story that George I forgave Handel after hearing his lovely 'Water Music' is now discredited.)

In 1717 Handel became director of music to the Duke of Chandos, at his palace at Edgware, north of London, where he maintained a large choir and orchestra for his private chapel. During the next 3 years Handel composed many works, chief among them being *Acis and Galatea*, *Esther* (his first oratorio), and the 'Chandos' Anthems. Meanwhile a company called the Royal Academy of Music was started to stage a season of opera under Handel's direction. In the course of its 8 years' existence Handel produced 14 operas, but the venture failed and left him bankrupt at the age of 52.

This misfortune caused a temporary breakdown, but Handel produced several more operas with varying success before he turned to the composition of his magnificent series of oratorios. In 1741 he achieved the greatest triumph of his life—the *Messiah*. The words for an oratorio on this subject were sent to him by a friend, and in 24 days he had composed the music. He took the score with him to Dublin, where he had been invited by the Lord-Lieutenant of Ireland, and the first performance took place there. The

Ashmolean Museum

GEORGE FREDERICK HANDEL

Terracotta model by Roubilliac for the monument in Westminster Abbey

profits were given to charity—a characteristic gesture, for although Handel could be rude and uncouth, he was always generous with his money. When the work was performed in London, George II, who was present, was so moved by the grandeur of the 'Hallelujah' Chorus that he rose to his feet and remained standing till the end of the performance—a custom which has prevailed ever since.

Handel's fame rests chiefly upon the wonderful oratorios of these last years, in which the lovely tunes of his arias are varied with noble, harmonious choruses. Beethoven used to say, 'Go to Handel's choruses if you want to learn broad, simple effects'. But his chamber music, his organ concertos, and his *concerti grossi* are also full of fine music. Eight years before his death Handel became totally blind, but with the help of his old friend and copyist, Christopher Smith, he continued to compose, and to play and direct his own music. One day, when he was 74, after directing the *Messiah*, he fainted, and shortly afterwards died. He was buried in Westminster Abbey.

See also Vol. XII: ORATORIO.

HANNIBAL (*c.* 247–183 B.C.). The son of the Carthaginian general, Hamilcar, Hannibal from the age of 9 swore to defeat Rome. He led the Carthaginians in the Second Punic War, and came very near to his ambition.

Carthage in North Africa, originally a colony of the PHOENICIANS (q.v. Vol. I), had grown powerful and was rivalling Rome for the control of the southern Mediterranean. Hannibal made very far-reaching plans which, with his genius for thinking farther ahead than his opponents, often gave him the advantage of surprise. Following up his father's successful campaigns in Spain, he sacked the Roman city of Saguntum in 218 B.C., and marched across southern France to the foot of the Alps. He then performed the extraordinary and quite unexpected feat of marching his huge army with all its equipment, including elephants (the Carthaginian equivalent of tanks), across the Alps. Although he lost half his army in the snow and ice, the reputation he won and the surprise of his attack enabled him to inflict crushing blows on the Romans as he marched south. After the Battle of Cannae in Apulia in 216 B.C. all southern Italy was in his hands.

This was the peak of Hannibal's success. Although later he reached within 3 miles of Rome, his striking power from this time onwards was weakened by the failure of supplies from Africa, because the Romans held command of the sea. In 208 B.C. his brother Hasdrubal tried to come to his support with another army, but he was defeated and killed. Finally, after a 15 years' campaign, Hannibal abandoned the war and returned to Africa.

His failure was largely due to the young Roman general Scipio, who had the wisdom to learn from his opponent. He avoided pitched battles in Italy, and instead himself invaded Africa. In 202 B.C. his army faced Hannibal at Zama. Before the battle the two generals, who had much in common, met and talked; then Scipio won the battle by the same tactics that Hannibal had used at Cannae.

Hannibal turned from war to reforming the government of his own city. This raised such fury that he fled into exile; but the Romans, dreading his hostility, demanded his surrender, and pursued him until finally to escape them he committed suicide with a poisoned ring which he always wore. Hannibal had outstanding military ability; he also had charm, a sense of humour, and, according to the cruel standards of the time, chivalry. He concentrated his life on a single unattainable object—the defeat of an enemy who would not admit defeat.

See also Vol. I: PHOENICIAN CIVILIZATION.

HAPSBURGS, *see* CHARLES V; PHILIP II; MARIA THERESA.

HARDIE, James Keir (1856–1915). This pioneer of political SOCIALISM in Britain (q.v. Vol. X) was founder of the Independent Labour Party and first leader of the party in Parliament.

His hard upbringing and early struggles explain the bitterness of many of his speeches and writings. He was born in a one-roomed house in Lanarkshire, the eldest of nine children, and, before he was 10 years old, he was put to work in a Lanarkshire coal-mine. Later he became a skilled hewer. At this time TRADE UNIONS (q.v. Vol. VII) were beginning to develop, but colliery owners were extremely hostile to them, and when Hardie began to agitate for an extension of trade unionism he was dismissed. As his name was placed on a 'black list' by owners of other collieries, he had to support himself by running a small shop and writing articles and pamphlets. In 1886 he became organizing secretary of the Ayrshire Miners' Union and the Scottish Miners' Federation, and worked hard for both unions for little or no payment. He also started a monthly periodical called *The Miner*, which later developed into *The Labour Leader*.

Hardie looked forward to the eventual improvement of the workers' lot by parliamentary action. He did not believe that this action could be looked for from the Liberal party, and came to realize that Labour must have its own party. At the Mid-Lanark by-election of 1888, he therefore stood as the first Labour candidate in any British constituency. The Liberals tried hard to prevent his candidature, offering him a

JAMES KEIR HARDIE IN 1892

in Britain. He spent the greater part of his life as a socialist speaker, writer, and agitator; his socialism owed little to MARX (q.v.) or any theory, and was largely the result of actual experience and personal conviction. He believed in PACIFISM and became unpopular for condemning the SOUTH AFRICAN WAR of 1899–1902 (qq.v. Vol. X). He hoped to develop socialism internationally, not realizing how basically Continental socialism differed from British socialism. He was greatly distressed that international socialism could not prevent the First World War, and his death within a year may have been hastened by disappointment.

See also Vol. X: SOCIALISM; POLITICAL PARTIES.

HARDY, Thomas (1840–1928). Hardy, the novelist and poet, author of *Tess of the D'Urbervilles* and other famous novels of the Wessex countryside, was born near Stinsford in Dorset where the families of both his parents had lived for many generations. Though sensitive and shy by nature, he loved, like his father, to enter into the life of the country people, and during his boyhood he stored up impressions which always remained fresh. A harvest-home supper, for instance, to which he was taken as a child, one of the last where the old traditional ballads were still sung, is described in *Far from the Madding Crowd*. Again, his father, continuing his grandfather's custom, used to take the Stinsford church choir carol-singing round the parish on Christmas Eve—an experience which enabled Hardy to create the vivid characters of the Mellstock choir in *Under the Greenwood Tree*. Hardy played the violin, as his grandfather had done, and he took delight as a young man in playing at all kinds of village functions. His life at this time had, as he said, 'three strands'. He got up early to read Greek and Latin books, studied architecture all day at an office in Dorchester, and, in the evenings, went off with his fiddle to play, sometimes all night, at some village party.

When Hardy was 22 he became an assistant architect in London; but his heart was in literature. Like most young writers, he preferred poetry to prose at this time, but he finally decided that he would try to become a novelist. He returned to Dorchester, where he took a part-time job in an architect's office, giving the rest of his time to writing. His first successful novel, *Under the Greenwood Tree*, appeared in 1872. It was an idyllic comedy of Dorset life. During

post worth £300 a year and a safe seat at the next general election; but Hardie turned a deaf ear to all such offers. He was defeated by the Liberal candidate, but he held tenaciously to the idea of a separate Labour party, and set to work to form a Scottish Labour party, the first to be formed in the kingdom.

In 1892 he succeeded in getting into Parliament for West Ham, Essex, constituting in the House of Commons a one-man party on his own. He refused to dress in the customary frock coat and silk hat worn by members of Parliament in those days, and his tweed suit and cloth cap figured in many a newspaper cartoon. He believed that the working-men's representative should not assume, even in political circles, the garb of those who were not working men. In 1900 he was elected M.P. for Merthyr Tydfil, South Wales, and in 1906 became leader of the new parliamentary Labour party, which by now had twenty-nine members in Parliament.

Hardie did more perhaps than any other man to consolidate the political Labour movement

Reece Winstone

WOOL MANOR, DORSET, DESCRIBED BY HARDY IN 'TESS OF THE D'URBERVILLES'
Angel Clare brings Tess to this house for the first night of their honeymoon

the next 25 years Hardy's other great novels followed in regular succession—*Far From the Madding Crowd*, *The Return of the Native*, *The Trumpet Major*, *The Mayor of Casterbridge*, *The Woodlanders*, *Tess of the D'Urbervilles*, and *Jude the Obscure*.

All Hardy's best novels are set in Wessex—the old name for the kingdom of West Saxons, which Hardy used especially for Dorset. He chose the old name because he loved his native county and understood its traditional ways. He thought of his characters—the woodlanders, shepherds, dairy-maids, pedlars, farmers—as the inheritors of traditions which had their roots in those far-off times when the Normans, or before them the Danes and Saxons, Romans and early Britons inhabited this part of the land. The landscape of Hardy's novels has the same unchanging quality; it is Egdon Heath, bare, desolate, and timeless, which provides the most dramatically fitting background to Hardy's lonely, tragic characters —characters who by their stoic acceptance of fate and their dignity in suffering remind us of the classical heroes and heroines of Greek plays.

During his later years Hardy returned to writing poetry and published many of his early poems for the first time. His most original poetry was written after the age of 70, though much of it

springs from incidents which impressed him as a very young man. In his poetry he uses—and even invents—words and rhythms which would seem hardly possible in lyric poetry; yet he succeeds in creating his effect—vivid, moving, and dramatic. His greatest poetic work is *The Dynasts*, a colossal epic-drama of the Napoleonic Wars which he had been planning for many years. Much of the material came from first-hand accounts he had heard as a boy from old soldiers who had served against Napoleon.

Hardy was a fatalist. He believed that life could be unjust and that Fate pursues its course relentlessly, indifferent to human suffering. He was a fearless writer—never false to his vision of the truth for fear of offending against the conventional beliefs of the day. Both *Tess of the D'Urbervilles* and *Jude the Obscure* caused great offence at the time. Hardy had fine humour, but a certain grim irony is more characteristic of him, and he uses it most effectively, perhaps, in his short stories.

HARGREAVES, James (died 1778), Inventor, *see* Vol. VII: WOOL INDUSTRY, MODERN.

HAROUN AL-RASCHID (*c.* 763–809). The hero of the half-mythical adventures in the

Arabian Nights was the most outstanding of the caliphs of Baghdad, who claimed descent from the prophet MOHAMMED (q.v.). After some 200 years of warlike expansion, the Mohammedan Empire extended from Armenia in the north-east to Carthage in the west (*see* ARABS, Vol. I). Haroun al-Raschid inherited these glories when he was only 22, but though he fought some successful wars, his chief claim to fame is not military. He attracted to his Court artists, poets, musicians, and learned men, and surrounded himself with wealth and luxury—a departure from the austere Moslem way of life which the Prophet had practised. He made his new capital, Baghdad, a magnificent city, stories of the splendour of which reached even to CHARLEMAGNE (q.v.), Emperor of the Franks, with whom Haroun al-Raschid exchanged gifts.

Haroun allowed political power to fall into the hands of foreigners, chiefly the Barmecides, a noble Persian family, whose influence in the long run was pernicious, and whom Haroun finally expelled. The phrase 'a Barmecide feast' is based on a story of one of the Barmecides who entertained a beggar to dinner and served him with nothing but empty dishes, pretending that they contained sumptuous food. The beggar humorously thanked his host for the excellence of each dish.

The ARABIAN NIGHTS (q.v. Vol. XII) is a series of stories based on Persian translations from Indian literature which took their present shape mainly in the 13th century. According to tradition, Haroun in disguise used to take walks in Baghdad and involved himself in adventures with the poorest of his subjects.

Haroun was a deeply pious Moslem, who is said to have made the pilgrimage to Mecca nine times. Arab history speaks of him as a man of great nobility and fine intelligence, an artist and a poet, but lacking in strength of will, and capable of behaving with extreme cruelty.

See also Vol. I: ARABS; ISLAM.
See also Vol. XII: ARABIAN NIGHTS.

HARVEY, William (1578–1657). This English doctor is honoured throughout the world as the discoverer of the circulation of the blood. By proving that the blood flows from the heart through the arteries, and back to the heart through the veins, he made possible the great discoveries of modern medicine and physiology. The book in which he proved this fact is one of the classics of modern scientific method and is the first in which measurement and mathematics are applied to biology.

The son of a successful merchant, Harvey was educated at King's School, Canterbury, and then at Cambridge, a noted centre for the study of ANATOMY (q.v. Vol. XI). Later, as several English doctors at that time had done, he went to the University of Padua, then celebrated throughout Europe for the brilliance of its medical teachers. Among these was Fabricius, whose own discovery of the valves in the veins led the way to Harvey's work. Harvey returned to England in 1602, not only with his doctor's diploma but also with the lines of his research already laid down.

Although Francis BACON (q.v.) was then preparing a grand plan for scientific research, which later resulted in the founding of the Royal Society in 1662, such investigation as Harvey proposed was not then regarded as of sufficient national importance to be supported by public money, but was looked on merely as a private hobby to be carried on at one's own expense. Harvey, therefore, could carry on his experiments only in what time he could spare from a busy London practice. His career followed the usual course of a leading doctor of his day. Before he was 30 he was elected a Fellow of the Royal College of Physicians, and soon after he became physician to St. Bartholomew's Hospital in London. His patients included Bacon, and he became physician to James I and Charles I. As royal physician Harvey went with Charles I to his coronation and was with him in the Civil War. It is said that at the Battle of Edgehill he looked after the two young princes, reading to them under a hedge while the battle raged in the adjoining fields. This royal patronage doubtless

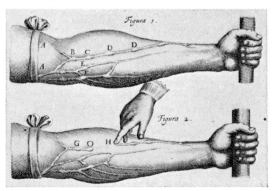

DEMONSTRATION OF THE FUNCTION OF VALVES IN VEINS
Figure from Harvey, *De Motu Cordis*, 1639

gave him more leisure for his scientific work, which he pursued to the end of his life.

He first made public his discovery of the circulation of the blood in 1616 in a course of lectures to the College of Physicians. When Harvey published his book on the movement of the heart and blood in 1628, this natural law, which we now take for granted, was hotly opposed by those who still believed in the age-old view that the blood only moved in the body like the ebb and flow of the tide. Some thought him a 'crank', and his practice suffered.

Harvey had a great deal of detailed knowledge of comparative anatomy. After years of experiment and observation, he wrote an important book on the reproduction of animals, in which he rejected the idea of spontaneous generation, a theory which held ground until it was finally disproved by PASTEUR (q.v.). An oration in his honour (the Harveian Oration) is still given every year by one of the leading physicians and Fellows of the Royal College of Physicians.

See also Vol. XI: MEDICINE, HISTORY OF; HEART; BLOOD, CIRCULATION OF.

HASTINGS, Warren (1732–1818). This great Governor-General of India saved British rule there from widespread disorder and corruption. By imaginative experiments in government, he went on to build, almost singlehanded, the first permanent and responsible British administration on the slender foundations laid by Robert CLIVE (q.v.).

At 18 Hastings was sent to Calcutta as a clerk in the EAST INDIA COMPANY (q.v. Vol. VII), and when he was only 25 he was appointed Resident at the Court of the Indian ruler of Bengal. There his attempts to put down free trading by Company employees and his forthright criticisms of the Company made him unpopular, and when he returned to England in 1765 he was given no employment for 4 years.

But in 1772, having returned to India, Hastings was appointed Governor of Bengal, where he took charge of an inefficient and almost totally corrupt administration. He at once set about the immense task of reform. He was one of the first to realize that if Britain was to rule effectively she must respect Indian law and combine with it a British sense of justice; he realized that strong measures were necessary to prevent outbreaks of violence amongst the native races; and he was determined to rescue India from the wrangles of party politics at home. He overhauled Bengal's financial system; replaced corrupt Indian tax-collectors by Englishmen; and took over all civil and judicial powers from the local ruler, the Nawab. To help famine-stricken peasants, he reduced customs duties. Finding some senior Indian administrators to be corrupt, he brought them to trial.

A year after he had taken office, the British Parliament passed the Regulating Act which transferred much of the responsibility for government from the East India Company to the Crown. Hastings was made Governor-General, assisted by a council of four. But he had little authority over the British governors of Bombay and Madras, and was thwarted by members of his own council. These, led by his senior councillor Philip Francis, were from the first opposed to Hastings, and soon encouraged a corrupt Indian official to bring charges of bribery against him. Then the Chief Justice, a friend of Hastings, promptly produced charges of forgery against the Indian and, after conviction, hastily had him executed, although forgery was not a capital offence. The feud went on, his enemies removing from office any officials loyal to Hastings. By 1780 relations with the council had become so bitter that Hastings challenged Francis to a duel; Francis was wounded, and returned to England to plot Hastings' downfall.

In the midst of these difficulties the French, who were at war with Britain in Europe, seized the opportunity to stir up trouble in India, and encouraged the Indian ruler of Mysore to attack southern India. Hastings sent troops to save Madras and to put down disturbances in other parts of India. Desperate for funds to keep his armies in the field, Hastings then demanded money from the ruler of Benares, and deposed him when he refused. He next turned to another Indian prince, and when he too refused, Hastings forced the prince's relatives to provide the money.

The disturbances were put down, but in 1784 Hastings resigned, and in the following year returned to England. BURKE, FOX, SHERIDAN (qq.v.), and other politicians were already preparing charges of corruption against him, and 2 years later his great trial began. It lasted 145 days over a period of $7\frac{1}{4}$ years, and cost Hastings £70,000—seven-eighths of his fortune. Like Clive, whom Hastings disliked and never trusted, but with much less cause, Hastings had been

WARREN HASTINGS, HIS WIFE, AND HER INDIAN MAID

The official residence of the Governor-General can be seen in the background. Painting by Zoffany, who was in India between 1783 and 1789. Reproduced by permission of the Trustees of the Victoria Memorial Hall, Calcutta

made the scapegoat for the growing indignation at corruption in India. Burke and Sheridan undid their cause by savage exaggeration, while Hastings defended himself frankly and with dignity. The accusations against him proved to be largely a matter of political hostility. Though some of his actions had been unjust, none had been for private gain, and he was acquitted on all charges. But the trial did show that though a man in immediate peril might be forgiven certain actions, these could never become the normal standard of British rule in India. The Company granted Hastings a generous pension, and though he failed to obtain the formal redress from Parliament which he wanted, he came very close to it some years later when, after giving evidence before a Parliamentary Committee, there was applause for his speech, and silent respect as he passed from the chamber.

Opposition and ingratitude made Hastings ruthless; isolation made him dictatorial; and his reforms created enemies, stirring up prejudice and vested interests. But he was imaginative, thorough, well-informed, self-disciplined, and generous. He had a good knowledge of Indian languages and he respected Indians. He looked after the welfare of the peasants, as very few of his contemporaries did, and he set an example of plain living in an environment of luxury. As J. S. MILL declared (q.v.), few public men could have survived so gruelling and minute a public scrutiny, and emerged so well and with their reputation enhanced.

See also Vol. X: IMPEACHMENT.

National Maritime Museum

THE BATTLE OF QUIBERON BAY, 1759

The ships of Hawke's fleet are shown chasing the French into Quiberon Bay in rough weather. In the centre the French ship *Thésée* founders. On the left of the picture Hawke's *Royal George* is attacking the French flagship. Painting by R. Paton

HAWKE, Edward (Baron) (1705–81). This great British admiral was the victor of one of the most daring and heroic naval actions ever fought, and his fine leadership did much to fashion the great navy that was later to play so vital a part in the NAPOLEONIC WARS. The system of close BLOCKADE (qq.v. Vol. X) which Hawke instituted not only ensured the success of Pitt's strategy in the Seven Years War (1756–63) (*see* CHATHAM), but remained the basis of British sea power until the time of Trafalgar.

Though Hawke joined the Navy when he was 15, he saw no action until he was 39, when he was concerned in a half-hearted action against the French–Spanish fleet during the War of the Austrian Succession. The British senior officers quarrelled amongst themselves, and only Hawke succeeded in capturing an enemy ship, gaining thereby a reputation as a fearless officer. Three years later he routed a French fleet convoying 252 merchant ships bound for the West Indies, for which action he was knighted. On the outbreak of the Seven Years War, after Admiral Byng had been court-martialled and shot,

Hawke for a short time took command of the Mediterranean fleet. Then he returned to command the Channel fleet in the blockade of Brest. This blockade was largely responsible for the success of WOLFE's army in Canada (q.v.), for the French were prevented from sending reinforcements to their garrisons there.

Hawke's greatest feat occurred in the autumn of 1759. A French army, supported by fleets from Brest and Rochefort, was waiting in Brittany to invade Britain. The Brest fleet of twenty-one ships was closely blockaded by Hawke's slightly larger fleet. On 14 November, however, a gale compelled Hawke to withdraw his ships for 6 days to Torbay, in Devonshire, during which time the French fleet slipped out of Brest to embark the invasion troops in Quiberon Bay. Though the coast is one of the most dangerous in the world, Hawke unhesitatingly signalled 'general chase'. He caught the enemy and engaged them in close action as his ships ran before another furious gale into the rock-strewn waters of the Bay. It is said that when the sailing-master of Hawke's flagship the *Royal George* protested at having to take the flagship into the Bay in such terrible conditions and in semi-darkness, Hawke replied: 'You have done your duty in pointing out the danger . . . now lay me alongside the French admiral.' By dawn next day ten of the enemy ships were aground and the remainder had scattered. In his dispatch Hawke wrote: 'Had we but two hours more of daylight, the whole had been totally destroyed.' The victory of Quiberon Bay was the finest chase in naval history. Coming so soon after the capture of Quebec by Wolfe, it inspired the toast: 'May all our officers have the heart of a Wolfe and the eye of a Hawke.'

See also Vol. X: BLOCKADE; SEA POWER.

HAWKINS, Sir John (1532–95).

Hawkins was Britain's first great naval administrator and, after DRAKE (q.v.), was the leading naval commander. He had a reliable and modest character—unusual in that age.

His father, William Hawkins, made Plymouth an important port by starting the ivory trade with the Guinea coast. His son started the 'round trip' pattern of trading: a mixed cargo was taken to the Gulf of Guinea (the Outward Passage), slaves were transported from Guinea to the West Indies (the notorious Middle Passage), and tropical products were brought back to England (the Homeward Passage). His third voyage to the Spanish Main in 1567, on which Drake also sailed, ended disastrously and in a sense began the war with Spain.

Later Hawkins became M.P. for Plymouth and Treasurer of the Navy; in that capacity he introduced a new type of galleon (see SAILING SHIPS, Vol. IV), ships such as the REVENGE and ARK ROYAL (qq.v. Vol. IV), which defeated the Spanish Armada. On that occasion he commanded the *Victory* under Lord Howard, who knighted him as the fleets passed up the Channel. Hawkins made Chatham a naval base, and at the same time founded the Chatham Chest for the benefit of wounded and aged seamen. He was later responsible for maintaining squadrons off the Azores to intercept the Spanish treasure fleets, and himself commanded one of their unsuccessful cruises. About the same time his son, Sir Richard Hawkins, in an attempt to sail round the world, was captured off Peru, though he returned home later.

When he was 63, Hawkins sailed with Drake in command of the largest expedition yet sent to the Spanish West Indies. The characters of the two commanders were quite different, and Hawkins, 'an old man and wary', disapproved of Drake's impetuosity. The expedition was a tragic failure; Hawkins died at sea off Puerto Rico, and Drake died soon after.

HAYDN, Franz Joseph (1732–1809).

The composer Haydn was born near the Austro-Hungarian border at a time when J. S. BACH was still alive and HANDEL had not yet written his *Messiah*. MOZART's entire life falls within the span of Haydn's, and when Haydn died, BEETHOVEN (qq.v.) had composed six of his nine symphonies. He was thus a living bridge between two musical generations. His boyhood was passed amid wars between his own Empress MARIA THERESA and FREDERICK THE GREAT of Prussia (qq.v.); he lived through the French Revolution and died in a Vienna occupied by Napoleon's armies. In music he wrought revolutionary changes, but in life he accepted employ-

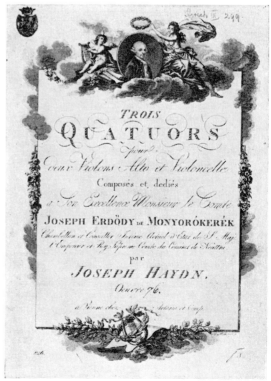

British Museum

FIRST EDITION OF THREE QUARTETS BY HAYDN
The medallion at the top of the title-page contains a portrait of the composer

ment, simply and modestly, with the noble
families whose cultured tastes provided work
for so many artists and musicians, and he wrote
immortal works for them as part of his duty.

From his father, a village wheelwright, Haydn
inherited his naturally good ear. When he was
5 he was sent away to a cousin, a choirmaster,
and at 8 was chosen for the choir-school of
St. Stephen's Cathedral in Vienna. He learned
a vast amount of church music; he played
the violin, and he struggled to teach himself
to compose. At 17, however, he was expelled
because of a practical joke he had played, and
was turned out, penniless, into the streets.

Haydn managed to earn just enough to keep
himself from starving by giving clavier lessons
and by playing the violin in the streets. He
succeeded in securing an attic and a piano, and
there he doggedly wrestled with composition.
Eventually he was engaged as music master by a
certain Baron von Fürnberg, and wrote his first
string quartets, probably about 1755, for members of the household to play; he wrote his first
symphony when musical director to another
nobleman who kept a small orchestra. In 1760
he made an unhappy marriage, and in the next
year was appointed assistant musical director
to the princely Hungarian house of Esterházy.

In 1766 Prince Nicholas Esterházy took up
residence at a new palace built in lavish splendour and complete isolation amid the Hungarian
swamps. Here Haydn worked for 25 years as
musical director, rehearsing and performing
operas and symphonies for the Prince and his
guests with his little group of singers and instru-
mentalists, keeping everyone happy, and composing his own operas, symphonies, and chamber
music in the early morning before the day's
work began. In 1781 he and Mozart met and
became friends in Vienna. Haydn, though much
the elder, was not too proud to be influenced by
Mozart's music, to the great enrichment of his
own.

When Prince Nicholas died in 1790, Salomon,
a German violinist working in London, persuaded Haydn to come to England to direct his
orchestral concerts (Haydn had already written
a set of twelve symphonies for Paris). Haydn's
inspiring leadership and the splendid new works
he wrote for Salomon's concerts ensured his
triumph. He was welcomed by the Prince
Regent, and the University of Oxford made him
an honorary Doctor of Music. During this visit,

O. V. W. Hubmann

THE BERGKIRCHE, EISENSTADT, WHERE HAYDN IS BURIED
Haydn performed many of his works in this church during
his service with the Esterházy family

which lasted until the summer of 1792, he wrote
the first six of his 'London' symphonies, including
the 'Surprise'. The 'Clock' and the remaining
six 'London' symphonies were among those he
composed on his return visit in 1794–5.

Haydn then returned to Prince Esterházy, and
with his greater maturity and wider experience
he wrote a splendid series of Masses for the
family chapel and his last and greatest string
quartets. Inspired by hearing Handel's *Messiah*
at Westminster Abbey, he produced his first
oratorio, *The Creation*, in 1798 when he was 66.
The Seasons followed 3 years later.

Haydn has been called 'the father of the symphony'. He was not the first to write symphonies,
but he discovered by experience the capacities
of the orchestra and its instruments, and the very
different capacities of the four single instruments
which make up the string quartet. This perception, with his gift of original melody and his
wonderful sense of design, transformed the
primitive symphony of his early years into something capable of expressing the widest range of
thought and feeling. His instrumental style was
at the root of Mozart's, and later of Beethoven's

style. The best of his own symphonies and string quartets are among the finest ever written.

See also Vol. XII: Music, History of; Symphony.

HAZLITT, William (1778–1830). This English essayist, the son of a Unitarian minister, spent part of his childhood in America and part in Shropshire. As a boy he heard Coleridge preach a sermon, an experience which he later described brilliantly in his essay 'My First Acquaintance with Poets'. Through Coleridge he met Wordsworth, and, later on, in London, he became one of Lamb's circle (qq.v.). Though Hazlitt had the gift of painting, he preferred a literary career; but he wrote many excellent essays on the fine arts. Intended for the Church, he had read widely in philosophy, and on any subject his reasoning was sharp and his choice of ideas original. In politics he was a passionate republican and loyal all his life to the idea of Revolution (q.v. Vol. X). This led him later to attack his early heroes, such as Wordsworth and Coleridge, who, he thought, had forsaken their ideals. Napoleon—the symbol of the French Revolution (q.v. Vol. X) and the enemy of hereditary kings—was his hero; but his *Life of Napoleon*, less of a masterpiece than he intended it to be, roused great antagonism, since Napoleon was England's enemy.

Hazlitt's *Spirit of the Age* (1825), a series of pen-portraits, mainly intellectual and political, is his true masterpiece. The eye of the painter is at work in these essays, still more the inquiry of the imaginative seeker after truth who flashed out his contempt for much that seemed to him despicable in the modern world. His direct and vehement prose reflects his honesty, his hatreds, and his generous enthusiasms. A passionate admirer of Shakespeare, he was one of the first, and best, English writers of modern dramatic criticism.

Hazlitt's personal life seemed to him largely a sequence of disenchantments; his marriages were unhappy, and in his later life he suffered from ill health and money difficulties. But the mysterious delight which in youth he had hoped to secure was never for him a dead dream.

See also Vol. XII: Essay.

HEGEL, Georg Wilhelm Friedrich (1770–1831). Hegel was, if not the most important, certainly the most influential of the long line of German philosophers deriving from Kant (q.v.).

He was born at Stuttgart and studied theology at Tübingen. After some years of teaching, at 48 he was appointed to a professorship at Berlin, where he remained till his death 13 years later. He was then at the height of his powers and fame.

The object of philosophy is to attempt to explain the universe. Each philosopher starts from his own viewpoint, and philosophies, therefore, differ widely. Hegel assumed what he called the Absolute—very much, though not quite, the same as that which other philosophers have called the First Cause and religious people call God. Hegel thought of the Absolute, as its title implies, as dependent on itself alone, yet expressing itself in an infinite number of differences, that is, in all the apparently separate things in nature. Its highest expression Hegel held to be man's mind, or reason; for in this the Absolute comes to be conscious of itself. Man, therefore, is a kind of union, or reconciliation, of the Absolute and nature. Hegel used for this process the terms *thesis*, *antithesis*, and *synthesis*. The *thesis* is what is given to begin with; the *antithesis* is the opposite of the *thesis*; and the *synthesis* unites the two.

Hegel derived this from reflecting on the human mind. Every idea, he said, is confronted by its opposite or limitation: positive irresistibly suggests negative. But as the mind cannot rest in a contradiction, it is driven to unite the opposites in a higher synthesis. Man, being mind and matter, unites the Absolute and nature. So for Hegel the laws of thought are the laws of reality; consequently the human mind, through its necessary mode of operation, can interpret the universe. Hegel was, therefore, what we call an Idealist. Thus the universe is conceived as a development of the Absolute through stress and strain. Hegel used the term 'dialectic' for this process—a term Plato had used to describe the process of pushing an idea or argument to its logical conclusion in order to detect and eliminate error or inconsistency. Hegel extended the application of the term.

Hegel, chiefly in his two books *The Philosophy of History* and *The Philosophy of Law*, used his method to interpret Christianity and the State. In the Trinity, according to him, the Father is *thesis*, the Son *antithesis*, and the Spirit, who unites them, *synthesis*. He exalted the State at the expense of the individual, and justified internal tyranny of the State over the individual, and external aggression towards other States. He glorified war as having a positive moral value. Hegel believed history to show that in every age one nation was dominant, and entrusted with the development of the world spirit. In his own age he saw that nation as Germany —in the future, as America. Hegel's theory of the State as a more complete form of life than that of the individual man, his belief that whatever action it takes is justifiable, and his glorification of Germany are the bases of the philosophy on which the modern TOTALITARIAN State (q.v. Vol. X) is based, and were used by HITLER (q.v.) as the philosophy of Nazi Germany.

See also Vol. I: PHILOSOPHY.
See also Vol. X: NATION AND STATE; TOTALITARIANISM.

HEINE, Heinrich (1797–1856), *see* Vol. XII: GERMAN LITERATURE.

HENRY II (1133–89). Henry, son of the Empress Matilda and Count Geoffrey of Anjou and grandson of Henry I, came to the throne of England in 1154 at the end of the long civil war between Matilda and her cousin Stephen. Henry's first task was to restore order in England, to demolish castles and punish rebels. Henry was lord over a vast domain—not only England, but more than half of France acquired through his parents and through his wife, Eleanor of

British Museum
HENRY II DISPUTING WITH BECKET
English 14th-century illumination (*Cott. MS. Claudius DII*)

Aquitaine. He was himself as much a Frenchman as an Englishman, and he spent a great part of his life on his French estates, where he inevitably came into conflict with the French King. He was also the first English King to attempt to conquer Ireland, which he gave to his youngest son, John. Henry attempted to divide control of his territories among his unruly sons; but, encouraged by their mother, they revolted against him, and his latter years were darkened by bitter family quarrels.

Henry II is chiefly memorable as one of the founders of English Common Law (*see* LAW, ENGLISH, Vol. X). He made general the use of juries both in criminal cases and in disputes about land; and as an increasing number of cases came to be heard before the King's judges, either at Westminster or on their circuits round the shires (*see* ASSIZES, Vol. X), something like a law common to the whole land began to emerge. The King's quarrel with Archbishop Thomas BECKET (q.v.) arose from his desire to bring within the scope of this law all clergymen guilty of secular crimes. But over this the King had to admit defeat, and for the rest of the Middle Ages the clergy continued to enjoy their privileges, few cases affecting clergymen coming before the King's judges.

In appearance, Henry II was sandy-haired, short, and stout. A man of restless energy, he ate and drank enormously, and rode and hunted vigorously to keep down his weight. But he never neglected his business as king, and he was a voracious reader who loved to gather scholars at his Court. His avarice was notorious, and he was not popular among his contemporaries, though many recognized his greatness. It was he, more than any other single ruler, who made England the best governed State in 12th-century Europe, and modern historians judge him a statesman and diplomatist of the first rank.

See also BECKET.
See also Vol. X: LAW, ENGLISH.

HENRY VII (1457–1509). This founder of the English royal house of Tudor was the son of a Welshman, Edmund Tudor, Earl of Richmond, and his wife, Margaret Beaufort, heiress of John of GAUNT (q.v.). Through his mother Henry was head of the house of Lancaster after the death of Henry VI in 1471, and could therefore lay claim to the crown of England.

During the reign of the Yorkist Edward IV,

Henry lived in France. But in 1485 he took advantage of the unpopularity of Richard III to land at Milford Haven and proclaim that he had come to free England from a usurper and a tyrant. Richard was defeated and killed in the battle of Bosworth, near Leicester, and the crown of England, found under a bush on the battle-field, was placed on Henry's head.

Henry's character fitted him for the task of restoring order and effective government, which had collapsed during the Wars of the Roses (*see* FEUDALISM, Vol. X). He was ambitious, cold, crafty, cautious, and methodical. Yet, in a cruel age, when human life and suffering counted for very little in affairs of state, he never shed blood if he could avoid doing so.

Soon after his coronation he extinguished the best Yorkist claim to the throne by marrying Elizabeth, Edward IV's daughter and heir. Most of the over-powerful lords who had been responsible for the Wars of the Roses had either fallen in battle or been executed. Henry then set up the Court of the STAR CHAMBER (q.v. Vol. X), which enforced obedience from the remaining nobles by imposing very heavy fines on all who flouted Henry's laws. He chose his ministers from the new middle class of wealthy traders whose prosperity depended on the order and strong government which Henry seemed able to give. He encouraged the development of the woollen-cloth trade, built a merchant navy, and made commercial treaties with foreign powers which enabled English ships to carry English goods into the Baltic and the Mediterranean. By these acts Henry laid the foundations of England's great commercial wealth in the centuries to come.

Henry early recognized that a rich king is a strong king, and he, therefore, set about making himself the richest man in his realm. His agents were ruthless in extorting money not only from rich nobles, monasteries, and city councils, but from any private subject who had infringed the law. What began as a statesman-like thrift ended in avarice.

In the years from 1485 to 1499 Henry had to deal with many plots and risings, such as those which supported the pretenders, Lambert Simnel and Perkin Warbeck. But with cool foresight he defeated every effort of his enemies. The last 10 years of his reign were peaceful. He restored order in Ireland and in 1502, with his usual prevision, married his eldest daughter

National Portrait Gallery

HENRY VIII AND HENRY VII

Drawing by Holbein for a mural painting in Whitehall Palace

Margaret to James IV of Scotland, a marriage which 100 years later united the crowns of the two countries in the Stuart kings (*see* SCOTS, Vol. I).

On his death he left his son HENRY VIII (q.v.) an unchallenged throne, useful foreign alliances, and a brimming treasury.

See also Vol. VII: MERCANTILE SYSTEM; MERCHANT ADVENTURERS.

HENRY VIII (1491–1547). Henry, the second son of HENRY VII (q.v.) and Elizabeth, daughter of Edward IV, united in one person the claims of both Lancaster (Red rose) and York (White rose). In order to preserve the alliance with Spain, he married Catherine of Aragon, his elder brother's widow, the Pope granting him a dispensation to enable him to marry his sister-in-law. At 17, when he became King, Henry was a very well-educated young man, good-looking and well-made, a great horseman and archer, and extremely popular because of his willingness to spend the vast wealth left him by Henry VII. His fame spread all over western Europe.

For a time Henry fell victim to the wiles and flattery of his father-in-law, FERDINAND of Aragon (q.v.), who led him to believe that he might recover the large French territories held by his ancestors, and at the same time win glory by defending the Pope from French aggression. He invaded France and won the Battle of the Spurs (1513); but he soon saw that Ferdinand was using him to further his own ends against France, so he made peace. In the meantime James IV of Scotland, in alliance with France, invaded England and was beaten and killed at the Battle of Flodden.

Thereafter, under the guidance of the brilliant Thomas WOLSEY (q.v.), Henry tried to exploit the rivalry between Francis I of France and the Emperor CHARLES V (q.v.), who succeeded Ferdinand in 1516 and became Emperor in 1519. Henry's famous meeting with Francis at the Field of the Cloth of Gold in 1520 was an empty spectacle, for he had already decided to join with Charles. In these wars Henry gained little, but Charles won complete ascendancy in Italy, even holding the Pope a prisoner.

About this time Henry began to wish to break his marriage because Catherine had given him no male heir. All their six children had died in infancy except a daughter, Mary. Henry convinced himself that God was frowning upon his marriage—a conviction which was strengthened by the fact that he had fallen in love with Anne Boleyn, the lively young niece of the Duke of Norfolk. He wanted the Pope to declare that his marriage with Catherine, his brother's widow, was null and void. He had every hope that the Pope would do what he wanted for he knew that he had deserved well of the Holy See. Not only had he supported the Papacy in the European quarrels, but he had written and dedicated to Pope Leo X in 1521 a book against the Protestantism of Luther, for which the Pope had given him the title *Fidei Defensor* (Defender

of the Faith), confirmed to him by Parliament and borne by his successors.

The Pope probably would have annulled the marriage had not Catherine, although herself not happy about the marriage, refused to make way for another bride. The Pope, who dared not offend the Emperor Charles, who was Catherine's nephew, refused to dissolve the marriage.

Henry's position was morally fortified by the opinions collected by CRANMER (q.v.) from the universities of Europe, which were upon the whole in his favour. He would, however, never have acted so boldly had he not known, with the sure sense the great Tudor monarchs had, that the nationalist sentiment of the English people was behind him, for they were tired of foreign interference and of ecclesiastical rule, especially as exercised by Wolsey. The 'Reformation Parliament', therefore, carefully managed by Henry's Minister, Thomas Cromwell, passed during the next few years a series of statutes directed against the papal power. The Act of Appeals, 1533, enabled the English Crown to settle all ecclesiastical cases in England itself without reference to the Pope; and consequently Cranmer, now Archbishop, separated Catherine from Henry, who promptly married Anne Boleyn. The next year the Act of Supremacy transferred to the English Crown all the powers hitherto enjoyed by the Pope in England, and a new Treasons Act made it possible to arrest and try anyone who refused to acknowledge the royal supremacy.

Henry now had absolute authority both in spiritual and temporal matters. There followed the suppression of most of the smaller religious houses, and the confiscation by the Crown of their land. This led to the Pilgrimage of Grace (1536-7), a rising in Lincolnshire and the northern counties in protest against the break with Rome, and in consequence the larger monasteries were also suppressed (*see* MONK, Vol. I). The landholding classes were alarmed, but Henry won them over by selling to them—for he seldom gave—much of the church property which he had acquired.

Probably the Pilgrimage of Grace warned the King that he must not go too far, and also his own good sense counselled caution. He did not join with the German Lutherans, and though some of his decrees at this time were Protestant in tone—for example, his decree in 1538 that the Bible in English was to be used—the Act of Six Articles of 1539 asserting the doctrine of the Mass, and the 'King's Book' of 1543 were definitely Catholic.

Henry did as he pleased without interference from abroad or from home. On the Continent the Emperor and the King of France could not sink their differences to unite in a grand crusade against Protestant England, and the Pope was not strong enough to launch a Bull of deposition; at home the King, who managed Parliaments well, had the Commons with him.

In 1536 Henry divorced Anne Boleyn and had her beheaded on the ground of infidelity, possibly because she also had no son but only a daughter, Elizabeth. He then married Jane Seymour, who died the next year in giving birth to the long-wished-for heir, the future Edward VI. In 1540 for diplomatic reasons he married Anne of Cleves, but got rid of her at once because he disliked her when he saw her and because an alliance with her brother was no longer necessary. Immediately afterwards he married another niece of Norfolk, Catherine Howard, but she also was executed for infidelity in 1542. His last wife, Catherine Parr, an experienced widow, managed to survive him.

Henry was ruthless not only against wives but also against nobles, especially those who challenged his authority. His Ministers also suffered. At the beginning of his reign he had executed Empson and Dudley, who had served his father faithfully. Wolsey later fell into disgrace and died while journeying to his trial in London; Sir Thomas More (q.v.) was beheaded in 1535, and Thomas Cromwell in 1540. Relying upon new men, who erected a competent machinery based upon the royal council, he brought all England under his control.

Henry was a tyrant. Yet he brought England in peace through a crisis which produced deadly struggles in much of Europe; and in all that he did he had the support of the most active part of the English people. He took the Commons into partnership, and in so doing he began the development which ended in the lower house of Parliament becoming the mainspring of the BRITISH CONSTITUTION (q.v. Vol. X).

See also Vol. I: CHURCH OF ENGLAND; REFORMATION.

HENRY OF NAVARRE (1553–1610).

Henry of Bourbon, King of Navarre, and later Henry IV of France, played an important part in

Ashmolean Museum

HENRY OF NAVARRE HUNTING AT FONTAINEBLEAU
Engraving published in 1600

French history by bringing France through the religious wars and restoring her prosperity and her position in Europe.

France was torn by the struggle between the Catholics, led by the great French family, the Guises, and the HUGUENOTS (q.v. Vol. I), of whom Henry became leader. The three sons of Catherine de Medici, all completely dominated by their mother, became kings of France in turn, and Catherine, by fair means or foul, tried to keep a balance between the Catholic and Huguenot power in France. In August 1572, fearing the growing strength of the Huguenots, she roused the Catholics to the terrible massacre of St. Bartholomew, in which in Paris alone some 3,000–4,000 Huguenots fell. Henry, who had just celebrated his marriage to the French King's sister, only saved his life by renouncing his faith, a faith he always held rather lightly. Soon, however, he returned to Protestantism and to the Huguenot leadership.

When the last of Catherine's sons died, the extreme Catholics bitterly opposed Henry's rightful succession; but he gained the support of

Paris by again accepting Catholicism, observing cynically 'Paris is well worth a Mass'. He was crowned in 1594. For a time the wars continued, but in 1598 peace was made and, by the Edict of Nantes, Henry secured for the Protestants considerable religious freedom and full civil rights.

Peace and unity being restored, Henry, with his Minister Sully, inspired by a genuine wish to promote the welfare of the common people, set to work to restore French prosperity. He reorganized the finances, encouraged agriculture, established certain industries, built roads and canals, and in general so restored France that, when he was stabbed by a Catholic fanatic in 1610, he left a country able to respond to the great leadership of Cardinal RICHELIEU and, later, of LOUIS XIV (qq.v.). Henry was mourned all over France for his wise leadership, and his humane, tolerant, genial character.

See also MEDICI.

HENRY THE NAVIGATOR (1394–1460).

This Portuguese prince, the fourth son of King John I of Portugal and great-grandson of King Edward III of England, inspired important explorations down the Atlantic coast of Africa in the 15th century, which paved the way for the seaborne trade of many nations with India and the Far East.

Prince Henry won his spurs as a knight at the capture of the Moorish stronghold and port of Ceuta in North Africa in 1415, a conquest which had far-reaching results in the history of sea trade, and which established the first overseas colony of a modern European State. The Portuguese hoped to continue from Ceuta the crusade against the Moors, and to secure the trade in ivory, gold, and slaves which were brought by caravans across the Sahara Desert from Central Africa. Although the shape and extent of Africa were unknown, the Portuguese began to think that if they sailed far enough along its shore they might discover a way round Africa to India, which would enable them to take part in the valuable spice trade, then a monopoly of the Venetians and Genoese who controlled the overland trade routes.

The search for this new route from Europe to India was the great work of Prince Henry's life, although he himself never sailed down the West African coast. In 1419 he became Governor of Algarve, the most southerly province of Portugal, and established an observatory and a school of navigation at Sagres close to Cape St. Vincent, overlooking the vast waste of the Atlantic. From there he organized voyage after voyage down the African coast. He had formidable obstacles to overcome: neither ships nor methods of navigation were adequate for such long voyages in unknown waters; and the superstitious sailors believed all sorts of terrifying legends, such as that the sun was so hot in the tropics that the sea boiled and white men were turned into Negroes. But he urged his sailors on, rewarding the adventurous and encouraging the timid.

Experience gradually overcame the sailors' fears and improved their ships and methods of navigation. Prince Henry organized and financed the expeditions, collected and studied the information each captain brought back, and saw that each new expedition profited from the information and experience of all earlier voyages. He was himself a scholar as well as a man of action, and had studied the geographical and astronomical writings of the ancient world. He surrounded himself with the best geographers, astronomers, cartographers, instrument-makers, and shipbuilders of his day. He was also a religious man and encouraged his captains to convert the heathen.

Progress was slow, because Cape Bojador, opposite the Canary Islands, was a formidable difficulty to primitive sailing ships and to sailors who needed to keep in sight of the shore so that they could navigate by it, and who believed that round every headland were the horrors of the legendary tropics. The navigators gradually became more adventurous, and in 1441 they brought back to Portugal the first gold and slaves, proving that a profitable trade could be opened up by the west coast route. In 1442 the first European trading warehouse overseas was established at Cape Blanco. By 1460, the year of Prince Henry's death, the explorers had reached the area now occupied by the British colony of Sierra Leone, and had also secured for Portugal the islands of Madeira, the Azores, and Cape Verde.

Prince Henry achieved great practical success in trading and colonization, and organized improvements in navigation and ship-building which, a generation after his death, made possible the long open sea voyages of Vasco DA GAMA and Christopher COLUMBUS (qq.v.).

See also Vol. IV: EXPLORATION; TRADE ROUTES.

HERBERT, George (1593–1633), *see* Vol. XII: METAPHYSICAL POETRY.

HEREWARD THE WAKE (11th century), *see* WILLIAM I.

HERODOTUS (*c.* 480–425 B.C.), Greek historian, *see* Vol. XII: HISTORIES.

HERRICK, Robert (1591–1674). Herrick, the son of a goldsmith of good family, began writing poetry when he was at Cambridge, and after leaving the University he joined Ben JONSON'S (q.v.) circle in London. But in 1629, perhaps desiring a regular livelihood, he took holy orders and was appointed to a living at Totnes, in South Devon. He was ejected during the Puritan Commonwealth, but in 1662 he returned and stayed there till he died.

FRONTISPIECE TO HERRICK'S 'THE HESPERIDES', 1648, WITH A PORTRAIT OF THE AUTHOR

Though he also wrote religious poetry, Herrick's fame rests on his secular poetry. He is one of the great lyric poets of our language because of his mastery of a wonderful variety of metre and rhythm. He has been called the English HORACE (q.v.); but though he had all Horace's urbanity and technical brilliance he had as well a colloquial directness and simplicity beyond the Roman poet. His poems, unique in tone, derive directly from the songs of Shakespeare and Campion, but combine an Elizabethan freshness with a Caroline sophistication; his *Hesperides* is one of the most perfect books of English lyric poetry.

See also Vol. XII: LYRIC POETRY.

HILL, Octavia (1838–1912), *see* Vol. X: HOUSING MANAGEMENT.

HILL, Sir Rowland (1795–1879). Hill, the originator of the penny post, was the son of a Kidderminster schoolmaster. As a child he became interested in mathematics, which he later taught in his father's school.

In 1837 he issued a pamphlet suggesting improvements in the postal system (*see* POST OFFICE, HISTORY OF, Vol. IV). He recommended a uniform rate of 1*d.* a half ounce for letters to any address in the United Kingdom irrespective of distance, and the prepayment of postage by adhesive stamps. After some opposition, his scheme became law in 1840. He held various posts at the Treasury and the General Post Office, and in 1854 became Chief Secretary of the Post Office. The general principles of his scheme were gradually adopted throughout the civilized world.

See also Vol. IV: POSTMARKS AND POSTAGE STAMPS.

HIPPOCRATES (*c.* 460–357 B.C.). This ancient Greek physician, 'the Father of Medicine', lived in the Golden Age of Greece at the same time as PLATO, SOCRATES, SOPHOCLES, and EURIPIDES (qq.v.). Even in such brilliant company he was called 'Hippocrates the Great' and was said to be a descendant of Aesculapius, the Greek god of medicine. He came of a medical family long established on the island of Cos. From his father he received a thorough training in medicine, which he supplemented by years of practice as a travelling physician throughout Greece.

Hippocrates was the first to separate the art and science of medicine from philosophy and superstition, and to base his practice on actual observation and experience. His treatment was cautious and founded on an appreciation of the healing power of nature. His clear and objective descriptions of diseases and his case-histories are still read. He has always been regarded as the ideal physician—wise, kindly, and humane, with a deep respect for his patient and a high sense of duty. Among the numerous medical writings which bear his name (though some were certainly written by others) there is the famous Hippocratic Oath which is the basis of medical conduct, and which is still generally included in the inaugural ceremony for newly qualified doctors.

See also Vol. XI: MEDICINE, HISTORY OF.

HITLER, Adolf (1889–1945). The Führer (leader) of the German Nazi State (*see* TOTALI-TARIANISM, Vol. X) was responsible for leading the world into the Second World War, and authorizing the murder of nearly 6 million Jewish men, women, and children.

Hitler was born at Braunau, a small town in Austria just over the German frontier, where his father was an Austrian customs official. Failing to get into the Vienna art school, he went to Munich and had a hard struggle earning his living by painting picture postcards. He bitterly resented the old Austro-Hungarian Government because it did not grant enough privileges to people, like himself, of Austro-German stock. Therefore, when the First World War broke out, Hitler volunteered enthusiastically to fight for Germany, not Austria. After the war he went back to Munich as a political spy for some officers of the defeated German Army. He attended all kinds of political meetings, and at one of these he discovered his extraordinary capacity to bewitch the public he addressed. It was on this remarkable personal magnetism that his success in the next 20 years largely depended.

In 1920 he joined and soon became leader of a new party which he renamed the 'National Socialist German Working-men's Party'. In 1923 he was arrested and sent to prison for trying to start a revolution. In prison he jotted down his ideas in a book called *Mein Kampf* ('My Fight'), in which he praised utter ruthlessness, showed his intention of reversing Germany's war defeat and making her dominate the world, and expressed his fanatical hatred of all Jews. Even when he began to carry out his intentions point by point, no one outside his own following would take him or his book seriously until it was too late.

On leaving prison in 1924 Hitler began to build up a party in the German Parliament. As he played very skilfully on everyone's discontent, his party gained enormously from the tremendous unemployment of the years 1929 to 1932. By 1933, so many Nazis had been elected to Parliament that the President of the German Republic, Field Marshal Hindenburg, was persuaded that the country could no longer be governed without the Nazi party's help. Hitler was invited to join the government, and was soon appointed Chancellor (Prime Minister). In a short time Hitler abolished all parties but his own, and reduced Parliament to a mere farce. He controlled the police, using them to enslave the people; and he established special Nazi forces, the S.A. and the S.S. Those who opposed the Nazis were arrested, sent to concentration camps and horribly maltreated or killed. Many escaped abroad. By stages the Jews in Germany were turned into social outcasts, thousands being sent to the concentration camps. Distinguished Jewish scientists, artists, and business men escaped, if they could, taking their talents to other countries. With such methods Germany was terrified into letting Hitler have his way.

Hitler immediately set about rearming Germany, and this provided jobs which did much to win Hitler popularity. He was determined to destroy the Treaty of Versailles, which had rearranged Europe after Germany's defeat in 1918. In March 1936 he marched his troops into the Rhineland, which, by treaty, had been demilitarized. The countries of Europe did nothing to stop him, so Hitler decided that in future he could risk anything. He invited MUSSOLINI (q.v.), the leader of Fascist Italy, to visit him, and assured himself of Italian support. In November 1937 Hitler at a secret meeting of his generals described his plan for the German conquest of Europe. In accordance with this, his armies seized Austria in March 1938 and Czechoslovakia in March 1939. At last the British and French Governments came to realize that Hitler meant to dominate Europe; so when he attacked Poland in September 1939 they declared war against him.

For the first 2 years of the SECOND WORLD WAR (q.v. Vol. X), Hitler seemed to triumph everywhere; he conquered most of Europe,

LOUIS XIV AND HIS HEIRS

Behind the King's chair is his eldest son, the Grand Dauphin, and to the right his eldest grandson, the Duke of Burgundy. The child on the left, led by a governess, is his eldest surviving great-grandson. Painting by Nicolas de Largillière

Radio Times Hulton Lib.

HITLER TAKING THE SALUTE AT A MARCH PAST OF THE NAZI
LABOUR CORPS AT NUREMBERG, 1938

isolating Britain. But in 1941 he attacked Russia and persuaded Japan to attack the United States, and those two giant enemies proved too strong. In 1942 he dismissed his leading generals and himself took over the supreme command. In July 1944 a despairing group of German officers tried to assassinate him in order to make peace, but he escaped from them and fought on the more desperately until he had nothing left of his Empire but his air-raid shelter in Berlin; there, on 30 April 1945, he killed himself.

HOBBES, Thomas (1588–1679). Hobbes, the philosopher who wrote the famous *Leviathan*, lived a long life, from Elizabeth's reign well into the reign of Charles II, during which time England faced the religious problems caused by the REFORMATION (q.v. Vol. I) and the political problems which resulted in the CIVIL WAR (q.v. Vol. X). It was an age of experiment and new thought; the discoveries of science were changing men's ideas of the constitution of the world.

Hobbes was born at Malmesbury in Wiltshire. He took his degree at Oxford, where he studied and conceived a lifelong dislike for the philo-

sophy of ARISTOTLE (q.v.). He then became tutor to William Cavendish, afterwards Earl of Devonshire, with whom he remained for 20 happy years. He continued his friendship with the Devonshire family all his life; he never married, but later became tutor to his former pupil's son, the young Earl of Devonshire. He made several tours of the Continent with his pupils, on one of which he met Galileo, aged and in retirement. At the outbreak of the civil war he fled with many other Royalists to Paris; but after the publication of the *Leviathan*, unpopular both with English Royalists and the French Government, he returned to England and made his peace with Cromwell. At the Restoration he came into royal favour again. He lived until he was 91.

The writings of the great men of his time, such as BACON, MONTAIGNE, and DESCARTES (qq.v.), and the scientific discoveries of men such as GALILEO and KEPLER (qq.v.), stimulated Hobbes to work out a new philosophy to replace the medieval philosophy still largely taught in the universities. The study of geometry appealed to him because of its method of presenting a clear proof for every problem. Hobbes, starting from man's experience through his senses, reflected that sensation is possible only through motion, and this led him to a mechanical explanation of nature and man, based upon the laws of motion. 'What is the heart', he says, 'but a spring, and the nerves but so many strings, and the joints but so many wheels, giving motion to the whole body, such as was intended by the artificer?' Hobbes originally planned to write his great philosophy in three divisions, the first explaining the physical nature of man and the universe; the second the intellect, will, reasoning process, and moral sense—what we should call psychology; and the third the State, its function and form, and all that we include under politics and religion. But before this could be completed civil war in England became imminent, and Hobbes retired to Paris. There he wrote the third of these sections, namely that concerning the State or Commonwealth. He made, however, an introduction on the elementary foundations of philosophy and the nature of man, and so he gives a fairly complete idea of his system. It was published in 1651 under the title, *Leviathan*, for Hobbes regarded the State as a monster, created by ordinary men for their protection and security.

Hobbes held that men were moved mainly by their personal desires, and that they had no thoughts themselves of justice or injustice. Nature gave every man the right to preserve himself and to use his power as he liked to secure this end. But clearly if everyone acted as he liked there would be anarchy, bringing satisfaction and security to none. So, to avoid chaos every citizen must agree to give up his rights to a sovereign (a person or assembly) with supreme power over all. This sovereign Hobbes called the Leviathan, 'a real unity of them all', to whom they must all submit. The sovereign judges what is best, what doctrines are to be taught and what books published, and none must accuse him. In answer to the criticism that the consequences of this might be bad for some citizens, Hobbes replied that the consequences of popular government were worse; for at any rate the sovereign cannot disagree with himself, thus causing civil war. He added that, in any case, it would never be possible to make life convenient for everybody. The only exception Hobbes made to Leviathan's supremacy was resistance in self-defence.

The Leviathan must also be supreme over the Church. Hobbes does not seem to have objected to the Church of England, and he continued to receive the Church's sacraments; but his doctrine, which would reduce religion to a department of State, naturally made him unpopular with the clergy, especially with Roman Catholics who insisted on the supremacy of Church over State. *Leviathan* was condemned by Parliament in 1666; indeed, his work caused an intense intellectual ferment.

Hobbes was not among the greatest of men intellectually: his ideas in mathematics, for example, were often quite indefensible. In philosophy and religion he was a materialist, regarding political laws as creating justice rather than as being imperfect expressions of an ideal law. His judgements on the Scriptures were sound; but they did not lead to any new or enlightening view of religion. His *Leviathan* repays reading, if only for Hobbes's pure and vigorous English and his frequent flashes of wit and wisdom.

See also Vol. X: NATION AND STATE.

TITLE-PAGE OF HOBBES'S 'LEVIATHAN'

Leviathan, made up of all the members of the community, dominates the State. Below are symbols of ecclesiastical and civil rule

HOGARTH, William (1697–1764). This English painter and engraver was born in London, the son of a schoolmaster, and became the earliest artist of the great 18th-century school of painting.

At an early age he was apprenticed to an engraver of heraldic designs on silver plate, and thus acquired the skill which enabled him to set up on his own account as an engraver of book illustrations. But he was ambitious and began to study painting, stimulated by admiration for the works of Sir James Thornhill, one of the few native-born English artists who practised large decorative paintings in the continental style of BAROQUE ART (q.v. Vol. XII).

Probably Thornhill's example as a history painter, and his own experience as a book illustrator, inspired Hogarth to turn from portrait-painting to a style of painting which uses as its subject the scenes of common life, a style akin to the Dutch GENRE PAINTING (q.v. Vol. XII) of the 17th century. Instead of seeking his themes in mythology and the great events of

THE LEVÉE: PAINTING BY HOGARTH

This is one of the 'Rake's Progress' series. The Rake, in fashionable dress, is surrounded by hangers-on, including a fencing master, a dancing master, and music masters

history, Hogarth sought them in the streets of London. In his early social satires in pictures he already reveals himself as an acute observer of life and a humorist. But he was also a story-teller and a great lover of drama. He wished to tell his story like a play, scene by scene, or rather picture by picture, until the climax was reached.

One of the most famous of these 'serial' works is the 'Rake's Progress', which unfolds the story of a weak young man who, after inheriting his father's wealth, falls a victim to his own folly and indolence, and ends in a lunatic asylum. Another is the 'Marriage à la Mode' series (*see* picture, Vol. XII, p. 405), in which six pictures tell the story of a young couple whose loveless marriage has been arranged by selfish parents

for reasons of money. This, too, ends in moral downfall and finally in death. There are many others, such as 'The Four Prints of an Election' and 'Industry and Idleness'.

Hogarth himself spoke of these narrative pictures as 'modern moral subjects'. He made engravings from the paintings which became immensely popular, for they appealed to an entirely new audience of middle-class people, just as did the novels of Daniel DEFOE and Henry FIELDING (qq.v.), a great admirer of Hogarth's work. Today these engravings are known to great numbers of people who have no knowledge of Hogarth's pictures or of his fame as a painter.

Towards the close of his life Hogarth wrote a treatise called *The Analysis of Beauty*, in which he tried to prove by argument and diagram that an undulating line forms the basis of artistic beauty. But although many of the observations are shrewd, the style is confused and illiterate.

Hogarth married the daughter of Sir James Thornhill, a runaway match which turned into a happy marriage. His career, however, was not uniformly successful, especially after 1750, partly because of his vain ambition to prove himself a master of history-painting in the grand manner.

See also Vol. XII: ETCHING and ENGRAVING.

HOLBEIN, Hans (1497–1543). This German painter and draughtsman was born at Augsburg, where he studied under his father, Hans Holbein the Elder, who was also an artist. He travelled in France and Italy and was thus able to combine in his work the realism of GERMAN ART with the main trends of RENAISSANCE PAINTING (qq.v. Vol. XII). He began by designing woodcuts and painting religious pictures at Basle in Switzerland, where he settled; but the Reformation movement made it difficult at that time to earn a living there as a religious painter. Holbein met in Basle, however, some of the greatest scholars of the time, including ERASMUS (q.v.). Erasmus gave him a letter of introduction to Sir Thomas MORE (q.v.) which in 1526 Holbein brought to England. More and his friends gave him commissions, and he painted the large group of the More family which was the first domestic group painted in Europe. This painting is now lost, but is known from a drawing and from copies (*see* p. 321).

Two years later Holbein returned to Basle; but, finding conditions still disturbed, he came back to England and remained there for the rest of his life. He depended mainly at first on the patronage of German merchants in London, for whom he painted some magnificent portraits, including that of George Gisz (*see* Vol. VII, opposite p. 32). Eventually he attracted court patronage, and Henry VIII gave him a studio in Whitehall Palace. There being no demand for religious painting by the Reformed English Church, Holbein devoted himself to portraiture and to designing clothes, jewellery, and plate, as well as decorations for palaces and displays for great occasions. His style, affected by English fashion, became more formal and severe, and the rich decorative accessories in his portraits were exchanged for a plain blue or green background. His insight into character, however, combined with his sensitive drawing, infused life and solidarity into even his most formal portraits, making them not only great works of art but also invaluable historical records. His working portrait-drawings have been preserved, and are now at Windsor Castle. He died of the plague in London when he was only 46. Holbein employed pupils but left no school of painters behind him.

See also picture, p. 219.

HOLINSHED, Raphael (died *c.* 1580), Chronicler, *see* Vol. XII: HISTORIES.

HOMER (*c.* 8th–7th century B.C.). According to ancient Greek tradition Homer was the author of many epic poems of which only the *Iliad*, the story of the siege of Troy, and the *Odyssey*, the story of Odysseus' wanderings, now survive. His date, birthplace, and ancestry were disputed even in Classical times; stories of his blindness, his failure to solve a fisherman's riddle, and his

TITLE-PAGE FROM CHAPMAN'S TRANSLATION OF THE *ODYSSEY*
George Chapman (*c.* 1559–1634) was the first English translator of Homer

THE BATTLE OF FRIGATE BAY, ST. KITTS, 1782

After luring the French from Frigate Bay, Hood anchored his fleet across the Bay. The French, seen approaching from the left, were repulsed and the British garrison on the island relieved. Painting by T. Maynard

gift of a poem to his daughter as her dowry are first told by writers of the 6th and early 5th centuries B.C., and Homer is mentioned as a poet by two writers of the early 7th century. We know too that towards the end of the 6th century there was a guild of bards on the island of Chios called *Homeridae* ('sons of Homer'). In the 5th century, a line from the *Iliad* is quoted as by 'a man of Chios', and the historian Herodotus (who is the first author to mention the *Iliad* and the *Odyssey* by name) estimates that Homer had lived some 400 years earlier. The poems themselves tell us nothing directly about their author (or authors); but it has lately been suggested that the *Iliad* was composed out of earlier ballads in about 700 B.C., and the *Odyssey* some years later, and that the author of each was an Ionian Greek who had been trained as a bard. The Greek word *Homeros*, which seems to mean 'fitter together' (i.e. 'com-poser'), is probably not a personal name, but rather a 'bardic' name which may have been borne by several people at different times. We cannot therefore assume that the same man composed both the *Iliad* and the *Odyssey* (though it is not impossible). Later Greeks admired the author of the *Iliad* so much that they often called him simply 'the poet'. A not entirely imaginary account of his life might run somewhat like this: born in Smyrna about 740 B.C., he was trained as a bard and travelled about the Greek world practising his profession.

Later (perhaps after becoming blind) he settled in Chios, where he either joined an existing guild or gathered pupils to form a new one. His works included the *Iliad* and perhaps the *Odyssey* (composed towards the end of his life); after receiving honours from the Chians, he died (perhaps about 670 B.C.) while on a visit to the Island of Ios, where he was buried.

See also Vol. XII: HOMERIC LITERATURE.

HOOD, Samuel (Viscount) (1724–1816). This British admiral, described by NELSON (q.v.) as 'the greatest sea officer I ever knew', was an inspiring leader and a brilliant tactician. He concentrated his whole life on defeating the enemy decisively at sea, and with something of Nelson's own intense devotion to the person of the Sovereign, he inspired in the ships he commanded a patriotic zeal and an eager, offensive spirit.

Hood was 57 when he won his most distinguished victory. In the war with France which occurred during the last years of the American War of Independence, Hood lured the French fleet from its anchorage at Frigate Bay in the island of St. Kitts, in the West Indies, outwitted and defeated them by a series of masterly manœuvres, and then so occupied the island himself that he could not be attacked. Later that year he commanded the rear of RODNEY's battle fleet (q.v.) at the Battle of the Saints, and it was to Hood's ship that the French admiral struck his colours.

At the beginning of the NAPOLEONIC WARS (q.v. Vol. X) Hood took command of the Mediterranean fleet, and was responsible for the capture of Toulon and Corsica. When he was at length recalled at the age of 69, Nelson wrote in his praise, 'Oh miserable Board of Admiralty, they have forced the first officer in our service away from his command.'

HOPKINS, Gerard Manley (1844–89), *see* BRIDGES. *See also* Vol. XII: MODERN POETRY; SONNET.

HORACE (65–8 B.C.). The Roman poet, Quintus Horatius Flaccus, was the son of a freed slave who had prospered. His father took him to a celebrated schoolmaster in Rome, Orbilius, and then he went to Athens for further study. He commanded a legion under the Republican Brutus, until the Republicans were defeated at Philippi in 42 B.C. by Octavius Caesar (*see* AUGUSTUS CAESAR). In the general pardon that followed he was given a clerkship at the Treasury. Soon his verse attracted the attention of VIRGIL (q.v.), who introduced him to Maecenas, Octavius' chief adviser. Maecenas invited him to join his circle of literary friends, and gave him an estate in the Sabine Hills, about 30 miles east of Rome (the remains of which still exist). This enabled Horace, now 32, to write without financial anxiety. He divided his bachelor existence between Rome, the farm, and pleasant resorts such as Tibur (Tivoli). His main interests were people and literature, conduct and conversation, but as Augustus Caesar's long reign of reform and prosperity continued, Horace gradually contributed more and more by his poetry to the expression of Augustan ideals. Horace, who was shocked by civil war and loved a simple life, could sincerely advocate a return to old Roman standards of duty, piety, and frugality; and in the extension of Roman power he saw both protection from civil strife and a chance of imposing world-wide peace and respect for law. In 17 B.C., Virgil being dead, he was chosen to compose the Hymn for the great Secular Festival, and from that time was something of a Laureate, although his poetry remained largely private and personal to the end.

Horace's verse is of two very different kinds. The *Talks* (*Sermones*) or *Satires* are in loose hexameter verse (*see* VERSIFICATION, Vol. XII). Each has a theme, but glides from point to point like real conversation. They poke fun at human foibles, illustrating moral sentiments by lively anecdotes, parables, and personal allusions. Some are autobiographical and some contain literary criticism; and this is also true of the *Epistles*. The Epistle to the Piso family (wrongly styled *Ars Poetica*) had exaggerated influence on the literary criticism of the 17th and 18th centuries. Of his lyric poetry the *Odes* (*Carmina*) are his chief title to fame. For the *Odes* he cleverly adapted intricate Greek metres, especially of the 6th-century poet Alcaeus and the poetess SAPPHO (q.v.); but the peculiar weight and sonority of the Latin language, and its flexible word-order, enabled him to compose unique artistic masterpieces which defy translation. Often he had some Greek poem in mind as he wrote, yet each ode bears the stamp of his individuality. His subjects vary from the ideals and majesty of Augustan Rome, the shame of civil war, the power of poetry, the brevity of life, and the finality of death to his private ideal of the 'golden mean', country life, friendship, wine, and (not too serious) love. The wit and disarming humour of the lighter poems are a foil to the moral intensity of the heavier. Above all he is human, so that he still makes countless friends as well as admirers.

See also Vol. XII: LATIN LITERATURE; ODE.

HOWARD, John (1726–90), *see* Vol. X: PRISONS, HISTORY OF.

HOWE, Richard (Earl) (1726–99). Admiral Earl Howe was a humane and generous-hearted officer, though as stern and 'as silent as a rock'. Popularly known as 'Black Dick the sailor's friend', it was said that he used 'to go below after an action, and talk to every wounded man, sitting by the side of their cradles'.

As a boy of 14, he went on ANSON's great voyage round the world (q.v.), but his ship was forced to turn back off Cape Horn. At 33 he was already a captain, and held the post of honour in HAWKE's chase of the French at Quiberon Bay (q.v.). In 1782 he commanded the Channel fleet, winning fame for his relief of Gibraltar after it had been defended for 3 years against French and Spanish attacks. A year later, when First Lord of the Admiralty, he improved the code of naval signals.

National Maritime Museum

GEORGE III AND QUEEN CHARLOTTE VISITING LORD HOWE'S FLAGSHIP AT SPITHEAD ON 26 JUNE, 1794
The King presented Howe with a diamond hilted sword. Painting by H. P. Briggs

On the outbreak of the NAPOLEONIC WARS (q.v. Vol. X) Howe was recalled to the Channel fleet, and in 1794 defeated the French in the battle known as 'the Glorious First of June'. Meeting the French fleet from Brest on equal terms in the Bay of Biscay, Howe, improving on the tactics that RODNEY (q.v.) had already made famous, tried to break the enemy's line at all points. Though in fact only six ships, including Howe's, got through, a complete victory resulted, seven of the enemy ships being destroyed and ten more dismasted.

Howe was recalled from retirement when he was 71 to deal with the naval MUTINY at Spithead (q.v. Vol. X), and his popularity with the seamen helped him to reach a peaceful settlement.

HUDSON, Henry (*c.* 1570–1611). Nothing is known of the private life of this English navigator and explorer, who devoted himself to the task of seeking a third way from Europe to the Spice Islands of the East Indies. The Portuguese controlled the route round the Cape of Good Hope. A route found by MAGELLAN (q.v.) round South America had proved impracticable; so there was a strong demand in England and Holland for a third route, which would enable the Portuguese monopoly of the valuable spice trade to be broken.

In 1607 Hudson was employed by the English Muscovy Company, which was founded in 1554 to trade with Russia by the newly discovered route round the North Cape to Archangel. Hudson was to test the belief that the Spice Islands could be reached by sailing straight across the North Pole, an idea first put forward in the reign of Henry VIII. The commonly held belief that the tropical seas were impassable because they boiled in the intense heat of the sun had been disproved, and so it was thought that the idea that the Polar seas were frozen solid was equally likely to prove untrue. Hudson sailed up the east coast of Greenland until he reached the ice barrier, which forced him eastwards to Spitzbergen. He explored the coasts of that island, and then returned to England.

The next year Hudson sailed again for the Muscovy Company to try to find a passage round the north of Russia—the North-East Passage—but ice blocked the way. In 1609 he again attempted the North-East Passage, this time for the Dutch East India Company, but in the Arctic Ocean the Dutch crews refused to go farther. Hoping to show something for his voyage, he sailed right across the Atlantic to investigate the belief that there was a strait leading to the Pacific about the latitude of modern New York. Hudson, having explored the coast, sailed about 150 miles up what we now call the Hudson river. He found no strait, but he enabled the Dutch to found a colony at the mouth of the Hudson river, where they built the town of New Amsterdam which, when later captured by the English, was renamed New York.

Hudson's fourth and last voyage in 1610 was round North America in search of a North-West Passage. He sailed in the *Discovery* through Hudson Strait into the vast Hudson Bay, where his ship was frozen in for the winter, and he and his men suffered extreme hardship from the bitter cold and shortage of food. When the melting of the ice freed the *Discovery* Hudson wished to continue exploring; but his men mutinied—a disaster which threatened most great explorers, and had happened to Hudson himself on his third voyage. There was a desperate fight in which the mutineers overcame Hudson and cast him, his son John, and seven sick or wounded men adrift in a small open boat. They were never seen again. The mutineers reached England after a terrible voyage, during which many of them died. The survivors were immediately imprisoned for their treachery, but were soon released on the grounds that the ringleaders had already perished.

Although Hudson did not, in fact, actually discover much that had not already been discovered by explorers such as CABOT, CARTIER (qq.v.) and Chancellor, his voyages were important because they contributed to the development of the Arctic WHALING industry (q.v. Vol. VI) and opened to the English a new approach to Canada, through which later passed the most valuable fur trade in the world.

See also Vol. IV: EXPLORATION.
See also Vol. VII: HUDSON'S BAY COMPANY.

HUDSON, William H. (1841–1922), *see* Vol. XII: NATURE WRITING.

HUGO, Victor (1802–85). Hugo's father was an officer in the Napoleonic armies, and he took his family about Europe with him when possible. Thus Victor Hugo had been to Corsica, Italy, and Spain by 1812, when his mother settled in Paris. He began writing poetry very early, publishing his first volume of poems, *Odes et Ballades*, when he was 20. From that time until his death there was a continual flow of publications—lyric and epic poetry, novels, plays, reminiscences, and political writings. He was early recognized as the leading figure among the French Romantics, and finally won a position of eminence in the literary world that few French writers have held.

After the Revolution of 1848 Hugo became a member of the Constituent and Legislative Assemblies; but when Napoleon III seized power in 1851, Hugo went into exile as a protest, and did not return to France again until the establishment of the Third Republic. He was regarded universally not only as a great writer but also as a tireless defender of liberty.

Today the splendid poetical quality of his plays *Hernani* and *Ruy Blas* still holds the stage. But his weaknesses as a dramatist and novelist were that he had little gift for characterization, little self-critical sense, and little ability in abstract thought; consequently even his best-known novels, such as *Notre-Dame de Paris* and *Les Misérables*, while containing remarkable descriptive passages and stirring narrative, are too far removed from human experience to be entirely successful. Hugo was perhaps most successful as a lyric and epic poet. Full of ennobling imagination and endowed with prodigious mastery over sound and rhythm, he was at his best in such collections as *Les Feuilles d'Automne* and *La Légende des Siècles*.

See also Vol. XII: FRENCH LITERATURE.

HUME, David (1711–76). This celebrated Scottish philosopher and historian, after a period of study in France, published in 1739, when he was only 28, one of the most influential books of English philosophy of modern times—the *Treatise of Human Nature*. It excited little interest, however, when it first appeared, and Hume turned to writing admirable *Essays* on a variety of topics. In 1752 he returned to Edinburgh as

National Galleries of Scotland
DAVID HUME
Painting by Allan Ramsay

impressions will be accompanied by certain other impressions, and so we grow to think that things are actually connected by cause and effect, quite apart from our own mental processes. But, he says, this belief is not supported by reason, and there is nothing in nature to justify it. 'If we believe that fire warms and water refreshes', he writes, ''tis only because it costs us too much pain to think otherwise.' Hume believed that even a human being is a bundle of different perceptions, and has no permanent identity. His criticism of man's belief that everything has a cause seemed to deny what we assume, not merely from ordinary experience, but from scientific knowledge; and since he wrote, philosophers have been trying to find answers to his penetrating doubts. Indeed, he has had more influence upon recent discussion in England about the principles of knowledge than any other philosopher of the past.

See also LOCKE.
See also Vol. I: PHILOSOPHY.

HUNT, James Henry Leigh (1784–1859). The writer Leigh Hunt, educated at Christ's Hospital, soon began a career of authorship. By his 21st year he was known as a slashing critic of plays and players. From 1808 to 1821 he edited the independent newspaper, *The Examiner*, founded by his brother John, a determined reformer. Both brothers suffered for their courageous criticism of abuses and for their daring liberalism by government prosecutions for political libels, by fines, and prison sentences; but both also won many admirers.

Leigh Hunt was by nature a poet, not a politician; but in his poetry he had more original ideas than he had mastery to express. His best work is his *Autobiography*, in which he heralds SHELLEY, KEATS, BYRON (qq.v.), and others, and in which he presents his generous philosophy of life, built up after painful experience. Hunt also wrote some very lively essays—character studies, criticisms, tales, and so on.

HUNTER, John (1728–93). Generally regarded as the founder of modern scientific surgery, Hunter was also a pioneer in the study and teaching of pathology, physiology, and biology.

He was the youngest of the ten children of a poor Scots laird. As a schoolboy, he found the Lanarkshire countryside and its wild life more

librarian of the Advocates' Library, and began to compose *A History of England*, the final volume of which was published in 1761. From 1763 to 1765 he was secretary to the British Embassy in Paris, where he was sought after by cultured society. For the rest of his life he lived in his native Edinburgh, the central figure of a distinguished group of writers. Hume was a generous, cheerful, modest man, who spoke with a broad Scottish accent, and had an extraordinarily clear and critical mind. His close friend Adam SMITH (q.v.) wrote that he approached 'as nearly to the idea of a perfectly wise and virtuous man as perhaps the nature of human frailty will admit'.

Hume's chief fame as a philosopher rests on the strict and logical way in which he applied the principle of LOCKE (q.v.), that all thought is built up from simple and separate elements, which Hume calls impressions. We may have, for example, two distinct and separate impressions—the sight of a fire and the feeling of heat; but from where do we obtain the idea that the fire causes the heat? Hume concludes that, since each impression is separate, the connexion cannot be in things, but in our minds. We have an expectation based on experience that certain

Wellcome Collection

THE HUNTER ANATOMY SCHOOL AT GREAT WINDMILL STREET, LONDON
Lithograph after Rowlandson's *The Dissecting Room*

Hunter was always fearless in handling animals, no matter how fierce; on one occasion he recaptured with his bare hands two leopards that were escaping, and on another, when attacked by a young bull given him by the Queen, he wrestled with it until help came.

He became the leading surgeon of his day, surgeon to St. George's Hospital and to George III. He published important books, and taught several pupils who later became famous. His portrait was painted by Sir Joshua Reynolds and his bust can still be seen on the gate of St. George's Hospital at Hyde Park Corner.

His scientific museum, on which he spent £70,000, was eventually bought by the nation for £15,000 and housed in the Royal College of Surgeons. Hunter's remains were moved to Westminster Abbey some 60 years after his death.

See also Vol. XI: SURGERY, HISTORY OF.

HUSS, John (*c.* 1369–1415), Bohemian religious reformer, *see* Vol. I: MORAVIAN CHURCH.

HUXLEY, Thomas Henry (1825–95). As well as being the champion of DARWIN's (q.v.) theory of evolution, Huxley was himself a distinguished and original scientist. He was made a Fellow of the Royal Society at the age of 25.

Huxley had to struggle against difficulties. He received little formal education. In his youth he wished to be a mechanical engineer, and then he trained as a doctor. In his teens he began to read Thomas CARLYLE's books (q.v.), and as an old man he wrote: 'To make things clear and get rid of cant and shows of all sorts—this was the lesson I learnt from Carlyle's books . . . and it has stuck to me all my life.'

He became a medical apprentice in the East End of London, and then won a scholarship to the Charing Cross Hospital. When he was 21 he went as surgeon to H.M.S. *Rattlesnake*, a survey sailing-vessel, on an expedition to Australian

attractive than the classroom, and by the time he was 20 he had a good knowledge of natural history and was clever at making things with his hands, but was trained in no profession or trade. His elder brother, William, who had settled in London as a doctor and ran a private anatomy school, suggested that he should come and help in the school. He soon showed himself so outstandingly skilful at dissection that he studied with the best surgeons and won a great reputation as an anatomist.

Later he joined the army as a surgeon and accompanied a military expedition to Brittany, from which he brought home many valuable notes on gunshot wounds, as well as many biological specimens from seashore life. When he was 35 he set up in practice as a surgeon in London. But he continued to collect specimens of animal life, and built a country house at Earl's Court to serve as a field laboratory and private menagerie. From his study of these animals he was able to work out the principles of comparative ANATOMY (q.v. Vol. II) and pathology, which he later applied to surgery. In pursuit of this knowledge he had dealings with the notorious 'resurrection men', who stole dead bodies from graveyards to supply anatomists; he once paid £500 for the body of a famous 'giant' of that time, an Irishman 8 feet tall, whose skeleton can still be seen in his museum.

waters. Huxley lashed his microscope to a table in a corner of the tiny chartroom, and studied intensively the anatomy of the sea-creatures that he dredged up in his improvised net. He wrote a striking report on his anatomical studies, which was sent to England and published. On returning home 4 years later, though hailed as a distinguished scientist, he was unable to obtain regular work for some years. At last he was appointed naturalist to the Geological Survey, and other appointments followed.

When Huxley first met Darwin he denounced his theory of evolution as a 'fallacious doctrine'. But after he had read Darwin's newly published book, *The Origin of Species*, he likened its effect to 'a flash of light . . . on a dark night', and from that time, regardless of prejudice and hostility, he was essentially a Darwinian, supporting Darwin's theories in the famous debate with Bishop Wilberforce. Huxley's own book, *Evidence as to Man's Place in Nature*, also brought him abuse from frightened people who usually misunderstood what he wrote.

A fundamentally religious man, Huxley coined the word 'agnostic' to distinguish an intelligent, thoughtful person who questions accepted belief from the atheist who denies the existence of God. Huxley did an enormous amount of work for educational reform, often lecturing to working people who had little opportunity to educate themselves.

See also DARWIN.
See also Vol. II: EVOLUTION.

T. H. HUXLEY

Caricature by 'Ape' published in *Vanity Fair*, 1871

I

IBSEN, Henrik (1828–1906). This Norwegian dramatist has been likened to a north-east wind suddenly entering the stuffy hot-house atmosphere of the English theatre during the 1890's. In fact, Ibsen was over 60 and had already had a long career as a poetic dramatist when he first became known in London. He was nearly 50 when he began to write his famous prose plays, his 'social documents' by which he is best known in England and which greatly influenced such writers as Bernard SHAW (q.v.).

Ibsen, the son of a wealthy business man, was born in a small timber-trading centre in southern Norway. We know that when Peer Gynt describes life on his father's farm in the old days, Ibsen was writing from his own early memories:

> Lights gleam from every window;
> They are feasting in the big hall.

When he was 8, his father became bankrupt, and the family had to move to a poor farm, where Ibsen became a lonely, reserved boy, spending much of his time playing with his toy theatre. At 14 he was apprenticed to a chemist. In 1850 he produced his first play, and though it was a failure, he obtained employment at the Bergen theatre as a literary assistant ('stage-poet'). 'He was more quaint than handsome', someone wrote of him at the time, 'There was something clumsy and anxious in his demeanour, and he seemed afraid of being laughed at or of making a fool of himself'. At Bergen he met Suzannah Thoresen, with whom he enjoyed almost 50 years of happy married life.

Both at Bergen and at Christiania (now Oslo), where he went as sub-director of the theatre, Ibsen wrote steadily for the stage: now a romantic medieval play, now a tragedy, now a satirical verse play. But success was slow in coming, and he was continually short of money. In 1863 he won a travelling fellowship which enabled him to visit Italy and Germany, and 3 years later, when his lyric drama *Brand* appeared, he was granted a State pension.

Angered by Norwegian politics, Ibsen spent much of his later life in Germany and Italy, writing the series of plays that finally established his reputation. *Brand* and the satirical fantasy, *Peer Gynt*, were vast poetic plays, the first the story of an indomitable idealist, unwavering in his chosen faith; the second an account of a man's life from extravagant youth to failing age. Ibsen himself regarded as his best work the 'double play' called *Emperor and Galilean*, a complicated study of the struggle between early Christian doctrine and paganism, which took him 4 years to write. But this difficult drama has never been professionally acted in Britain.

Ibsen is best known by his 'social dramas', written in the early 1880's, in which he showed superb stage craftsmanship. He sought always for the truth. In *Pillars of Society*, *Ghosts*, and *An Enemy of the People*, he shows how deceit and corruption can damage communities and individual lives. *A Doll's House* shows the awakening of a

Norwegian Official Photo

HENRIK IBSEN

sense of individual responsibility in a woman who has been a spoilt child.

In his later plays, such as *Hedda Gabler*—the portrait of a self-seeking woman, a study in frustration—he reinforces the meaning of his dramatic story by using symbols. It has been said that to watch an Ibsen play of this period —*The Wild Duck* or *Rosmersholm*—is like looking into a two-storey house: straightforward drama is being acted on the ground floor and, at the same time, one more complex goes on upstairs. His last work became much more difficult. Critics have long tried to explain fully the close-woven thought of *The Master Builder*, which is, however, extraordinarily dramatic in the theatre. He finished his last play, *When We Dead Awaken*, in 1899, though he lived for another 7 years, an honoured figure in Christiania—Norway's 'grand old man'.

Ibsen was irritable and often difficult, with a tight, severe expression that repelled strangers; but his family life was happy. Until he grew too ill, he kept a regular routine, and was to be seen day by day in the streets in frock-coat and silk hat, or sitting at his usual place at a café table— the customers rising in respect when he entered. His reputation has grown steadily; the ideas that seemed advanced in his day are now generally accepted, and he is recognized as one of the world's great dramatists.

See also Vol. XII: DRAMA.

INGRES, Jean (1781–1867), *see* Vol. XII: FRENCH ART.

IQBAL, Mohammed (1873–1938). This distinguished poet, who was also lawyer, politician, and educationist, was born in West Punjab. Iqbal went to the Government College, Lahore, and then to Cambridge in 1905. After a period at the Universities of Heidelberg and Munich, where he took his Doctorate in Philosophy, he returned home, was called to the Bar in 1908, and practised law as a profession until his death. During his stay in Europe, Iqbal developed a deep dislike for Western materialism and for the narrow and selfish nationalism which seemed to him to be at the root of most political trouble in Europe.

Iqbal wrote poetry in Urdu and Persian, and was planning to write the *Book of a Forgotten Prophet* in English when he died. His prose works were published in English and Urdu. As a poet

he became the leader of the modernist movement in Asia, and as a philosopher was recognized as the best interpreter of contemporary Western philosophy and as an original thinker. But Iqbal was not only a great writer, he was also a practical politician. Elected President of the All India Moslem League in 1930, he first conceived the idea of a self-governing Moslem State. This idea led eventually to the foundation of PAKISTAN (q.v. Vol. III) and to the emergence of the Moslems as a separate nation.

See also JINNAH.

IRVING, Sir Henry John (1838–1905). The English actor H. J. Brodribb was born in Somerset and became a clerk in the City of London. But he was determined to become an actor, despite certain physical disabilities, and he devoted all his spare time to the study of acting. When he was 18, taking the stage-name of Henry Irving, he faced his first audience, playing Romeo with a cast of amateurs at the Royal Soho Theatre. As a result, he threw up his job and joined a company in Sunderland, where he made his first professional appearance in Bulwer Lytton's *Richelieu*.

For the next 10 years Irving played in the provinces, and though he had little success, he had the invaluable experience of playing more than 600 different parts. Eventually he came to London, to the St. James's Theatre, and soon won recognition, first as an interpreter of villains in melodrama, and later as a character actor with a gift for comedy.

Irving's first great triumph came with his performance of the Burgomaster, Mathias, in *The Bells*—a part which his genius transformed from melodrama to tragedy. Immediately he received recognition as a tragedian of power and originality. His performance of Hamlet in 1878 revealed the full scope of his genius and established him at the head of his profession. In the same year he became manager of the Lyceum Theatre, where his policy was to alternate Shakespearian productions with works by modern playwrights and poets. With his partner, Ellen Terry, a fine actress of great intelligence and beauty, he reigned in splendour until 1902. With his extraordinarily forceful personality, his acute dramatic intelligence, and wonderfully expressive face, he excelled in parts into which he could project his personality without straining his limited physical resources. His interpretations of Hamlet, Richard III, Shylock, and Iago were recognized to be the finest of his time, while on the other hand his Macbeth, Lear, and Othello lacked force and clarity of conception.

For 30 years he was without a rival as actor and actor-manager. He raised the standards of the theatre and the status of his fellow players by his own integrity and his single-minded devotion to his art, for which he was knighted by Queen Victoria in 1895; he was the first actor to receive that honour.

Irving was lavish, even extravagant, in the conduct of his theatre; in private, his only indulgence was the entertainment of his friends, among whom were numbered most of the distinguished men of the day. After 1897 a series of misfortunes robbed him of his financial reserves, his stock of scenery on which his repertory depended, and finally of his health. In 1899 he gave up his financial interest in the Lyceum Theatre. He played his last London season at Drury Lane in the summer of 1905—a season especially remarkable for the perfection of his performances and for public demonstrations of admiration and affection.

See also Vol. IX: Acting, History of.

Victoria & Albert Museum

IRVING AS WOLSEY IN 'HENRY VIII'

ISAIAH (*c.* 760–690 B.C.). We know that Isaiah received his call to be a prophet 'in the year that King Uzziah died', namely 740 B.C., and that he was alive in 701 B.C., when Sennacherib invaded Judah; those are the only dates we have. The historical record of the reigns of Uzziah, Jotham, Ahaz, and Hezekiah, through which Isaiah lived, is found in 2 Kings xv–xx.

Isaiah is an outstanding figure among the Hebrew prophets or visionaries (*see* PROPHECY, Vol. I), who played so important a part in developing the simple faith of the early nomadic Israelites into the highly civilized worship of one God, with its high code of morality, its religious literature, priests, temple, and ritual. When Isaiah was born, the united kingdom which DAVID and SOLOMON (qq.v.) had established had been disrupted by tribal jealousies, and had so become an easy prey to the neighbouring powers.

Isaiah's call came one day when he was in the temple in Jerusalem. Falling into a trance, he saw the vision which is described in the Book of Isaiah vi. At the climax of the vision, Isaiah heard the voice of Jehovah cry, 'Whom shall I send, and who will go for us?' Isaiah answered, 'Here am I; send me.' In his vision Isaiah was charged to tell the Israelites of the coming destruction of their land as a judgement on them for their sins.

Isaiah's mission to the Israelites lays its stress on moral conduct. Injustice, murder, bribery, and oppression of the poor and helpless—these are the things condemned. Religion without right conduct, Isaiah says, is valueless. God is tired of their fasts and feasts and sacrifices. Let them cease to do evil and learn to do good. This was not new teaching. Elijah had asserted it against the despotic Ahab, and Amos had proclaimed it in Samaria only a generation before Isaiah. But none had spoken with such passion, weight, and eloquence as Isaiah. He made it plain for all time that no ceremonial worship could make up for the lack of right conduct. God was holy and good, and man must be like him.

Isaiah prophesied that the ASSYRIANS (q.v. Vol. I) would bring the judgement of the Lord upon the Israelites. The first threat came from Syria, and the Hebrew King Ahaz in fear appealed to Assyria for help. Isaiah protested vigorously, telling Ahaz to cease following false gods and to trust in the Lord; but Ahaz preferred to pay tribute to Assyria. The Assyrians, as Isaiah knew they would, soon attacked Hebrew territory, capturing Samaria. Meanwhile Ahaz's son, Hezekiah, on succeeding his father, made an attempt to bring about reform; but in 701 B.C. the Assyrian leader Sennacherib marched against Judah and ordered Jerusalem to surrender. Hezekiah wanted to seek help from Egypt; but Isaiah declared that Egypt was a broken reed, and boldly prophesied that the Assyrians would never capture Jerusalem. In fact, they never did, for some disaster caused Sennacherib to withdraw his troops, and Jerusalem was for the time saved. After Hezekiah's death, his son, Manasseh, went back to the idolatry and immorality of the past, and Isaiah may have fallen victim to the persecutions of this reign.

Isaiah was the champion of the weak and poor at a time when power was used without pity. His thought about God was exalted and noble, and he was a poet of a high order, using abundant and varied imagery. He believed that God destroyed only to purify, and that from a surviving remnant God would raise a new nation. He prophesied the coming of 'The Prince of Peace' and of a time when 'They shall not hurt nor destroy in all my holy mountain: for the earth shall be full of the knowledge of the Lord . . .'.

A great part of the Book of Isaiah was clearly written by another and later prophet, generally known as the Second Isaiah. In 587 B.C., more than 100 years after the death of Isaiah, Nebuchadnezzar, King of Babylon, captured Jerusalem and took the people of Judah into exile. The second part of Isaiah, beginning with the famous Chapter xl, is a message of hope, promising deliverance. 'Comfort ye, comfort ye, my people, saith your God. Speak comfortably to Jerusalem, and cry unto her, that her warfare is accomplished, that her iniquity is pardoned.' In fact, in 538 B.C. the Persian leader CYRUS (q.v.) captured Babylon and brought the Babylonian power to an end (*see* BABYLONIAN CIVILIZATION, Vol. I). Soon after this, many of the Hebrew exiles returned to their own land and re-established their national life in Judah.

The oracles of this second prophet, about whom we know nothing, not even his name, became attached to those of the great Isaiah, and so were preserved. Both their poetic beauty and their religious thought are of supreme value. Four poems, known as the 'Servant Songs', are

Archives Photographiques
THE PROPHET ISAIAH
Stone figure, *c*. 1110, from the portal of Souillac Abbey, France

to be found in Chapters xlii. 1–4, xlix. 1–6, l. 4–9, and lii. 13–liii. 12. These speak of a 'servant of God', appointed for a special purpose, and accepting suffering because it will ultimately be to the advantage of the world. This 'servant' has been taken by Christians to be a prophecy of the ministry of Jesus Christ; but the prophet was probably thinking of the Jewish exiles as being collectively God's servant who, having been purified by suffering, would go back to serve God more sincerely. The last chapters of Isaiah from lvi to the end are by yet a third and later writer. They are not of outstanding importance.

See also JEREMIAH.
See also Vol. I: PROPHECY; HEBREW CIVILIZATION.

IVAN THE TERRIBLE
From Thevet, *Cosmographie Universelle*, 1575

IVAN THE TERRIBLE (1530–84). Ivan IV became Grand Duke of Muscovy when he was 3, and in 1547, when he was 17, he was crowned first Emperor (Tsar) of Russia.

Muscovy was the small principality around Moscow from which has developed the modern Russian State. Another Ivan, 'the Great', had started this growth about 1450 by conquering the land northwards and eastwards of Muscovy as far as the Arctic Ocean and the Ural Mountains, and making Archangel, on the White Sea, Russia's first sea-port. Ivan IV had three main objects during his reign: to subdue the great nobles of Russia (*boyars*); to extend his dominions eastwards and southwards, driving back the nomadic Mongol peoples; and to open direct contact with western Europe by seizing an outlet to the Baltic Sea. Against the Mongols he won complete success, adding the whole basin of the river Volga to his dominions. Westwards he was at first successful, but Poland and Sweden proved too strong for him, and he failed to win his outlet to the Baltic.

It was his treatment of his subjects, especially the *boyars*, which has earned Ivan the title 'Terrible'. During the second half of his reign, crazed with suspicion, fear, and ungovernable rage, he committed terrible cruelties on individuals and communities. In 1580, in a moment of frenzy, he struck his adored eldest son a blow so severe that he died, and this filled him with such remorse that he would have retired to a monastery had there been anyone else strong enough to rule. When he died 3 years later, Russia fell into the kind of chaos which often follows the death of a tyrant.

See also Vol. I: RUSSIANS.

J

JACKSON, Thomas ('Stonewall') (1824–63), American General, *see* LEE.

JAMES, Henry (1843–1916), American novelist, *see* Vol. XII: AMERICAN LITERATURE.

JEFFERIES, Richard (1848–87), *see* Vol. XII: NATURE WRITING.

JEFFERSON, Thomas (1743–1826). Jefferson was the author of the famous American Declaration of Independence (*see* AMERICAN CONSTITUTION, Vol. X), which Americans celebrate every year on 4 July, its anniversary. He played a leading part in the struggle of the American Colonies to gain freedom from Britain (*see* AMERICAN WAR OF INDEPENDENCE, Vol. X), and became third President of the United States.

Jefferson was born in Virginia, the son of a planter of Welsh descent, and became a successful lawyer before taking to politics. When quarrels over taxation between Britain and her American Colonies broke out, Jefferson became a leader of the revolutionary group in the Virginia House of Burgesses, in spite of threats of prosecution for high treason by the British Government. As the crisis grew, the Virginians sent Jefferson to Philadelphia to attend a special meeting of representatives of the Colonies (known as the Continental Congress) which was determined to win self-government.

Jefferson, 'frank, explicit, decisive' in the debates, won the respect of the Congress, and was appointed chairman of a committee of five members charged with drawing up a document declaring the colonists' intention to break from Britain. This document, known as the Declaration of Independence, was written by Jefferson himself with only small amendments by others. On 4 July 1776, Congress voted to accept the Declaration.

Jefferson then busied himself with drawing up a constitution for Virginia, and introducing various reforms. Among these reforms were religious freedom, the disestablishment of the Anglican Church, and the abolition of the English feudal law which gave an eldest son the right to inherit all his father's estate—a law which remained in force in England until the 1920's. Jefferson was twice elected governor of Virginia, and founded the University there. He was called upon to defend his State against the attacks of the British army in the last years of the War of Independence.

In 1785 Jefferson was appointed American Minister (Ambassador) in France and, though in sympathy with the French revolutionary movement, he carried out his duties with great tact. Four years later, when the Americans set up a federal government under George WASHINGTON, Jefferson became its Secretary of State, with Alexander HAMILTON (qq.v.) as Secretary of the Treasury. Jefferson was strongly opposed to giving greater power to the central government, and the support he gave to farmers as against town traders, and his sympathy with revolutionary France, caused several clashes with Hamilton. Jefferson later became the leader of the Democratic party, and Hamilton of the Republican party; these, in spite of many changes in name, have remained the two traditional American political parties.

When he was 57 Jefferson was elected President of the United States and later was re-elected for a second term. Perhaps his greatest achievement then was the purchase from Napoleon of the territory of Louisiana, which had been ceded to France by Spain.

Jefferson had many interests and talents: he was a good classical scholar, a musician, a dashing horseman, and a man of wide scientific interests. He was tall, with a fine, broad forehead, and, in his youth, a mop of red hair. He was unaffectedly simple in all things. As President he did away with all ceremony, believing that the head of the State should not be artificially distinguished from the people. Instead of driving to the capital in a coach he rode on horseback 'in a suit of plain cloth' without a guard or servants. He did away with all titles of honour, even 'Mr.' being distasteful to him.

See also HAMILTON; WASHINGTON.
See also Vol. X: AMERICAN WAR OF INDEPENDENCE; AMERICAN CONSTITUTION.

The Lord Chancellor taken disguised in Wapping

Ingraven for the Devills Broker

Ashmolean Museum

THE CAPTURE OF JUDGE JEFFREYS AT WAPPING
From a contemporary broadside

JEFFREYS, George (Baron) (1648–89). 'Infamous Jeffreys', who became Lord Chief Justice of England, was notorious for his harshness—which was sometimes attributed to the pain he suffered from an internal malady.

Jeffreys is best remembered for the 'Bloody Assize', an ASSIZE COURT (q.v. Vol. X) which he held at Taunton and elsewhere in 1685, to try the followers, mainly simple countrymen, of the Duke of Monmouth in his rebellion against James II. The trials were a mockery of justice, but 320 prisoners were executed and hundreds more transported, whipped, or fined. The King rewarded Jeffreys by making him Lord Chancellor. When James fled during the REVOLUTION OF 1688 (q.v. Vol. X), Jeffreys fled also, but was captured in the docks near London disguised as a seaman, and died in the Tower of London.

JENNER, Edward (1749–1823). This English country doctor was the discoverer of vaccination and a pioneer in modern preventive medicine. The almost universal adoption of vaccination succeeded in reducing SMALLPOX (q.v. Vol. XI) from a persistent world-wide plague to a disease with rare and limited outbreaks.

Jenner was the son of a Gloucestershire parson, who died when his son was only 5. Jenner left school when he was 13 and served an apprenticeship (as was then usual) with a doctor near Bristol, before spending 2 years at St. George's Hospital, London, to finish his training. There he was the pupil of the famous John HUNTER (q.v.), and between them there sprang up an affectionate and lasting friendship which did much to stimulate Jenner's naturally lively and inquiring mind. Hunter might have helped Jenner to an important career in London; but Jenner, a naturally simple person, fond of music, poetry, conversation, and above all of a quiet country life, preferred to be a country doctor. Having turned his back on London and its wealth of opportunities he found his greatest opportunity awaiting him in his native village.

From time to time the dairy herds in the rich farming country round his home developed 'pocks' or sores on their teats which sometimes spread to the hands of the milkmaids. It was noticed that, for some unexplained reason, these milkmaids did not seem to catch smallpox as other people did, a fact which Jenner studied carefully for about 20 years. Nobody then knew of the existence of germs, but Jenner was able by patient and careful observation to discover the true explanation—that the sick animals gave some form of protection to the milkmaids. He found that only the sores that were true 'cowpox' appeared to give protection against smallpox, and that cowpox itself only gave such protection when passed on at a certain stage in its development. He had to wait for all the conditions to be right before he could test the truth of his conclusions. On 14 May 1796 he performed the first vaccination by inserting cowpox matter into two scratches made on the arm of a healthy 8-year-old boy named James Phipps. A few months later the same boy was inoculated with the disease of smallpox, and the disease failed to 'take'.

All Jenner's hopes were justified, and in 1798 he published his discovery. At first it aroused fierce opposition from the medical profession, but was received by the public with more enthusiasm. Even in days when news travelled slowly, vaccination was accepted more spontaneously and more universally than any medical discovery of modern times before PENICILLIN (q.v. Vol. XI). The wealthy in all countries, including many kings and queens, were its strongest supporters, and its almost miraculous effects made them acclaim Jenner as a benefactor of humanity. Many public honours were paid to him, and a grateful Parliament made him two grants of money, one of £10,000 and the other of £20,000. There are statues and memorials to Jenner in many parts of the world. But fame did not spoil the simple country doctor. He continued living at Berkeley, carrying on his practice in what time he could spare from his work for the cause of vaccination, until he died at 73.

Jenner was also a gifted naturalist; he was the first to describe how the baby CUCKOO (q.v. Vol. II) ousts the other nestlings or eggs from the nest, a fact only recently confirmed by cinematography; and he anticipated Charles Darwin in appreciating the importance of the role of the EARTHWORM (q.v. Vol. VI) in the maintenance of good arable soil.

See also Vol. XI: INOCULATION AND VACCINATION.

Wellcome Collection
EDWARD JENNER
From the mezzotint by J. R. Smith

JEREMIAH (*c.* 650–580 B.C.). The introduction of the Book of Jeremiah says that this Hebrew prophet began his work in the thirtieth year of Josiah's reign, that is, 626 B.C. His call is described as an inward revelation, unaccompanied by visions of God such as those seen by ISAIAH (q.v.) and Ezekiel.

Jeremiah's home was at Anathoth, a village just outside Jerusalem. His family was a priestly one. When Jeremiah was a young man, King Josiah concerned himself with reforming Hebrew religious practice according to the 'Book of the Law' which had been recently discovered in the Temple. But Jeremiah took little interest in Josiah's reform, good as it was, for his teaching went deeper than a right performance of ritual; he insisted on the obedience of the heart to God's moral demands—an individual response to God rather than a communal obedience to tribal laws.

At this time there was rivalry between Egypt and the powerful nations of the East, Assyria and Babylonia. Judah was not strong enough to remain completely independent of these powers. In 608 B.C., when the Egyptian army marched east, Josiah, King of Judah, tried to stop it and was defeated and killed. Two years later, the Babylonians, under Nebuchadnezzar, defeated the Assyrians and then turned on the Egyptians, whom they also defeated. Babylon was then the leading nation.

During this time of desolating warfare Jeremiah came to the front, both as religious and political adviser. He preached that Judah, having turned from God and accepted the lower standards of the Baals, the local gods of the CANAANITES (q.v. Vol. I), must expect disaster. His continual prophecies of disaster have resulted in the coining of the modern word 'jeremiad', meaning a doleful recital of troubles. Jeremiah's religious ideas were far in advance of his time. He taught that men should replace the old covenant given to Moses with a new covenant written in men's hearts, and establishing a relationship between God and man so intimate that men would not need to be taught about God.

Early in the reign of Jehoiakim, Josiah's son, Jeremiah preached a famous sermon in the Temple in which he declared that God would destroy the Temple and Jerusalem unless the people changed their ways. This aroused great anger, and Jeremiah narrowly escaped death.

He was forbidden to preach, and so he wrote out his prophecies and bade his secretary read them to the people. The King destroyed the writings, but Jeremiah, in hiding, wrote them again and added to them. The threatened destruction did not come in Jehoiakim's reign; but on his death Nebuchadnezzar descended on Jerusalem, took the city, and carried off to Babylon the new King and his family and all the soldiers and skilled craftsmen. He appointed a new King over those left behind. Jeremiah declared that Judah's only hope lay in repentance and submission to Babylon; but the nobles refused to listen. Then, as Jeremiah warned them, Nebuchadnezzar returned, and after a 2 years' siege, destroyed Jerusalem, took a cruel vengeance on the King, and carried off to Babylon the remaining inhabitants, except the very poor. Jeremiah he treated with courtesy and allowed to remain in Judah, though later he was forced to join a large migration into Egypt. What happened to him in the end we do not know, but as he continued to preach the same message, he probably ended with a martyr's death. Jeremiah believed that one day a remnant would return from exile in Babylon and build the nation anew, and this happened about 40 years later when the Persian CYRUS (q.v.) destroyed Babylonia and freed the subject peoples.

See also ISAIAH.

See also Vol. I: HEBREW CIVILIZATION; PROPHECY; BABYLONIAN CIVILIZATION.

JERVIS, Sir John (Earl of St. Vincent) (1735–1823). The admiral who won the Battle of Cape St. Vincent was the sternest disciplinarian the ROYAL NAVY (q.v. Vol. X) has known. 'Old Jarvie' fought and did much to stamp out the easy corruption, 'frippery and gimcrack' that were prevalent in the Navy of his time, and by strict discipline he made the fleets he commanded invincible. He cared for the welfare of his seamen, and his unerring eye for merit led him to press, among others, NELSON'S claims for promotion (q.v.).

Jervis joined the Navy when he was 14 without money or connexions to help him. In 1759 he was in charge of the boats which landed WOLFE's men below the Heights of Abraham at Quebec, and he later served under HOWE (qq.v.) during the relief of Gibraltar. At the outbreak of the NAPOLEONIC WARS (q.v. Vol. X) he was commanding the West Indies station, and captured from France the islands of Martinique and Guadaloupe.

In 1795, by then a full Admiral, he became commander-in-chief in the Mediterranean, where his outstanding ability for training and for improving efficiency had full scope. He never hesitated to attack inefficient officers: for example, when a ship's captain complained that his crew were below strength, Jervis wrote: 'There are men enough at Gibraltar, and you and your officers would be better employed in picking them up than laying upon your backs and roaring like bull-calves'; and he checked the spread of naval mutiny in 1797 by ruthlessly hanging the first mutineer at the yard-arm of his flagship, the *Victory*, on a Sunday morning (*see* MUTINY, Vol. X).

The great battle from which Jervis took his title was fought on 14 February 1797. Britain had been forced to surrender the Mediterranean to the fleets of France and Spain, and Jervis had withdrawn his ships to Lisbon. A Spanish fleet of twenty-seven ships was ordered to join the French fleet at Brest; Jervis, with only fifteen ships, and determined to prevent the enemy fleets from joining, met the Spanish fleet off Cape

National Maritime Museum

ADMIRAL JERVIS, EARL OF ST. VINCENT, IN ADMIRAL'S UNDRESS UNIFORM

Mezzotint after the portrait by J. Keenan

St. Vincent. As the enemy fleet hove into view the captain of Jervis's flagship reported that their strength was nearly double his own. Jervis replied: 'Enough of that, Sir, if there are fifty sail, I will go through them. A victory is very essential to England at this moment.' Though the action was distinguished by the brilliant conduct of Nelson, who for a time engaged single-handed three of the biggest enemy ships, Jervis's whole fleet fought heroically, and won a complete victory. The Spanish fleet was split into two and the rear scattered with severe losses. Three years later Jervis took charge of the Channel fleet, closely blockading the French at Brest, and by unsparing energy held the enemy inactive for the rest of the war.

As First Lord of the Admiralty, his active service being over, Jervis tried to stamp out corruption in the dockyards as ruthlessly as he had eliminated inefficiency at sea. Though his strictness and outspoken criticism was notorious, and made him many enemies, he won, as the playwright SHERIDAN (q.v.) said, a 'triple laurel over the enemy, the mutineer, and the corrupt'. George III referred to him affectionately as 'my Old Oak', and after the Battle of the Nile Nelson wrote to him as his commander-in-chief: 'We look up to you as our father, under whose fostering care we have been led to fame.'

See also NELSON.
See also Vol. X: ROYAL NAVY.

JESUS CHRIST, *see* Vol. I: JESUS OF NAZARETH.

JINNAH, Mahomed Ali (1876–1948). Jinnah was the leader of the Indian Moslems in their long political struggle with the Hindus which preceded the foundation of the new Moslem Dominion of PAKISTAN (q.v. Vol. III). The Moslems, though opposed to British rule, feared being overshadowed by the large Hindu majority among the INDIAN PEOPLES (q.v. Vol. I).

Jinnah, the son of a wealthy merchant in Karachi, went to London when he was 16 and studied law at Lincoln's Inn for 4 years. Tall, immaculately dressed, with a fine face, and a strong, powerful voice, Jinnah on his return to India soon became one of the leading lawyers in Bombay, and active in Indian politics. At 30 he was private secretary to the President of the Indian National Congress—the main political party in India, in which the overwhelming majority were Hindus. Seven years later he joined the Moslem League (the principal Moslem political party), while at the same time remaining a member of Congress. During the next few years he worked to bring about an alliance between the League and Congress, who were already bitterly hostile to each other; but he was soon persuaded that co-operation was impossible unless the Moslem minority was protected by effective legislation. When, in 1916, be became President of the League, he was determined to win them greater political rights.

For the next 30 years Jinnah and Mahatma GANDHI (q.v.) dominated Indian politics. India, determined to win independence, seized every opportunity to attack the British Government. But the Hindus and Moslems, hostile and suspicious of each other, tore the country in two and appeared to make any solution impossible. When in 1928 the British Government sent a commission to India to attempt to solve these differences, Jinnah drafted the League's 'fourteen points' which for the first time set out the Moslem point of view to the British Government. At further conferences in London Jinnah acted as the Moslem spokesman, and stayed on to attend the Commons' debates on the Government of India Act (1935), which awarded self-government to the Indian Provinces (*see* INDIA, GOVERNMENT OF, Vol. X).

Jinnah then toured India, determined to persuade all Moslems to rally to the League, and thus to compel Congress and the British Government to accept their co-operation in administering the new Act. Jinnah feared that in the self-governing Provinces Moslems would not only be barred from holding office but might also suffer political persecution. When the Moslems were in fact excluded from office, Jinnah led the Moslem agitation for a separate, independent State of their own. He became known as *Quaid-i-Azam* ('the Great Leader'). But the League and Congress being unable to agree, the struggle dragged on bitterly for another 10 years. At length in 1947 the British Parliament passed the India Independence Act, setting up the independent Moslem Dominion of Pakistan and the mainly Hindu Union of India. Jinnah was appointed governor-general of Pakistan, but he died after only one year in office.

See also GANDHI; IQBAL.
See also Vol. X: PAKISTAN, GOVERNMENT OF; INDIA, GOVERNMENT OF.

JOAN OF ARC (1412–31). The appearance of this young, uneducated, peasant girl from the remote village of Domrémy in Lorraine as the saviour of France near the end of the HUNDRED YEARS WAR (q.v. Vol. X) is one of the most remarkable events of French history. Joan's father cultivated a little land, and until she was 17 she led a normal country life, spinning, ploughing, minding the cattle, and learning her religion from the village priest. But one summer day, as a child of 13, when she was in her father's garden, she heard a voice beside her coming out of a great light and speaking to her. She believed the voice to be that of the Archangel Michael, and it seemed to her that he told her to go to the French Court and save the nation from the English.

France at this time was in a very unhappy position. In the years following the defeat of the French army at Agincourt in 1415, Henry V of England had married the French princess, and the poor old French King Charles VI had signed a treaty cutting out his own heir, Charles, the 'Dauphin', from the succession in favour of the English King. The French barons and princes thought only of their own gain and not at all of their country, and the army was utterly discouraged When, in 1422, both the French King and Henry V died, the English claimed the throne of France for Henry's son, the boy Henry VI. Several of the powerful French barons, including the mighty Duke of Burgundy, joined the English, and the Dauphin Charles was faced with both civil war and a foreign invasion.

Joan, meantime, though she continued to have visions and hear voices, went on living at home for another 4 years, growing more devout and more apart from other people. The voices continued, becoming more insistent, and urging her to seek the help of the commander of the local garrison. Finally she went to him and succeeded in persuading him to give her an escort to take her to the Dauphin, at the castle of Chinon on the river Loire.

The appearance at the Court of a sturdily built country girl of 17, dressed in man's clothing, declaring that she was sent by God to lead the army and to bring Charles to be crowned at Rheims, must have seemed to the Court an absurdity. But Joan supplied what the Dauphin and his followers lacked—courage and faith. She had natural courtesy combined with unshakeable conviction and a direct manner of speech. When she entered the hall, she at once won his confidence by recognizing him even though he was disguised as a courtier. His situation was desperate. The English were at the walls of Orleans, the strategic key to central France; and the French had lost all confidence that they could save the city. Joan declared that she would lead the army to raise the siege. For weeks Charles hesitated, influenced by powerful Ministers who feared and hated Joan; but at last, there being nothing else to do, he followed her lead, and the army marched to the relief of Orleans in April 1429. Joan rode at the head of her army, wearing a coat of mail and carrying a great sword and a white banner embroidered with the *fleur de lys*.

Musée Historique, Orléans

JOAN OF ARC ARRIVING AT THE CASTLE OF CHINON

The Dauphin comes out to the drawbridge to meet her. 15th-century German (or possibly Swiss) tapestry

Orleans lies on the north bank of the river Loire, connected with the other bank by a bridge, at the southern end of which was a fort. The English had occupied the fort and destroyed the bridge. They had also built a chain of forts encircling Orleans to the north. The town could not be relieved until the English had been thrown out of these forts. This feat Joan, with no knowledge of soldiering at all, achieved in 9 days, where experienced soldiers had failed. She succeeded because she saw that attack rather than passive defence was the best way to defeat the English, and because she inspired with courage the soldiers and townspeople, who genuinely believed that she came from God. With surprisingly little difficulty the relieving army entered Orleans, and then Joan led the soldiers and townsmen to attack the main fort. Though wounded, she fought from early morning until late in the evening, when on the last attack panic spread among the English, who abandoned the fort with heavy losses.

The moral effect of the day's fighting was so great that the English withdrew from Orleans, and the immediate threat to the French cause was ended. Joan led the French on to drive the English from several other towns on the Loire and routed them at the Battle of Patay. The whole military situation was changed. The soundness of the English position had depended on their being victorious; they had neither men nor money enough for a real occupation, nor for fighting a defensive war on a dangerously extended front. Their advantage had lain in the confidence inspired in them by victory and in the weaknesses of the French leaders. But after Joan had given both leadership and faith to the French, fear spread among the English. Within 3 months, in July 1429, the Dauphin was crowned King of France in the cathedral at Rheims, Joan herself standing proudly beside the kneeling King, holding the royal banner.

This was the peak of Joan's achievement. She then decided that the capture of Paris must be the next step. But the King was more concerned with diplomacy than with battles; therefore, listening to enemies who were jealous of Joan, he refused to support her attack. Finally, when she went to the relief of a city which was being attacked by the Duke of Burgundy, she and some followers were surprised and captured. The King, who owed everything to her, made no attempt to save her; but the English, being determined that she should die discredited, in order to destroy the sense of confidence which she had given the French, paid a large ransom to her captor. They handed her over to the Court of the INQUISITION (q.v. Vol. I), and bribed the Bishop of Beauvais, by promise of rich preferment, so to dominate her trial that she should be found guilty of heresy and witchcraft.

Probably her trial was no more unfair than that of many people accused of heresy before the Inquisition. She was kept chained in a cell for many weeks. She was allowed neither counsel nor adviser, but had to defend herself against the ceaseless questioning of skilled clerical lawyers. To all their interrogations she answered boldly and frankly, often making her examiners look foolish. After a 2 months' trial, during which she was accused of absurd crimes, even of having flown through the air like a witch, her prosecutors drew up twelve charges against her. She was chiefly accused of acting according to her private desires and of denying the authority of the Church. The verdict of guilty was inevitable. At one point, after incessant persuasions from the clergy, and terrified by the threat of death by burning, Joan broke down and confessed to guilt. But when she heard that she would be saved from burning only to be condemned to perpetual imprisonment, her anger restored her courage, she withdrew her confession, and again declared her faith in her voices. She was condemned to be burnt as a heretic, and the sentence was carried out in Rouen, the English headquarters, on 30 May 1431. She died holding a rough cross of sticks, given her by an English soldier, and calling on the name of Jesus.

The war dragged on for more than 20 years. But Joan had captured the initiative for the French, and eventually the English were expelled. The legend of Joan grew with the centuries. In 1456 the verdict at her trial was reversed by the Pope and the calumnies wiped out. She became the heroine of France, and, in 1920, nearly 500 years after her death, the Church declared her a Saint.

See also Vol. X: HUNDRED YEARS WAR.

JOHN (1167–1216), King of England, *see* Vol. X: MAGNA CARTA.

JOHN, St., Apostle, *see* Vol. I: BIBLE.

JOHNSON, Samuel (1709–84). The great Doctor Johnson was born at Lichfield, the son of a bookseller. He was a heavy, ungainly child, infected with scrofula, or the 'King's Evil', which left him scarred and caused him much suffering all his life. At school he was a brilliant but unreliable scholar and, despite his ugliness, gained a certain popularity and earned considerable respect by sheer force of personality.

In 1728 Johnson went up to Pembroke College, Oxford; but though he made friends and worked hard, he felt his poverty keenly. He could not afford to attend all the lectures and used to go across the road to Christ Church to copy a friend's notes until the dreadful state of his shoes was noticed. When a new pair was left at his door he returned them with angry pride, and at the end of the year, without a degree, he returned to Lichfield. At the age of 26 he married a widow 20 years older than himself, to whom he was devoted. After a short period as a schoolmaster near Lichfield, he set

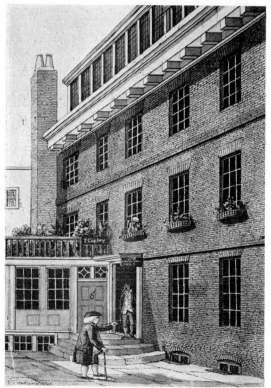

British Museum

BOLT COURT, FLEET STREET, WHERE DR. JOHNSON LIVED IN HIS OLD AGE

He occupied this house from 1777 until his death. From Pennant's *London*, vol. VIII

out for London with his pupil, David GARRICK (q.v.), to seek his fortune. Talking to Garrick in later years, Johnson said, 'I came with twopence halfpenny in my pocket, and thou, Davy, with three halfpence in thine.'

In London he and his wife lived in utmost poverty, but he fell in love with the city. 'When a man is tired of London', he said later, 'he is tired of life.' He earned his living by writing articles for *The Gentleman's Magazine*, and wrote a fine life of the poet Savage, with whom he had often walked the streets all night for want of a lodging. His poem *London*, published in 1738, was much praised; but it was not until 1746 that he began on the work which was to make him famous—his *Dictionary of the English Language*. For 9 years he laboured with a few helpers at this huge task. During this time he wrote his finest poem, *The Vanity of Human Wishes*, and published a series of periodical essays mainly on moral subjects, called *The Rambler*, which established his reputation. But in 1752 he lost his wife—a profound and enduring grief to him.

The appearance of the great Dictionary in 1755 assured his fame. Johnson describes a writer of dictionaries as 'a harmless drudge . . . bearing burdens with dull patience, and beating the track of the alphabet with sluggish resolution'. But where earlier dictionaries had been mere vocabularies Johnson's was—and remains to this day—a work of literature. He was ignorant of the early history of the language, but he had a genius for definition, and his literary references show the amazing range of his reading and his prodigious memory. The Dictionary was more complete than any before it, and had no rival till the end of the 19th century.

In 1759, wanting money to pay for his mother's funeral, he wrote a book during the evenings of a single week, sending it to the printers sheet by sheet as it was ready. The book, which was an immediate success, was *Rasselas, Prince of Abissinia*, a parable to prove the truth that 'Human life is everywhere a state in which much is to be endured, and little to be enjoyed'.

When he was 53, Johnson was granted a government pension of £300 a year and, though he had defined a pension as 'pay given to a state hireling for treason to his country', he accepted it and was never short of money again. He had said that 'No man but a blockhead ever wrote except for money', and now he was able to indulge himself in the one real joy of his life—conversation. Except for two great works still to come, it is as a conversationalist that we think of him for the rest of his life.

In 1765 he brought out his edition of Shakespeare—the first edition in which any real attempt was made to establish exactly what Shakespeare wrote. Though Johnson knew just what an editor ought to do, he did not always do it thoroughly enough, and later scholars soon made his text out of date. But the literary criticism in the notes, and especially in the great *Preface*, in which he clearly recognized (as Dryden had done before him) the great genius of Shakespeare, has lost nothing of its value.

In 1777 a group of booksellers asked him to write introductions to a collection of British poets, and so originated his most-read work *The Lives of the Poets*. Written in Johnson's magnificent prose, the biographies, though not always entirely accurate, are lively, prejudiced by his own political and religious convictions (as in the life of Milton), and full of anecdotes. The criticism is penetrating, sane, and forthright, combining all that was best in the standards of his time with a personal freshness and common sense which never allow him to become dry and pedantic.

Johnson was a huge, untidy figure in an uncombed wig and with wrinkled stockings; he had a curious way of twitching his face and body and peering short-sightedly at the company. He was often rude and overbearing, especially where he suspected any false sentimentality; but people put up with his roughness and grotesque appearance for the sake of the wit and wisdom of his conversation. He was, in fact, both generous and tenderhearted: he would put pennies in the hands of destitute children as they slept in the street so that they could at least buy some breakfast in the morning. He supported for many years an odd and quarrelsome household which included an ex-waiter, a liberated Negro slave, and his cat, Hodge, for whom he bought oysters. He took especial pleasure in good food, once saying, 'For my part I mind my belly very studiously and very carefully'. Tea was his favourite beverage; he described himself as one 'who with tea amuses the evening, with tea solaces the midnight, and with tea welcomes the morning'. On one occasion at a lady's tea-table, he drank twenty-five cups of tea rather than talk to his hostess. He loved above all things a tavern

Victoria & Albert Museum
BOSWELL AND DR. JOHNSON CONVERSING
Drawing by Samuel Collings

and a circle of intelligent men with whom he could enjoy good food and good talk, and in 1762 he founded 'The Club', with Sir Joshua REYNOLDS and Oliver GOLDSMITH (qq.v.) among its many famous members.

For the last 20 years of his life he chiefly relied upon his friends, the Thrales, a rich brewer and his wife, and it was in their house at Streatham, among an ever-widening circle of friends, that he held court. When Mr. Thrale died and Mrs. Thrale married again, Johnson quarrelled with her and lost a friendship he had grown to rely on. By good talk and constant company he had tried to keep at bay the extreme melancholy which had oppressed him all his life, and which he feared would drive him insane. But gradually the periods of gloom increased, and the illness he had always suffered from grew worse, until on 13 December 1784, he died, attended to the last by his faithful Negro servant.

James Boswell, who first met Johnson in 1763, almost at once began to collect material for his biography. He and Johnson had together paid a visit to Scotland, which Johnson delightfully described in his *Journey to the Western Islands of Scotland*. It is through Boswell that we know Johnson the man, the supreme conversationalist, so well—incomparably better than we should ever have known him through his work. Vain, garrulous, a not very admirable character, Boswell was, like PEPYS (q.v.), a fascinatingly frank diarist; but it is to his *Life of Johnson*, published in 1791, that he owes his immortality.

See also Vol. XII: BIOGRAPHY; DICTIONARIES.

THE BANQUETING HOUSE, WHITEHALL (NOW THE ROYAL UNITED SERVICE MUSEUM)

It was designed by Inigo Jones in the Italian manner; Jones borrowed ideas from Palladio, but put them together in his own way, so that the building is by no means a copy. (By permission of the Comptroller, H.M. Stationery Office)

JONES, Inigo (1573–1652). This great architect and stage designer is one of the most important and influential figures in the history of English art. He was the first English artist who understood the principle of Italian RENAISSANCE ART (q.v. Vol. XII), and under his influence English art rose from the low position it had occupied in the reign of Queen Elizabeth. By the beauty and distinction of his work he raised the position of the artist above that of a mere craftsman, and he was also the first English architect as that word is now understood—a single controlling mind, responsible for the whole of a building and its decoration.

Jones was the son of a London cloth-worker. He visited Italy about 1600, where he trained himself by studying Renaissance and Classical art. He made himself a good scholar, learning Italian and reading Italian books on architecture and also on history and philosophy. He was particularly interested in the buildings, writings, and drawings of the architect PALLADIO (q.v.). He copied many Italian drawings and engravings, and probably worked, for a time at least, as a painter.

Jones's first employment by King James I was as the designer of the scenery and costumes for Court MASQUES (q.v. Vol. IX), on which he worked almost continuously from 1605 to 1640. In the lavish staging of these entertainments Jones, imitating what he had seen in Italy, made great advances on the simple Shakespearian stage. Before long, however, he quarrelled with the poet Ben JONSON (q.v.), who thought the words of the masques were more important than the settings.

In 1614 Inigo Jones was made Surveyor to the Crown, a post he held until the Civil War. In 1616 he began for James I's Queen Anne the Queen's House at Greenwich (now the National Maritime Museum), which was finished in 1635 for Queen Henrietta Maria. The design was revolutionary, for it was in the greatest possible contrast to the usual confused, over-decorated buildings of the period. It is like an Italian villa, very simple and clear-cut in its lines; and both inside and out the proportions of all the parts are logically related to each other and to the whole.

His most famous building, the Banqueting

House for Whitehall Palace, was completed in 1622, and soon afterwards he built Marlborough House Chapel, a little building with a splendid decorated roof imitating an antique vault—the first church in England in the classical style.

Much of his work as Surveyor was connected with complaints and committees, though he sometimes advised Charles I about the purchase of pictures. In the 1630's he undertook the repair of Old St. Paul's, recasing the nave in a classical manner and building a grand portico at the west end, which was destroyed by the Great Fire of London in 1666. Probably about this time he also carried out the first piece of town-planning in England, Covent Garden 'Piazza', which was surrounded by arcades with a church at its west end. It is now much altered. About 1638 he designed a series of schemes for the rebuilding of Whitehall Palace on a vast scale, but these were never carried out. The book on architecture which he almost certainly planned, and for which many drawings were made by his pupil John Webb, was never actually written.

In the Civil War he supported the King, and was taken prisoner in 1645 at the siege of Basing House; but as he was old and sick he was soon released. At the end of his life he and John Webb built a great suite of rooms at Wilton House, Wiltshire. The Double Cube Room—its length is twice its height and width—is one of the finest rooms in England, and shows how, in decoration as well as in architecture, Jones revolutionized English style.

Inigo Jones died at the age of 79. Since his death the influence of his work has been enormous. In the 18th century the architect Lord Burlington and his circle greatly admired his work, and published many of his drawings. The 19th-century government buildings in Whitehall also owe much to his example.

See also Vol. XII: BRITISH ART.

JONSON, Benjamin (1572–1637).

Upon Jonson's gravestone in Westminster Abbey are cut the words: 'O rare Ben Jonson', a fitting epitaph for the man who was bricklayer, soldier, scholar, actor, poet, dramatist, critic, Shakespeare's friend, and one of the great writers of English comedy.

Jonson in his plays set out to record the contemporary scene, using 'deeds and language such as men do use'. His characters are for the most part types, dominated by a particular 'humour' —such as meanness, credulity, hypocrisy. His first notable play, *Every Man in His Humour* (in which Shakespeare is said to have played), is characteristic of his satiric, realistic method. Among his best plays are *Volpone, or the Fox*, a brilliant, cynical comedy, *The Silent Woman*, a farce which Dryden said he preferred 'before all other plays', and *The Alchemist*, in which Sir Epicure Mammon, his greatest comic character, appears. Apart from *Bartholomew Fair* with its vivid picture of life in Elizabethan London, his other plays are less remarkable. He wrote sometimes in prose, sometimes in blank verse; but

CHLORIS IN THE MASQUE 'CHLORIDA' BY BEN JONSON
The costume was designed by Inigo Jones for Queen Henrietta Maria in 1631. (From the Devonshire Collection, by permission of the Trustees of the Chatsworth Settlement)

apart from occasional great lines, as in *Volpone*, 'Where she came in like star-light, hid with jewels', the dialogue is too packed and realistic for poetry. Jonson wrote some poetry, however—love-poems, elegies, epitaphs, and satiric verses; and some marvellous songs such as 'Drink to me only with thine eyes'. The MASQUES (q.v. Vol. IX), in some of which he collaborated with Inigo JONES (q.v.), reveal his true poetic genius.

Jonson's shrewd criticism of Shakespeare, and especially the poem which prefaces the first collected works of Shakespeare (1623), 'He was not for our age but for all time', will always be remembered.

See also Vol. XII: COMEDY.

JOYCE, James (1882–1941).

This Irish novelist, who wrote very few books and has been little read by the general public, has had an extraordinary influence on 20th-century literature. Joyce, brought up as a Catholic in Dublin and educated at Jesuit schools, soon left Ireland for good, preferring to live in Paris and Switzerland.

His first important work was an autobiographical novel, *A Portrait of the Artist as a Young Man*, in which he shows his hatred and contempt for respectable suburban life in Dublin and his criticism of priests and religion. His masterpiece, *Ulysses*, published in Paris in 1922, was a revolutionary book, which tried to set out at great length, and without any reserve, all the thoughts that pass through the minds of the characters during a period of 24 hours.

Joyce brought into fashion what writers call the 'internal monologue' or 'stream of consciousness', in which words spoken aloud are deliberately interwoven with the unspoken secret thoughts which go on at the same time. In his language Joyce ignored verbs, punctuation, and other accepted conventions in order to express his ideas in words with the brilliant shorthand of a poet and the humour of a satirist. He invented thousands of new words, usually half-words or composite words made up of scraps of many languages. The freshness of his method, despite its difficulty, constantly surprises the reader into taking notice of what he is really saying. Joyce developed his own style and language so far that many passages in a later book, *Finnegans Wake*, are incomprehensible to most people.

Joyce died an exile, poor, half-blind, ignored by the general public; but he had given a vital stimulus to writers of prose and poetry in many tongues.

See also Vol. XII: NOVEL.

JULIUS CAESAR (c. 102–44 B.C.).

Like Napoleon, Caius Julius Caesar has become an historical legend. 'Why, man, he doth bestride the narrow world like a Colossus', Shakespeare said of him. Caesar felt himself born to greatness. The Julian family, to which he belonged, believed that it could trace its ancestry to the legendary Aeneas, the Trojan founder of Rome. But though Caesar was an aristocrat himself, he was opposed all his life to the nobles of the Senate, and rose to power in politics by his skill in winning popularity with the common people.

Caesar had a noble presence; he was tall and had thin features. He was known to all for his elegant manners, personal charm, and diplomatic ability; the Senate feared his political ambition and his popularity with the people; but, though he was Rome's greatest soldier, he won no warlike renown until after he was 40 when, as governor in Spain, he had to fight the fierce mountain tribes. He returned to Rome, and very much strengthened his position against the hostile Senate by making a political alliance with the popular military hero POMPEY (q.v.), with whom the Senate were also quarrelling, and with Crassus, the chief of the Roman financiers.

With Caesar's political skill, Pompey's prestige, and Crassus' money, these three strong men, the First Triumvirate, were irresistible. Caesar was elected consul, which gave him political position, and he won a long military command, which gave him real power.

Caesar went out to Gaul, where he remained nearly 10 years, conquering the numerous Gallic tribes and uniting them under Roman influence. Caesar himself wrote the account of these brilliant military campaigns in his superb *Commentaries on the Gallic Wars*. During this period he invaded Britain twice. In the meanwhile, Crassus having been killed, Pompey became jealous of the rising reputation of Caesar. He allied himself with Caesar's opponents in the Senate, and they demanded that Caesar should lay down his military command and disband his army. This would have meant his political downfall, so Caesar decided to take drastic steps. He 'crossed the Rubicon', a small

Anderson

JULIUS CAESAR
Head of a statue in the Conservatori, Rome

stream lying between him and Italy, marched on Rome, and set himself up as dictator. In the civil war which followed Caesar finally defeated Pompey at Pharsalus in Greece, destroyed the remaining Pompeian armies in Africa and Spain, and then emerged the master of the Roman world.

Caesar used his supreme power to restore order and prosperity. He settled a great many soldiers and poor citizens on land where they could make a future for themselves, especially in Gaul, Spain, and Africa. He improved conditions in the provinces and granted Roman citizenship to non-Romans. He overhauled the administration of Rome itself and of Italy, reformed the calendar and planned to codify the laws and to carry out large engineering projects. His programme was one of great imperial development.

But although Caesar was an outstanding statesman as well as soldier, he had an aristocratic impatience with men who hindered him and made little attempt to conciliate his opponents in the Senate. His sense of his own high destiny led him to live with pomp and ceremony and even to set his statue in the temple of Romulus among the statues of the kings of

Rome. These extravagant gestures seemed to show that he thought of himself as more than a leader—almost as a king and god. When in 44 B.C. he took the dictatorship for life, many feared that he would become a tyrant.

So on the Ides (15th) of March, a band of sixty conspirators led by Brutus and Cassius assassinated him for threatening the republican traditions of Rome, hoping that, if they removed the dictator, Rome would return to her old political condition. In fact, Rome was plunged again into 'domestic fury and fierce civil strife'.

Caesar was a fine diplomat and decisive in politics—well fitted to command. He was a brilliant general and, except for CICERO (q.v.), the greatest orator of his time. He wrote simple, direct, elegant prose, and was a man of much knowledge in many directions. But he tried to press forward too far and too fast. Whether his power had gone to his head, or whether he felt that Rome's problems were too serious for delay, he finally ignored the traditional Roman way of doing things. Rome was not ready for the autocracy of a Caesar, and so he fell.

See also AUGUSTUS CAESAR.
See also Vol. I: ROMAN CIVILIZATION.

JUNG, Carl (born 1875), *see* Vol. XI: PSYCHOLOGY.

JUSTINIAN I (*c.* 483–565). This Emperor, the greatest of the late Roman Emperors, reigned for 38 years, and is remembered because with his brilliant general Belisarius he restored the boundaries of the Empire, and because he revised the Roman laws, both civil and ecclesiastical, and encouraged building and the arts (*see* ST. SOPHIA, Vol. XII).

Since CONSTANTINE (q.v.) had transferred the capital of the Empire from Rome to Constantinople, the western part of the Empire had been subject to attacks by HUNS, GOTHS, and VANDALS (qq.v. Vol. I) who had gained control of large areas. Justinian set himself to recover these territories. Belisarius carried out a magnificent campaign which drove the Vandals from North Africa. Then he recaptured Sicily and, crossing to Italy, fought his way to Rome, which he took from the Gothic King. When, later, the Goths revolted under their leader Totila and recaptured most of Italy, Justinian sent another army which defeated and killed Totila. Meanwhile Justinian fought the Persians, though with

Anderson

THE EMPRESS THEODORA, WIFE OF JUSTINIAN, AND HER COURT
6th-century mosaic from the church of San Vitale, Ravenna

less spectacular success, and drove back enemies from his long, unprotected northern frontiers. In 559 a horde of barbarians fought their way to the very walls of Constantinople; but the veteran Belisarius drove them off. All these wars, successful as they were, necessitated heavy taxation, which made Justinian very unpopular and left the land desolate. There were serious riots in Constantinople in 552 against the Emperor's oppression, but they were severely repressed.

Justinian's legal reforms were undoubtedly his best work. Many of the old laws had become obsolete, largely because of the establishment of Christianity as the State religion; and an overhaul of the whole legal system was badly needed. Justinian was personally interested in framing a new Code of Laws (*see* LAW, HISTORY OF, Volume X). His laws covered the whole life of Roman citizens, ecclesiastical as well as civil.

The law expected everyone to be Christian, and pagans and heretics were harshly treated. The appointment and duties of the clergy and the rules of the monastic life were regulated by law. Justinian, by prohibiting the teaching of law and philosophy at Athens, and confiscating the property of Plato's Academy, brought the famous University of Athens to an end.

Justinian's reputation as a great ruler depends largely on his tremendous industry: he seemed to take no pleasure in anything except his work. But competent as he was, he had no vision for the future; and the many buildings, both civil and ecclesiastical, which he put up, were so costly that they added greatly to the already crushing burden of taxation. It is interesting to remember that it was Justinian who first introduced silkworms to the West (*see* SILK INDUSTRY, Vol. VII).

See also Vol. X: LAW, HISTORY OF.

K

KANT, Immanuel (1724–1804). This philosopher, generally considered one of the greatest of modern times, was the son of a poor tradesman of Scottish descent in Königsberg, East Prussia. Kant went to Königsberg University, where he was so poor that he gave lessons to buy food and often had to borrow a coat from a friend. Physically he was always undersized and feeble. He became a tutor to various families in the neighbourhood, but soon returned to the University as a lecturer, and stayed there for the rest of his life, becoming Professor of Philosophy when he was 46. He published books on astronomy and other subjects; and as his fame began to spread, officers, professional men, and merchants alike flocked to hear his lectures on mathematics and physics. His days, starting at 5 a.m., were precisely regulated between his study, his lecture-room, and his afternoon walk; it is said that the citizens of Königsberg used to set their clocks by him. He was no recluse, but enjoyed the company of many friends and delighted in genial conversation on politics and literature. He was fond of reading English novels.

Kant's fame rests on his book, the *Critique of Pure Reason*, which appeared in 1781, when he was 57. In this book he put forward ideas concerning the foundations of our knowledge of the physical world which have been turning-points in the history of human thought. His style is difficult and dry, and his meaning has been interpreted in different ways. From his doctrine sprang a number of important movements in philosophy, notably the movement led by HEGEL (q.v.). It deeply influenced English thought in the 19th century, and is still closely studied. He wrote several other books, in two of which, the *Critique of Practical Reason* (1788) and the *Critique of Judgment* (1790), he completed his system of thought, expressing original and striking ideas on moral, scientific, and artistic principles. Kant believed profoundly in moral freedom, in man's ability to choose what is right. Although some of his doctrines have been much criticized, they are always being revived wherever men search into the basis of our knowledge in science, conduct, and religion.

See also HUME; HEGEL.
See also Vol. I: PHILOSOPHY.

KEAN, Edmund (1787–1833). Though only 46 when he died, Kean had established an extraordinary reputation on the English stage as the greatest tragic actor of his day. He had a career as theatrical as any drama; his performances excited the audience to immense enthusiasm. 'He was not at a single fault', wrote William HAZLITT (q.v.), the critic, after Kean's famous study of Sir Giles Overreach, the usurer, in Massinger's *A New Way to Pay Old Debts*, 'the conclusion was quite overwhelming'. Kean's acting on that night is said to have rendered its

Victoria & Albert Museum
EDMUND KEAN AS RICHARD III
Theatre Royal, Drury Lane, 12 February 1814.
Painting by George Clint

audience speechless with real terror, and several ladies in the boxes fainted.

The circumstances of Kean's birth are obscure. He was the illegitimate son of a young itinerant actress, who made no attempt to bring him up. He appears to have spent a wild, uncared-for childhood on and around the stage, as a cabin-boy on a vessel bound for Madeira, singing and dancing at tavern doors or at country fairs, and to have had practically no schooling. On one occasion, when acting as an acrobat, he fell and broke both his legs. When he was 21, he married an Irish actress, and together they acted in the provinces in great poverty with little professional success. The actor-manager Macready, who saw Kean act in Birmingham at this time, said in later years: 'How little did I know, or could guess, that under the shabby green dress was hidden one of the most extraordinary theatrical geniuses that have ever illustrated the dramatic poetry of England.'

On 26 January 1814, Kean was playing Shylock in London, with a poor cast, before a small audience at Drury Lane. It was a remarkable night in the history of the theatre when this man who, in Coleridge's later phrase, could reveal Shakespeare 'by flashes of lightning', first acted to a London audience. At the end of the trial scene the audience, mesmerized by the power of the small man with the fierce black eyes, was shouting itself hoarse. From that moment Kean's place on the stage was assured. Critics wrote of him as Hazlitt did on his performance in the death scene in *Richard the Third*: 'He fights like one drunk with wounds; and the attitude in which he stands with his hands stretched out after his sword is wrested from him, has a preternatural and terrific grandeur.' He was less good in any character that called for virtue or sustained nobility. But as Macbeth, Shylock, or Iago he was unmatchable.

Kean's life was as fierce as much of his playing. He drank to excess and was often absent from the theatre; he was driven off the stage for a while because of an affair with the wife of a city alderman. By the late 1820's his sun was setting. He acted for the last time on 25 March 1833, playing Othello at Covent Garden to the Iago of his son, Charles. It was a tragic night. Just as he reached the line, 'Othello's occupation's gone', he collapsed in pain, whispered to his son, 'O God, I am dying; speak to them for me', and fainted. He died a few weeks later.

His reputation was enormous, and he soon became a legend of the English theatre.

See also Vol. IX: ACTING, HISTORY OF.

KEATS, John (1795–1821). The poet Keats, who during the five short years of his adult life wrote some of the finest poems in the English language, was born at the Swan and Hoop Livery Stables, Finsbury Pavement, London. He was the eldest son of the head ostler, who had married the daughter of the proprietor of the stables. His father died in a riding accident when Keats was only 8, and his mother died of consumption when he was 14. John, his two brothers, and his sister Fanny were left in charge of a guardian. Until his mother's death, John was a rowdy, cheerful schoolboy with a passion for fighting in spite of being very small for his age. Now he was seized with an even greater passion for books, which he read without stopping at meals or even on walks. When nearly 16, he was apprenticed to a surgeon to train as a doctor; but he still returned to his school at Enfield every week to see his brother Tom, and to read with his friend Charles Cowden Clarke, the headmaster's son. He was just 18 when Clarke lent him Spenser's *Faerie Queene*, which he went through 'as a young horse through a Spring meadow—ramping!' and imitated in his first verses. Soon afterwards his brother George, who was working in their guardian's counting-house, introduced him to a set of young City people interested in literature, and he began to write regularly. When he was nearly 20 he entered Guy's Hospital, where his fellow students noticed that he thought about nothing but poetry. At 21, to his guardian's horror, he gave up medicine, and he published his first book of poems in March 1817.

This book, which contains the famous sonnet 'On First Looking Into Chapman's Homer', was a failure, but it was admired by Leigh HUNT (q.v.), to whom it was dedicated, and by other writers and artists whom Keats had now met. One of these introduced Keats to a publishing firm who commissioned the long poem he had planned to write on the classical legend of the love of Cynthia, the Moon Goddess, and a mortal, Endymion. Full of enthusiasm, Keats completed 4,000 lines in just over 7 months. Keats knew that *Endymion* was hasty and immature, as he admitted in his introduction. This admission, and the disclosure by a tactless

THE DUKE OF MARLBOROUGH ON HIS WHITE HORSE AT THE BATTLE OF
DONAUWÖRTH, 1704

One of thirteen tapestries at Blenheim Palace depicting the Duke's campaigns. Designed by Josse de Vos and
completed about 1720

friend that Keats had until recently been a medical student, was seized upon by the reviewers. The powerful *Blackwood's Edinburgh Magazine*, which was conducting a series of attacks on Leigh Hunt and his friends entitled 'The Cockney School of Poetry', ridiculed both the *Poems* and *Endymion*, and ended its article: 'It is . . . better . . . to be a starved apothecary than a starved poet; so back to the shop, Mr. John, back to the "plasters, pills, and ointment boxes".'

Keats was at first undisturbed by this abuse, and by an equally critical though less brutal review in *The Quarterly Review*. 'I think I shall be among the English Poets after my death', he wrote to George. Life, however, began to deal him a series of blows. He and his brothers, of whom he was intensely fond, lived in lodgings together until, in the summer of 1818, George married and emigrated to America. By the autumn, Tom, always delicate, was obviously dying of consumption. He was nursed by John, who was himself ill, until he died at the end of the year. Though Keats had many kind friends in Hampstead, where he now lived, he had very little money, his guardian put every obstacle in his way, and he had fallen in love while still without any prospect of worldly success. Yet the poems written between September 1818 and September 1819—the most amazing year's work by any English poet—include *The Eve of St. Agnes*, *Lamia*, the fragment of *Hyperion*, and the famous *Odes*. All these, together with an earlier poem, *Isabella*, were published in the summer of 1820 in one incomparable volume. By that time, Keats knew that he himself was dying. Worry over George, who had borrowed nearly all his money, and the struggle to earn enough to marry Fanny Brawne, to whom he was now engaged, had brought on the consumption which he had probably contracted while nursing Tom. As a last hope, his friends and publishers sent him to Rome with a young artist, Joseph Severn, but the change proved disastrous, and he died in Severn's arms on 23 February 1821. He is buried in the English Cemetery, at Rome, and his tombstone bears the words he chose for himself: 'Here lies one whose name was writ in water.' Keats died at the age of 25, an age at which few even of the greatest poets have accomplished anything of value.

Keats was one of the most loved and loving of men, and the affection, philosophy, and humour

that he poured into his letters to his brothers, his sister, his friends, and his fiancée show him to be as great a genius in prose as in poetry. Indeed, some of his finest verses such as *La Belle Dame Sans Merci*, were scribbled in these letters.

Victoria & Albert Museum
JOHN KEATS
Drawing by Joseph Severn

To his friends he appeared an inspired creature —'the humming of a bee, the sight of a flower, the glitter of the sun, seemed to make his nature tremble'—yet until his last illness he was hardy and manly, playing cricket, taking long walks, boxing, and enjoying practical jokes. His companions and others have blamed the reviewers, Fanny Brawne, and even George for his unhappy death. The truth is that he was a victim to the family disease, which later carried off George as well, and that his own passionate nature drove him too hard for happiness.

See also Vol. XII: ROMANTIC MOVEMENT.

KEBLE, John (1792–1866), *see* NEWMAN.

KELVIN, Lord (1824–1907). The great scientist, William Thomson or Lord Kelvin (the name he chose when he was made a peer), devoted the first part of his life to physics and the latter part to engineering. Born in Belfast, he was brought up in Glasgow, where he was educated by his father, a mathematics teacher, till he was 11. He then studied at Glasgow University until he went to Cambridge at 17. There he was triumphantly successful, and at 22, having published twelve original papers in physics, he returned to Glasgow as professor, a post he held till he was 75.

Kelvin began his life's work as a disciple of FARADAY (q.v.) in electricity and magnetism. Unlike Faraday, however, he was an expert mathematician, able to work out the fullest consequence of any idea that occurred to him. One of his investigations gave Clerk MAXWELL (q.v.) the clue to his electro-magnetic theory of Light. Another early experiment suggested a way of producing certain electric waves that Hertz later used in WIRELESS TELEGRAPHY (q.v. Vol. IV).

Kelvin's interpretation of earlier work on heat engines was an independent discovery of what are now known as the Laws of Thermodynamics (see ENERGY, Vol. VIII). It had been shown that heat, the nature of which was then little understood, could be only partly converted into work by an engine. Kelvin, meditating upon this, concluded that it was impossible for a source of energy (a steam-engine, for example) to give off energy if it was cooler than its surroundings, for heat can flow only from a hot object to a cold one and not the other way round. This, in simplified form, is the Second Law of Thermodynamics, and is still accepted as true. One of Kelvin's important deductions from this Law was that the Universe cannot be infinitely old; it must have had a definite beginning. In 1871 he calculated the age of the earth as a hundred million years, but modern scientists put the figure at between two and three thousand million years (see EARTH, HISTORY OF, Vol. III). When investigating thermodynamics with J. P. Joule, Kelvin made the important discovery that an expanding gas can cool itself, a principle which forms the basis of REFRIGERATION (q.v. Vol. VIII).

The laying of the first telegraph cable across the Atlantic in 1857 turned Kelvin from a physicist to an engineer. He solved the enormous difficulties of transmitting messages over long distances by cable; he invented galvanometers, voltmeters, gyrostats, sounding-machines, microbalances and improved ships' compasses; he made the navigation of steamships safer, and improved TELEGRAPHY (q.v. Vol. IV). He was

one of the earliest to suggest the harnessing of Niagara Falls for electric power.

Towards the end of his life Kelvin found it hard to accept some of the more revolutionary discoveries of younger men, especially the existence of the electron, finally isolated in 1897 by J. J. THOMSON. His firm faith in the unchangeability of the chemical atom also prevented his acceptance of RUTHERFORD's disintegration theory of radioactivity (qq.v.).

Kelvin was honoured by the Presidency of the Royal Society, the Chancellorship of Glasgow University, a peerage, and the Order of Merit.

See also Vol. VIII: ELECTRICAL ENGINEERING, HISTORY OF.

KEPLER, Johann (1571–1630). Kepler, the German scientist who established the laws governing the movements of planets, started life with many handicaps. His mother, an almost illiterate woman of ungovernable temper, was in later life nearly condemned for witchcraft. His father was a reckless adventurer who, after several years of soldiering, returned home to the German Duchy of Württemberg to keep the village inn, but later quarrelled with his wife and left home.

Kepler was a weakly child, who in infancy almost died of smallpox and was left with sight and hands permanently injured. His early education was constantly interrupted by illness or by the need to help his parents in the inn. But he won his way to the university and passed his examinations there brilliantly. His life was dogged by ill-health, financial difficulties, and persecution of his Protestantism in a Catholic part of the world.

When he was 25 he published a book about the planets which was unimportant except that it won him the friendship of GALILEO (q.v.) and of Tycho Brahe, a famous astronomical observer. In 1600 Kepler became assistant to Brahe at his observatory in Prague, where he began to study the orbit of Mars, the movements of which could not be fully explained, even by the revolutionary new theory of COPERNICUS (q.v.). Kepler, after trying one theory after another, discovered his famous Laws of Planetary Motion, describing the movements of the planets, which he published in 1609 and 1619 (see PLANETS, Vol. III). These laws formed the basis on which NEWTON (q.v.) built his theory of universal GRAVITATION (q.v. Vol. III). In fact, the most important evidence for Newton's theory was that it explained why the planets should move as Kepler's laws said they did.

Kepler also made discoveries in optics, general physics, and geometry. Towards the end of his life he became astrologer to WALLENSTEIN (q.v.) and died at Ratisbon.

See also Vol. III: ASTRONOMY, HISTORY OF.

KEYNES, John Maynard (Baron) (1883–1946). Keynes, a Fellow of King's College, Cambridge, was one of the leading economists of the century, and has had a great influence on the work of present-day political economists. During the First World War he worked at the Treasury, and was principal Treasury representative at the Versailles Peace Conference. He resigned because he considered the proposals for German reparations too harsh, and he wrote a famous book: *The Economic Consequences of the Peace*. His later works on monetary theory supplied the basis for the Beveridge plan for full employment (*see* SOCIAL INSURANCE, Vol. X). In the Second World War he acted as financial adviser to the government, and in 1942 was made a peer. In 1943 he became a regular financial ambassador to North America, where he did much to establish the International Monetary Fund (*see* INTERNATIONAL FINANCE, Vol. X) and to negotiate the American reconstruction loan to Britain. His speech on the loan agreement in the House of Lords was an outstandingly fine one.

Keynes was a man of sensitive taste and great personal charm. He married Lydia Lopokova, formerly of the Russian Imperial Ballet, and the two did much to develop English ballet. He also built and endowed the Cambridge Arts Theatre, and was a great patron of all the arts.

See also Vol. VII: ECONOMICS.

KHAYYÁM, Omar (11th century). The work of this Persian poet, famous in his own country, was first made known throughout the Western world by the publication in 1859 of *The Rubáiyát of Omar Khayyám*, translated by the English poet and scholar Edward FitzGerald (1809–83). FitzGerald's poem, which had a phenomenal success, sent oriental scholars searching for the actual works of Omar, for some thought that he had never really existed and that the works ascribed to him were by a number of other poets. Manuscripts only recently discovered, however, prove beyond doubt that Omar's poetry is his own. A brilliant man and a distinguished mathematician, he was a sceptic in religion and outspoken enough to get himself into trouble. The *rubái* (*rubáiyát* is the plural) was a four-line verse in which Persian poets expressed their thoughts and feelings. The best were passed round by word of mouth and often never written down by the poet himself. Omar's *rubáiyát* were witty and cynical and often mocked the rather flowery language of other poets. He was a fine craftsman, and his use of words was fresh and colloquial. FitzGerald's version is a very free paraphrase of selections from the original; it does not convey the essence of Omar's genius at all closely, but taken as a poem in its own right it is a masterpiece. Whatever Omar truly was himself he is likely to live in our literature as FitzGerald's Omar.

KINGSLEY, Charles (1819–75). This writer and social reformer, the son of a clergyman, himself took orders and became rector of a small parish in Hampshire, where he died and was buried. When he was 25 he came under the influence of a fellow clergyman and writer, F. D. Maurice, who was the leader of a group of social reformers, later called the Christian Socialists. Kingsley wrote many political pamphlets and two novels, *Yeast* about the rural worker, and *Alton Locke* about the London worker, all designed to show up the terrible conditions in which working-men lived. His famous

MRS. BEDONEBYASYOUDID
Illustration to Charles Kingsley's *The Water Babies*, 1869

children's story *The Water Babies* (1863), about Tom, a little chimney sweep, was written partly with the intention of rousing people's sympathy for these cruelly ill-treated children. He retained his deep feeling for the poor and oppressed all his life, though in later years he concerned himself with more fundamental remedies for social evils—for example, he helped to secure the passage through Parliament of the first General Education Act in 1870.

Kingsley's best-remembered novels are *Hypatia*, a tale set in 5th-century Alexandria; *Westward Ho!*, a story of Elizabethan sailors; and *Hereward the Wake*. He wrote a certain amount of religious poetry, and some charming songs such as *The Three Fishers* and *Sands of Dee*.

Kingsley's enthusiasm and sympathy made him loved by many people. But he was a man more often led by his emotions than his reason. For example, he made a wholly unjust attack on the integrity of John NEWMAN (q.v.) because Newman's conversion to Catholicism offended his rather narrow patriotism and fervent Protestantism. On the other hand he was an ardent admirer of the rationalist writings of John Stuart MILL (q.v.). At the end of his life he was made a canon of Westminster and Chaplain to the Queen.

KIPLING, Rudyard (1865–1936). Kipling, the author of *The Jungle Books*, *Kim*, and many other well-known stories and ballads, often about India, was born in Bombay. From his father, an artist and a scholar, he learnt to understand and respect the traditional pattern of Indian civilization. After a happy young childhood in India, Kipling was sent home to England because of his health, and was boarded out with people who for 6 years treated him not just unkindly but cruelly. This treatment frightened and confused him, a fact Kipling bitterly resented all his life. The story *Baa Baa, Black Sheep* and the autobiographical *Something of Myself* are vivid and painful records of this period. He used to spend happy Christmas holidays, however, with his aunt, the wife of the artist Burne-Jones.

Kipling went to a tough school, the United Services College at Westward Ho, where, although he was no good at games, he and two or three friends with courage and high spirits contrived the sort of life glorified and exaggerated in *Stalky & Co.*

National Portrait Gallery

RUDYARD KIPLING IN 1899
Painting by P. Burne-Jones

When he was 17, Kipling returned to India as a journalist, and within 10 years he had made his name as a writer. India fed Kipling's imagination in two ways. First, he was fascinated by her vastness and variety, her mystery and beauty, as well as by her squalor, superstition, and confusion; secondly he was inspired by the spectacle of his own countrymen in the midst of this chaos, for the most part with orderly, efficient industry, governing, protecting, and educating this great medley of peoples whom Kipling, in common with almost everyone else, believed incapable of doing these things for themselves. He had a vision of a British Empire even greater than the Empire of ancient Rome, and like it, charged with guarding civilization from the dangers of barbarism and chaos. When he finally left India at the age of 24, he brought back a passionate belief in the virtue and necessity of law and order. But there is an element of aggressive imperialism, a toleration of violence, and a racial arrogance which make it difficult for people brought up to popular 20th-century ideas of democracy to do him justice.

Although widely travelled, Kipling remained intensely English. In 1892 he married an American and they made some attempt to live in America; but Kipling could not settle there, and soon they returned to England and lived first in Rottingdean, near Brighton, and finally, in 1902, at Burwash, Sussex. Their only son was killed in the First World War. Kipling was shy of public occasions and accepted no honours from any government, considering that to do so would be to limit his right of criticism. He received the Nobel Prize, however, in 1907. He died at the age of 71.

Kipling's deepest belief was in duty, responsibility, and personal honour, and this has given his books a powerful moral force, just as his brilliant powers of description and command of atmosphere and suspense has given them artistic appeal. His poetry readily appeals to anybody with an ear for powerful rhythms and rapid, vigorous language, to be found in such straightforward ballads as 'Clampherdown' and 'Bolivar'. He also wrote more complex dramatic monologues (influenced by Browning), such as 'M'Andrew's Hymn' and 'The "Mary Gloster"'.

Kipling's greatest genius lay in story-telling. Owing little to his predecessors and nothing to his contemporaries, he was an original and went his own way. His earliest collection of short stories, *Plain Tales from the Hills*, already shows that sure touch, that passion for fact and accurate detail, that love of 'knowing how' about an astonishing number of things, which provide vivid settings for his innumerable stories.

In *The Jungle Books* (and, less successfully, in *The Just So Stories*) Kipling's genius is entirely free to create his own world. The story of Mowgli, the man-child adopted by the Wolf family and brought up in the jungle, is intensely real. Baloo the bear, Bagheera the panther, Kaa the serpent, Shere Khan the tiger, though they speak as men, obey the law of the jungle and do not for an instant lose their true animal natures; nothing is sentimentalized. *Kim*, his successful full-length novel, tells the story of an orphan who attaches himself to a

Lama, or holy man of Tibet, and goes on his wanderings with him; and the descriptions of life in India seen through Indian eyes are unforgettable and are perhaps the best thing Kipling ever did. In his later books, *Puck of Pook's Hill* (1906) and *Rewards and Fairies* (1910), Kipling recreates incidents in English history with an equally scrupulous attention to detail and great imaginative power.

See also Vol. XII: SHORT STORIES.

KITCHENER, Horatio Herbert (Earl) (1850–1916). Kitchener, who became a national symbol of resistance in the FIRST WORLD WAR (q.v. Vol. X), first won fame by his reconquest of the Sudan. In 1884–5 rebels had seized the Sudan and had murdered General GORDON (q.v.) at Khartoum. Thirteen years later Kitchener, in command of an Anglo-Egyptian army, fought his way down the Nile in scorching heat for over 1,000 miles, and in a day of savage fighting against fanatical opponents destroyed the Dervish army at Omdurman. Kitchener later served as chief-of-staff and then as commander-in-chief in the SOUTH AFRICAN WAR (q.v. Vol. X), and afterwards as commander-in-chief in India. On the outbreak of war in 1914 he became Secretary of State for War.

Kitchener had had no previous political experience. To his colleagues he was often

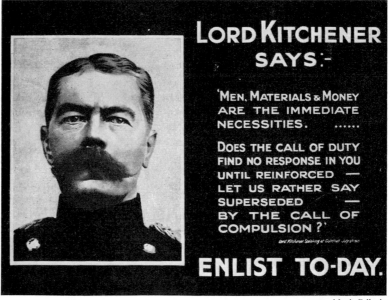

Meade Collection

RECRUITING POSTER OF THE FIRST WORLD WAR

reserved in manner, autocratic, inarticulate, inflexibly obstinate; but those whom he once trusted he trusted absolutely. By the public he was regarded with immense respect. His portrait, with its heavy moustache and piercing eye, looked down from recruiting posters all over Britain, with the caption 'Your Country Needs You'. The raising of the 'Kitchener armies'—3 million volunteers—was a feat unparalleled in military history, and in a matter of months many were in France in the trenches from which few returned.

Kitchener lost his life when the cruiser *Hampshire*, in which he was travelling to visit the Russian armies, was sunk by a mine off the Orkneys.

KNOX, John (*c.* 1505–72). This leader of the Scottish REFORMATION (q.v. Vol. I), whose forceful, dogmatic personality made a lasting impression on the religion and national character of Scotland, was mainly responsible for establishing and shaping the Presbyterian Church (*see* CALVINIST, Vol. I). Scotland at this time was under the domination of Catholic France. As a result of his reforming activities, Knox was sent to France for 18 months as a galley slave—an experience which undermined his health. On release, he spent some time assisting CRANMER in the work of the English Reformation, and then, on the accession of Mary Tudor, he fled to the Continent where he worked with CALVIN and other reformers (qq.v.).

In 1559, at the request of the Protestant party, he returned to Scotland, and spent the rest of his life using his relentless energy, his fiery and outspoken eloquence, and his shrewd, worldly sense in opposing Roman Catholicism and establishing the Protestant religion. In 1560, with help from England, the reformers drove out the French, and the Presbyterian form of Protestantism became the official religion. Knox and other Ministers drew up a *Confession of Faith* and the first *Book of Discipline*, with its wise suggestions for the organization of religion and education in Scotland. In 1561, however, MARY, QUEEN OF SCOTS (q.v.) returned to her country from France, intent on restoring Roman Catholicism. Knox opposed her with such violence that he was forbidden to preach. He continued, however, boldly to denounce Mary's party. When he was reinstated after Mary's abdication, his health had failed; he preached

his last sermon at St. Giles, Edinburgh, in November 1572, and died the same month.

Though for the most part 'oppressed with melancholy', Knox showed surprising tenderness in his letters; he was twice happily married and had many lifelong friendships with women. His great work was the *History of the Reformation in Scotland*, though more notorious is his *Monstrous Regiment of Women*—a diatribe against the rule of queens.

See also Vol. X: SCOTTISH EDUCATION.

KRUGER, Paul (1825–1904). This famous Boer leader was President of the Transvaal during the bitter quarrels with the British that led to the SOUTH AFRICAN WAR (q.v. Vol. X). When he was 10 he had accompanied his parents on 'The Great Trek' to escape British rule in Cape Colony and to found new independent territories north of the Orange River. This left him with bitter feelings against the British which lasted all his life. Kruger had little education, and was brought up mainly on the Bible. At 39

PRESIDENT KRUGER
Photograph taken just before the outbreak of the Boer War

he became Commandant-General of the Transvaal army, having had much experience of guerrilla warfare against African tribes. He strongly opposed Britain's annexation of the Transvaal in 1877 and, 3 years later, took the lead in the first Transvaal war of independence (1880–1). Kruger was elected President in 1883 and, a year later, Britain recognized the independence of the Transvaal, though retaining the right to control the Republic's foreign policy.

When large numbers of British settlers entered the Transvaal in search of gold, Kruger, concerned at this new threat to his country's security, refused to allow them political rights. The British appealed for help to Cecil RHODES (q.v.), Prime Minister of Cape Colony; negotiations came to nothing, and fresh outbreaks of violence, including the notorious 'Jameson Raid', led eventually to the South African War. Kruger was too old to take any active part in the fighting, but he remained in political control until 1900 when he went to Europe to try to win help in the war against Britain. His mission failed and, completely broken in health, he retired to Switzerland and died there 2 years after the defeat of his country.

See also RHODES; SMUTS.
See also Vol. III: SOUTH AFRICA.

KUBLAI KHAN (1216–94). Qubilai, or Kublai, grandson of GENGHIS KHAN (q.v.), was proclaimed *Qa'an* ('Great Khan') of all the Mongols by his armies in 1260, when his elder brother died. After Kublai had secured himself in his position, he proceeded to carry out his brother's ambition, to make himself master of China. By 1279 the whole of China was in Kublai's hands, thanks largely to a military commander of genius, Bayan of the Hundred Eyes. Kublai then made two unsuccessful attempts to invade Japan, unsuccessful because the Mongols, though matchless cavalrymen, were less good mariners. The rulers of Annam and Burma, though not completely conquered, judged it prudent to become vassals of Kublai.

Kublai Khan was nominally sovereign over all the Mongol lands, his brother Hulagu ruling Persia as his vassal, and consequently the ancient maritime trade-route between Persia and China was reopened (see TRADE ROUTES, Vol. IV). But Kublai had to wage almost incessant war in Mongolia against his cousin Qaidu. Qaidu, remaining true to his birth and

Bodleian Library

KUBLAI KHAN

Miniature of Kublai Khan at the feast which he gave annually on his birthday. From a 14th-century French manuscript of the travels of Marco Polo

upbringing, lived the life of a Mongol prince, and so regarded himself as better qualified to bear the title of *Qa'an* than Kublai, who was becoming more and more an emperor on the classical Chinese pattern.

Kublai was an enthusiastic admirer of CHINESE CIVILIZATION. He adopted BUDDHISM and followed the Chinese custom of ANCESTOR-WORSHIP (qq.v. Vol. I). But he was tolerant of other faiths, and exempted ministers of all religions from taxation. He probably did not care greatly how men worshipped God so long as they remembered their duty to their sovereign. China prospered under his reign; even historians of the conquered Chinese testify to his love of justice and to his benevolence towards his subjects. He clothed the needy, and instituted State granaries which bought surplus grain in good years and sold it cheaply to the public in time of dearth. He encouraged scholarship. He built himself a new capital, Cambaluc, across the river from Peking, and established there a magnificent court. Among his other residences was the Summer Palace at Shangtu, the 'Xanadu' of Coleridge's poem.

The best source of information about Kublai and his reign is that most readable of all travel-books, the *Travels* of MARCO POLO (q.v.).

See also GENGHIS KHAN; MARCO POLO.
See also Vol. I: CHINESE CIVILIZATION.

L

LA FONTAINE, Jean de (1621–95), *see* Vol. XII: FABLES.

LAMB, Charles (1775–1834). This English essayist and critic was the son of a servant to Samuel Salt, a bencher of the Inner Temple in London, where Charles was born. Lamb was educated at Christ's Hospital at the same time as COLERIDGE (q.v.), his lifelong friend. He was a promising classical scholar, but a bad stutter made it impossible for him to consider entering the Church, and instead he became an accountant, and gained a safe post in the India House.

Victoria & Albert Museum
CHARLES LAMB
Drawing by Daniel Maclise

At first his love of literature and his own early verses contended with his business prospects; but when his sister Mary, in one of her fits of insanity, killed their mother, Lamb at the age of 22 chose decisively—and heroically—to make authorship his spare-time pleasure only, so that he might be her lifelong guardian.

Nevertheless he wrote much and in many kinds. His exquisite sympathy with his sister's nature made it easy for them to write together such books for young readers as the *Tales from Shakespeare*. His *Specimens of English Dramatic Poets*, an annotated anthology from Elizabethan sources, was an original work of rediscovery, and established Lamb as a fresh and imaginative critic. When he was 45, he began publishing in the *London Magazine* the essays signed 'Elia' which were gathered in two series (1823, 1833). These are on widely differing subjects and in many manners—sometimes Lamb seems to speak directly, sometimes in the person of a fictitious old-fashioned being. But whether the essays are reminiscent or fantastic, the tone and style are distinct—the touch unmistakably Elia's. They often reveal their full subtlety only to those who penetrate beneath the surface to discover the literary or artistic message underlying them. Their poetical quality is deeper, or freer, than that of Lamb's actual verse, even such a poem as 'The Old Familiar Faces'.

Lamb retired from the India House in 1825, but the larger work, which Wordsworth for one expected from him, never came. He was a great letter-writer all his life and a most generous friend. He wrote many small things for the pleasure of his own circle, especially its younger members, and insisted on life before literature. His pretence of disliking nature in comparison with the city must not be taken too seriously any more than many of his 'attitudes'; his apparent resistance to music, for example, masked a considerable understanding of it. Many who knew him called him 'gentle', and this was one of the few things Lamb resented concerning himself; it is, indeed, a doubtful description of a spirit and an intelligence so invincible.

See also Vol. XII: ESSAYS.

LAS CASAS, Bartolomé de (1474–1566). This Spanish priest from Seville devoted his life to missionary work among the Indians of Central and South America and to their protection from slavery and exploitation by the cruel and selfish

Spanish colonists. He wrote many books on the American Indians, in particular his famous *History of the Indies*. He, like Francis Xavier, is often known as the 'Apostle of the Indies'—Xavier of the East Indies and Las Casas of the West.

Las Casas first went to the New World in one of Columbus's expeditions. In 1502 he went to Hispaniola (now Haiti), where he was ordained priest. Some years later he joined a missionary expedition to Cuba, and was so much horrified by the Spaniards' plunder and massacre of the natives that he resolved to try to help them. He freed his own slaves and returned to Spain to plead the cause of the Indians. The Spanish authorities were impressed by his story, but the directions that were issued to improve conditions were not obeyed by the colonists. Las Casas in his elaborate plan for a South American colony suggested that African Negroes should be imported to replace the Indian slaves, a suggestion which he afterwards bitterly regretted. But Las Casas's wise and humane plans for colonization were opposed and disregarded by the settlers, and even though he returned to Spain to demand stronger measures, he could make no headway. Deeply depressed he returned to Hispaniola and joined a Dominican order, where he spent 8 years working on the material for his *History*.

Then he was sent on missionary expeditions to Mexico and Nicaragua. Everywhere he denounced the cruel treatment of the Indians and incurred the anger of the settlers. He learned the native language and wrote a book to show that Christians could be made by persuasion only and not by force. He and other brave Dominicans put their theories to proof in a settlement they made in a wild district known as 'the land of war'. They planted a Church there and changed it to a land of peace.

The Pope and the Emperor Charles II both forbade the settlers to hold Indians as slaves, but the orders were ineffective. In 1540 Las Casas returned to Spain to enlist more clergy as missionaries. He persuaded Charles to issue a set of New Laws; but when he returned to Mexico as Bishop of Chiapa, he was received with such hostility that Charles revoked the New Laws. Three years later, when he was 73, Las Casas resigned the bishopric and returned to Spain to spend the rest of his life fighting the cause of the Indians both by writing and by speaking. When

he was 92 he left his home to plead with Philip II for the Guatemalans, who were threatened with further injustice. This effort, though successful, caused his death.

Las Casas is a splendid example of indomitable and selfless energy and courage. He had the rare capacity to persevere against hostility and apparent failure, and never to give up hope, even in this heart-breaking task.

See also Vol. I: American Indians, Central and South.
See also Vol. X: Slavery.

LATIMER, Hugh (*c* 1485–1555), *see* Cranmer.

LAUD, William (1573–1645). Laud, as Archbishop of Canterbury, was one of Charles I's principal advisers (q.v.). Like Charles, he regarded the Anglican Church as a branch of the Catholic Church, and endeavoured to suppress Puritanism by enforcing the strict observance of the Prayer Book, both in relation to doctrine and in the ordered arrangement of churches and services. To the Puritans this was tyranny. It aroused deep resentment and caused many Puritans to emigrate to America. When Laud tried to force his rule on Presbyterian Scotland, the Scots rebelled and the 'Bishops' War' broke out. Parliament, refusing to support the war, impeached both Laud and Strafford (q.v.) for high treason. Laud, after 4 years' imprisonment, was condemned by a special Bill of Attainder, there being insufficient evidence at his trial, and was beheaded in 1645.

Laud was a sincerely religious and courageous man and an extremely able administrator. While Chancellor of Oxford University (q.v. Vol. X) he codified the statutes, revived the college system, and founded the University Press and two professorships. He was, however, over-zealous, narrow-minded, and intolerant. His policy became identified with the King's administration and helped to bring about the Civil War of 1642 (q.v. Vol. X).

See also Charles I.
See also Vol. X: Impeachment.

LAVOISIER, Antoine Laurent (1743–94). This scientist and reformer was one of the outstanding personalities in France in the period immediately before the French Revolution (q.v. Vol. X). He was a pioneer in chemistry and physics, in physiology, agriculture, geology, education, and statistics.

Giraudon

LAVOISIER AND HIS WIFE IN THEIR LABORATORY
Relief from the Lavoisier statue in the Place de la Madeleine, Paris

His logical, systematic mind gave chemistry its modern character. Unlike others of his time, he used the laboratory balance to measure the changes in weight that accompany chemical reactions. He gradually exposed the fallacies underlying the theory of combustion known as the 'phlogiston theory' (*see* CHEMISTRY, HISTORY OF, Vol. VII). In this he was helped by the discoveries of such contemporaries as Joseph PRIESTLEY (q.v.), but he alone saw the significance of their discoveries. Lavoisier quickened the advance of science in all fields by giving not only chemists but workers in physics, biology, and medicine their first clear view of the various forms of MATTER (q.v. Vol. III) that we call elements, and of the distinction between chemical and physical changes.

Trained as a lawyer, Lavoisier was a member of a corporation which collected taxes for the French Government. He was always ready to turn his knowledge to some practical purpose, and in 1775 he took charge of the French gunpowder factories, where he made great improvements. But during the French Revolution he and others doing similar work were attacked because they had worked for the pre-revolutionary government, and in 1793 they were arrested on various charges. Their trial was a mockery of justice, and Lavoisier and twenty-seven of his colleagues were guillotined a few hours later.

See also Vol. VII: CHEMISTRY, HISTORY OF.

LAWRENCE, David Herbert (1885–1930). This English novelist and poet, the son of a Nottinghamshire miner, has had a social as well as a literary influence. Lawrence's works are largely autobiographical and were written to express ideas and beliefs which were important to him. *Sons and Lovers*, an early novel and perhaps his best, gives a vivid picture of his early life in a small mining town in the last years of the 19th century, a life from which Lawrence escaped by becoming a teacher. By 1914 he was recognized as a writer of great promise. But because he had married a German wife and was himself unfit for military service, he suffered much humiliation during the War, and by 1918 his one idea was to escape from England. After trying Europe, Ceylon, and Australia (as a result of which he wrote *Kangaroo*, a strange half-mystical, half-political novel on the theme of leadership), the Lawrences settled in Mexico.

Lawrence believed in the unity of nature: his feeling for landscape, for trees, birds, and animals, is not distinguished from his feelings for men and women. His power to identify himself with nature is expressed with outstanding success and originality in his best poems. Belief in the essential unity of things convinced him that spirit and body were of equal importance in any true relationship between a man and woman, and since he felt that in England the physical side of the relationship was usually despised or abused, he deliberately and challengingly emphasized its importance in his books. This led to an outcry against novels such as *The Rainbow* and *Lady Chatterley's Lover*, both then banned in England. Lawrence despised the conventions and deliberately offended public opinion, yet through his writing he succeeded in breaking down much unreasonable prejudice.

LAWRENCE, John (Baron) (1811–79). Lawrence, an Irish protestant, was one of three brothers to become famous in Indian affairs. He was chief commissioner of the Punjab in northern India when the Indian Mutiny broke out in 1857. His firm rule enabled him to retain control of the Punjab when it seemed that all India would be lost to Britain. When British rule was re-established, he was hailed as 'the saviour of India'.

Lawrence ruled with vigour and an intense assurance that God was on his side. He was masterful, hot-tempered, unconventional in dress and manner. After leaving school he joined the EAST INDIA COMPANY (q.v. Vol. VII) in Delhi. Illness brought him back to England for 4 years, but declaring, 'If I cannot live in India, then I must go and die there', he returned, and eventually, with his elder brother Henry, was appointed to rule the Punjab. Together they created an efficient system of government, drew up a new legal system, put down the murder and banditry that was common, built roads, and promoted agriculture. When his brother left the province, Lawrence became chief commissioner.

When the Indian Mutiny broke out, Lawrence acted promptly and at great personal risk. He quickly disarmed the rebels, and the province, which had become devoted to him, remained loyal. The British were thus able to maintain communication with Delhi, and to use the Punjab as a secure base for operations and for raising troops. Eventually, at the head of 60,000 troops, Lawrence himself marched against Delhi and relieved the city after a 3 months' siege. The mutiny was put down, and Lawrence came back to England a popular hero.

When appointed Viceroy of India in 1863, Lawrence devoted all his energies to preserving peace and establishing a wise and tolerant British rule. He created a forests department, extended railways, started irrigation and sanitation schemes, and reorganized the whole Indian judicial system. When he retired he was made a peer, and in the Lords devoted the last 10 years of his life to opposing DISRAELI's aggressive and flamboyant Imperialism (q.v.).

See also Vol. I: INDIAN PEOPLES.
See also Vol. X: MUTINY.

LAWRENCE, T. E. ('Lawrence of Arabia') (1888–1935). This scholar-turned-soldier won renown for his leadership of the Arabs in their revolt against Turkey, then allied to Germany, during the FIRST WORLD WAR (q.v. Vol. X). He wrote a magnificent account of his adventures, the *Seven Pillars of Wisdom*, and then, refusing rewards, deliberately retired into seclusion.

Lawrence first learned Arabic and Arab ways while travelling in the Middle East to collect material for a thesis on Crusader castles. On the outbreak of war he was sent to Cairo as an intelligence officer, and was later attached to the Arab leader, Feisal (afterwards King of Iraq), to assist in leading Arab troops against the Turks. His influence over the Arabs, whom he combined and trained into a wonderfully efficient force, was a triumph of personality. He learnt 'that no man could be their leader except he ate the ranks' food, wore their clothes, lived level with them, and yet appeared better in himself'. In a whirling campaign against the Turkish lines of communication, Lawrence himself led dashing, surprise raids on camel-back, forcing the Turks to retain troops urgently needed to counter the British offensive in Palestine. He showed particular ingenuity in blowing up railway lines, and the Turks put a price of £20,000 on the head of 'Al Urans, destroyer of engines'. Eventually the Turks were routed, and Lawrence led his Arabs in triumph to Damascus.

The war over, Lawrence retired to write his classic *Seven Pillars of Wisdom* (which he refused to publish in his lifetime). He returned to public

T. E. LAWRENCE IN ARAB DRESS
Painting by Augustus John

life in 1921 to help solve difficult problems arising from the grant of independence to the new Arab States. Lawrence was bitterly disappointed with the Allies' failure to fulfil promises made to the Arabs—promises for which he felt himself largely responsible. Therefore in 1922 he gave up his rank, refused all honours, and, changing his name to T. E. Shaw, enlisted as a mechanic in the Royal Air Force. When his service expired, he returned to Dorset and became interested in high-speed travel on motorcycles. He eventually crashed and was killed.

Lawrence was only 5 ft. 5 in. in height, with long, unruly hair and beautifully formed hands. When he chose, he could hold his own in conversation with his friends Bernard SHAW and Winston CHURCHILL (qq.v.); at other times, it was difficult to induce him to speak. Intensely proud, he was bitterly disillusioned when his high hopes for the Arabs were not fulfilled.

See also Vol. I: ARABS.

LEE, Robert Edward (1807–70). General Lee, who commanded the Southern forces in the

AMERICAN CIVIL WAR (q.v. Vol. X), was associated with 'Stonewall' Jackson, his second-in-command, in one of the most brilliant partnerships in military history.

Lee served with distinction in the Mexican War (1846–7) as chief engineer of the army, and later was superintendent of the U.S. Military Academy at West Point. When the Civil War broke out in 1861, President LINCOLN (q.v.) offered Lee command of the Federal army; but Lee, who was a Southerner, after a great struggle with conflicting loyalties, refused and offered his services to the South.

A year later Lee was appointed to command the Confederate army in northern Virginia, with Thomas Jackson as one of his subordinates. Jackson, a Professor of Science at the Virginia Military Institute, had quickly established himself as a most able military leader, winning the nickname of 'Stonewall' for his stubborn resistance against the North at the Battle of Bull Run. Lee and Jackson were utterly opposed in character and temperament; Lee was a grave, simple Virginian of distinguished family, and an experienced professional soldier; Jackson was an orphan without social graces, a militant, earnest Presbyterian, who came late to war.

Lee's strategy, and Jackson's execution of it, saved the Southern capital of Richmond. While Lee's army guarded the approaches to the town, Jackson, by audacious manœuvres, extraordinarily rapid marching, and determined fighting, whirled a small force up and down the Shenandoah Valley, threatening the Northern lines of communication, and eventually forcing back the enemy to defend their own capital of Washington. It was this type of fighting—with Lee the pivot, Jackson the moving arm hammering at the flanks and rear of the Northern armies —which baffled the enemy during the next few months. But in May 1863, following the victory of Chancellorsville, which threw open the Northern States to invasion, Jackson, reconnoitring at night between the lines, was accidentally shot by his own men.

Jackson's death was a heavy blow to the South. Though Lee took the offensive and invaded the Northern States of Maryland and Pennsylvania, he was soon checked and defeated at Gettysburg—though Lee always maintained that Gettysburg would have been a Southern victory had Jackson been present. For the next year and a half Lee was forced back on the defensive, and a series of bitter, defensive actions against General GRANT (q.v.) culminated in the surrender of his hungry, ragged army at Appomattox Courthouse in April 1865.

After the war, Lee was appointed President of Washington College, Virginia, and devoted the rest of his life to trying to heal the breach between North and South.

See also GRANT.
See also Vol. X: AMERICAN CIVIL WAR.

LEIBNIZ, Gottfried Wilhelm (1646–1716).

Leibniz was a German philosopher who belonged to the Rationalist school of philosophers, to which also belonged DESCARTES and SPINOZA (qq.v.). But Leibniz was not only a philosopher, he was also a considerable authority on law, a diplomat, an historian, and an outstanding mathematician—as is proved by his discovery in 1676, independently of Newton, of the Differential CALCULUS (q.v. Vol. VIII).

Leibniz was the son of a Professor of Philosophy of Leipzig University, who died when his son was only 6, but who left behind a fine collection of books which the young Leibniz read eagerly. Leibniz studied law at the University, and then, while in the service of the Elector of Mainz, he visited Paris and London and became acquainted with the learned men of his time. When he was 30 he became official librarian of the Brunswick family at Hanover, where he remained till he died.

His philosophy is set out in a short paper, *The Monadology*, which he wrote 2 years before his death. Otherwise, except for one or two famous essays (including a criticism of LOCKE's great *Essay* (q.v.)), his philosophical and scientific ideas have had to be assembled from his various papers and letters which, fortunately, have survived. They show Leibniz's brilliant intellect, especially in his attempt to relate mathematics and logic so that problems of philosophy could be exactly calculated and no longer be under dispute. He held that everything from a table to man's soul, and even to God himself, is made up of 'monads', or atoms, each of which is a simple, indivisible, imperishable unit, different from every other monad and constantly changing. But the monads which make up, for example, a table, though of the same stuff as our souls and minds, are unlike them in being unconscious, whereas the individual person can be directly conscious of the monad which is his own mind.

Monads, however, are never directly aware of one another. This theory of monads, Leibniz claimed, showed the true nature of real substance and the relation between body and mind —physical things which we call bodies being, in fact, made up of points of mental energy. Although each monad, being an individual unit, develops on lines of its own, the activities of all are co-ordinated to form the best of all possible universes, because God, according to Leibniz, has established and preserves a universal harmony.

See also Vol. I: PHILOSOPHY; RATIONALISM.

LENIN (1870–1924).

The Russian revolutionary and statesman, Vladimir Ilyich Ulyanov, better known as Lenin, was the creator of the Russian Soviet dictatorship, and a man who impressed his personality upon the 20th-century world to a remarkable extent. It is probable that there would have been a Russian Revolution even if Lenin had never lived, but the form the revolution took, and the new State—the Soviet Union—that was established out of the ruins of the old Russian Empire, were both deeply affected by Lenin's outlook and character. The lack of restraint, the rejection of any factor in human affairs except power, the ruthlessness and disregard for human life, the contempt for adversaries, the intolerance, and the readiness to use any means to secure an end, all the things that have come to be associated with the conduct of affairs by the Soviet Union, were features of Lenin's own character. The makers of the new Russia and the leaders of world COMMUNISM (q.v. Vol. X) have continued to look for their inspiration much more to his writings than to those of his teachers, Karl MARX (q.v.) and Engels. Lenin belongs to that small category of great men in history whose lives are inseparable from the cause they served, and whose stature as human beings must rank low except by the standard of service to that cause.

Lenin was the son of an important local official in the provincial town of Simbirsk (now Ulyanovsk) on the Volga river, and he had the normal education of a middle-class boy of the Russian Empire in the 19th century. Russia was one of the most backward countries in Europe, and masses of the people lived miserable lives. To become a revolutionary in the environment in which Lenin grew up was not an unusual thing, but the particular violence of his revolt against

LENIN ADDRESSING A MEETING IN PETROGRAD ON
7 NOVEMBER 1917

At this meeting he issued a proclamation announcing that
Kerensky's government had fallen and that the Soviets
had assumed power

Communist party, and which is Lenin's most abiding monument.

The study, propaganda, and personal intrigue directed towards this end occupied the whole of Lenin's adult life until war caused a crisis in Russia in 1917. In 1895 he was exiled to Siberia; but the conditions there were not strict enough to interfere with his revolutionary planning. Afterwards he went abroad, living mainly in London. He returned to Russia during the revolutionary upheaval of 1905, though he played no prominent part; and when that revolutionary movement was suppressed, he went abroad once more.

When the FIRST WORLD WAR (q.v.) began in 1914, he was one of the small group of Socialists who refused to acknowledge the obligations of patriotism and continued to work against their own governments. For this reason, the Germans made use of him in 1917. At that time Russia, an ally of Britain and France, had suffered appalling casualties, and its inefficient and corrupt government was collapsing. A Liberal revolution in the spring led to a democratic experiment in government under Kerensky; but this was threatened by the plots both among the former ruling class and among the extreme Marxist revolutionaries (*see* RUSSIAN REVOLUTION, Vol. X). Lenin, who was living in Switzerland, a neutral country, was taken across Germany in a special train to enter Russia through Sweden, in the hope that his influence would stop the Russians fighting, and thus free several German armies to fight the British and French.

Lenin found that many of his old friends were satisfied not to carry the Revolution any further. He saw and was able to convince others that the new Russian Government could be easily overthrown by revolutionary workers in the capital because the government would not be able to depend on the support of the army. The army, the bulk of which consisted of peasants, would support the revolutionaries if they promised to confiscate for them the lands belonging to the rich landowners. In November 1917, when the revolution broke out, the armed workers, as Lenin had foretold, achieved a rapid victory, and Kerensky's Government was overthrown.

Lenin, as chairman of the Council of People's Commissars, became the real ruler of Russia. After this date the story of his life is identical with Russian history. It was he who persuaded his new government to accept a harsh peace

his own society and class may be accounted for by the execution at the age of 19 of his elder brother, who had been implicated in a plot against the Tsar. He followed the usual practice of revolutionaries, and adopted the special name 'Lenin' in place of his own surname.

Lenin did not believe that acts of individual terrorism, such as the throwing of bombs or the assassination of hated individuals, could overthrow the Russian system of government. Only a mass movement of the people could bring this about. Yet he did not believe, as many revolutionaries did, that the people would take matters into their own hands without leadership. When, about 1900, he became a prominent figure among the Russian followers of Marx's Communist theories, he devoted himself to building up among them a group of skilled, professional revolutionaries. These were prepared to exploit the grievances of the town workers and the peasants and of the minor nationalities within the Russian Empire for the purpose of organizing and carrying out a revolution according to their own ideas. Such was the Bolshevik party which, after the Revolution, became the Russian

from the Germans in order to get a breathing space to complete the revolution. And when the revolutions which he hoped and worked for in other countries failed to happen, he rallied his supporters for eventual triumph in the civil war, which took place within Russia. He laid the foundations of the new social order, dominated by the needs of the State, and ruled by the party he had created.

Lenin's health gave way at the end of 1922, weakened by a wound from a would-be assassin, and he died in 1924, at the age of 53. His body was preserved and is encased in a great tomb in the Red Square in Moscow, as an object of public veneration.

See also MARX; STALIN.

LEONARDO DA VINCI (1452–1519). Leonardo was a universal genius, whose interests ranged over every subject and whose extraordinary gifts of mind and body enabled him to tackle every problem. This wide interest was typical of the RENAISSANCE (q.v. Vol. I), when new ways of thought were leading to new discoveries in every branch of learning.

Leonardo was the illegitimate son of a Florentine lawyer who acknowledged him as his son and brought him up. He was said to have been exceptionally handsome and also extremely strong—he could bend a horse-shoe with his hands. Leonardo worked in Florence until he was nearly 30. He was trained in the studio of Verrocchio, a versatile artist who practised in painting, sculpture, and goldsmith's work, and Leonardo seems to have spent these earlier years chiefly in painting. This was not sufficient to engage his many talents, and in 1481 he sent a letter to the ruler of Milan, Lodovico Sforza, asking for employment, and claiming in his letter that he could do almost everything better than anyone else. He was employed apparently in the capacity of a musician, in which he is said to have excelled. During the 20 years he spent at Milan he made good his promises by carrying out the most varied kinds of work—organizing theatrical entertainments, preparing plans for rebuilding Milan and for finishing the cathedral, undertaking military engineering, as well as preparing the model for a gigantic statue of Lodovico's father on horseback, and painting court portraits and murals.

When Milan was captured by the French in 1499 and Lodovico expelled, Leonardo returned to Florence. For a few months he was in the service of Cesare BORGIA (q.v.), as military engineer. At this time he started an ambitious scheme for making a canal from Florence to the sea, but after some months of work the idea was abandoned. He also worked on a huge battle picture called 'The Battle of Anghiari' for the council-chamber of the Republic of Florence. MICHELANGELO (q.v.) was to paint a similar picture, but neither work was ever finished. Leonardo invented a new system for painting in oils on the wall, but he was not satisfied with the result and abandoned the undertaking. The failure of this and of the canal project was doubtless responsible for his returning to Milan in 1506, where he stayed for 7 years working in many different capacities for the French, who occupied the city. In 1513 Leonardo went to Rome, where he enjoyed the patronage of the Pope's brother, Giuliano de' MEDICI (q.v.). But he was now an old man and did little work, probably feeling that he could no longer compete with the young Michelangelo and the even younger RAPHAEL (q.v.), both of whom were then at the height of their fame. About 1517, he left Italy for the first time in his life and went to France, at the invitation of King Francis I. It was there (near Amboise on the Loire) that he died some 2 years later.

In the 20th century, when knowledge in every field has become highly specialized, it would be impossible for a single man to master every branch of knowledge as Leonardo did. Leonardo was born with an insatiable curiosity about the workings of nature in every form. He was not interested in the works of man, and in contrast to the other great Italians of the Renaissance, he had only a limited interest in Roman art, and taught himself Latin only in order to be able to read scientific books. His love of nature was intense: he became a vegetarian, and is said to have bought caged birds in order to have the pleasure of setting them free. Nature interested him first as an artist: he wanted to copy, in drawings or paintings, the beauty of the world around him, not merely human beings, but all animals, fish, and flowers, trees, mountains, and blades of grass He constantly sought ideally beautiful people, but was also fascinated by those who were supremely ugly, and he did a famous series of caricatures of such people. Then his interest led him to explore the workings of the human body, and he made many anatomical dissections.

ST. JAMES THE GREATER

Drawing by Leonardo for his painting *The Last Supper*.
The architectural sketches are probably connected with
the castle of his patron, Lodovico Sforza, at Milan

He almost, but not quite, discovered the principle of the circulation of the blood—more than a century before HARVEY (q.v.) did so. He studied rocks and fossils and made prolonged researches into the movement of water, which fascinated him all his life. For a long time he occupied himself with studying the flight of birds in the hope of building an aeroplane or glider (*see* FLYING, HISTORY OF, Vol. IV).

In Leonardo's scientific researches he had the field almost to himself. Scientists before his day had generally been content to rely on the authority of the ancients. Leonardo took nothing for granted and only trusted what he himself had actually observed. This is a truly scientific attitude in the modern sense, but it was an extraordinary novelty in the Renaissance. By one of the ironies of fate which followed him all his life, Leonardo's actual discoveries in science led nowhere, and they all had to be rediscovered by later scientists. He wrote down the results of his researches in notebooks (written in mirror-writing, from right to left, which is a more natural way of writing for a left-handed man, as he was). These notebooks have survived, but they were unknown for many years after his death.

It is as an artist that Leonardo is chiefly remembered, and even in this sphere fate and his own temperament have been unkind to him. He aimed at perfection and saw faults in what appeared marvellous to everyone else; consequently he left many of his pictures unfinished, or started a second or even a third version, instead of finishing the first. For this reason, too, he sometimes ruined his pictures by experimenting in a new and improved way of painting or kind of paint. His great battle-piece was an example of this, as was also his most famous painting, the 'Last Supper'. Leonardo liked to work slowly, which is not possible with the fresco technique (*see* PAINTING, Vol. XII). When commissioned to paint the 'Last Supper' on the wall of the refectory of the church of S. Maria delle Grazie in Milan, he wanted to paint in oils, and so he invented a new method for applying oils to a wall-surface. But the preparation on which he laid the colours gave way, and they started to flake off even in Leonardo's own lifetime. Since then the picture has been repainted many times.

Even in its ruined state we can see what a great work of art the 'Last Supper' must have been, for the perfection of its design remains. At the time it was painted it made so great an impression that without it much of the art of the 16th century in Italy would have been quite different. The same can be said of Leonardo's most famous portrait, the 'Mona Lisa' in the Louvre. Since it was painted people have been fascinated by the mysterious smile on the face and by the strange background of fantastic rocks. It was the first portrait which showed the sitter at half-length and in an easy and graceful attitude. Before then portraits had shown merely the head and shoulders of the sitter, nearly always giving an impression of stiffness. The pose of the 'Mona Lisa', or something similar to it, became the normal way of painting portraits for a long time to come.

In all his work as an artist Leonardo was fascinated by a few themes to which he returned again and again. The smile of the 'Mona Lisa' occurs in all his later pictures; an arm pointing upwards is a recurrent subject; moving water,

THE LAST SUPPER
Wall-painting by Leonardo in the refectory of the monastery of Santa Maria delle Grazie, Milan

especially a breaking wave, rocks, and rocky mountains occur in nearly all his pictures and were also studied by him as a scientist. He was interested all his life in horses and made numerous drawings and models of them. The vast full-size model for the statue of Francesco Sforza on horseback, on which Leonardo had worked for about 15 years, was destroyed soon after it was finished, and was never cast in bronze. There is no surviving work of sculpture which is certainly by Leonardo, and no building carried out according to any of the many designs which he made.

The few ruined or unfinished paintings which survive would hardly be sufficient in themselves to justify Leonardo's reputation. It is chiefly in his drawings that we can appreciate his real quality. Fortunately a very large number of these have been preserved, nearly all the best being at Windsor Castle; and in them and in the notebooks we can see the extent of Leonardo's interests and his skill as a draughtsman. The notes were intended as material for learned books which were never in fact written and, apart from a connected fragment of a treatise on painting, are only a very incomplete monument as they stand. But the drawings are probably the most beautiful and the most skilful ever drawn by anyone at any time, and if all the rest of Leonardo's life-work had perished they would

still be sufficient to establish him as one of the greatest of all artists.

See also Vol. XII: DRAWING; FLORENTINE PAINTING; ITALIAN ART.

LINCOLN, Abraham (1809–65). Lincoln was elected President of the United States of America when a bitter quarrel over SLAVERY (q.v. Vol. X) was tearing apart the Northern and Southern States. Within a year the quarrel had led to the outbreak of the AMERICAN CIVIL WAR (q.v. Vol. X). Lincoln led the North through 4 years of bitter fighting to final victory. In those years he introduced legislation which gave freedom to some 4 million Negro slaves; and (perhaps his greatest concern) he saved the Union from the dissolution with which it was threatened when the Southern States broke away. He was a remarkable orator and his eloquent speeches ('with malice toward none, with charity for all') would alone ensure his fame.

Lincoln was born on a farm in Kentucky. His father, who had little money, moved restlessly from State to State. For a time he settled in the deep forests of Indiana, and there the boy Lincoln became an expert woodsman and tree feller. As a young man, he made trips with a cargo-boat to New Orleans, where his first contact with slavery made a lasting impression on his mind. When he was 21 his family moved to Illinois, and there Lincoln lived and worked until he was elected President.

Lincoln, a sensitive child who suffered from spells of brooding melancholy, had received only a most elementary education in the schools of the backwoods; but he had a passion for self-improvement. After failing in various jobs, he was at length persuaded to study law. This was the turning-point in his career, for he soon became a successful lawyer. At 25 he was elected to the legislature of the State of Illinois, and 13 years later he won a seat in the House of Representatives of the United States Congress. But at that time he showed no unusual qualities of leadership; in fact, the success of his legal practice was tending to direct his attention away from politics.

In 1854, however, Congress passed a Bill allowing for the extension of slavery into the new Western territories if the majority of the people wanted it. In the North, where slavery had long been prohibited, this caused a storm of indignant protest. The Senator responsible for the Bill defended his action in a public speech, and

Radio Times Hulton Lib.

LINCOLN IN 1862, VISITING THE BATTLEFIELD OF SHARPSBURG

Lincoln was persuaded by his friends to reply. There followed a series of heated debates, which attracted nation-wide attention and established Lincoln as a powerful speaker and one of the acknowledged leaders of the anti-slavery movement.

In 1860 the Republican party, which had been reorganized to fight the extension of slavery, elected Lincoln ('Honest Abe') as its candidate for the Presidency. Although Lincoln had made it clear that in opposing the extension of slavery he did not mean to interfere with it in those States where it was already legally sanctioned, on his election the States of the extreme South broke away from the rest of the United States. They were later followed by others. These States reorganized themselves as an independent nation, called the Southern Confederacy. Lincoln, faced with this break up of the Union, declared that no State was legally free to leave the Union; and his determination to uphold this constitutional principle led to the outbreak of civil war. Many of the 'slave' States who were loyal to the Union wanted to remain neutral, but Lincoln declared that this was impossible: that the American Constitution demanded the complete loyalty of the States to the federal government.

In the first 18 months of the war the North suffered severe setbacks. The Southern armies under General LEE (q.v.) pressed forward against Washington, the Northern capital, and all the Northern States seemed threatened with invasion. But late in 1862 the tide began to turn. The Northern forces under General GRANT (q.v.) won important victories, and Grant himself inspired his troops with new courage. During this time Lincoln took whatever powers he considered necessary to win the war—powers greater than any President has taken before or since. He took advantage of the vague authority which the constitution gave to the President as commander-in-chief, leaving Congress to approve his actions afterwards. Sometimes he stepped outside the conventional limits of the constitution: in 1862, for example, he issued on his sole authority as President the Emancipation Proclamation, by which the slaves in the rebellious States were declared free. A year later, at the opening of a military cemetery to commemorate the Northern victory of Gettysburg, Lincoln delivered his most famous speech, beginning 'Fourscore and seven years ago our fathers brought forth on this continent a new nation conceived in liberty and dedicated to the proposition that all men are created equal'. His concluding sentence—the resolution that 'this nation, under God, shall have a new birth of freedom, and that government of the people, by the people, for the people, shall not perish from the earth'—has become the watchword of democratic governments throughout the world.

In November 1864 Lincoln was elected President for a second term; but only 5 months later, when a Northern victory was already assured, he was shot dead in his box at the theatre by a fanatical Southern supporter, an actor called Booth. Lincoln had scarcely begun to consider the new problems that would be thrown up by the peace, and the whole work of reconstruction devolved upon his successors. But as the war had drawn to a close his sympathy had more and more extended to the Southerners, and had he lived they would almost certainly have been spared much of the humiliation they later endured.

Lincoln was unusually tall, nearly 6 ft. 4 in. in height, muscular, with long ungainly limbs, a dark complexion, and thick, coarse, black hair. He had extraordinary physical endurance, and great patience. He was gentle, unaffected, and loved laughter and people. But beneath this there was an undercurrent of sadness, and he was given to long periods of deep silence and introspection. His humble beginnings, his great awkward frame, and his unaffected dignity had won the hearts of the American people, and news of his death was received with profound sorrow throughout the world.

See also GRANT; LEE.
See also Vol. X: AMERICAN CONSTITUTION.

LINNAEUS, Carl (1707–78). This Swedish naturalist was a pioneer in the naming and classifying of plants and animals. His father, a poor clergyman, kept a little private botanical garden in which the boy interested himself, and the family doctor gave him his first instruction in botany. His exceptional talent for this subject was soon recognized when he went to a university to study medicine.

As a young man Linnaeus made a scientific expedition to Lapland, suffering great hardships and dangers during his travels through sparsely populated districts. Afterwards he spent some years in Holland, where he published

CARL LINNAEUS
Frontispiece from *Species Plantarum*, 1762

several important books on natural history. Then he returned home and practised as a doctor, before long becoming Professor of Medicine in Upsala University. But in fact what he actually taught and studied was natural history; he organized collecting expeditions to various parts of the world and supervised the study of the plants and animals obtained.

Linnaeus had a genius for providing short, accurate definitions that separated one kind of plant or animal from another. There existed at the time no generally agreed system of classification, and different botanists and zoologists gave different names to the same plant or animal. Linnaeus's chief service to science, therefore, was the institution of a universal system for classification. His system was not new; it had been used by a botanist named Bauhin a century earlier; but it was Linnaeus who brought a single system into universal use. This system, made popular by Linnaeus and developed more fully later, is described in the article SCIENTIFIC NAMES (q.v. Vol. II).

Linnaeus wished to make it as easy as possible to name plants and animals, and so, wherever possible, he classified according to some easily noticed external feature—such as the number of stamens in a flower—and he paid little attention to internal anatomy. This made his classification of animals particularly unsatisfactory, and led him, for example, to place an extraordinary variety of very different animals in the single group AMPHIBIA (q.v. Vol. II).

Linnaeus's affable, humorous nature inspired the devotion of students. He used to make excursions into the country on Saturdays with about 150 students, who dispersed to look for specimens. When a rare plant was found a trumpet was sounded to assemble the whole party to hear the Professor describe it.

His own collection was sold after his death to an English buyer and shipped abroad. The King of Sweden hearing of this loss to the fatherland, sent a frigate to give chase and recover the treasure; but the English ship outsailed it, and the collection is preserved to this day by the Linnean Society at its rooms in Piccadilly, London.

See also Vol. II: SCIENTIFIC NAMES; CLASSIFICATION OF ANIMALS AND PLANTS.

LISTER, Joseph (Baron) (1827–1912). Lord Lister, one of the greatest of English surgeons, was the first to establish the need for antiseptic methods in surgical operations. He made it possible for surgeons to operate on any part of the body with almost complete safety from outside infection by germs, and consequently there are now no longer the large proportion of deaths after operations from this cause.

Joseph Lister, born at Upton, Essex, was one of the seven children of Quaker parents. His father was a prosperous wine-merchant and amateur scientist. Their family circle was a happy one, with the quiet and serious atmosphere usual among QUAKERS (q.v. Vol. I), and with a deep respect for all kinds of learning.

From his earliest years Joseph and his brothers and sisters were encouraged in a love of natural history and drawing. His father had been made a Fellow of the Royal Society for his invention of a greatly improved microscope; thus at a time when few doctors or scientists owned a microscope, the Lister children were able to use one. Joseph became very skilful at fine and delicate dissection, and before he was 14 he had already determined to be a surgeon.

After his Quaker boarding-school Lister went to University College, London, where he remained for 9 years, took the highest surgical degree, receiving the Fellowship of the Royal College of Surgeons, and did much brilliant research work. In 1846, when he was 19, he was present at the first operation ever performed in England with the aid of ANAESTHETICS (q.v. Vol. XI), carried out in University College Hospital by the well-known surgeon, Robert Liston. This was a great event in British surgery. Up to that time, a patient could not be 'put to sleep' but, rendered semi-conscious with brandy or rum, had to be held down by force. A surgeon had to work so fast that he could not always work with sufficient care. By making the patient unconscious, a surgeon, no longer disturbed by his sufferings, could take adequate time. But although the use of anaesthetics made operations easier, it did not make them safer, for the patient's wounds, instead of healing, still often became inflamed and more patients died of this poison than of the operation itself. Nobody knew how the infection was caused or how it could be avoided.

It took Lister 12 years of hard work before he found the answer to this problem. He spent 7 of these years in Edinburgh gaining valuable experience from working with the famous surgeon, James Syme, whose daughter Agnes became Lister's devoted wife. Then, in 1860, he became Professor of Surgery at Glasgow, and the Royal Infirmary in that city, which had an appalling record of deaths from surgical infection, was the place where he proved his theory—which was to save the lives of countless sick people. In 1865, Lister read how the French chemist, PASTEUR (q.v.), had discovered that putrefaction (decay of the flesh) is caused by living germs carried everywhere on the dust in the air, and that these germs breed and multiply like other kinds of animal life. Lister began to look for a method of killing drifting germs before they were able to multiply in vast numbers in the wounds of his patients; and he chose the powerful disinfectant carbolic acid. He used this liberally on his hands, instruments, dressings, and the patient's skin, and he also tried to purify the air with a carbolic spray. The result was dramatic. Patients recovered without any of the usual dangerous infections, and the number of deaths fell rapidly. But Lister soon found that crude carbolic acid was too strong (it is in fact a dangerous burning acid), so he mixed it with oil or water to make it less irritating. He also found that the chief carriers of infective germs were the hands, the

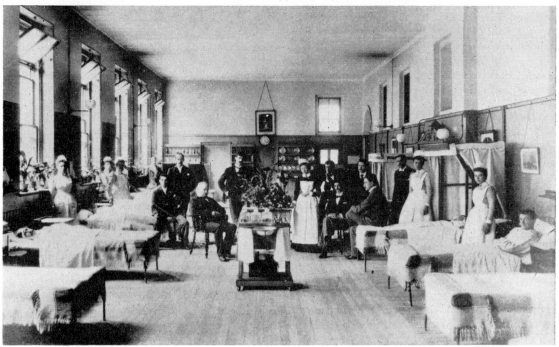

LORD LISTER AND HIS STAFF IN THE VICTORIA WARD, KING'S COLLEGE HOSPITAL, 1893

instruments, and the dressings, and that if these were disinfected the spray was unnecessary.

Thus the wonderful demonstration of applied science known as the 'Listerian revolution' went through two stages in getting rid of the danger of sepsis (Greek for 'putrefaction') in wounds. First came 'antisepsis', when everything was flooded with carbolic to kill any germs during an operation; then 'asepsis', when everything was made so clean to start with that no germs were present at the operation, and so no carbolic was needed. The aseptic routine for an operation today, in which heat and soap and water have replaced chemical antiseptics, is merely a logical development of Lister's methods (*see* SURGERY, Vol. XI). The modern operating-theatre, with its gleaming white tiles and table (all easily washed down) and its hygienically gowned and masked surgeons and nurses, is his finest memorial, and is to be found in every hospital in the world.

Lister published the first detailed account of his new methods in *The Lancet* in 1867, and surgeons in other lands were quick to copy them. For some years he worked in Edinburgh, and then in 1877 he returned to London, where from King's College Hospital he was able to convert those who still clung to the old ways. Honours were paid to him from all over the world; Pasteur acclaimed him as the co-founder of the new science of bacteriology. He became President of the Royal Society, and in 1897 he was made a baron, the first British medical man to be raised to the peerage. He was also one of the twelve original members of the Order of Merit.

Always modest and gentle, Lister was much loved by his patients, and when he died the country mourned the passing of a great scientist and a noble man.

See also Vol. XI: SURGERY, HISTORY OF; ANTISEPSIS.

LISZT, Franz (1811–86). This Hungarian composer, probably the greatest pianist the world has known, inherited his gifts from his father and gave his first concert when he was 9. The tenderness and fire of his performances and the delicacy and richness of sound which he produced from the piano made him sought after all over Europe. For some time when he was not touring he lived in France, and often thought of himself as a Frenchman, putting into his music some of the clarity and grace of the French spirit. From 1848 he was employed as music director to the Duke of Weimar. When he was 54 he received minor orders in the Catholic priesthood,

LISZT CONDUCTING HIS ORATORIO, *ST. ELIZABETH*, AT BUDAPEST IN 1865
Engraving from the *Illustrated London News*

and was often known as Abbé. He divided the rest of his life between Weimar, retirement, and concert tours, and died at Bayreuth.

Liszt was a musical thinker as well as a performer. His symphonic poems for orchestra are unusual in their design, which is shaped by the story of each piece; and his Piano Sonata is an exciting work in one movement broken into three main sections. He wrote symphonies inspired by the works of GOETHE and DANTE (qq.v.), and much sacred music—some of it very original—as well as songs, two piano concertos, and an enormous amount of piano music, including the brilliant and glittering *Hungarian Rhapsodies*. To display his skill as a pianist he also arranged for piano organ fugues by Bach, Beethoven symphonies, and Schubert songs. Liszt was a strong champion of WAGNER's music (q.v.), and several of Wagner's most striking ideas came first from Liszt. Nobody questions his greatness as a pianist, but his importance as a composer is only now beginning to be realized.

See also Vol. XII: SONATA.

LIVINGSTONE, David (1813–73). This Scottish medical missionary, of saintly character and phenomenal physical endurance, explored the basin of the river Zambezi and the great lakes of East Africa. Livingstone was a man of humble origin who secured a good education by his own efforts, and was selected in 1838 by the London Missionary Society for training as a medical missionary. He qualified in 1840, and was sent to Bechuanaland.

For over 10 years Livingstone worked as a missionary, often accompanied by his wife and children; but during this period he became convinced that his duty was to open up the vast unexplored centre of Africa to missionaries; he would pioneer, and others would follow and consolidate. The rest of his life was devoted to three great expeditions into the unexplored interior of the continent.

The object of his first expedition (1852–6) was to find a practical route from the coast to the area of his missionary activity around the headwaters of the Zambezi river. He crossed Africa from the Atlantic to the Indian Ocean, tracing the course of the Zambezi from its source to its mouth, and discovering the VICTORIA FALLS (q.v. Vol. III). His account of this journey (*Missionary Travels and Researches in South Africa,*

1857) was so popular that he could have retired on the proceeds had he wished to do so.

In 1858 Livingstone was commissioned as a consul by the British Government to explore eastern and central Africa. On this expedition he discovered and explored Lake Nyasa, and entered for the first time a region devastated by the SLAVE TRADE (q.v. Vol. VII) carried on by the Arabs from Zanzibar. Livingstone's mind became increasingly dominated by the absolute necessity of abolishing this horrible trade in human beings.

In 1866 Livingstone left Zanzibar on his third and most important expedition, almost entirely privately financed. His objects were to carry on the fight against the slave trade, to discover the watershed between Lakes Nyasa and Tanganyika, and to find out if the source of the Nile was situated so far south. The party of thirty-six Indians and Africans with whom he started soon dwindled to four or five, but in spite of this he travelled vast distances among the great lakes, discovering Lake Bangweulu. He suffered dreadful hardship, especially after the theft of his medicine chest in January 1867 deprived him of the means of controlling his fever, and he was in constant danger from the Arab slave traders. In Europe he was given up for lost, but an American newspaper organized an expedition under H. M. STANLEY (q.v.) to seek him. In November 1871 the two men met at Ujiji, on the eastern shore of Lake Tanganyika, and Stanley greeted him with the now famous words, 'Dr. Livingstone, I presume.'

Stanley left Livingstone with ample supplies of medicine and trade-goods, and a reliable party of fifty-seven natives. But Livingstone's health had been shattered by the hardships and disappointments of his long journey, and on 2 May 1873 his faithful servants found him dead, in an attitude of prayer beside his bed. So great was their devotion that they carried him and his precious journals 1,000 miles back to Zanzibar. His body was buried in Westminster Abbey.

After Livingstone's death, Stanley continued to explore Africa; the two men between them explored and opened to Christianity and to European trade the whole of equatorial Africa south of the equator. Through their work the brutal Arab slave trade, the last extensive trade of its kind in the world, was at last suppressed.

See also STANLEY.
See also Vol. III: EAST AFRICA.

LIVY (59 B.C.–A.D. 17). Titus Livius, the Roman historian, was born at Patavium (Padua), a wealthy city in North Italy. His parents were reasonably rich, and he received a good education, studying philosophy and, as his work shows, rhetoric.

The first 30 years of Livy's life were years of civil war, ending in the downfall of the Roman Republic which he supported. In consequence he turned his attention to the study of literature and to the writing of a history of Rome, in which he emphasized her past grandeur. His undertaking had the approval of AUGUSTUS (q.v.), the first Roman Emperor, with whom Livy became friends on his arrival at Rome as a young man.

The history, consisting of 142 books, recorded the achievements of Rome from its foundation to 9 B.C. Only the first 35 books have survived in full, though there are short summaries of almost all the rest. Since this colossal work was didactic in purpose—that is, designed to teach—Livy gave examples, wherever possible, of the virtue and bravery of Rome's ancestors, and emphasized how a decline in morals had brought about the troubles of the 1st century B.C.

Livy's didactic purpose often caused him to be biased and partial. He had little knowledge of political, social, or military matters, and was less interested in historical accuracy than in the much wider poetic kind of truth. Indeed his lucid prose, exalted and dramatic in quality, contains much that is poetic both in rhythm and in diction. He had immense enthusiasm for his subject, and much will-power—both necessary for the execution of so tremendous a task. The great patriot-historian spent most of his life in Rome; but returned to his native city in his old age, and died there.

See also Vol. I: ROMAN CIVILIZATION.
See also Vol. XII: HISTORIES; LATIN LITERATURE.

LLOYD GEORGE, David (1863–1945). Lloyd George was the first man to make his way up by his own efforts from poverty and obscurity to the position of British Prime Minister. He was the most active figure, in the face of great hostility, in laying the foundations of social security in Britain in the years before the FIRST WORLD WAR (q.v. Vol. X); and during the second half of that war he became Prime Minister.

Lloyd George was a Welshman, born in Manchester and brought up in the village of Llanystumdwy, in Caernarvonshire. His family was Welsh-speaking, Nonconformist, and strongly Nationalist in politics. Helped by family savings Lloyd George struggled to be a solicitor, and then, at the age of 27, entered Parliament. He represented Caernarvon Boroughs for 55 years. Dark, sturdy, with flashing blue eyes, he soon proved a magnetic orator. His early interests were Welsh Home Rule and the Disestablishment of the Church of England in Wales, and he risked his career by condemning the SOUTH AFRICAN WAR (q.v. Vol. X).

In the General Election of 1906 the Liberals, with their policy of social reform, swept the country. Lloyd George became President of the Board of Trade and later succeeded Asquith as Chancellor of the Exchequer. His first Budget was framed to supply large sums of money for social services; but the taxes he proposed and his stinging speeches stirred deep animosity, and the House of Lords, contrary to long tradition, rejected the Budget. The resulting conflict ended in curbing the power of the Lords, and Lloyd George then carried through the National Insurance Act, making the State, workers, and employers partners in schemes of SOCIAL INSURANCE (q.v. Vol. X).

When war with Germany broke out in 1914, Lloyd George threw all his energy into finding money to pay for it, and then, as Minister of Munitions, into enormously increasing the output of armaments. Controversy about the conduct of the war came to a head when he wanted to set up a small War Cabinet, with himself as Chairman. Asquith, the Prime Minister, naturally felt that he should be Chairman, but finding how strong a following Lloyd George had in the government, Asquith resigned, and Lloyd George became Prime Minister in December 1916. This caused a lasting split in the Liberal party.

Lloyd George took over the prosecution of the war with great vigour, reorganizing the Cabinet to increase its efficiency. His tireless energy and kindling eloquence made him a great war leader. He felt convinced of the necessity of placing all the Allied armies on the Western front under one supreme leader, and fought long and hard battles with British generals and politicians on this issue. Finally the series of defeats in the early part of 1918 brought about an agreement to his proposals, and the French commander, Marshal Foch, became commander-in-chief.

Lloyd George had always affirmed that the Allied war aims included only acts of restitution and justice; but in the elections immediately after the war in December 1918, he made extremely vengeful speeches against Britain's beaten enemies, especially in regard to German reparations. At the Paris Peace Conference, however, he mediated between Clemenceau, leader of ravaged France, who wished to adopt severe measures against Germany, and the visionary American President WILSON (q.v.), whose country had never had first-hand experience of the German menace, and who wished to be lenient. Later, by a series of conferences, he strove to restore prosperity to Europe.

To Britain the aftermath of war brought, not the better world that Lloyd George had forecast, but disillusion and devastating UNEMPLOYMENT (q.v. Vol. VII). In Ireland the Government of Ireland Act, designed to pacify Ireland, separated Ulster from the South and brought the country to the edge of civil war. In December 1921, after an appeal by King George V for tolerance, Lloyd George negotiated a treaty with the Irish leaders of both sides which led to the setting up of the Irish Free State. In the following year the majority of the Conservatives withdrew their support from Lloyd George's Coalition, and Lloyd George resigned. He never again held office.

Lloyd George spent his remaining 23 years in vain efforts to persuade the country to support his plans for conquering unemployment. Though at first deluded by Hitler's apparent success in improving social conditions in Germany, he later consistently attacked Neville Chamberlain's policy of appeasement. When the Second World War broke out, Lloyd George was too old for active politics. He retired to Llanystumdwy and died in April 1945, 3 months after he had been created Earl of Dwyfor.

See also Vol. X: FIRST WORLD WAR.

LOCKE, John (1632–1704). This greatest of English philosophers, author of the famous *Essay Concerning Human Understanding*, has had a profound influence on philosophical and political thought. He concerned himself in particular with problems of society, of education, of the relation of Church and State, and especially of religious toleration in an age when this was far from an accepted ideal.

Locke was a Somerset man, born at Wrington. In the CIVIL WAR (q.v. Vol. X), which broke out in his boyhood, his family took the Parliamentary side. He was educated at Westminster School and Christ Church, Oxford, where he remained as a Fellow until expelled for political reasons in 1684. The second half of the 17th century witnessed the beginnings of a great scientific movement. Locke, a scientist and Fellow of the newly founded Royal Society, was chiefly interested in medicine—though every scientific discovery interested him. In the 17th century it was still possible for one person to acquaint himself with a great deal of what was known in every field of learning, and Locke was one of the most learned men of his age. At the same time he took an active part in practical affairs, assisting the great Whig leader, Lord Shaftesbury. When, in the last years of Charles II's reign, Shaftesbury fell into disfavour and fled to Holland, Locke followed him, and remained there till 1689, when William and Mary of Orange came to England to take the throne.

Throughout his life Locke had been pondering over certain general problems in politics, economics, religion, and philosophy, and during this $5\frac{1}{2}$ years of exile in Holland he brought his reflections to a head. On his return to England in his late fifties he published a number of books which gave him lasting fame. After the REVOLUTION OF 1688 (q.v. Vol. X), which drew much of its inspiration from Locke's own writings, he took no further active part in government, though he gave advice to his friends, the Whigs. He himself spent his days reading, writing, and entertaining in his Essex retreat at Oates, and there, when he was 72, he died.

Locke was wise and far-seeing in his actions and counsel—a wisdom so obvious in his writings that Voltaire and his school talked of *le sage Locke*. He loved truth, honesty, and fair dealing between men; he enjoyed also good company and good talk. He loved children and young people, and spent much time instructing them and advising their parents. He was practical and utilitarian, and would advise young people to seek recreation not in wasteful activities such as games, but in gardening, carpentry, or other useful crafts. He considered music, poetry, and painting as pleasant but trifling occupations, not worthy of a man's main energies. He believed in 'enlightened self-interest', that is, in doing things for pleasure and because they will be useful. Finally, he was truly religious and combined a deep piety with a broad spirit of toleration.

JOHN LOCKE
Portrait by Kneller. Reproduced by permission of the Governing Body of Christ Church, Oxford

His first publication, in 1689, was a defence of religious toleration called *A Letter Concerning Toleration*. No one, he wrote, be he priest or ruler, has the right to compel another to believe any doctrine. No human being knows the whole truth, and, if he did know it, the use of force would not make another believe it. In the long run intolerance is as ineffective as it is immoral. In the *Two Treatises of Civil Government* (1690) Locke makes a further defence of the liberties of the individual. Government is necessary, he says, and for this purpose power must be vested in the hands of a few, even the power of life and death over others; but this power must be wielded only for the good of the community. The people put power into the hands of rulers in trust to safeguard, and not to limit, their own rights and liberties. If the rulers fail in their trust, the people have the right to rebel and seek other rulers. Locke justifies his view of government in the second *Treatise* with the famous dictum: 'He who attempts to get another man into his absolute power does thereby put himself into a state of war with him.' This philosophy has ruled the political thought of Britain in the last two centuries, and profoundly influenced the formation of the AMERICAN CONSTITUTION (q.v. Vol. X). The same liberal, humane influences can be traced in his books on education and religion, particularly *Some Thoughts Concerning Education* (1693) and *The Reasonableness of Christianity* (1695).

In Locke's most famous work, *An Essay Concerning Human Understanding* (1690), he sets out to examine the character and limitations of human knowledge. In this profoundly original essay he first considers the materials out of which our knowledge is made. These, he holds, are ideas in the mind, which are all derived from the senses—of seeing, hearing, and so on—and from our awareness of our own mental experiences (introspection). This view that all knowledge is derived from sensation and experience of the mind is termed 'empiricism', and Locke, though not the first empiricist, laid down the basic doctrine upon which modern empiricism rests. Locke does not identify knowing with seeing or hearing; he thinks knowing is 'seeing' in another sense, as when one 'sees' that two and two are four. But in all such cases we are 'seeing' connexions and making comparisons between materials or ideas ultimately derived from sensation or introspection. Because of this, and because, too, we express these ideas in words which are frequently misleading, Locke concludes that our certain knowledge is very limited; the most we can hope for is probable knowledge.

See also HUME.
See also Vol. I: PHILOSOPHY.
See also Vol. X: GOVERNMENT; EDUCATION, HISTORY OF; JUSTICE AND LAW.

LONGFELLOW, Henry Wadsworth (1807–82).

This well-known American poet was born at Portland, Maine, of an old New England family. After completing his education he went to Europe to study languages in preparation for an academic career. He finally became professor of modern languages at Harvard University, where he remained for nearly 20 years. During this time Longfellow produced a great deal of poetry; *Evangeline*, a long novel in hexameter verses (*see* VERSIFICATION, Vol. XII), being his greatest success. In 1854 he resigned his professorship to devote his whole time to poetry, and next year published his most famous poem, *Hiawatha*, about the Red Indians. This poem was based on the rather sing-song metre of an old

Finnish saga, the *Kalevala*, and has lent itself to countless parodies.

Though he is not one of the greatest poets, Longfellow was an excellent and fluent story-teller, and even his little ballad *The Wreck of the Hesperus* has its own kind of immortality. He was widely acclaimed in his lifetime both in America and in Europe, and he was the first American poet to have a memorial in Westminster Abbey.

See also Vol. XII: AMERICAN LITERATURE.

LOUIS IX, (Saint) (1214–70).

The saintly Louis IX became King of France when he was only 12, and his beautiful and capable mother, Blanche of Castile, ruled for him during his minority. Apart from a revolt at the beginning of his reign, and at a later period a baronial rebellion aided by Henry III of England, Louis' reign was peaceful. Though peace-loving and generous, he was a strong king, and the moral force of his character exercised a remarkable influence on his times. Louis sought always to do justice to all men and was never willing to take advantage of the weakness of an adversary. He maintained neutrality in the age-old contest between the Emperor (*see* HOLY ROMAN EMPIRE, Vol. I) and the Pope, though when he feared that the Emperor intended to imprison the Pope he interfered strongly. In this way he won a great reputation in medieval Europe for his wisdom and saintliness.

Louis was in many ways a conservative king. For example, when Simon de MONTFORT (q.v.) asked him to arbitrate in the dispute between the English barons and Henry III, he strongly denied the barons' right to set limits on the King's power. He was not an aggressive nationalist ruler, set on increasing the wealth and power of his country, as was his grandfather Philip Augustus. For example, in 1259 he signed the Treaty of Paris, by which the territorial claims of Henry III of England were peacefully and generously settled. He was more concerned with France's place as part of Christendom than with her worldly power. He cared about the welfare and happiness of his people, but when it came to a question of choice, he put first his urgent desire to lead a CRUSADE (q.v. Vol. I) against the Moslems.

Louis embarked on two lavishly prepared crusades, the first in 1248 and the second in 1269. In both cases he acted in opposition to the advice of his wise mother and his councillors, who realized that these crusades were harmful

LOUIS IX HOLDING A MODEL OF THE SAINTE CHAPELLE

This church, which formed part of the palace of La Cité in Paris, was built by St. Louis in 1248. From a 14th-century manuscript. (Bédier et Hazard, *Littérature française* Larousse)

to France. Louis, though personally brave, was not a good general, and both crusades were lamentable failures. On the first occasion his army was destroyed, and he was taken prisoner. On the second he fell ill and died of plague in Tunisia before he could achieve much. He was canonized some 27 years after his death.

LOUIS XIV (1638–1715). Louis XIV of France is sometimes referred to as *le grand monarque*. Besides asserting French supremacy in Europe to a greater degree than any other French ruler before NAPOLEON (q.v.), he also raised the splendour of the French monarchy to its greatest height within the State. He gave expression to the idea of absolute MONARCHY (q.v. Vol. X), the monarch claiming to have absolute power over the lives and property of his subjects. When Louis came to the throne in 1643, the powers of government were largely in the capable hands of Cardinal Mazarin; but when Mazarin died in 1661, Louis suddenly took over complete control, announcing the change to his council on the following day in a speech supposed to have contained the famous phrase '*L'État, c'est moi*' (I am the State)—a concise statement of the theory of Absolute Monarchy.

Believing the State to be his personal property entrusted to him by God, Louis worked hard and regularly at the task of kingship. With an almanac and a watch, said a contemporary writer, 'one could always know what the King would be doing'. He supervised all State business personally, working through the machinery of government which Cardinal RICHELIEU (q.v.) had set up. He was fortunate in his Ministers, among whom was the great administrator Colbert; but he never allowed them to make important decisions. In spite of Louis' determination to serve the State—and thereby his own glory —and in spite of the magnificence of his reign, he conferred few lasting benefits on France.

Louis' quest for absolute control of his subjects had some directly bad effects. Richelieu had broken the political power of the Huguenots (the French Protestants); but Louis, unwilling to rule over heretics, tried by bullying and bribery to convert them to Catholicism, and finally in 1685 he revoked the Edict of Nantes which had assured the Huguenots of toleration. The effect was disastrous for France: thousands of the most able Protestants left the country, to the great benefit of Holland, Great Britain, and Prussia, where many of them settled. He exercised so rigorous a censorship of religious and political views that men such as DESCARTES (q.v.) could not publish their works in France. In spite of his Catholic zeal, however, Louis himself quarrelled with the Pope over his own control of the French clergy.

Although Louis' ambitions soon made him feared by his neighbours, they were also impressed by his success, or apparent success. His enormous prestige was built in part on his genius for showmanship. He acted ceaselessly the role of kingship on the European stage, no opportunity for adding ceremony and splendour to his surroundings being overlooked. His background, and his best monument, was the great palace built at enormous cost at VERSAILLES (q.v. Vol. XII), a few miles outside Paris. In the splendid decoration and furniture were repeated the monogram and the symbols of *le roi soleil* (the sun king), about whom the complicated ritual of the Court revolved. He called the nobility of France to Versailles to provide his retinue (incidentally, thereby, keeping a watch on them). The splendours of the Court enabled Louis to win a cheap reputation for patronizing the arts (*see* MOLIÈRE and RACINE). But the centre of the

Archives Photographiques

LOUIS XIV IN 1701
Portrait by Rigaud in the Louvre

the throne of Spain for his grandson, by 1713 he had thrown away France's dominant position in Europe by exhausting her.

When Louis died in 1715, extravagance, neglect of commerce, casualties in war, and the loss of many of the best brains of France by religious persecution had ruined France. The French peasant, on whom the burden of taxes ultimately rested, was worse off at the end of the reign than he had been at the beginning. After the longest reign in European history it was said that Louis had reduced France to a great hospital. By making the nobles courtiers at Versailles he cut them off from their tenants and their real responsibilities, and paved the way for the bitter class hatred which finally exploded in the French Revolution in 1789. His ambitions, in fact, broke the power of the monarchy which he had built up. His success lay in the hold which he had on the imagination of his age, and can be measured by the many princelings who paid him the tribute of imitation and the many small copies of Versailles which were built in the next century.

See also Vol. I: HUGUENOTS.

LOYOLA, Ignatius de (1491–1556). Inigo Lopez de Recalde, the founder of the Jesuits, was a Basque, the son of a nobleman of Spain. He became a soldier and enthusiastically pursued a military life until, in 1521, a serious wound rendered him unfit for further military service. During a long convalescence, shortage of other reading material led him to read the lives of Christ and of the saints. He was intensely moved, and as soon as he recovered, he went to the monastery of Monserrat to leave his armour on the Virgin's altar and to dedicate himself henceforth as a Christian knight. He began to plan his book of *Spiritual Exercises*, a manual of training involving the most rigorous self-discipline and hardship, which he practised himself, and afterwards used for all who joined his society.

After making a pilgrimage to Jerusalem he studied at a university, and then went to Paris to prepare for the priesthood, all the time keeping to the severe rule of life which he had himself drawn up. A company of enthusiastic young men gathered round him, many of whom afterwards became famous in the Church, in particular St. Francis Xavier, the great missionary to Japan and India. In 1537 Loyola was ordained priest.

spectacle was always Louis himself, of whose power Versailles was the setting and the symbol, a setting as much designed to impress observers as were Louis' magnificent wigs, or the diamond-studded heels of his shoes (*see* Colour Plate opposite p. 224).

Though Versailles as a piece of showmanship was completely successful, the real France suffered heavily from Louis' lavish expenditure, as she did also from his ambitious foreign policy, which in course of time overreached itself. The peak of his success abroad was reached with the Peace of Nijmegen (1678), by which time France had gained large territories in the Netherlands, Lorraine, and Savoy. Then the balance of European power began to turn against Louis. William III threw English sea-power into the struggle against France, and the other European powers, whether Catholic or Protestant, leagued together against her. At the Treaty of Ryswick (1697), which ended this war, Louis had for the first time to surrender territory. Although in the war of the Spanish Succession which followed (*see* MARLBOROUGH) Louis succeeded in winning

Loyola, now certain that he wanted to fight for the Church, went to Pope Paul III to secure his authority to form an order founded on the three chief monastic rules, poverty, chastity, and obedience, but which would work in the outer world rather than in monasteries. The order was called the Company, later the Society, of Jesus, and Loyola planned it on a military pattern. He thought of Jesus as a supreme Chief calling for volunteers to fight in a crusade against the devil to rescue the world. The head of the Society, which position Loyola held, was called the General, and was subject only to the Pope—but absolutely to him. Discipline was strict, and Loyola's men had to be ready to do any kind of work which promoted the greater glory of God.

At that time two dangers faced the Roman Catholic Church: the low standard of morals in the Church itself, and the growth of the Protestant REFORMATION (q.v. Vol. I), begun by LUTHER and CALVIN (qq.v.). The Society of Jesus played a vigorous part in bringing about the Counter-Reformation. Its members were often sent as teachers and confessors to the houses of the ruling classes, thus gaining considerable political power. The Jesuits were so anxious to keep people within the Catholic Church that they acquired the reputation of defining sin and granting absolution too leniently, of having, in fact, a political rather than a religious motive and of using their power somewhat unscrupulously. This led to bitter controversy.

The Society of Jesus increased rapidly, and by the end of the 17th century there were some 20,000 members of the Order, besides numerous pupils in their colleges training for membership. The Society has specialized in education, especially in the higher branches, and Jesuits have conducted many famous schools for boys, including English schools such as Stonyhurst. Its missionary work throughout the world, especially in South America, Canada, Japan, and Africa, has been a story of enterprise and courage.

But dislike and suspicion always followed the Jesuits, and in 1773 Pope Clement XIV suppressed the Society. It was, however, restored in 1814, and is still a notable monument to Loyola's inspiration and genius.

See also Vol. I: MONK; ROMAN CATHOLIC CHURCH.

LUCRETIUS (1st century B.C.), Roman poet, *see* EPICURUS.

LUKE, St., *see* Vol. I: BIBLE.

LUTHER, Martin (1483–1546). Luther, the leader of the Protestant Reformation in Germany, was the son of a Saxon peasant miner, who was ambitious for his son and educated him for the law. But a deep consciousness of sin, quickened by a friend's death at his side from lightning, turned Luther to the religious life. He was ordained priest in 1507, and proved so able a scholar that he became a lecturer on religious philosophy at the University of Wittenberg.

Luther soon found himself in opposition to some of the practices of the Church, particularly on the question of the forgiveness of sin. Pope Leo X, in order to get money to build the magnificent new church of St. Peter at Rome, offered 'indulgences', that is, promises of forgiveness of sin, to all who gave money; and he authorized a Dominican friar, Tetzel, to preach about the pains of hell which could be escaped by buying an indulgence. Luther, in 1517, protested by nailing to the door of Wittenberg church a list of ninety-five theses, denying the Pope's right to forgive sins in this way. He offered to support these in open argument.

A storm of controversy arose, and Luther was summoned to Rome. But the support of Frederick, the Elector (ruler) of Saxony, deterred the Pope from taking action against him. Luther followed up his attack at a conference at Leipzig, as well as in his famous address to the *Christian Nobles of Germany* and in other writings. In these he called for a thorough reformation of the Church, especially in its teaching and practice in regard to the sacraments. The Pope sent him a 'Bull', or order of excommunication, and Luther had this publicly burnt in Wittenberg. He continued his teaching and writing with his characteristic energetic fire and vivid perception of the truth as he saw it. In 1521 the Emperor Charles V summoned a 'diet' or council at Worms, and there he called upon Luther to recant. But Luther refused saying: 'Here I stand. I cannot do otherwise. God help me, Amen.' Charles was angry, and Luther was outlawed by the Edict of Worms. But German sympathies were mainly with Luther, and for a year he remained under the protection of Frederick of Saxony in his castle at Wartburg. During this time he translated the New Testament from Latin into German for the first time,

MARTIN LUTHER
Woodcut from Beza, *Icones*, 1580

a work which was important in determining the literary language of Germany.

In the meantime some of his more irresponsible followers carried the reform movement much further, denouncing the Mass, destroying church ornaments and altars, and encouraging monks and nuns to forsake their vows. Although Luther on returning to Wittenberg tried to check these excesses and divisions, he could not altogether do so. In 1524 many of the German peasants used his teaching as a reason for revolting against their serfdom. This revolt was put down mercilessly by the princes with Luther's approval.

In 1525 Luther married Katharina von Bora, a former nun, and lived happily with her for the rest of his life. In the meantime tension increased between those German states that accepted the reformed doctrines of Luther and those that remained Catholic. All efforts at bringing about union only widened the gulf, but after a conference in 1529, when he quarrelled with the Swiss reform leader ZWINGLI (q.v.), Luther took little further part. In 1546, the year of his death, civil war broke out between the German Protestant and Catholic princes, and peace and official acceptance of the Lutheran church were not reached until the Peace of Augsburg in 1555.

See also Vol. I: LUTHERAN; REFORMATION.

M

MACADAM, John (1756–1836), *see* Vol. IV: MACADAM ROADS.

MACAULAY, Thomas Babington (Baron) (1800–59). The historian, Macaulay, was the son of Zachary Macaulay, one of the leaders of the anti-slavery movement. A very precocious child, he could read when he was 3, at 7 began to write a *Universal History*, and at 8 wrote a treatise to convert the natives of Malabar to Christianity. At Cambridge he became an excellent classical scholar, and later studied law, which he never cared for.

In 1825 Macaulay wrote his famous article on Milton, the first of many essays contributed to the *Edinburgh Review*, and his obvious ability and distinctive style won him immediate recognition. At 30 he entered Parliament as a Whig (*see* POLITICAL PARTIES, Vol. X), where his oratory made a great impression. Throughout his parliamentary career, which lasted with various intervals till 1853, Macaulay sincerely interested himself in social welfare and progress and opposed abuses and injustice. He spent 3 years in India as legal adviser to the Supreme Council, and still found time to read voraciously and to write, despite the tremendous amount of official work, which included the composition of a criminal code for India and the foundation of the Indian educational system. On his return from India he visited Italy, and this led to the writing of his *Lays of Ancient Rome*. *Horatius* and his poem on the Armada are among the finest ballads in existence. In 1838 he began his *History of England from the Accession of James II*, a much more detailed account than any so far existing. He had intended to continue it to his own times, but he died before he had completed further than 1697. In 1853 he was made a baron, and when he died 6 years later, he was buried in Westminster Abbey. He never married, but remained strongly attached to his family. He was short and stout and never cared for exercise. Once when offered a horse at Windsor, ne replied that if he rode it must be on an elephant. He was frequently to be found among the distinguished political and literary guests at the great London houses.

Macaulay is one of the most readable of authors, his greatest quality lying in his power of arrangement. Whatever his subject—biography, literary criticism, or a complex historical narrative—there is throughout an intelligible and orderly sequence. In detail his style is clear and precise, but sometimes mechanical, and frequently too positive. (Lord Melbourne, the Prime Minister, wished he 'could be as cocksure of anything as Macaulay is of everything'.) To his great natural gifts, his ability to read very rapidly, and a memory so retentive that he knew *Paradise Lost* by heart, he added very hard work. His most serious limitation was a dislike of speculative thought. He sometimes made mistakes, and was sometimes unfair in the moral judgements which he passed on the people or events he described. His essays are rather uneven in quality, among the best being those on Chatham, Clive, and Sir William Temple.

Macaulay is the first historian to have combined social and economic with political and religious history—to have described, in fact, the whole life of the nation; and his method has affected the scope of all later historical study. While his researches for his *History* were extensive and thorough, his lack of professional training resulted sometimes in rather crude scholarship; he was, however, a master of the literature of public opinion (newspapers, ballads, and the like), and this, with his penetration and political experience, enabled him to reconstruct the whole movement of the time. The change of outlook which has now taken place, and the publication of documents unknown to Macaulay, have naturally affected its value as history, but as literature it is one of the greatest historical compositions of all time.

See also Vol. XII: HISTORIES.

MACHIAVELLI, Niccolo (1469–1527). The son of a well-known lawyer, Machiavelli was descended on both sides from aristocratic legal families in Florence. His portrait bust, in painted terracotta, shows a man with sharp features, a

MACHIAVELLI
15th-century terracotta bust

Alinari

Machiavelli, who seems to have been temperamentally insensitive to the good in other men's natures. He held that in politics 'the end justifies the means'. These are some of his typical precepts. 'Men ought to be well treated or utterly crushed, since they can avenge small injuries but not great ones.' 'A prince who wants to hold his own must know how to do wrong when necessary.' 'It is unnecessary for a prince to have all the virtues, but very necessary to appear to have them.'

It has naturally been the custom for politicians to hold up their hands in horror at the name of Machiavelli; even FREDERICK THE GREAT (q.v.) of Prussia, one of the most unscrupulous followers of Machiavellian policy, thought it politic to publish a tract, the *Anti-Machiavel*. Although we now use the term 'Machiavellian' to denote unscrupulous scheming, in fact, without some of Machiavelli's unpalatable honesty we cannot see man's life in society as it really is.

See also BORGIA FAMILY.

long, inquisitive nose, and keen eyes. He was employed as an envoy by the Florentine Republic for 14 years, during a time in many ways like our own, when the nations of Europe were combining, invading, and quarrelling, and when the old political order seemed to be collapsing (*see* CITY STATE, Vol. X). During these years Machiavelli, as he says, 'reaped experience at the expense of others', until his own party fell from power, and he found himself at the age of 43, restless and ambitious, forced into exile on a small farm in the country, where all day he had to work hard on the land. There in the evening he wrote his masterpiece *The Prince*, the book which is the result of his watchful years of political experience.

The Prince discusses in terse, vigorous Italian the methods by which a 'new prince'—we should now call him a dictator—can build up his power. For the first time in history, with the possible exception of Aristotle's *Politics*, it applied to politics the methods of experimental science. Machiavelli was original in forming his opinions of men in society solely from what he saw on his travels or from facts he read in history. He rejected altogether the medieval dream of an ideal unchangeable social order, and based his political theories on men's behaviour as he saw it to be. This method of cold, realistic observation yields startling results, especially in the hands of

MADISON, James (1751–1836), American statesman, *see* HAMILTON; *see also* Vol. X: AMERICAN CONSTITUTION.

MAGELLAN, Ferdinand (*c.* 1480–1521). This Portuguese explorer, in the service of Spain, found the long-sought westward route from Europe to the Spice Islands of Asia by sailing round the south of South America. A ship from this expedition circumnavigated the world for the first time. It was Magellan who named the Pacific Ocean.

Magellan was brought up as a page at the Portuguese royal court, and then fought for Portugal on land and sea until he was lamed for life in Morocco. In the year 1517, having quarrelled with the King of Portugal, he migrated to Spain. There he gained the support of the King for a scheme to discover the westward route to the Spice Islands, which would enable Spain to compete with the Portuguese who controlled the sea-route round South Africa. In 1519 he sailed in command of five ships and about 270 men.

It had been realized since the death of Columbus that the American continental coastline was broken by no gap, at least as far south as the river Plate. Therefore Magellan sailed south, looking for the southernmost tip of the American continent. Having sheltered for seven miserable winter months on the coast of Patagonia, during which time he lost a ship and had to suppress a dangerous mutiny, he set off again, and almost immediately entered the strait now named after him. It took 5 weeks to navigate the 300 miles of tortuous strait, where the prevailing wind is westerly. One of his ships gave up hope and turned back for Spain without his authority. By November 1520 the three remaining ships cleared the stormy strait and came out into a vast and comparatively calm ocean, which they named the Pacific.

Although Magellan knew the latitude of the

AN ALLEGORICAL REPRESENTATION OF MAGELLAN DISCOVERING THE MAGELLAN STRAITS
Engraving from De Bry, *Peregrationes in Americam*

Spice Islands, he had no idea of their longitude, which could not at that time be accurately measured (*see* NAVIGATION, HISTORY OF, Vol. IV). He calculated that he was close to them, but in fact he had to sail for 98 days before he reached any inhabited island, during which time he and his crews were reduced to eating rats when they could get them and leather and sawdust. At last he reached the Philippines, where he learned that he was at the longitude of the Spice Islands. Thus Magellan had achieved the unique feat of joining up the areas explored by the westward and eastward routes. It now became possible to check by actual experience the circumference of the earth, previously calculated by astronomical methods, and to prevent in the future such gigantic errors as misled Columbus and Magellan himself.

Magellan never reached home; he was killed taking part in a fight between the Philippine islanders. One ship, the *Victoria*, laden with spices, sailed home by the South African route, and nineteen survivors reached Spain 3 years after leaving there, the first men to circumnavigate the world.

See also COLUMBUS.
See also Vol. IV: EXPLORATION.

MALORY, Sir Thomas (died 1470), *see* Vol. XII: ARTHURIAN LITERATURE.

MANET, Édouard (1832–83). Manet, forerunner of French IMPRESSIONIST PAINTING (q.v. Vol. XII), was the son of a rich magistrate who at first opposed his son's ambition to be a painter. Manet travelled in Holland, Italy, and later in Spain, studying and copying the work of old masters. In this way he built up a remarkable technical skill: he has been called 'the greatest manipulator of oil paint who ever lived'. He was particularly interested in the work of the Dutch painter Frans Hals and the Spaniards VELAZQUEZ and GOYA (qq.v.), who were pioneers in realistic painting.

Manet, like COURBET (q.v.), preferred to paint those things which he could actually see before his eyes, and he was one of the first open-air painters. He delighted in painting the contemporary scene, race-courses, bars, and crowded public gardens. When he painted a picnic scene he painted it from life, though he based the composition on a picture by GIORGIONE (q.v.). No one objected to Giorgione's figure of a nude woman sitting with shepherds, but they were outraged when, in Manet's 'Déjeuner sur l'herbe', the same subject was given a contemporary setting. Manet's brilliant colours, which were then so unusual as to appear garish and crude, also aroused criticism. One of his nude portraits, 'Olympia', which was hung in the Salon in Paris, aroused such anger that the public had to be restrained from attacking it with umbrellas. But, in spite of public indignation, Manet's originality inspired an important group of younger painters.

See also Vol. XII: IMPRESSIONIST PAINTING; illustration, p. 163.

MANNING, Henry (1808–92), Cardinal, *see* NEWMAN.

Anderson

ST. GEORGE: PAINTING BY MANTEGNA
Accademia, Venice

MANTEGNA, Andrea (*c.* 1430–1506). This Renaissance painter came from Padua in northern Italy, and married the sister of Gentile and Giovanni BELLINI (q.v.). Many great Renaissance scholars taught at the University of Padua, which was famous for its study of the classics; and this probably inspired Mantegna's great eagerness to learn from the art of ancient Rome. He went to Rome to study classical sculpture and architecture only fairly late in life, but he would have been familiar with the work of the Renaissance sculptor DONATELLO (q.v.) in Padua. Even in his earlier works, which are mostly religious, the figures look like statues of Roman gods and goddesses; and he was most at home when painting a classical subject such as the 'Triumph of Caesar', which is now at Hampton Court. Whatever the subject, his pictures are always magnificent and often adorned with splendid architectural backgrounds or with garlands of flowers and fruit.

Mantegna spent the last 40 years of his life at Mantua as court painter to the Gonzaga family, famous patrons of the arts. In one room of the palace he painted frescoes which for the first time achieve an astonishing illusion of reality, as though the figures were real figures seen through a window, and the painted ceiling was really the open sky.

See also Vol. XII: ITALIAN ART.

MARCONI, Guglielmo (1874–1937). The inventor of the first practical method of WIRELESS TELEGRAPHY (q.v. Vol. IV) was an Italian with an Irish mother. As a young experimenter he developed the early work of Clerk MAXWELL (q.v.), Hertz, Sir Oliver Lodge, and others, and in 1895 succeeded in sending wireless signals to a distance of slightly over a mile. In 1896 he came to England, took out the first British wireless patents, conducted demonstrations for the Post Office, and increased his range to 10 miles; and the following year he formed a British company to develop his patents. In 1898 he succeeded in arranging wireless communication between ships and the shore, and the next year established the first wireless communication between Britain and the Continent, and increased the range for naval communication to 75 miles. Marconi's invention was put to practical use by the British Army in the South African War. In 1901 communication was established between Europe and America.

During the First World War Marconi concentrated on short-wave military transmission (*see* WAVE-LENGTHS, Vol. IV), which resulted in the first wireless communication between Britain and Australia. In 1929 the King of Italy made Marconi a marquis, and the next year he became President of the Italian Royal Academy.

See also Vol. IV: WIRELESS TELEGRAPHY.

MARCO POLO (1254–1324). The Venetian, Marco Polo, was one of the few Europeans in the Middle Ages to penetrate the fabled Empire of China. In his famous book are descriptions of the splendours of the Court of KUBLAI KHAN (q.v.) and of the countries he visited.

At that time Venice was the greatest trading centre in Europe, and specialized in the import of Oriental goods, such as silk and pearls. Marco Polo's father and uncle, Nicolo and Maffeo Polo, were leading Venetian merchants and often visited Constantinople. On one visit, when Marco was only 6, they learnt in Constantinople that better business could be done at Sarai, on the river Volga, north of the Caspian; so they decided to journey on to that city. Sarai was within the vast Empire of the MONGOLS (q.v. Vol. I), who during the previous 50 years had conquered China and a great part of Asia, as far west as Persia. Their Emperor, whose capital was Cambaluc (now Peking), was called the Kublai Khan. He was grandson to the great GENGHIS KHAN (q.v.). One business matter leading to another, the two Venetians continued eastwards and came to Bokhara. There they met envoys from Persia on their way to Peking. They made friends with the Polos and invited them to join the caravan to Peking, saying that very good business could be done in China, a land then quite unknown to white men. The Polos were enterprising enough to accept this invitation, and set out with the envoys on their tremendous journey. The caravan went by the northern branch of the famous Silk Road, through Samarkand and the oases of Turfan and Hami, which lie to the north of Tibet (*see* TRADE ROUTES, Vol. IV), and at last reached Peking. Here the Polos met the great Kublai Khan, who was kind to them and put business in their way. When they decided to return home, he gave them a letter to the Pope in which he asked for friars and men learned in the arts and sciences to teach the Mongols Christianity and culture. They promised to return with these teachers if

British Museum

NICOLO AND MAFFEO POLO SETTING OUT

They are seen before the Byzantine emperor, then before the Patriarch of Constantinople, and finally sailing for the Black Sea. 14th-century French manuscript (*Royal MS. 19 D. 1*)

they could. When they got back to Venice they had been away 9 years.

The Polos spent some 2 years at home, preparing for their journey, and buying goods for which the Khan had asked. Then they set out again for China, taking Marco, who was now 17 years old, with them. So began his travels, of which he gives so vivid a description in his famous book.

They had intended, this time, to do a large part of the journey by sea, so they went to Hormuz on the Persian Gulf, the nearest port reached by Chinese ships. But there, perhaps when they saw the ships in Hormuz harbour, they changed their minds and decided that it would be less dangerous to go by land. This time they took the southern branch of the Silk Road through the Pamir Mountains, Kashgar, and Khotan. The entire journey took $3\frac{1}{2}$ years; at an early stage the friars they were escorting lost their nerve and went back.

The Khan was delighted to welcome the Venetians again. He took special notice of Marco, now about 21, and offered him a post in his service. The young man accepted the post, and for 17 years he remained in China working industriously for the Khan and filling several important posts. He became Governor of the large city of Yangchow, Imperial Commissioner on a tour to Yunnan and Burma, and Envoy Extraordinary to Ceylon. In his book, most of which is not a story of his personal adventures but a careful description of the almost unknown Mongol Empire, he begins by describing the Kublai Khan, and the magnificent state in which he lived. He has chapters telling of the Summer Palace, the great dinners in the Winter Palace, and the hunting parties in the country south-east of Peking. There are fascinating chapters too about his travels inside China, particularly his visit to Hangchow, which was the native capital before the Great Khan conquered the country. He mentions, among other things, how he was sent to Ceylon to buy a tooth of the Buddha.

In course of time the Polos (who had become very rich) began to long for home. At first the Khan refused to let them go, but finally they obtained his permission in 1292 on condition that they took charge of a Mongol princess whom he wished to send as wife to his grand-nephew, the ruler of Persia. On this occasion they went by sea, by way of Singapore, Ceylon, and the Persian Gulf. When they had safely delivered the princess, the three Polos returned to Venice, having been away altogether 23 years. They brought back great wealth in precious stones.

A year after his return Marco Polo was captured in a sea fight between the Venetians and their trade rivals, the Genoese, and thrown into prison in Genoa. There he met a literary man called Rustichello, and to while away the hours he dictated to him the famous book relating his adventures. After his release he returned to Venice, and lived for another 25 years in the big family house, parts of which still exist.

See also Vol. I: CHINESE CIVILIZATION; MONGOLS.

MARCUS AURELIUS (A.D. 121–180).

This Roman Emperor, author of the *Meditations*, came from a distinguished Roman family of Spanish origin. He was carefully instructed in Greek and Latin literature by various tutors, the chief of whom was Fronto, and much of the delightful correspondence which he carried on with this tutor has survived. When Marcus was about 17, he was adopted by the Emperor Antoninus as his successor, according to the directions of the Emperor HADRIAN (q.v.); and so, much against his inclinations, he was drawn more and more into public life and the work of government. He married Antoninus' daughter, Faustina, with whom he seems to have lived happily.

As a young man, Marcus had adopted Stoicism (*see* ZENO), then a popular philosophy, and he pursued its rigorous ideal of elevated thought and simple living till his death. He was a lifelong student and a serious-minded thinker, as well as an enlightened and peace-loving emperor. His name is now best remembered for the small Greek volume of his *Meditations*, in which he reveals his own most intimate reflections in the form of a kind of spiritual diary. These *Meditations*, which express a view of life moulded largely by Stoicism, have been translated into many European languages.

Marcus Aurelius was of a peace-loving nature, but his reign, unlike that of Antoninus, was disturbed by frontier wars, which placed a severe strain on the national resources and on Marcus' own limited reserves of energy. The first war, against an eastern state called Parthia, embracing most of modern Persia and Iraq, though successful, ended in an outbreak of plague among the troops. They carried the infection home, and it spread widely through the Empire. The second war was conducted against the Germanic tribes which threatened the long northern frontier from modern Hungary to southern Ger-

MARCUS AURELIUS RECEIVING THE SUBMISSION OF TWO BARBARIAN CHIEFTAINS
Relief in the Capitoline Museum, Rome

Kunsthistoriches Museum, Vienna

THE SCHÖNBRUNN PALACE, OUTSIDE VIENNA, BUILT BY MARIA THERESA IN 1744
Painting by Bernardo Bellotto (called Canaletto)

many. Towards the end of one of these campaigns, when Marcus Aurelius seemed at last on the point of securely establishing Rome's northern frontier, death overtook him. Commodus, his son, broke off the campaign and returned to Rome, thus throwing away the great military advantage won by his father.

Apart from these frontier campaigns and a short-lived military insurrection, Marcus Aurelius' reign is regarded as one of the happiest periods that the Roman Empire enjoyed. In general there was peace over the Empire, under an administration that was on the whole wise and beneficent. Times were prosperous, and the people enjoyed a comparatively high standard of civilized living. During this period there was a remarkable spread of the CHRISTIAN CHURCH (q.v. Vol. I), though even in Marcus Aurelius' reign there was a certain amount of persecution. After Marcus Aurelius' death, however, Commodus proved ineffective and depraved, and before long the Empire was torn by civil strife. For this Marcus Aurelius must be held partly to blame, for he failed to continue the policy of his predecessors of adopting and training a successor who could be relied on to govern wisely.

See also Vol. I: ROMAN CIVILIZATION.

MARIA THERESA (1717–80). Charles VI of Austria-Hungary, having no son to succeed him, endeavoured to secure the throne for his daughter by the 'Pragmatic Sanction', an agreement accepted by all his territories, and guaranteed by the great powers of Europe. When Charles died in 1740, however, FREDERICK THE GREAT of Prussia (q.v.), one of the guarantors, immediately demanded Silesia from Austria and invaded the country. Most of the European powers supported Frederick; only Britain honoured her guarantee. The young Queen, to the surprise of Europe, gallantly and energetically rallied her peoples, especially the Hungarians, and though at the Peace of Aix-la-Chapelle, which ended the War of the Austrian Succession in 1748, Maria Theresa had to cede Silesia to Prussia and lost certain Italian dominions, her right to Austria was recognized, and her husband, Francis I of Tuscany, was elected Emperor. In the Seven Years War which followed in 1756, Maria Theresa's chief Minister, Prince Kaunitz, secured an alliance with France and Russia; but Frederick retained his gains.

Although Maria Theresa lost some territory, her reign was a happy one for Austria, and she was a well-loved ruler. She introduced many reforms, particularly to relieve the oppressed peasants. She so stimulated agriculture, industry, and commerce that she greatly increased the national revenue while decreasing taxation. She was personally very attractive, especially in her youth, with a vivacious and natural manner. Her many letters to her ten surviving children (one of whom was Marie Antoinette, the unfortunate Queen of France) reveal her charming personality and are full of love and wisdom.

MARIE ANTOINETTE, Queen of France (1755–93), *see* Vol. X: FRENCH REVOLUTION.

MARK, St., *see* Vol. I: BIBLE.

MARK ANTONY (*c.* 82–30 B.C.). Few men had better chances than Mark Antony of gaining supreme power in the Roman Empire, or lost them more disastrously. Mark Antony seemed the natural successor to JULIUS CAESAR (q.v.), but on Caesar's death he was ruined first by Octavian's opposition (*see* AUGUSTUS CAESAR) and later by his love for Cleopatra.

Antony had served Caesar with distinction as a soldier and administrator, and when Caesar was assassinated in 44 B.C. he was well placed to succeed him; but Octavian, Caesar's heir, forced him into a political alliance. Together they destroyed the party who had assassinated Caesar, and divided the Roman world between them, Antony taking the East. At first he co-operated with Octavian, and married Octavian's sister, Octavia. But in 41 B.C. he fell in love with Cleopatra, the Queen of Egypt, a brilliant and beautiful woman, who was also politically very ambitious. She succeeded in captivating Antony in order to further her policy for Egypt, and her influence over him grew until finally, deserting Octavia and breaking with Octavian, Antony decided to establish his power independently in the East.

Antony became a Greek king rather than a Roman general. He restored the old importance of Egypt, making Cleopatra 'Queen of Kings'. But he was severely defeated by the Parthians in Mesopotamia, and since he could no longer reinforce his legions with good soldiers from Italy, he was at a disadvantage in his struggle with Octavian. Octavian also built up opposition to Antony by pointing out the danger to Rome of a powerful Egypt, making the war seem not a civil war, with divided loyalties, but a united resistance against a foreign enemy. Even

Antony's troops were affected, and he lost the great naval battle of Actium (31 B.C.).

After his defeat Antony committed suicide, and when Cleopatra knew Egypt was doomed, she followed his example. A bold soldier and a brilliant woman had raised the Greek East against the Roman West, and Rome had won, a drama which Shakespeare describes in his *Antony and Cleopatra*.

See also JULIUS CAESAR; AUGUSTUS CAESAR.

MARLBOROUGH, Duke of (1650–1722). John Churchill, first Duke of Marlborough, was perhaps the greatest of all British soldiers. In the War of the Spanish Succession (1702–13) he led the British and Dutch armies against LOUIS XIV (q.v.) in ten victorious campaigns; 'he never fought a battle which he did not gain, nor besieged a place which he failed to take'.

Marlborough's family had suffered in the Civil War, and he was brought up in some poverty. But with the Restoration the family fortunes changed, and Marlborough rose in royal favour. As a young man he served under the great French general, Turenne, in Flanders, and distinguished himself by his courage and personal charm. Turenne is said to have won a bet that the 'handsome Englishman' would recapture an enemy post with only half the men who had lost it. At 28, Marlborough married the beautiful and talented Sarah Jennings, then a lady-in-waiting to Princess Anne (later Queen Anne).

James II, his friend and patron, raised Marlborough to the peerage and, at 32, he became a general. At the REVOLUTION OF 1688 (q.v. Vol. X) Marlborough, putting Church before King, attached himself to William III; but the new King suspected him of treasonable relations with the exiled Stuarts. For a short time he was imprisoned, and for 5 years stripped of his offices. But in 1698 he was restored to favour, and later chosen to take over the military and diplomatic leadership of the Grand Alliance (Britain, the Netherlands, and Austria) which Britain was building against France.

Marlborough and his wife had by now won the close confidence of Anne, and when she became Queen in 1702, 'the sunshine day' started for them both. Sarah's influence was paramount with the Queen, and Marlborough, as master-general of the ordnance, captain-general of the English forces, and deputy commander of the forces of Britain's chief ally, the

Dutch, had power at home and great influence abroad.

During the next 10 years Marlborough's diplomacy held together the Grand Alliance, while his superlative military talents won for them some of the greatest victories in the history of war. His task was difficult. The Allies were torn by political jealousies and intrigue. The Dutch, suspicious of Marlborough and more concerned with the security of their frontiers than with victories, clogged his strategy and on more than one occasion prevented battles that might have ended the war.

In 1704 the French, having advanced into Austria, had already reached the Danube. Marlborough marched the Anglo-Dutch army from the Low Countries to the Danube, and there joined hands with the Germans under Prince Eugene of Savoy. Now began one of the greatest military partnerships in the history of war. Marlborough and Eugene, each a great soldier, each a generous ally, won three great victories together. Of these, the first, the Battle of Blenheim, was the most resounding. It was the first major victory won by a British general in Europe since the days of Henry V. The French were beaten back to their own frontiers, and the war was saved. In recognition of this victory, Marlborough was granted the manor of Woodstock, and Blenheim Palace was built for him (*see* VANBRUGH).

Marlborough and Eugene were the victors at Oudenarde (1708) and at the 'very murderous' Battle of Malplaquet (1709). Marlborough, in sole command, had already won the great Battle of Ramillies in 1706. In this battle he was once ridden over when his horse fell, was attacked by French sabres, and again narrowly escaped death when a cannon-ball severed the head of an officer holding his stirrup. But as the fighting flared round him, he directed his troops with icy detachment, showing the highest tactical genius. In the middle of the battle he concentrated his cavalry, by brilliant use of cover, in overwhelming force on the French right flank, and then unleashed them in one of the greatest cavalry attacks in history. In all 25,000 horsemen were engaged, plunging and slashing in grim combat. A final charge, perfectly timed, turned battle into victory and victory into rout.

But in the Netherlands it was difficult for even the most aggressive commander to force a pitched battle upon a reluctant opponent, for the many

Duke of Marlborough

MARLBOROUGH WRITING THE DISPATCH WHICH ANNOUNCED THE VICTORY OF BLENHEIM

He is writing on a kettledrum which a soldier holds for him. Silver statuette in Blenheim Palace

fortified towns commanded the roads and waterways (*see* FORTIFICATIONS, Vol. X). Moreover, though Marlborough more than once wished to thrust forward into the heart of France, he could not carry his Allies with him, and these four great battles remained the only major engagements between the rival armies in 10 years of war. But Marlborough carried through his SIEGE operations (q.v. Vol. X), of which there were eighteen, with remarkable thoroughness, and as the campaigns dragged wearily on, town after town was captured from the French.

In the meantime England had become tired of the war. Political intrigue at Court and in Parliament undermined the great position which Marlborough had once held. Sarah quarrelled with the Queen, and accusations multiplied against Marlborough. The Tory party accused him of prolonging the war for his own advantage, and of embezzling public money; stories grew of his meanness and greed; it was even suggested that he was using his military position to threaten the throne. At the end of 1711 he was dismissed from his position, and a year later he left the country. In 1713 peace was at last declared by the Treaty of

Utrecht. In 1714, when the Queen died, Marlborough returned as commander-in-chief, but stricken with paralysis he survived only 6 painful years.

It is difficult to see Marlborough's character in perspective. The historian MACAULAY (q.v.) has painted a bitter portrait of him in the *History of England*; Thackeray blackened him in *Henry Esmond*, and others have accused him of treason and embezzlement. Certainly, he was not disinterested; but, on the other hand, he could place principle above personal advantage. He made a great fortune, and was careful how he spent it. His diplomatic and political skill were both marked by a cleverness which his opponents distrusted. Though his correspondence with James II and the exiled Stuarts, while he held office under William III and Anne, was unwise, the charge that he gave them valuable military information has now been discredited. But there is no dispute whatever about Marlborough's military genius. He was one of the greatest commanders in history—the peer of Hannibal, Caesar, and Napoleon.

See also Colour Plate opposite p. 256.

See also Vol. X: LAND WARFARE, HISTORY OF; TACTICS AND STRATEGY.

MARLOWE, Christopher (1564–93). Little is known of the life of this Elizabethan poet and dramatist save that he was the son of a Canterbury shoemaker, that after leaving Cambridge University his name was associated with that of Sir Walter RALEIGH (q.v.) and others as a dangerously free thinker and suspected atheist, and that he was stabbed to death in a tavern brawl at Deptford, possibly in Queen Elizabeth's employ as a secret agent. Marlowe's work, full of violence and rhetoric, has a superb lyrical quality which, at its best, only Shakespeare could equal. He created dramatic BLANK VERSE (q.v. Vol. XII) as we know it and his 'mighty line' (in Ben Jonson's phrase) bore little relation to the stilted verse of his predecessors. Marlowe, very much of the Renaissance and the world of MACHIAVELLI (q.v.), was obsessed with the problem of earthly power and its effect upon men. In *Tamburlaine the Great*, *The Jew of Malta*, and above all *Dr. Faustus*, his heroes are equally villains; yet they battle against fate with such magnificent defiance that they become tragic figures. *Edward II*, the first historical play of its kind, lacks the grandeur of the earlier plays.

As a poet, Marlowe is remembered for his lyric, *The Passionate Shepherd*, and for his unfinished *Hero and Leander*, one of the richest, most sensuous poems in the language, from which comes the famous line, 'Who ever loved that loved not at first sight'. But Marlowe is remembered not only for what he wrote, but as the man out of whose work SHAKESPEARIAN DRAMA sprang (q.v. Vol. XII).

MARSDEN, Samuel (1765–1838). This English missionary, chaplain to the convict settlement in Sydney, Australia, first brought Christianity to the MAORIS (q.v. Vol. I) in New Zealand. Marsden was persuaded to become a missionary by William WILBERFORCE (q.v.), and left for Sydney when he was 28. There, besides his work among the convicts, he founded an orphanage and a reformatory for women, and earned a reputation for severity both as preacher and magistrate. It was said that the petty criminals who were brought before him used to pray earnestly 'Lord, have mercy upon us for His Reverence will have none'.

Marsden soon grew to respect the Maori seamen who visited the colony from New Zealand; and when he met their ageing chief, Rautara, he was fired with the idea of evangelizing the natives. He believed that prayers and sermons could do little to transform Maori pagan culture, unless he could teach crafts and industry as well. So to his mission station in the North Island he sent tools, a horse, some cows, and helpers trained as carpenters, cobblers, and schoolmasters. Though Marsden went to New Zealand in 1814 to preach a Christmas sermon, he did not himself work in the New Zealand mission, but always took a personal interest in its progress. The mission did much for the development of New Zealand and the good relations between natives and Europeans.

See also Vol. I: NEW ZEALANDERS; MAORIS.

MARVELL, Andrew (1621–78), *see* Vol. XII: METAPHYSICAL POETRY.

MARX, Karl (1818–83). This political philosopher, economist, and international revolutionary, the author of the *Communist Manifesto* and *Das Kapital*, was the founder of Marxian SOCIALISM and the prophet of COMMUNISM (qq.v. Vol. X). Communist parties all over the world look to Marx's writings for the ultimate truth on matters of economics, politics, science, and philosophy, and all the details of his life and every scrap that he wrote have been treasured devotedly.

Marx was born at Trèves in the Rhineland, the son of a middle-class Jewish lawyer. The family had been converted to Christianity when Marx was a child; but Marx always had nothing but contempt for his own people and for their religion. He was sent to Bonn and Berlin Universities to study law, but turned to philosophy and came under the influence of the philosopher HEGEL (q.v.). At that time a rebellious political outlook made a university career impossible, so Marx turned to journalism, and in 1843 he went to Paris to study socialist economics. He also went to Brussels and met many socialists who had emigrated there, among them Friedrich Engels, who remained his devoted friend all his life. It was here that he wrote, together with Engels, the famous pamphlet, the *Communist Manifesto*, published early in 1848, in which they detailed a programme for socialist revolution to be led by the workers of the more industrially advanced States. This pamphlet appeared at a time when the industrial workers were suffering the worst results of the INDUSTRIAL REVOLUTION (q.v. Vol. VII), and it naturally made a strong appeal to them.

Marx based his theories on what he believed to be the scientific evidence of human history, which made a Socialist revolution inevitable. He denied the commonly held view that the course of events was dictated by ideas in men's minds as to what should be done. He held that men's ideas are the product, not the cause, of their material circumstances, and that the evidence of history shows that as these change society must change to suit them. He declared that since the idea of private property was unsuitable in the new world of great industries, it would have to give way to some sort of common ownership by the workers of all the sources of wealth. He did not believe this change could be effected without a violent revolution, in which the property-owning classes would be overthrown by the proletariat or workers. Marx at no time concerned himself very much with the practical problems of how such a society should be run; he was interested only in the first stage— the Revolution itself.

The Revolution of 1848 in Germany gave Marx a chance to show how he could put his

Meade Collection

KARL MARX
Engraving from *The Secular Chronicle*, 1878

theories into practice; but the Revolution failed, and Marx was expelled from Prussia. France also refused to accept him, and in 1849 he came to England, where Engels was already settled, meaning to stay only a few weeks but in fact staying for the remaining 34 years of his life.

The usual picture people have of Marx is of a learned German exile with a bearded face (familiar on Communist hoardings)—the Marx of this latter stage. He was extremely short of money, a fact which caused hardship to his beautiful and devoted wife and their children. He made some money by journalism and borrowed much from the faithful Engels, who continued to collaborate with him but who also made a reasonably good living as a manufacturer in Manchester. Engels bore patiently with his friend's vain, spiteful, and quarrelsome nature, and supplied the more practical mind in their joint work. Marx spent much of his time reading and writing in the British Museum, where he studied industrial and economic history, and where he enlarged the theory of the *Communist Manifesto* into a series of books, the most important being the three-volume *Das Kapital*.

Marx was largely responsible for founding in 1864 the International Working-man's Association, generally known as the International—a union of socialist or communist movements in all countries. The International very soon split, however, mainly because Marx could not bear any rival leaders and quarrelled fiercely and often unscrupulously with all prominent socialists except Engels. The influence both of his personality and his theories on the working-class movement of modern times has been greater than that of any other man.

See also Vol. X: Socialism; Communism; Revolution.

MARY, QUEEN OF SCOTS (1542–87). When the young James V died, broken-hearted at the defeat of his army by the English, the Crown went to his daughter Mary, then a week old. Henry VIII of England offered his young son Edward (later Edward VI) as husband to the child Queen. When, however, the Scots, fearing English domination of their country, finally refused this offer, Henry again attacked Scotland. Scotland's long-standing ally, France, came to her help, and the little Queen was betrothed to France's heir (later Francis II), and was sent to the French Court for safety. There she grew up a strict Roman Catholic and a Frenchwoman rather than a Scot. When she was 16, her husband became King of France. Mary, therefore, was Queen of Scots, Queen-consort of France, and in the eyes of Catholics, as Henry VIII's legitimate great-niece (see table), also lawful Queen of England, for Catholics considered Elizabeth I (q.v.) illegitimate and therefore not legally able to inherit.

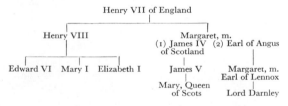

Meanwhile, Mary's mother, Marie de Guise, ruled Scotland as Regent, and finally the Scots forced the English to peace. But then the struggle of Protestants and Catholics that was shaking all Europe brought civil war to Scotland. When Marie de Guise died in 1560 the Protestant lords, backed by England, seized the government. In 1561, the young French king Francis II having died, his widow Mary, now 18 years old and very beautiful, came back to Scotland to face the task of ruling her shattered kingdom.

Though the Protestants had seized power, in fact most of Scotland was still Roman Catholic. Both the Catholic and the Protestant powers of Europe alike desired to have Scotland on their side; but Mary wanted peace in which Scotland could recover. She refused many offers of royal marriage that might have dragged Scotland into wars abroad, and tried to make Catholics and Protestants live freely in harmony together. She hoped, too, to end the long, bitter feud with England by using, not her claim to the English throne, which only Catholics admitted, but her position as Elizabeth's nearest kinswoman and heiress, about which both Catholics and Protestants were agreed.

Mary genuinely sought these good and wise aims, but she was inexperienced, and did not understand the people with whom she was dealing, many of whom were greedy and ambitious. Both Catholics and Protestants, in Scotland and elsewhere, were angry at her policy of toleration and justice. The English, who for generations had been trying to annex Scotland, resented the thought of a Scots Sovereign, while Elizabeth hated and feared Mary. Outwardly she returned Mary's friendship, but secretly she stirred the Scottish Protestants against her, promising them support if they overthrew her. For 5 years Mary succeeded in keeping Scotland at peace, and the young Queen was loved by her people of both religions. Mary's enemies knew, therefore, that to attack her openly would be dangerous, unless the nation could first be turned against her.

In 1565 Mary married her cousin Lord Darnley, whose father had Protestant leanings, and whose mother (see table) was a Catholic and a niece of Henry VIII; Mary, therefore, hoped that both Scots and English, Catholics and Protestants, would approve. But Darnley was stupid, vain, and selfish. Mary's enemies easily made him jealous of her secretary, David Rizzio, and induced him to share in the murder of Rizzio in Mary's presence. They hoped that even if the shock did not kill her, there would be a scandal and people would despise her. Mary succeeded, however, in inducing Darnley to return to her side, and they escaped to Dunbar. For a time the Protestant chiefs, who were her enemies, fled. In 1566 Prince James was born.

Then a house at Kirk o' Field near Edinburgh, to which Darnley (who was ill) had been conveyed by the Queen and her favourite, the Earl of Bothwell, was blown up, and Darnley was

THE TRIAL OF MARY, QUEEN OF SCOTS, IN FOTHERINGHAY CASTLE

The trial was held in the hall of the castle on 14 and 15 October 1586. Mary is standing on the platform. Drawing by an unknown Flemish artist

found murdered. Almost certainly Bothwell was among those responsible; but it is quite possible that Mary knew nothing about it, and that Bothwell, a Protestant, was suborned by Mary's Protestant enemies so that they could throw the blame of the murder on the Queen. Bothwell then carried Mary off, and within 3 months of Darnley's murder Mary married Bothwell and made him a duke. It is probable that Mary was for a time infatuated by Bothwell, although recognizing his worthlessness.

At this, many of the chief Scottish nobles rose against Mary. Horrible stories were put about, and Mary was imprisoned at Lochleven Castle and made to abdicate in favour of her baby son James VI. A year later she escaped, but the army that rallied to her was defeated and, trusting Elizabeth, she sought safety in England. Elizabeth inquired into Darnley's murder, but Mary was not allowed to appear to answer her accusers. The case against her largely depended on the famous 'Casket Letters', several of which are now known to be forgeries. The court, suspecting this, refused to convict Mary, but Elizabeth, fearing that Mary would become the centre of plots against herself, kept her a prisoner for 19 years. At length Mary was tricked by Elizabeth's Secretary, Walsingham, into becoming involved in Catholic plots to overthrow Elizabeth with Spanish help. When he had his evidence, Walsingham arrested the leaders, and Mary was tried again, condemned, and beheaded at Fotheringhay, Northants, in 1587. She died bravely, as became a Queen of Scots.

See also ELIZABETH I; KNOX.

MARY TUDOR, Queen (1516–58), *see* ELIZABETH I; CRANMER.

MASACCIO (*c.* 1401–28). The name of this Italian painter means 'clumsy Thomas', and he was said to have been untidy and unworldly. Most of his very short life was spent in Florence, and he died when visiting Rome.

Masaccio was the first who completely solved the painter's basic problem of how to represent solid objects in a lifelike way on the flat surface of a wall or of a canvas, and to relate them in space to their background. Before his time neither perspective nor anatomy was properly understood by painters, and their ideas of representing light and shade were entirely unscientific. Masaccio made great advances in all these subjects. He received help in perspective from his friend BRUNELLESCHI (q.v.), and probably learnt from him the details of classical

ST. PETER ENTHRONED
Mansell

Detail of a fresco by Masaccio in the Brancacci Chapel of the Carmine Church, Florence

architecture which he sometimes introduced into his paintings. He used his technical knowledge to give dramatic force to his subjects. For example, in his wall-paintings (frescoes) in the Brancacci Chapel of the Carmine Church at Florence, all the light in each scene appears to come from the direction of a real window in the Chapel. This gives the greatest dramatic emphasis to the lifelike and majestic figures. That so much which was entirely new could have been discovered and perfected by a youth in his 20's, even the greatest genius, is hardly short of a miracle.

Apart from these frescoes, a Trinity in another Florentine church, and a number of altar-pieces, there are hardly any paintings by Masaccio still in existence.

See also Vol. XII: FLORENTINE PAINTING.

MASARYK, Thomas Garrigue (1850–1937). The nationalist leader of the Czechoslovak people under Austrian domination became their first president when, after the First World War, they won their freedom. Masaryk's son, Jan Masaryk (1886–1948), was also a leader of his people until the Communist domination.

The Czechs and Slovaks are a Slav people whose country, the old kingdom of Bohemia, was part of the Austro-Hungarian Empire from the 17th to the 20th century (*see* CZECHOSLOVAKS, Vol. I). During this time the speech and culture of the upper classes were mainly German; only among servants and peasants was the native language spoken, and the native culture was almost lost.

Masaryk's father was a Slovak and his mother a Czech. His father was a coachman on one of the estates of the royal Hapsburg family. The boy was apprenticed to a locksmith in Vienna, and then worked as assistant to his home village blacksmith, before he was able to go to college at Brno. He proved a brilliant scholar, helping to pay his way by giving lessons in his private time. He gained a degree at Vienna University and did post-graduate work at Leipzig University. There he met an American girl studying music, whom he followed to the U.S.A. and married.

The young couple settled in Vienna, where Masaryk became a lecturer in philosophy. Soon afterwards the University of Prague was divided into German and Czech parts as a concession to the Slav people, and Masaryk was made a

Czech professor. His pupils found him an inspiring teacher who taught them to be proud of their Slav origins and of their Czech nationality. He wrote fourteen books which won for him a wider audience. He sat for 2 years in the Imperial Parliament, but resigned because he believed that he could help his fellow Slavs better outside Parliament, and he did not become a member again for some years. He formed a progressive political party, and was active as a courageous and fair-minded critic of the 'ramshackle Empire' which held unwieldy and uncertain sway over Czechs, Magyars, and other subject peoples.

Masaryk was already 64 when the First World War broke out, yet he flung himself with the energy of a young man into the task of arousing international sympathy for the cause of the Czechoslovaks, who, being Austrian subjects, had to serve in the Austro-Hungarian imperial army. Masaryk, pleading for his people, travelled in Holland, Italy, France, England, Russia, and America. As a lecturer at King's College in London, he made British public opinion aware of his national aspirations. His claims for Czechoslovakia were recognized by Britain and others when a Council he had formed in Paris with his friend and fellow patriot Dr. Edward Beneš was officially accepted, towards the end of the war, as a Provisional Government for his country.

Many Czechs, as Austrian soldiers, had been captured by Russia or had fled there. Masaryk was largely responsible for organizing these into an army, to help Russia against Germany. When the Russian resistance to Germany collapsed, Masaryk and his followers managed to make their way, in spite of considerable opposition, to America via Vladivostok and Japan. In this way they were able to continue their support of the Allied cause. The Czechoslovak people still within the Austro-Hungarian Empire, heartened by this news and by Masaryk's great work in establishing their claims, rose against the tottering Austrian Government during the last days of the war.

When peace came, the free Republic of Czechoslovakia was established, with Professor Masaryk as its President, and he entered Prague in triumph. For the next 16 years he sought to build up his own and the neighbouring little countries without ill will to his former enemies, and on the basis of alliance with France and close friendships with Britain and America. In this he had the help of Dr. Beneš, who later succeeded him as President.

The Liberator-President, as his people called Masaryk, never lost, in days of power, the principles of reasoned liberalism that had sustained him through all his struggles and setbacks. Vast learning—he could hold his own in half-a-dozen languages—combined in him with complete simplicity. He lived an abstemious life, neither drinking nor smoking. On his old horse, Hector, he was a familiar sight to the citizens of Prague. Happily for this most civilized of scholar-statesmen, he died before the Second World War began.

His son, Jan Masaryk, was less fortunate. From 1925 to 1938 he was Czech Minister in Great Britain, where his gay, fiery spirit, lack of convention, and sense of humour won him many friends. During the Second World War, while his people were under the oppression of Germany, he worked for them abroad and made inspired broadcasts to them. He was Foreign Minister in the free Czechoslovak Government which Dr. Beneš established in London. After the war, he helped to reconstruct his country. 'We must either make our children secure', he said, 'or become the remnant of a once great race, undignified troglodytes living under the ground.' But soon after the free government in Czechoslovakia was overthrown by Communism, Jan Masaryk was found dead beneath a high window in Prague. It seems probable that he killed himself in despair.

See also Vol. I: CZECHOSLOVAKS.
See also Vol. III: CZECHOSLOVAKIA.

MASSÉNA, André (1756–1817). Napoleon's most brilliant marshal, the son of a poor wine merchant, was born in Nice (then part of Italy). After being a ship's cabin-boy, he enlisted in an Italian regiment attached to the French army, and served 14 years in the ranks. When the FRENCH REVOLUTION (q.v. Vol. X) began, Masséna rejoined the French army, where there was now no bar to the promotion of men of humble birth. He became an officer at once, and within 3 years was commanding a division.

When NAPOLEON (q.v.) was in Egypt, Masséna commanded the French army in Switzerland, and there won his greatest victory. The Russian general SUVAROV (q.v.), having defeated the main French armies in Italy, was racing northwards to the Alps. Another Russian and an Austrian army were converging from the east. Only Masséna stood between France and invasion. When the second Russian army pressed too far ahead of its allies, Masséna, who was watching for such a chance, struck and scattered them, drove a wedge between the converging armies, and ended at a blow the threat of invasion (*see* NAPOLEONIC WARS, Vol. X).

In 1809, in a battle against the Austrians, Masséna, with an army corps, was directed to cover the Grand Army's crossing of the Danube. Driving about in a wagon, for he was too ill to ride his horse that day, he courageously and skilfully drew the full weight of the Austrian attack upon his corps, thus enabling Napoleon to cross the river in safety.

In 1810, Masséna, who was already ageing, was sent to oppose WELLINGTON (q.v.) in the Peninsular War, with orders to 'drive the English into the sea'. He advanced into Portugal, but found Lisbon strongly guarded, and the land swept bare of supplies. A less resolute commander might have retired, but Masséna hung

Radio Times Hulton Lib.

MARSHAL MASSÉNA

on for nearly 4 months before retreating. After further defeats by Wellington he was recalled, and never held active command again.

Masséna, though a brilliant general, with a commanding eye which made men tremble, often squandered his great talents by fits of indolence and licentiousness; his relations with both officers and men were sometimes awkward: the men, for example, often accused him with some justification of appropriating their pay.

See also NAPOLEON.
See also Vol. X: NAPOLEONIC WARS.

MATTHEW, St., *see* Vol. I: BIBLE.

MAUPASSANT, Guy de (1850–93), French writer, *see* Vol. XII: SHORT STORIES.

MAXWELL, James Clerk (1831–79). This great Scotsman was one of the outstanding physicists of the 19th century. His book, *Electricity and Magnetism* (1873), which embodied in mathematical form his original ideas on light, electricity, magnetism, and the supposed 'ether' of space, is one of the most splendid books ever written by a man of science.

Maxwell, like NEWTON in the past and EINSTEIN in our day (qq.v.), was a man both with original ideas and the ability to express them in their fullest and most accurate form by mathematical equations. His greatest achievement was the proof that LIGHT is not some kind of special radiation 'on its own', but a form of a general RADIATION (qq.v. Vol. III) that arises in space owing to the rapid motion of electric and magnetic units. All radiation is waves, he said. All waves are in essence the same. They all obey the laws that waves of light obey. The difference between one kind of radiation and another lies only in the length of the wave. In consequence of this, Maxwell predicted that there must be waves longer than the longest light-waves and shorter than the shortest light-waves. These ideas of Maxwell's gave Hertz the knowledge from which he was able in 1888 to produce wireless waves (*see* WAVE MOTION, Vol. III).

Maxwell went to Edinburgh University before he went to Cambridge. In both universities he carried all before him in mathematics and science. With his brilliance and originality went a great modesty about his achievements, perpetual high spirits, and an entire lack of envy and jealousy. He was made professor in Aberdeen and later in London, and in 1871 became the first professor of experimental physics at Cambridge and director of the Cavendish Laboratory there. That laboratory has since become the most celebrated centre of experimental physics in the world, its policy having been created by Maxwell.

Besides his work on electro-magnetism Maxwell did important work on the theory of probability, on the statistical motion of particles moving irregularly, on colour, and on thermodynamics. FARADAY (q.v.) was his master. Like KELVIN (q.v.), Maxwell believed that without the higher mathematics, physics could never progress properly. Even the theory of RELATIVITY (q.v. Vol. III) has not rendered unsound 'Maxwell's equations' in electro-magnetism.

See also Vol. III: LIGHT; RADIATION.

MAZZINI, Giuseppe (1805–72).

This Italian patriot was the leader of the Italian movement for national independence which ended in a united Italy. He prepared the way for the soldier GARIBALDI and the statesman CAVOUR (qq.v.). Mazzini was also the first man who consistently preached the doctrines of nationalism in general.

Mazzini, born in Genoa, grew up in an Italy divided into many small States under foreign influence or control. The old Genoese Republic had been absorbed into the Kingdom of Sardinia, a change resented bitterly by many, among them the young Mazzini. Fired by the patriotism of his student friends, and by the example of the death of BYRON (q.v.) in the cause of Greek independence, Mazzini joined the *Carbonari*, a revolutionary secret society (*see* SECRET SOCIETIES, Section 5, Vol. X). He was arrested, and while in prison awaiting trial his ideas took permanent shape. He inherited from his mother an unflinching sense of duty which dominated his view of life. 'Life is a mission', he wrote: his mission being to further the cause of those nations, or groups of people, marked off from others by history, geography, and language to be the agents of God in the world; among these was the divided and oppressed Italy. Such a doctrine was a revolutionary one for the Europe of his day.

Mazzini was acquitted and released from prison. He then abandoned the *Carbonari* as useless, and founded instead his own secret

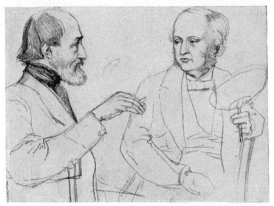
Balliol College, Oxford
MAZZINI AND BENJAMIN JOWETT, MASTER OF BALLIOL
Drawing by George, Earl of Carlisle

revolutionary society, 'Young Italy' (*Giovane Italia*), with the aim of a national united Italian republic to be achieved by popular revolution; its motto was 'God and the People'. 'Young Italy' tried to stir Italy by attempting insurrections on its own, but these attempts all failed, and the movement lost much of its early prestige. Mazzini was exiled in London from 1836 to 1848, and communicated with his agents by courier and post. He made his living by journalism, and also found time to run a school for the Italian organ-grinder boys of the London slums. His friendships among the English, and the respect which his character inspired, won support in Britain for his cause. But his long exile put Mazzini out of touch with the situation in Italy, and the revolutions which broke out in 1848 took him completely by surprise.

He hurried to Italy, and went to Rome where, in March 1849, the Pope having fled, the citizens set up a Republic. Mazzini with two others formed a triumvirate to rule the Republic, and they held the city for 9 months against a French army sent to restore the Pope. During this time Mazzini's qualities of integrity, leadership, and devotion to duty were seen at their best; but Rome was the only place apart from Venice where the people rallied to the revolutionary cause, and when Rome at last fell Mazzini went once more into exile.

The failure of the 1848 revolutionary movement embittered his remaining years. He hated Cavour, who considered popular revolution to be useless, and used instead diplomatic methods which Mazzini considered dishonest. He regarded as a national disgrace the achievement of 1860, when Italy was united under a king, and even more the diplomatic bargain with the French which gave Venetia back to Italy in 1866. When at last he returned to Italy to die, he disguised himself as an Englishman, and would have no dealings with the new kingdom.

But although his practical attempts failed, Mazzini by his inspiration is as much the founder of Italian nationalism as Cavour is the founder of the Italian State.

See also CAVOUR; GARIBALDI.
See also Vol. I: ITALIANS.

MEDICI FAMILY. This illustrious Florentine family was probably the most brilliant and powerful of the many families, such as the Sforzas and Viscontis in Milan, the Estes of Ferrara, and the BORGIA FAMILY (q.v.) in Rome, that contributed to the cultural splendour and political history of the RENAISSANCE (q.v. Vol. I) in Italy.

The Medicis were originally middle-class merchants in Florence; but in the 15th century they became prominent in the public affairs of the CITY-STATE (q.v. Vol. X). Giovanni, born in 1360, amassed their immense fortune and made them the leading bankers in Italy, and distinguished patrons of the arts (*see* FLORENTINE PAINTING, Vol. XII). From his sons, Cosimo and Lorenzo, descended the two main branches of the family. Cosimo, during a war between Florence and the neighbouring city of Lucca, became involved in political quarrels in Florence, and was exiled in 1433 as an enemy of the State. The next year, however, Cosimo's rivals were in turn exiled, and he himself returned to become, in fact though not in name, ruler of Florence. Under him Florence prospered and became a considerable force in Italian politics. He supported the arts, founded libraries, and erected many splendid buildings. When he died in 1464 the words *Pater Patriae* (Father of his Country) were engraved on his tomb.

A few years after his death the rulership of Florence fell to his grandson, Lorenzo, an extremely talented young man of 20, who, as a boy, had already shown promise of the greatness that was later to earn him the title 'Magnificent'. He was widely educated and fond of the company of scholars. He was the patron of the young MICHELANGELO, BOTTICELLI (qq.v.), and other great painters, and was himself a talented poet. He gathered round him distinguished men of all sorts, painters, poets, and philosophers, and Florence was the scene of both gay carnival and grave philosophic discussion. He strove to maintain peace among the Italian States, and in the process came into conflict with the Pope and the King of Naples. Eventually those jealous of his power conspired to kill him, and although he escaped, his brother was murdered. The Pope then excommunicated Lorenzo, and war broke out between Florence on the one hand, supported by France, Milan, and Venice, and the Pope on the other, supported by the King of Naples. When the war went against Florence, Lorenzo gained a great personal triumph by himself travelling to Naples to negotiate for peace.

His position in Florence was now more powerful than ever. Though officially a private citizen, all government decisions were his, and the city's treasury was, in fact, the bank run by the Medici family. For the rest of his life he struggled to maintain peace in Italy, and for this, as much as for his government and the cultural splendour of Florence, he deserves the title 'Magnificent'. He used his great power wisely, but its concentration in the hands of one man weakened rather than strengthened the government for his successor. (*See* Colour Plate, opp. p. 336.)

Lorenzo's son Pietro was unequal to following his great father, and could not deal with the situation when the French invaded Italy in 1494. He was expelled by the Florentines who returned for a time to a republican government. In 1512, however, Giuliano, another of Lorenzo's sons, was restored to Florence, and a third son about this time became Pope as Leo X. In 1530, after a period of political upheavals, a great-grandson of Lorenzo was made hereditary ruler by the Emperor Charles V, but he was assassinated by a cousin who took his place. In 1560 the two branches of the family were united under Cosimo, who took the title Grand Duke of Tuscany.

In the next 200 years the Medicis became linked by marriage with various royal houses of Europe, including the imperial Hapsburgs of Austria and Spain and the kings of France. Catherine de Medici (1519–89), Lorenzo's unscrupulous and ambitious great-granddaughter, for example, married Henry II of France and was responsible for the Massacre of Protestants on St. Bartholomew's Eve. Marie de Medici

ADORATION OF THE MAGI: PAINTING BY BOTTICELLI
The kneeling Magi are portraits of Cosimo de Medici and his sons Pietro and Giovanni. Standing behind Giovanni is Pietro's son, Giuliano, and on the extreme left his other son, Lorenzo the Magnificent

Alinari

(1573–1642) married HENRY OF NAVARRE (q.v.) and supported RICHELIEU (q.v.) in the early days of his rise to power, while she was regent for her young son. She was a worthless regent, and when her son took over the government she left France and died in obscurity.

The main branch of the Medici family died out in the 18th century, but descendants of other branches still live in Italy today.

See also Vol. I: RENAISSANCE.
See also Vol. XII: ITALIAN ART.

MELBA, Dame Nellie (1861–1931). This Australian soprano singer's real name was Helen Mitchell; she adopted a stage-name derived from Melbourne, near which she was born. She studied first as a pianist, and did not make her operatic début until she was 28, when she had been studying singing for only a year with the great teacher Mathilde Marchesi in Paris. Her exceptional voice and singing were immediately recognized. She sang mostly the great Italian florid soprano roles, such as Gilda in VERDI's *Rigoletto* (q.v.) or Lucia di Lammermoor in Donizetti's opera; but in her later years she was considered without an equal in the lyric soprano roles, such as Mimi in *La Bohème*. It was in this part that she appeared on the stage for the last time at Covent Garden in 1926. In 1918 she was made a Dame of the British Empire.

Melba sang in concerts as well as in opera, and from the gramophone records she made we can still admire the purity of her voice, and the neatness with which she executed shakes and runs.

MENDEL, Gregor Johann (1822–84). This Bohemian monk, who discovered the laws of biological inheritance known as the Mendelian laws or Mendelism, is now recognized as the founder of the science of genetics.

The son of a poor peasant, Mendel was educated in an Augustinian monastery at Brno, Moravia, and at 25 was ordained a priest. He then went to Vienna University and took a degree in the physical sciences. In 1853 he returned to the monastery at Brno and taught science in the High School until he became Abbot in 1868. He spent his spare time in carrying out a long series of plant-breeding experiments in the monastery garden. Using the common garden pea as his experimental plant, he worked out the simple laws of HEREDITY (q.v. Vol. II) based on the existence of the determining factors later known as 'genes'. His work, although published in 1866, remained little known until the beginning of this century.

The Russian geneticist Lysenko has recently cast doubt on the scientific validity of Mendelism, but it is still accepted by scientists outside the Soviet Union.

See also Vol. II: HEREDITY.
See also Vol. VI: PLANT BREEDING; STOCK BREEDING.

MENDELSSOHN, Jakob Ludwig Felix (1809–47). This German composer was born into a well-to-do and highly cultured Jewish family who had become Protestant Christians. Felix began to learn the piano from his mother when he was 4 and, with his brother and two sisters, had a thorough musical and general education. He first played the piano in public when he was 9; a year later he became a member of the Song-Academy at Berlin and at that time began to compose seriously. He was able to hear and conduct his own pieces in the Mendelssohn family's Sunday morning concerts. At 16 he composed a lovely octet for strings, and at 17 the Overture to Shakespeare's *A Midsummer-Night's Dream*: works which some musicians think more inspired than any of his later compositions.

One of his first professional acts was to conduct the *St. Matthew Passion* of BACH (q.v.), its first performance since the composer's death 75 years before; Mendelssohn did much to show the world what a great composer Bach had been. He then toured Europe for 3 years, making friends everywhere. He travelled several times to England, making happy visits to Scotland, which inspired the overture *Fingal's Cave* (The Hebrides) and the 'Scottish' Symphony, just as his journey through Italy produced the 'Italian' Symphony. In London he published the first book of his famous *Songs Without Words* for piano.

He returned to Germany and eventually became conductor of the Leipzig orchestra. During these years he wrote what are probably his two most popular works: the Violin Concerto in E minor, and the oratorio *Elijah*, first performed in 1846 at the Birmingham Festival with Mendelssohn conducting. In the following year the shock of the death of his beloved sister Fanny (almost as gifted a musician as he) caused him to burst a blood-vessel, and a few months later he died.

Mendelssohn's charm enabled him to make friends quickly, and his wealth gave him an easy life—an ease which some people hold prevented his touching deep feelings in his music. But music can be good without being deep, and Mendelssohn is most himself when he is being charming and lovably human. He could be dramatic too, as in *Elijah*, an oratorio which choirs always enjoy singing. His music is always perfectly suited to its medium, for he was an expert practical musician, whose strict musical training gave him a sure hand at the shaping and ordering of his musical ideas. Every climax, every point of repose, every newly appearing tune is perfectly judged. This 'tidiness' was part of his mind, one of the four or five most musical minds that ever lived. He composed a huge quantity of music in his 37 years of life, some of which is dull and some rather pompous, but much of which is too lovely ever to be forgotten.

See also Vol. XII: OVERTURE.

MERCATOR (1512–94), Flemish geographer, *see* Vol. IV: MAPS, HISTORY OF; MAP PROJECTIONS; CHARTS.

METTERNICH, Clement (Prince) (1773–1859). This Austrian statesman is significant for two reasons to later generations: as the statesman who drew together the countries of Europe into a coalition to check the headlong career of NAPOLEON (q.v.), and who strove to restore a peaceful balance in Europe after the upheavals caused by the FRENCH REVOLUTION (q.v. Vol. X); and as the statesman who, in Austria and wherever Austrian influence could reach, held up the general movement towards DEMOCRACY (q.v. Vol. X) and the claim of national groups to govern themselves. So successful was he that his name came to signify the very essence of conservatism. His final overthrow in the revolutions of 1848 seemed to be a portent of a new age.

Metternich, as a diplomat, stands for the methods of an aristocratic age, by which negotiations are carried on and bargains struck in the intimacy of a narrow social group, without the necessity of explaining their subtleties to masses of uneducated voters. His success was largely based on personal acquaintance with eminent people in his own aristocratic world and upon his handsome presence, his personal charm, and his great social gifts. Contemporaries speak of him as being both indolent and conceited. The stabilizing of Europe, however, after the Congress of Vienna of 1814–15 (see NAPOLEONIC WARS, Vol. X), the greatest achievement of his career, is a tribute to the virtues of his system of diplomacy, and to his belief that the European States had a common interest in peace. His life spans the whole era between the old days before the French Revolution and the modern world of conflicting nations.

Metternich was born and brought up in the Rhineland, but he followed his father into the Austrian diplomatic service. In his youth he visited England, where he met such men as PITT, FOX, and BURKE (qq.v.). After serving as Austrian Minister at the courts of Dresden, Berlin, and Paris, Metternich became Minister for Foreign Affairs in 1809, when he was 36, and held the post for nearly 40 years.

Under his guidance Austria, which had suffered crushing defeats at Napoleon's hands, adopted a policy of armed neutrality. Metternich even arranged for the Emperor's daughter, Marie-Louise, to marry Napoleon. He waited for Napoleon's ambitions to drive him to destruction, and then he played a leading part in organizing the countries of Europe to attack Napoleon before he could recover from his defeat in Russia. At the Congress of Vienna Metternich took good care that the Russian Emperor should have no opportunity of dominating Europe in Napoleon's stead.

In later years the ageing Metternich succeeded, but only for a time, in suppressing Italian nationalism and liberalism (see CAVOUR), in strengthening Austrian influence in Spain and Portugal, and in discouraging any radical or progressive spirit in the various German States. Austria itself stood in much need of reform, but Metternich was handicapped by the Emperor's obstinate hatred of progress. When the Emperor Francis I died, Metternich was too old to do anything but wait for the storm to break. His attempt to continue shaping the affairs of Europe by a series of international congresses failed, partly because of the increasing reluctance of Britain to be involved in suppressing liberalism. Yet he managed to hold together the three most reactionary powers—Russia, Prussia, and Austria—until 1848, when revolutions broke out all over Europe.

The revolution in Austria immediately brought about Metternich's fall, and he sought refuge in England. He and his young wife (his third) were much sought after by English society, including such men as the Duke of Wellington and even Lord Palmerston, a former antagonist. Disraeli wrote glowingly of the wit and wisdom of Metternich's conversation. He finally

Archives Photographiques

METTERNICH AT THE CONGRESS OF VIENNA
Metternich stands on the left, addressing the Congress. Drawing by Isabey. Louvre

returned to Vienna, where he died soon after the beginning of the Franco-Austrian War of 1859, which marked the real end of his political system.

MICHELANGELO (1475–1564). A member of the Buonarroti, an old Florentine family who had lost their wealth, this sculptor, painter, architect, and poet is always known by his Christian name. He never married and devoted his whole life to his art, caring less and less for worldly comforts. Being so much on his own, Michelangelo is said to have grown suspicious and irritable. He was apprenticed to Ghirlandaio when he was 13, and trained both as a sculptor and painter. His master recommended him to the patronage of Lorenzo the Magnificent (*see* MEDICI), for whom he worked till Lorenzo's death in 1492.

Michelangelo was only 29 when he carved his gigantic statue of David from a great block of marble which had lain about in Florence for years because no other sculptor had had the courage to touch it. The success of this work made him famous through Italy, and for the rest of his life each Pope in succession claimed his services and tried to prevent his working for anyone else. Pope Julius II diverted him from finishing (in rivalry with LEONARDO (q.v.)) a great battle-picture in the council-chamber of the Republic of Florence, and ordered him to prepare a magnificent tomb for the Pope, to be ready before he died. The tomb, adorned with statues and reliefs, was to stand in the new church of St. Peter's at Rome, then being rebuilt.

Michelangelo executed the marble Moses, now as famous as the David, and several figures of slaves for this tomb. But to his bitter disappointment he was never allowed to finish it, for the Pope switched him on to making a huge bronze statue of himself for Bologna (which was destroyed a few years later). When this was finished, he ordered him to paint the ceiling of the Sistine chapel in the VATICAN (q.v. Vol. XII). Michelangelo spent over 4 years painting the Sistine ceiling (*see* Vol. I, p. 221). He undertook it very much against his will, because he said he was a sculptor and not a painter and he wanted to finish the Pope's tomb. These frescoes, which contain some of the most beautiful nude figures ever painted, are now considered among the greatest of his achievements. They reflect the young Michelangelo's faith in the

Mansell

STATUE OF A SLAVE BY MICHELANGELO
This statue, now in the Louvre, was intended for the tomb of Pope Julius II

greatness and nobility of man. The figures are truly human and yet they have something of the power of godlike heroes.

After Julius's death the new Pope, Leo X, engaged Michelangelo on work in the church of S. Lorenzo at Florence, so that he still had no chance of continuing with the tomb. This, however, gave him his first opportunity as an architect, and in the last of his works at S. Lorenzo— the chapel built to contain the tombs of the Medici family—Michelangelo not only carved the statues on the tombs but also designed the architecture of the chapel. Of all his many masterpieces this is perhaps the greatest. The details of the architecture are extremely original and blend perfectly with the statues; but, like the rest of the chapel, they were never entirely finished.

In 1527 the city of Rome was sacked by the army of the Emperor CHARLES V (q.v.), a calamity which made a terrible impression on Michelangelo and other artists who had lived and worked there. The first major work which

Michelangelo undertook after the outrage on the Holy City was the painting of a vast fresco of the Last Judgement on the end wall of the Sistine chapel. This picture shows clearly the change which had come over him since he painted the ceiling of the same chapel more than 20 years earlier. The figures are no longer shown in easy and graceful attitudes; they appear angry and their bodies are contorted, because the painter, no longer interested in beauty for its own sake, is expressing very violent religious emotions.

As he grew older Michelangelo's religious feelings grew more and more intense until, in a sonnet which he wrote in his old age, he declared that he no longer had any use for the beautiful works of art which he had spent his whole life creating; they seemed to him to hinder rather than help a human being in his efforts to draw closer to God. Before this he had painted one more set of frescoes—in the Pauline chapel of the Vatican—and designed a number of buildings in Rome, of which the most important was the dome, choir, and transepts of the new ST. PETER'S (q.v. Vol. XII).

People who lived at the same time as Michelangelo realized that his genius was so immense as to seem superhuman, and even in his lifetime he was referred to as 'the Divine'. He died in Rome, but his native city of Florence insisted on claiming the honour of burying him. The journey from Rome was in every way like the funeral procession of a king. At all times since then it has been recognized that Michelangelo Buonarroti was one of the greatest men who have ever lived.

See also Vol. XII: ITALIAN ART.

MILL, John Stuart (1806–73). Mill, writer on politics, economics, and philosophy, was the last great leader of the Utilitarian school of philosophy, and one of the principal intellectual thinkers behind modern Liberalism. The earlier Utilitarian philosophers, such as BENTHAM (q.v.) and also Mill's father James, declared that the guiding principle of political conduct should be to promote the greatest happiness of the greatest number. By 'happiness' they generally meant 'pleasure', or material well-being, but they made no distinction between one pleasure and another, and tended to disregard spiritual values. Mill edited many of Bentham's unpublished papers; his own contribution to Utilitarianism was his insistence that some pleasures rank higher than others; that the pleasure of serving society was of more social value, or utility, than the pleasure of caring for oneself.

Mill was educated entirely by his father, who tried to bring him up as a cold and unemotional reasoning machine, which would carry on and develop his own rather rigid ideas. By the time Mill was 20 his reading was deep, though on rather narrow lines. But he then went through (as he tells us in his *Autobiography*) a spiritual crisis, from which he emerged with a broader and less mechanical view of human happiness, a delight in poetry (especially Wordsworth's) and the arts, a greater toleration of the opinions of others, and a hatred of narrow and intolerant religious views. This more humanitarian outlook was deepened and widened by his friendship with Harriet Taylor, whom he married in 1851 after the death of her husband. It was she who inspired and helped him to write his famous essay *On Liberty*, which was published in 1859, a year after her death. The rest of his life was devoted partly to politics—he was elected M.P. for Westminster in 1865—and partly to writing on the social, economic, and political problems of the day.

National Portrait Gallery

JOHN STUART MILL
Painting by G. F. Watts

Many of Mill's ideas are nowadays held almost as a matter of course by democratically minded people; for example, the arguments in favour of freedom of thought, speech, and discussion, and the recognition of the dangerous tendency of democratic majorities to tyrannize over MINORITIES (q.v. Vol. X). 'We can never be sure', he wrote in the essay *On Liberty*, 'that the opinion we are endeavouring to stifle is a false opinion; and if we were sure, stifling it would be an evil still.' In matters of practical politics, nearly all Mill's suggestions—such as votes for women, proportional representation, and the recruitment of a civil service by open competitive examination—are now accepted ideas. He has profoundly influenced his own and later generations, and his advice to the young men and women of his circle might be adopted today without any sense of its being out of date: 'Keep yourself in the free air of the world; do your best in the world's affairs; study the active rather than the passive.'

See also BENTHAM.
See also Vol. I: PHILOSOPHY.

MILTON, John (1608–74). This great English poet, patriot, and pamphleteer of the English Protestant Revolution was born in London. The family came from Oxfordshire, but Milton's father, disinherited of his Oxfordshire estate for his Protestantism, had moved to London, where he prospered, and was able to give his son the best possible education. Milton himself writes, 'My father destined me from a child to the pursuits of literature; and my appetite for knowledge was so voracious that, from twelve years of age, I hardly ever left my studies or went to bed before midnight.'

At 11, Milton went to St. Paul's school, and at 16, to Christ's College, Cambridge. He had already a wide knowledge of Greek, Latin, and English literature; he had a great taste for music, was well versed in the scriptures, and soon knew Italian well enough to compose Italian poems. The Latin poems which he wrote between the ages of 16 and 20 are far more than mere brilliant imitations of the classics, and contain much valuable autobiographical material. His first really great poem in English, *On the Morning of Christ's Nativity*, was finished in 1629.

There is no doubt that Milton kept constantly before him the aim of becoming a great poet. He retired for 5 years to his father's estate near Windsor to study, and during this period, between the age of 23 and 28, he wrote some of his best-known poems, including *L'Allegro*, *Il Penseroso*, *Lycidas* (written in memory of his friend, Edward King, who was drowned), and *Comus*, a MASQUE (q.v. Vol. IX). These poems are among the greatest in our language; but still Milton was not satisfied. Towards the end of this period he wrote to a friend: 'Do you ask what I am meditating? By the help of heaven an immortality of fame. But what am I doing? . . . I am letting my wings grow and preparing to fly . . .' To describe these splendid achievements as 'preparing to fly' is a measure both of Milton's self-confidence and of his modesty.

After this long period of study Milton, still feeling his education was incomplete, travelled abroad, mostly in Italy, until news from England that civil war was about to break out decided him to return home. Up to this point in his life everything seems to have gone according to plan, but the outbreak of the CIVIL WAR (q.v. Vol. X) disrupted his plans. A Latin poem written at this period makes it clear that he intended to write a great national epic on the subject of King Arthur and his Knights. But for the next 20 years he was actively engaged in politics—on the side of the Protestant revolution against the bishops and the King—and most of his literary output was in prose. His first political pamphlet, *Of Reformation in England*, appeared in 1641. This and the political works which followed it show what high hopes Milton built on the ideas of freedom of conscience, freedom of inquiry, and freedom of choice in politics. He thought that the Reformation in England would spread to Europe and lead to a new Golden Age of free God-fearing men.

In 1642 he married Mary Powell, a girl of 17 belonging to a Royalist family. But his young wife, after a very short trial of a life utterly different from that she was used to, left her husband and returned to her father's house. Two years later, when Cromwell's armies were victorious and the Royalist Powells were facing ruin, Milton took both his wife and her family into his house. Immediately after the shock of the separation Milton wrote *The Doctrine and Discipline of Divorce*, a pamphlet which argues his belief in personal freedom and his high ideals for married life. He also wrote at this time two important essays, *Of Education* and *Areopagitica*. *Areopagitica* is the most eloquent appeal for free-

National Portrait Gallery

JOHN MILTON
Engraving by William Faithorne

dom of publication and of thought ever written in English. In 1649, when CHARLES I (q.v.) was executed, Milton, addressing a European audience, defended the action of the revolutionaries in two Latin pamphlets. At the same time he was appointed Latin Secretary to the Council of State, where he undertook work of propaganda and diplomacy which brought him into contact with Cromwell and the leading statesmen of the Commonwealth.

For some time Milton's eyesight had been failing, and in 1651 he became totally blind. But for 9 more years, until the Restoration in 1660, he continued vigorously to defend the Revolution and to press forward his own ideals for an expanding liberty. Just before the Restoration, when indeed the cause was lost, he published his last political pamphlet *The Ready and Easy Way to Establish a Free Commonwealth*. Shortly afterwards he went into hiding, fearing for his life. Though *Paradise Lost* was already begun, it was still 7 years short of completion, and it is likely that at this time Milton felt that all his hopes, both in poetry and politics, had failed.

Both this despair and the calm resignation with which he faced his position left their mark on his later work. Though the new government banned him from political life, he was otherwise left untouched and able at last to devote himself to the literary tasks which he had begun to plan in early youth.

His first wife had died in 1652, leaving him with three daughters. In 1656 he married again, but his wife with her infant daughter died a year and a half later. For several years he lived unhappily with his daughters who resented bitterly his demands on them, until in 1663 he married for the third time. His wife, Elizabeth, brought comfort again to his house. In 1665 he finished PARADISE LOST (q.v. Vol. XII), the greatest English epic poem and one of the greatest in any language.

This poem, the long-matured fruit of learning, passion, and experience, is described by Milton as an

> adventrous Song,
> That with no middle flight intends to soar.

His theme is the loss of the happy innocence of the Garden of Eden. Adam and Eve, the central figures, are surrounded by the stupendous forces of good and evil and the whole landscape of Heaven and Hell. Both in structure and style Milton borrowed something from VIRGIL (q.v.), but the result is a unique work, great in itself and as much a monument to the age of Milton as the *Aeneid* is to the age of Virgil. The first two books describing the fallen angels and Book IX describing the fatal disobedience of Adam and Eve are perhaps the most moving, but the grand, individual, and impassioned style is sustained throughout.

Paradise Regained (1671) is a shorter and a quieter epic on the theme of Christ's temptations in the wilderness. Its beauty lies in its slow movement, its deliberation, and its dignity. But *Samson Agonistes* (published in the same year) shows the same fire and vigour as *Paradise Lost*. Milton tells the story of the blinded Samson finally triumphant over the Philistines, in the form of a Greek tragic drama, but the result is unique and something peculiarly characteristic of Milton's own age and experience. The poem ends with the words 'And calm of mind all passion spent'—a calmness reached only after enormous mental disturbance and many scenes and words of passion. So it was in Milton's own life, in his continual following of the ideas of individual freedom and in his belief in the possibility of real happiness for men and women.

Milton wrote many magnificent sonnets, very different from the conventional Elizabethan love sonnets, for Milton used them, as Wordsworth did later, to express personal, political, and general ideas with the greatest force and economy (*see* Sonnet, Vol. XII).

Three years after the publication of *Samson Agonistes* Milton died. He had qualities of greatness and sublimity. His industry and his learning were immense; yet it would be wrong to see in him the type of a severe unbending Puritan. He wrote not only some of the grandest but some of the most sensuous poetry in English. This is the impression he made on a contemporary: 'His deportment was sweet and affable; and his gait erect and manly, bespeaking courage and undauntedness.'

See also Vol. XII: Paradise Lost; Epic.

MIRANDA, Francisco de (1750–1816). Towards the end of the 18th century and beginning of the 19th, the impetus given by the French Revolution (q.v. Vol. X) to new forms of government everywhere, and the decline of Spanish imperial power, led to powerful revolutionary movements in the Spanish colonies of southern and central America. Leaders of these movements, such as Bolívar (q.v.) and San Martin (q.v.), are justly famous, but the forerunner of them all, and as such recognized in Latin America by the title 'Precursor', was Francisco de Miranda.

Miranda was born in Venezuela of Spanish ancestors, and when he was 21 he went to Spain to become a soldier. In Spain he felt that his American birth was against him, a belief which influenced him strongly all his life.

When he was 30 he returned to Cuba, but growing differences with the Spanish authorities soon decided him to flee to the United States. After 2 years there, he went to Europe, where he made many friends who later supported his ventures in Venezuela. He became a well-known figure in revolutionary circles in France, though he made a personal enemy of Robespierre (q.v.). In consequence he had later to flee again, this time to England, where his home became a meeting-place for all South Americans.

Miranda saw that, though freedom from Spanish rule must be won by the Latin-Americans themselves, they should have at least the tacit support of the great European powers. By writing and speaking he worked enthusiastically to rouse this support. In 1805 he returned to the U.S.A., thinking that he would find more backing there than in Europe. The first liberating expedition sailed for Venezuela in 1806; but when this failed Miranda returned to England, to try to win support there. The government promised him military help, but a rising of the Spanish people against Napoleon's rule in Spain resulted in the British force being sent to Spain to help the Spaniards against the French, instead of to South America to fight the Spaniards.

Miranda stayed in London where he had many friends, never losing hope. At last in 1810 news came that, encouraged by Napoleon's domination of Spain, Venezuela had declared a revolt against the Spaniards and had appointed an independent government. Miranda returned to Venezuela, and in 1811 the independence of that country was proclaimed. The liberators, however, were still not strong enough, and Miranda's forces were defeated and had to sue for an armistice. The terms of this armistice were soon broken, and Miranda himself was captured as he was trying to leave the country. He was finally transported to Spain and imprisoned at Cadiz. Though plans for his release were made by his English friends, they were unsuccessful, and Miranda died in prison.

He was a man of charming personality and of great powers of speech, to which his many friends of all nationalities testified. Though a patriotic Venezuelan, he was one of the first to feel himself a citizen of South America.

See also Bolívar; San Martin.

MOHAMMED (*c.* A.D. 570–632). The founder of the religion called Islam (q.v. Vol. I) was born in Mecca, an important city of Central Arabia. The people of Arabia for the most part believed in many nature deities. One of their great sanctuaries was at Mecca, where a famous black stone was regarded as extremely holy. The care of this sanctuary belonged to the Quraish tribe, of which Mohammed's family were members. To this day the Quraish wear green robes, green being the Arabian colour of royalty, as red or purple is in England.

Both Mohammed's parents died when he was

THE DOME OF THE ROCK, JERUSALEM
This mosque, built in 691, replaced one founded soon after the death of the Prophet

young, and he seems to have had a fairly hard youth, working with the caravans along the desert routes. When he was grown-up he entered the service of Khadija, the rich widow of a Meccan merchant, and when he was 25 he married her. He was devoted to his wife and managed her business affairs with considerable success and great integrity. He probably made several long journeys on her behalf, thus coming into contact with various peoples and religions, and was able to compare the religions of the Jews and Christians with the more primitive beliefs of the Arabs. He was a Semite, and of a race which had produced spiritual leaders such as the Hebrew prophets. It is not surprising that Mohammed, a thoughtful man, should gradually conceive the idea of being a sort of Moses or Christ to his own people.

When he was about 40 he went into complete retirement for a time. His message was growing within him, and was becoming a burden to him, and he seems to have suffered from nervous seizures. He ceased to eat regularly, and grew unkempt and feverish. His favourite spot for solitary meditation was a cave at the foot of a mountain near Mecca. One day in a moment of revelation a Presence seemed to approach him and speak. At first he doubted the reality of the vision, and returned home in great anxiety to tell Khadija what had happened to him. After some time he had another similar experience, accompanied by a physical convulsion, in which he cried to his wife: 'Cover me, Cover me.' She spread a mantle over him, and then there came to him, so he declared, the words:

> O Thou that art covered with a mantle,
> Arise and preach!
> Magnify thy Lord!
> Purify thy garments!
> Depart from all uncleanness!

Mohammed was then sure that he was intended to be the prophet, apostle, and preacher to teach men about the Living God. His early revelations were certainly influenced by his contacts with Jews and Christians, but Mohammed had little first-hand knowledge of these religions and their sacred literatures, and his early utterances dealing with God, the Resurrection, Judgement, Heaven, and Hell bear the stamp of his own vital and original personality. His intimate friends profoundly believed in his divine mission, fully accepting his commands to put away all idols and to surrender entirely to the supreme will of God, whom he called *Il Allah*, 'He who is greater than all else.'

At first Mohammed had a hard struggle, made all the harder by the death of his wife—a great loss to him. He had only a small following, and his wish to destroy the idols of Mecca and change the national religion of his people brought him many enemies. Indeed, at one point Mohammed agreed to accept a few of the ancient deities; but his new followers, indignantly insisting that 'there is no God but Allah', persuaded him to retract. Then, in 621, Mohammed preached to some pilgrims from the neighbouring town, Yathrib, and converted several, who invited him to visit their town. His new disciples prepared his way by preaching his message in advance so successfully that the leaders of Yathrib promised to support him. With a band of his Meccan disciples, he escaped thither, after some exciting adventures, and henceforth Yathrib became known as *Medinatan-nabi* (Prophet's town) or more shortly Medina ('the town'); and Moslems date their calendar from this flight to Yathrib (the *Hijra*).

During the next 18 years there began one of the most remarkable expansions of a religious movement ever known in history, which during the next 8 centuries carried the new faith as far west as Spain and as far east as China.

As a member of the Quraish, Mohammed was bound to become not merely a religious but a national leader; and so he did. At first, there was some idea of making Jerusalem the centre of the movement, and of including the Jews in it. But, when the Jews at Medina plotted with the Meccans against the Prophet, calling him an impostor, Mohammed and his followers overthrew the conspiracy with relentless severity and defeated the Meccans—a victory which Mohammed regarded as a sign of Divine favour. After that, in spite of setbacks, the Arabian tribes flocked to his standard. He entered Mecca as a conqueror, destroying all the idols there except the Black Stone, the shrine of which he made the central sanctuary of his new religion.

It seems that at first Mohammed's intention was to convert only the citizens of Mecca, as he thought that it was to them alone that he had been sent as a prophet; within 10 years, however, Mohammed had become the master of the whole Arabian peninsula. He was completely confident about his New Order for the world. In 628 he actually sent letters to the neighbouring States of Byzantium, Egypt, Persia, and Syria, urging their rulers to embrace Islam, and sometimes threatening war if they refused. Indeed, a year after his death, an Arab army won a crushing victory over the Byzantines, and the expansion of Islam outside Arabia began in earnest (*see* ARABS, Vol. I).

Mohammed spent his later years putting his message into writing, and the Koran (*Qur'an*) has become the sacred book of Islam (*see* SACRED BOOKS, Section 8, Vol. I).

In the large Islamic world of today the Koran is still looked upon to guide Moslems in their way of life, although a great many of them also accept Hadith, or tradition, as amplifying it. It is important to remember that Mohammed never claimed to be divine, and even his most ardent followers neither worshipped him nor treated him as any other than human and possessed of certain human frailties, especially in later years. Apart from his theological revelations Mohammed believed in the great importance of consolidating his empire and of reforming the pagan customs of the Arabs. For example, he attacked the practice of blood feud by urging offended people to take money instead of a life, if they could not forgive the crime entirely. This led to a far more orderly form of government.

Mohammed lived very simply. Tradition paints him as a man of striking appearance, with a large head, an intelligent face, large black piercing eyes, a flowing beard, and broad shoulders. Taciturn in ordinary speech, but with unusual insight, he could be stirred at times to a kind of rugged eloquence. His personality was so overwhelming that he could win even his strongest enemies to his side. At his best he was kindly and loved children, even teaching kindness to animals at a time when such an idea was very strange.

See also Vol. III: ARABIA.

MOLIÈRE (1622–73). Jean Baptiste Poquelin (Molière was his stage name) was a playwright, theatrical manager, and actor, and the greatest writer of French comedy. He was born in Paris, 6 years after the death of Shakespeare. His father, an upholsterer by appointment to the king, had his shop in the very heart of Paris, close to the Market Place and the Pont Neuf—favourite haunts of all street-singers, quacks, and mountebanks—so that Molière was well acquainted with many of the types whom he later used in his plays. His father was quite well off, and at 15 Molière was sent to a fashionable Jesuit college, where he met quite a different type—the sons of nobles and courtiers.

A feature of the Jesuit educational system was the study and acting of Latin plays, more especially of comedies, and it was probably here that Molière himself had his first experience of acting—later he took lessons from the famous comic actor, Scaramouche. As a child, too, his grandfather had often taken him to the Hôtel de

Bourgogne, a theatre where every kind of play was produced. On leaving college, Molière studied law and philosophy, because his father hoped to get him a Court appointment. But when he was 21, he inherited his mother's money, and on the strength of this announced that he and his friends were going to form a theatrical company, which they proceeded to do. They called themselves *L'Illustre Théâtre*, and began to produce tragedies in Paris. Forced to compete, however, with the old-established companies who had the monopoly of the best plays, their own third-rate tragedies attracted no audiences, and after 3 years Molière found himself in prison for debt. On his release, the company set out to try their luck in the provinces. For 12 years, from 1646 to 1658, they toured France as strolling players, with a wide repertoire of plays, most of which were probably farces. During these years, Molière gained valuable experience in theatrical management and acting, as well as in writing plays; this experience was all the more valuable because he had to conform to the limitations of his little company. At Pézénas, in the south of France, where they often played, there is a statue to the memory of Molière, and at the barber's an armchair is preserved in which he is said to have spent much time listening to the conversation of the customers—getting to know provincial types as well as he already knew Parisian ones.

The first of Molière's own plays which he produced was a farce, *L'Etourdi*, which had such a success that the now well-trained and prosperous company ventured back to Paris, where they found favour with LOUIS XIV (q.v.). The remaining 15 years of Molière's life were spent in writing, producing, and acting in his own plays in Paris. In 1673 his last play, *Le Malade Imaginaire*, was produced. Molière himself acted the title-role, but was taken ill on the stage and although he managed to finish the performance, he died that night.

Molière created French comedy, raising it from farce to the level of serious art. Like Shakespeare, he was a poetic dramatist, but where Shakespeare used blank verse, Molière used rhymed couplets. The comedy of his plays lies not only in the absurdity of the plot and the wit and gaiety of the words but in the characters themselves—for like all great comic writers he found his subjects in the everyday life around him, and his concern was not only to make

'LE MALADE IMAGINAIRE'
Engraving from Molière, *Œuvres*, 1682

people laugh but to make them think. In each play he ridicules some fashionable absurdity and makes laughable some human weakness or passion. In *Les Précieuses Ridicules* he mocks the prevalent fashion of affected speech and manners —for example, calling teeth 'the furnishings of the mouth'; in *Les Femmes Savantes*, the exaggerated passion for learning which makes Bélise say she would embrace anyone 'for love of Greek'; in *Le Misanthrope*, the absurdity of a society which demands that everyone should slavishly follow whatever is fashionable. And he creates a vast range of characters—the miser in *L'Avare*, the weak fool and the hypocrite in *Tartuffe*, the bore, the snob, the knave, the ignorant doctor, the stupid little country shopkeeper aspiring to be a fine gentleman—all of whom are slaves to a ruling passion. Yet because they are so real, they are pathetic as well as ridiculous. For Molière the first essential in writing a comedy was to entertain, and through entertainment to hold up to scorn the affectations, follies, and vices he hated. 'No truth without comedy and no comedy without truth.'

See also Vol. XII: Comedy; French Literature.

MONET, Claude (1840–1926), French painter, *see* Vol. XII: Impressionist Painting.

MONTAIGNE, Michel de (1533–92). Montaigne, the first writer to use the Essay form (q.v. Vol. XII), wrote detailed descriptions of almost every aspect of his daily life and private thoughts —an original theme for a 16th-century writer. He was a wealthy man, and a magistrate in Bordeaux, but when he was 37 he retired to his country house, built a tower in a corner of his courtyard so that he could work undisturbed, and devoted himself to study. On the ground floor of his tower was a chapel, from which he could conveniently hear mass as he lay in bed on the second floor; and in between was his library of a thousand books in Greek, Latin, Italian, and French. Here, as he read his favourite authors, he jotted down ideas which were later elaborated in his essays, the first two volumes of which were published in 1580.

Montaigne set out to discover himself; and, through himself, mankind in general. '*Tout le monde me reconnait en mon livre et mon livre en moi*' ('All the world may recognize me in my book and my book in me'). Reading his essays is like listening to the conversation of a cultivated, humorous, and very likeable man. He wrote to no plan, and whatever the subject he set out to consider, he usually came back to himself. He tells us, for instance, that he liked to scratch his ears, that he gobbled down his food so quickly he sometimes bit his tongue, that he preferred a hard bed and never used a warming-pan, and that his memory was so bad that he could not remember his servants' names. But besides such trivial personal details, he tells us what he thought—and Montaigne was interested in the deepest questions on which men have speculated. He lived through the cruel wars between French Catholics and Protestants which culminated in the terrible massacre on St. Bartholomew's Eve. He was not convinced by the arguments on either side, and hated any form of persecution or constraint; he was a doubter and a sceptic. This tolerance and lack of dogmatism was rare in his day, and his essays had a civilizing effect on his contemporaries. An English translation was published in 1603, and may have influenced Shakespeare.

Montaigne had a great influence on the development of French prose. Writers before him, imitating the long, complicated pattern of the Latin sentence, wrote in an artificial and cumbersome style. Montaigne, who wrote for his own pleasure and for everyone to read, used the words of everyday speech. He gave French prose a new simplicity and the tones of ordinary conversation.

MONTESSORI, Maria (1870–1952). Modern methods of educating small children have largely grown out of the teachings of this great Italian educationalist, whose experimental work in trying to fit educational methods to the natural needs and interests of the growing child has had a profound effect on teaching methods generally.

Maria Montessori showed as a young child so much ability in mathematics and engineering that her parents sent her to a boys' school in Rome, since the young ladies' schools of those days did not cater for such tastes. Here her interests turned to biology and medicine, and she took a degree in medicine at Rome University and later became a professor—both unique achievements for a woman at that time.

From the University she became a doctor in Rome at a psychiatric clinic (a clinic for treating psychological troubles). Here her interest in human behaviour led her to an understanding of the scientific value of careful observation of children's behaviour. She quickly saw that mentally defective children could not learn satisfactorily if left with mentally ill adults, as many were at that time; so she obtained permission to set up a special school for them. She discovered that children at certain stages of development would repeat over and over again particular exercises; so she devised sense training apparatus to suit these different stages. With this training she enabled several 8-year-old mental defectives to pass the State examination in reading and writing as well or even better than many normal children. She then proceeded to apply her methods to normal children in the Roman slum district of San Lorenzo, where she had charge of a crèche for children from 3 to 6, which she called *Casa dei Bambini* (Children's House).

Dr. Montessori knew that children needed the right environment in which to make proper mental, physical, and spiritual growth. She provided light, colourful rooms equipped with furniture of the correct size and type. She devised suitable material for training the senses and teaching early skills, allowing the children to choose their own activities and work at their own pace. She was soon able to prove that by these methods the children reached a high scholastic level, and developed self-discipline which made rewards and punishments unnecessary. They became busy, peaceful, and happy.

By 1911 Montessori methods were spreading, and schools were set up in Switzerland and then in England and America. In 1917 a research institute was founded in Barcelona. Her methods were found to work equally well with children of different colour, race, creed, or social position. She went on to study the phases of development from birth right through to the University, preaching that true education, supplying the real needs of the child, would produce a well-balanced adult—and consequently a peaceful world.

Madame Montessori died in Holland when she was 82, her work on education, psychology, sociology, and philosophy having become well-known all over the world.

See also FROEBEL.

See also Vol. X: EDUCATION, MODERN; NURSERY SCHOOLS; SPECIAL SCHOOLS.

MONTEVERDI, Claudio (1568–1643), Italian composer, *see* Vol. XII: OPERA, HISTORY OF.

MONTFORT, Simon de (*c.* 1208–65). Montfort, who led the barons in their quarrel with King Henry III, was the first man to call together a representative assembly which was one of the early beginnings of the modern British PARLIAMENT (q.v. Vol. X).

Montfort, born in Normandy, came to England as a young man, having inherited the earldom of Leicester from his Anglo-Norman grandmother. He married Henry III's sister, and afterwards spent some years as the King's representative in Gascony, where his harsh rule provoked many complaints.

The barons' quarrel with the King was pro-voked by the corruption of the royal officials, by Henry's extravagant favouritism of certain foreigners at Court, and by his ill-judged foreign policy, which caused the country to pay huge sums of money to the Pope. In 1258, a 'Council of Fifteen', of which Montfort was a member, was set up at Oxford to control the King's Ministers and to effect reforms.

Five years later Montfort, as leader of the barons, was largely responsible for an appeal to LOUIS IX of France (q.v.) to arbitrate between the King and the barons. When Louis declared for Henry III and annulled the barons' demands Montfort took to arms. At the Battle of Lewes (1264) he captured and imprisoned the King and his son Prince Edward. The barons then drafted a constitution setting up a 'Council of Nine', with Montfort at its head—virtually Protector of the realm. But his successes and his power aroused the jealousy of some of the barons. Indeed it was probably in the hope of gaining the support of the middle-classes against the barons that he summoned representatives of shires and towns to the famous Parliament of 1265. Shortly afterwards Prince Edward escaped from prison, rallied an army, and defeated and killed Montfort at Evesham.

Montfort is a puzzling character. He was ambitious and self-centred, with no real roots in England. Yet he had an interest, though fitful, in political ideas. There is little reason to think that his famous Parliament was more than an emergency measure: but by summoning for the first time the knights and burgesses to Westminster he set an example which was followed by Edward I. His reform movement failed to impose any permanent check upon the King, but it did pave the way for many necessary improvements in law and local government. In a contemporary poem, *The Song of Lewes*, he appears as a popular hero, and two generations after his death Montfort was still remembered as a champion of popular rights.

See also EDWARD I.

MONTROSE, Marquis of (1612–50). The Scottish hero and poet, James Graham, Marquis of Montrose, fought loyally and with brilliant leadership for CHARLES I (q.v.) against the domination of the Scottish Covenanters. Montrose, the head of an ancient Scots family, was handsome and accomplished, with a courteous charm that won most men's friendship.

THE MARQUIS OF MONTROSE

Ashmolean Museum

His execution is shown in the background. Contemporary
Dutch engraving

When Charles tried to force the Scottish Church into line with the Church of England, in particular to use the English Prayer Book, most of Scotland supported the Scottish Church against the King, and signed a protest called the National Covenant. Montrose took a leading part in asserting the freedom of the Scottish Church. When Charles tried to crush the opposition by force, Montrose captured the Royalist city of Aberdeen. Charles then yielded to the Covenanters' demands.

The Presbyterian section of the Scottish Church then assumed control of both Church and State, and began to force a far more rigid uniformity than the King had attempted. They signed a Solemn League and Covenant with the Puritan Roundheads of England, agreeing to force the people of Scotland, England, and Ireland to a Puritan type of religion. Montrose feared this tyranny far more than that of the King, and still strove to achieve a just and peaceful settlement between the Scots and Charles. He spoke out so boldly against his own associates that the Covenanters imprisoned him for several months in Edinburgh Castle. After the alliance with the Roundheads, however, Montrose, believing that the only hope of freedom for Scotland lay with the King, joined Charles

in England. But Charles, who was already approaching defeat in England, distrusted Montrose. Eventually he sent him north to reconquer Scotland. He could give him no support, however, and Montrose took with him the King's appointment as Viceroy of Scotland and two men, four horses, and no money.

In the year which followed (1644–5), known as 'Montrose's Year', he led a small force of Highlanders and Scots-Irish, without any permanent base, money, or guns, and with never more than a handful of cavalry, through a series of astonishing victories. In his first battle, at Tippermuir, his front rank had only one round of ammunition, the rear rank none; yet they broke a much larger force, fully armed and with cavalry and guns. At Inverlochy Montrose lost only four men in killing 1,500 of the enemy. His rugged Highlanders were admirably suited to the rapid marches and highly flexible tactics that Montrose devised. His final victory at Kilsyth, near Glasgow, made him the master of Scotland. Montrose was a natural soldier, who could see immediately how best to adapt his slender resources to meet the great odds against him; he was a born leader, who not only won his men's devotion, but drew from them more than they knew was in them.

But disaster followed quickly. Only a month later, his small force was surprised in a fog in the Border country and utterly destroyed. Montrose himself escaped abroad. In spite of offers of high commands from France and Germany, he remained loyal to the King. When news reached him of Charles's execution, he swore support for the young Prince, later Charles II.

In 1650 Montrose again tried to raise the Highlands. But only a few supporters rallied to him, and his dispirited army pressed on only to be caught and cut to pieces at Carbisdale. Montrose escaped, and after nearly starving to death in the desolate mountains of Sutherland, he was captured by a Highland chieftain and sold to the Scottish leaders. He was taken to Edinburgh, condemned to death, and treated with the greatest insult. On his dignified journey to the scaffold, the crowds, who were expected to stone him, watched him in silent respect; even the hangman wept as he did his work. Eleven years later his remains were recovered and buried in St. Giles' Cathedral.

See also CHARLES I.
See also Vol. X: CIVIL WAR.

MOORE, Sir John (1761–1809). Moore, who died a hero's death during the defence of Corunna against Napoleon's forces, is famous for the new training methods he introduced to the British army. The success of these was first proved in battle by WELLINGTON's armies (q.v.) in the Peninsular War, and many of Moore's principles of training are still in force today.

Moore joined the army when he was only 15; in the first years of the NAPOLEONIC WARS (q.v. Vol. X) he fought bravely in the capture of Corsica, and then in the West Indies and Egypt. He was promoted rapidly, and at 42 was given command of a training brigade at Shorncliffe, near Dover. There he trained regiments which, as the Light Division, were among the most famous of Wellington's forces. At that time the private soldier was generally thought of as the scum of the earth, to be disciplined only by the lash and the threat of the gallows; but Moore concentrated with remarkable success on building up his troops' self-respect. He punished little, but his men were superbly disciplined and devoted to him. He left his mark on the lives of many brilliant young officers, who all their lives were proud to be known as 'John Moore's men'.

After 5 years at Shorncliffe, Moore was sent with a small British force to Sweden, then threatened by the French and Russians. When the King of Sweden proposed to use the British forces for wild schemes of conquest, Moore objected, and the King placed him under arrest. Moore was forced to escape disguised as a peasant. On his return to England he found that an army was to be sent to the help of the Spanish and Portuguese who had risen in revolt against Napoleon. He accepted an appointment as third in command of the expedition, though he considered such a rank an insult to an officer with his record.

Soon after Moore's arrival in Portugal, in the autumn of 1808, the senior officers were recalled to face a court of inquiry (*see* WELLINGTON), and Moore was left in command of an army of nearly 40,000 men. Napoleon, determined to smash Spanish resistance, himself led the Grand Army into the Peninsula. Moore advanced into Spain, but his Spanish allies were everywhere defeated, and in the mountainous country he soon ran short of supplies. In response to Spanish appeals for help, however, he pressed on in an attempt to strike at Napoleon's lines of communication with France. But on the eve of battle with a French army in northern Spain, Moore heard

Parker Gallery

THE BATTLE OF CORUNNA
Aquatint by M. Dubourg after W. Heath

that Napoleon himself was marching against him at the head of 70,000 men, and had already cut him off from his base. Moore at once retreated fast for the coast, ordering ships to be ready to embark the British troops at Corunna.

During the next 3 weeks, the army covered 250 miles of desolate, mountainous country in driving rain and snow. There is no doubt that, after the first few days, when Napoleon had left the pursuit to his subordinates, Moore's army would have suffered less had they made less haste and fought more rearguard actions. As it was, they reached Corunna in poor spirits, ragged and hungry, to discover that the ships had not arrived. For 3 days, until the ships came in and his army was safely embarked, Moore gallantly defended the town against the advancing French, and at the height of the battle himself led a valiant charge to revive the spirits of his flagging infantry. In this action he was mortally wounded, and at his own request was buried in the ramparts of the town.

See also WELLINGTON; NAPOLEON.
See also Vol. X: NAPOLEONIC WARS.

MORE, Sir Thomas (1478–1535). More, author of *Utopia* and the Chancellor who had the moral courage to protest against Henry VIII's break with Rome, was the son of Sir John More, Justice of the King's Bench. He was born and educated in London, and when he was about 13, according to the custom of the time, he was put as a page into the household of Cardinal Morton, Archbishop of Canterbury, to learn manners and the ways of the world. Morton sent him to Oxford University. At this time Oxford was becoming a centre of the 'New Learning' or Humanism, that is, the study of Greek and of ancient books and manuscripts brought from Italy. These were gradually replacing the exclusively theological studies of the older scholars.

When he was 16, More's father brought him home to study law at the New Inn in London, and at 18 he was admitted to Lincoln's Inn. But he did not give up his Oxford studies and his literary interests, which were much stimulated by a growing friendship with the great European scholar ERASMUS (q.v.), who first came to England in 1499. Erasmus records that it was More who first introduced him to the future Henry VIII, then a boy of 8. The two scholars continued to meet and correspond with each other all their lives, and when More died Erasmus wrote, 'I seem to have died myself; we had but one soul between us'. They both wished for reform in the Catholic Church brought about by better education, but neither wished to break with the Church, and both disapproved of the violence of Martin LUTHER's movement (q.v.).

During the next few years More tried to make up his mind whether or not to throw up the study of law and become a priest. He had a severe, self-mortifying side to his nature which was concealed by the gaiety and wit more familiar to his friends. For a time he took lodgings near the Charterhouse in London and shared as far as possible in the life of the monks there, fasting and scourging himself and sleeping little.

More was elected a member of Parliament and got into serious trouble by eloquently and effectively opposing a demand of Henry VII's for a financial grant on the marriage of his daughter Margaret to the King of Scotland. As a result More was forced for a time to withdraw from public life. The next year he married the eldest daughter of John Colt, thus resolving his indecision about taking Holy Orders, since priests were not allowed to marry. It was said that More admired all three of Colt's daughters 'for their honest conversation and virtuous education', but that, though he really favoured the second, he married the eldest, not wishing to humiliate her by preferring her junior. They lived together happily until her death in 1511, when More within a month married Alice Middleton, a widow with one daughter. More had four children by his first wife, one of whom, Margaret, was a charming and highly cultured woman devoted to her father; she married his biographer, William Roper.

When the young Henry VIII succeeded to the throne in 1509, More was able to follow a public career again, and he served under Wolsey in several capacities. In 1516 the *Utopia*, More's most famous book, was published. Utopia (Greek for 'nowhere') is an imaginary commonwealth with an ideal government. More's book was probably written partly in protest against *The Prince* by MACHIAVELLI (q.v.), which describes the ideal autocratic ruler of a nationalist State, and partly against the system of land enclosure which was causing great distress in England (*see* OPEN FIELDS AND ENCLOSURES, Vol. VI). The *Utopia* was written in Latin in the form of an imaginary conversation with a voyager called

The Trustees of the late Lord St. Oswald

SIR THOMAS MORE AND HIS FAMILY

More is in the centre between his father and son. His second wife, Alice, sits at the right with two of his daughters, Margaret and Cecilia, in front of her

Ralph Hythlodaye. It describes an imaginary island, the inhabitants of which have devised a kind of community life, despising gold and all individual property, rejecting war—though they are willing to fight for their country in the last resort—and showing tolerance of all religious views. (More as Chancellor was himself far from tolerant of heretics.) The *Utopia* has had a far-reaching effect; it was translated into several languages, and even as late as the 19th century it played its part in forming the socialism of people such as William MORRIS (q.v.). More also wrote a *History of Richard III*, the first modern English historical writing (*see* HISTORIES, Vol. XII), and used by Shakespeare as the source of his play.

More became a member of the Privy Council in 1518, and later he was knighted, sent on various diplomatic missions, elected Speaker of the House, and in 1529, much against his will, was made Lord Chancellor as Wolsey's successor. Trouble soon started between Henry and his Chancellor. More would not support the divorce of Catherine of Aragon, and steadfastly refused to recognize any supreme head of the Church except the Pope. In 1532 he resigned the Chancellorship; and when in 1534 he and Bishop Fisher were summoned to take the Oath of Supremacy acknowledging the King, not the Pope, as head of the Church, they both refused and were both committed to the Tower. A year later they were both tried under a new Act of Treason, and beheaded on Tower Hill. More died with courage and dignity, proclaiming from the scaffold that he died 'the King's good servant but God's first'. In 1935 he was canonized by the Roman Catholic Church.

More was a friend of all the leading scholars of his day, and of the painter HOLBEIN (q.v.). His writings and the example of his life have earned him an important place in the history of the English RENAISSANCE and REFORMATION (qq.v. Vol. I).

See also HENRY VIII.

MORRIS, William (1834–96). William Morris, artist, poet, and socialist, stands out from among his fellows like a giant. He was a big, handsome man with great bodily strength and an equally vigorous mind. He had a violent temper, his anger being especially kindled against insincerity and incompetence. His interests were amazingly broad, and whatever he did he mastered thoroughly. At the same time he possessed great tenderness, and a love of beauty which dominated all he did.

Morris went from Marlborough College to Oxford intending to study for the Church. At Oxford he read the works of RUSKIN (q.v.) who believed that beauty and goodness could not exist independently and that a work of art could not be beautiful unless the artist had enjoyed making it. Morris, with a group of friends, determined to devote his life to the creation of beautiful things, and so decided to become an artist, not a clergyman.

Morris realized that the arts were interdependent, that it was no good having good pictures if you did not have good furniture and, most important of all, a good house in which to enjoy them. Architecture, therefore, seemed of primary importance; and with characteristic impetuosity he started working in an architect's office. But after a year he joined his friend Burne-Jones in London where he met Rossetti, the founder of the Pre-Raphaelite Brotherhood. The PRE-RAPHAELITES (q.v. Vol. XII) were in sympathy with many of Morris's ideas, and Rossetti encouraged him to paint. He was at the same time writing poetry and published his first book of poems, *The Defence of Guenevere*, in 1858. In the following year Morris married Jane Burden, often painted by Rossetti, and built the 'Red House' designed by his friend, Philip Webb, at Upton in Kent. The red brick walls shocked many people as brick was always stuccoed at that time, but Morris would have nothing sham. After searching vainly for beautiful furniture and hangings, Morris realized he must make them himself.

While building and furnishing his house he had gathered round him a group of artists and craftsmen, and with these he formed the firm of Morris, Marshall, and Faulkner (later Morris and Company). Their first productions were stained-glass windows and wall-papers. Morris was the chief designer, though his patterns often included figures by Burne-Jones. Morris studied the shape of plants and flowers most carefully, combining a love of accuracy with a strong sense of design. Above all he loved colour; he turned from the prevalent gloomy dirty reds and browns and hard chemical greens to brilliant and pure colours, experimenting with vegetable dyes to get the colours he wanted for the yarn for his tapestries and stuffs.

His poetry has the same qualities as his designs, and he took great pleasure in describing the colours of the landscape, of his heroine's dress, or of the birds and animals. His poems are the work of a first-rate craftsman rather than a great poet. Though most of his writing was done at the end of a day's work in office or workshop, he wrote with the greatest ease. Many of his poems are stories similar to the old ballads: he wrote about the medieval heroes, Arthur and his knights, whom Rossetti and the Pre-Raphaelites loved to paint; *The Earthly Paradise* tells the stories of various heroes. Later, becoming interested in Scandinavian SAGAS (q.v. Vol. XII), he visited Iceland, translated many of the sagas from Icelandic and Danish, and wrote his own version in *Sigurd the Volsung*, the most satisfying of all his long poems.

In 1877 Morris began lecturing on art, but gradually his interests shifted from his own art

Victoria & Albert Museum

PART OF THE TITLE-PAGE OF A MANUSCRIPT BOOK OF VERSE
BY WILLIAM MORRIS

The decoration is by Morris and the portrait by Charles Fairfax Murray

to the social conditions around him. Morris was a Socialist because he was an artist. Like Ruskin, he believed men could be happy only if they enjoyed their work and, conversely, that the products of their labour could be good only if they were happy. Neither of these conditions could be satisfied in factories where men, women, and children worked at tasks which had no interest because they were purely mechanical, where conditions were horrible, and pay barely sufficient to keep them alive. Happiness was equally impossible for the rich capitalists who had no interest in things into which they had put no creative labour, but only money. The only solution was for everyone to own the means of production and equally for everyone to help produce. Socialism was a growing idea in the 1880's, though it had as yet no political party. Morris preached Socialism, wrote his *Chants for Socialists*, and hoped for a Socialist revolution. His serious Socialist writings include *The Dream of John Ball*, a vision based on the Peasants' Revolt in the 14th century, and *News from Nowhere*, which was a Utopian vision of the future Socialist world.

Morris's last new interest was in printing. Dissatisfied with the poor quality of contemporary printing, he studied types and designed his own, based on the best examples of 15th-century Italian books. He also designed a gothic type. The Kelmscott Press, named after his house in Oxfordshire, was set up at Hammersmith and produced a number of his own books as well as editions of Chaucer and other classics. The pages were decorated with Morris's designs, with figures by Burne-Jones and others.

Morris's influence is still felt. The best modern designs for furniture and hangings owe much to his insistence on good design, suitability, and quality; and present-day educational ideals owe much to his belief that men can be happy only if they enjoy the work they do.

See also Vol. XII: Pre-Raphaelites.

MOSES (14th century B.C.), *see* Vol. I: Bible.

MOZART, Wolfgang Amadeus (1756–91). Although he lived only 35 years Mozart wrote a vast amount of music and was one of the greatest, some would say the greatest, musical genius the world has ever known. He was the son of Leopold Mozart, an Austrian musician employed by the Archbishop of Salzburg and author of a famous book on violin playing. Mozart started his musical life at a very early age; he was picking out chords when he was 3 and composing little pieces by the time he was 5. His sister, Nannerl, who was 5 years older than Wolfgang, also showed unusual promise. Leopold was very ambitious for both children and made them work very hard. But they were carefully and lovingly trained, and the children were devoted to each other and to their parents. Wolfgang was extremely sensitive as a child, but he was also gay and good-natured, and all his life had an irrepressible sense of humour.

From 1762 until 1766, Wolfgang and Nannerl toured Europe with their father. They played before the Empress Maria Theresa in Vienna, before Louis XV at Versailles, and at the court of George III in London. The tour was a great success, and Wolfgang won much admiration for his piano, organ, and violin playing, and for his sight-reading and improvising. In London he read at sight everything which the King placed before him. All the time Wolfgang was learning from the music he heard in the big cities. In London he met Bach's son, Christian, who was music-master to Queen Charlotte. At this time, when he was only 8, he wrote his first symphonies, and his first oratorio was produced in Holland with great success.

In 1769 father and son went to Italy for a two-year visit. There Wolfgang learnt much about Italian opera and especially about writing for voices. In Rome he astonished the Papal musicians by writing out from memory a whole *miserere* by Allegri which he heard during Holy Week.

When the Mozarts finally returned to Salzburg, their patron, the Archbishop, had died, and his successor was a harsh man who cared nothing for music. The young Mozart was appointed director of concerts, but he was unhappy and wanted to find work elsewhere; so he made many trips abroad with either his father or mother in search of another post. At Mannheim he made friends with the four daughters of Weber, a penniless music copyist. He fell in love with one sister and later married another, and he wrote some brilliant music (including the part of the Queen of Night in the *Magic Flute*) for a third, who had a high soprano voice.

He reached Paris in 1778, and there he had a success with his 'Paris Symphony'. But he could

MOZART, AGED 7, WITH HIS FATHER AND SISTER
Contemporary French engraving

find no permanent post. He was saddened by the death of his mother and also by the failure of his courtship of Aloysia Weber. Finally he returned reluctantly to Salzburg.

In 1780 the ruler of Bavaria asked him to compose a new opera for Munich; it was *Idomeneo*, the first of Mozart's great operas and the only wholly serious one that can be called a masterpiece, and it had a triumphant success. Elated by this he had a violent quarrel with his master, the Archbishop, was literally kicked out of the palace, and went to live in Vienna. He soon after married a younger Weber sister, Constanze.

For the rest of his life Mozart had no regular post. In those days it was difficult for a composer to live without a settled post as a court or church musician, for his work was not then protected by any law of COPYRIGHT (q.v. Vol. IV). Mozart received occasional presents from wealthy patrons to whom he dedicated work, and he earned some money from the public performance of his operas. Apart from this he had to eke out a living by teaching and giving concerts. Neither he nor his wife were practical managers, and they had a constant struggle against poverty.

Shortly before his marriage Mozart wrote *Die Entführung*—an opera often known by its Italian title, *Il Seraglio*—which was a great success. During this period Mozart gave concerts at which he often played his own piano concertos; he greatly developed the piano CONCERTO (q.v. Vol. XII) and wrote brilliantly for the piano. About this time he made friends with HAYDN (q.v.), and both learned much from each other. Mozart was led by Haydn to treat his symphonies with far more care and thought, and especially to develop his musical ideas in a richer and more elaborate way. The six symphonies (from the 'Haffner' to the 'Jupiter') and the last ten string quartets which he wrote after meeting Haydn are generally considered his finest.

Mozart continued to work with extraordinary fluency and speed, the last three of his great Symphonies being composed within the incredibly short space of two months. His mind never rested from music. The actual composition of his music usually took place late at night when he was alone; then, with it already perfect in his head, he could write it down anywhere—even in the middle of a crowded room. He wrote the D minor Quartet while his wife was giving birth to a son.

In 1785 he had the good fortune to meet Lorenzo da Ponte, the poet who wrote for him the texts (or librettos) of his comic operas *The Marriage of Figaro*, *Don Giovanni*, and *Così fan tutte*. Da Ponte could provide Mozart with convincing plots and sensible, often amusing words that sounded well when set to music. Mozart, as well as his musical genius, had a sense of humour and drama and an understanding of the theatre. Together they could create comic operas of unsurpassed beauty and wit. Both *Don Giovanni* and *The Marriage of Figaro* were produced at Prague with triumphant success. In 1791 an old theatre-manager friend, Schikaneder, asked Mozart to write music for a sort of pantomime which he had concocted from various plays, and which was a mixture of broad farce and religious mystery. Mozart was the ideal composer for such a subject since he knew perfectly how to mix laughter and solemnity without making either appear out of place. The result was *The Magic Flute*.

Shortly before *The Magic Flute*'s first performance, a mysterious stranger called on Mozart, asking him to compose a Requiem Mass. Actually he was a servant of a nobleman who wanted to pay Mozart to write the work and then to pass it off as his own. Mozart, who was already ill, became convinced that the stranger was Death and that the Requiem was for his own funeral. While writing the Requiem he became increasingly ill, and in December 1791 he died, leaving the Requiem unfinished. There being no money to pay for the funeral, he was buried in a pauper's grave, the exact place of his burial being unknown.

Mozart wrote music of all kinds, from dance tunes to church masses. He left such an enormous amount of music that it was difficult to distinguish one title from another. There are, for example, fourteen symphonies in D major and several concertos in B flat. A German, named Köchel, catalogued all Mozart's works, giving each a number. Nowadays Köchel's numbering is used to identify Mozart's music, the letter K standing for Köchel: for example, we would say Symphony in C, K. 551. Among much other music Mozart has left more than forty symphonies and twenty piano concertos, six concertos for violin, two for flute, three for horn, one for clarinet, and several for other instruments; there are twenty-three string quartets, six string quintets, thirty-seven violin sonatas, about sixteen piano sonatas, and at least seven outstanding operas and thirteen masses.

'Composition is my one and only passion and joy', Mozart once wrote to his father, and throughout his short life he devoted himself entirely to his musical ideals. Mozart was a classical composer in the sense that he wrote within the accepted forms of his time, his originality lying in his fresh treatment of old ideas. His music, exquisite for its grace and elegance and perfect in its craftsmanship, has also great emotional depth. This is true particularly of the great G minor Symphony and of many of the wonderful arias from the operas.

See also Vol. XII: MUSIC, HISTORY OF; OPERA.

MUSSOLINI, Benito (1883–1945). Mussolini was the leader (*Il Duce*) of Italian Fascism (*see* TOTALITARIANISM, Vol. X), and dictator of Italy for more than 20 years.

He was born in the Romagna province. On leaving school he became an elementary school-teacher, but soon took to politics and journalism. He became a leader of the revolutionary and pacifist wing of the Italian Socialist party, and editor of the chief Socialist newspaper. After the outbreak of the First World War in 1914,

Mussolini broke with those Socialists who wanted peace, and agitated for Italy to join the Allies, which she did in 1915. He was above everything an agitator.

After the war Italy was in the kind of distracted state which made her vulnerable to a revolutionary movement. In 1919, in Milan, Mussolini founded his new party, which he called Fascist (meaning 'a group'). The party was both extremely nationalistic and socialistic, and therefore attracted many different kinds of people; it was also ready to use force unscrupulously. At first Mussolini's most powerful weapon was his gift of oratory. He worked up enthusiasm in his party with uniforms (black shirts), badges, drilling, salutes with a raised arm, and slogans, and impressed the general public by displays. In October 1922 the Fascists made a spectacular 'march on Rome', as a result of which the King of Italy asked Mussolini to become Prime Minister with a coalition government. In the next few years the Fascists terrorized the Italian people, in 1924 murdering the chief Socialist leader, Matteotti. By 1926 Mussolini was able to establish Fascist one-party rule, and to prevent the expression of all anti-Fascist opinions.

Mussolini's chief aim was to increase Italy's power as a nation. For this reason, defying the protests of the League of Nations, he attacked Abyssinia in 1935 and proclaimed it as part of the Italian Empire. The opposition of the other European Powers compelled Mussolini to draw closer to the Germany of HITLER (q.v.), with whom he made an aggressive military alliance in May 1939. When Hitler set going the SECOND WORLD WAR (q.v. Vol. X) a few months later, Mussolini held back for a time, for Italy was still exhausted from her Abyssinian campaign and her interference in the Spanish Civil War. But in June 1940 he declared war against Britain and France, and later in the year attacked Greece.

The war, always unpopular in Italy, went badly from the beginning. When the Allies invaded Sicily in July 1943 much of the Fascist Party turned against Mussolini, and the King decided to arrest him. But the Germans rescued him and put him at the head of a north Italian Republic, which they were able to defend against the Allies and the anti-Fascist Italian volunteers for the next 18 months. In April 1945 Mussolini was shot by Italian Communists as he was trying to escape to Switzerland.

See also HITLER.

N

NANSEN, Fridtjof (1861–1930). This Norwegian explorer, and later statesman and humanitarian, set an example of ideal leadership—strong, skilful, hardy, and expert—which was followed by men such as SCOTT, SHACKLETON, and AMUNDSEN (qq.v.).

Born near Oslo (then called Christiania), he became expert at ski-ing, sledging, and all outdoor sports, and specially loved to go on fishing and hunting expeditions, alone with his dog. At the University he studied zoology, and then for practical experience joined a sealer going to Greenland. On the voyage he made scientific observations, sketched, acted as gunner, hunted Polar bears, and got his first taste of the Arctic. He determined to explore the unknown interior of Greenland, and in 1888–9 made the first successful crossing, an extremely hazardous journey, in which it took him 2 months to reach the highest point (9,000 ft.) before beginning the easier journey down to the inhabited west coast.

On his return to Norway Nansen, now famous, resumed his job as curator of the Zoological Museum at Bergen and gave lecture tours in most countries of Europe.

Nansen conceived a bold and original plan of crossing the Pole, based on two bits of evidence —an American yacht *Jeannette*, having become frozen in the Arctic, had drifted with the ice across the Polar regions, and a piece of Siberian larchwood was also known to have drifted right across the Pole. He therefore planned a ship so strong and of such a shape that, instead of being crushed by the ice when the sea froze, she would rise above it like an orange pip when pinched between the fingers. The result was the famous polar ship *Fram*, built in a Scottish shipyard. She was schooner-rigged and fitted with engines—a ship of 400 tons, 128 ft. long, 36 ft. broad, and with sides 2 ft. thick.

The *Fram* sailed from Christiania in June 1893 with a crew of thirteen and thirty sledge-dogs. By September she had got as far as Cape Chelyuskin, the most northerly point of Siberia. Soon the ice was 30 ft. thick. Then came 'the nip'; the ship groaned and trembled and then broke from the terrifying grip of the ice and rose upward until she was safe on top of it. The drift of the *Fram* had begun, and there was no going back. Nansen, as a good leader, knew that at this time all his crew must be fully occupied, so the scientific instruments were set up, a camp built on the ice for the dogs, and hunting expeditions organized.

The ship drifted slowly northward for a year, and then began to drift westward. Nansen decided that the moment had come to make a dash for the Pole, and with one companion, twenty-eight dogs, three sledges carrying their two kayaks (Eskimo canoes), a tent, sleeping-bags, scientific instruments, and stores he parted from the *Fram* and set off. By April 1895 the two men had reached a point only 200 miles from the Pole—farther north than any previous explorers; but with temperatures 40° below zero, clothes and sleeping-bags frozen stiff, and the dogs exhausted, Nansen decided to turn back. They travelled for 4 months, on one occasion being nearly killed by a bear that took them unawares. Their canoes went adrift when they climbed an iceberg to get their bearings, and Nansen had to swim in his heavy furs through icy water to retrieve them. Then a huge bull-walrus attacked Nansen's canoe, nearly destroying it. Finally they had to dig themselves in for the winter, building themselves a hut with tools made from walrus tusks. They spent the winter hunting, talking, and writing. In May they set off again, and a month later ran into a party of British explorers who had been out 2 years and were waiting for a ship to take them home. It was a dramatic meeting.

When the two Norwegians reached Norway they had been away more than 3 years. They found no news of the *Fram*; but a week later she turned up, having drifted right round the Pole and come safely back, just as Nansen had hoped. He wrote an account of his adventures in his book, *Farthest North*.

Nansen then found himself drawn into politics and international affairs. He would have preferred to have pursued his scientific work, but he felt it his duty to serve first his own country in its struggle for independence from Sweden (*see* NORWEGIANS, Vol. I), and later, through the League of Nations, to serve the victims of the First World War, in which Norway had remained neutral. He did great work in repatriating prisoners of war, for whom he ran the famous Nansen Relief Committee. In 1921 he organized relief for the victims of the terrible Russian famine; he worked for the Armenians; and he devised the Nansen Pass, the League of Nations PASSPORT for people such as REFUGEES (qq.v. Vol. X) who had been deprived of their right to a nationality. He was awarded the NOBEL Peace prize (q.v.) in 1922. His worst struggles were always against political indifference and prejudice.

In 1930, he planned to celebrate his 69th birthday by flying over the North Pole in an airship; but he died that year at the age of 68— a man famed for great endeavour in many different fields.

See also Vol. III: POLAR REGIONS (EXPLORATION).

See also Vol. X: INTERNATIONAL CO-OPERATION, SOCIAL AND ECONOMIC.

NAPOLEON I (Bonaparte) (1769–1821). This titanic figure, one of the greatest soldiers and administrators who have ever lived, changed the history of Europe.

Bonaparte, the son of a Corsican noble, was born in Corsica only a year after the French had taken that island from the Italian Republic of Genoa. His father, like many Corsicans, at first resented the change of government. Bonaparte himself, though he spoke French, retained an Italian accent all his life. He entered a French military school at 10, and was commissioned in the French royal army at 15. When the FRENCH REVOLUTION (q.v. Vol. X) broke out, he accepted its principles but was sickened by its disorders. At 24 his leadership as an artillery officer won him promotion to brigadier, and 2 years later, when France was ringed by powerful enemies, he was given supreme command of the French army opposing the Sardinians and Austrians in Italy. Thus, at the age of 26 his terrifying genius burst fully formed on the world.

Bonaparte's first great Italian campaign (1796–7) provided France with some of the most spectacular victories of the NAPOLEONIC WARS (q.v. Vol. X), and was as brilliant as anything he ever accomplished. Within a short time he had transformed the army's spirit by lightning successes, and within a month the Sardinians were compelled to make peace. Later he repeatedly defeated the Austrians. He became a national hero and one of the first soldiers in Europe. Thus began 16 years of French military conquest during which Bonaparte became the terror of Europe.

He next led an army to Egypt, intending to create a French Empire overseas and to threaten the British overland route to India. But NELSON (q.v.), by destroying the French fleet at the Nile, prevented his carrying out this plan. The next year Bonaparte abandoned his army, and made a perilous journey back to France, arriving at a critical moment in French politics. The forms of government of the old kingdom had been swept away by the Revolution, and the new, complicated institutions of government set up in their place were not working. The ambitious Bonaparte realized that this was his opportunity to achieve power. He joined a conspiracy hatched against the constitutional government by politicians who hoped to use for their own ends Bonaparte's prestige and standing with the army. The revolutionaries attacked, overthrew the government, and set up a new constitution under which the executive was in the hands of three Consuls. Bonaparte as First Consul gradually began to draw the supreme power into his own hands.

Theoretically his power was based upon the will of the people. He was accepted by a PLEBISCITE (q.v. Vol. X) of the great majority of Frenchmen as First Consul for 10 years, then for life, and finally, in 1804, as Emperor. But once they had given their approval, the people's share in the government had ended.

The first years of Napoleon's rule saw his most spectacular and most enduring achievements. He laid down an administrative framework which, in great part, still exists. The government was strictly centralized. Prefects, appointed directly from Paris and responsible to Napoleon himself, administered the provinces. The laws of France were codified in a number of *Codes Napoléon*. The system of finance and taxation was reorganized, and a national bank was created. A national university directed higher education, ensuring that the young were educated in principles useful to the Emperor's purpose. A highly efficient secret police checked political agitation dangerous to the State.

Archives Photographiques

NAPOLEON I CROWNING THE EMPRESS JOSEPHINE AT HIS CORONATION IN NOTRE DAME, PARIS, ON 2 DECEMBER 1804
Painting by J. L. David, in the Louvre

Catholicism was recognized as the 'religion of the majority of Frenchmen', though the Church was strictly controlled by the government. Napoleon invited the Pope to Paris for his coronation; but he placed the crown upon his own head, saying 'God gave it to me. Woe to him who touches it!' Napoleon, too, created a new nobility, most of whom were soldiers created marshals and given titles taken from their battles. Behind all this Napoleon himself was the driving force. He had superb powers of concentration and a gift for choosing subordinates, picking their brains, guiding their work, and transferring to them something of his own energy.

Napoleon was a small man—no more than 5 ft. 2 in. in height, with small delicate hands and feet. His lean figure and fine-drawn, sallow features were, by the time he was 36, beginning to fill out and show signs of plumpness. He would work at his papers for long hours, sometimes rising at 2 a.m. and working on until late at night. He would dictate pacing up and down his study, his steps growing faster as the torrent of his thought gathered momentum, while his harassed secretaries strove to keep up with his dictation. He

could, when he wished, display an almost magical charm, a charm which captivated his enemy, the Tsar Alexander, and won the admiration of the poet GOETHE (q.v.). In anger, he could quell the roughest and most arrogant of his marshals. Yet, beneath the trappings of Imperial majesty, he never lost some of the crude habits of the Corsican. He sometimes grossly insulted ambassadors, and once poured on the head of his Minister TALLEYRAND (q.v.) a flood of filthy abuse. He had a remarkable memory, and often stopped during his military inspections to remind some grizzled warrior of a victory they had shared. His sense of humour was crude: one of his favourite methods of showing approval was to pinch the ears of his subordinates. His tastes in music and art were narrow, though he wished to make Paris the capital of European culture. His museums were filled with art treasures pillaged from his conquered countries; he encouraged architecture, and would have encouraged literature had not many of the greatest French writers preferred to live in exile.

Napoleon's power rested, in the last resort, upon the Grand Army, which he forged into one of the most effective military weapons in the history of war. His great victories were the result of the skill, endurance, and courage of the men who fought under him and of his own wonderful talents as a strategist. He could move whole armies by separate, often distant, routes to converge in paralysing force on the enemy's weakest point. He could enforce great speed on the march (he once covered 400 miles in 25 days), driving his soldiers in a frenzy of controlled energy. He inspired confidence and admiration in his officers and blind devotion in his troops, to whom he appeared invincible. He left minor tactics and methods of advance to his brilliant corps commanders—MASSÉNA (q.v.), Ney, and others—while he himself directed where and when their troops should strike. In battle he always kept part of the Grand Army in reserve. When the battle was 'ripe' and the enemy exhausted, Napoleon would hurl in his reserves in storming columns, supported by the terribly destructive fire of his light artillery. As his columns broke through the enemy's ranks they were followed by the cavalry, matchlessly commanded by Marshal Murat, to turn defeat into rout. Once, at Jena, he swept away the entire enemy army in a swirling pursuit over half north Germany. Scarcely a fortress, regiment, battery, or squadron of cavalry of the whole Prussian army remained in the field. Indeed, in these campaigns it was Napoleon's annihilation of the enemy's power (his 'thunderbolts of victory') that was so decisive militarily and politically, and which enabled him to rearrange the map of Europe at his will.

As his ambition grew, Napoleon set up a dynasty—a House of Bonaparte. His brother Joseph, at first King of Naples, was transferred to Madrid as King of Spain, and his sister Caroline and her husband Marshal Murat became joint sovereigns of Naples. Other brothers were installed as Kings of Westphalia and Holland. In 1809, Napoleon's first wife, the Empress Josephine, having failed to provide him with an heir, he divorced her and married the Archduchess Marie-Louise, daughter of the Austrian Emperor and a descendant of countless kings; their baby son was given the title King of Rome.

In every part of Europe, wherever his armies fought and conquered, Napoleon introduced his efficient administration, and the scientific principles of his legal code. Ecclesiastical and feudal

Marlborough Fine Art, Ltd.
NAPOLEON I IN LATER LIFE
Drawing by Théodore Géricault (1791–1824)

privilege vanished; men of talent pushed themselves to the front. But in spite of all this, Napoleon's statesmanship seemed to have no settled purpose, to be merely an appendage to his military power. He interpreted treaties to his own advantage; he changed the instructions, sometimes from month to month, of the brilliant officials who administered the new Imperial lands; he seemed incapable of making peace. He often burdened the subject States with taxation, stifled freedom of thought, and made them feel that they existed only for the advantage of France. Many of these subject peoples awoke for the first time to a sense of their own nationality, and the surge of popular feeling which this produced stimulated the reaction against Napoleon and eventually brought about his defeat.

In 1807 Napoleon's struggle with England drew him into an attempt to exclude all English goods from the Continent. This led him into further expansion so that he could control the European coasts. He seized Spain, which led to a bitter national uprising against him and to the disastrous Peninsular War (*see* WELLINGTON). Then he attacked Russia, but lost nearly half a million men in the terrible retreat from Moscow through a Russian winter. This so weakened him that Europe was able to combine to defeat him and to force his abdication in 1814. But a year later he escaped from exile on the island of Elba to make a last bid for power. French armies rallied to him, but he was finally defeated by Wellington at the great Battle of Waterloo. The British then imprisoned him for life on the island of St. Helena, in the south Atlantic, where he died of cancer 6 years later.

In France, the legend of Napoleon grew in the hearts of Frenchmen. For years after his death men of every shade of political opinion could claim him as one of their patrons, and in 1852 his nephew Louis Napoleon (Napoleon III) used the popularity of the legend to create the Second French Empire. In 1840 Napoleon's remains were brought back to France amid a tremendous outburst of public enthusiasm to be buried under the great dome of Les Invalides in Paris.

NASH, John (1752–1835). This Regency architect was born in London but in his youth worked mostly in Wales. About 1796 he returned to London and became the architect partner of Humphrey Repton, a famous landscape gardener (*see* LANDSCAPE ART, Vol. XII). In 1798 Nash married a lady of some fortune, and they lived either in Dover Street, London, or at East Cowes Castle, Isle of Wight, a house which was designed by Nash to look like an ancient castle. About 1810 Nash must have met the Prince of Wales (later GEORGE IV (q.v.)), and it was then that his real career began. The Prince's grandiose ideas gave Nash a chance to work on a really big scale. Nash's greatness lay in his ability to plan whole districts of London as if they were a landscape garden, contrasting formal streets of houses with villas set among trees. His greatest achievement was the layout and building of what are now called Regent's Park, Regent Street, Waterloo Place, and Carlton House Terrace, all planned and built between about 1810 and 1830. The effect was spoilt when much of Nash's Regent Street was pulled down in the 1920's and replaced by modern buildings.

In Regent's Park, villas are dotted about among trees, and an artificial lake gives a country effect; this is set off by the formal terraces of town houses on three sides of the park, which link it with the rest of London. Most of these houses were designed for professional men who worked in Westminster, and Regent Street was made to provide a direct road for them, for there was then no other; but it was also intended to form a magnificent approach to Carlton House, where the Prince Regent was then living. Carlton House was pulled down before Regent Street was finished, and Nash then began building Buckingham Palace. His designs for this were expensive and unsuccessful, and after his death the palace was remodelled. Nash's triumphal arch which formed the en-

A. F. Kersting

CUMBERLAND TERRACE, REGENT'S PARK, LONDON, DESIGNED BY JOHN NASH, AND BEGUN IN 1826

What seems to be one huge palace is really a whole street of houses

trance, now known as Marble Arch, was removed and placed at the top of Park Lane.

Nash used classical features in most of his designs, but he was also interested in other styles of decoration. He built Brighton Pavilion for George IV by adding 'Chinese' and 'Indian' fantasies to a plain Georgian house; this was meant to be a fairy-tale palace by the sea, and as such it is charming.

Nash was often careless in the details of his designs, and did not try to copy classical models exactly. To give a good effect cheaply he used stucco—a layer of painted plaster on brick walls—setting a fashion which lasted for many years.

See also Vol. XII: REGENCY ARCHITECTURE.

NASH, Richard (1674–1761). The dandy 'Beau' Nash, as Master of Ceremonies to the city of Bath, changed the manners and habits of fashionable English society. The penniless son of a good Welsh family, he had tried soldiering and the study of the law before becoming, like others of his kind, a professional gambler. He went to Bath, which the nobility was beginning to visit for the sake of its healing waters, and soon he was employed by the corporation to direct the social entertainments, in which gambling held a prominent place.

For 40 years Nash practically ruled Bath. He had the roads repaired, the streets cleaned and lit, a Pump Room and spacious Assembly Rooms built, and made keepers of lodgings accept fixed prices. He imposed rules of behaviour at public dances and other social gatherings, forbade the wearing of swords, persuaded gentlemen to wear shoes and stockings instead of rough riding-boots, and caused duels and challenges to be regarded as bad manners. He also saw that young girls were protected from penniless adventurers and gamblers. His influence, and the work of John Wood and other architects, transformed a squalid little town into a beautiful and fashionable city. Nash himself, with a magnificent white hat and heavily laced clothes, set a spectacular standard of elegance.

In 1745 a new Act of Parliament against gambling ruined Nash's livelihood, and he fell into comparative poverty.

See also Vol. IX: SPA; GAMBLING.

NEBUCHADNEZZAR, King (died 562 B.C.), *see* ISAIAH; JEREMIAH.

National Maritime Museum
NELSON AS A CAPTAIN, 1781
Painting by J. F. Rigaud

NELSON, Horatio (Viscount) (1758–1805). Nelson, whose restless energy and brilliant seamanship twice broke the naval power of France, is probably the greatest tactician in naval history. He was an inspired leader, devoted to the Crown and to his country's service. His dispatches ring with memorable phrases: 'The order of sailing is to be the order of battle'; 'Almighty God has blest His Majesty's arms.' He bound his captains to him by regular conferences aboard his flagship, in which every move and detail of an expected engagement was planned. His battle tactics, though often surprisingly unorthodox, were brilliantly executed. He was outspoken, and often obstinately self-willed; and although he was impatient of inefficiency in his superiors, he was always most generous to his subordinates.

Nelson, the son of a Norfolk clergyman, joined the navy as a midshipman when he was 12, and before he was 16 had served in the East Indies and made an expedition to the Arctic. At 19 he served in a frigate in the West Indies, and finding life insufficiently active, he was already confident enough to ask for the command of a schooner. He later said that this experience gave him 'that confidence in himself among rocks and shoals which was afterwards to be so great a comfort'. He was a commander at 20, and was sent to protect the Honduras coast from raiding parties of American privateers. His success in this enterprise won him the rank of captain and the command of a frigate before he was 21. Unlike many of his contemporaries, Nelson won his remarkably early promotion not by patronage but by professional skill and outstanding leadership alone.

When he was 22 Nelson was appointed naval commander of a combined military and naval force sent to Central America to seize a Spanish stronghold on Lake Nicaragua. But the little army was soon decimated by fever, and 145 of Nelson's 200 men fell victims to it. It took all Nelson's inspired leadership to save the expedition from disaster. The officer commanding the troops wrote: 'A light-haired boy came to me in a little frigate . . . and afterwards he directed all the operations.' After many hardships, the Spanish fort was captured, but Nelson, worn out with dysentery and fatigue, had already been ordered home.

After a period fighting widespread smuggling in the Leeward Islands, Nelson returned to 6 years of restless inactivity on shore. But on the outbreak of the NAPOLEONIC WARS (q.v. Vol. X) in 1793, he was given command of the battleship *Agamemnon*. His commander-in-chief, Lord HOOD (q.v.), placed him in charge of the operations against the French island of Corsica, an important base if the Mediterranean was to be held against France. After 7 months of hard fighting ashore, during which Nelson lost his right eye, the island was taken.

In 1796 the British Government decided to abandon the Mediterranean, and Sir John JERVIS (q.v.) gave Nelson the difficult task of evacuating Corsica and, 3 months later, Elba. He rejoined Jervis's fleet on the eve of the great Battle of Cape St. Vincent. It was Nelson's brilliant manœuvre at a critical moment in that engagement that led to the rout of the Spanish. Quitting the line as the fleets drew towards each other, Nelson threw his ship against the Spanish centre, offering himself to the attack of at least seven of the enemy, including the *Santissima Trinidad*, the largest fighting ship in the world. The Spanish were thrown into confusion, and Nelson himself led a boarding-party to capture two of the ships. After the battle every man in the fleet, on sighting Nelson's broad pennant, saluted him with cheers.

Not long afterwards Nelson, now a Rear-Admiral, was selected by Jervis to command an expedition against the Spanish base of Santa Cruz in the Canary Islands, an assault which failed with heavy loss of life, and cost Nelson his right arm. Nelson, as always highly self-critical, wrote: 'I am become a burden to my friends and useless to my country.' But after a period in England his spirits revived, and he rejoined Jervis's fleet, with his flag in the *Vanguard*.

It was then obvious that Napoleon was planning a great expedition into the Mediterranean, and Jervis gave Nelson his twelve best ships to blockade the port of Toulon, already filled with enemy transports. When Nelson learnt that the French fleet had sailed, he at once gave chase. He swept the Mediterranean from end to end, on one occasion missing the enemy almost by minutes, and eventually found the French fleet lying at anchor at Aboukir Bay, near Alexandria. Nelson had already explained to his captains his method of attack for every possible circumstance in which he might sight the enemy. The fleet, therefore, was able to attack at once to the pre-arranged plan. Nelson took grave risks, for he planned to enter a strange, reef-strewn bay at nightfall, without charts or pilots. But speed was essential, and not a ship hesitated. His victory was complete: in the fierce battle that raged all night, of the thirteen French ships nine were taken prize and two burnt. With the fleet destroyed, Napoleon's army in Egypt was cut off from supplies and reinforcements, and his dream of an eastern empire was shattered.

For the next 2 years Nelson commanded a detached squadron ordered to support the King of Naples and to blockade Malta. Nelson, who was suffering from a severe head wound he had received at the Nile, seemed content to waste his days at the Neapolitan Court, where he had fallen deeply in love with Lady Hamilton, the wife of the British Ambassador. Twice he disobeyed orders to remove his ships from Naples and suffered censure from the Admiralty. His love for Lady Hamilton, which endured to the end of his life, withstood the strongest disapproval of the highest in the land. He was greatly concerned that 'my beloved Emma' and their daughter Horatia should not suffer poverty, and almost his last words before his death 7 years later were 'I leave Lady Hamilton and my

National Maritime Museum

NELSON FATALLY WOUNDED AT TRAFALGAR

The scene on the quarter-deck of the *Victory* after Nelson had been shot from the tops of the *Redoutable*. A midshipman is shown replying to the shot. Painting by L. Dighton

daughter as a legacy to my country—never forget Horatia.'

On his return to England Nelson's old strength of purpose returned. In 1801, as second-in-command of the Channel Fleet under Sir Hyde Parker, he sailed for the Baltic either to negotiate a settlement with the Danes, Swedes, and Russians, who were in alliance with Napoleon, or to destroy the enemy fleets should the negotiations fail. The Danes were obdurate, but Parker hesitated to act. At length Nelson wrung from him grudging permission to attack with twelve ships. As at the Nile the risks Nelson took were enormous; he had not only to negotiate a difficult narrow passage into Copenhagen harbour, but had to face fire from a column of dismasted Danish ships mounting over 600 guns. The battle opened disastrously, three of his ships going aground and the remainder coming under heavy fire from the Danish batteries. Parker, realizing that Nelson had met with mishaps,

ordered the engagement to be broken off; but when Parker's signal was pointed out to Nelson, he raised his telescope to his blind eye and announced 'I really do not see the signal'. An hour later the Danish fire began to slacken, and after another hour the action had closed. Though British losses had been heavy, hardly a Danish ship remained intact, and the Battle of Copenhagen prevented powerful fresh forces joining Napoleon. Soon after, the Treaty of Amiens was signed with France, and Nelson was able to enjoy his first long rest for many years.

When war broke out again 2 years later, Nelson was appointed commander-in-chief in the Mediterranean, hoisting his flag in the *Victory*. Again he blockaded the French fleet at Toulon; but when he learnt that the French had escaped, Nelson began the longest and most dramatic chase in naval history. Crowding on sail, he pursued his quarry across the Atlantic to the West Indies, where, narrowly escaping him, the enemy turned back for France, and having gained a considerable start, they reached safety in Cadiz. Nelson expressed himself 'very miserable', but to have covered nearly 7,000 miles in a little over 8 weeks, after months of wearying blockade duties, was a remarkable feat of sustained endurance. Nelson himself had set foot on shore for only one day in nearly 2 years.

After a period of leave in England, Nelson departed from Portsmouth with a great crowd to bid him farewell, and arrived off Cadiz on September 28. For nearly a month he waited for the combined French and Spanish fleets to emerge. At last, on October 21, 1805, off Cape Trafalgar, the enemy were caught and brought to battle, and there followed the great victory of TRAFALGAR (q.v. Vol. X) which ensured British naval supremacy for more than 50 years. Nelson himself, his backbone shot through, died of wounds soon after Hardy, his flag-captain, reported to him 'a brilliant victory, which is complete'. 'May the great God, whom I worship', he had written, 'grant to my country, and for the benefit of Europe in general, a great and glorious victory; and may no misconduct in any-one tarnish it; and may humanity after victory be the predominant feature in the British fleet.' His last words were 'Thank God, I have done my duty'. At home, news of the death of Nelson was received with profound sorrow. His body was carried home in the battered *Victory*, and 2 months later, on a day of bright winter sunshine, he was buried with great ceremony in St. Paul's Cathedral.

See also Vol. X: SEA WARFARE, HISTORY OF; ROYAL NAVY.

NERO (A.D. 37–68). Nero succeeded his step-father Claudius as Emperor of Rome when, in A.D. 54, his ambitious and unscrupulous mother Agrippina poisoned her husband. At first, while under the influence of his tutor Seneca, he was popular. But in 59 he brutally murdered his mother with whom he had been struggling for power; then he divorced and executed his innocent wife. Seneca, unable to restrain him, left him to the evil influence of his favourites.

Nero thought of himself as an artist rather than an Emperor, his dying words being 'What an artist perishes with me!' He antagonized Roman society by his preference for Greek culture and by his self-display as a poet, actor, musician, and charioteer, which was thought

Alinari

THE EMPEROR NERO
Marble bust. Uffizi Gallery, Florence

unbecoming. So unpopular was he that when a great fire broke out in Rome, Nero was rumoured to have caused it. To avert suspicion he accused the Christians and had hundreds of them murdered. He then taxed the provinces heavily in order that he might rebuild on a lavish scale.

The discovery of a conspiracy against him made Nero so bloodthirsty and suspicious that in 68 the generals in Gaul and Spain revolted, one of them, Galba, declaring himself Emperor. When the Senate, supporting Galba, condemned Nero to death, he fled, and committed suicide outside the city.

In the Eastern Empire Nero's memory was revered because of his enthusiasm for Greek art, but Christian tradition and many historians have painted him as a monster of iniquity.

See also Vol. I: ROMAN CIVILIZATION.

NEVSKI, Alexander (1220–63). This military and religious hero of Russia ruled the principality of NOVGOROD (q.v. Vol. III). He was forced to fight almost continually against German, Swedish, and Lithuanian invaders, and when only 20 won a great victory over the Swedes on the River Neva (where Leningrad stands today), for which he earned the surname of Nevski. Two years later he fought a famous battle against the Germans over the frozen lake Peipus. Other great victories over the Teutonic knights (*see* KNIGHTS, ORDERS OF, Vol. I) made his territory secure.

Large parts of Russia were then under the domination of the TARTARS (q.v. Vol. I), who had invaded Europe under GENGHIS KHAN (q.v.). There were constant threats of war, generally about the tribute-money which the Russians had to pay. Nevski devoted the rest of his life to teaching his people to live at peace with the Tartars. Finally, he himself journeyed to the great Tartar Khan, and by personal intervention managed to preserve peace. On the return journey he died. His people venerated him so much that he was made a Saint. PETER THE GREAT (q.v.), 400 years later, built a magnificent monastery in his memory on the banks of the Neva, and instituted a knightly order of Alexander Nevski. The Soviet have revived this order, and award it to commanders of the Red Army.

See also Vol. I: RUSSIANS.

NEWMAN, John Henry (1801–90). In the second quarter of the 19th century there began in the CHURCH OF ENGLAND (q.v.) what is called the Oxford Movement, because most of its leaders came from Oxford. This group of people, of whom Newman was the most conspicuous, included Edward Pusey, John Keble, and, to a lesser extent, Henry Manning. Newman was brought up in a religious but rather Calvinistic home; he revealed early in life that mystical tendency which led him to regard God and the spiritual world as the most real of all things. He went to Oxford, and in 1822 became a Fellow of Oriel College. He was ordained in 1824, and in 1828 became Vicar of St. Mary's, the University church.

These were the days when 'reform' was in the air, both political and ecclesiastical. At Oxford Newman grew out of the rather narrow teachings of his youth, and came to believe that the Church was a divine society, whose creeds, liturgical services, and regularly ordained bishops and priests were necessary to its existence. He felt that the Church of England needed rousing out of its indifference to these matters. In 1827 Keble published a book of poems, *The Christian Year*, in order to revive that personal holiness which he, like Newman, felt to be lacking. Keble and Newman met at Oxford and became close friends.

In July 1833 Keble preached a sermon at Oxford on 'National Apostasy' which became famous for starting off what was later called the Tractarian movement. Several friends gathered together and began to write a series of pamphlets called *Tracts for the Times*. Newman wrote the first, and later Keble and Pusey wrote others. These pamphlets, defending the Catholic character of the Church of England, were scholarly in form and intended chiefly for the clergy. At the same time Newman preached a series of famous sermons at St. Mary's, which vigorously reinforced the message of the tracts and had a tremendous influence.

During this time Newman began to have doubts about the position of the Church of England. The world-wide nature and the long unbroken history of the Church of Rome, its clear doctrine and, as he saw it, its holiness appealed more and more to him. In 1841 he wrote the famous Tract 90, in which he set out to claim that the Church of England's Thirty-nine Articles, to which all clergy must agree, although anti-Roman when casually read, were really designed to condemn not the ancient Catholic doctrines themselves but medieval Roman corruptions of them. This tract provoked an explosion of indignation, which brought the *Tracts for the Times* to an end. On all hands Newman was attacked. He resigned from St. Mary's in 1843. Finally, after 3 years of inner conflict which gradually changed into calm certainty, he was received into the Roman Catholic Church. Newman's conversion broke up the original Oxford Movement, and it was largely due to Pusey's loyalty and determination that the Anglo-Catholic movement continued without going over to Rome, though later Manning, afterwards Cardinal Manning, and several other leading figures followed Newman.

After a visit to Rome for study and ordination, Newman was made head of the Oratory of St. Philip Neri in Birmingham, where he spent most of the rest of his long life. An attack by Charles KINGSLEY (q.v.), suggesting that the Church of Rome, and Newman also, did not value truth for its own sake, led him to write his *Apologia*, describing his spiritual pilgrimage. This book did much to reinstate Newman in the regard of English people. In 1878 he was made a Cardinal. He wrote a number of theological works,

Oriel College, Oxford
JOHN HENRY NEWMAN
Engraving after the painting by Sir W. C. Ross

though the work most likely to give him immortality is *The Dream of Gerontius*, a poem on death and judgement, which ELGAR's music (q.v.) has helped to make known. Newman is also the author of the hymn *Lead, Kindly Light*, written in 1832 when he was journeying home after a dangerous illness in Sicily.

NEWTON, Sir Isaac (1642–1727). Newton, perhaps the greatest scientist of all time, was born on Christmas Day, 1642, at the little village of Woolsthorpe, near Grantham, in Lincolnshire. His father, a farmer, died before he was born; his mother was a woman of intelligence and character for whom Newton retained a great affection all his life. But on neither side of the family had there been anyone of outstanding brilliance. Newton's schooldays were not remarkable. At 18 he went to Trinity College, Cambridge, to study mathematics, taking his degree in 1665. Then, the University being closed because of the danger of plague, Newton went home to Woolsthorpe for a period of 18 months: a most significant period, for during that time Newton, between the ages of 22 and 24, made his three great discoveries—the dis-

covery of the differential CALCULUS (q.v. Vol. VIII), of the nature of white LIGHT, and of the laws governing the forces of GRAVITATION (qq.v. Vol. III). These three tremendous discoveries have altered the course of human thought and have influenced the course of science from that day until our own. Newton's greatest work was actually done or in mind before he was known in the world at all, and before he had had an opportunity of meeting any of the great men of science of his day. He soon gained recognition, however, and was elected Professor of Mathematics at Cambridge before he was 27.

Newton had always been interested in the problem of light. Most people have seen the colours of the rainbow reflected in a drop of dew or from an edge of cut glass; but it was Newton who, by his experiments, showed how ordinary white light is made up of these various colours (*see* COLOUR, Vol. III). Connected with these experiments was his work on LENSES, which he ground himself, and his experiments with TELESCOPES (qq.v. Vol. VIII). He made his own reflecting telescope, and later made a replica for the Royal Society, which is still one of their most treasured possessions. Today, two of the mightiest telescopes in the world, those on Mount Wilson and Mount Palomar in the United States, are made on the very same principle. In 1704 Newton collected together all his papers on light, many of which had been read to the Royal Society, and published them in a book called *Opticks*.

Through his work on gravitation, he discovered the laws governing the movements of the PLANETS round the sun; the action of the moon on the TIDES; how to predict the courses of COMETS (qq.v. Vol. III), and many other things. One day, when Newton was an old man, sitting drinking tea with the antiquarian Stukeley in the orchard of his house in Kensington, he told how the idea which led to these discoveries first came to him. 'It was occasion'd', Stukeley records, 'by the fall of an apple, as he sat in a contemplative mood. Why should that apple always descend perpendicularly to the ground, thought he to himself? Why should it not go sideways or upwards, but constantly to the earth's centre? Assuredly, the reason is, that the earth draws it. . . . And thus by degrees he began to apply this property of gravitation to the motion of the earth and of the heavenly bodys . . . and thus he unfolded the Universe.'

LORENZO DE MEDICI

Detail from the fresco of the Adoration of the Magi by Benozzo Gozzoli in the Medici Palace, Florence. Lorenzo is portrayed as one of the Kings, and other members of the family are included in the fresco

The greatness and originality of Newton's genius lay in his power of seeing beyond the simple happening to its farthest implications. An apple falling was no unusual event, but only Newton drew from this sight the inspiration and practical demonstration which led to a great scientific discovery. Up to Newton's day, explanations of scientific phenomena were usually mere general speculation. Newton, the first great scientist in the modern sense, sought to establish simple laws which agreed with what actually happened, and his theories, to satisfy him, had to be capable of exact mathematical proof.

Newton's greatest work, the *Principia*, embodying all his work on gravitation, might never have been written or published but for his friend, the astronomer Halley. Apparently, Sir Christopher Wren offered a 40*s.* book to his friends Halley and Hooke if either of them could produce a mathematical proof for a complicated problem concerning the motion of the planets. Neither could. Halley went up to Cambridge to ask Newton, who immediately gave the correct answer, but when asked for the calculation could not find it. He found it afterwards, or re-worked it; but it is typical of Newton's astounding indifference to the world's opinion that he could work out one of the fundamental problems of science and never bother to tell anyone or keep the proof. Halley urged Newton to work out his results fully, and publish them, and finally in 1687 Newton sent to the Royal Society for publication the manuscript (which they still have) of the greatest single work of science in the world and the supreme achievement of Newton's genius—the *Principia*.

Newton's secretary, also called Newton although no relation, has left some account of him. 'His carriage then was very meek, sedate and humble, never seemingly angry, of profound thought, his countenance mild, pleasant and comely.' He records also that Newton rarely laughed, and took no exercise except sometimes a brief turn or two in the garden of Trinity College, from which he would break off suddenly to dash up to his room where, without troubling to sit down, he would start making notes on some idea which had just occurred to him. He never bothered about eating or drinking, often forgetting his meals altogether and, when reminded, taking a mouthful or two standing. He was unconcerned about his clothes and appear-

Royal Society

NEWTON'S REFLECTING TELESCOPE

ance, but he enjoyed the few parties he went to and would return hospitality most generously. He was constantly at work in his laboratory, often staying up all night over one of his experiments.

When he was 45, the fatigue of frequent journeys to London occasioned by his being member of Parliament for Cambridge University, together with grief at his mother's death, caused Newton to have a nervous breakdown. In one of his periodic moods of reaction against science, he grew more than usually depressed and eccentric, and he became morose and extremely suspicious of even his best friends. But within 4 years he was so well recovered that when a famous Swiss mathematician published two problems as a challenge to European mathematicians, Newton received the problems one day and solved them the next. His solutions were sent anonymously to the challenger, who immediately recognized them as Newton's from the unmistakable style. Some time later LEIBNIZ (q.v.), another famous mathematician, set a problem, and this Newton solved between afternoon and bedtime.

In 1696, through the good offices of Charles

Montague (later Lord Halifax), a great friend and admirer, Newton was appointed Warden of the Mint at a salary of £500–£600 a year, a very considerable sum in those days. Three years later he became Master of the Mint, and responsible for an urgently needed reform of the coinage. In this position he showed himself both practical and efficient.

By 1700 Newton was famous and highly respected, with many friends at court and in the government. He lived in Jermyn Street, and his niece Catherine Barton, a great beauty and a wit, ran his household for him. Many fashionable and distinguished men came to the house. In 1703 he became President of the Royal Society, and in 1705 he was knighted by Queen Anne. Not long afterwards he moved out of London to the village of Kensington for the benefit of the country air. When Newton was an old man he still kept up his interest in Lincolnshire, and Stukeley tells how he attended a Lincolnshire feast held at a London tavern. The important guests upstairs, hearing that Newton was sitting below, sent to ask him to come up to the chief room. Stukeley, who was with him, sent back a message that 'the chief room was where Sir Isaac Newton was. Upon which the upper room was immediately left to the ordinary company, and the better sort came to us.'

Newton died when he was 84, and was buried in Westminster Abbey, where his monument is today.

There are few records of Newton's personal life. He shunned publicity, and evidently would have been content to have lived and died without communicating a single one of his discoveries to his contemporaries. Whenever he was persuaded to speak or write of them he found himself involved in argument and dispute, which he detested. He deliberately made the *Principia* difficult in order 'to avoid being bated by little smatterers in mathematics'—and good mathematicians today still find the book difficult. He quarrelled violently with several famous men of his day, and yet he was not ungenerous and was the first to recognize his own debt to the work of his predecessors: 'If I have seen further than most men it is by standing on the shoulders of giants.' In his old age his mind, as active and original as ever, turned chiefly towards theology and chronology.

Newton was not only a great creative genius but also a scholar and a man of considerable practical and administrative ability; yet only a little while before his death he wrote, in words which show that like all truly great men he had remained humble, and which show also that he was poet and mystic as well as man of science: 'I do not know what I may appear to the world; but to myself I seem to have been only like a boy, playing on the sea shore, and diverting myself in now and then finding a smoother pebble or a prettier shell than ordinary, whilst the great ocean of truth lay all undiscovered before me.'

Warburg Institute

SIR ISAAC NEWTON

Monument designed by William Kent and executed by J. M. Rysbrack. Westminster Abbey

NIETZSCHE, Friedrich Wilhelm (1844–1900). This German philosopher was the son of a Lutheran pastor in Saxony who died when his son was only 4. Nietzsche's upbringing consequently suffered from an excess of feminine care which further weakened his naturally unstable temperament. His precocious brilliance secured him the chair of Philology at Basle in 1868; but he was unsuited for university life, and resigned in 1879. He made many friends, among whom was the composer WAGNER (q.v.); but he quarrelled with them all. He possessed the type of character which exalts instinct against reason and wild romance against ordered life. He divided mankind into a small 'master-class' and a large 'herd', and he regarded it as his mission to prepare the way for the 'superman'. Men such as Napoleon and Frederick the Great, possessing the energy of greatness, were his heroes. All his works are collections of aphorisms on the subject of power. He attacks teachers such as SOCRATES (q.v.) and JESUS (q.v. Vol. I) as preaching 'the virtues of the weak'. The 'master-class', he said, must not be peaceful and compassionate, but must fight, lie, be cruel, and unrestrained—a doctrine which became part of the Nazi culture (see TOTALITARIANISM, Vol. X), after Nietzsche's death. His contempt for women was as violent as his hatred of religion. In *Beyond Good and Evil* he attempts to change human ideas of what is good and bad. About 1889, the mental stress which Nietzsche endured, coupled with his loneliness, caused his mind to break down, and for the last 12 years of his life he was mad.

See also Vol. X: TOTALITARIANISM.

NIGHTINGALE, Florence (1820–1910).

The creator of modern nursing was born in Florence while her parents were on a visit to Italy. She and her sister were brought up partly at Lea Hurst in Derbyshire and partly at Embley in Hampshire. Her parents were wealthy, and when young, Florence was much admired in London society for her beauty and her wit. Even so, from the age of 17, she felt that she was called to serve God in a special way, and it soon became clear to her that her vocation was to nurse the sick.

Her parents were horrified when she asked permission to enter a hospital for training. The hospitals of those days were filthy, fever-ridden places, and most of the nurses were ignorant and drunken. It was an unheard-of thing for an educated young woman to wish to be a nurse. Florence had to give up her wish to train, and instead she did what nursing she could in the

National Portrait Gallery

FLORENCE NIGHTINGALE (SEATED), AGED ABOUT SIXTEEN, AND HER SISTER PARTHENOPE
Water-colour by William White

villages near her home, and studied hospital reports when she could get them. She travelled abroad with friends, visiting hospitals in many places, and in 1851 she managed to train for 3 months in a hospital run on model lines at Kaiserwerth, in Germany.

When their daughter had refused a most suitable proposal of marriage for no other reason than that she meant to be a nurse, the Nightingales reluctantly accepted the fact that nothing would keep her from her career. In 1853 Florence became Lady Superintendent of the Institute for Sick Gentlewomen in Harley Street, London.

In 1854 Britain was involved in the CRIMEAN WAR against Russia (q.v. Vol. X). Horrifying reports reached England about the British army hospital at Scutari, near Constantinople, to which thousands of sick and wounded were sent from the Crimean battlefields. The building was not properly equipped, and there were only untrained medical orderlies to nurse the patients. Sidney Herbert, the Secretary of State for War, an old friend of Florence Nightingale's, wrote to ask her if she would take a party of nurses out

THE MILITARY HOSPITAL AT SCUTARI

Engraving from the *Illustrated London News*, December 1854

to Scutari, and his letter crossed with one from her offering to go.

In November 1854 she arrived at the hospital with about thirty nurses. They found terrible conditions: there were no medicines, no beds, and no bedding; the huge building was filthy, and desperately overcrowded; there was no proper drainage system, and the smell was frightful; there was no hot water. Worst of all, the doctors had no authority to make the government departments provide what was needed.

Florence Nightingale was received with suspicion. Nurses were unheard-of in a military hospital; the doctors thought they would only be a nuisance. But she had brought medical supplies with her, she had a fund of money raised by *The Times* at her disposal, and she was not afraid of regulations. She provided medicines, blankets, shirts, soap, and scrubbing-brushes. By her orders, an entire wing of the hospital was repaired and equipped in time to receive 800 new patients. As well as carrying out her enormous task of organization, Florence Nightingale nursed the worst cases herself. She was known to spend 24 hours at a stretch on her feet in the wards. At night she made her rounds with a lantern, to attend to the patients. The soldiers worshipped her, calling her 'The Lady with the Lamp'. The doctors now turned to her for everything they needed.

Meanwhile the army in the Crimea was desperately short of supplies and winter clothing, and in consequence thousands of sick men

poured into the hospitals. In January 1855 there were 12,000 men in Scutari and 42 per cent. of them died. Florence Nightingale's masterly organization and determined insistence in getting her own way greatly improved conditions, and after the drainage and water supply had been attended to the death-rate began to fall immediately. By June it was only 2 per cent.

Later, Florence Nightingale travelled through the Crimea fitting out and organizing hospitals. The physical strain was terrific, and she fell desperately ill; but when she recovered, though her friends urged her to go home, she insisted on returning to work. She extended her activities by providing recreation rooms, books, and lectures for the convalescents, and later for soldiers who were well. Their officers accused her of 'spoiling the brutes', but, as a result, drunkenness among the men decreased, and they began to save their pay and to send home their savings through a scheme suggested by her.

When peace came in September 1855, she did not leave Scutari until the hospital was empty. When she came home the nation longed to honour her publicly, but she would not allow it. In 1856 she was received by Queen Victoria and the Prince Consort, who were much impressed by 'her powerful clear head and simple modest manner' and by her suggestions for improving the army hospital system. Ill and exhausted as she was from 2 years of terrible strain and hardship, she yet determined to start new work— the improvement of conditions in the army, so that the death-rate among the troops in peace-time should not be twice the civilian rate.

Supported by the Queen, a Royal Commission with Sidney Herbert as chairman was set up to inquire into the health of the troops. Florence Nightingale worked for it night and day, collecting information and drafting plans for reform, the house in which she lived being nicknamed 'The Little War Office'. Her aunt, who lived with her, wrote, 'She alone has both the smallest details at her fingers' ends and the great general view of the whole.'

In 1857 her health collapsed entirely, but after a short rest she was back at work again. Health, comfort, friends, were all sacrificed to her task, and when she was too ill to travel she directed reforms in hospitals and barracks all over England from her London home. Gradually many of the things she fought for were achieved. Barracks and army hospitals improved, and an

Army Medical School was founded. Many army chiefs thought her ideas molly-coddling, but by 1861 the death-rate in the army had been halved. In 1861 Sidney Herbert, her faithful friend and supporter, died, worn out with overwork. His death was a severe loss; but Florence Nightingale continued to advise the army on health and sanitation, and also did a great deal of important work for Indian Public Health.

In 1860 a sum of £50,000, which had been collected in gratitude for her services in the Crimea, was used to found the Nightingale Training School for Nurses attached to St Thomas's Hospital, London. The training, which was planned by Florence Nightingale, set a new standard of discipline, good behaviour, and skill in nursing. Soon hospitals all over the country were asking for Nightingale nurses, and as the years passed nursing became established as an honourable profession for women of every class.

During the second half of her life Florence Nightingale was a semi-invalid, often bed-ridden for months at a time. But statesmen, nurses, and viceroys of India came to her house in South Street, Mayfair, to consult her; letters arrived from all over the world asking her advice on hospital affairs. As she grew older the desperate, often bitter, energy that had possessed her changed to serenity. She continued to work for many years, until first her eyesight faded, and then her memory. In 1907 the King awarded her the Order of Merit. Her only comment was, 'Too kind, too kind.' Three years later she died.

See also Vol. X: HOSPITALS.
See also Vol. XI: NURSING.

NIJINSKY, Vaslav (1890–1950). Nijinsky, the most famous male ballet dancer, was born in Russia of Polish parents, both of whom had been dancers. He trained at the Imperial Ballet School in St. Petersburg, then the capital of Russia, and immediately attracted attention. But it was in Paris, when dancing with Diaghileff's Russian Ballet Company, that he became famous. His daring leap out of the window in *Le Spectre de la Rose* set the world talking, and so great was his popularity that his dresser is said to have made a small fortune by selling the rose petals off his costume. Diaghileff said of him 'so light is Nijinsky that he looks like a butterfly painted on the ceiling'. In contrast to this

aerial dancing he added to his reputation by his wonderful portrayal of the tragic figure of the puppet Petrouchka in Fokine's ballet of that name. In 1912 Nijinsky started to design ballets himself, and *L'Après-midi d'un faune* (with Debussy's music) and *Le Sacre du Printemps* (with Stravinsky's music)—works right outside the then accepted tradition of ballet—caused such stir and controversy that smart people in evening dress shouted insults at one another on the first nights. These incidents served their purpose in drawing attention to the Russian Ballet Nijinsky became a legend during his lifetime, and all sorts of absurd stories began to be circulated—that his legs were shaped like a bird's, or that he could leap into the air and remain there. The truth was that Nijinsky was so great an artist that he could create such illusions.

Nijinsky's career only lasted for a few years and had a tragic ending. During the First World War, after undergoing the hardships of internment, he lost his reason. He was nursed by a devoted wife. Then, in 1945, he was caught again by the horrors of war and was rescued by the Russian army in Hungary. He died in London in 1950 and is buried in Paris. Although his career was so short, the legend that grew up round him has persisted; and largely through Nijinsky the male dancer has come into his own again.

See also DIAGHILEFF.
See also Vol. IX: BALLET.

NOBEL, Alfred Bernhard (1833–96). This Swedish chemist, who founded the famous Nobel prizes, was the son of an explosives manufacturer. He spent most of his life studying explosives, and invented dynamite, blasting gelatine, and the first smokeless explosive—the forerunner of the modern cordite cartridge (*see* EXPLOSIVES, Vol. VIII). He made a great fortune from these inventions and from investments in Russian oilfields and, as he had no family, he left the money in trust to found five international money prizes. Four of these prizes are awarded each year to the person or persons selected by Swedish learned societies as having done the best work during the year in physics, chemistry, medicine, and literature. The fifth, the peace prize, is awarded to the person chosen by the Norwegian Parliament as having best served the cause of peace.

O

OATES, L. E. G. (1880–1912), Explorer, *see* SCOTT, R. F.

O'CONNELL, Daniel (1775–1847). 'The Liberator', as this great Irish patriot was called in Ireland, was a boisterous, good-humoured, hard-swearing lawyer who devoted his life to political agitation in the hope of removing the worst injustices of British rule in Ireland.

O'Connell's two great ambitions were to win emancipation for Irish Catholics (who were denied all political privileges) and to abolish the union with England, under a single Parliament, which had been imposed on the country in 1798. As the result of agitation in Ireland by the Cauldric Association which O'Connell organized, the Catholic Emancipation Bill was passed in 1829. In an attempt to win independence for his country O'Connell then travelled all over Ireland, addressing crowded meetings with great eloquence. In 1843 Peel, the British Prime Minister, declared one of these proposed meetings illegal; despite this O'Connell attended the meeting, and was arrested and sentenced to imprisonment, though the conviction was later set aside.

In 1845–6 the Irish potato crop failed, and the disastrous FAMINE (q.v. Vol. VI) which followed turned the attention of Irishmen away from politics. At the height of the famine O'Connell died on his way to Rome, and the movement for independence temporarily collapsed, to be renewed some 30 years later by PARNELL (q.v.).

Meade Collection

O'CONNELL CARICATURED AS A NAUGHTY BOY

O'Connell was the *enfant terrible* of the politics of his time. Caricature by John Doyle

OVID (43 B.C.–A.D. 17). Publius Ovidus Naso was a Roman poet who came from a well-to-do family of hereditary land-owners, and his father, intending him for the law, sent him to Rome to be educated.

As a young man he travelled to Greece, Asia Minor, and Sicily. He came back to Rome at the time of the first Emperor AUGUSTUS (q.v.), and took his place in a society which was almost entirely pleasure-seeking and extremely free-living. The young poet, who was gay, volatile, and amiable, wrote his first poem, the *Ars Amatoria*, for just such a society. Unluckily Augustus, angered by a scandalous love-affair of his daughter Julia, disapproved of it strongly, and 10 years later, on the pretext of this poem and of some other unnamed indiscretion, Ovid was banished to Tomi at the mouth of the Danube. He had, however, already written the poem by which he is best remembered, the *Metamorphoses*. It is a long poem telling the stories of all kinds of mythical transformations, or changes of shape, such as Jupiter's transformation into a bull or a shower of gold. The last story is of Julius Caesar's transformation into a star. This poem, full of romantic and lively stories, had a great influence upon the poets of the Renaissance in Italy and in England, when Ovid's poetry was better known and more admired even than VIRGIL's (q.v.). Ovid in his miserable exile at Tomi wrote his elegies, the *Tristia*; but he was never recalled, and after 8 years died there. Ovid, with Catullus and Propertius, stands in Roman literature as a romantic, much as Byron, Shelley, and Keats do in our own.

See also Vol. XII: LATIN LITERATURE; ELEGY.

OWEN, Robert (1771–1858). Owen, the social prophet and leading reformer of the early 19th century, was a man with ideas far ahead of his time. He devised schemes to remedy evils which other people accepted as inevitable—poverty, overcrowding, drunkenness, long working hours in bad conditions, the exploitation of children, and the absence of schools. He became, by his own efforts, a successful and rich factory owner, and so could put some of his theories into practice, and consequently greatly influence public opinion.

Owen, the son of a small tradesman in Newtown, Montgomeryshire, had an early history typical of his class: a brief schooling till he was 9, an early start at work, and a period of hardship and struggle. He went to Manchester at a time when the cotton industry was developing; and when very young became manager of a spinning-mill employing 500 workers. He greatly increased his employer's profits, in spite of his opinion that his employer paid more attention to his 'dead' than to his 'living' machinery. Owen later became partner and manager of a group of Manchester mills. He fell in love with the daughter of a millionaire from New Lanark, near Glasgow, so he persuaded his Manchester partner to buy the New Lanark mill. He married the girl and himself settled there as manager and part-owner.

Owen now saw a chance of putting into practice his ideas on social and economic reform. Of his 2,000 employees, some 500 were pauper children who had been sent there at the age of 5 or 6 years as Poor Law apprentices from parish workhouses (*see* CHILD WELFARE, Vol. X). Owen ceased employing children under 10, and reduced the working day for all his workers to 10½ hours. He started welfare schemes to help his people to live better and healthier lives, and opened a shop at which they could buy sound goods at low prices. He set up some of the first infant schools in the country, making a rule, startling at that time, that no child should be

Meade Collection

ROBERT OWEN AS A YOUNG MAN

Engraving from *The Percy Anecdotes*, 1821, which were dedicated to Owen

beaten in school. Owen also won his workers' allegiance by a characteristic act: while the mill was closed because of an American embargo on the export of raw cotton, Owen continued—at a cost of over £7,000—to pay full wages. His partners soon began to object to his schemes, and Owen realized that if he wished to carry on his social work he would have to buy out the partners. He drafted and published a pamphlet, *A New View of Society*, and soon obtained from sympathizers, including Jeremy BENTHAM (q.v.), enough money to purchase the business outright. A new agreement was signed making the profits of the business available for general educational schemes and for the improvement of the workers' conditions.

New Lanark and its model village soon became famous in Europe and America, and all kinds of eminent people became interested in Owen's social experiments. The exiled Napoleon wrote for information, and a future Emperor of Russia visited the mill. The Duke of Kent, father of Queen Victoria, was also a supporter.

Owen believed that human character was not inborn but formed by circumstances and environment, so that if the environment could be improved the person would also improve. There are objections to such a doctrine, but in Owen's own mills it seemed to work. Wishing to see his welfare schemes extended to the whole country, he called a meeting of manufacturers to press for parliamentary legislation limiting children's hours of work; this resulted in the Factory Act of 1819. Owen went on a triumphal progress of lectures and conferences in Europe, where he was honoured by most of the political and industrial leaders of the time.

After 1819, Owen's schemes, which had hitherto been practical and successful, became more idealistic and less realistic. He had been much struck by a scheme for collective industry described by a 17th-century Quaker, John Bellers; and he started a small experimental venture of the same kind near Glasgow. His idea was that a community of about 1,200 people should settle on a large plot of land and live and work on primitive communistic lines. There should be one large living centre in which all work should be done in common, and the children should belong to and be brought up by the community, not by their parents.

In 1824 he heard of a colony of German emigrants who had settled in Indiana, U.S.A., in a place they called New Harmony. The next year he bought this village with 20,000 acres of land, in order to found another experimental communal colony. The scheme broke down because the colony contained too many restless, unhappy people whose past misfortunes had left them slack and useless. The enterprising and hard-working members soon became discontented because they received only the same share of the profits as those who did not work. In 1828 Owen abandoned the scheme, having lost altogether £40,000 on it.

About the same time Owen began to offend public opinion and made enemies of his supporters by fiercely attacking religion and all organized Churches. This and the apparent failure of his practical business sense resulted in contemporaries, such as COBBETT (q.v.) who shared many of his views, treating him with ridicule or shunning him as a champion of immorality.

On his return to England, Owen quarrelled with his partners at New Lanark, and left the mills. He came to London and gave himself wholly to political and social propaganda. The word SOCIALISM (q.v. Vol. X) first arose in an organization founded by him in 1835. In his remaining years he greatly assisted the early movements to organize CO-OPERATIVE SOCIETIES (q.v. Vol. VII).

From a distance of 100 years, modern sociologists and historians look back on Owen as one of the major social prophets of his period, remembering, not his errors, but his humane and highly successful work as a factory employer, his part in promoting the Factory Acts, and his help in launching nation-wide trade unions and the vast co-operative trading movement.

See also Vol. VII: INDUSTRIAL REVOLUTION; CO-OPERATIVE SOCIETIES; TRADE UNIONS.
See also Vol. X: SOCIALISM; CHILD WELFARE.

P

PADEREWSKI, **Ignace Jan** (1860–1941). This famous pianist and composer was also a Polish statesman and patriot. There have been many famous pianists—Liszt, Rubinstein, Busoni, and Rachmaninoff—but none was so popular in England as Paderewski. He had been a wonder-child as pianist and composer, but did not come forward as a performer until he was 27. From then on he was welcomed everywhere, partly for his powerful technique and his lovely

touch in tender music, partly because his Minuet in G was known and played everywhere, and partly because he cut a striking figure with his long hair and romantic appearance. Though he composed many pieces besides the minuet, including a symphony and many piano pieces, only the minuet is famous.

During the First World War Paderewski travelled in Britain, America, and elsewhere, pleading that Poland should no longer be divided and the Poles subjects of the German, Austrian, and Russian Empires, but that Poland should again become independent. When his country was freed at the end of the war he became its first Prime Minister. When the Germans and Russians occupied Poland at the start of the Second World War, Paderewski vowed not to play the piano until Poland was free. He died before the end of the war.

See also Vol. I: POLES.

PAINE, **Thomas** (1737–1809). Paine, the son of a Quaker workman, after a meagre education and a series of lost jobs, abandoned his debts in England and became a political journalist in America. He returned to England in 1787, and later published *The Rights of Man*, in answer to BURKE's (q.v.) *Reflections on the French Revolution*. Paine's book declared that all hereditary government by king or lords was 'an imposition on mankind', and that the people, the source of all power, should be governed only by their chosen representatives.

At the time when the terrible example of the FRENCH REVOLUTION (q.v. Vol. X) was making everyone afraid of revolutionary ideas, William PITT (q.v.), the Prime Minister, said, 'Tom Paine is quite in the right, but what am I to do? As things are, if I were to encourage Tom Paine's opinions we should have a bloody revolution.' As it was, Paine had to flee to France to escape a trial for treason, and was never able to return to his own country. He died in New York.

The Rights of Man had an enormous circulation in spite of the government's attempts to suppress it. It passed secretly from hand to hand in the factories and industrial slums of Britain's great cities, and for the next 40 years it was the bible of the working-class movement.

See also Vol. X: CHARTISM.

PADEREWSKI AS A YOUNG MAN
Caricature from *Vanity Fair*, 1899

PALESTRINA, **Giovanni da** (1525–94), *see* Vol. XII: MUSIC, HISTORY OF, Section 3.

Alinari

THE VILLA ROTONDA, VICENZA, DESIGNED BY PALLADIO

PALLADIO, Andrea (1518–80). This Italian architect, born at Vicenza in north Italy, worked chiefly in and around Venice. Like other architects of the RENAISSANCE (q.v. Vol. I), he modelled his style on that of ancient Roman buildings, studying the ruins in Rome and the books of the Roman architect Vitruvius. He followed these models closely in the details of his buildings, though he used the classic forms in a new way. For instance, he used columns of different sizes and kinds on one building, some running the whole height of the building, others only one storey high, and others smaller still to frame windows. In Roman buildings each storey has its own kind of column, or 'order' (*see* ORDERS OF ARCHITECTURE, Vol. XII).

Palladio built churches and palaces, but his most original buildings were the villas designed as country residences for Venetian nobles. It was these which chiefly impressed the 17th-century English architect Inigo JONES (q.v.) and the early 18th-century English architects who so closely imitated Palladio's work that their style is called Palladian. Inigo Jones published a translation of Palladio's book on architecture.

See also Vol. XII: CLASSICAL ART.

PALMERSTON, Viscount (1784–1865). Palmerston, who held ministerial office for 45 years, represents the confidence of Victorian Britain at the peak of her power. He gave his name to his own brand of foreign policy, which sought to uphold Liberalism abroad and to protect British interests in every corner of the world. His opponents, however, claimed that his policy involved unwarrantable interference in the affairs of foreign governments, and brought the country to the brink of war.

Palmerston, as an Irish peer, did not sit in the House of Lords but spent all his political life as a member of the House of Commons. When he was 25 he became Secretary at War in the Tory Government, and was responsible for the army's finances in the last years of the NAPOLEONIC WARS (q.v. Vol. X). In 1830, having broken with the Tories, he became the Whig Foreign Secretary, and with two intervals remained in charge of foreign policy for 16 years. His first great success was the setting up of Belgium as an independent State, its neutrality guaranteed by the Great Powers, as a buffer against French expansion. Sympathetic with liberal governments abroad, he criticized the repressive policies of Russia, Prussia, and Austria, and made alliances with the liberal governments in Spain and Portugal. In 1848 the revolutions which flared up in almost every country in Europe gave Palmerston further opportunities to aid

Liberalism, especially in Italy and Hungary, where risings against Austrian rule were taking place.

In 1850 Palmerston's aggressive policy was violently attacked in the House of Commons. Don Pacifico, a British subject living in Greece, had made extravagant demands to the Greek Government for compensation after a mob had pillaged his house. Palmerston supported Don Pacifico and when the Greek Government appeared unwilling to pay the large sums Pacifico demanded, Palmerston sent the British fleet to blockade the port of Athens. The angry debate that followed this incident ranged over every aspect of Palmerston's foreign policy, and his opponents included some of the ablest speakers of the day—PEEL, GLADSTONE, DISRAELI, COBDEN (qq.v.). Palmerston defended himself in the greatest speech of his life, which lasted nearly 5 hours from 'the dusk of one day to the dawn of the next', and won a resounding vote of confidence. In his speech Palmerston declared that just as a Roman need only say 'civis Romanus sum' ('I am a Roman citizen') to be secure under the majesty of Rome, so a British subject should find the long arm of Britain stretching out to protect him from injustice wherever he might be.

A year later, however, Palmerston's struggle with Queen VICTORIA (q.v.), who objected to his independent methods and aggressive temper, reached a climax when he gave the British Government's recognition of a change of government in France without the Queen's or the Cabinet's knowledge or authority. He was dismissed, but by this time he was too powerful for any stable government to be formed without him, and a year later he joined a coalition government as Home Secretary. At the height of the CRIMEAN WAR (q.v. Vol. X) public opinion turned to him as the only man capable of leading the country to victory, and at the age of 70 he became Prime Minister.

In 1859 he again became Prime Minister of the first government bearing the name 'Liberal'—a coalition of Whigs, Peelites (see PEEL), and Radicals. A common sympathy for the movement for Italian independence (see CAVOUR) won him the support of Gladstone, previously a bitter critic. The combination of Gladstone's finance and Palmerston's popularity produced 6 years of stable, prosperous government for the first time since the defeat of Peel. It was a period of increasing wealth, domestic harmony, and bounding national confidence, though Palmerston had little real sympathy for reform and held up much of the progressive legislation that his party supported.

Palmerston was a great 'character': bluff, jaunty, always ready for a joke or for an adventure. He was generally liked even by people who disapproved of his policy; and he never took himself too seriously. When he died in office at the age of 81 he was as gay and energetic as ever.

See also Vol. X: POLITICAL PARTIES.

PARK, Mungo (1771–1806).

This pioneer of African exploration was one of the thirteen children of a Scots farmer. His unusual ability procured him education at Edinburgh University as a doctor. After a voyage to the Far East as ship's surgeon, he was asked by the African Association, when only 24, to explore the Niger basin.

Meade Collection

THE YOUNG QUEEN VICTORIA WITH MELBOURNE AND PALMERSTON
Caricature by John Doyle entitled *Susannah and the Elders*

The Association was founded in 1788 to promote exploration in the interests of commerce. Europeans had heard of rich areas around Timbuktu on the middle Niger, but they did not know in which direction the river flowed or where it reached the sea. Major Houghton, the first explorer sent out by the Association, had been murdered by the natives.

Park was strong, enterprising, far-sighted, persevering, and a stern Calvinist, calmly accepting success or failure as ordained by God. In his last letter home before his death he wrote, 'Though all the Europeans who are with me should die, and though I were myself half dead, I would still persevere; and if I could not succeed . . . I would at least die on the Niger.'

His first expedition was undertaken almost single-handed. Riding a horse and wearing a top hat and a blue coat, Park set out from the mouth of the Gambia in June 1795 accompanied by six Negroes who soon died or deserted him It took him over a year of incredible hardships and difficulties with tribesmen to reach the Niger—the first white man to see it. Then he explored its middle course for 300 miles. On his return home he wrote an exciting book, *Travels in the Interior of Africa*, the first reliable account of African tribal life and customs.

For 5 years Park practised as a doctor in Scotland, married, and had a family; then he was appointed leader of another expedition to the Niger. This time he struck inland from the African coast with forty-five Europeans, including soldiers and naval boat-builders. Within three months, when they reached the Niger, thirty-four of the Europeans had died of fever. They succeeded in building a boat, and at length the survivors, now reduced to five (Park, a lieutenant, and three soldiers, one of whom had gone mad) set sail down the mighty river. From this point Park sent back his journal and last letters by a messenger.

What happened next was not discovered until long afterwards. The party sailed 800 miles down the river, beset by dangerous rapids and attacked by hostile natives. During this time the mad soldier and another died. Then, at the Busa rapids, while under native attack, the boat was wrecked, and all were drowned.

It was many years before other explorers succeeded in completing Park's work.

See also Vol. III: AFRICA.
See also Vol. IV: TRAVEL BOOKS AND GUIDE BOOKS.

PARNELL, Charles Stewart (1846–91). Parnell continued the struggle, begun by O'CONNELL (q.v.), to win independence for Ireland. Though a Protestant he was supported, at first, by the Irish Catholics.

As a member of Parliament Parnell organized the Irish members of the House of Commons into a compact, disciplined party. By deliberately obstructive tactics he forced the House into wearisome all-night sittings, often ending in stormy scenes and even outbreaks of violence. On one occasion, after a particularly bitter debate, he was ejected from the House. In 1881 he was for a time imprisoned. In 1882 Irish terrorists murdered the Chief Secretary and Under-Secretary for Ireland as they were walking across Phoenix Park in Dublin. Parnell was honestly horrified by the Phoenix Park murders, with which he dissociated himself in the House of Commons. Even more severe measures were taken against crime in Ireland, but GLADSTONE (q.v.) began to realize that the only solution was Home Rule.

The struggle continued for years. In 1886 with Parnell's support Gladstone brought before the House of Commons a Bill giving Ireland limited Home Rule; but Gladstone's party was divided and the Bill rejected. Had the alliance between Parnell and Gladstone continued, the Bill might have been passed at the second attempt. But Parnell became involved in a sensational divorce suit, and Gladstone, a High Churchman, and with him most of the leaders of the Liberal party, turned against him, and his influence vanished. When Parnell died suddenly a few months later, his funeral was attended by a great crowd of 200,000 people.

PASCAL, Blaise (1623–62). Pascal was born at Clermont-Ferrand in central France, but he lived in Paris for most of his life. His genius first showed itself in mathematics when at 16 he composed an original treatise on conic sections. Also, seeing his father spending hours over his accounts, Pascal thought out and constructed the first calculating machine. He then began to experiment in physics, and might well have become a scientist of the first rank.

But Pascal, educated in the Catholic religion, believed that neither science nor philosophy could answer the questionings of the soul, for above the visible world was a supernatural one which could only be apprehended by faith.

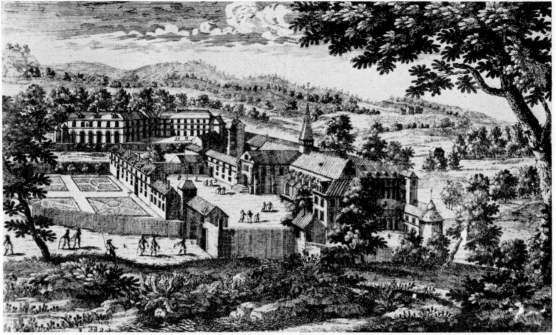

Bibliothèque Nationale, Paris

THE ABBEY OF PORT-ROYAL DES CHAMPS

Pascal frequently visited this convent of Cistercian nuns which was closely connected with the Jansenist movement.
It received lay persons desiring to live in religious solitude

'The heart', Pascal wrote, 'has its reasons which the reason does not know.' In 1646, he read and was much moved by the writings of Bishop Jansen, who stressed personal goodness, the Evangelical rather than the institutional side of religion. Jansenists taught that man was a sinful creature who could do no good without God's grace; this he could not get by his own effort but only by God's gift. The man who has received God's grace will dedicate his life wholly to God.

Pascal went on with his scientific work for a time, but he was sick in body and soul alike. Then, in the night of 23 November 1654, an inward illumination came to him, which he afterwards described. The message which this vision brought to him was 'Forgetfulness of the world, and of everything save God'. Henceforth he was at peace, and religion filled his life.

Inevitable controversies, much mixed up with French politics, arose between the two sections of the Catholic Church, the Jansenists and the Jesuits, the followers of Ignatius LOYOLA (q.v.). Pascal supported the Jansenists by publishing pamphlets called *Provincial Letters*, in which,

writing under an assumed name, he attacked those Jesuit doctrines which he felt were attempting to secure the Church's power rather than God's. The brilliant phrasing and delicate irony of these *Letters* made them eagerly read, and filled the Jesuits with fury.

Pascal wished also to appeal to the many educated people who were estranged from religion; and for this purpose he proposed to write a defence of the Christian faith. He died before the work was finished, but from the notes found among his papers his *Thoughts* were published—the book by which he is now best known. Pascal is a master of epigrammatic writing, able to present in a few words an unforgettable picture. His main subject is man, so great and yet often so vile, whose condition, he claimed, the Christian religion alone can meet and whose true destiny and happiness he can find only in God. Pascal's view of life was one-sided, perhaps because of his constant ill-health; but so deep is his insight and so intense his feeling that we think of him as one of the great spirits of history.

See also Vol. I: CHRISTIAN RELIGION.

Wellcome Collection

LOUIS PASTEUR

THIS PORTRAIT SHOWS PASTEUR IN HIS LABORATORY DURING
THE PERIOD OF HIS WORK ON RABIES

Painting by Edelfeldt

PASTEUR, Louis (1822–95). This French chemist was one of the greatest of modern scientists. His theory of germ life revolutionized medical science and made it possible to cure or to prevent many diseases formerly considered incurable. One result has been the opening up of tropical countries by the conquest of many tropical diseases. His work has also been largely responsible for the tremendous growth of the industries dependent upon food preservation. He spent his life in untiring devotion to the cause of science as the servant of mankind.

Louis Pasteur was born in a little town in the Jura mountains, the son of a tanner, with a passion for self-education. His mother was a hard-working and religious woman, imaginative and sympathetic. His father's greatest hope was that one day his son would be a teacher in a local school; and so with his headmaster's encouragement Louis, at 16, was sent to Paris to train. There he grew so homesick that his father brought him home, but he soon entered the Royal College of Besançon, where he became assistant mathematics master in 1840.

The only special talent which Pasteur had so far revealed was for art, but at Besançon he became enthusiastic about science. He worked hard, and with this new conviction of his need to acquire knowledge, he returned to Paris, took a degree in physics, and at 25 became a doctor of science. Within a year Pasteur published an account of his first important discovery, which helped to establish the new branch of chemistry dealing with the composition of MATTER (q.v. Vol. III), and led to a rapid increase in knowledge of the structure of the chemical molecule.

Hailed as a leading scientist at 26, Pasteur spent 5 years at Strasbourg, teaching and continuing his experiments, and there he married the daughter of the rector of the University. He became professor at the important University of Lille, a city with many large breweries and distilleries, a fact partly responsible for his studies on FERMENTATION (q.v. Vol. II) and thus for his greatest discovery.

Fermentation and similar processes such as putrefaction (rotting) were described in all the textbooks of that time as purely chemical reactions, and any suggestion to the contrary was ridiculed by scientists. Pasteur's researches led him to conclude that these were not chemical but living processes, caused by microscopic living organisms in the air. These 'little animals', as they were sometimes called in the 17th century, were thought to be the result of decomposition, not its cause, and to be examples of spontaneous generation—that is, new life springing from nothing. This belief was challenged by Pasteur, who set up the principle that all life, no matter how small, must spring from living parents (*see* REPRODUCTION IN ANIMALS; REPRODUCTION IN PLANTS, Vol. II).

In 1857, Pasteur published the first of many accounts of his researches. In the same year he was made assistant director of scientific studies of the École Normale in Paris; but though this gave him some opportunity for spreading his scientific ideas, the College gave him no facilities for research, no laboratory, and no grant. So, spending what could be spared for equipment from his meagre salary, Pasteur fitted up a tiny attic in the College as a laboratory. This was so small that he had to enter it on his knees; yet it was there, with his simple and cheap apparatus, that he carried out the numerous ingenious experiments which, aided by his skill and determination in argument, proved his case. In the course of his work he also found that germs can be killed by moderate heat, and from this he devised the process now known as PASTEURIZATION (q.v. Vol. VII) as a means of preventing beer and wine—and later milk—from turning bad. Pasteur's researches also showed that INFECTIOUS DISEASES (q.v. Vol. XI) were caused by living organisms called germs. Working from his discoveries, the English surgeon LISTER (q.v.) was able by the use of antiseptics to counteract the infection of wounds by germs.

Between 1865 and 1871, Pasteur saved the important French silk industry from ruin by isolating the germ of a disease attacking the silkworms. He began to investigate 'anthrax', a deadly disease then widespread among sheep and cattle (see ANIMAL DISEASES, Vol. VI), but which also attacks man. In the midst of these labours he had a stroke which paralysed his left side, but which, fortunately, hardly affected his tremendous capacity for work. A serious outbreak of chicken cholera led him to study the germ responsible for it. He found that his cultures of this germ gradually became weaker and that fowls which were inoculated with this weak culture did not catch chicken cholera. Pasteur named this process of inoculation 'vaccination' in honour of JENNER (q.v.), the first user of vaccines. Later Pasteur made a similar vaccine for anthrax and proved its value in a sensational public demonstration on sheep and goats in 1881.

His last triumph was won against hydrophobia, or rabies, then responsible for the deaths of people bitten by mad dogs. He succeeded in making a rabies vaccine which not only protected dogs from the disease but which also cured dogs and humans already bitten. In 1885 he inoculated a boy whose life was despaired of, and the boy recovered. This discovery was immediately taken up and widely used, and grateful people from many countries subscribed to build the famous Pasteur Institute in Paris, opened in 1888 as a centre for the production of the rabies vaccine, and as a research institute for Pasteur and others. There are now over 60 Pasteur institutes in various parts of the world.

Pasteur was honoured in his own and many other countries during his lifetime, and when he died at the age of 72 he was given a State funeral. His body lies in a marble and granite vault beneath the Pasteur Institute in Paris. Pasteur was always conscious of his mission in life, summed up in his own words: 'Science, in obeying the laws of humanity, will always labour to enlarge the frontiers of life.'

See also Vol. II: BACTERIA; VIRUS; FUNGI.
See also Vol. XI: INOCULATION AND VACCINATION.

PATRICK, St. (c. A.D. 389–461). The patron saint of Ireland was born in western Britain, possibly in Glamorganshire. His grandfather was a priest and his father a deacon, so the family had been Christian for two generations at least. They prided themselves on being Roman citizens. But Roman power was declining. When he was 16, Patrick and many others were carried off by Irish pirates to what he calls the 'outermost places of the earth'. He lived as a slave in north-eastern Ireland for 6 years, tending cattle for a local chieftain, until at last he contrived to escape. But the only ship he could find took him to Italy, and he was forced to wander many years before he reached home again.

Patrick, however, could not settle down. He dreamed that he was called to preach the Gospel to the pagan Irish. To fit himself for this task he studied in France under the Bishop of Auxerre for 17 years. At last, the missionary bishop who had been sent to Ireland having died, Patrick was consecrated bishop and went in his place. He visited the people among whom he had been a captive, and won them and many others to Christianity. He went also to Southern Ireland, where there was already a Christian settlement. There was indeed no part of Ireland untouched by Patrick's influence.

Though he spoke to the people in their own tongue, Patrick introduced the Latin language into the Irish services, and this gave Ireland a share in the culture of Western Christendom. Monasteries, schools, and a native ministry were established. The *Confession*, Patrick's simple narrative of his life, is still preserved in the Book of Armagh in the library of Trinity College, Dublin. Patrick's sincerity, zeal, and love for men explain the great esteem in which he has always been held.

See also Vol. I: IRISH.

PAUL, St. (c. A.D. 16–c. 64). In his letter to the Philippians Paul says that he was an Israelite, of the tribe of Benjamin, a Hebrew of Hebrews, a Pharisee, a strict keeper of the Law, and formerly an eager persecutor of the Christian Church. He was proud of his descent and status.

Born at Tarsus, in Cilicia, he was named Saul after the first King of Israel, also a Benjaminite. (He took the name Paul after he became a Christian.) He learnt a trade, tent-making, a common occupation in Cilicia, where goats' wool was woven into canvas. But his ability marked him out to become a rabbi, or teacher of the Law, and so he was sent to Jerusalem to learn from Gamaliel, a famous rabbi of the time. This was after Jesus' death, for Paul, speaking of himself as 'born out of due time', makes it clear that he never actually saw Jesus.

We first hear of him at the stoning of Stephen. Stephen had been teaching that there was an Authority greater than the Temple and the Law, and that Moses, through whom the Law was given to the Hebrews, had foretold the coming of a prophet with authority greater than his own. This infuriated the strict Jews, who dragged Stephen out of the city and stoned him to death. Saul, then a young man whose religious training had been very narrow, believed that he was witnessing the death of a blasphemer. Saul took a leading part in a cruel persecution of the Christians; but his real nature was gentle, not cruel, and this period of persecution was short.

One day, when coming towards Damascus, he saw a light brighter than the noonday sun. Stunned and blinded he fell to the earth and heard a voice: 'Saul, Saul, why persecutest thou Me?' He cried: 'Who art Thou, Lord?' The reply came: 'I am Jesus, whom thou persecutest.' Then followed the command that he must extend, without limit of land or race, the faith he had tried so hard to destroy.

Still blind, Saul was led by the hand to the Christian community in Damascus, where he was initiated into its membership by baptism. After a period of retirement and meditation, he returned to Damascus; and 3 years later he paid a fortnight's visit to Peter in Jerusalem, where he also saw James, Jesus' brother. There followed a period of considerable expansion and development in the early Church. The flourishing Christian community of both Jews and Gentiles at Antioch grew eager to carry the faith farther afield—to Cyprus and perhaps Asia Minor. Barnabas and Saul were appointed as missioners, and Saul, who at this point took the name Paul, soon became the leader. On this first journey they travelled as far as what is now southern Turkey. Although the Jews were hostile, the Gentiles welcomed the new faith. Paul accepted

Archives Photographiques

ST. PAUL

In the Middle Ages St. Paul was shown holding a book. 14th-century statue. Musée des Augustins, Toulouse

gladly all who believed in Jesus; but this seemed a serious mistake to the original apostles, who still thought of Christianity as an exclusively Jewish religion. Paul, therefore, returned to Jerusalem to discuss this controversy, and at a meeting of the leaders of the early Church Paul's principle, that Gentiles could become full Christians without accepting Jewish customs, was agreed to. It was decided that PETER (q.v.) was to be the leader in work among Jews, and Paul among Gentiles.

But a large section of the Christian Jews never accepted the idea of an equal and complete brotherhood with the Gentiles, and for many years they tried to undo Paul's work and, if possible, to kill him. Nothing could stop Paul's determined energy, and in two further journeys he visited every important city in the Roman provinces of Asia, Macedonia, and Greece. His preaching made so great a stir that he was charged with 'turning the world upside down'. Yet he was also a careful organizer. In each city he left a brotherhood with officers called elders (in Greek, 'presbyters', later shortened to 'priests'). These were also called *episcopoi*, or overseers, or as we now say, bishops. To each church Paul wrote letters of teaching, warning, and encouragement. His *Epistles* must be but a small surviving remnant of his correspondence. These scattered brotherhoods came to think of themselves as parts of one universal Church, which one day, strange as it might seem, would embrace all mankind.

Paul still thought of Jerusalem as the centre of a united Church. His long-cherished desire was to visit Rome; but first he must return to Jerusalem. He took with him a number of Gentile friends, including Luke, whose records give us vivid pictures of incidents on this journey. More than once Paul was warned not to enter Jerusalem, but he would not change his purpose. His presence with his Gentile friends in the city led to a riot in the Temple in which, but for the intervention of the Roman soldiery, he would have been killed. Being by birth a Roman citizen Paul could claim a trial by Roman law. He came before the Roman governor Felix, who kept him in prison at Caesarea for 2 years. When brought before his successor, Festus, Paul appealed to the Emperor. So he did go to Rome, though not in the way he had hoped.

The events of this voyage, the shipwreck, the three months' stay at Malta, and other happenings are vividly described by Luke in The Acts. When they finally approached Rome in A.D. 50, the Roman Christians, who already knew him because of his great epistle to them, came out to meet him. The Acts ends by stating that Paul lived for 2 years as a prisoner in his own hired dwelling, during which time he apparently taught with complete freedom. But the book ends here, and what finally happened to Paul we do not know for certain.

The concluding paragraphs of two Epistles, Titus and 2 Timothy, indicate that Paul was released and travelled again to Greece, Asia Minor, and Crete. Then he was arrested again, and this time was not released. The words, 'I am already being offered, and the time of my departure is come', and, 'Only Luke is with me', have a final ring about them. Tradition says that he was martyred under Nero about A.D. 64.

Paul believed that by the life, death, and resurrection of Jesus the old Jewish system of a religion depending on law, sacrifice, and national exclusiveness had been brought to an end. In its place had come a religion in which man could live by the power of the Spirit, an inward instead of an outward authority. Jesus could supply this power because he was still alive. This was, in Paul's view, a change from bondage to freedom, from being a servant to being a son of God. Such a religion made men equal, and was by its nature universal. Paul's character touched two extremes: he was brave, masterful, and capable of unlimited endurance; yet courteous, patient, and gentle—and he made many friends, by whom he was loved.

See also Vol. I: JESUS OF NAZARETH; CHRISTIAN CHURCH.

PAVLOV, Ivan Petrovich (1849–1936). This great Russian physiologist made original discoveries concerning the digestive system and the brain and the nervous system.

Pavlov was the son of a poor Russian priest in a remote village. An accident at the age of 8 left him with a physical disability from which he freed himself by a rigid programme of physical exercises, and this may have influenced the direction of his later researches into the nervous system. When he was 15, and in a theological college, he read a book on physiology by G. H. Lewes, which determined him to become a physiologist. He pursued his aim with his usual unswerving concentration, and he graduated in both science and medicine at St. Petersburg University. In 1891 he became director of physiology in the St. Petersburg Institute of Experimental Medicine, and in the next 12 years he carried out important researches on the physiology of Digestion, and won the NOBEL Prize for Medicine (q.v.) in 1904.

He then devoted himself to the study of conditioned reflexes, that is, automatic physical responses to certain outside stimuli, such as mouth-watering at the sight of good food (*see* PSYCHOLOGY, Vol. XI). Pavlov carried out experiments on dogs, which enabled him to learn a great deal about the physiology of the brain. His theory that many (if not most) of the important activities of life are automatic responses had a great influence on psychology.

Pavlov was kind, impulsive, and sincere, and was much loved by all who worked with him. Honoured at home and abroad, he was made an honorary Fellow of the Royal Society.

Radio Times Hulton Lib.

ANNA PAVLOVA

The search for the North Pole was engaging the attention of explorers of many nations. Peary's method was to travel light and fast, without the bulky equipment and food reserves favoured by other explorers. In 1909 he started from Cape Columbia, in Grant Land, on a 500-mile dash across the icefloes of the Arctic Ocean, in the centre of which the North Pole is located. He used a series of relay parties, and on the last lap reached the Pole on 6 April, accompanied only by his Negro servant and four Eskimoes. His speed (130 miles in 2 days without skis) was so incredible that, in the absence of independent witnesses, it has raised doubts whether he ever reached the Pole. His claim, however, is generally acknowledged today, though the inaccuracy of his charts and observations has rendered much of his work valueless.

See also NANSEN; AMUNDSEN; SCOTT, R. F.; SHACKLETON. See also Vol. III: POLAR REGIONS.

PAVLOVA, Anna (1885–1931). This famous dancer was born in St. Petersburg, the delicate daughter of poor parents. When she was 10 she entered the Russian Imperial School of Ballet, and by 16 she had attracted considerable attention. Though she had become strong she still seemed fragile and ethereal, the ideal heroine of the romantic ballets of sylphs and fairies. In 1906 she earned the coveted title of *prima ballerina* (first dancer). At first she joined the DIAGHILEFF Ballet (q.v.), but she soon started her own company and travelled all over the world, bringing ballet not only to the great European and American cities but to India, Africa, and South America. She specialized in the portrayal of frail and ephemeral creatures, The Dying Swan, The Californian Poppy, The Dragon-fly, and, greatest of ballet heroines, Giselle.

Although her ballets had neither the music nor the scenery of Diaghileff's historic productions, her own genius was so outstanding that she could transform even the commonplace into something great. From 1912 she made her headquarters in London. We owe her a special debt of gratitude, for she was the first of the Russians to recognize the talent of English dancers, and the majority of her company was English.

See also Vol. IX: BALLET.

PEARY, Robert Edwin (1856–1920). The first man to reach the North Pole was Peary, an American naval officer born in Pennsylvania.

PEEL, Sir Robert (1788–1850). Peel was responsible for many important reforms, and did much to fashion the early Conservative party (*see* POLITICAL PARTIES, Vol. X). He is also remembered for his work, when Home Secretary, in reorganizing the London police (*see* POLICE, HISTORY OF, Vol. X).

Peel never feared to change his mind when circumstances altered, or when he found he had been mistaken. This often brought him criticism, as when he assisted WELLINGTON (q.v.) in passing the Catholic Emancipation Bill, a measure he had previously opposed. In 1841 Peel became Prime Minister with a clear Conservative majority. He began to reorganize the financial policy of the government, simplifying and reforming the tariff, and then moving towards free trade. Many of his own party, anxious to protect English farmers by keeping the taxes on imported corn, opposed him; but when the Irish potato crop failed in 1845–6, Peel carried through the repeal of the Corn Laws, even though a section of his own party, led by DISRAELI (q.v.), broke away from him. The next year he was defeated, and he spent the last 4 years of his life, with a group of brilliant disciples, known as the Peelites, as an independent force in politics. He died in 1850 after falling from his horse.

Peel was a shy, reserved man. 'I have no small talk, and Peel has no manners', Wellington once said. Peel's greatest achievement was in recognizing the need to bring the country's institutions into line with changing forces and demands in society. Consequently 'there were revolutions on the Continent, and reforms in Britain'.

See also DISRAELI; GLADSTONE.
See also Vol. VII: INTERNATIONAL TRADE, Section 4.

PENN, William (1644–1718). Penn was the founder of Pennsylvania. The son of an admiral, he was born in London, and went to school in Essex. He then went to Oxford, where he was first influenced by Quaker teaching, and later to France. He grew into a handsome and athletic young man and seemed, as Mrs. Pepys remarked, 'a most modish person'. When he was 22, being in Ireland on family business, he went to Cork to hear a Quaker preacher, and from that day he became a devout Quaker, his faith never wavering. He spent the next few years preaching and writing, often from prison, for Quaker meetings were at that time forbidden by law. He worked with obstinate energy for freedom of worship among all Christians: 'Whoever was in the wrong', he wrote from prison, 'those who used force for religion could never be right.'

His father's death made Penn wealthy, and in 1681, in payment of a debt, Charles II granted him Pennsylvania, a tract of virgin country in America as large as England. Penn immediately planned to establish there a State founded upon religion, and he directed all his energies to this 'Holy Experiment', which offered complete religious freedom to settlers, and to planning his capital, Philadelphia, the City of Brotherly Love.

In 1682, with some hundred fellow Quakers, Penn set sail for Pennsylvania. Immediately he held a great meeting with the local Indians, walking unarmed among the tribesmen in all their war paint, and sitting down with them to read his promises of peace and friendship. This peace was kept so long as the Quakers ruled Pennsylvania, and was Penn's greatest achievement as a statesman and a Christian. Immigrants arrived, land was bought from the

WILLIAM PENN MEETING THE INDIAN TRIBES AT SHACKA MAXON IN NOVEMBER 1682
Painting by Benjamin West (1738–1820). Pennsylvania Academy of the Fine Arts

Indians, wooden houses appeared on the plains, and the colony prospered.

After 2 years Penn had to return to England to settle a boundary dispute. He stayed on, hoping to persuade the new king, James II, to give the Quakers religious toleration. James II was willing to extend toleration to everyone for the sake of his fellow Roman Catholics, but Penn did not realize how unpopular the King's policy was. When the reign ended disastrously, and the King fled, Penn was ruined, and was forced to hide in order to escape arrest.

When at last he was able to return to Pennsylvania, he found that things had gone very wrong in his absence, and that his constitution for the colony had proved unworkable. The Holy Experiment had become a political wrangle. He returned to England and became ill while negotiating the sale of his governorship to the Crown, and 6 years later he died.

See also Vol. I: QUAKERS.

PEPYS, Samuel (1633–1703). This famous English diarist (*see* DIARIES, Vol. XII) was also a distinguished naval administrator (*see* ADMIRALTY, Vol. X). His father was a London tailor, a poor member of a well-connected East Anglian family. After attending Huntingdon grammar school, Pepys went to St. Paul's School in London, and then to Magdalene College, Cambridge. When he was 22 he married a frivolous girl of 15, a French inventor's penniless daughter, to whom he was devoted. By then he had entered the service of a powerful relative, Edward Montagu, a rising admiral and friend of Oliver CROMWELL (q.v.). Pepys accompanied him to Holland to bring back CHARLES II (q.v.) from exile, and became an enthusiastic royalist.

After the Restoration Pepys became Clerk of the Acts to the Navy Board, which looked after the business side of naval affairs, and had to guide the Board through a difficult period of reorganization. He had to see to the provision of ships, material, and pay during the Dutch War of 1665–7. Pepys worked hard, mastered his job, carried through a series of reforms, and by the end of the war had proved himself a very capable administrator, well able to defend his office against criticism in Parliament. With considerable courage he stayed in London during the year of the PLAGUE (q.v. Vol. XI), and by his advice helped to limit the spread of the FIRE OF LONDON (q.v. Vol. X) in the following year.

National Maritime Museum
SAMUEL PEPYS
Painting by Kneller

Pepys was by now well established and comfortably off; he knew almost everyone who mattered, and began to consider entering Parliament, which he eventually did in 1673. Being a man of abounding energy, curiosity, and friendliness, he enjoyed life in London to the full. He composed and sang, as well as playing a number of instruments; he collected and read all sorts of books, in several languages; and he dearly loved an afternoon at the theatre. Like most intelligent men of his generation, he was fascinated by the new scientific discoveries, and in 1665 he was elected to the Royal Society, of which he later became President. In 1669 his eyesight began to give him trouble, and for a rest he went on a brief tour of Holland and France with his wife. Shortly after their return, she died, and he never married again.

In 1673 the Duke of York (later James II), who was Lord High Admiral, had to resign because of his Roman Catholicism. Pepys was then appointed Secretary to the Admiralty and was largely responsible for the great shipbuilding programme of the late 70's. In 1679, his association with the Duke of York led to his being falsely charged with participation in a Popish Plot; he was imprisoned and forced to resign.

Although he was later recalled to the Admiralty, he again fell under suspicion at the time of the REVOLUTION OF 1688 (q.v. Vol. X), and resigned finally. By this time he had become a grand personage—the friend of WREN, NEWTON, and DRYDEN (qq.v.)—and in his retirement at Clapham he played the part of patron of the arts and sciences.

At his death the Crown owed him £28,000, but the debt was never paid. His property passed to a nephew, for he had no children, and his books and papers went ultimately to his old college at Cambridge, where the six volumes of his *Journal*, written in a small but clear shorthand, remained undiscovered till shortly after 1818. They were deciphered in 1825 and published in a very incomplete form. Pepys's fame rests far more on his authorship of this unique diary than on his other achievements. It is an exciting book because Pepys recorded all he did and thought; what clothes he and his wife wore; what food they ate; what he saw and heard; and all his intimate relations with his pretty, silly little wife. He began the diary when he was 27, and ended it just over 9 years later when the strain of these daily or almost daily entries became too great for his eyes. It is the work of a young man, overflowing with exuberance and vitality. Its fullness and lack of reserve have led to a misunderstanding of the author. Pepys faithfully recorded all his faults and weaknesses—weaknesses not in the least unusual, though few people have the inclination, the courage, or the frankness to confess to them. He reveals himself as a sensualist, indulging his feelings when he can, greedy, deceitful, and vain; but a proper study of the diary and of his life shows us another Pepys—the trusted and responsible civil servant, the friend of kings and politicians, and of the greatest scientists, authors, and painters of the day; in fact, a distinguished and respected man. To historians, the diary is valuable as disclosing not only the man but also the times in which he lived. Our knowledge of the London of the 1660's—of its gossip, its taverns and churches, its homes and its streets—is largely due to this lively young man who went everywhere, spoke to everybody, and wrote down everything.

See also Vol. XII: DIARIES.

PERICLES (*c.* 500–429 B.C.). The greatest of Athenian statesmen, so great that we speak of the 'Age of Pericles', was of a noble family. We know little of his youth. In politics he first emerges as a democrat and opponent of Cimon, an aristocrat, who favoured the rival city of Sparta. He combined with the leader of the democratic party in attacking Cimon's policy of helping the SPARTANS (q.v. Vol. I) to crush a rising of their serfs, and in proposing measures which brought Athens nearer to complete democracy. These proposals attacked the Council of the Areopagus; this formerly powerful body was stripped of nearly all its rights, and the higher offices of State were opened up to the lower classes. Pericles proposed that all State offices, including service on the jury in the people's law courts, should be paid. By 461 B.C. Pericles was the most influential man in Athens.

After the Persian Wars (*see* XERXES) the Greeks turned to Athens for leadership. A League was formed for the protection of Greece against Persia, member-States contributing ships or money; but Athens so dominated the League with her large fleet (*see* THEMISTOCLES) that the League soon became an Athenian Empire. Pericles' foreign policy, which always aimed at increasing Athenian power, won such success that other Greek States became jealous, especially Corinth and Aegina, her great commercial rivals. A League of Peloponnesian States with Sparta at the head was formed in opposition to Athens. During the struggles in which Athens built up her Empire and warded off Peloponnesian hostility, Pericles was active in subduing any State that revolted from the Athenian League, until finally in 445 B.C. a Thirty Years' Peace with Sparta was made which left Athens free to pursue her imperialistic policy.

Pericles extended Athenian influence by planting settlements at important points on the Aegean islands and the Hellespont; he established a new city-state, Thurii, on the south coast of Italy and another, Amphipolis, on the north Aegean, and he tried to establish settlements on the Black Sea. Pericles' only official position was that of Commander, one of the ten military leaders who were elected annually, all other officials being chosen by lot. The success of his policy and his known integrity inspired confidence, and he was so eloquent that he could almost always persuade the Assembly to vote for his proposals.

When the Peloponnesians, alarmed at the

growth of Athenian power, called on Sparta to intervene, Pericles encouraged Athens to resist, and war was declared in 431 B.C. Pericles' advice was to ignore land invasion and rely upon the fleet to protect the sea route on which Athens' food supply depended. So, when the Peloponnesians invaded, the farmers took refuge within the city walls. But a plague brought from overseas caused terrible havoc in the over-crowded city, and Pericles became so unpopular that he was dismissed from office and fined. Although he was soon afterwards restored, he died in 429 B.C. of after-effects of the plague, in which he had lost two of his sons.

Pericles, besides being a patriot and a demo-crat, was also highly cultivated, handsome, and dignified. He was a brilliant speaker, famous for clarity and force. He not only extended Athen-ian power abroad but he made Athens the intellectual leader of Greece. He planned the adornment of the Acropolis (q.v. Vol. XII) with beautiful buildings, the chief being the Temple of Athena called the Parthenon. He invited distinguished men from other Greek city-states to live in Athens, and though some-what aloof towards the crowd, he loved the society of poets, philosophers, and artists, such as Sophocles (q.v.) the tragic dramatist, Anaxa-goras the scientific philosopher, Phidias the sculptor, Damon the musician, and others. After an unhappy first marriage, he entered upon a lifelong union with Aspasia, a brilliant woman from Miletus whom, according to the Athenian law, he could not legally marry since she was not an Athenian. In his famous Funeral Speech on the first of those who had fallen in the war, which is reported by Thucydides, Pericles gave a wonderful description of the Athenian ideal and way of life. He said that Athenians should be proud to die for their city: 'The survivors should . . . actively enjoy the daily spectacle of her power and become her lovers, realizing that her greatness was won by the courage and devotion to duty of men whose deeds were governed by a sense of honour.'

See also Vol. I: Greek Civilization.
See also Vol. X: City-State; Democracy.

PETER, St. Simon Peter was the leader of the twelve original disciples of Jesus of Nazareth (q.v. Vol. I). When Jesus came into Galilee to prepare men to enter the kingdom of God, he needed helpers—men of tough and enduring

fibre. One day, seeing Simon with his brother Andrew fishing, he called to them, 'Come ye after me, and I will make you to become fishers of men.' The Fourth Gospel says that they had met Jesus before, which is not unlikely. They followed him for the same reason which led thousands of young Galileans to follow other leaders before and after the time of Jesus, because they hoped for some event which would free the Jews from Roman rule and make them the sovereign nation on earth. For this is what they understood by the 'kingdom of God'.

Jesus gave Simon the name *Cephas*, a stone. 'Peter' comes from its Greek form *petra*. Although young, Peter was already married: 20 years later Paul mentions that his wife accompanied him on his missionary journeys. Peter's home was in Capernaum, probably a good-sized house, for Peter's mother-in-law lived there, and perhaps his own parents also. Jesus seems to have used the house for a time as his headquarters. Peter and Andrew's family most likely owned their boats and employed assistant fishermen. We should call them middle-class folk; the men, though not highly educated, were intelligent and by no means illiterate.

Peter, with two other disciples, James and John, often accompanied Jesus when the others did not. From the first Peter was the most active and vocal of the disciples, being nearly always their spokesman. When Jesus, at Caesarea Philippi, asked them who they thought he was, it was Peter who said, expressing the belief of them all, 'Thou art the Christ.' Jesus warned them that he would be arrested and killed at Jerusalem, and Peter at once declared that this should not happen. He was severely rebuked, but not convinced. Later on he protested that he would stand by Jesus to the end, but was warned that he would deny Jesus; and in a moment of panic he denied him three times. Peter was really brave and loyal, but he had not yet overcome the fears and impulsiveness of youth. After the Crucifixion Jesus appeared to Peter before the other apostles and from this time he became a wiser and stronger man.

In the formation and early growth of the Christian Church (q.v. Vol. I) Peter was pro-minent. He proclaimed openly and fearlessly that the crucified Jesus was alive and would re-turn to earth in glory. He was twice imprisoned, though he escaped each time, and went on boldly preaching. Peter, however, had the limited outlook of the Jews, and still thought of Jesus as the Messiah (in Greek, the Christ) sent to the Jews and not to the rest of the world. It took the new disciple, PAUL (q.v.), to teach the early Church that its mission was world-wide. At the Council held in Jerusalem about A.D. 49 it was agreed that Peter should confine himself to work among the Jews, while Paul should go to the Gentiles.

According to some accounts we are told that Peter visited and associated freely with Gentile Christians; according to others we learn that Peter, when he visited Antioch, kept himself apart from the Gentiles, refusing to join in the common meals, for which Paul blamed him.

We know nothing more for certain about Peter's life. There is a strong tradition, though no actual evidence, that Peter went to Rome and was martyred there, being crucified head downmost as he did not think himself worthy of dying as Christ had died. This must have been after Paul was taken to Rome, and if both men died in the persecution by NERO (q.v.) in A.D. 64, the havoc wrought in the Church might have prevented any record from surviving.

The Epistle entitled 2 Peter is generally admitted to be a 2nd-century work issued in Peter's name, a practice not uncommon in those days; but many scholars accept 1 Peter as Peter's own composition, though others doubt it. There is also a tradition that Mark wrote his Gospel from Peter's dictation; and certainly that Gospel does give more description than any of the others of Peter's personal contact with Jesus.

National Gallery

ST. PETER

St. Peter is wearing the papal tiara as the first head of the Church, and carrying the keys of the kingdom of heaven. Detail from the 'Demidoff' altar-piece, by Carlo Crivelli (*c.* 1435–*c.* 1495)

more advanced countries of Europe. Her Church, a branch of the ORTHODOX EASTERN CHURCH (q.v. Vol. I), was ignorant, slothful, and ruled by superstition; the masses of her people lived in servitude on the edge of starvation, and her nobles were corrupt, brutal, and uneducated. There was no Parliament, no justice, no civil service capable of carrying out a fair system of taxation. The army was medieval, and there were no industries. Russia was isolated from Europe, and she lacked access to any sea except the Arctic Ocean (*see* RUSSIANS, Vol. I).

Peter's upbringing was a mixture of brutality and complete neglect, and he narrowly escaped death in the murderous feuds between the families of his father's first and second wives. It is not surprising that he developed a savage character and uncouth manners.

During his wild youth Peter spent much of his time in the foreign quarter of Moscow, where lived those foreign experts which the Russian Government had begun to employ. From these foreigners and from the few enterprising merchants who had ventured abroad Peter learned how far his country lagged behind Europe. He learned of the wonders of European industry, of mighty armies and navies, and of efficient governments.

For shipbuilding in particular he developed an intense and practical enthusiasm. He determined to break down Russia's isolation, so that European example and help could raise her to the level of prosperity, efficiency, and strength of the leading European States. He became convinced that, to secure this free communication with Europe, she must win an outlet to the Baltic Sea from Sweden and build a navy. For this she must have an efficient professional army, and to equip the army, she must develop industries. To control and pay for all this activity,

PETER THE GREAT (1672–1725). Peter, the founder of the Russian Empire, became sole and absolute ruler of Russia when he was 22. Russia at this time was barbaric compared with the

National Maritime Museum

PETER THE GREAT AT AMSTERDAM INSPECTING A SHIP HE HAS JUST BOUGHT

He is standing in front of the mast of the small sailing vessel towards the right of the picture. Painting by Abraham Storck (1636–1710)

the government must be radically reformed and a civil service started. Thus Peter found himself led on inevitably, step by step, to revolutionize the social, economic, and political life of Russia.

In 1697 Peter set out on a visit to western Europe to learn all he could of Western crafts, particularly shipbuilding. While he was at Deptford, on the Thames, the King sent the Bishop of Salisbury to tell him about the government and religion of England. The bishop was greatly impressed by the huge strength and gigantic size of the Tsar (he was over $6\frac{1}{2}$ feet tall). 'He is a man of very hot temper', reported the bishop, 'soon inflamed and very brutal in his passion. . . . He wants not capacity, and has a larger measure of knowledge than might be expected from his education, which was very indifferent. . . . He is mechanically turned, and seems designed by nature rather to be a ship carpenter than a great prince.'

Peter had to return home hastily to subdue a mutiny against his radical reforms, which deeply offended the profound religious conservatism of the Russians. He punished this resistance with the terrible cruelty which was part of his character. The obstinacy and stupidity of his subjects often goaded him into fits of almost insane rage,

during which he kicked and thrashed everyone who crossed his path.

In 1700 Peter started a war with Sweden, which lasted almost until his death. On land conquered from Sweden he founded his new port and capital St. Petersburg (now Leningrad), the 'window towards the west' which had been the object of all his reforms and wars.

The closing years of his reign were marked by his brutal execution of his only son, Alexius, who was involved in the conservative opposition to his reforms. Peter feared that after his death Alexius would undo all his work; but, in fact, the confusion into which his death without an heir threw Russia was almost equally disastrous.

Peter's great work of Europeanizing Russia was carried out with small reforms as well as large. Not only did he reform the Church, the government, and the armed forces, and set up institutions of education, but also he reformed the currency and the alphabet, brought the Russian calendar into line with the European, and introduced, often by force, European customs and dress, even forcing the *boyars* to shave their Eastern beards.

See also IVAN THE TERRIBLE; CATHERINE THE GREAT; ALEXANDER II.

PETER THE HERMIT (died 1115). This French monk by preaching the Holy War in Europe raised the first crusading army to rescue the Holy Places from the Moslem Turks. It is said that he had been prevented by the Turks from making a pilgrimage to Jerusalem, and so he enthusiastically received Pope Urban II's call to the CRUSADES (q.v. Vol. I). Peter, called 'the Hermit' because he always wore a hermit's cap, was a small, dark man with a long, bony face, who wore no shoes and poor clothes, and rode everywhere on a donkey. He was an inspired preacher, and he collected an enormous rabble army, mostly peasants, perhaps some 20,000 in all, whom he led from Cologne to Constantinople. The venture was, not surprisingly, entirely disastrous. The army had no way of getting food except by plundering the countries through which it passed, and it was untrained and inadequately armed. Those who were not killed on the way to the Holy Land were almost wiped out in the first battle with the Turks.

PETRARCH (1304–74). Francesco Petrarca, the Italian poet, was the creator of the SONNET (q.v. Vol. XII), a poet who mirrored the griefs of love in words as clear as running water. He took the language of everyday speech, the Tuscan he had learnt as a boy in the streets of Florence, and used it to make the first lyrical poems of the modern world. Petrarch was a true product of the RENAISSANCE (q.v. Vol. I), and although he knew little Greek and was forced to admit that Homer was dumb to him and he deaf to Homer, he loved the ancient world with an intense passion. With his friend BOCCACCIO (q.v.) he collected coins and manuscripts, annotated classical authors, and explored the half-forgotten ruins of Rome. In all this he set a fashion—a fashion for the romantic rediscovery of the past—which the Renaissance was to carry across Europe. But for many people it is not as a poet or scholar, but as the lover of Laura, that Petrarch is remembered.

Petrarch was the son of a Florentine lawyer driven by political quarrels to exile in Provence. From his writings we learn how, as a young poet at church in Avignon, he first saw the beautiful fair-haired woman who became the Laura of his sonnets. She was married to someone else, but she inspired him with a pure and constant love. As a scholar in his 30's he retired from the world for a time to his country house at Vau-

cluse, where a fountain rose among the fig and olive trees in his garden. He loved the country and solitude, yet longed for fame.

His reputation for scholarship grew, and in 1341 he visited Rome at Easter and, having delivered an oration, was crowned in the Capitol among cheering crowds with the laurel crown of a classical poet. As he grew older, the rulers of Italy invited him to their courts and received him with honour—though his long friendship with Boccaccio was still his greatest delight. He died when he was 70, near Padua, his servants finding him one morning dead among his books.

See also Colour Plate opposite p. 400.

PHILIP II OF SPAIN (1527–98). Son of the Emperor CHARLES V (q.v.) and husband of Mary, Queen of England, Philip became, when

Anderson

PHILIP II
Painting by Titian. Prado, Madrid

his father abdicated in 1556, a very powerful prince in Europe, the ruler of Spain and the Spanish American possessions, together with Naples and Sicily, the duchy of Milan, and the Netherlands. Spain, where he had been educated, was the only country Philip understood or cared for. Mary died in 1558, and Philip, when he left the Netherlands in 1559, never returned to the northern part of his dominions.

His long reign of nearly 40 years was dominated by two great ambitions, the wish to make Spain the most powerful nation in Europe, unified under his personal sovereignty, and the wish to be champion of the Roman Catholic faith and the destroyer of heresy. Though he governed through a complicated system of Councils, Philip kept the decision of all important affairs in his own hands. He had intimate advisers such as the priest Diego de Espinosa, who became President of the Council of Castile and Inquisitor-General (see INQUISITION, Vol. I), and the luxurious Antonio Perez; but such favourites fell as rapidly as they rose. Philip was determined to brook no challenge to his rule. He suppressed free institutions in his dominions and set to work to unify the Spanish peninsula. After his nephew, King Sebastian of Portugal, had been killed in Morocco, Philip himself secured the throne of Portugal by bribery, by calculated generosity, and by the strength of General Alva's occupying army.

Philip's ambition to be an equal partner with the Pope in a movement to crush heresy, which would redound to the glory of Spain, led him to encourage an internal heresy hunt which brought even St. TERESA (q.v.) herself under suspicion. His bitter persecution of the MOORS of Granada (q.v. Vol. I) in southern Spain destroyed much profitable commerce which depended upon the Moors. Philip would have done better to have concentrated his crusading zeal against the infidels in the Mediterranean and to have followed up the splendid victory of Lepanto by his half-brother, Don John of Austria, in 1571, at which the Turkish navy was destroyed. Instead, he tried to enforce Roman Catholicism and his own oppressive rule on the Netherlands, which led to a revolt under the heroic leadership of WILLIAM THE SILENT (q.v.) and a bitter and ruinous struggle which lasted for the remainder of Philip's reign. England's aid to the Netherlands and new raids on Spanish domains in the New World drove Philip at last to send

out the ill-fated SPANISH ARMADA (q.v. Vol. X) to attack this stronghold of Protestantism (see ELIZABETH I).

The disaster of the Armada, the failure of his attempts finally to subdue the Netherlands, and the losses caused by the raids of British seamen in the Spanish main, cast a gloom on the last years of Philip's reign, which was deepened by the financial ruin which his policy had brought upon Spain. The ordinary economic activity of the country was throttled by Philip's taxation and forced loans. In spite of his great industry and considerable ability, his rule was unwise, and his insistence on dealing with detailed administration himself led to delays and confusion.

Philip had a sombre nature, capable of terrible fanaticism and cruelty. To most people he is associated with the Inquisition, with the merciless Duke of Alva, who boasted when he left the Netherlands that he had executed 18,000 men, and with the wretched Don Carlos, his weak and vicious son who was found guilty of conspiring against his life. But he was a tender husband and father, and his charming letters to his daughter Isabella reveal a more attractive side of his character. In these he showed himself a man who could jest with children and who thought roses were perfection.

Jallatin Collection, Philadelphia Museum of Art

SELF-PORTRAIT BY PABLO PICASSO, PAINTED IN 1906

PICASSO, Pablo (born 1881). Picasso is the most versatile artist of the 20th century, famous not only for his paintings but for his engravings and book illustrations, his sculpture, his designs for ballet, and his pottery.

Picasso, who very early revealed his extraordinary talents, was first taught drawing and painting by his father, an art teacher in Barcelona, Spain. While still a schoolboy Picasso studied contemporary French art, and he paid his first visit to Paris when he was 19. Soon after he began the first of a long series of artistic explorations.

In 1901 Picasso began painting subjects such as starving mothers and blind beggars, using chiefly tones of blue. The pathos of this 'blue period' was perhaps the outcome of his own poverty at that time. In 1904 he settled permanently in Paris and, in a mood of less anguished sadness, painted clowns and acrobats—favourite subjects with the Paris artists of the time. Next he developed a classical style, borrowing from Greek art, and painting predominantly in shades of rose. The 'rose period' was followed by harsh barbaric works inspired (like the Self-portrait shown here) by primitive Spanish sculpture and Negro wood carvings, in which he found a tendency to reduce things to simple geometrical shapes. It was this tendency that suggested to Picasso and the French painter Braque the development of the style of painting called 'cubism', in which natural objects are represented by constructions of geometrical forms alone (*see* MODERN ART, Vol. XII).

Picasso's vigorous genius could not long be bound to a single artistic method. About 1915 he began a series of naturalistic portrait drawings of his friends; two years later he designed brilliantly for DIAGHILEFF's Russian ballet (q.v.), and in 1920 he produced huge paintings with a calm sculptural quality. But as the political persecutions which led to the Spanish Civil War and the Second World War intensified, Picasso's paintings became more and more violent and distorted. He regarded painting as a weapon against barbarism; in his mural painting *Guernica*, a Spanish town destroyed by bombs in 1937, for example, he revealed the brutal horror of war.

Since 1945 he seems to have become more light-hearted, designing and often modelling with his own hands delightful pottery in shapes both classical and fantastic. These reveal clearly

Anderson

THE ANNUNCIATION

Painting by Piero della Francesca. Church of San Francesco, Arezzo

the streak of mischief which has long been an element in his art and the vitality and inventiveness which have made him the dominant figure in the art of our time.

PIERO DELLA FRANCESCA (*c.* 1416–92). Piero came from central Italy and spent most of his life painting in the different cities of that region until in his old age he went blind. He died an old man, but the date of his birth is not known.

Piero was an artist of the RENAISSANCE (q.v. Vol. I), and, like his contemporaries, was interested in the study of man, of nature, and of antiquity. He was trained in Florence, the chief centre of art and scholarship; he studied the work of artists such as DONATELLO and MASACCIO (qq.v.), and became so much interested in PERSPECTIVE (q.v. Vol. XII) that he wrote a book about it.

With the exception of a few portraits, Piero's work consists mainly of religious frescoes and altar-pieces in churches. But the majestic and solemn treatment of the figures, which are sometimes dressed as Roman soldiers, reminds one of antique statues; while accurate perspective and the pearly light in which the figures and landscape are bathed give a feeling of space and reality. After his death, Piero's work aroused little interest, but recently he has come to be considered among the greatest of Italian painters.

See also Vol. XII: ITALIAN ART.

PITT, William (1759–1806). William Pitt 'the Younger' holds as high a place as his famous father, the elder Pitt, Earl of CHATHAM (q.v.). The younger Pitt became British Prime Minister before he was 25. He was at the head of the government for 19 years, and not only led Britain through the worst perils of the Napoleonic Wars but was responsible for many important reforms at home.

'Pitt', said a contemporary, 'never was a boy.' From an early age he trained himself seriously for a political career. He entered Parliament at 22 and, scorning offers of junior posts, became Chancellor of the Exchequer at 23. Less than 2 years later he had formed his own Ministry. He began his first period of office almost single-handed, but when the 'schoolboy's' administration was seen to be strong and trusted by GEORGE III (q.v.) support rallied to him. Pitt believed his special mission was to put right a worn-out political system. Though he failed to persuade the Commons to alter the corrupt electoral system, he did succeed in getting rid of many of the useless but well-paid posts both at Court and in the government which Ministers often sold for votes. Pitt also freed Britain's trade from many restrictions and arranged a trade treaty with France. He remodelled the system of taxation, and set up a fund for the reduction of the NATIONAL DEBT (q.v. Vol. X). Later, he introduced Income Tax into England for a

National Portrait Gallery

PITT ADDRESSING THE HOUSE OF COMMONS, 1793
Painting by K. A. Hickel

short time at the rate of 2s. in the £ to pay for the war.

In 1793, with the outbreak of the NAPOLEONIC WARS (q.v. Vol. X), Pitt was faced with a war against France. His real interest lay in domestic and economic reform, and he was not, as his father was, a brilliant war minister. Nevertheless he showed in his management of affairs qualities of heroic determination and endurance that carried Britain past the perils of invasion and defeat. Pitt had to put fresh heart (and money) into Britain's allies each time they were overwhelmed by the military genius of Napoleon; he had to maintain Britain's command of the sea against the combined fleets of France and Spain, and at the same time to guard against revolutionary movements at home. The suppression of these movements (which were due mainly to industrial disturbances and the dislocation of trade by war) made people think that Pitt had abandoned his youthful reforming ideas. In fact he was still anxious for reform if it could be achieved gradually and peacefully, but he felt the country could not afford serious domestic upheavals at such a time.

In 1801, after his struggle to win emancipation for Catholics in Ireland had been defeated by the opposition of the King, Pitt resigned the premiership. Three years later, however, when Britain was threatened by invasion from Napoleon, the country demanded his return. But his health was already broken, and he died of premature old age at 46, 3 months after Nelson's great victory at TRAFALGAR (q.v. Vol. X) had saved the country from immediate danger, and given Britain decisive supremacy at sea.

Though Pitt always considered himself a Whig, his great coalition government of members of all political parties, committed to maintaining a strong government and to winning the war before all else, laid the foundation of a new sort of Toryism (see POLITICAL PARTIES, Vol. X). In public Pitt's manner was cold and repellant, and as an orator he spoke too much in the clear, careful terms of an official document. But he had courage, efficiency, and superb practical good sense. His young disciple CANNING (q.v.) called him the 'pilot who weathered the storm' of the wars. But equally important is his claim to fame as the reformer who remodelled the old 18th-century system of government, meeting the fury of attacks in Parliament with an appeal to hard facts and cool reason.

PIZARRO, Francisco (c. 1471–1541). The Spanish discoverer and conqueror of Peru was the illegitimate son of a poor officer in the Spanish army, and was brought up like a peasant, unable to read or write. He sailed to the New World, the newly discovered American continent, with other Spanish pioneers, and was a member of Balboa's expedition which crossed the isthmus of Panama and reached the Pacific Ocean in 1513, the first Europeans to do so.

The conquest of Mexico by CORTÉS (q.v.) had shown what a handful of Spaniards could do against a whole empire. Ever since Balboa had reached the Pacific there had been persistent rumours of a great civilized land of fabulous wealth far to the south. So Pizarro and another adventurer, Almagro, who came from a Spanish peasant family, borrowed money to explore the west coast of South America. After early failures and terrible hardships, they reached the outposts of the great Inca Empire of Peru (see INCA CIVILIZATION, Vol. I), but two expeditions fitted out and financed from Panama failed to conquer it. Pizarro went back to Spain to get the King's support for the final conquest of Peru. The King appointed him governor of Peru in advance, and in 1529 Pizarro returned to America with his reinforcements, among whom were his four brothers.

The Inca Empire stretched over 2,000 miles from north to south along the great plateau of the Andes at a height of 9,000 to 13,000 feet above sea-level, and protected from the outside world by the still higher mountain ranges of the Cordilleras. It possessed vast stores of gold and silver, and was ruled by fierce warrior kings, the Incas, who dominated numerous subject peoples by means of a network of roads and posting-houses. But recently this powerful Empire had been disastrously weakened by a quarrel over the succession to the throne. The successful usurper, Atahualpa, had established his capital at Cajamarca, some 600 miles north of the traditional capital, Cuzco.

Pizarro sailed from Panama to Peru and marched to the usurper's capital, with a force of about 62 horsemen and 106 infantry, armed with twenty crossbows and three muskets. Although Atahualpa was protected by an army of over 30,000 men, the Spaniards took him prisoner by treachery. They then set him up as a puppet ruler under their control, and proceeded to plunder the Empire. The booty taken

THE INCAS BRINGING GOLD AND SILVER TO PIZARRO
Engraving from De Bry, *Americae*

by Pizarro's men was so vast that each horseman received as his share about 90 lb. of gold and 180 lb. of silver and each foot soldier about half these amounts. Having infamously extorted an enormous ransom from the Inca, the Spaniards killed him, thus destroying the basis of their authority and causing themselves endless trouble. But the conquests and the plunder went on, and Pizarro founded a new Spanish capital, Lima, and became governor. Just as the conquest seemed complete, the Incas rose in desperate revolt against the cruelty and greed of the Spaniards, who defended themselves bravely and skilfully until reinforcements arrived to crush the revolt. The next year, 1537, a long-smouldering quarrel broke out between Pizarro and his partner Almagro over the division of their conquests, and this led to civil war among the Spaniards. Almagro was taken prisoner in 1538 and was beheaded. But his followers never settled down under Pizarro's rule, and in 1541 they rose in revolt and murdered him.

See also Vol. I: INCA CIVILIZATION; PERUVIANS.

PLATO (*c.* 428–347 B.C.). This great philosopher of ancient Greece was born of aristocratic Athenian parents. During his early life Athens was carrying on a long war with Sparta, and Plato must have served the usual 5 years in the army. In his youth he was active in the political affairs of the city and appeared to be a rising statesman. But he became disgusted with the tyrannical violence of the party in power, and when he saw the conviction and death of his dearly-loved master, SOCRATES (q.v.), he withdrew from public life, and devoted himself to systematic thought concerning the principles of politics and personal conduct. The dialogues he wrote at this time, such as the *Protagoras*, carried on the teaching and method of Socrates, though he was already extending his questions into new fields. The *Apology*, which is a reproduction of the wonderful defence put forward by Socrates at his trial, belongs also to these early years.

When he was 40 Plato visited Sicily and Italy, where he conversed with mathematicians. Soon after his return he founded in Athens the famous school of education and advanced studies known as the Academy (*see* UNIVERSITIES, HISTORY OF, Vol. X). We know little about the organization of the Academy. It is probable that a wide range of scientific and social subjects was discussed, and there seems to have been special emphasis on mathematics and the art of logical thinking. Plato believed that students should study these subjects in order to train their minds so that they could, when more mature, take up the higher studies of philosophy. The glory of the Academy lay in the number of original thinkers, especially in the fields of mathematics and astronomy, who gathered round Plato and received encouragement from him—thinkers whose influence was to spread far over the Greek world. The Academy existed for 8 centuries in various forms, until it was closed by Justinian I in A.D. 529.

In his middle age Plato was persuaded to go again to Sicily to give advice to a well-intentioned but weak young ruler, Dionysius II, whom he had tried to help on his earlier visit. Dionysius, however, failed to profit from Plato's teaching and was a bitter disappointment to him. Meanwhile Plato was writing the great dialogues of his middle and later years, such as the *Phaedo*, the *Philebus*, and the *Timaeus*. He died at the age of 81, and was buried in the grounds of the Academy that he had served for 40 years.

The dialogues still provide the most attractive introduction to PHILOSOPHY (q.v. Vol. I). Socrates, who always appears as the principal speaker, seeks the real meaning of friendship or courage or knowledge, and moves by question and answer from vague and superficial statements to clearer and deeper understanding. The conversation is often amusing; Socrates pokes fun at the other speakers, and they in turn enjoy drawing him out. The living tones of keen, good-natured discussion are presented with delightful skill. In the whole series of dialogues can be found the outlines of a great scheme of thought, but the scheme is never fully stated.

Plato asked questions about numerous ideas which people usually take for granted because he believed that the resolute attempt to clarify beliefs would make life better. He was chiefly concerned about two fundamental problems— the real nature of goodness and the real nature of knowledge. The problem of the meaning of the ideas of right and good was forced on him by serious contemporary criticisms of moral and religious beliefs. In his most famous work, the *Republic*, he answers these attacks in the course of a long inquiry into the best form of life for men and States. A notable feature of his ideal commonwealth is the view that its rulers should be only those men and women who have, by long training, reached a supreme state of spiritual and scientific understanding. In his search for what we can really know, Plato was led to the famous doctrine of Ideas or Forms. These are not ideas in our minds, but complete and independent standards, or abstracts of reality and goodness, in the light of which we come to understand the real nature of the imperfect and changing things we see and handle, and the true character of what is good and beautiful.

Plato's thought has profoundly influenced Christian theology and the philosophy of the West. In the realm of theology, certain of his doctrines, especially his beliefs concerning an eternal and spiritual existence, the immortality of the soul, and the creation of the world, were early associated with the Christian faith; and some of the leading Fathers of the Church, such as St. AUGUSTINE (q.v.), drew deeply on the thought of Plato. In the history of philosophy, his ideas on many problems have continuously influenced thinkers in every period, and as philosophers have come to understand him better, they have continued to find the dialogues full of valuable reasoning and insight. In the development of science, also, Plato has played a powerful role, for the study of his writings led to the view that physical science should be based on mathematics. His influence can be seen, too, in wide ranges of literature. For the dialogues contain passages of sheer poetry, as well as passages of hard logic and science; and Plato's visions have moved poets of all periods, including many English poets such as Spenser and Shelley. To describe all that civlization owes to Plato would require a history of the thought and literature of the Western world.

See also Vol. I: PHILOSOPHY; GREEK CIVILIZATION.

PLUTARCH (*c.* A.D. 46–*c.* 120). This Greek writer, best known by his book of *Lives*, was educated in Athens, and spent most of his life in his native city in northern Greece. He visited Rome several times as a political representative and made distinguished friends there, though he never perfected his knowledge of Latin. Plutarch's most famous work, *Parallel Lives*, has been a model for biographers ever since. He was more concerned with giving a true portrait of a man's character, good or bad, than in recording his actions. He published the *Lives* (forty-six in all) in pairs, choosing for each pair a Greek and a Roman whose careers were similar—DEMOSTHENES, for example, is paired with CICERO, ALEXANDER with JULIUS CAESAR (qq.v.). Plutarch's writings on religion, politics, and history, and those essays tell us much about the beliefs and doings of his age which we should not otherwise know. He was a man of considerable knowledge, a generous friend, and a great admirer of genius and goodness wherever he found it.

See also Vol. XII: BIOGRAPHY.

POMPEY THE GREAT (106–48 B.C.). In Pompey's lifetime the Senate's monopoly of power in Rome was challenged by several great leaders. To challenge it successfully a man needed an army and a flair for politics. Pompey, like his rival JULIUS CAESAR (q.v.), was a great soldier, but unlike Caesar he was no politician and could make no use of his military triumphs.

His rise was extremely swift. His brilliant generalship won him the title 'Magnus' and an early consulship. In 67 B.C. he cleared the Mediterranean in 4 months of pirates who had been active for many years. The next year he defeated Mithridates, King of Pontus on the Black Sea, who had defied Rome for 40 years. Then he went on to settle the whole Eastern Empire.

When he came home in 62 B.C. his power was overwhelming. But as a politician he was inept. Tactless and vacillating, he failed to win the support of the Senate, which consequently would neither ratify his settlement of the East nor give him land for settling his troops. To gain his ends he joined Caesar and Crassus in the First Triumvirate; but whereas this gave Caesar the opportunity of winning glory in Gaul, in the long run Pompey, outwardly the greatest of the three, gained little. By 50 B.C. Caesar was the more formidable, and the leaders of the Senate decided to use Pompey to crush him. But when civil war broke out, Caesar easily won over Italy, and Pompey withdrew to Greece. Caesar followed him the next year, and Pompey, who could still, had he waited, have assembled the larger army, was foolishly persuaded to join battle at Pharsalus in Thessaly, and was utterly defeated. He fled to Egypt, where he was stabbed in the back as he stepped ashore.

POPE, Alexander (1688–1744). Pope was the greatest poet of the period which we call the AUGUSTAN AGE (q.v. Vol. XII). He brought the poetry of argument and satire to a new level of brilliance and power, and developed the heroic couplet (*see* VERSIFICATION, Vol. XII) into an instrument of amazing flexibility.

The son of a Roman Catholic linen-draper, Pope was a most precocious child. He had little formal education but, alone in his parents' house on the edge of Windsor Forest, he read most of the English poets, especially Spenser and Dryden. Almost as soon as he could write, he began composing poetry and in later years he wrote of these youthful efforts, 'I lisped in numbers, for the

Parker Gallery

POPE'S HOUSE AT TWICKENHAM

Pope bought this house in 1718 out of the early proceeds from his translation of the *Iliad*.
Coloured aquatint by I. Farington

numbers came' ('numbers' here means 'verses'). When he was 12, Pope contracted a disease of the spine and never grew more than 5 feet high. His back was so crooked that all his life he had to wear a steel frame to keep himself upright, and he suffered continually. He suffered, too, from the malice of his enemies who called him 'Hunch-backed toad', 'Apollo's maggot', and other outrageously cruel things, which provoked many of his own savage retorts.

With the publication in 1709 of his first poems, the *Pastorals*, Pope made his entry into the brilliant circle of London wits and poets among whom he was later to play a leading part. His poem called an *Essay on Criticism* (1711) widened his reputation, and his most famous early poem *The Rape of the Lock* established him as a writer of the first rank. It is a brilliant, delicate satire written with extravagant fantasy as a mock-heroic account of the stealing of a lady's ringlet by a young nobleman of Pope's acquaintance. It was followed by his translation of Homer's *Iliad*, which was so successful that he was able to settle in a house at Twickenham and keep himself comfortably for the rest of his life.

His success brought fame and friends, friends such as Gay and Swift (q.v.), Lord Bolingbroke, and Lady Mary Wortley Montagu with whom he later quarrelled bitterly. He also made many enemies—Addison (q.v.), Dennis the critic, Theobald the scholar who savagely but in many ways justifiably criticized Pope's edition of Shakespeare, and a host of smaller jealous enemies. In 1729 Pope returned the attack savagely and wittily in his satirical poem *The Dunciad*.

For the rest of his life he wrote satirical and moral poetry; though he often said he longed for peace and quiet to cultivate his garden at Twickenham, complaining 'Heavens! was I born for nothing but to write?' The satirical *Epistles* of unsurpassed wit and force precipitated many quarrels. In 1733 he published *An Essay on Man*, a long philosophical poem to 'vindicate the ways of God to man'. It discusses in polished and sometimes magnificent verse the philosophical ideas of the age, and though much of the thought has dated, the verse remains. With its marvellously varied and skilfully arranged rhythm, its incisive and clear-cut expression, it has probably provided us with more aphorisms ('The proper study of mankind is man', 'Hope springs eternal in the human breast') than any other poem in the English language.

National Portrait Gallery
ALEXANDER POPE
Portrait by J. Richardson (1665–1745)

Pope's character and work have been the subject of endless controversy. To his enemies he was an intriguer; a creature of spite, meanness, dishonesty, and vanity. To his friends he was generous, loving, and witty. His poetry too has had a varied reputation. From his position as the undisputed literary leader of his day, his reputation declined as the romantic movement gained power. In our own day his poetry has received perhaps its first balanced examination and appraisal. In the Augustan Age poets and artists sought to express the ideals of CLASSICAL ART (q.v. Vol. XII), and few would dispute that of the English 'classical' poets Pope is the supreme example.

See also Vol. XII: AUGUSTAN AGE; SATIRE.

POUSSIN, Nicolas (1594–1665). The French painter Poussin was born at Les Andelys in Normandy, and came to Paris when he was about 16. He learnt to paint in the style made fashionable by the painters who had decorated the Palace of Fontainebleau for Francis I. His interest in antique art and in the Italian painters of the Renaissance took him to Italy in 1624. He visited Venice, and then went to Rome, the artistic centre of the time, where many French

DANCE TO THE MUSIC OF TIME
Painting by Poussin. From the original in the Wallace Collection, by permission

painters were already working. He stayed in Rome for most of his life. Poussin was not in sympathy with the BAROQUE ART (q.v. Vol. XII) of the time, but developed a classical style of his own based on the study of TITIAN and RAPHAEL (qq.v.) and also of antique statues, for in these he found the serenity and perfection which he considered the basis of art (*see* CLASSICAL ART, Vol. XII). His pictures are not scenes from ordinary life but ideal compositions of classical or religious subjects.

Poussin became well-known in France and began to receive commissions from wealthy patrons; and in 1640 he reluctantly accepted the French King's invitation to Paris where he was greatly fêted. He was asked, however, to paint large altar-pieces and decorations for the Long Gallery in the Louvre, whereas he preferred to do small easel-paintings. Consequently he soon returned to Rome. His style became yet more classical, his tones cold and clear. His themes, frequently of stoical subjects from Plutarch, were more suited to the seriousness and 'Roman' gravity of his new patrons. He began to paint more landscapes, at first heroic compositions based on noble subjects such as the death of the Greek hero, Phocion. Later he turned to allegorical and mythological subjects with magnificent backgrounds. The figures give the impression of statues, with cool and silvery colouring and classical features very accurately rendered.

Poussin's approach to art was intellectual; like his contemporary, the dramatist CORNEILLE (q.v.), he held that the aim of art was not to give pleasure but to ennoble the mind. 'First of all it is necessary that the subject be in itself noble', he wrote in the year of his death.

Poussin had a great influence on FRENCH ART (q.v. Vol. XII), especially on those painters who thought that classical art was the highest form of expression.

PRAXITELES (4th century B.C.). The later Greeks and the Romans thought of the sculptor, Praxiteles, as a master unsurpassed for delicacy and charm, and they constantly imitated the types of physical beauty which he created—as did later artists during and after the Renaissance. Yet we know almost nothing about his life. He came of a family of sculptors, and inherited, perhaps through his father, the skill which had been learned in the previous century, when his native Athens had been an imperial city and had set up majestic images of the gods who had favoured her. In Praxiteles' time the great age of Greece was over. His gods, though still mysterious, are no longer enthroned or on guard over their worshippers, but absorbed like mere humans in their private occupations. His 'Aphrodite of Cnidus' is a lovely woman about to bathe, and his 'Apollo' is a graceful young man lazily waiting to stab a lizard with an arrow for sport. These two statues are known to us only by inferior copies made in Roman times, but the 'Hermes with the infant Dionysus' is probably an original work—perhaps the only one we have by any really great Greek sculptor.

See also Vol. XII: GREEK ART.

Alinari

HERMES WITH THE INFANT DIONYSUS
Statue by Praxiteles. Olympia Museum

PRESTER JOHN (*c.* 12th century). This legendary Christian ruler was believed to reign over a great kingdom somewhere in Asia or Africa. He was supposed to be both king and priest—hence 'Prester', from the Greek *presbyter* (priest). In fact there was no such person, and the fame attributed to him really belonged to a number of different Eastern rulers.

The name was first given to the Gur Khan of China, and appears in 1145 in the chronicle of a German bishop. About 20 years later news spread of an extraordinary letter supposed to have been sent by Prester John to the Emperor of Byzantium. In it Prester John boasted that he was the greatest king on earth, and that he ruled over the three Indies and seventy-two subject kings. A river whose sand was priceless gems ran through his kingdom, and there could be found huge ants that dug up gold, and pebbles that had the power both to give light and make objects invisible.

In 1177 the Pope wrote a letter to a king whom he evidently believed to be the same Prester John. He addressed him as 'John, dearest son in Christ, illustrious and magnificent King of the Indies'. Historians think the Pope was probably writing to the Christian King of Ethiopia (*see* ABYSSINIA, Vol. I). In the 13th century the victories of GENGHIS KHAN (q.v.) were attributed to a descendant of Prester John, called David.

PRIESTLEY, Joseph (1733–1804). This scientific experimenter was a Unitarian minister, a schoolmaster, and a radical politician, as well as a versatile and prolific writer. He wrote over a hundred books covering a wide range of subjects as well as natural science. Today he is chiefly remembered for his work in discovering and identifying most of the common gases, showing that a number of substances could exist in the gaseous state and play an important part in chemical reactions. He was the author of the famous phrase 'the greatest happiness of the greatest number', which he was the first to associate with the principle of DEMOCRACY (q.v. Vol. X). He had an amazingly quick mind. He left school at 16 knowing Latin, Greek, and Hebrew, and before going to a theological college 3 years later he had taught himself some oriental languages as well as French, Italian, and Dutch.

Although Priestley had had no scientific training he had a genius for making experiments, and the chance fact of living next to a brewery at Leeds determined the nature of some of them and incidentally led to his inventing soda-water. In 1774 he discovered oxygen (*see* MATTER, Vol. III). His experiments were among those that contributed to LAVOISIER's exposure (q.v.) of the fallacies of the phlogiston theory (*see* CHEMISTRY, HISTORY OF, Vol. VII), though Priestley himself continued to support that theory which his own experiments were helping to discredit.

In 1780 Priestley moved to Birmingham where he found a congenial circle of friends in the Lunar Society, so called merely because it met once a month at the full moon. Among its members were James WATT, Josiah WEDGWOOD the potter (qq.v.), and Erasmus Darwin. After the French Revolution there was strong popular feeling against political radicals, and Priestley, who had written a pamphlet vindicating the principles of Revolution, became very unpopular. On one occasion in Birmingham a mob wrecked his chapel and burnt his home, destroying all his instruments and papers. Although Priestley himself escaped, he found himself so much shunned for his political and religious opinions that in 1794 he followed his sons who had emigrated to America. He lived in Pennsylvania until his death.

PROUST, Marcel (1871–1922). This French writer came of a rich Parisian family. As a young man he frequented fashionable society, which he later described extensively. Suffering acutely from asthma, he ultimately became an almost permanent invalid. His renown is based upon one long novel in fifteen volumes, *À la Recherche du Temps Perdu*. Another long novel, *Jean Santeuil*, was discovered almost by chance, and published in 1952.

Proust's originality lies above all in his investigation of the processes of memory, and in his minute examination of motives in human conduct. A fleeting sensation, a sound, taste, smell, may suddenly awaken in us a whole clear remembrance associated with the same sensation experienced long ago. Proust reaches the conclusion that our most intense, most pleasurable experiences are not those of the present, but those of the past, preserved intact in our memories, subconsciously.

Proust's language is difficult at first sight, for he uses immensely long and complex sentences to convey the subtle associations of ideas thrown up in his mind. But once at home in this Proustian world, the style is seen to be as supple and fastidious as the author's intelligence.

PTOLEMY DYNASTY. When the conqueror ALEXANDER THE GREAT (q.v.) died, his Empire was divided up among his chieftains, the satraps (governors) of the various provinces which had fallen under his control. One of the most capable and ambitious of these governors was Ptolemy, Satrap of Egypt. Ptolemy soon acquired absolute power in that country, and he took the title of King, founding a dynasty which lasted from 323 B.C. to 30 B.C. There were altogether fourteen monarchs of the Ptolemaic line, the last being Cleopatra and her son Ptolemy XIV. Their rule came to an end only when the Roman Empire under AUGUSTUS CAESAR (q.v.) brought Egypt under its sway.

The Egypt of the Ptolemies was part of the Greek world rather than the Roman, patronizing Greek culture and Greek art. Although portraits and statues show them wearing the traditional dress of the Pharaohs, Egyptian art became much modified by Greek influence. Ptolemy IV even built a temple to the poet Homer and himself wrote a tragedy in the Greek style. The first three Ptolemies were much the most important as rulers, many of the later members of the family being decadent and dissolute, no doubt largely the result of intermarriage. It was an Egyptian custom for the King to marry his own sister.

Ptolemy I (367–283 B.C.), called Ptolemy Soter ('saviour'), was the most remarkable of all Ptolemies. He was a genial soldier of great administrative ability, who succeeded in attracting to his service the most efficient of the soldier-class of Greece and Macedon. He led these troops in a series of campaigns against his fellow satraps, the most formidable of whom was Antigonus, master of Alexander's former Eastern dominions. Ptolemy's primary ambition was to get possession of Palestine and Cyprus. He

AERIAL VIEW OF THE ISLAND OF PHILAE, IN THE NILE, NOW SUBMERGED

Many of the buildings were the work of the Ptolemies, including the temple of Isis in the middle of the island

formed a coalition with three other of Alexander's former chiefs against Antigonus, but when Antigonus was killed, Seleucus, another member of the coalition, secured Palestine and founded there the Seleucid Dynasty, rivals of the Ptolemies for many generations. After 301 B.C. Ptolemy interfered little in Asia, but concentrated on Egypt and the neighbouring territories.

Ptolemy did much for Egypt, building roads and canals, and founding the famous Library of Alexandria (*see* LIBRARIES, Vol. IV). He was an accomplished writer himself, and wrote an accurate and scholarly account of Alexander's campaigns, in which he had played a prominent part. In 285 B.C. he abdicated in favour of one of his younger sons, Ptolemy II, and died 2 years later at the age of 84.

Ptolemy II (309–246 B.C.), surnamed Philadelphus, was a brilliant king and a cultivated man, but not a soldier like his father, having a delicate constitution. However, he supported Rome in her war with Carthage, and continued the struggle with the Seleucids. Egypt still remained the dominant power in the eastern Mediterranean, and Alexandria became the centre of commerce and Greek culture. Many Greek poets, including Theocritus, visited Ptolemy's Court, which in its brilliance and artificiality

has been compared to that of the French King Louis XIV (q.v.) at Versailles. Ptolemy II adopted the Egyptian custom of marrying his sister, and from this time the Ptolemies began to conform more closely to the customs of their adopted country.

Ptolemy III (281–221 B.C.) was far more like his grandfather, the great Ptolemy I. A vigorous man and a warrior, he reopened war with the Seleucids and marched victoriously into the heart of their realm, as far as Babylonia. This marked the peak of Ptolemaic power. Though the Seleucids regained control of northern Syria and the eastern provinces, Ptolemy III had still the supreme power in the eastern Mediterranean. Domestically the King seems to have been a just ruler and is noted for having given more freedom to Egyptian religion and customs.

His successor, Ptolemy IV, was a weak and dissolute man; and the next 150 years are a record of shameful family intrigue and bloody struggle for power, with the Roman Empire gaining ever more control. The last period of greatness, under Queen Cleopatra (*see* MARK ANTONY), ended in disaster, and when she committed suicide and her young son, Ptolemy XIV was murdered, Egypt became a Roman province.

See also Vol. I: EGYPTIAN CIVILIZATION.

PTOLEMY, Claudius (*c.* 2nd century A.D.). This famous Greek astronomer and geographer lived in Alexandria, a city of culture and learning built by the Greek rulers of Egypt. Much of Ptolemy's work consisted of co-ordinating and improving the work of earlier scientists. He was, however, an important astronomer. According to the Ptolemaic system, the sun and moon moved round the earth, which was believed to be the centre of the universe. This belief remained unchallenged until the time of Copernicus (*see* ASTRONOMY, Vol. III). Ptolemy's *Geography*, a treatise in eight books containing many maps, was based on an earlier theory that the world can be accurately mapped only by observing the lines of latitude and longitude. But because of difficulties in obtaining information about distant places the *Geography* is inaccurate in detail; for instance, Ptolemy greatly underestimated the distance between eastern Asia and western Europe, and omitted the American continent altogether. This misconception led COLUMBUS (q.v.), 15 centuries later, to seek a direct route to India westwards from Spain.

About 1400 the *Geography* was brought from Byzantium to Italy, where it was translated into Latin, and became the highest authority on geography all over Europe—the standard textbook for explorers—until the discoveries of the 15th and 16th centuries and the development of scientific knowledge made it out of date.

See also COPERNICUS.
See also Vol. IV: MAPS, HISTORY OF.

PURCELL, Henry (*c.* 1659–95). Purcell, a great figure in English music, was born in London, where both his father and uncle were professional musicians working as Gentlemen of the Chapel Royal. A year after his birth CHARLES II (q.v.) was restored to the throne. The Court then offered employment to musicians as singers, players, and composers; the revived Anglican Church required both music and organists; and the theatres, founded in the West End of London under royal patronage, included much music in their entertainment. This greatly increased the opportunities for musicians.

Purcell, as a boy, was appointed a chorister in the Chapel Royal. This not only gave him the best possible training, but brought him into personal contact with the King and with the most prominent musicians, including John Blow who taught him. Purcell became one of the

National Portrait Gallery
HENRY PURCELL
Portrait by J. Closterman

King's composers when he was only 18, and within 2 years he succeeded Blow as organist of Westminster Abbey. In 1682 he became one of the three organists of the Chapel Royal itself. During these years of increasing success he married. Finally he was given the important post of maker, repairer, and tuner of the King's organs and wind instruments.

As a court composer, the Chapel Royal provided him with a string orchestra and the finest male singers in the country, and he wrote for them splendid anthems with orchestral parts and elaborate solos, the most famous being 'Rejoice in the Lord alway'. It is a pity that this and others, such as 'My beloved spake' or 'Praise the Lord O my soul', cannot now be performed in church with the orchestral accompaniment which Purcell intended. His masterpiece in this form is the anthem 'My heart is inditing', written for the coronation of James II. He also wrote many odes in praise of members of the royal family, the very best of which were written for the birthdays of Queen Mary II. In one of them, 'Come, come, ye sons of art, away', occurs the fine duet, 'Sound the trumpet'. His ode in celebration of St. Cecilia's Day in 1692 was the magnificent 'Hail, Bright Cecilia'.

Probably he liked writing for the theatre better than any other work. In his wonderful opera *Dido and Aeneas*, written for a girls' dancing academy in Chelsea when he was about 30, the singing is continuous and is nowhere interrupted by the speaking voice, as was the custom in English opera at the time. He wrote other dramatic music for the professional theatres which called for much singing and dancing not related to the main plot—somewhat as in modern pantomime. It is in his theatre music that many of his loveliest songs are found, such as 'Nymphs and Shepherds' or 'Music for a while'.

Among his finest songs are 'Fairest Isle' from Dryden's *King Arthur*; 'I attempt from love's sickness to fly' from *The Indian Queen*; 'Come unto these yellow sands' from *The Tempest*; and 'Hark the echoing Air' from *The Fairy Queen*. The theme by Purcell which Benjamin Britten uses for his variations called *The Young Person's Guide to the Orchestra* is found amongst the dances in a play called *Abdelazar, or The Moor's Revenge*. Finally Purcell wrote a quantity of music for amateurs—songs such as the famous 'Evening Hymn', harpsichord pieces, and sonatas for two violins, 'cello, and harpsichord—one called 'The Golden Sonata'.

When Purcell was alive there were no public concerts such as we have today, so he wrote hardly anything suitable for performance by a modern orchestra. Unfortunately, also, many of the plays to which he supplied music are no longer attractive. He wrote, however, with equal greatness in every form of music known in his day. His finest qualities are beauty of melody, wonderful expressive power, and, above all, skill in writing music to fit English words exactly.

Purcell died of consumption when he was only 36, and was given a splendid burial in Westminster Abbey.

See also Vol. XII: SACRED MUSIC; OPERA; ANTHEM; SONGS.

PUSEY, Edward (1800–82), *see* NEWMAN.

PUSHKIN, Alexander (1799–1837). This great Russian poet, the creator of the modern Russian literary language, had already won some reputation as a poet when he left school at 18. Before long he got himself into trouble by expressing his too liberal political views in his verses, and he was exiled from St. Petersburg.

In 1825, the new Tsar, Nicholas I, despite Pushkin's open sympathy with the revolutionary movement, permitted him to return to St. Petersburg (now Leningrad), and himself undertook to censor Pushkin's work. Nicholas, who had no literary taste nor appreciation of Pushkin's genius, meant to make use of him, and this personal obligation to the Tsar later became a great source of embarrassment to Pushkin.

In 1831 he married Natalia Goncharova, a beautiful but commonplace and frivolous young woman, who soon ran him heavily into debt. Natalia became one of the ornaments of the Court, and Pushkin, who wished for nothing but to leave Petersburg and settle down to a steady life of writing, had to accompany her regularly to the palace balls. The Tsar gave him financial aid, but never enough to enable him to clear his debts and be able to leave the Court; so he remained, almost like a prisoner.

Towards the end of 1836 a young French adventurer paid such attentions to Natalia that early in 1837 Pushkin had to challenge him to a duel, in which Pushkin was mortally wounded. He died 2 days later, at the age of 37.

Although Pushkin's place in Russian literature may be said to correspond to Shakespeare's in English, his greatness is not easy for foreigners to recognize. Few western Europeans can read Russian easily enough really to appreciate Russian poetry; in addition, Pushkin's poetry, characteristically optimistic and sane, differs profoundly from that which English people have learnt to regard as the greatest poetry. It has neither the splendour of the Elizabethans, nor the musical quality of the Romantics. It is precise and bare in style, having those classical qualities of lucidity, freedom from rhetoric, and a concreteness of expression, through which it achieves the effect rather of sculpture than of painting or of music.

Pushkin is not only the greatest of Russia's lyric poets, he is also a master of narrative verse. The poem which made him famous was *Ruslan and Liudmila* (1820), a light-hearted romantic epic which owes much to Byron, whom Pushkin admired; while his verse novel *Eugene Onegin* seems to many people his greatest achievement. His tragic story of St. Petersburg, *The Bronze Horseman*, is another masterpiece, as is the *Tale of Tsar Saltan*, one of his six enchanting verse fairy-tales. He also wrote tragic dramas, and was the first great Russian writer of prose

S.C.R.

ALEXANDER PUSHKIN IN 1827
Portrait by V. A. Tropinin

fiction, *The Queen of Spades* being one of the greatest Russian short stories. His prose, both in his stories and critical writings, has the qualities which he himself judged to be essential to good prose: precision and brevity.

See also Vol. XII: RUSSIAN LITERATURE.

PYM, John (1584–1643), Leader of the Long Parliament, *see* CHARLES I.

PYTHAGORAS (6th century B.C.). This Greek philosopher and mathematician lived about 100 years before the great age of PERICLES and about 200 years before the mathematician EUCLID (qq.v.). He migrated to Croton, a rich Greek city in southern Italy, and founded a brotherhood there. The Pythagoreans believed in the immortality of the soul, and also in transmigration—that is, that after death the soul goes to inhabit some other body. Pythagoras' mystical and religious ideas have had a profound influence on the development of man's thought.

Pythagoras kept his mathematical work largely separate from his philosophy. He collected and invented many of the earliest propositions in geometry and tried to make this subject part of the liberal education of his day. He is said to have created the proposition recorded by Euclid that the square on the longest side (hypotenuse) of a right-angled triangle is equal to the sum of the squares on the other two sides. He developed and stressed the importance of the simple science of arithmetic, his greatest arithmetical discovery being the dependence of the musical intervals on certain arithmetical ratios of the length of a wire at a fixed tension (*see* MUSICAL INSTRUMENTS, Section 3, Vol. IX). His theory, that 'all things are number', was an early shot at what is now the QUANTUM THEORY in physics (q.v. Vol. III). Anticipating the scientists of today, Pythagoras suggested, though only vaguely, that the universe was not endless, but finite; and he also anticipated COPERNICUS (q.v.) by suggesting that the earth possibly went round some fixed point in the heavens.

PYTHEAS (4th century B.C.). This great Greek explorer from the Greek colony of Massalia (Marseilles) lived in the time of ALEXANDER THE GREAT (q.v.). His own accounts of his voyages are lost, and we know of him mainly from other classical writers.

Pytheas sailed through the Pillars of Hercules (Straits of Gibraltar) into the unknown ocean (the Atlantic) to try to find the northern lands from which tin was being brought by wandering traders. Pytheas, who lived before the science of astronomy had developed, was the first Greek to realize the connexion between the moon and TIDES (q.v. Vol. III), and one of the first to fix latitudes (*see* MAP PROJECTIONS, Vol. IV). During his first voyage he fixed the latitudes of five different places by measuring the length of their longest days, from which calculations we can map his journey. He sailed round Spain and Brittany and across to Britain, where he landed to inspect the tin mines in Cornwall. He described the methods of mining and various customs of the natives, their wood and thatch houses, and their war chariots. Afterwards he sailed up the east coast to somewhere near the Shetlands, where he heard tales of frozen seas and of a land called 'Thule' (the 'Ultima Thule' of later legend)—possibly Norway or Iceland. He made further explorations along the coast of Gaul as far as the mouth of the river Elbe. Pytheas' account, disbelieved by the ancients as altogether too fantastic, has been verified by modern historians and scientists and shown to be the first full account of Britain given to the Ancient World.

R

RABELAIS, François (*c.* 1494–1553). This great French story-teller was the son of a fairly prosperous lawyer and landowner in Touraine. He was educated at an abbey and later became a monk at a Franciscan monastery at Fontenay, where he studied the writers of ancient Greece and Rome and also medieval writers. When, however, the Franciscans interfered with his study, he left the monastery and thereafter pursued an active, wandering career which took him, at one time and another, over much of Europe. He studied medicine in Paris and Montpellier, and for a period practised medicine.

Rabelais's great books, *Gargantua* and *Panta-*

'LA VIE TRÈS HORRIFICQUE DU GRAND GARGANTUA'
Grandgousier, while feasting, hears of the birth of his son, Gargantua. Woodcut from the edition printed in Lyons, 1542

gruel, recount the lives and adventures of the giant Gargantua and his son Pantagruel, together with those of their followers, notably the uproarious and bawdy monk Frère Jean, and the witty but cowardly Panurge. Beginning as an almost purely humorous account of the giant's prowess, Rabelais gradually incorporates more and more of his prodigious knowledge of the range of human experience.

Rabelais was the true founder of the novel in France. He had remarkable narrative powers, an acute and vivid flair for observation and characterization, and above all a joyous intellectual curiosity and a riotous and often coarse sense of humour—a coarseness which has given rise to the adjective 'Rabelaisian'. He was a true man of the Renaissance, one who believed in the innate goodness of mankind, which he distinguished from the rest of creation because 'only men know how to laugh'.

See also Vol. XII: FRENCH LITERATURE.

RACHMANINOV, Serge (1873–1943). One of the greatest pianists since LISZT (q.v.), this Russian musician is most famous as the composer of the popular Piano Concerto in C minor (the second of four concertos) and the Prelude in C sharp minor (one of twenty-four preludes). The first three piano concertos, the brilliant *Rhapsody on a theme of Paganini*, and several of the preludes are often performed. Rachmaninov also composed operas, symphonies, and works for chorus and orchestra, besides many songs and short piano pieces.

Rachmaninov was making a name for himself in Russia as a conductor and composer-pianist when the Revolution broke out in 1917. He was able to leave the country, and thereafter spent half his time touring the world as a pianist, and half in Switzerland resting and composing. When the Second World War began, he settled in America. His best music, with its bitter-sweet sadness and touches of sentimentality, written before he left Russia, owes much to his friend and helper TCHAIKOVSKY (q.v.). Rachmaninov had a real gift for melody and for orchestral scoring. His popular Second Piano Concerto is a fine and brilliantly written piece.

See also Vol. XII: CONCERTO; SONGS.

RACINE, Jean (1639–99). The great French dramatist, Racine, the son of a solicitor, was born near Paris. Left an orphan, he was brought up by relations and was fortunate in receiving an exceptionally wide education at the Abbaye de Port-Royal where, in addition to the strict religious instruction, he studied Greek, mathematics, geography, and history, as well as the traditional Latin. It was to his knowledge of the Greek poets and dramatists that Racine owed most.

At 19 he came to Paris, where he began to frequent literary circles and to make his first efforts in poetry. But his uncle, wishing to dissuade him from being a writer, sent him for 2 years to a little town in Provence where, under the guardianship of another uncle, a priest, they hoped he would forget his literary ambitions and enter the Church. But Racine, though a sensitive young man, was not submissive, and this exile only developed in him a bitter resistance.

By 1663 he was back in Paris, embarked on a literary career. He wrote his first play *La Thébaïde* when he was 25, and a second *Alexandre* in the following year. About this time he quarrelled with the Abbaye de Port-Royal over a public attack on dramatic poets made by one of its teachers. From 1667—the date of his first great success with *Andromaque*—until 1677—the date of *Phèdre*—he was entirely involved in his career as a dramatist, writing altogether six great tragedies and one comedy (*Les Plaideurs*). There is little record of his personal life at this period, but he seems to have lived a life of fashionable dissipation. *Phèdre*, perhaps the greatest of his tragedies, had at first a cool reception, largely because certain enemies bought up many of the seats in the theatre for the first performances. This setback, together, perhaps, with a growing feeling of uneasiness about his way of life and his break with Port-Royal, may have led him to give up writing plays, to marry, and to settle down to the sober duties of Historiographer to the King. He wrote two more plays, however, *Esther* (1689) and *Athalie* (1691), both on biblical subjects and written for performance by the schoolgirls of Saint-Cyr. Towards the end of his life Racine appears to have lost favour with the King, Louis XIV, who for years had cherished and protected him. When he died, he was buried at Port-Royal, with which he had been reconciled.

Racine soon outstripped his rival CORNEILLE (q.v.) in popular esteem. Racine had an original conception of tragedy in which the characters usually suffer an inner conflict and strive in vain to overcome the power of passionate love. They

FRONTISPIECE TO RACINE'S 'BÉRÉNICE', 1676

are driven on by a force beyond their control—perhaps Racine's version of the Fates which pursued the heroes and heroines of Greek drama. It is this presentation of a struggle against overwhelming odds that stirs and touches the spectator in such plays as *Andromaque*, *Phèdre*, and *Athalie*. In *Bérénice*, where he attained a remarkable degree of concentration of plot, Titus loves and is loved by Bérénice; but when he becomes Emperor of Rome they have unwillingly to part, for reasons of State. Racine's treatment of such a situation is much more simple than is Corneille's: Racine concentrates on the analysis of his characters' feelings at moments of acute stress, and his understanding of human emotions is true and realistic. But the language is the formal language of the 17th century, clear and capable of great variety in rhythm and intensity, yet never the language of real life. The great passionate speeches in Racine are like incantations, or operatic arias whose music resides in the sounds and rhythms themselves, ranging from climaxes of tortured violence, through exalted lyricism to the stillness of resignation. With few playwrights are dramatic intensity and poetry so completely inseparable. It is difficult, therefore, for foreigners to understand Racine's genius, which cannot be fully appreciated without a knowledge of the elements of French versification.

See also Vol. XII: FRENCH LITERATURE; TRAGEDY.

RAFFLES, Sir Thomas Stamford (1781–1826). This English colonial administrator and scholar was the founder of the colony of Singapore and of the London Zoological Society. His father commanded a ship trading between England and the West Indies, and Raffles was born at sea off Jamaica. When he was 14 he started to earn his living as a clerk in the London headquarters of the EAST INDIA COMPANY (q.v. Vol. VII), where his industry and accuracy attracted favourable attention. He had a remarkable talent for languages, and taught himself French in his spare time.

In 1805 he was sent out to the Company's colony of Penang, on the west coast of the Malay peninsula, where he soon mastered the language and was promoted secretary to the governor and council of the colony. When a breakdown of health forced him to visit Malacca, he persuaded the Company to give up its intention of abandoning this port, a public service which gained him the confidence of the Governor-General of India whose authority extended over the East Indies.

Relying on Raffles's local knowledge, the Governor-General undertook the conquest of the great island of Java, its Dutch masters being under the French, with whom England was at war; and in 1811 Raffles was appointed its Governor. He soon brought the whole island under British authority, treating the natives with kindness, humanity, and trust, and abolishing many cruel and oppressive institutions and practices.

At the end of the Napoleonic Wars in 1815 the British Government decided to return all its war-time conquests in the East Indies, including Java and Malacca, to their original owners, the Dutch. Raffles was recalled to England and knighted in 1816. He was an acknowledged authority on the East and for some 2 years he studied in England the history, natural history, geography, and archaeology of the East Indies—

to which he had devoted nearly as much time and energy in the tropics as to his official duties, often working from 4 a.m. to 11 p.m. He also had to carry on incessant disputes with his employers, the East India Company, whose sole interest was in commercial success and who looked with suspicion on his originality and independence, on his passion for the well-being of the natives, and on his interest in their languages and customs.

Raffles returned to the East in 1818 as Governor of a wretched little port in Sumatra. Finding the Dutch busy re-establishing their old monopoly of East Indian trade, Raffles circumvented them by buying the almost uninhabited island of SINGAPORE (q.v. Vol. III) from the Sultan of Johore, and founding a port at this strategic point. He had the vision to see that Singapore could become the meeting-point of all the trade routes east of India, the most important commercial centre between Calcutta and Hong Kong, and the pivot of the defence of the vast British interests in the Far East. He also established there a native college which has developed into the University of Singapore.

Raffles's first wife died in the East and four of the five children of his second marriage died in the tropical climate of Sumatra. During his return to England in 1824 the ship caught fire and all his possessions, including thousands of specimens and all his papers, were destroyed. He died when only 45, worn out by his arduous life in the tropics. The most important achievement of his last years was the foundation of the Zoological Society. Raffles, though physically small and not strong, was a giant in energy, vision, and scholarly and humanitarian activity.

See also Vol. X: COLONIES, HISTORY OF.

RAIKES, Robert (1735–1811), *see* Vol. X: SUNDAY SCHOOLS.

RALEIGH, Sir Walter (*c.* 1552–1618). This explorer, sailor, poet, and courtier, one of the spectacular figures of the Elizabethan age, combined the love of learning and of fearless adventure that typified Elizabethan England. Like DRAKE (q.v.) and other sea-captains of the time, Raleigh came from Devon, near Budleigh Salterton. When he was about 17 he and some others volunteered to fight in support of the HUGUENOTS (q.v. Vol. I) in France, where he learnt the art of war. He then went to Oxford

National Portrait Gallery
SIR WALTER RALEIGH
Portrait by an unknown artist

and, in 1574, to London to finish his education and to train as a courtier.

Raleigh dominated the Queen's personal circle at Court—a tall, imposing figure, elaborately dressed, with dark, curling hair, a long face and a high forehead, and with an arrogant, self-confident manner. There are many stories of Raleigh's gallantry as a courtier. The Queen showered favours upon him, knighting him, giving him charge of the rich tin-mines of Cornwall, and making him Lord Lieutenant of that county and Vice-admiral of Devon and Cornwall. In 1587 she made him Captain of the Guard, an office of high honour and responsibility.

But Raleigh was already planning to explore and build an overseas empire. His voyage to North America in 1578 as captain of the Queen's ship *Falcon*, with his half-brother Sir Humphrey GILBERT (q.v.), failed; but in 1584 he sent an expedition which founded Virginia, named in honour of the Queen, and the next year he sent Sir Richard Grenville to settle the first English garrison on Roanoke Island, North Carolina. This garrison, however, came home with Drake the next year. In 1587 he sent settlers under John White to build a new city in Virginia, but they had disappeared when, 3 years later, two privateers called to bring them help. This, for a time, ended Raleigh's colonizing efforts, though he encouraged Richard HAKLUYT (q.v.) and others to publish the journals and surveys of the expeditions. Raleigh himself never visited Virginia, and he was not the first, as is often supposed, to introduce tobacco to England. He did much, however, to increase its popularity, and he may have introduced potatoes in his Irish estates.

During the whole course of the war at sea with Spain (1585–1603) Raleigh sent his ships on privateering (pirating) ventures, and contributed to those expeditions organized by the government. As the Queen's favourite, he could not always go to sea himself: for example, during the great battle with the SPANISH ARMADA (q.v. Vol. X) he was kept busy with tasks on land. The ARK ROYAL (q.v. Vol. IV), Lord Howard's flagship, had been built for Raleigh in 1587.

The Queen in the meantime had transferred her favours to the young Earl of Essex, and there followed 5 years of fierce rivalry between the two. In 1592 Raleigh angered the Queen by marrying without her permission her maid of honour, Elizabeth Throckmorton, and after some months of imprisonment, he was exiled from Court. This left him free to carry out his own plans. His imagination had been fired by splendid descriptions of Guiana in the north of South America, where in the valley of the Orinoco river was thought to lie the rich INCA kingdom (q.v. Vol. I) of El Dorado (the Golden One) with its capital, Manoa. Raleigh determined to explore this region, and hoped by making an alliance with El Dorado to strike a blow at Spain, and so to restore himself in the Queen's favour. He set out in February 1595 with four ships, capturing on the way the island of Trinidad from the Spaniards. For his voyage up the Orinoco he stripped a small sailing-ship and re-equipped her as an oared galley. Having travelled up the mouth of the river, he led a party inland to within sight of the great Caroni waterfalls which made an apparently insuperable barrier. Tropical rains forced him to turn back, and he returned to England with some gold-bearing quartz and precious stones, and a firm belief that Manoa and the gold-mines could indeed be reached. At home, however, his discoveries were treated with scepticism, and he failed to get support for his schemes of conquest.

In 1596 Raleigh sailed under Howard of Effingham and Essex in an expedition to Cadiz. In command of the leading ship, the *Warspite*, Raleigh, though severely wounded, greatly distinguished himself, and the Spanish fleet was again shattered. After a second, though this time unsuccessful, expedition against the Spanish islands of the Azores, he was reconciled with the Queen, and 3 years later was made Governor of Jersey.

For the rest of Elizabeth's reign Raleigh remained a prominent, though not well-trusted, member of the Court; but he failed to win James I's favour. Raleigh's well-known hatred of Spain was not enough to prevent his enemies persuading the King that he was plotting with Spain to depose him; and Raleigh was arrested, given a notoriously unjust trial, and sentenced to death. On the scaffold, however, the sentence was remitted to life imprisonment in the Tower. There he remained in a sort of imprisonment, visited by his wife and children, for nearly 13 years, writing his *Historie of the World*, making chemical experiments, and keeping in touch with English venturers who continued to explore northern South America.

At last, James's greed for gold persuaded him to permit Raleigh to make another expedition to Guiana. His fear of offending Spain, however, led him to promise the Spanish ambassador that Raleigh would be punished if he molested Spanish ships or settlements. Raleigh, now aged 65, set sail with fourteen ships on his last tragic expedition in April 1617, and reached the South American coast in November, after a disastrous voyage of storm and sickness. Being too ill to ascend the Orinoco himself, he sent his lieutenant, Laurence Keymis, with 400 men to search for the gold-mines. Keymis, ignoring his orders, attacked a Spanish post and went on to capture and burn a Spanish town, during which engagement Raleigh's son was killed. Keymis, demoralized, lost control of his men, and later, unable to bear Raleigh's reproaches, stabbed himself. Raleigh desperately tried to enlist volunteers for a final venture, but failed. The fleet broke up, and Raleigh returned to Plymouth to be arrested immediately for attacking the Spaniards. In October 1618 his suspended sentence of 1603 was enforced, and he was executed without further trial. On the scaffold he showed great courage and dignity. Touching the edge of the axe he said: 'This gives me no fear. It is a sharp and fast medicine to cure me of all my diseases.' And his moving words, 'It is no time to flatter or to fear princes, I who am subject only unto death', served to underline the injustice of his sentence.

Raleigh's greed and pride made him many enemies, and his sceptical attitude to religion—although he was a loyal member of the Church of England—led Catholics to accuse him of atheism. He was undoubtedly a gallant and courageous leader and a fine sea-captain. His efforts at colonization, prompted by a desire for wealth and fame and in the outcome tragically unsuccessful, nevertheless set Britain unwittingly on the road to building an empire overseas (*see* COLONIES, HISTORY OF, Vol. X). Raleigh was the friend of poets: he knew SPENSER well, and Ben JONSON tutored his son for a while (qq.v.). Though few of his poems survive, there are some excellent lyrics in the conventional Elizabethan style, some brilliant and cynical verses, and one or two longer poems of great force and originality. In his *Historie of the World*, which is written in superb prose and which he carried as far as 130 B.C., Raleigh wrote of Death, 'thou hast drawn together all the far-stretched greatness, all the pride, cruelty, and ambition of man, and covered it all over with these two narrow words, *Hic jacet*' ('Here lies').

See also ELIZABETH I.

RAMESES (*c.* 1350–1115 B.C.). This was the name of twelve Egyptian Pharaohs of the 19th and 20th dynasties (*see* EGYPTIAN CIVILIZATION, Vol. I). Rameses II, the Great, is much the most important.

Rameses II ruled Egypt for about 77 years, and lived till he was over 90. In his prime he was an able and vigorous ruler who carried on his father's policy of imperial expansion, reaching far into northern Syria and recovering territories in Asia from the HITTITES (q.v. Vol. I). During his long reign he built magnificent temples filled with statues of himself and obelisks to commemorate his many jubilees. At Tanis he built a temple with a statue over 90 feet high hewn from a single block of granite. At Thebes he erected a great mortuary temple, the Rameseum. At Karnak (Luxor) he finished the vast hall begun by Rameses I. In Nubia (the Sudan) the famous temple at Abu Simbel was hewn out of the rock-face.

Rameses loved luxury and ceremonial display;

he kept a sumptuous court and had a tame lion which accompanied him on his campaigns. He had an enormous harem and some 100 sons and 50 daughters. His mummy and statues show him to have been handsome and well-built. As he got old his rule weakened, and his court became full of intrigues and conspiracies. On his death anarchy broke out and lasted some 25 years or more until Rameses III took control.

Rameses III restored order and revived commercial prosperity. But Egypt was suffering from fundamental decadence, and after a series of weak rulers and a period of domination by the priests and by foreigners, she was finally conquered by the PERSIANS (q.v. Vol. I) in 525 B.C.

See also Vol. XII: EGYPTIAN ART.

Egyptian Museum, Turin

RAMESES II HOLDING A SCEPTRE

RAPHAEL (1483–1520). Raffaello Santi, called Raphael, is one of the greatest and most famous of all painters. He came from Urbino in central Italy, his father also being a painter. He lived at the same time as LEONARDO and MICHELANGELO (qq.v.), but he was younger than either, and with a genius quite different from theirs. Unlike them, he did not show striking originality at an early age, although he always painted beautifully. But he possessed an unequalled talent for learning, which enabled him to absorb all that was best in other painters and to make it a real part of himself. He built up in this way a talent which was almost the equal even of Michelangelo's. He was said to have possessed irresistible charm and gentleness of manner.

His earliest master was Perugino, whose tender and beautiful pictures of the Holy Family, usually set in a rolling landscape, had made him the most sought-after painter in central Italy at the time. When he was 21, Raphael had learnt all that he could from Perugino, and so he moved on to Florence, at that time the greatest art centre, where he stayed about 4 years. Here he fell under the spell of Leonardo, who inspired some of his most famous paintings of the Virgin with the Holy Children—such as 'La Belle Jardinière'. Having learnt all he could from Leonardo, Raphael went to Rome about 1508–9 and here he remained for the rest of his short life. His kinsman, the great architect BRAMANTE (q.v.), who was already installed at the Pope's court, welcomed Raphael's arrival, as he thought he could turn him into a formidable rival of his enemy Michelangelo. Bramante seems to have done his best to stir up trouble between Raphael and Michelangelo, but that did not prevent Raphael learning all he could from Michelangelo's art, as he had done before from that of Perugino and Leonardo.

The first important work which was entrusted to Raphael after his arrival in Rome was to decorate with wall paintings a small room in the VATICAN (q.v. Vol. XII), the Stanza della Segnatura—used by the Pope for signing documents. Raphael was told exactly what he had to paint—which was a series of historical, mythological, and religious subjects to illustrate a kind of learned encyclopaedia of general knowledge. A more unpromising subject for a painter could hardly have been thought of. Most of the subjects were abstract, and in none of them was any real event taking place. There was nothing to

Mansell

THE SISTINE MADONNA
Painting by Raphael. Dresden Gallery

do but to represent groups of figures in conversation. In painting them Raphael accomplished the impossible: he produced a series of masterpieces, of which the one called the School of Athens, representing Philosophy, is perhaps the greatest. The other large scenes were of Apollo and the Muses on Mount Parnassus, representing Poetry, and the Discussion of the Sacrament, representing Theology (*see* Vol. I, pp. 215, 402). In these works Raphael showed a mastery of grouping equal to that of Michelangelo, together with a skill in painting draped figures which Michelangelo never cared to exercise.

During the last 6 years of Raphael's life he was forced to work much too hard by Pope Leo X, who made him a kind of artistic director at the Papal Court. Not only did he continue his frescoes in the Vatican by painting other rooms adjoining the first one; he also painted frescoes in a private house (the Villa Farnesina) and in several Roman churches; he painted a number of portraits and altar-pieces (including the famous Sistine Madonna, for the town of Piacenza); and he made designs for tapestries (now in the Victoria and Albert Museum, *see* Vol. I, p. 320). As well as all this he was made director of the archaeological investigations then being carried out in Rome; he was appointed architect, in succession to Bramante, for the rebuilding of St. Peter's; and he designed a number of smaller buildings. It was not possible for one man to do so much unaided and, although Raphael had many pupils who helped him (and painted considerable portions of his later pictures to his designs), his early death was almost certainly due to general ill-health as a result of overwork.

See also Vol. XII: ITALIAN ART.

REMBRANDT (1606–69). Rembrandt Harmensz van Rijn, the Dutch painter and engraver, usually known by his Christian name only, was a near contemporary of RUBENS (q.v.). The contrast between Rembrandt's style and that of Rubens illustrates the different outlook between Protestant Holland and Catholic Flanders. Rembrandt received little official patronage during most of his life, and so seldom had the opportunity of carrying out important commissions; he worked either on his own or for a few private patrons. His mature art is penetrated by his profound and intimate understanding of human nature.

Born in Leyden, the son of a miller and a baker's daughter, Rembrandt, after studying for a few months at the University there, persuaded his father to let him take up painting. When he was 17, having completed his preliminary training with a painter in Leyden, he went to Amsterdam to study under a painter of historical subjects, whose rather arid style Rembrandt imitated for a time and then rapidly surpassed. When his father died in 1630, he settled permanently in Amsterdam where his first big portrait group, 'The Anatomy Lesson of Dr. Nicholas Tulp', established his reputation. For the next 10 years he was in much demand as a painter of portraits and was able to ask the highest prices. As he was also a successful teacher with many pupils, and his etchings enjoyed a wide circulation, he was prosperous enough to indulge his extravagant tastes as a collector of rare and beautiful things. In 1639 he bought a large house where he lived with his young wife, Saskia, who was the daughter of a burgomaster, or chief magistrate, of a social standing higher than his own.

The turning point in Rembrandt's career

Rijksmuseum, Amsterdam

THE NIGHT WATCH. PAINTING BY REMBRANDT

came in 1642 when he painted the 'Night Watch', a very large picture showing a captain and his company of soldiers making a sortie. As the figures, lighted by the flare of torches, move through the dark town, we can almost hear the sound of voices and the bark of a dog, so well has Rembrandt conveyed an impression of bustle and excitement. The picture, however, failed to please his patrons, who expected a conventional portrait group and not the exciting subject picture which Rembrandt gave them. His beloved wife died the same year. For the rest of his life, although his art was always admired by people discerning enough to appreciate its extraordinary originality and though he still received a few important commissions, Rembrandt's worldly career was unsuccessful. In 1656 he was declared bankrupt, and his house and collection of pictures, drawings, and prints

were put up for auction. In this crisis, however, his second wife, the faithful Hendrickje Stoffels, and Titus, his son by his first wife, undertook the management of his affairs, and formed a company, a device which prevented all his property and work being taken in payment of his debts. Hendrickje died in 1661, and when, 7 years later, Titus at the age of 24 also died, Rembrandt was left alone with a little daughter, until his own death in the following year. Public taste had never caught up with the originality of Rembrandt's vision and manner of painting. A few years before his death, he had had the humiliation of seeing a large historical picture, which he had painted for the new Town Hall at Amsterdam, removed and replaced by the work of one of his pupils.

Rembrandt's misfortunes and the lack of official recognition which kept him from becoming better known probably enriched his personality and developed his immense powers of insight and self-contemplation. No other artist has left a comparable record of his spiritual growth. His paintings have been called 'a continuous self-portrait'; he did, in fact, paint a self-portrait almost every year of his working life, and these are supplemented by many etchings and drawings of himself. These self-portraits show Rembrandt's personality evolving from the exuberant young man, surrounded by the ostentatious luxury which a successful career and marriage had brought him during his early life in Amsterdam, to the lonely old man of the final period, who contemplates his experience-laden features in humorous detachment. He seems to have enjoyed working in solitude or in the intimacy of his home. Besides the self-portraits there are many paintings and sketches of Saskia, Titus, and Hendrickje Stoffels, sometimes in mythological or biblical guise. The Old and New Testaments were his favourite sources of imagery. Had he lived in Flanders, it is possible that, like Rubens, he would have been commissioned to paint large altar-pieces for churches, but the Reformed (Calvinist) Church of Holland did not believe that the Bible should be represented in pictures, and some of Rembrandt's most vivid interpretations of biblical scenes are etchings only a few inches in size. The influence of Rubens, however, was inescapable, and many of Rembrandt's earlier works have the theatrical quality of the baroque style. Particularly characteristic of Rembrandt is his management of light and dark areas which he indirectly derived from Caravaggio (*see* CHIAROSCURO, Vol. XII). In his most dramatic works the strong oppositions of light and dark suggest the eternal conflict of Good and Evil in the universe, while in more placid ones a twilight effect evokes the studious thoughts of an old philosopher seated in a dimly lighted room. In middle life Rembrandt sought consolation in the countryside around Amsterdam, and some of the landscapes he did in this neighbourhood are among the loveliest of all his etchings.

See also Vol. XII: DUTCH ART.

RENOIR, Auguste (1841–1919), French painter, *see* Vol. XII: IMPRESSIONIST PAINTING.

REYNOLDS, Sir Joshua (1723–92). Reynolds, one of the great figures of the English

traditional school of painting, did much by his wise rule of the Royal Academy to revitalize English painting with the traditions of Continental art (*see* ACADEMIES, Vol. XII).

Reynolds was born at Plympton, in Devon, and as a young man trained in London under Thomas Hudson, the most fashionable portrait painter of his day. In 1749 he visited Italy and stayed there about 3 years studying the great masters. In 1753 he settled in London and quickly built up a great reputation and a prosperous studio. Portraiture was greatly in demand, and his patrons, who had themselves travelled, were quick to see that he had assimilated fashionable trends into his style. His first pictures were a justification of his travels and a forceful proof of his ability. In 1753 he painted one of his greatest canvases, depicting Admiral Keppel walking along the sea-shore, a picture full of movement in contrast to the static postures favoured by earlier painters. This vitality, combined with variety of posing, is found in nearly all the full-length portraits (which he painted to ornament the large houses of his clients), whether his sitters are in their everyday clothes in their own parkland, or whether they are dressed in classical draperies in the style of the historical painters. His smaller portraits, including those of children, such as 'Master Bunbury' and 'The Strawberry Girl', combine a shrewd insight into character with a detached yet intimate approach to the individual problems set by each sitter.

The Royal Academy was founded in 1768 under the direct patronage of George III out of the wreck of the Incorporated Society of Artists. Reynolds, being considered the most fitted by his abilities, both social and artistic, to promote the arts in England, was elected the first President and was knighted. At the Academy, Reynolds was able to influence public taste both by the annual exhibits on the walls and also by the fifteen *Discourses* he delivered there. His intention was to build up a strong native school of artists in line with contemporary thought, and to instil into them the principles of academic art. In this he was successful, and the *Discourses* remain among the most lucid and well-written contributions to the theory of art as well as reflecting the taste and aspirations of the time. The combination of Reynolds's talent with the foundation of an Academy where it could be displayed was a most important and far-reaching

National Maritime Museum
·AUGUSTUS, FIRST VISCOUNT KEPPEL
Painting by Sir Joshua Reynolds

event in English painting. Reynolds painted some of the greatest men and women of his day, among them the portrait of Mrs. Siddons as the 'Tragic Muse'. His friends were drawn from the circle of Dr. Johnson and Oliver Goldsmith. His output was enormous, but the failure of his sight prevented his painting for the last 3 years of his life. Much of his work remains in the houses for which it was painted, but most of his main styles can be studied in the National and Tate Galleries.

See also Vol. XII: PORTRAITS; ENGLISH ART.

RHODES, Cecil John (1853–1902). This business pioneer and colonial administrator played a vital part in the history of South Africa towards the end of the 19th century. He founded the territory of Rhodesia, and as Prime Minister of the British Cape Colony was concerned in the quarrels with the Boer leader KRUGER (q.v.) which led up to the SOUTH AFRICAN WAR (q.v. Vol. X).

Rhodes went to South Africa at the age of 17 to restore his health after a severe illness. After a time he made his way to Kimberley, and for the next 10 years worked at the newly discovered diamond fields, returning to England for brief periods in order to study at Oxford.

Though Rhodes himself prospered in the diamond fields, he realized that there was no real future for the industry unless competing interests joined together and regulated the supply of the stones. He therefore set out to gain control of the largest mining and trading companies, and at the age of 35 had not only amassed a considerable fortune for himself, but had formed a combine which today practically controls the mining and sale of diamonds throughout the world. At the same time he obtained a controlling interest in a company working in the South African goldfields.

Rhodes, whose ambition was to see the four South African provinces united under the British flag, then turned his attention to politics. To counter the policy of Kruger, President of the Boer Republic of the Transvaal, and to prevent German expansion in Southern Africa, he succeeded in getting the southern part of Bechuanaland, to the west of the Transvaal, annexed to Cape Colony and the northern part taken over as a British protectorate. North and east of Bechuanaland lay the vast territories of Matabeleland and Mashonaland, and Rhodes persuaded the King of the Matabele to grant him the mineral rights in this territory. The British Government refused to grant Rhodes a protectorate, but agreed that the territory might be administered and developed by a chartered company on the lines of the old EAST INDIA COMPANY (q.v. Vol. VII). The charter of the British South Africa Company was signed in the following year, and the new territory was eventually named Rhodesia.

When Rhodes was still only 37 he became Prime Minister of Cape Colony. At this time the Boers in the Transvaal were much concerned at the growing number of foreigners, or *Uitlanders* (mostly British), who had entered the country in search of gold. Kruger refused to grant the *Uitlanders* political rights, and they appealed for help to Rhodes. Rhodes provided them with arms and money, and at the same time concentrated his Rhodesian police force on the Transvaal frontier. His assistant and friend, L. S. Jameson, a Scots doctor, then led a raid of 500 mounted troops against Johannesburg, where the *Uitlanders* were concentrated, in an attempt to capture the city. The force was surprised by the Boers and defeated; and Jameson was later sent to prison. The 'Jameson Raid' brought Rhodes's political career to an abrupt end. Though Jameson certainly acted ahead of instructions in making the raid, Rhodes acknowledged his share in the movement to arm the *Uitlanders*, and was rebuked by the House of Commons in England. He resigned his Premiership the following year.

The last 6 years of Rhodes's life were devoted to the development of Rhodesia, to establishing a permanent peace with the Matabele, and to promoting a 'Cape to Cairo' railway. Seven years after his death in Cape Town, the Union of South Africa, in which Boers and British had equal rights, was established (*see* SOUTH AFRICA, GOVERNMENT OF, Vol. X), and Rhodes's dream had been realized. In his will he left enough money to provide some 200 scholarships for Dominion, American, and German students to study at Oxford University.

See also KRUGER.
See also Vol. III: SOUTH AFRICA.

RICHARD I, King of England (1157–99), *see* Vol. I: CRUSADES.

RICHARDSON, Samuel (1689–1761), *see* Vol. XII: NOVEL.

RICHELIEU, Cardinal (1585–1642). As Louis XIII's Prime Minister, Richelieu set out to win greatness for France by concentrating all authority and power in the hands of the King and of himself as chief minister. He abandoned any pretence of ruling constitutionally, and used his power to pursue an aggressive foreign policy. He was the real founder of the despotic MONARCHY (q.v. Vol. X) which reached its height under LOUIS XIV (q.v.). He was an important patron of FRENCH LITERATURE (q.v. Vol. XII), and founded the Académie Française in 1635.

Richelieu was consecrated bishop at the age of 22. Seven years later, at a meeting of the States-General (the feudal parliament of France), Richelieu acted as orator for the clergy, and came to the notice of Marie de MEDICI (q.v.), then acting as Regent for her son, Louis XIII. Through her influence Richelieu won a place at Court, and later was made a Cardinal.

When he was 39 Richelieu became Prime Minister. He realized that the French Crown had lost much of its authority since the reign of

THE RHODES MEMORIAL ON TABLE MOUNTAIN, NEAR CAPE TOWN

National Gallery

CARDINAL RICHELIEU
Painting by Philippe de Champaigne (1602–74)

HENRY OF NAVARRE (q.v.) and, believing that 'kings are the living images of God', his first aim was to restore the monarchy to its former power. Throughout his years of office Richelieu never once summoned a meeting of the States-General, and as Louis was weak and helpless without him, he remained the absolute ruler of France.

Richelieu's first problem was to curb the strong and ambitious nobles, who enjoyed virtual independence from royal authority. He ordered the destruction of the nobles' castles, and when a plot to depose Louis and kill Richelieu was discovered, the leader was executed. He forbade duelling and private warfare, and had executed one of the most powerful nobles in France who defiantly fought a duel under his window. In 1630 he foiled an attempt by the Queen Mother and the leading nobles to bully the King into dismissing him: Marie de Medici fled to Brussels, and many of the nobles were imprisoned or executed. Richelieu continued to crush with merciless severity other such intrigues.

In the midst of these difficulties the Protestant HUGUENOTS (q.v. Vol. I), who had been granted certain favours by Henry of Navarre, rose in rebellion in protest against Richelieu's attempts to reduce their power. Eventually Richelieu decided to attack their great stronghold of La Rochelle, and after a siege of 15 months, which he directed in person, the fortress was taken Though the Huguenots lost many of their privileges, they were allowed to retain freedom of worship.

Richelieu's foreign policy was directed towards restoring French influence and power in Europe, especially against Austria and Spain. During the early campaigns of the Thirty Years War (*see* WALLENSTEIN), he could do little more than help the enemies of Austria with money. But in 1635, Richelieu felt that France was sufficiently strong to declare war on Spain. At first the Spanish army invaded France from the Netherlands and threatened Paris itself. But Richelieu with an army of some 40,000 men threw the invaders back; 2 years later they were decisively defeated. Further great victories against the Emperor's forces in Germany in the last years of Richelieu's life and the collapse of Spanish power enabled the French to dominate the peace negotiations which ended the war in 1648 with the Peace of Westphalia.

Richelieu restored the power of the French Crown, gave order and unity to the country, and won for France a leading position in European affairs. But his belief that the interests of national greatness justified any means, good or bad, led him without fear or pity to destroy many of the local liberties of France, to oppress the country with taxation, and to crush any form of constitutional government. French interests, however, were never sacrificed to Richelieu's personal ambition. 'I have been severe to some', he said, 'in order to be good to all.' Indeed he seemed to identify himself wholly with the State, and when he died he exclaimed: 'I have never had any other enemies than the State's.'

RIDLEY, Nicholas (*c.* 1500–55), *see* CRANMER.

RIMBAUD, Jean Arthur (1854–91). Rimbaud's career as a poet lay entirely between his 16th and his 19th year. Thereafter he renounced literature, spent 7 years travelling around Europe holding various jobs, and then, when he was 26, went to Aden and Abyssinia where he had a fairly successful career as a trader until illness forced him to return to France in 1891. Rimbaud's life was deeply affected by his passionate friendship with the poet Paul Verlaine.

The poems written when Rimbaud was 16 and 17—such as *Le Bateau Ivre*—together with the slightly later prose-poems, *Les Illuminations*, rank among the most original and moving in FRENCH LITERATURE (q.v. Vol. XII). Influenced by BAUDELAIRE (q.v.) for his themes, and by his friend Verlaine for certain of his effects of verbal harmony, Rimbaud was yet a most individual poet, excelling in the creation of startling images and in the transmission of the acutest emotions from despair to ecstasy.

ROBESPIERRE, Maximilien Marie Isidore

(1758–94). Robespierre was the merciless leader of the extreme revolutionary party in the later stages of the FRENCH REVOLUTION (q.v. Vol. X). He was small, anxious-looking, melancholy, with a deathly pale, almost greenish complexion. He was trained as a lawyer, and like many young men of the time was greatly influenced by the ideas of the philosopher ROUSSEAU (q.v.).

In his native town of Arras Robespierre's reputation as a lawyer quickly grew, and when the States-General (the feudal parliament of France) was summoned in 1789, he was elected to represent the province, and at once sided with the revolutionaries. In the National Assembly (the States-General) his speeches were at first not a success; but his enthusiasm and boasted incorruptibility soon took him to the front of the extreme revolutionary party. In 1793 he played a leading part in expelling the 'Girondins', or moderates, from office.

The 'Mountain' (as the extreme revolutionaries were called), led by Robespierre and DANTON (q.v.), was then left in power. Dictatorial powers were given to a Committee of Public Safety, of which Robespierre later became a member. The Committee declared that anyone who was not for the Republic deserved to die, and in the Reign of Terror which followed hundreds of innocent people were guillotined. Robespierre used his power to rid himself of any possible rivals, and in 1794 he had the more moderate Danton and his followers guillotined.

But Robespierre, with supreme power in his hands, frightened members of the National Convention (the new Assembly) by refusing them legal protection from the Terror. Others were angered by his puritanical moralizing and by a preposterous new religion which he introduced, with himself as high priest. Meanwhile the terrible slaughter of the guillotine went on. Soon his enemies began to plot Robespierre's downfall. He himself brought about a crisis by demanding a purge of the Committee. Then his enemies, realizing that they must strike quickly, violently attacked him at a meeting of the Convention. Robespierre's voice was drowned by wild cries of accusation, and the deputies were encouraged to vote for his arrest. Later that evening he and his associates were set free by the Paris mob, only to be recaptured by soldiers before they had had time to organize a revolt. Robespierre tried to shoot himself, but only smashed his jaw, and was guillotined without trial the next day. His fall marked the collapse of the extreme revolutionary party.

Robespierre's character and motives are still disputed. Most people now believe that he was driven forward further and further into bloodshed by the fanatical pursuit of an ideal. This ideal was the establishment of a perfect republic, by means of 'virtue and terror'.

ROBIN HOOD

(*c.* 13th–14th century). This hero of English legend and ballad was the champion of the poor and enemy of the rich, greedy barons, officials, and churchmen. His fights with his enemies brought him exciting adventures and many thrilling escapes. Most tales connect Robin with Nottingham, where the sheriff was his chief enemy. Robin was supposed to live in Sherwood Forest with his band of devoted followers—'Little John', 'Maid Marian', and others.

But whether Robin really existed is very doubtful. The stories may have begun with a Robin Hood who was in prison in 1354 awaiting trial for offences committed in a forest in Northamptonshire; but both 'Hood' and 'Robinhood' were common medieval surnames, and there is no other evidence to support the legend. The many hills, old oak-trees, and other objects in England and Scotland which bear his name only show us how popular the legend became, and how quickly it spread. He was undoubtedly an outlaw and something of a highwayman: but the romantic atmosphere of the greenwood and Robin's own chivalrous character are typified in an early rhyme:

> I never hurt woman in all my life,
> Nor man in woman's company.

THE MOONLIGHT BATTLE, 16 JANUARY 1780

Rodney engaged the Spanish fleet off Cape St. Vincent just before sunset. His 90-gun flagship, *Sandwich*, a three-decker,
is shown in the centre alongside a Spanish two-decker

RODNEY, George Brydges (Baron) (1719–
92). Lord Rodney, one of England's naval
heroes, was an aristocrat by birth and of distinguished appearance and manners. As an
admiral he imposed a strong sense of duty and
discipline in the fleets he commanded. Apart
from gallant service during the Seven Years War
(1756–63), however, his career was not unduly
notable until, when he was already in his 60's
and stricken with gout, he won two great
victories, the last of which, the Battle of the
Saints, revolutionized naval tactics and ringed
his name with glory.

In 1780, during the war with France and
Spain, Rodney was instructed to break the
Spanish blockade of Gibraltar and then to take
up command of the West Indies station. On
his way out he not only captured an entire
convoy of Spanish store-ships but, in a battle
fought by moonlight, soundly defeated the
Spanish blockading squadron, capturing seven
out of eleven ships.

Two years later, hearing that the French fleet
was about to join the Spanish fleet for an attack
on Jamaica, Rodney immediately gave chase
and brought the enemy to close action in the
Saints' Passage (between the islands of Guadaloupe and Dominica). Sea battles were then
usually fought with the fleets in tight formation
in line ahead, sailing on opposite tacks. The
result was frequently an indecisive cannonade.
The Battle of the Saints began in the usual way,
but a sudden shift of wind enabled Rodney to
break through the enemy's line near the centre,
while HOOD (q.v.), commanding the rear,
divided the enemy's centre from his van in a
similar way. Many enemy ships were thus
'raked'—that is, swept by broadside fire from
astern, causing heavy casualties. Seven French
ships including the French flagship were captured. Thereafter 'breaking the line' became
a recognized means of gaining decisive victories which had not been possible for a hundred
years. Nelson used somewhat the same tactics
at TRAFALGAR (q.v. Vol. X).

Rodney's victory, coming after the British had

lost their American colonies, had great political importance, for it enabled Britain to bargain with France at the peace conference, and to retain other parts of her Empire.

See also NELSON.

See also Vol. X: SEA WARFARE, HISTORY OF.

ROLAND (8th century), Legendary hero, *see* Vol. XII: CHANSON DE ROLAND.

RONSARD, Pierre de (1524–85). The French poet Ronsard was early obliged to abandon a military and diplomatic career because of deafness. He turned instead to a study of Greek and Latin literature. He and Joachim du Bellay were the leaders of *La Pléiade*, the group of poets who re-created French lyric forms in the 16th century. Ronsard, justly called *Prince des Poètes*, was admired universally and favoured by the kings of France, by Queen Elizabeth of England, and by Mary Queen of Scots. On his death in 1585 he was mourned as France's greatest poet.

His first important poems were five books of *Odes* in imitation of Greek and Latin poets such as Pindar and Horace. Some are grave and exalted, others light and amorous: most were designed to be sung to the lute, on which Ronsard himself was an accomplished performer. Co-operation between poets and musicians was encouraged by *La Pléiade*. Ronsard also wrote three famous collections of *Amours*—to Cassandre (mostly imitated from PETRARCH (q.v.)), to Marie (gay and sensuous for the most part), and later in life, in 1574, to Hélène (passionate and sometimes sad). He also wrote political poems (*Discours*), and part of an epic (*La Franciade*).

See also Vol. XII: FRENCH LITERATURE; ODES.

ROOSEVELT, Franklin Delano (1882–1945). Roosevelt, four times President of the United States, led the American people through the grave economic crisis of the 1930's and through the Second World War. He came, on both sides, from families long established in the U.S.A. His immediate family was Democratic, and he was always loyal to that party. Born at Hyde Park in Dutchess County, New York State, an only son of rich parents, he often visited Europe in his boyhood. He wanted to enter the navy, but went instead to Harvard, and then studied law at Columbia University. He was called to the bar in New York in 1907 and practised there in the courts, entering public life as a Senator for New York State in 1910.

Under President WILSON (q.v.), Roosevelt became Navy Assistant Secretary and, during the First World War, visited England and France, making many friends in both countries. During the Republican government after the war, he returned to his legal practice, but found leisure to concern himself with the Boy Scout movement. In 1921 a grim affliction overtook him—he fell a victim to INFANTILE PARALYSIS (q.v. Vol. XI). His reaction was to vow, 'I'll beat this thing'. Although he could never walk again—and he had been a powerfully athletic man—he was able to swim, to drive a car, and to go on long fishing trips. He was a tall, handsome man, with a fine head and a compelling voice that won him confidence and affection.

New York State elected Roosevelt a Governor in 1928, and he then began to learn the art of broadcasting, of which he became a master. His 'fireside chats' later brought home to the American people both the personality of their leader and the realities behind the issues of peace and war. He was first elected President in 1932 with a large majority. He won 480 out of 531 State votes in the electoral college—an unprecedented result. At this time the United States was in the throes of a financial panic: banks had been closing all over the country, and it was feared that even some in New York and Chicago might follow. Roosevelt restored public confidence. Supported by advisers whom he called his 'Brain Trust', he brought in a 'New Deal for the American People'. He declared that 'every man has a right to live; and this means that he has the right to a comfortable living'.

Vast schemes of reform were introduced, including public relief works to provide jobs for millions of unemployed. The New Deal had three aspects. It aimed at averting abuses by bringing in drastic limitations on big business. It sought to develop the national resources by building dams and hydro-electric plants and by other schemes. It involved 'social security', that is, those who are in misfortune can look to the State for help, either by SOCIAL INSURANCE (q.v. Vol. X) or other means. Roosevelt, with the support of a majority of citizens, faced strong opposition in financial and industrial quarters. He came into conflict with the Supreme Court and was accused of tampering with the Constitution. His critics protested that he was setting

Fox Photos

PRESIDENT ROOSEVELT SIGNING THE DECLARATION OF
WAR IN DECEMBER 1941

himself up as a dictator. Yet in 1936 he was again elected President, with a very greatly increased majority, in spite of the opposition of three-quarters of the Press and other powerful interests.

As the shadows of approaching war darkened, he threw himself into the task, first of trying to avert it by personal appeals to Hitler and Mussolini, and then by giving all help that he could to the democratic nations, short of actual fighting. 'Let no one imagine that America will escape,' he warned his countrymen, 'that this western hemisphere will not be attacked, and that it will continue tranquilly and peacefully to carry on the ethics and the arts of civilization.' He built up a 'good neighbour' policy with South American countries, which helped him when Japan suddenly attacked the U.S. and he needed South American co-operation.

In the early part of the war, he devised a 'Cash and Carry' plan which brought munitions to the democratic cause, and he transferred to Britain fifty sorely needed destroyers in exchange for naval bases in the West Indies. In 1940 he became President for the third time, which had never happened before in American history, and he took two leading Republicans into his Cabinet. After Japan had attacked the American fleet in Pearl Harbour in 1941, Roosevelt was able to come out in open partnership with Churchill against the dictators. As commander-in-chief of the United States forces, he inspired his countrymen with the will to victory. In spite of his physical handicap, he travelled as far as Casablanca in North Africa, to Cairo in Egypt, to Teheran in Persia, and even to Yalta in south Russia, where he and Churchill met Stalin. His concentration on winning the war did not prevent his looking forward to the establishment of a stable and prosperous world after victory had been won. But he did not live to face the practical difficulties which arose from Communist hostility to the democratic way of life, and he has been accused of failing to foresee that the wide gulf between Soviet Russia and Western Europe and the United States could not be bridged by gestures of friendship. He died suddenly after he had been elected President for the fourth time. Even his most bitter Republican opponents honoured him as a great war leader and one of the greatest citizens in American history.

See also CHURCHILL; STALIN.
See also Vol. X: SECOND WORLD WAR.

ROSSETTI, Dante Gabriel (1828–82), Painter and poet, *see* Vol. XII: PRE-RAPHAELITES.

ROTHSCHILD FAMILY. The famous Jewish banking family of Rothschild started business in a small way in 18th-century Germany, and rapidly rose to importance in the world of finance, particularly in 19th-century England. Its founder, Mayer Amschel Rothschild of Frankfort (1744–1812), a dealer in old coins and medals, originally meant to become a rabbi, and it was largely by chance that he became a banker. His sons, later known as 'the five Frankforters', enlarged his business into an international one. Amschel, the eldest, succeeded his father in Frankfort; Solomon went to Vienna; Nathan to England; Carl to Naples; and James opened up in Paris.

Nathan, perhaps the greatest financial genius that the world has ever seen, arrived in London about 1805. During the NAPOLEONIC WARS (q.v. Vol. X) he carried out immense and profitable deals. He invented a daring scheme, with the help of his brother in Paris, for conveying through enemy France the money to pay Wellington's troops in Spain and Portugal. His highly efficient international news service brought to his London office the first news of the victory of Waterloo, which enabled him to sell and buy stock at enormous profit. He began to specialize in loans to foreign governments, and popularized these securities by making their interest payable in London in English money, thus helping to make the pound sterling the international currency of the 19th century (*see* INTERNATIONAL FINANCE, Vol. VII).

When Nathan died in 1836, he passed on to his sons a powerful and established position in the City of London. Lionel, the next head of the firm, greatly developed his father's business in foreign loans, bringing their total, before his death, to £200 million. Lionel preferred not to make money out of human misery. In 1861, for example, he refused to float a loan for Russia when that country was repressing the Polish struggle for national freedom. He was elected an M.P. for the City of London, but he refused to take his seat until Parliament altered the form of oath which members had to take to one that was possible for a man of Jewish faith. One of Lionel Rothschild's most spectacular business deals was in answer to the British Prime Minister Disraeli's appeal to him to find £4 million to enable Britain to purchase a proportion of the SUEZ CANAL shares, and so to keep control of the Canal (q.v. Vol. IV). Rothschild arranged the business within 24 hours.

Lionel's three sons (the eldest of whom became a peer in 1885) developed a warm friendship with the Prince of Wales—afterwards King Edward VII; the brothers were well known in fashionable society, and allied themselves to other great Jewish families through marriage.

Political changes over 100 years brought to an end the Rothschild houses in Naples, Frankfort, and Vienna, but the London and Paris houses still flourish. The red shield (for which *Rothschild* is the German name), bearing the family arms with the motto *Concordia, Industria, Integritas*, still swings over the entrance to New Court, St. Swithin's Lane, in London, where the first Nathan set up his business during the wars of Napoleon.

See also Vol. VII: INTERNATIONAL FINANCE.

ROUSSEAU, Jean Jacques (1712–78). This French philosophical writer, like VOLTAIRE (q.v.), has had an extraordinary influence on political opinions in many countries for nearly 200 years. His revolutionary views on freedom

and equality had an effect on the American Declaration of Independence, and were wildly acclaimed during the FRENCH REVOLUTION (q.v. Vol. X), when his body was brought to Paris and reburied with pomp in the Pantheon.

Rousseau was born in Geneva, the son of a poor watch-maker descended from French Protestant emigrants. He was brought up by relations, as his mother died at his birth. He had an unhappy childhood, to which can be attributed some of his faults of character and his morbidly over-emotional nature. In his early unhappiness, Rousseau wandered from place to place, trying and failing at the careers of engraver, lawyer, priest, and musician. He exploited his friends, sometimes showing little gratitude, or even behaving with positive meanness. His longest settled period was in the household of a young widow, Madame de Warens, with whom he stayed for some years, partly as servant, partly as intimate friend, and where he studied Latin and philosophy, read the works of Voltaire, and learnt to love nature.

When he was 29, Rousseau drifted to Paris to pick up a living, and made friends with writers and with several great ladies of the court. He settled down to live with an inn servant, Thérèse, an uneducated and simple woman who was the companion of most of his life. She later claimed

National Gallery of Scotland

JEAN JACQUES ROUSSEAU
Portrait by Allan Ramsay

that she had five children by him, all of whom she handed over to a Foundlings' Home.

Rousseau's first real chance came when DIDEROT (q.v.) asked him to write articles on music and politics for his celebrated Encyclopaedia, to which most of the great writers of the time were contributing. Rousseau's reputation as a writer came only after he was 38, when he won a prize for an essay in which he declared that the arts and sciences had corrupted the simple and honest nature of primitive man—the 'noble savage'.

After further literary success, Rousseau went to a cottage near Paris, the Hermitage, belonging to one of his benefactresses. There he wrote *Julie, or the New Héloïse*, a novel in letter form about two parted lovers, which was immediately popular, partly because it satisfied the need for emotion in literature of which the 18th century had been starved, and because it described the effect of nature on human feelings. This romantic attitude towards nature seemed very original to the writers of the next generation, such as Byron, and Rousseau's influence on the development of the ROMANTIC MOVEMENT (q.v. Vol. XII) was great.

In 1762 Rousseau published his most important work, the *Social Contract*. This short, eloquent book begins with the famous statement, 'Man is born free and everywhere he is found in chains.' Rousseau, following the philosopher LOCKE (q.v.) but going further, argued that consent, not force, should be the basis of all GOVERNMENT (q.v. Vol. X), that those who govern are the officers, not the masters, of the people, and that each individual sacrifices himself and his natural rights to the general will of the whole community on condition that he gets protection in return. The idea of the sovereignty of the people, so attractively presented in the *Social Contract*, was adopted by all who were working for freedom. After the American and French Revolutions there grew up from Rousseau's doctrine the idea of the almost divine authority of the democratic nation-states.

Rousseau's next book, *Émile*, is really a tract on the education of a boy—a plea for training a child by direct experience rather than by excessive book-learning. It inspired modern educationalists such as FROEBEL and MONTESSORI, and profoundly impressed KANT (qq.v.), but it offended opinion at the time, especially its doctrine that if a child learns to believe in God

and to see Him in the universe, he does not need the intervention of Bible, Church, or priest. Rousseau was, in fact, a sincerely religious man; but so unconventional an attitude to religion was unacceptable to the Church, and he escaped arrest only by flight to Switzerland.

In 1766 Rousseau accepted the invitation of David HUME, the philosopher (q.v.), to go to England, and there he received a pension from George III. Rousseau, however, suffered from a suspicious nature, always quick to take offence. As Byron said of him, 'His life was one long war with self-sought foes.' Now he believed that his friends were plotting against him, and he quarrelled, among others, with Hume. Similar delusions overtook him more and more frequently until his death at Ermenonville in France—a death which may possibly have been suicide.

The best picture of him as a man is to be found in his *Confessions*, though much of the detail is inaccurate. In an age of hard sophistication he preached a cult of feeling and simplicity; in an unjust and aristocratic society he insisted on equality and the value of the common man.

See also LOCKE; VOLTAIRE.

Alte Pinakothek, Munich

RUBENS AND HIS FIRST WIFE, ISABELLA BRANT
Painting by Rubens

AUTUMN: THE CHÂTEAU DE STEEN
Painting by Rubens

RUBENS, Peter Paul (1577–1640). One of the most superbly gifted painters, Rubens was the greatest exponent of BAROQUE ART (q.v. Vol. XII) in Northern Europe. He worked chiefly in the service of the Roman Catholic Church in Spanish Flanders.

Rubens was born at Siegen, near Cologne, the son of a Protestant lawyer who had sought refuge from religious persecution. His father died during the year following his birth, and the family, having adopted the Roman Catholic faith, returned to Antwerp. Rubens was given a good education; he spent a few months as a page in a noble household, and then studied in the workshops of three Flemish painters until he was 23. He spent the next 8 years in Italy, where he entered the service of the Duke of Mantua. He had ample opportunities for studying and copying the Italian masters of the Renaissance in Venice, Rome, Genoa, and other centres. As well as carrying out a number of commissions for the Duke, he was sent to Spain with a caravan of gifts for King Philip III.

Rubens was recalled to Antwerp in 1608 by the sudden illness of his mother. He then became court painter to the Spanish ruler of Flanders, Archduke Albert. He married, and built himself a magnificent house which he filled with pictures and costly works of art. He made his studio the centre of a prodigious artistic activity by employing numerous apprentices—of whom the most famous was VAN DYCK (q.v.), at that time a mere boy—to carry out his pictures from sketches prepared by himself. He also collaborated with artists of established reputation such as Jan, son of Pieter BRUEGHEL (q.v.). This was the only way he could cope with the number of commissions he received for the decoration of churches and palaces. By 1621 he had acquired an international reputation. The following year he was in Paris, making arrangements for the decoration of two halls in the Luxembourg palace with scenes from the life of the Queen Mother, Marie de Medici (*see* Vol. X, p. 365).

When Archduke Albert died in 1623 and his widow, the Archduchess Isabella, was appointed by Spain to rule in his place, Rubens became her trusted counsellor. At intervals for the next 10 years he played the dual role of artist-diplomat. His first mission was to Holland to renew a treaty of friendship. He was also engaged in trying to strengthen the friendship between Spain and England. In 1628 he went to Madrid where he painted portraits of Philip

IV and the Duke of Lerma and spent much of his time in the company of the young VELASQUEZ (q.v.). From Spain he was sent to London, where he was entertained on a lavish scale at the Court of King Charles I, who knighted him and commissioned him to decorate the ceiling of the Banqueting House in Whitehall.

Rubens's first wife died in 1626, and 4 years later he married a girl considerably younger than himself and a noted beauty. Though ageing, Rubens's intense activity continued unabated. After the Archduchess Isabella's death he was put in charge of the decorations for the new Regent's triumphal entry into Antwerp, and he continued to work on a large series of mythological pictures for the King of Spain almost to the day of his death. The last 5 years of his life were spent in the castle of Steen, which forms the subject of one of his magnificent landscapes, now in the National Gallery in London.

The foundations of Rubens's style were laid by studying the works of Italian painters during his stay in Italy; but he developed an entirely distinctive style, ideally fitted for the decoration of large palaces and churches. Only a man of intense vitality could have carried out the enormous number of tasks which he undertook, and this vitality is evident in every brush-stroke he applied to canvas. From the Flemish tradition he inherited an instinctive feeling for the surface qualities of texture, and the roundness and weight of solid bodies. He exercised a decisive influence on French and English painters of the following century, particularly on WATTEAU and GAINSBOROUGH, and later on CONSTABLE (qq.v.). He thus forms the link between the art of the 18th and 19th centuries and that of the Renaissance, where his own origins lay.

See also Vol. XII: BAROQUE ART; FLEMISH ART.

RUPERT, Prince (1619–82). Rupert, a nephew of CHARLES I (q.v.), distinguished himself as one of the Royalist leaders in the CIVIL WAR (q.v. Vol. X). His mother, a daughter of James I, married Frederick, the Elector Palatine and King of Bohemia, and Rupert was brought up as a German prince.

As a young man Rupert studied mathematics and languages at Leyden, in Holland, then trained as a soldier. He saw fighting in the Thirty Years War (*see* WALLENSTEIN), and by the time he was 23 was already a veteran. When he

National Portrait Gallery
PRINCE RUPERT
Portrait attributed to Lely

placed his sword at the service of his uncle, Charles made him his General of Horse. He proved himself a brave though reckless cavalry leader, and in the early battles of the Civil War gained spectacular successes. But at Marston Moor (1644) his thrusting tactics were at last mastered by the steadiness of the Parliament horse under CROMWELL (q.v.). Two years later he surrendered to Fairfax's troops at Oxford and was ordered to leave England. After Charles's death Rupert took charge of the remains of the Royalist fleet, and for 3 years succeeded in keeping it afloat. Eventually his ships were destroyed by BLAKE (q.v.), though Rupert himself escaped to the West Indies, where he lived as a buccaneer. He later returned to the Continent.

After the Restoration Charles II soon made use of Rupert's sea experience against the Dutch. He fought with success at the Battle of Lowestoft, and in 1666 shared with Monk the burden of a bloody but indecisive 4-day battle against the Dutch admirals DE RUYTER (q.v.) and Tromp. In another engagement he and Monk won a clear-cut victory over De Ruyter. Later, Rupert held supreme command, but could win no decisive victories. He spent the last years of his life in retirement in London and Windsor, engaged in scientific pursuits, and he was honoured with a Fellowship of the Royal Society. He was also instrumental in founding the HUDSON'S BAY COMPANY (q.v. Vol. VII).

Though proud and imperious when young, experience of defeat and adversity softened Rupert's character. Cardinal Mazarin called him 'one of the best and most generous princes that I have ever known'. He has passed into legend as a pattern of reckless courage, and indeed to the end of his life he was an outstanding leader of men. He had many other gifts. He loved to make chemical experiments; and he learnt to engrave in mezzotint so well that his prints are still prized as works of art.

See also Vol. X: CIVIL WAR, ENGLISH; CAVALRY.

RUSKIN, John (1819–1900). This great Victorian writer, artist, moralist, and social reformer, taught the English to value and enjoy beauty in an age of commercialism. Ruskin was the only child of a well-to-do Scottish sherry merchant in London: the child of rather old parents. His mother, a devout Evangelical Christian, brought him up to read the Bible every day; he had few toys and no friends and was the inseparable companion of his parents, never living apart from them except for a brief period of married life. His father, who had a taste for literature and painting, took his wife and child with him when he drove round England in the summer, soliciting orders; so Ruskin saw fine scenery and visited many great country-houses. They also began to travel in Europe, and Ruskin's first visit to Switzerland and the Alps was a revelation to him. He filled his journal with descriptions of great literary promise, and with geological notes and sketches which revealed his keen powers of observation.

When he was 18 Ruskin went up to Christ Church, Oxford, and his mother took lodgings in the town, to which his father came every week-end. In spite of an unhappy love-affair, he did well at Oxford, winning the Newdigate Prize for poetry and taking his degree in 1842.

Ruskin was a great admirer of the painter J. M. W. TURNER (q.v.) who, as an old man, was making new experiments in an impressionist technique at which the critics mocked. Ruskin, infuriated by their lack of understanding and in a mood of 'black anger', set out to expose their

stupidity and to glorify Turner. The original essay, written when he was 17, grew into the five volumes of *Modern Painters*; the first volume published when Ruskin was 24, the last, 17 years later. Into this book, beside his magnificent defence of Turner, he put his passionate enjoyment of scenery—particularly mountain scenery, his love of the early Italian school of painters (*see* ITALIAN ART, Vol. XII), his admiration of the great Venetian painters such as TITIAN (q.v.), his hatred of the false and pretentious in art, and above all his belief in those moral truths which he felt to be the basis of all beauty. The book was very well received and exerted a great influence, especially on William MORRIS (q.v.).

In 1846 he married; but the marriage came to an end in 1854. Ruskin, during this period, went to Venice to study medieval architecture; there in 1849 he wrote the *Seven Lamps of Architecture*, an extremely personal study of the aesthetics of building, and, later, *The Stones of Venice*, in both

Ashmolean Museum

PART OF THE BAPTISTERY, FLORENCE
Drawing by Ruskin

JOHN RUSKIN
Self-portrait. The Fogg Museum of Art, Harvard University

of which he expressed his belief that the true qualities of a nation can be discovered in its architecture. In 1849, the PRE-RAPHAELITE painters (q.v. Vol. XII) first exhibited at the Royal Academy and met the same kind of unfair and prejudiced criticism that Turner had met. Ruskin championed their cause, and was a most generous patron to the movement, especially to Rossetti. Ruskin wrote a great deal at this period, including *Sesame and Lilies*, a collection of lectures on good literature.

Ruskin's interest was gradually turning from the study of art to the study of the social conditions that made its production possible. He had come to the conclusion that the happiness of the workman in his work was an essential condition, and this belief led him to write a series of essays, published under the title *Unto This Last* in 1862. It was Ruskin's own favourite work and expounds many of his views: that 'there is no wealth but life'; that it is not the getting of money but the wise spending of it that matters; that to

employ people in something useless and uncongenial is immoral and destructive of a man's human dignity; that the doing of one's duty is more important than the assertion of one's rights. He wished to recapture the best in the medieval system of apprenticeships (*see* CRAFT GUILDS, Vol. VII). He suggested the setting up of vocational schools, national enterprise alongside private enterprise, full employment, and social services for the old and destitute. These ideas, in the tradition of such reformers as Robert OWEN (q.v.), were revolutionary at the time, and Ruskin was labelled a Socialist, though he himself disliked the term.

In 1869 Ruskin was appointed first Slade Professor of Fine Art at Oxford. There he worked indefatigably but unsuccessfully to establish the study of art as a real part of the Oxford curriculum. In the following year he fell seriously ill, and for the rest of his life he was subject to recurrent attacks of insanity. He was still able to lecture and write when he was well, and he wrote many interesting letters, including those addressed to the workmen of Britain and published as *Fors Clavigera*. These became the organ of his Guild of St. George, an idealistic company of people which vowed to establish medieval communities, and, among other things, to cultivate the land without mechanical aid.

In 1872 Ruskin went to live at Brantwood, a house on the shores of Coniston Lake in Lancashire, where he spent much of his later life. There he began to write the most delightful of his books, an autobiography entitled *Praeterita*, and there he died. Though outwardly successful, Ruskin's private life was unhappy and frustrated, and in old age he became increasingly gloomy. He was not always wise, being impetuous and easily angered, but he was generous and magnanimous and a great personality.

See also MORRIS; OWEN.
See also Vol. XII: PRE-RAPHAELITES.

RUTHERFORD, Ernest (Baron) (1871–1937). The great New Zealand physicist, Ernest Rutherford, devoted his life to establishing the science of radio-activity, which is concerned with the way one chemical element may change or be changed into another. He made all the big discoveries in this subject before 1932. He showed for the first time that an atom has a regular structure, and he found the various particles that form this structure. He was the first to split the atom and to reveal the importance of this act. As the result of his work we can now get energy from the atom; we can make atoms and elements that nature herself has never made; we have made for good or ill the atomic bomb (*see* NUCLEAR ENERGY, Vol. VIII).

Rutherford, one of twelve children, came from a happy home. He grew up a strong, boisterous, cheerful boy who was good at everything he did. He was a great reader and clever with his hands. He had an all-round education, and went to Canterbury College, New Zealand: then he began to specialize in physics.

When he was 24 he went to Cambridge with a scholarship and worked there with Sir J. J. THOMSON (q.v.). At this time the study of physics was particularly exciting. In that year the X-rays were discovered in Germany, and the next year radio-activity was discovered in France. In 1897 the electron—the basic unit in electricity—was isolated at Cambridge, and in the following year radium and other radio-active elements were discovered by Pierre and Marie CURIE (q.v.). Rutherford could hardly have come to Europe at a better time.

In 1898 he became Professor of Physics at Montreal in Canada, and for the next 9 years he and his colleagues studied radio-activity. This was shown to be a property of the very heaviest elements in nature, in which one kind of atom became changed into another kind by the expulsion of a minute particle. Rutherford's theory of atoms and their structure is explained in the article ATOM (q.v. Vol. III). Unlike NEWTON, FARADAY, and EINSTEIN (qq.v.), who were solitary workers, Rutherford loved working in a team, and he had the right qualities to attract and guide one. In 1907 he became professor at Manchester, where he remained for 12 years. There his principal work was to reveal the structure of the atoms of all the elements; this has been the foundation of all later work on atomic energy.

In 1919 he became professor at Cambridge, succeeding Sir J. J. Thomson, who had, in turn, followed Clerk MAXWELL (q.v.). There he remained till his death in 1937. During that period many of the difficult problems arising in radio-activity were cleared up. The atom was shown to split in ways that were quite new. In Rutherford's laboratory Sir John Cockcroft (later head of the British Government's atomic research laboratory) found that swift particles of hydrogen could do what particles of helium formerly had done. In the same laboratory another of Rutherford's pupils, Sir James Chadwick, discovered a new particle, the neutron, which was found to split the atom best of all. Rutherford died a year or two before the processes that gave Britain the atomic bomb were fully known.

All who worked with Rutherford speak of his generous, unselfish, vivacious character, as well as of his great work. He had a fine imagination, which he kept well in check No one since Newton has had such wonderful insight into the processes of nature. He went almost instinctively, and always in the simplest way, for the truth. He gained all the honours a man of science can attain—a peerage, the Order of Merit, the Presidency of the Royal Society, and others. He was buried in Westminster Abbey.

See also Vol. III: ATOM.
See also Vol. VIII: NUCLEAR ENERGY.

S

SALADIN (1137–93). This great Sultan of Syria and Egypt, whose name means 'Honouring the Faith', led the Moslems against the Christians in the Third CRUSADE (q.v. Vol. I).

Saladin, having served in the Syrian army, ruled Egypt for the King of Syria until, when the latter died, he made himself Sultan of both Egypt and Syria. He then conquered Mesopotamia and added it to his dominions. He was a good administrator, building citadels, roads, and canals, and instituting law and justice.

In 1187 Saladin led the Moslems in a religious war in the Holy Land, and having won a great victory near Tiberias, he drove the Christians out of Jerusalem and all the coast towns excepting Tyre. The sovereigns of France, England, and Germany then personally led the Third Crusade, but in spite of some successes, they failed to recapture Jerusalem. At last, having quarrelled among themselves, they had to accept a truce on Saladin's terms, which he made chivalrously generous, allowing among other things facilities for pilgrimages to the Holy City.

When Saladin died the next year, this wise king, courageous soldier, and gentle and devout man was deeply mourned by his subjects. There are many stories of his chivalry. When his enemy Richard I of England, whom he much admired, lost his horse in battle, Saladin sent him two to replace it. When Richard lay ill with fever, Saladin sent him fruit and snow brought from the mountains.

SAN MARTÍN, José de (1778–1850). The liberator of the southern States of South America in the Spanish-American War of Liberation was born at Yapeyú in Argentina. He was educated mainly in Spain and entered the Spanish army as a cadet, serving with it for 20 years and winning a high respect for his soldierly qualities. He was modest, attractive in appearance, and of martial bearing. He returned to America in 1812. San Martín disliked popular risings and liberal forms of government, but in spite of this he felt the call to liberate his native country from Spain. He introduced a rigorous military training and firm discipline into the revolutionary armies which, until his arrival, were mainly of a guerrilla type. He never became a popular leader, but was a fine professional soldier with a gift for leading men. He had no political philosophy, as had BOLÍVAR (q.v.), but was concerned solely with the task of driving the Spanish from Latin America.

In 1814 San Martín was ordered by the Argentine authorities to train an army in the Andes to defend Argentina against Spanish aggression from Chile and Peru. He centred his forces at Mendoza, on the slopes of the Andes near the Argentine-Chilean frontier, realizing that the Spanish could never be expelled from their strong base in Peru, except by an attack from Chile, for the more direct route from the north-west went over extremely difficult mountainous country. San Martín opened his campaign by misleading the Spaniards as to which of the very difficult passes over the Andes he would take. On reaching Chile, he joined the Chileans under their liberator, Bernardo O'Higgins, and defeated the Spaniards in two battles, which ended Spanish rule in Chile.

At this point San Martín depended on the English Lord Cochrane, who played his part in the defeat of the Spanish forces by taking command of the Chilean navy. With the help of Lord Cochrane's ships San Martín made a landing in Peru, and quickly assumed the title of 'Protector' of Peru. After trying to negotiate with the Spanish viceroy, he occupied Lima, the capital, in July 1821 and proclaimed the independence of Peru. He had not, however, enough forces to defeat the Spaniards entirely, and so he made an unexpected visit to Ecuador in the hopes of inducing Bolívar, the liberator of the northern States, to join in a final attack on the Spaniards. The negotiations, however, came to nothing, and San Martín, realizing that there was not room for two leaders, generously decided to leave the field free for Bolívar, retired from Peru, and took no further part in the wars of liberation.

The end of San Martín's life was sad. He

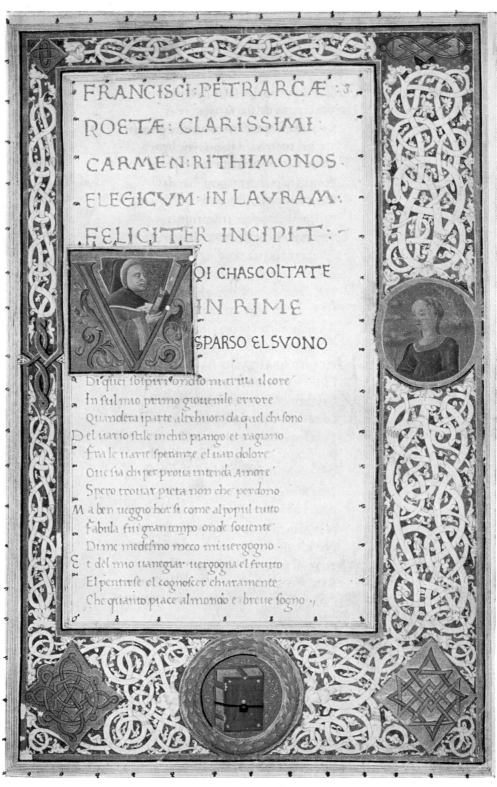

FRANCISCI·PETRARCÆ·3·

ROETÆ·CLARISSIMI·

CARMEN·RITHIMONOS·

ELEGICVM·IN·LAVRAM·

FELICITER·INCIPIT·

OI CHASCOLTATE

IN RIME

SPARSO ELSVONO

Di quei sospiri ondio nutriua ilcore·
In sul mio primo giouenile errore·
Quandera iparte altrhuom da quel chi sono·
Del uario stile inchio piango et ragiono·
Fra le uarie speranze el uan dolore·
Oue sia chi per proua intenda Amore·
Spero trouar pieta non che perdono·
Ma ben ueggio hor si come alpopul tutto·
Fabula fui gran tempo onde souente·
Dime medesmo meco mi uergogno·
Et del mio uanegiar uergogna el frutto·
El pentirse el cognoscer chiaramente·
Che quanto piace almondo e breue sogno·

PAGE FROM PETRARCH'S SONNETS AND TRIONFI
The portrait in the initial is of Petrarch. Laura appears in the medallion on the border.
Written in Ferrara, c. 1470–80

Chile National Historical Museum

JOSÉ DE SAN MARTÍN

Portrait by José Gil

returned to Argentina in 1823 to find that his wife had just died, and to be accused by the Argentine Government of having disobeyed orders. He departed in bitterness for Europe. Refusing to allow himself to be used as a rallying point for civil war, he lived with his daughter in Brussels in great poverty until his death.

See also MIRANDA; BOLÍVAR.
See also Vol I: ARGENTINES.

SAPPHO (*c.* 600 B.C.). Practically nothing is known for certain about Sappho's life, and little of her poetry survives. Yet she is without doubt the most famous poetess of the ancient world, and her name and the legend of her greatness have become symbols inspiring innumerable poets who have come after her. She lived, it is thought, on the island of Lesbos in the Aegean Sea, and, according to the legend, she is supposed to have thrown herself into the sea from the Leucadian rock because Phaon did not return her love. What survives of her poetry shows her to have achieved what only the very greatest poets do achieve: the expression of the deepest emotions in ordinary, simple, everyday language.

SAVONAROLA, Girolamo (1452–98). This Italian preacher and martyr lived at a brilliant period in the history of Florence—the period of BOTTICELLI, LEONARDO DA VINCI, MACHIAVELLI (qq.v.), and many others. Florence had once been a republican CITY-STATE (q.v. Vol. X), in which merchants, bankers, writers, and artists struggled for control. This did not make for a stable government, and the MEDICI (q.v.), a powerful family of bankers, became despotic rulers. Though their methods were ruthless, they gave the city peace and prosperity, in which the genius of its great men could flower.

Savonarola was born at Ferrara. From early manhood he was disturbed by the wickedness which flourished in Church and State alike. Prosperity and artistic achievement could not, he felt, atone for the luxury, bribery, and sensuality which most men accepted without question. So in 1475 he became a Dominican monk at Bologna, and after some years of preparation he began to preach. He meditated on the threats of coming judgement which the Old Testament prophets uttered to their people, and he saw visions of a like doom about to fall on Italy unless there was a return to God. In 1489 he began to preach about this impending doom at the church of San Marco in Florence. His fervent words and evident sincerity attracted large crowds, who were deeply moved, and he was hailed as an inspired prophet.

Savonarola felt that both in Church and State power was held by wicked men; so he supported the party who wished to expel the Medici and restore the old free government. He was even more vehement against the princes of the Church. In 1492 Alexander VI, a crime-stained member of the BORGIA FAMILY (q.v.), had become Pope by bribery. Shocked at this, Savonarola told his excited listeners that he had seen a divine hand pointing a sword towards the earth. When King Charles VIII of France prepared to invade Italy, Savonarola openly welcomed him as the agent of God's vengeance, and the citizens of Florence rose and drove out the Medici. For 4 years, from 1494 to 1498, Savonarola controlled the government. He tried to raise the city's morality by calling for a great purge of all vices and frivolities. His followers held a public 'bonfire of vanities' into which the people were urged to throw all their ornaments and other vanities. For a time, stirred by Savonarola's eloquence and earnestness, the people responded;

Alinari

THE BURNING OF SAVONAROLA IN THE PIAZZA DELLA SIGNORIA, FLORENCE

On the right is the Town Hall and at the extreme left, the Cathedral. Painting by an unknown 16th-century artist.
Museum of San Marco, Florence

but his discipline was too exacting, and the French soldiers too unpopular. He disregarded the Pope's orders to stop preaching, and even the Pope's sentence of excommunication pronounced against him in 1497. Instead he tried to get Charles VIII to call a general council of the Church and depose Pope Alexander VI. But by this time Savonarola's authority was waning, and his enemies seized their chance to arrest him. Under terrible torture he confessed to heresy, but afterwards withdrew, and he and two fellow monks, declaring their loyalty to the Catholic Church, were hanged and burned.

George Eliot's novel *Romola* gives a vivid picture of Florence in the time of Savonarola.

SCHILLER, Johann Friedrich von (1759–1805). Schiller, one of Germany's greatest dramatists and a stirring lyric poet, was born in south Germany, the son of an army surgeon in the service of the Duke of Württemberg. The Duke compelled Schiller to prepare for the same career as his father, and much of his youth was spent in misery at a military academy. He escaped from Württemberg at the first opportunity, married in 1790, and died in Weimar at the age of 46. During the last 10 years of his life he became close friends with GOETHE (q.v.).

Schiller's first play was a fiery tragedy, *Die Raüber*, an eloquent and deeply felt attack on tyranny. *Don Carlos*, set in 16th-century Spain, also deals with political freedom but in a more nobly restrained manner. The trilogy *Wallenstein*, perhaps his greatest achievement, is an immense historical tragedy, full of action and colour, and illumined by an exalted idealism. The last play, *Wilhelm Tell*, powerfully reiterates the plea for freedom. Though over-simple in characterization and too often bombastic, his works are stamped with nobility and ardent hope, and couched in language that is at once moving, sonorous, and passionate.

See also Vol. XII: GERMAN LITERATURE.

SCHUBERT, Franz Peter (1797–1828).

The Austrian composer, Schubert, was born in Vienna. His father, a schoolmaster, was his earliest music teacher; but it soon became clear that a boy who 'had learned his music from God', as a later teacher put it, must have professional instruction. When he was 11, he was fortunate in being chosen as one of the Vienna Boys' Choir, where he received a free general education as well as music teaching. He began to compose in these years, mostly instrumental or orchestral compositions, but also a few songs. He spent more time in covering sheets of paper with these compositions than at his other studies, and consequently, when his voice broke, though known to be an excellent musician, he was considered not hard-working enough to be kept on.

On leaving the choir school, Schubert became a schoolmaster to avoid being sent into the army. When only 17, he wrote his first great song 'Gretchen at the spinning wheel', and during the next 2 years he wrote many of his finest songs, including 'The Erl King'. After his 3 years' teaching, he lived with various friends, all as penniless as himself, composing all the time, sometimes writing eight songs in a day, and even sleeping in his spectacles in case he might have an idea for a song during the night. Although he hated teaching, he earned some money by giving piano lessons, and he spent some enjoyable months as instructor to the princely Esterházy family at their summer country residence near Vienna. Though very shy, Schubert had many good friends who helped him in various ways, and who are remembered through their connexion with him. He dedicated his song-cycle 'The Maid of the Mill' (*Die Schöne Müllerin*) to one of them.

The songs which Schubert wrote in such numbers during these years are his most wonderful and original contribution to music. This kind of song composed for voice and piano—which is generally known by its German name *Lied* (plural *Lieder*)—had hardly been touched by earlier composers; there are a few by Haydn, Mozart, and Beethoven, none of them so carefully worked out nor so far developed as Schubert's.

He had in addition written six symphonies by the time he was 20, and also much chamber music, piano sonatas, church music, and operas. The seventh is an uncompleted one, though the famous Unfinished Symphony is the eighth. The great C major Symphony, sometimes called the seventh, is actually the last and therefore the ninth or, if we include the Gastein Symphony which seems to have vanished, the tenth.

Among Schubert's best-known chamber music is the delightful 'Trout' Quintet for Piano and Strings written on one of his few holidays; the Octet for Wind and Strings, written in 1824; the three string quartets in A minor, G major, and D minor, and a heavenly Quintet for Strings, one of Schubert's last works. He wrote a quantity of piano duets (one piano, four hands), a form of music which has attracted few composers; some of them, like the Hungarian Divertimento, the Fantasy, and the Grand Duo, are among his most splendid pieces.

E. O. Hoppé

FRANZ SCHUBERT AGED 28
Portrait by his friend, August Rieder

Schubert never became widely famous outside Vienna during his life. It was late in his short life, and only after much persuasion, that publishers began to print and sell any of his compositions; and Schubert received very little money for these. He had been able to be happy and free to compose, though extremely poor. But a cloud of sadness hung over him in his last years. In 1827 he wrote his song-cycle for voice and piano, 'The Winter Journey' (*Winterreise*), and its sadness reveals his own state of mind. In the autumn of 1828 he fell ill for the second time in his life and died of typhoid fever. Almost his last words were of Beethoven, whom he loved and admired above all other composers; he was buried beside him.

Although Schubert died when only 31, he wrote a prodigious amount of music. Much of his finest work he never heard performed, and he died full of projects. One friend wrote most truly for his epitaph, 'Music has buried here a rich treasure but much fairer hopes.'

See also Vol. XII: CHAMBER MUSIC; SONG, HISTORY OF.

SCHUMANN, Robert (1810–56). The German composer, Schumann, was born in Saxony, the son of a cultured bookseller and publisher. Encouraged in an early love of music and literature, he played the pianoforte well by 11 and by 15 showed an equal talent for composition. At Leipzig University he met Friedrich Wieck, a well-known pianoforte teacher; after a brief period at Heidelberg University, he decided to become a concert pianist and returned to Leipzig where he lived as a pupil with Wieck. But, while over-exercising on a small 'dummy' keyboard, Schumann permanently injured one of his fingers; so he changed his career of pianist for that of composer. In 1834 he started a musical magazine, intending to encourage better performances and, more important, to help young, progressive composers such as CHOPIN and BRAHMS (qq.v.). Schumann's writings on music are sensible and understanding. During these years he also composed much music, chiefly for the piano. He had a special fondness for collections of short pieces, each suggesting its own mood. The *Scenes from Childhood* and the suite *Carnaval* are popular piano works of this time.

In 1840 Schumann married Wieck's daughter, Clara, who was a brilliant pianist. He began to pour forth songs in rapid succession, including the well-known song-cycles 'A poet's love, (*Dichterliebe*) and 'A woman's love and life' (*Frauenliebe und Leben*). After a year of song-writing he turned to orchestral music again. He composed two symphonies and began the Piano Concerto in A minor; in the following year he turned to chamber music, writing three fine string quartets and the lovely Quintet for piano and strings.

In 1844 he undertook a concert tour with his wife in Russia, but he was taken ill and had to return home. After a short rest he completed his Piano Concerto. Five years later he unwisely accepted the post of conductor at Düsseldorf, for which he proved quite unfitted. For years he had suffered from a brain illness, and early in 1854, worried by the responsibilities of his new post, he threw himself into the Rhine. He was rescued but had to spend the last 2 years of his life in a private asylum.

The spirit of Schumann's music can be summed up as glowing and enthusiastic. Of all the composers between Beethoven and Wagner, Schumann was most keenly devoted to the cause

Macmillan & Co., Ltd.

ROBERT AND CLARA SCHUMANN
From a contemporary daguerreotype
(Grove, *Dictionary of Music*)

of new art (whether books, pictures, or music) and to the expression of the inmost feelings. All his music reflects his personality, and since that personality was warm, friendly, and generous, the music which he created is always lovable.

See also Vol. XII: SONG, HISTORY OF.

SCHWEITZER, Dr. Albert (b. 1875). This great humanitarian, musician, and thinker was born in Alsace Lorraine, then part of Germany. He was the eldest son of the pastor of Günsbach, a little town in the Vosges mountains, and he went to the village school. He was strong and brave, but did not appear to be particularly clever, although he was unusually thoughtful and determined. Certain conclusions he came to as a boy influenced his whole life. For instance, while he was still at school, he made up his mind never willingly to kill any living thing —a determination which found full expression in his great book, *The Philosophy of Civilization*. He was still very young when he discovered his love of music, and he became a famous performer on both organ and piano.

Schweitzer studied philosophy and theology at Strasbourg University, during which time he was slowly thinking out his plans for his own future. He decided that until he was 30 he would enjoy the pursuit of learning and music, but that after 30 he would give his life to the service of others. In those first 9 years he achieved as much as others have done in a lifetime. He became President of his old college, a renowned writer and thinker, and a famous musician. An article in a missionary paper suggested to him how he could best fulfil his pledge of service. He determined to serve the very poorest Negroes in the unhealthiest part of Africa, and since a doctor was what they most needed, he trained to be one. One person alone fully understood his decision at this time—Helène Bresslau (later his wife). While he trained as a doctor, she trained as a nurse, and in 1913 they set off together for Lambaréné, an unknown missionary station in French Equatorial Africa.

They completed their journey far up the Ogowe river in dugout canoes, and by canoe came his medical supplies, stores, books, and finally his piano. Even before the packing cases arrived, patients in every stage of misery and disease began to pour in, travelling hundreds of miles by river to see the new doctor. In the first 9 months he and his wife treated over 2,000 people. At first there was nowhere to store medicines, let alone anywhere to perform operations; but gradually some primitive buildings were erected with the help of the friends and relations who accompanied the sick. It was a heroic task demanding dauntless courage, and there were many setbacks. During the First World War the Schweitzers were interned in France, and when Schweitzer returned in 1924 he found the jungle had destroyed most of his work. Next year, after a terrible epidemic followed by famine, Schweitzer decided to find a new site with room for an isolation hospital and ground to grow fresh fruit and vegetables for patients and staff—for by now he had some devoted helpers. Between the wars he paid frequent visits to Europe, where he lectured and gave concerts to earn money for the hospital. During the Second World War, isolated and short of supplies, he still managed to carry on at the hospital.

When he was 75 he began to build a separate settlement for his leper patients, where he could make use of a new drug which, for the first time, gave hope of cure (*see* TROPICAL DISEASES, Vol. XI). As usual he was short of funds, but in 1953 he won the Nobel Peace Prize and was able to complete the work.

In 1957 Schweitzer made a personal appeal to the great powers to stop testing nuclear weapons—an appeal on behalf of the human race by the greatest humanitarian of our time.

SCOTT, Robert Falcon (1868–1912). Scott, the leader of the British expeditions to the South Pole in 1901–4 and again in 1910–12, became a British national hero at a time when public attention was eagerly focused on the exploration of POLAR REGIONS (q.v. Vol. III) and when Scott and SHACKLETON were in keen competition with the Norwegian explorers NANSEN and AMUNDSEN and the American PEARY (qq.v.). Wireless and aviation were still in their infancy, and these expeditions on foot over unexplored regions of ice can be compared with the great explorations of the 15th and 16th centuries into unknown seas.

Scott was born at Devonport. He entered the navy, and when he was 31 he was selected to command the National Antarctic Expedition organized by the Royal Geographical Society and the Royal Society. Scott had no Polar experience, but was a brilliant naval officer and

Paul Popper

CAPTAIN SCOTT ON A DEPOT-LAYING JOURNEY DURING HIS
LAST EXPEDITION

also a first-class scientist, and soon mastered the early history of antarctic exploration. He sailed from the Thames in the summer of 1901 in the wooden research ship DISCOVERY (q.v. Vol. IV) with a well-chosen company which included Ernest Shackleton, E. A. Wilson (doctor, artist, and zoologist), and Petty Officer Edgar Evans. After 6 adventurous months they reached the Ross Sea and saw for the first time the Antarctic continent, over 100 miles away. They had sailed through pack-ice, captured all kinds of seal, and grown familiar with whales, penguins, and other Antarctic birds.

On this expedition Scott discovered and named King Edward VII Land, and from his winter quarters off Hut Point and McMurdo Sound he led and organized several important sledge journeys into the interior. With Shackleton and Wilson he penetrated farther south than anyone had yet been. At the end of 2 years the *Discovery*, and two relief ships which were sent out to find them, returned home with much valuable information.

Scott was promoted captain and resumed his

duties in the navy. In 1909 he announced plans for an attempt to reach the South Pole, and in 1910 he sailed in the *Terra Nova* with a company of fifty-nine, together with three motor-sledges, nineteen Siberian ponies, and thirty-four sledge-dogs. His second-in-command was Lieut. E. R. Evans (later Admiral Lord Mountevans), while also among the party were Scott's old comrades Petty Officer Edgar Evans and Dr. Wilson.

In November, which is springtime in the southern hemisphere, Scott set out overland from Cape Evans, with his sledges and food stores, on a journey of some 950 miles to the South Pole. Depots of food and oil were established along the route, each containing one week's food for one of the several parties into which the expedition was divided. At intervals, parties were sent back to the base, according to plan. Scott pressed on, and at the foot of the Great Beardmore Glacier, 400 miles from the Pole, the surviving ponies were killed, and a food depot named Desolation Camp was made from their carcasses. Then the dogs were sent back across the Great Ice Barrier to the base at Cape Evans. Three man-hauling teams, dragging 140 lb. per man, toiled up the Beardmore Glacier, 140 miles in length. On 4 January 1912, when about 200 miles from the Pole and 750 miles from the base, Scott sent back the last supporting party, under Lieut. Evans. Then he, with Dr. Wilson, Captain L. E. G. Oates of the Inniskilling Dragoons, Lieut. H. R. Bowers, and Petty Officer Edgar Evans, set out on the last stretch.

These five were never seen alive again, but Scott kept a diary of their last gallant journey, which was later found with his body. On 16 January they sighted the Pole and 2 days later reached it, only to find a Norwegian flag already there; the explorer AMUNDSEN (q.v.) had beaten them by little more than a month—a bitter disappointment. They also found the Norwegian party's tent and records. 'What a terrible place', Scott wrote in his diary.

The five men then set out on their tragic return journey. A succession of blizzards, frostbite, and treacherous surfaces hindered the party, and then they ran into a blizzard which lasted for 9 days and nights without cessation. Petty Officer Evans, considered the strongest man, fell and injured himself; and although his companions did their utmost to help him, he eventually died, having seriously delayed the party. A month later, Captain Oates, too badly frost-bitten to go on without delaying his companions still further, deliberately walked out from the tent into a driving blizzard, a grand act of self-sacrifice in an attempt to save his three companions. Scott wrote, 'We all hope to meet the end in the same fine spirit—and assuredly the end is not far.'

Scott, Wilson, and Bowers struggled another 20 miles in 4 days, and then were compelled to stop when only 11 miles from a big food depot at One Ton Camp. Fearful blizzard weather overtook them, and after 8 days without food the three died from starvation and exposure about 29 March. Yet one of the last entries in Scott's diary reads, 'How much better has all this been than lounging in too great comfort at home.' A relief party had actually reached One Ton Camp in March but had to turn back. It was not till 8 months later that a search party succeeded in finding the tent and the bodies, and in bringing back the notebooks, letters, and specimens which the explorers had continued to carry despite the extra weight.

The story of Scott's expeditions can be read in his own book, *The Voyage of the Discovery*, and in his journals, *Scott's Last Expedition*, published the year after his death.

See also Vol. III: POLAR REGIONS (EXPLORATION).

SCOTT, Sir Walter (1771–1832). Scott, the great romantic novelist and poet, creator of the Waverley novels, was born of Edinburgh middle-class parents when the ROMANTIC MOVEMENT (q.v. Vol. XII) and the Industrial Revolution were beginning. As a child, he was fascinated by his family history, and many of his best stories are based on actual reminiscences. He was brought up at home in his grandfather's country house because of an accident which had made him lame almost from birth. There he grew strong and active, becoming a great rider and, in spite of his lameness, a great walker; he was a delightful companion and while still at school acquired a reputation as a story-teller.

Scott was trained for the law, and his historical studies provided invaluable material later for his novels. At 28 he seemed settled as a moderately successful lawyer with literary leanings; he was married and already Sheriff-Depute of Selkirkshire, in the Scottish Border country from which his ancestors had come. As a boy, he had fallen under the spell of the traditional poetry of the Border and discovered for himself Percy's *Reliques*, a famous early collection of ballads. With James Hogg, the self-educated 'Ettrick Shepherd', he published a collection of *Border Minstrelsy* (1802) including such now-famous ballads as 'The Wife of Usher's Well' and 'Sir Patrick Spens'. Scott restored many of the ballads which he found incomplete, and these additions form a real part of his literary achievement. Three years later he produced a narrative poem of his own, *The Lay of the Last Minstrel*, written in the metre of Coleridge's *Christabel*, which he greatly admired. It was an immediate and resounding success.

Scott now turned seriously to literature and became a partner in the printing firm of James Ballantyne. *Marmion* (for which the publisher Constable paid 1,000 guineas without even seeing it), is another romantic narrative poem, in Scott's 'light horseman metre', and culminates in a superb account of the Battle of Flodden. *The Lady of the Lake*, a romantic tale set on the shore of Loch Katrine, followed. Scott's poetry was so successful that he was able to buy an estate on the banks of the Tweed where he began building the gothic mansion he called Abbotsford, which was finished in 1824. His popularity for a time rivalled Byron's, though he himself thought little of his own poetry.

In 1814, when he was 43, Scott published his first novel, *Waverley* (which, with *Redgauntlet*, is based on first-hand stories from survivors of the '45 Rebellion). It was published anonymously, though Scott's authorship was widely guessed. It made 'an instant and universal impression', wrote a contemporary, 'the unexpected newness of the thing . . . struck us with an electric shock of delight'. For *Waverley* was the first historical novel ever written. It was followed in the next 12 years by nineteen other novels. Scott was raised to a baronetcy, and became a great national figure, organizing George IV's visit to Edinburgh—the first visit of a British Sovereign to Scotland since before the Union of the two countries in 1707. At Abbotsford he worked and entertained his friends. Each day Scott rose at 5 a.m. and, having completed most of his day's work before the family was ready for breakfast, was free to see to his estate, entertain his friends, and amuse his children. But in 1826, by a combination of his own lack of business sense, the irresponsibility of his partners, the Ballantynes, and the national economic crisis, he was financially ruined. For the remaining 6 years of his life he wrote doggedly to pay off his enormous debts, work which for the most part falls far below the standard of his earlier writing. It includes, however, his *Tales of a Grandfather*, stories from history written for his grandson. In 1832, the year of the Reform Bill, which as a life-long Tory he had bitterly opposed, Scott died at Abbotsford.

Scott's influence both on English and European literature is immeasurable. He 'released the past for fiction' as none had done before, though many have done since: the whole conception of the imaginative reconstruction of the past derives from Scott. His novels are of two kinds—the Scottish novels, nearly all of which, set in the 18th century, draw on memories still living in Scott's own day, such as *Rob Roy*, *The Heart of Midlothian*, *Guy Mannering* (the most autobiographical), and the *Antiquary*

(Scott's own favourite); and the books set in the more remote past with non-Scottish subjects, such as *Ivanhoe*, *Kenilworth*, and *Quentin Durward*. All the novels show Scott's power of creating character, but the Scottish novels, with their skilful use of the Scottish dialect in portraying poor and middle-class Scots, contain his finest creations. These characters have a humour and often a dignity in adversity which is unrivalled.

Scott's output was prodigious; he wrote twenty-eight novels, apart from his poems, his life of Napoleon, his editions of Dryden and Swift, and his work for periodicals. Standing as he does between the old, feudal Scotland which he loved and modern Scotland, he transmitted a legend about his country which, whatever its inaccuracies and romantic colouring, is now firmly embedded in Scottish national tradition.

See also Vol. XII: NOVEL; BALLAD.

National Galleries of Scotland

THE SCOTT FAMILY AT ABBOTSFORD
Sir Walter Scott is seated in the centre, with Lady Scott on the far left. His two daughters are dressed as milkmaids.
Painting by Sir David Wilkie

SHACKLETON, Sir Ernest Henry (1874–1922). This great Irish explorer of the Polar regions had a magnificent physique and great moral courage; he was capable of outstanding feats of endurance, and his exhilarating, genial personality made him a great leader.

Shackleton was born in Co. Kildare and educated at Dulwich College, London, from which he joined the Merchant Service. In 1901 R. F. SCOTT (q.v.) engaged him as a junior officer on board the *Discovery*, which sailed from New Zealand to the Ross Sea. Shackleton was one of the sledge party which reached 82° South —the farthest south yet—but the party had to turn back on account of scurvy.

In 1908 Shackleton set out himself to try to reach the South Pole by the same route. He sailed in command of the 200-ton whaler *Nimrod* for the Ross Sea and landed three parties, one to discover the Southern Magnetic Pole, another to climb Mount Erebus (13,000 feet), and a third, led by himself, to find the Beardmore Glacier route up to the 10,000-foot Antarctic plateau, which he called 'the blackest and most horrible place of the earth'. He reached a point 88° 23′ South, about 100 miles from the Pole, before blizzards forced his sledge party to turn back. The return was a race with death, with only a few cups of cocoa between the explorers and starvation before the glacier base was reached.

Shackleton's account of his expedition, *The Heart of the Antarctic*, made him famous. He was knighted, and his lecture tours, at which the first cinematographic films of Polar exploration were shown, were very popular. At that date many nations were competing in the race for the Poles: PEARY (q.v.) reached the North Pole in 1909; AMUNDSEN (q.v.) the South Pole in December 1911, and Scott a month later.

Since the Poles had been conquered, Shackleton decided that his next expedition, in the *Endurance* (named after his family motto 'By endurance we conquer'), should attempt a sledge crossing of the 1,800-mile-wide Antarctic continent from the Weddell to the Ross Sea. The *Endurance* sailed at the outbreak of the First World War in August 1914. Soon after reaching the Weddell Sea she was caught in the ice, but the current took her 570 miles in 281 days before she broke up under the pressure of the surrounding ice. All hope of crossing the continent was over; the question was whether the party (which included F. R. Worsley, who described the

Royal Geographical Society

THE 'ENDURANCE' CRUSHED BY ICE IN THE WEDDELL SEA

journey in his book, *Endurance*) could regain safety by floating north on an ice floe with their boats, sledges, and dogs. The ice floe broke up beneath their camp, so they took to the boats and reached Elephant Isle after a fearful journey during which Shackleton's capacity for leadership was tested to the uttermost. 'The Boss' and five others then sailed one of the boats 800 miles to the island of South Georgia to obtain a boat to rescue the main party left on Elephant Isle. The 22-foot boat, which effected the rescue after four attempts through the stormiest seas in the world, is preserved at Dulwich College.

In 1921 Shackleton proposed to chart 2,000 miles of Antarctic coastline in the *Quest*, but he died of a heart attack on reaching South Georgia on 5 January 1922. Almost his last words were 'I grow old and tired, but must always lead on.' He was a real Elizabethan in his zest for adventure. His 1914–16 expedition, as he describes it in his book *South*, is a grand epic of endurance worthy of a leader of great strength and imagination—by nature a fighter.

See also Vol. III: POLAR REGIONS.

SHAFTESBURY, Earl of (1801–85). Anthony Ashley Cooper, 7th Earl of Shaftesbury, was perhaps the greatest social reformer of the 19th century. As Lord Shaftesbury's eldest son he was

Mrs. W. King

'LOST AND FOUND'

Two waifs looking at the portrait of their benefactor, Lord
Shaftesbury. Painting by William Macduff

known as Lord Ashley until his father died in
1851. As a boy he was neglected by his own
father and mother, and was largely brought up
by Maria Millis, an old family servant, who
gave him a religious upbringing and took the
place of a mother to him. All his life he carried
no other watch than the gold one she left him
when she died. He was sent to Harrow School
where, when he was 14, he witnessed a party
of drunken coffin-bearers carrying a pauper's
coffin to the churchyard. He was so shocked
that anyone should suffer such a mockery of a
funeral that he took a solemn vow to dedicate
his life to uplifting the downtrodden and oppressed. A tablet on the wall of Harrow School
still commemorates this resolution.

At Oxford, Lord Ashley did well in classics,
and after the customary European tour of
fashionable young men, he entered Parliament
in 1826. WELLINGTON (q.v.), then Prime Minister, appointed him to the India Board of Control.
In this post he started his first political agitation:
against 'suttee'—the Hindu widow's practice of
committing suicide by throwing herself on her
husband's funeral pyre. It was made illegal
3 years later.

The first social abuse in Britain to attract
Lord Ashley's interest was the cruel and inhuman
treatment of lunatics and the feeble-minded (*see*
MENTAL HOSPITAL, Vol. X). He was made a
member of a House of Commons Committee of
Inquiry, visited many homes and asylums, and
got an Act passed to amend the law. Before his
death he had secured an almost complete reform
of the Lunacy Acts. He also took a considerable
share in WILBERFORCE's agitation for the abolition of slavery (q.v.).

He then turned his attention to the mines and
factories, and was largely responsible for the
movement leading to the Factory Acts of 1833
and 1844, for the law forbidding women and
children to work underground in mines, and
for the famous Ten Hours Factory Act of 1847
(*see* INDUSTRIAL WELFARE, Vol. X). He became
an ardent supporter of the Early Closing Association, founded in 1842 to limit the working hours
of bank clerks, office workers, and shop assistants
—though this had no immediate effect. He was
made President of the Ragged School Union,
which ran schools financed by charity for the
poor children of city slums. One of his most
picturesque 'self-help' activities was the London
Shoeblack Brigade, recruited from children educated in the ragged schools who were supplied
with uniforms and cleaning outfits. He also
championed the cause of the 'climbing boys'
who were sent up chimneys to sweep them;
though this practice was not made completely
illegal until 1875 (*see* CHILD WELFARE, Vol. X).

Lord Ashley, as Chairman of the Central
Board of Public Health, did much to check
epidemics, and also to improve camp and
hospital conditions during the CRIMEAN WAR
(q.v. Vol. X). He agitated against the appalling
housing conditions in London and other cities
(*see* SLUMS, Vol. X), and in 1851 secured the
passage of the Lodging Houses Act, considered
by Dickens to have been the best piece of legislation that ever proceeded from Parliament. The
Peabody housing scheme for erecting model flats
and tenements for the working classes owed
much to Shaftesbury.

After he became an earl in 1851, he made the
village on his estate in Wimborne St. Giles a
model for all housing societies to follow. This
was the year in which the old Window Tax was
repealed: a tax which Shaftesbury had described
as a direct attack on fresh air and sunshine,
health and sanitation. He pleaded for parks and

playgrounds, and for reducing working hours, and providing a Saturday half-holiday for all workers. He co-operated closely in Dr. BARNARDO's emigration schemes (q.v.).

Shaftesbury's manifold philanthropic activities were based on a sincere and practical Christianity, a belief that human personality was more sacred than property, that all men were brothers under the common fatherhood of God, and that a selfish use of wealth, privilege, and ability was a flagrant denial of that brotherhood. He always insisted on first-hand information, and made it a rule to study personally every social problem in which he became interested. His wife, Lady Emily Cowper, was always an enthusiastic partner in all his schemes, and her mother's second marriage with Lord PALMERSTON (q.v.) gave him considerably more political power. Shaftesbury himself spent so much on philanthropic schemes that he was always in debt, and lived mainly on borrowed money.

Shaftesbury inevitably came up against criticism and made enemies. His opposition to the Reform Bills of 1832 and 1867 and to the development of trade unionism was strongly criticized. Shaftesbury argued that education for political responsibility should precede and not follow the granting of votes; and he feared that the development of trade unions might start class warfare. Among his fellow peers he was often considered to be unduly proud and self-contained. But among the poor he moved freely as a friend and brother, and he exercised a magic fascination over children, who called him 'our Earl'.

His place in the hearts of the people became obvious at his death, when a memorial service was held in Westminster Abbey. All his eight pall-bearers were humble men, and the congregation included factory workers, ex-chimney sweeps, women liberated from the mines, children from the ragged schools, and the London costermongers who had once made him a present of a donkey. On the coffin, beside a wreath from a princess, lay one given as 'the loving tribute of the flower-girls of London'. A biographer wrote of this memorial service that 'for no other man in England or in the world could such an assembly have been drawn together'.

SHAKESPEARE, William (1564–1616).

Shakespeare, whose name is better known than that of any other dramatist in history, and whose words are more often quoted, is himself a

THE SHAKESPEARE MONUMENT IN STRATFORD ON AVON CHURCH

shadowy figure. Some writers, indeed, deny his authorship of the plays, claiming that they were the work of Sir Francis BACON (q.v.), or the Earl of Oxford, or one of half a dozen other candidates presumed to have had a more fitting education and general background. But genius ignores the usual boundaries. We have no reason to suppose that William Shakespeare, first son and third child of a Stratford on Avon glover, could not have written the plays attributed to him both in his day and during the last three and a half centuries.

We know that he was born in the little meadow-fringed, riverside market-town of Stratford on Avon in Warwickshire during the spring of 1564, and that 23 April is said to have been the date. He was educated, it is presumed, at the local grammar school. After this, for a time, most things are vague, though there are various unproved traditions about his departure from Stratford after a deer-stalking episode in the park of Sir Thomas Lucy at the neighbouring village of Charlecote. In 1582 the young Shakespeare married Anne Hathaway, of Shottery, by whom he had a daughter, Susanna, and twins, Hamnet and Judith. When we hear of him next, he is both an actor and a dramatist; and if we like, we can believe that he began his career in the London theatre by holding horses at a playhouse door. The main thing is that he appeared suddenly as a dramatist of remarkable power, one able to move from early crudities and drum-and-trumpet historical chronicle, through comedies of light and delicate verbal quibbling (such as *Love's Labour's Lost*), and through poetic tragedy (*Romeo and Juliet*), towards the utterance of his great middle period when—at the Globe Theatre on Bankside—he climbed the peak of the drama with *Hamlet*, *Macbeth*, and *King Lear*.

He had become an actor with the company known as the Lord Chamberlain's Men (and later, after the accession of James I, as the King's Men). Tradition does not report that he was an especially good actor, but his reputation as a dramatist grew steadily during the 1590's, and he became a 'sharer' or partner in his company. Earlier, in 1593 or 1594, he dedicated his poems, *Venus and Adonis* and *The Rape of Lucrece*, to the Earl of Southampton in terms of affection. Although his Sonnets were not published until 1609, it is thought that they were written much earlier. Many of the poems are addressed to a man, but several record the writer's love for a faithless dark beauty, the unknown Dark Lady of the Sonnets.

Very much is conjecture. We are sure that by 1600 Shakespeare had considerable worldly success; that he had bought the great house of New Place at Stratford; and that—though continuing to live in London—he had various business dealings with Stratford people. Even so,

the man himself remains a flitting shadow among the documents. He was living at New Place for most of his last 6 years—by now he was breaking away from the theatre—and it was there that he died on 23 April 1616, 52 years exactly after the presumed date of his birth. He was buried in the chancel of Holy Trinity Church at Stratford on Avon. He left a detailed will, his elder daughter, Susanna, being the chief legatee.

One of his children, the boy Hamnet, died young. His wife and two married daughters survived him, but by the end of the 17th century the Shakespeare line had almost gone. We are left now with only a skeleton record and with the plays that show the man to have been what Ben JONSON (q.v.) called him after his death, 'the applause! delight! the wonder of our Stage!' He was a poet of genius who happened also to be an actor and to be writing for the stage he loved. His plays are eternally young and eternally actable. Their tragedy is profound; their comedy can be wise or gloriously foolish; they have grandeur and the common touch. Though we know next to nothing about their author, he lives on in his work, and the name of William Shakespeare has become a symbol of dramatic poetry at its unexampled best.

See also Vol. XII: SHAKESPEARIAN DRAMA; SONNET; LYRIC POETRY.

SHAW, George Bernard (1856–1950). This remarkable Irishman, the most influential British dramatist of his day, was also a critic, socialist, and lifelong propandist. He won a great reputation during his lifetime, and when he died, at the age of 94, he had already become an almost legendary figure. Shaw was born and grew up in Dublin, the son of an ineffective and unsuccessful father and an independent, unromantic, musical mother.

When he was 20, Shaw came to London, a tall, lean young man with blue eyes and sandy hair—at that time his favourite author was SHELLEY (q.v.), atheist and revolutionary. Between 1879 and 1883 he produced five novels —'heavy brown-paper parcels which were always coming back to me from some publisher and raising the very serious financial question of the sixpence to be paid to the carrier for passing them on to the next publisher'. But he had other matters to occupy his mind. He became, along with Sidney and Beatrice WEBB (q.v.), one of the early members of the Fabian Society. He

GEORGE BERNARD SHAW

Portrait by Augustus John

admired. In 1892 he produced the first of nearly fifty plays, *Widowers' Houses*, an attack on slum landlordism.

His record was one of tireless output, continuous crusading, and, once he had become accepted, of heartening commercial success. But recognition came slowly, and it was not until 1904 that any play of Shaw's was performed in the London West End. In fact, he was famous in Germany and America long before he was generally known in England, and his early plays, including the theatrical masterpiece *Candida*, were mostly published before they were acted. It took English audiences some time to become accustomed to plays with so strong a didactic purpose, conversation pieces in which the author debates on the stage so lucidly and with such conviction. Only the most brilliant technique and wit could have carried it off successfully. Shaw, in his plays, attacked such fallacies as the idea that war is romantic; he wrote on parents and children, on doctors, on politics, on marriage, on education. People found that the plays acted well and were excellent entertainment, and that with their long, closely argued, brilliantly written prefaces, they were also good to read.

From 1892 to 1950 he produced a series of great plays: the early comedy of *Arms and the Man* (1894), *Caesar and Cleopatra* (1898), the philosophic comedy *Man and Superman* (1903), *Heartbreak House* (1919), which symbolized 'cultured, leisured Europe' before the First World War, the five plays of the *Back to Methuselah* cycle (1921)—a lengthy statement of Shavian ideas, the moving and superbly dramatic chronicle of *Saint Joan* (1923), and many others. In his later plays the propagandist won over the dramatist, and his work grew less actable. At the age of 88 he produced a massive book called *Everbody's Political What's What*—a survey, so it seemed, of practically everything. His 90th birthday was acclaimed throughout the world, and his last play, *Far Fetched Fables*, was presented in London in 1950, only 2 months before his death.

Shaw enjoyed being an international *enfant terrible*; he delighted in being provoking, dogmatic, even contradictory. Personally, he was a man of abounding vitality, charm, and kindness. He had many enduring friendships. He was an indefatigable correspondent: the letters between Shaw and the actress Ellen Terry show his delightful, extravagant gift for letter-writing. He

determined to overcome his acute shyness of public speaking, and did so with such success that he was soon a familiar figure on every platform and at every open-air political meeting. He remained an active socialist all his life, and recorded many of his beliefs in *The Intelligent Woman's Guide to Socialism and Capitalism* (1928). Once established as a leading socialist, he began to make another reputation as a shrewd music critic. Music, especially opera, always had a strong influence upon Shaw; WAGNER (q.v.) was one of his idols. Later, writing in the *Saturday Review*, he became a famous dramatic critic, writing a great deal that was original and provocative about the theatre. He had already written a penetrating treatise on the Norwegian playwright IBSEN (q.v.), whose plays dealing with contemporary social themes he greatly

was happily married, fairly late in life, to Charlotte Payne-Townshend, who died in 1939. As a dramatist, he had certain limitations—propaganda too often triumphed over art. Unlike Ibsen who, while dealing with social problems, created real people, Shaw's characters remain his mouthpieces, however brilliantly they talk. It is as a great personality, above all as a superb entertainer, that Shaw will live.

See also Vol. XII: DRAMA.

SHELLEY, Percy Bysshe (1792–1822). Shelley, one of England's greatest lyric poets, came of a family of some importance and power. His father was a Sussex country gentleman and a Whig member of Parliament; his grandfather, who became a baronet, had amassed a great fortune. Shelley, the eldest son, accordingly grew up with the prospect of becoming a man of wealth and title. At Eton, he proved a good classical scholar, but was not very happy, for he was by nature revolutionary and unconventional. He was known as 'mad Shelley' and 'Shelley the atheist', and his enthusiasm for studies in electricity, chemistry, and astronomy, and the exciting experiments he conducted, gave rise to many stories. The persecutions which he endured and witnessed at school gave him a life-long detestation of tyranny and violence.

Shelley went to Oxford full of plans for changing the system of society—ideas partly picked up from the literature of the FRENCH REVOLUTION (q.v. Vol. X). Being convinced that religious faiths were harmful to man's happiness, he and his friend, T. J. Hogg, put forth a small study in logic, called *The Necessity of Atheism*. The Oxford authorities objected, and when Shelley and Hogg declined to discuss the matter, they were expelled from the University. This to Shelley at 18 was a disaster, for he lost a valuable education at Oxford.

He fell out with his father and became a wanderer; though he would eventually inherit a fortune, he had no ready money. When he was 19, he eloped with Harriet Westbrook, a girl of 16 whom he scarcely knew but whom he thought he should rescue from a tyrannical family. They were married in Edinburgh, and went to Keswick, where Southey was kind to them. From there Shelley, always full of schemes, went on a quixotic expedition to redress the wrongs of the Irish; from Lynmouth shortly afterwards he distributed a seditious pamphlet

called *A Declaration of Rights*, scattering some copies by balloon and putting others into bottles and throwing them into the sea. In 1813 he printed and published privately an extraordinary poem, *Queen Mab*, which expressed his protest against religion, his hatred of all forms of tyranny, and his belief in a new golden age. This won a reputation as an infamous and damnable book, and did Shelley much harm.

In his glorification of revolutionary ideas, Shelley had sought out William Godwin, author of *Political Justice*, who had married Mary Wollstonecraft, author of *A Vindication of the Rights of Woman*. His marriage with Harriet having proved a complete failure, Shelley eloped with Godwin's 15-year-old daughter Mary. But later that year Harriet was found drowned in the Serpentine, and her two children by Shelley became the subject of a lawsuit. Shelley was not only deeply shocked by the tragedy but also bitterly regretted losing his children. He married Mary Godwin, and they tried to settle at Marlow, on the Thames. There, in 1816, he wrote *Alastor, or the Spirit of Solitude*, the first long poem to show his true genius; next year he wrote a long imaginative poem on liberty and love, *The Revolt of Islam*, which was inspired by the French Revolution and contains many fine passages of description and dramatic narrative.

By this time Shelley had become a friend of Leigh HUNT and Peacock and had met KEATS (qq.v.), and his friends had come to realize that his troubles were due not to any wickedness but to a passionate and hasty idealism and an inherited sense of power which made him feel he should do something to redress the world's wrongs. Finally in 1818, partly to escape prejudice and insult, and also Godwin's constant demands for money, and partly because of Shelley's illnesses, the Shelleys decided to seek peace in Italy. There Shelley gave up his dream of reforming the world by direct political action and decided that he could accomplish most by passing on his own inspiration to others through his poetry. In this belief he composed his *Prometheus Unbound*, a poem to be enjoyed for its incomparable music, its colour and story, as well as because it contains Shelley's noblest ideas. To this period, too, belong his *Lines written in the Euganean Hills* and *Julian and Maddalo*, an autobiographical poem based on a happy visit to Byron in Venice. At this time Shelley wrote his finest lyrics—*The Cloud, The Skylark*, the *Ode to*

National Portrait Gallery

PERCY BYSSHE SHELLEY

Portrait by Amelia Curran

the West Wind, and others, the music and intensity of which show Shelley to be entering on a new stage of imaginative greatness.

The Shelleys moved restlessly from place to place suffering much unhappiness, including the misery of losing both their much-loved children, William and Clara. The strain of constant travelling told on his health, and they also found that the calumny and hate from which they had hoped to escape followed them even to Italy. In daily life Shelley was gay enough, however, the leading figure in their circle of friends in Pisa, where they eventually settled.

In the summer of 1822 Leigh Hunt came out to Italy to discuss a new periodical, proposed by Byron, in which Shelley was to take part. Shelley with a companion sailed in his yacht to greet him; but on the return voyage, Shelley's yacht capsized in a sudden squall and he and his friend were drowned. Shelley's body was identified by the volumes of Keats and Sophocles found in his pockets. The bodies were cremated on the shore, and Shelley's ashes were buried not far from Keats in the Protestant cemetery in Rome. It was for Keats that Shelley had written his elegy, *Adonais*, in 1821, in which he seemed

to predict his own death. Shelley was 30 when he died, leaving unfinished the most original of all his poems, *The Triumph of Life*, in which his realism appears in all its sharp strength. As we have it, this fragment presents life as a vanity of vanities, but it is almost certain that Shelley meant in the second half to assert the splendours which human beings could attain.

Mary Shelley, who was only 25 when Shelley died, wrote his biography and edited and published his poetry, comparatively little of which had appeared during his lifetime and that little received with almost universal abhorrence or indifference. He left much fine prose also, including his famous *Defence of Poetry*, containing his analysis of the way in which poetry is written and his defence of poets as the 'unacknowledged legislators of the world'.

See also Vol. XII: ROMANTIC MOVEMENT; LYRIC POETRY.

SHERIDAN, Richard Brinsley (1751–1816). Sheridan, author of *The Rivals* and *The School for Scandal*, was an Irishman born in Dublin. In his early 20's he eloped with and then married the beautiful Miss Linley, a singer known as 'the Maid of Bath', on whose behalf he fought two duels. Sheridan's plays were remarkable because they were neither sentimental nor coarse, as was most contemporary drama. *The Rivals* was at first a failure, but Sheridan largely rewrote it; it became a great success and has remained popular ever since. The Malaprop joke—that of the wrong word in the wrong place—was old even in Sheridan's day, but no one ever used it more brilliantly. *The School for Scandal* is Sheridan's masterpiece, its invention and its quick wit being as fresh today as ever. Sheridan's third comedy, *The Critic*, is an ingenious burlesque of the absurd tragic dramas of his day.

Sheridan then gave up writing and entered politics as a Whig, his gift of oratory making him conspicuous. Towards the end of his life Drury Lane Theatre (of which he was manager) was burned down; he then lost his seat in Parliament, and spent his last days in miserable circumstances. He was, however, given a magnificent funeral in Westminster Abbey.

See also Vol. XII: COMEDY.

SIBELIUS, Jean (1865–1957). This Finnish composer is regarded by many as the greatest composer of the century. He was intended for a lawyer, but at 20 decided to be a musician. He was trained in Germany, but began to find his own musical language after returning to Finland. The orchestral piece *En Saga* ('A Story') first made him famous. When he was 32 the Finnish Government granted him a pension so that he could give his whole time to composition.

In his seven published symphonies, several tone poems (including *Tapiola*), and a violin concerto, he has turned ancient legend or the bare, stormy Finnish landscape into powerful, sometimes terrifying music whose wild tunes, crisp rhythms, and atmosphere of cold, lonely grandeur grip the listener. His way of letting each short idea in a symphony suggest the next, until they all roll together into one long idea, is original and has since been adopted by other composers. No new work by Sibelius was published after 1929. The tone poem *Finlandia* and the *Valse Triste*, though probably his most popular pieces, represent neither his best nor his most typical work.

Sibelius also composed some very fine songs and much light music; he seemed to find light, popular music as necessary to his creative gifts as the serious music for which he is famous.

See also Vol. XII: SYMPHONY; MODERN MUSIC.

SIDDONS, Sarah (1755–1831). Sir Joshua Reynolds painted this famous English tragic actress as the Tragic Muse, and William Hazlitt, the dramatic critic, said that to have seen Mrs. Siddons was an event in everyone's life. She came of a distinguished theatrical family, the eldest of the twelve children of Roger Kemble, a provincial actor-manager. She reached the heights the hard way, acting in provincial companies and not venturing into a London theatre before she was 20. When she was 18, she married William Siddons, an actor employed in her father's company.

In 1775 she was invited to play at Drury Lane by GARRICK (q.v.), but, owing largely to miscasting and to the jealousy of the other actresses, and partly to nervousness, her first London appearance as Portia in *The Merchant of Venice* was a failure. But Sarah, determined to succeed, spent another 7 years in the provinces, and then returned to London in *The Fatal Marriage*, the beginning of 30 years' triumphant success. She was intelligent and beautiful, splendidly built, dignified and tall, with a long face, fine eyes, a sensitive mouth, and the large 'Kemble nose'. Moreover, she had a wealth of gesture and a deep, swelling voice. Lady Macbeth was regarded as her best part, an extraordinary blend of power and passion. She left behind her a long roll of 'Siddons parts': Constance in *King John*, Volumnia in *Coriolanus*, Katharine in *Henry the Eighth*, and Belvidera in Otway's *Venice Preserved*.

Mrs. Siddons was never popular with her fellow actors because she was arrogant and rather mean; in society she was courted by the most famous people of her day, but always remained somewhat aloof. Wisely she retired from the stage in 1812 when her powers began to decline. Her last performance was as Lady Macbeth, and the play was brought to an end at her last exit: the spectators had come not for the play but only for Mrs. Siddons. When she died the painter, B. R. Haydon, wrote: 'The greatest, grandest genius that ever was born! Peace to her immortal shade!'

See also Colour Plate opposite p. 176.
See also Vol. IX: ACTING, HISTORY OF.

SIDNEY, Sir Philip (1554–86). There are some people whose influence derives from an irresistible personality. Sidney—poet, scholar, soldier—was one of these: to meet him, to know him, was to come under a spell. Regarded simply from the point of view of what he, in fact, achieved, there is little reason why he should be remembered more than many other Elizabethan gentlemen whose names are now forgotten. But Sidney was a man whose upright and forthright character compelled attention, admiration, and devotion wherever he went. Born at Penshurst in Sussex, he was educated at Shrewsbury and Oxford, and as a young man travelled in Europe. His sister became Countess of Pembroke, and it was at Wilton, her home, that he wrote his charming romance, *Arcadia*. Sidney was essentially a man of action and a man of simple beliefs: for him Protestantism represented all that was good, Catholicism all that was oppressive and bad. The various diplomatic missions which he undertook for Queen Elizabeth were almost all to further the ends of Protestantism, and his final appointment in Holland to bring help to the Netherlanders against Spain was one after his own heart. He could at last fight for his faith. He rode out against the Spaniards in a small action near Zutphen. Quixotically he had put on no leg-armour simply because Sir William Pelham his commanding

A YOUNG MAN, SAID TO BE SIR PHILIP SIDNEY
Miniature by Isaac Oliver

officer had not done so; and he received a bullet wound in the leg. It was in this action that he passed a helmet of water to a dying soldier with the famous words 'Thy necessity is yet greater than mine.' He himself, aged only 32, died some 3 weeks later at Arnhem. There was an almost European sense of grief and loss at his death, for he was the perfect type of scholarly courtier and diplomat.

None of his writings was published until after his death; during his lifetime they were circulated in manuscript among his friends. The prose *Defense of Poesie*, the sonnet-sequence *Astrophel and Stella*, based on an early and unhappy love-affair, and *Arcadia* are his best-known works.

SMITH, Adam (1723–90). This Scottish political economist, author of the *Wealth of Nations*, was educated at Glasgow and Oxford. He became Professor of Moral Philosophy at Glasgow University in 1752, and in 1759 published his first important book, *The Theory of the*

Moral Sentiments. In 1764 he resigned to become tutor to the young Duke of Buccleuch, with whom he travelled abroad, meeting many eminent men, including Voltaire, and comparing his own views with those of a French school of economists called the Physiocrats. When he returned to Britain 2 years later he started to write his famous book on political economy, *An Inquiry into the Nature and Causes of the Wealth of Nations*, which was published in 1776, and immediately earned for its author an international reputation. It originated the study of political economy as a separate science. For a time Smith lived in London and was a member of Samuel JOHNSON's club (q.v.). Then he was appointed a Commissioner of Customs in Edinburgh, where he lived for the rest of his life.

In the *Wealth of Nations* Smith argues that wealth does not consist in money, but in the goods men use and their skill in getting or making them. Smith was the first real advocate of free trade. He exercised a considerable influence over 19th-century economic thought.

See also Vol. VII: ECONOMICS; INTERNATIONAL TRADE, Section 4.

SMUTS, Jan Christiaan (1870–1950). This South African leader, a farmer's son who once fought against the British, became Prime Minister of his own country, a member of the British War Cabinet, a Commander of the Imperial Army on active service, and a British Field-Marshal.

Smuts's father came from Dutch forebears and his mother from French Huguenot. When he was born at Malmesbury, a little country town near the Cape, British and Boers were living together in friendship, unclouded as yet by the SOUTH AFRICAN WAR (q.v. Vol. X). Diamonds and gold had not yet turned South Africa from a quiet agricultural community into an industrial centre of world-wide importance.

Young Smuts showed early that he had brains and a passion for reading. He went to the Victoria College, now the University, at Stellenbosch, where he first met Cecil RHODES (q.v.). After graduating, he came to England with a scholarship to Christ's College, Cambridge, where he took a double first in the Law Tripos. He studied for a while in Germany, was called to the English Bar, and then went home to practise as a lawyer, first in the Cape Colony and later in the Transvaal. He became State Attorney and a member of the last government of the famous Boer leader, President KRUGER (q.v.).

Smuts, known as a rising lawyer and politician, was prominent on the Boer side in the negotiations that led to the war with Britain, and then in the war itself. He was conciliatory so long as he saw a chance of peace, but later he won a reputation as a daring guerrilla soldier. After the war, at the peace conference, he acted as assistant to General Louis Botha, who was 8 years older and whom he served until Botha's death in 1919. At the peace conference, too, was another older fellow countryman, Christiaan de Wet, and the diverse fates of these three leaders of Afrikaans-speaking South Africa bring out the strains and stresses under which the new Union was shaped. Botha was a shrewd, great-hearted son of the soil, uncultured in the literary sense but rich in character and strong in the confidence of his followers, who worked loyally to heal the wounds left by the war. De Wet, a master of

Radio Times Hulton Lib.

FIELD-MARSHAL SMUTS IN LONDON DURING THE SECOND WORLD WAR

open warfare, was a champion of extreme Boer nationalism. When the First World War broke out, he led a rebellion, and Botha and Smuts unflinchingly accepted the responsibility of fighting him and taking him prisoner.

Smuts then took command of the British, South African, Indian, and native troops in East Africa, and in that huge and remote area he struggled vigorously against determined German opposition, bad climate, and worse lines of communication. In 1917 he was summoned to represent the Union of South Africa at the Imperial Conference in London, and he remained there as a member of the War Cabinet. With Botha, he went to the Paris Peace Conference to represent South Africa, and threw himself whole-heartedly into the creation of the League of Nations. The death of Botha left Smuts the most important representative of South Africa both at home and abroad. But although de Wet was dead, the forces of nationalism in South Africa were still alive.

Smuts spent the years between the wars sometimes leading the South African Government and sometimes in opposition, but always seeking to build up a South Africa in which Dutch and British should work together as they had done in his youth, and on equal terms. He never lost sight of the greatest South African problem—the relations between white and black. He did not agree entirely with those who wished to see the black and coloured races rapidly advanced: there was in Smuts a strong element of the old Boer tradition that regarded the black man as destined to play a humble role in society. As Prime Minister, he aimed at keeping a balance of colour which, after he had fallen from power, was upset by his Nationalist successors with their policy of *apartheid* or segregation for all non-whites (*see* COLOUR PROBLEM, Vol. X).

His last great period of authority began with the Second World War, into which he brought South Africa in spite of the fierce opposition of General Hertzog. As an honoured elder statesman, Smuts addressed both Houses of Parliament at Westminster in 1942. He was again a strength to the War Cabinet, and it was he who sent South African troops for a second time into action alongside the British. He was defeated in the South African General Election of 1948, and ended his days, still optimistic and full of zest for life, struggling against extreme nationalism.

This fine man of action found strength in a happy family life, was cherished by a devoted wife, and surrounded by children and grandchildren. He had, too, precious resources of the mind. His philosophic study, *Holism and Evolution*, and his Rhodes Memorial Lectures at Oxford were among the proofs of his power of thought and of expression. Honours came to him thick and fast, among the most valued being the Chancellorship of Cambridge University. A small, spare man, he kept his wiry, athletic figure and his pleasure in walking up Table Mountain almost to the very last. Statesman, soldier, scholar—Smuts remained always a good citizen of South Africa and of the world.

See also Vol. I: SOUTH AFRICANS.
See also Vol. III: SOUTH AFRICA.
See also Vol. X: SOUTH AFRICA, GOVERNMENT OF.

SOBIESKI, John (1629–96). Sobieski, elected King John III of Poland in middle life, is one of the outstanding military leaders of the 17th century. He was a highly intelligent man, devoted to books and learning, a shrewd statesman, and a fervent Catholic.

In the 17th century POLAND (q.v. Vol. III) was much larger than it is today: it included the Ukraine and stretched eastwards almost as far as Moscow. But the country was torn by rebellion, and constantly threatened with invasion by the Russians, Tartars, and Turks; the power of the selfish nobles made any strong central government impossible.

Sobieski, descended from a great Polish warrior who had once brought the Tsar of Russia captive to Warsaw, proved himself a vigorous and determined soldier, and rose to be Grand Marshal of Poland. In 1672 a disastrous war resulted in the surrender of the Ukraine to the Turks, who threatened to overrun Poland itself. Sobieski was looked to as the only man who could save the country, and in the following year he routed the Turks in a great battle in south Ukraine. He was then elected king, and for the next 10 years managed to preserve an uneasy peace with Turkey.

In 1683, however, an immense army of 200,000 Turks invaded Europe, laid siege to Vienna, and threatened to conquer, and convert to the Moslem faith, the whole Continent. The Pope appealed to all Christian countries to defend Europe from the infidel; but Sobieski was the only European leader who responded.

Ashmolean Museum

JOHN SOBIESKI
17th-century engraving

He raced from Warsaw with an army of 18,000 men, and, collecting a further 50,000 German troops on the way, descended on the great Turkish army from the heights above Vienna. He raised the siege and routed the Turkish army, splintering the Turkish power at a blow.

The Austrians, however, showed only hostility to their deliverer, fearing, perhaps, that he might claim part of their territory; and Sobieski returned in disgust to Poland. There he made a treaty with Russia, selling part of Poland's overlarge eastern territory. He tried to develop Poland's industry and waterways, as well as her literature and science; but many of his efforts were frustrated by the intrigues of his own nobles, and even of his wife. Sobieski died on his 67th birthday, worn out and saddened by the hostility around him.

See also Vol. I: POLES.

SOCRATES (469–399 B.C.). This famous Greek philosopher, who lived in Athens in the 5th century B.C., wrote nothing himself, but owing to his influence on PLATO (q.v.) he is one of the main forces in the history of Western thought. He is also one of the moral heroes of the world.

SOCRATES
5th-century B.C. Greek statuette

British Museum

how to think carefully and logically in order to discern the real nature of the principles to which they appealed. The charm and skill of his method can be seen in the earlier writings of Plato, where he shows Socrates exposing the confused thinking of his young friends with unvarying kindliness, humour, and modesty. He was fond of declaring that he himself knew nothing. A delightful feature of his conversation was his habit of drawing comparisons from the practical skill of craftsmen in the streets and shops of Athens, cobblers, harness-makers, ship-wrights, and cooks; indeed he taught that goodness is a kind of expert knowledge, which should be applied to the art of living.

Socrates' custom of exposing the ignorance and hypocrisy of people who set up to be wise naturally made him enemies. At length, at the age of 70, he was attacked by a powerful group in Athens who accused him of disrespect to the gods worshipped by the city, and of leading young men astray by his teaching. Indeed, some of his young pupils, such as ALCIBIADES (q.v.), later inflicted great evils on Athens; but then Alcibiades stood for everything that Socrates warned men against. Nevertheless, Socrates was ruthlessly condemned to death. The wonderful speech that he delivered at his trial is reported in Plato's *Apology*, and the *Phaedo* and *Crito* describe the noble discourses that he gave while awaiting death in prison, and the last touching scenes of his life. As was the Greek custom, the cup of hemlock was given to him to drink himself; and with his friends gathered round him he took the poison as if it were a goblet of wine at a dinner, and awaited his death with complete tranquillity.

In the British Museum there is a remarkable little statue of Socrates by a sculptor of his time. It shows his broad nose and thick lips and his gentle and wise expression.

See also Vol. I: GREEK CIVILIZATION; PHILOSOPHY.

Men of very different types who met him described him as the best man they ever knew. He devoted his life to thinking about questions of conduct, politics, and religion; he was frequently to be seen in public places in the city, surrounded by a group of young men, eagerly discussing moral and social principles. Xenophon, who expressed his profound admiration for him in a book written soon after his death, says that 'nothing could be more beneficial than to be in the company of Socrates and to talk with him at any time on any subject'. What distinguished his conversation was the way in which he sought, by persistent questions, to reach clearer understanding of ideas that men used in ordinary speech—ideas such as justice, happiness, knowledge. This method of searching into the truth by questions and answers is called the 'Socratic method'. He showed his hearers how little they really understood their customary and commonly accepted beliefs, and he taught them

SOLOMON (10th century B.C.). Solomon, the son of King DAVID (q.v.) by his most influential wife Bath-sheba, succeeded his father about 970 B.C. He was not the eldest son, but David on his death-bed gave orders that Solomon should be anointed as his successor. Solomon was about 20 when he became king, and he reigned over Israel and Judah for some 40 years.

David had left the kingdom united and strong, and Solomon's reign was, with a few minor exceptions, a time of peace. He strengthened the territory under his control by fortifying a number of cities in vulnerable positions, especially Jerusalem. He also developed David's bodyguard into a standing army, adding to it horsemen and chariots. He made an alliance with the King of Tyre, by which he supplied the Tyrians with corn in exchange for timber and the services of skilled craftsmen for his various buildings. He is said also to have allied himself with Egypt by marrying an Egyptian princess. In these ways he consolidated his kingdom.

In religion Solomon was, like his father, a worshipper of Yahweh, or JEHOVAH (q.v. Vol. I), the national God of the Hebrews. But Solomon did not recognize Jehovah as the one and only God any more than his father did, for he built 'high places' or sanctuaries not only for Jehovah but also for the gods of the various other foreign lands from which his numerous wives came. It is unlikely, however, that he worshipped these gods himself. His real fault lay in his determination to enjoy all the luxury of an eastern monarch. The number of his wives and the splendour of his surroundings are probably exaggerated, but they were nevertheless completely out of harmony with the traditional simplicity of Israelite life.

Solomon was a despot, whom not even the

Bibliothèque Royale de Belgique

THE JUDGEMENT OF SOLOMON

Solomon settles the dispute between the two women who both claim the child as their own. From Guyant des Moulins, *Bible Historiale* (French, early 15th century)

prophets dared to reprove as they had reproved David. He had many more political officers than David did, but they were servants, not advisers. When Solomon needed advice, he sought it through dreams. What he sought was wisdom, not devotion or personal goodness; and the wisdom he sought was shrewdness and practical business capacity rather than a deep understanding of life. Doubtless Solomon possessed this practical wisdom in a high degree. Whether any of the Proverbs, a collection of pithy sayings reflecting on life and conduct, were actually invented by Solomon is doubtful, but he must have had some insight and power of epigrammatic speech to account for the reputation he gained.

His supreme work was the building of the Temple, which made Jerusalem a holy city and formed a focus for Israelite devotion which has never died, and which played its part in purifying the Hebrew religion (*see* TEMPLE, Vol. I). On the other hand the cost of all this building fell on the people, and taxation was heavy. What was most resented was the levy, or system of forced labour. Solomon divided the country into twelve divisions under officers who were responsible for conscripting the needful labour.

The account of Solomon's reign in I Kings was compiled from documents written at a time when the Israelites were in captivity, and consequently they tend to exaggerate vanished glories. The visit of the Queen of Sheba, made probably for reasons of trade or politics, is presented with a touch of oriental legend. The truth is that Solomon brought to the edge of disruption the kingdom which David had held together by capable administration and leadership. The Jews a thousand years later followed a true instinct when they looked back beyond the glory of Solomon to 'the kingdom of our father David'.

See also Vol. I: HEBREW CIVILIZATION; JUDAISM.

SOLON (*c.* 640–559 B.C.). This Athenian political reformer and poet has been called the founder of DEMOCRACY (q.v. Vol. X.) Solon gained popularity by leading a successful expedition which recovered for Athens the island of Salamis; and about 594 B.C. he was elected archon, or chief magistrate, with unlimited powers. Athens at that time urgently needed both political and legal reform. Solon abolished the system whereby a debtor who could not pay his debt or his rent became the slave of the creditor, a system which had resulted in a population of a few rich moneylenders and landowners holding all political power, and a mass of slaves, with no middle class. He established a code of criminal law and made many other legal reforms. His most important work, however, was the reform of the constitution. Solon defined four classes of people, each with certain political rights. Only the upper class could be archons, though the two middle classes could hold all other public offices, and all classes were admitted into the ecclesia or national assembly.

Solon also established courts of justice, with magistrates elected annually by the ecclesia and responsible to it. It is probable that he also instituted the Council of the Four Hundred, whose members were chosen by lot, and which acted as an advisory body to the ecclesia.

Though all classes shared to some extent in control of the State, Solon did not create a true democracy, but rather a modified OLIGARCHY (q.v. Vol. X.) It was, however, a forerunner of the truer democracy which reached its peak at the time of PERICLES (q.v.).

Solon's reforms were so bitterly resisted that he had to leave the country for 10 years. Conditions did not improve until his friend, Peisistratus, seized power and carried out his reforms by force—in fact, a tyrant was needed to enforce the first measures of democracy.

See also Vol. I: GREEK CIVILIZATION, Section 4.

SOPHOCLES

SOPHOCLES (c. 495–406 B.C.). Few great writers can have lived so varied, so distinguished, so fortunate, and so full a life as did Sophocles, the great Greek playwright. He was born near Athens of a wealthy family, and as a boy was remarkable for his beauty and his skill in music and dancing. After the Battle of Salamis in 480 B.C. he was chosen to lead the choir which sang the hymn of victory.

His lasting fame rests on his work as a dramatic poet; but he also distinguished himself in other walks of life. Twice at least he was elected as one of the ten generals who controlled the military and naval affairs of Athens, in one of which commands he was associated with PERICLES (q.v.). He was also a friend of the historian Herodotus, and won the deep respect of both ARISTOPHANES and PLATO (qq.v). Sophocles is remembered as one who was wise, tolerant, and brilliant, and as far as we know he made no

Photographic Services (Berkshire)

A SCENE FROM 'ANTIGONE' PERFORMED AT BRADFIELD COLLEGE

Creon is shown the body of his wife Eurydice, who has killed herself. Near her lies their son, Haemon. In the foreground is the Chorus

enemies. As an old man shortly before his own death he appeared on the stage with his chorus to honour the memory of his great rival EURIPIDES (q.v.), who had just died.

When he was about 27, Sophocles won the first prize in the Athenian dramatic contest, defeating the elder poet AESCHYLUS (q.v.) and from that time becoming the leading figure in Athenian drama. He distinguished himself also as an actor in several of his early plays. In the course of his long life he composed 123 plays and won the first prize more often than any other dramatist.

In his work, and probably also in his life, Sophocles seems to have conformed more closely than any of his contemporaries to the ideal of the classical tradition as it was understood in later times. He was brilliant but not eccentric, his poetry does not show the new rationalistic thought or the human pity of Euripides, nor the sense of grandeur and insecurity of life shown in Aeschylus' plays. Where Euripides blames and questions the gods, and Aeschylus searches for a meaning that underlies human crime and suffering, Sophocles accepts what is outside the control of man and concentrates his attention on human beings themselves. His characters are dignified and, in a way, larger than life. There is much excitement in his plays, but also a perfect balance; he seems able to do exactly what he sets out to do.

His chief contribution to the development of the Athenian drama was in the introduction of a third actor, which made it possible to manage an intricate story more effectively on the stage, and to make the action move more quickly. Before Sophocles' time no more than two actors ever appeared on the stage at the same time (*see* GREEK DRAMA, Vol. XII).

None of Sophocles' early plays survives: the earliest we have is thought to be *Ajax*, followed by *Antigone, Oedipus Tyrannus*, and the *Trachiniae*. Later came *Electra* and *Philoctetes*. *Oedipus Coloneus*, the latest, was produced after the poet's death; it contains choruses of extraordinary beauty and serenity, celebrating the poet's own birthplace and the Athens in which he had lived. During his lifetime Sophocles saw and served Athens at her greatest; he also witnessed her utter defeat in the Peloponnesian war with Sparta. But his art remained strangely untouched either by the glories or the miseries of his times. It rests on its own perfection, and scarcely invites the mind to wander further than itself.

See also AESCHYLUS; EURIPIDES.
See also Vol. XII: GREEK DRAMA; TRAGEDY.

SPENCER, Herbert (1820–1903). This English philosopher, physical scientist, and sociologist was the son of a Derby schoolmaster. He trained for some years as a railway engineer and then took up journalism, and largely educated himself. He wrote many essays on scientific and philosophic subjects. When he was 40 he announced his *Programme of a System of Synthetic Philosophy*, a major work in five main parts— namely, *First Principles, Principles of Biology, Psychology, Sociology*, and *Ethics*. This work took him the rest of his life to write, and even then he did not complete his whole plan. In it he outlined a theory of EVOLUTION (q.v. Vol. I) 7 years before DARWIN (q.v.).

Spencer, who lived in an age in which unlimited progress seemed possible to human society, thought that the State should allow the utmost freedom to the individual. 'Every man', he wrote, 'is free to do that which he wills, provided he infringes not the equal freedom of any other man.' In modern times Spencer's

theories are out of favour, and equality rather than freedom is sought.

SPENSER, Edmund (*c.* 1552–99). Nobody is quite sure of the circumstances of this English poet's birth, but it is generally agreed that he was born in London, that his parents were poor, and that his family came probably from Lancashire. He went to the Merchant Taylors' School and then to Cambridge, where his great friend and mentor was a don named Gabriel Harvey, who encouraged his astonishing facility for writing verse. On leaving Cambridge, Spenser determined to try his luck at court, and the publication, in 1579, of *The Shepherd's Calendar* won him immediate recognition. It is a brilliantly clever, very artificial piece of work, written in a deliberately old-fashioned or archaic style, and it was rightly appreciated for its sheer novelty and command of words. Sir Philip SIDNEY (q.v.), to whom the poem was dedicated, and the Earl of Leicester, Sidney's influential uncle, were favourably disposed towards Spenser, and through their patronage he was appointed

ILLUSTRATION FROM SPENSER'S 'THE FAERIE QUEENE'
Engraving from the edition of 1590

secretary to the Lord-Deputy of Ireland. The outbreak of rebellion in Ireland showed that Spenser was not in the least a dreamy poet, but a hard-headed, efficient organizer, whose proposals for the ruthless and pitiless destruction of the rebellious Irish were set down in *A View of the Present State of Ireland*. In the next century, Oliver CROMWELL (q.v.) found them much to his taste. Spenser got 3,000 acres and a castle as a reward for his services, and was made Clerk to the Council of Munster.

All this time he was working at a long allegorical poem called *The Faerie Queene* (*see* ALLEGORY, Vol. XII), which was to glorify his country and his Queen and to set forth his system for human behaviour. The poem was planned in twelve books, but never completed. In it, King Arthur represents the perfect knight of chivalry, but, except in rare passages, the allegory never comes to life; for Spenser, in his earnestness to instruct, forgets all too often to tell the story. Raleigh, when he visited Spenser in Ireland, read the first three books with great enthusiasm and urged Spenser to come to London and publish them. He did so, and they were very successful. But his patrons, Sidney and Leicester, were dead, and he failed to obtain a post in England, which was what he desired. He returned gloomily to Kilcolman Castle and wrote a bitter autobiographical pastoral poem, called *Colin Clouts Come Home Againe*, which contrasts the viciousness of court life and the simple goodness of Colin Clout the honest countryman. In 1597, rebellion again broke out, and Spenser's castle was sacked with everything in it. Spenser was ruined; he returned to London and died, some said of starvation, certainly very poor, in 1599.

Spenser will always be remembered as the author of *The Faerie Queene* and for his two great lyrics *Prothalamion* and *Epithalamion*. He has often been called the 'poets' poet', for he has exerted a considerable influence on many of our greatest poets. He was, moreover, a supreme technical master of the art of verse and the inventor of the wonderful Spenserian stanza (*see* VERSIFICATION, Vol. XII).

See also Vol. XII: PASTORALS; ALLEGORY.

SPINOZA, Benedictus de (1632–77). The philosopher Spinoza was born in Amsterdam of parents of strictly Jewish faith who had left Portugal in fear of the INQUISITION (q.v. Vol. I). He was given a Hebrew education in a Jewish school, but he learnt languages, mathematics, and physics out of school. He was an independent thinker and when he was 18 found himself unable to accept the Jewish beliefs. He refused, even when offered a bribe, to keep his doubts to himself, and an attempt was made to assassinate him. He was then excommunicated from the synagogue, and stood alone. He found shelter with a friend, and made the little money required to meet his simple needs by grinding and polishing lenses, at which craft he acquired considerable skill.

Holland at this time was a refuge for freethinkers—DESCARTES (q.v.), whose work had a great influence on Spinoza, had come there to write and to think. Spinoza, therefore, had the opportunity to meet various interesting people. In the period from 1660 to 1675 he wrote his main great work, the *Ethics*, which sets out his philosophical theories. But even in Holland it was difficult for a scholar to get his work published without influential patrons to shield him from those who saw danger for themselves in his ideas; and Spinoza never saw the *Ethics* published. His high-principled determination to say always what he believed, however unpopular it might be, had the consequence that for a century he was widely considered the embodiment of wickedness.

Spinoza was above all a rationalist (*see* RATIONALISM, Vol. I). He believed that God, and man, and the physical world were all part of one substance, and that everything, both physical and spiritual, was an extension of God —a doctrine called pantheism (all-God). He thought of a world where everything happens in a rational manner according to law, and where, in the end, God is all and all is God, a state which man instinctively seeks, and in which he loses his own identity. The *Ethics* sets out to prove this theory as one would prove a theory in geometry, for his system depended on the fact that everything could be demonstrated. In the light of modern science, people cannot now accept his theory of the physical world, but the wisdom and deep human understanding of the *Ethics*, and the examples given to show how it is possible to live nobly and without hate, whatever may befall, are as valuable as they ever were. His doctrines were most fully accepted by German philosophers, and considerably influenced the thought of GOETHE (q.v.).

See also Vol. I: GOD; RATIONALISM.

STALIN (1879–1953). Joseph Vissarionovich Djugashvili, who succeeded LENIN (q.v.) as leader of the Russian Communist State, was always known as 'Stalin' ('Steel'). His father was an obscure shoemaker, and his grandparents had been serfs. He was born at Gori, a small town in Georgia, in the Caucasus, a colonial fringe of the old Russian Empire. Stalin went to a training-school for priests in the Georgian capital, Tiflis, where he was an unsuccessful student. His early apprenticeship in the revolutionary movement was at the Black Sea port of Batum, and later at the great oil-centre of Baku. He thus early experienced the conflict of different races and religions which intermingle in the Caucasus, and whose rivalries with each other and with the Russians were an important factor in the Russian Revolution.

Stalin's background, that of someone who was not Russian by race, nor of the middle class, nor an 'intellectual', helped to cut him off from the inner circle of the party which commanded his political allegiance at an early age. This was the Bolshevik party, which believed in COMMUNISM (q.v. Vol. X) as set out by Karl MARX (q.v.). And although Stalin had the usual experience of the Russian revolutionaries of his generation, of being banished to Siberia, he spent hardly any time abroad, and thus had little of the broad European background of men like Lenin and TROTSKY (q.v.). Some people have thought that his jealousy of the largely foreign-trained 'intellectuals' explains some of the ruthlessness with which in later years Stalin persecuted most of his early associates.

It was only after the RUSSIAN REVOLUTION of 1917 (q.v. Vol. X) that Stalin's gifts as an organizer began to be recognized, and that he started to move rapidly upwards in the Communist party, which held the power in Russia. His first post as Commissar (Minister) for Nationalities made him responsible for the relations between the Russians proper and the other nationalities of the old Empire. But during the bitter Russian civil war of 1918–20 he was called upon to fulfil a variety of functions, civil and military. The decisive moment in his career was when he was appointed General Secretary of the Russian Communist party in 1922. This enabled him to take the lead in running affairs after Lenin's death, in company with Kamenev and Zinoviev. With their help he got rid of his great opponent Trotsky; then he turned against Kamenev and

S.C.R.

STALIN IN 1946

Zinoviev, and with the help of the faithful adherents he had established within the party he made himself the absolute ruler of Russia.

By 1929 he wielded far greater power than the old Tsars. In the 1930's a series of 'treason trials' killed off all possible rivals. At this period Stalin was still, officially, only the Party Secretary. It was not until the Second World War, when a German attack was nearing Moscow in 1941, that he took over the premiership. As Marshal Stalin, he held supreme responsibility for both military and diplomatic affairs, and despite Russia's early catastrophic defeats, the end of the war found him, at the age of 66, more powerful than ever at home and abroad. He continued to hold this exacting office until his death at the age of 73.

See also MARX; LENIN.
See also Vol. X: COMMUNISM; RUSSIAN REVOLUTION.

STANLEY, Sir Henry Morton (1841–1904). Stanley did more to open up central Africa than any other explorer; but he is best remembered for his dramatic meeting with David LIVINGSTONE (q.v.) in the heart of Africa. He was a first-rate writer and his book, *How I Found Livingstone*, and others, such as *In Darkest Africa*, are exciting reading.

Stanley had a hard and unhappy youth. He was the illegitimate child of Welsh parents, orphaned at the age of 7. He was brought up

'DR. LIVINGSTONE, I PRESUME?'
Stanley, beneath the American flag, greets Livingstone at Ujiji on Lake Tanganyika, 10 November 1871.
From *How I Found Livingstone*

in a harsh workhouse in North Wales. When he was 16 he thrashed his cruel master and then worked his way to America as a cabin-boy. His real name was Rowlands, but he assumed the name Stanley in gratitude to an American merchant, named Stanley, who befriended him. After many adventures in the American Civil War and in other troubled parts of the world, he won a reputation as a journalist, adopted American citizenship, and in 1869 was sent to central Africa by an American newspaper in search of the lost Dr. Livingstone. In November 1871 he found Livingstone (for which Queen Victoria rewarded him with a gold snuff-box), and together they explored the north end of Lake Tanganyika.

Between 1874 and 1889 Stanley led several expeditions, financed by British and American newspapers, to explore tropical Africa south of the Equator; and during these he traced for the first time the course of the CONGO River (q.v. Vol. III). The appalling hardships of these journeys were conquered only by Stanley's courage and relentless will; he allowed no one to weaken, though many died on the way. He

hacked a path across the uncharted African continent, enduring the dangers of climate, disease, and constant attacks by natives. One of Stanley's expeditions was under the auspices of the Belgian King, during which he established the foundations of the BELGIAN CONGO Free State (q.v. Vol. III), a vast land rich in ivory, rubber, copper, and uranium. Stanley also opened East Africa to British trade.

Before Stanley's explorations the European colonies in Africa were confined to the coast. By 1914, however, the whole of Africa had been claimed as colonies by European countries, except inaccessible Abyssinia and American-protected Liberia. This 'scramble for Africa' among the great powers of Europe caused much international tension in Europe, and was one of the causes of the First World War.

Stanley himself, when he was 50, settled in England, became renaturalized, and married an English artist, Dorothy Tennant. He received honours from Oxford and Cambridge Universities, entered Parliament, and was knighted.

See also LIVINGSTONE.
See also Vol. III: CONGO RIVER; EAST AFRICA.

STEELE, Sir Richard (1672–1729), Essayist, *see* ADDISON. *See also* Vol. XII: PERIODICALS.

STENDHAL (1783–1842). This French novelist, whose real name was Henri Beyle, was born in Grenoble. He fought under Napoleon in Italy, and later served on the Imperial staff. Afterwards he lived mainly in Italy. Stendhal believed that the chief purpose of life was the pursuit of happiness, and that man's chief motive was, therefore, self-interest. These ideas are to be found in *Le Rouge et le Noir* and *La Chartreuse de Parme*, stories which are in part autobiographical. His heroes are deliberately larger than life, and conduct their destinies through a series of adventures that lie between reality and melodrama.

Stendhal was not appreciated in his day, but has since been universally acclaimed for his sense of truth, his insight into the complexities of behaviour and character, his penetrating social satire, and his prose style.

STEPHENSON, George (1781–1848). The inventor of the first successful railway locomotive and the 'Father of Railways' was born near Newcastle, the son of a fireman who tended the steam pumping-engine at a coal-mine. At that time steam-engines had been developed by James WATT (q.v.), but they were few, and were used only for stationary work. A set of rails ran by the Stephensons' cottage, but the coal-wagons on it were drawn by horses.

George did not go to school, and started work when he was 8, pulling turnips at 4*d.* a day. But from the time he was very small he was fascinated by steam-engines, and used to make clay models of them. When he was 14 he became his father's assistant, and worked continually with colliery engines for the next 20 years. He studied every detail of them, patiently taking them to pieces in his spare time. He taught himself to read, and then read eagerly everything he could about all kinds of machinery.

When Stephenson was 20, the first movable steam-engine or 'locomotive' to run on rails was designed in Cornwall by Richard Trevithick, a mining engineer. This was followed by other experimental locomotives (generally built for hauling coal at collieries), but these locomotives nearly always broke down, or blew up, or were too slow and cumbersome to be of any practical use. George Stephenson also worked towards making a successful locomotive. He was very poor, but he saved every shilling and earned extra money by mending watches and cobbling shoes. At last in 1814, when he was engine-wright at Killingworth Colliery, he completed his first locomotive, which was used for hauling colliery wagons.

The engine's success was partly the result of chance. The steam was pumped into the locomotive's chimney in order to lessen the noise of its escape from the cylinders; and this device incidentally so increased the draught as almost to double the power of the engine. So this big, gawky steam-kettle became a landmark in locomotive history.

In 1823 Stephenson and his son Robert started a factory for locomotives at Newcastle. Stephenson persuaded the backers of a projected new railway from Stockton to Darlington to make him chief engineer, and to allow steam locomotives to be used. In 1825, in spite of local opposition, the first railway in the world to carry goods and passengers was opened—a railway planned and built by Stephenson. The trains were drawn by engines built in Stephenson's own factory at Newcastle.

The railway was such a success that Stephenson was asked to oversee the building of a railway between Liverpool and Manchester. This idea aroused even more opposition. Canal companies feared for their trade, the gentry for their game preserves, and the farmers thought their cattle would be terrified by the noise of the trains. An Act of Parliament had to be passed before the railway could be built, and Stephenson was called to defend the scheme before a Committee of the House of Commons. His opponents jeered at his north-country speech and at his wild ideas, doing their best to make the scheme seem absurd. But, though at first they were successful, in 1826 the Railway Bill became law, and work on the line began.

Stephenson worked like a giant, designing tunnels, cuttings, and bridges. Part of the railway had to cross Chat Moss, a great bog too deep to drain; and this was done by building a causeway of brushwood and hurdles to carry the track. Stephenson travelled continually from end to end of the line, encouraging the workmen with his energy and his cheerful watchword, 'Persevere'. Once, when a party refused to go on digging a tunnel after a dangerous fall of earth, Stephenson walked into the tunnel alone,

A LOCOMOTIVE OF THE LIVERPOOL AND MANCHESTER RAILWAY CROSSING CHAT MOSS
Engraving by Ackermann in the Science Museum, South Kensington

calling to the men to come after him. His confidence induced them to follow, and work began again.

It took some time for even the railway directors to believe that steam locomotives were safe. In 1829, however, they held a competition, with a prize of £500 for the best engine, and five engines took part. George and Robert Stephenson's 'Rocket' was the only one that proved efficient, and it succeeded in travelling at an average speed of 15 miles an hour.

The Liverpool–Manchester Railway was opened in 1830 by the Duke of Wellington, then Prime Minister. The triumph of the day was spoilt by the accident to William Huskisson, a member of Parliament who had come to the opening, who was knocked down and killed by one of the engines. Nevertheless, this day marked the beginning of the 'railway age'. Though Stephenson designed other railways, this one remained his most famous achievement. He became both renowned and wealthy, but he never lost his energy and simplicity of character.

See also Vol. IV: RAILWAYS, HISTORY OF.
See also Vol. VIII: STEAM ENGINE.

STERNE, Laurence (1713–68). This humorous Irish novelist, famous as the author of *The*

Life and Opinions of Tristram Shandy, Gentleman, became an Anglican parson. It is typical of Sterne's odd humour that the Tristram of the title is an unborn baby for most of the nine volumes of the book. The two main characters, My Uncle Toby and Corporal Trim, somewhat resemble in type and in their relationship CERVANTES's Don Quixote and Sancho Panza (q.v.). Sterne's Continental travels are drawn on at the end of *Tristram Shandy* and in his shorter but artistically finer work, *A Sentimental Journey through France and Italy.*

At the time Sterne wrote, the English novel, after its elaboration in the portrayal of character by Richardson and FIELDING (q.v.), was reverting with Smollett to the sheer chronicle of exciting events begun by DEFOE (q.v.). Sterne, by showing that adventures of the mind can be as thrilling and entertaining to read about as external action, appears as the forerunner of 20th-century novelists such as PROUST and JOYCE (qq.v.). Sterne's mind was original and sensitive enough for this intensely personal kind of writing, which is called subjective; but his work is marred by his sentimentality, his striving after effects of pathos, and his often doubtful humour.

See also Vol. XII: NOVEL.

STEVENSON, Robert Louis (1850–94). The author of *Treasure Island* was a Scotsman born in Edinburgh. He came of three generations of lighthouse-builders and engineers, and was intended to follow the family profession. He was an only child, delicate and imaginative; and the stories told to him by his nurse, Alison Cunningham, gave him bad dreams, but also many ideas for stories. Though he studied engineering, and later the law, his heart lay in writing. With his thin, pale face, dark eyes, long, straight hair, and velvet jacket, he had the appearance expected of an artist. He did, in fact, suffer from tuberculosis.

Stevenson was rarely well in Scotland, and on leaving the university he went abroad. His wanderings through France, on foot and by canoe, are described in his first published books, *An Inland Voyage* and *Travels with a Donkey in the Cevennes*. In France he met an American, Fanny Osbourne, and later he journeyed to America in an emigrant ship to marry her. They returned to Scotland with Fanny's son, Lloyd, who became Stevenson's devoted companion and friend. But Stevenson could not stand the severe Scottish climate, and for several years lived mostly in Switzerland, the South of France, and Bournemouth. During this time he published *Virginibus Puerisque*, a collection of essays; *A Child's Garden of Verses*, perhaps the best collection of poems about children in the English language; *The Strange Case of Dr. Jekyll and Mr. Hyde*, a terrifying allegory with a London setting; and *Kidnapped*, an adventure story of the Scottish Highlands.

Treasure Island, his first popular success, was written in 1883 during a rainy holiday at Braemar to amuse his stepson Lloyd. 'It was to be a story for boys; no need of psychology or fine writing; and I had a boy at hand to be a touchstone. . . . On a chill September morning, by the cheek of a brisk fire, and the rain drumming on the window, I began *The Sea Cook*, for that was the original title.'

In 1887, when his father died, Stevenson, now a very sick man, set out for America with his wife, his mother, and Lloyd. There he was greeted as a famous author. After cruising among the Pacific islands, he finally settled in Samoa, where he lived with his family like a Scottish laird, busying himself with reforming the confused island government, receiving those of his many friends who were able to make the

National Galleries of Scotland

ROBERT LOUIS STEVENSON
Portrait by Count Nerli

journey, and writing many more stories. *Weir of Hermiston* (the tale of a harsh Scottish judge and his son), which is generally considered his greatest novel, was still unfinished when he died suddenly at the age of 44.

An invalid for so much of his life, Stevenson loved to read and write of adventure and action —fights, duels, escapes, deeds of heroism. He believed that adventure best revealed character. Even places suggested striking events to him. 'Certain dank gardens', he wrote, 'cry aloud for a murder; certain old houses demand to be haunted; certain coasts are set apart for shipwreck.' Yet he was a careful and elegant writer; with a polished, sometimes rather artificial, style. He wrote best about Scotland, and there are few more vivid accounts of his native country and its people than in *Kidnapped*, *Weir of Hermiston*, and certain of the poems.

See also Vol. XII: NOVEL; ESSAY.

STRAFFORD, Earl of (1593–1641). Thomas Wentworth, Earl of Strafford, was chief adviser to CHARLES I (q.v.) immediately before the CIVIL WAR (q.v. Vol. X). Though a man of warm affections and great integrity, his haughty, intolerant manner made him many enemies.

In the early quarrels between King and Parliament Wentworth, while strongly supporting the monarchy and the established Church, opposed any attempt at unconstitutional government. He tried to control Charles I's attempts to rule without the consent of Parliament, and in a violent attack on Charles's Ministers pledged himself to 'vindicate our ancient, sober, and vital liberties'. At the same time he tried to modify Parliament's extreme demands set out in the Petition of Right.

In 1632 Wentworth was appointed Lord Deputy of Ireland, and in 7 years of harsh but extremely effective rule stamped out disorder and corruption. Then Charles, faced with rebellion in Scotland, summoned Wentworth to England and made him Earl of Strafford and his chief adviser. Strafford tried to raise an army against the Scots, but Parliament refused to support the war and imprisoned Strafford in the Tower. At his IMPEACHMENT (q.v. Vol. X) for high treason, he was accused of trying to introduce tyrannical government against law. He made a brilliant and dignified defence; but his enemies believed with some justice that he stood between them and success, and the Lords were persuaded to pass a special Bill of Attainder condemning him to death. The King, who had given him a safe conduct, signed his death warrant, and he was beheaded on Tower Hill. He met his death before a vast crowd of people with outstanding dignity and courage.

See also CHARLES I; LAUD.

STRAUSS, Johann (1804–49), father; (1825–99), son; *see* Vol. XII: DANCE MUSIC.

STRAUSS, Richard (1864–1949). This most popular German composer of the 20th century, the last in the long line of German song-writers, is the undisputed successor of WAGNER (q.v.) as dramatic composer and master of orchestration. Born in Munich, he began his career as a conductor, and at 24 startled Germany with the passionate music of *Don Juan*, one of ten symphonic poems which tell stories in music.

Strauss had written beautiful songs and two successful operas when, in 1905, he shocked the world with his *Salome*, soon followed by *Elektra*. Their subjects are highly unpleasant and the music often deliberately ugly, but they are brilliant and exciting, full of marvellous writing for voices as well as for orchestra. But *Der Rosenkavalier* and the ten remaining operas proved far more charming. Clear, glowing sounds and smooth, long-drawn melodies are characteristic of this period, and his skill as a musical craftsman is outstanding. His last composition was a set of four songs, as moving as anything he ever composed.

See also Vol. XII: OPERA; PROGRAMME MUSIC.

STUART, Charles Edward ('The Young Pretender') (1720–88). 'Bonnie Prince Charlie' was the grandson of James II who fled to France after the REVOLUTION OF 1688 (q.v. Vol. X). When Charles was born George of Hanover was already established on the throne of Britain, though the Stuarts still considered themselves to be the rightful royal family. Charles's father, James Edward ('The Old Pretender'), maintained in exile the title 'James III', and tried, in 1715, to establish his claims by a rising in Scotland, known from its date as 'the '15'.

Under the Hanoverians, Britain began to enjoy a period of peace and prosperity, and for a long time her friendship with France deprived the Stuarts of the French support on which they had previously counted. But when Britain entered the War of the Austrian Succession (*see* MARIA THERESA) and sent an army out of the country, the Stuarts seized their chance. In 1745 Charles set sail with a few friends for the Western Highlands of Scotland, intending to rally the clans and invade England (the rebellion known as 'the '45'). He landed in July, and raised his standard in Glenfinnan, near Fort William. A Highland army rallied to him, but was never more than a few thousand strong and represented only certain clans, chiefly the Macdonalds. Others remained neutral or supported the House of Hanover. Moreover, Charles received little help from the Scottish Lowlands, or from England where there were now few Stuart supporters (or 'Jacobites').

In spite of these handicaps Charles was extraordinarily successful—indeed, he showed himself to be a brilliant natural leader. He captured Edinburgh without fighting, and in September he routed the panic-stricken government forces

National Galleries of Scotland

PRINCE CHARLES EDWARD STUART
Portrait by an unknown 18th-century painter

at the Battle of Prestonpans. At Edinburgh he proclaimed himself Prince Regent on behalf of his father, and announced his intention of dissolving the Union of England and Scotland. He then began his advance into England. Avoiding battle, he passed through Carlisle and Manchester towards London, and in December reached Derby.

But by this time his army had lost its first flush of enthusiasm. The Highlanders began to desert, and there were few English recruits. A government force was assembling in the Midlands under the Duke of Cumberland, George II's son; and Charles, instead of pressing on to London, which some think he might have occupied with little opposition, turned back for Scotland to gather strength in the Highlands for another campaign. He won a further battle at Falkirk, but in April 1746 he was overtaken by Cumberland near Inverness, and at Culloden his dispirited and shrunken army of barely 3,000 men was annihilated. After the massacre of Culloden, the clan system with its passionate loyalties was destroyed, and the Jacobite cause died with it.

After several months as a fugitive in the Western Highlands Charles, with the help of Flora Macdonald, escaped to the Continent, and spent the rest of his life in ineffective intrigue. When he assumed the empty title of 'Charles III' on his father's death in 1766, the once charming prince was a drunken, middle-aged failure.

STUBBS, George (1724–1806). This English animal painter, born in Liverpool, was almost entirely self-taught. Like most English artists of the period he went to Italy as a young man; but unlike his contemporaries, he took no interest in the ancient monuments and the time he spent there seems only to have strengthened his opinion that 'nature was and is always superior to art'. It was the sight of a lion seizing and devouring a white Barbary horse outside the walls of a North African city, rather than the ancient monuments, that made a lasting impression on him; and years later this formed the subject of one of his most notable pictures.

Soon after his return from Italy, Stubbs began the drawings for an ambitious series of designs, *The Anatomy of the Horse*, for which he both made the engravings and wrote the text. He worked in a lonely farmhouse in Lincolnshire where a dead horse was suspended from the ceiling of a room and methodically dissected. His book, which took 9 years to complete, established his reputation both as anatomist and draughtsman. He received many commissions from wealthy owners of fine horses and other prized and valueable animals, and became recognized as the most distinguished animal painter of his time, not only for accuracy but for charm of composition and colour. Stubbs experimented with painting in enamel colours on copper plates, and later on large earthenware panels especially made for him by WEDGWOOD (q.v.).

See also Colour Plate, Vol. VI, opposite p. 32.

SULEIMAN THE MAGNIFICENT (1494–1566). This Sultan ruled Turkey for 46 years, during which the Ottoman Empire reached the height of its power. The Ottoman Turks had first appeared some 200 years earlier—a few thousand people with their slaves and flocks driven from central Asia by the Mongols (*see* TURKS, Vol. I). The descendants of these people established an empire which, by the time of Suleiman the Magnificent, extended from the frontiers of Persia in the east to the frontiers of Germany in the west (*see* Map, INDEX, p. 53). Even the north coast of Africa acknowledged the supremacy of the Sultan, and his navy was so strong that Christendom itself was threatened.

The Sultan's title 'The Magnificent' was given him by Europeans who had visited his Court and marvelled at its splendour. In his own country he is best remembered as a wise lawgiver, who completely reorganized the administration of his country, and among other things organized a kind of civil service, introduced wise land reforms, and mitigated the severity of the laws governing the Christian minority in his country.

Like some of his predecessors, he loved poetry and the arts, and was a talented poet himself, writing under the name 'Muhibor'.

Suleiman was fortunate in inheriting from his father, Selim I, an orderly and wealthy State with a powerful army. The army, however, offered a problem. For generations the Sultans had relied on a highly disciplined standing army of 'janissaries' (*geni cheri*, new troops), originally a yearly forced levy of picked Christian youths. In the course of centuries this body of highly disciplined soldiers, fanatically devoted to their leaders, became a power to be reckoned with, even by the Sultan who employed them. Unless they were actively employed in warfare they might easily become a menace. Suleiman, to occupy his janissaries, embarked on a not entirely successful war with Persia.

In spite of his many gifts, Suleiman appears to have lacked force of character. Particularly in his later years he was too easily swayed by the advice of power-seeking Ministers, who often led him astray. He was also harmfully influenced, as were other of the Ottoman Sultans, by the women of his harem. None the less, he greatly added to his domains, bringing the power of Turkey to its culminating point.

See also Vol. I: TURKS.

SULLIVAN, Sir Arthur Seymour (1842–1900). This composer, who with W. S. Gilbert created the Gilbert and Sullivan operas, was the son of a bandmaster at the Royal Military College, Sandhurst. At 8 he could play all the wind instruments in his father's band, and at 12 he entered the Chapel Royal as a chorister. From there he won a scholarship to the famous Leipzig school of music, and later became a church organist in London.

His music to Shakespeare's *Tempest*, performed at the Crystal Palace in 1862, made him famous overnight. He became organist at Covent Garden, where he produced his own ballet. Then he was appointed Principal of what later became the Royal College of Music. He wrote cantatas, oratorios, grand opera, popular songs (including 'The Lost Chord'), and much sacred music (including the hymn tune 'Onward Christian Soldiers').

Soon his association began with William Schwenk Gilbert (1836–1911), the playwright and humorist who, like Sullivan, was later knighted. Gilbert, born and educated in London, had worked for 4 years as a civil servant ('one of the worst bargains any Government ever made', he said); then he joined the army, and finally, after trying the law, earned his living by contributing to magazines both articles and verse which he illustrated; his famous *Bab Ballads* first appeared in a magazine called *Fun*. He worked as a dramatic critic, wrote fairy plays, serious drama, romantic and sentimental plays and comedies, most of which enjoyed considerable success.

Gilbert and Sullivan had already met and worked together when Richard D'Oyly Carte, manager of the Royalty Theatre, Soho, suggested they should collaborate in a piece for his theatre, and *Trial by Jury* was produced there as a short 'after-piece' in 1875. It was an immediate success. *The Sorcerer* and *H.M.S. Pinafore* securely established their reputation, both in England and America (where some of their work was pirated). In 12 years the two produced a remarkable series: *Pirates of Penzance, Patience, Iolanthe, Princess Ida, The Mikado, Ruddigore, The Yeomen of the Guard*, and *The Gondoliers*. The Savoy Theatre, specially built by D'Oyly Carte, was opened in 1881, and all those concerned with the Gilbert and Sullivan productions became known as the Savoyards.

The two men, of very different temperaments, found it increasingly difficult to get on; at last a stupid but violent quarrel over the cost of a new carpet for the Savoy Theatre during the run of *The Gondoliers* ended their triumphant collaboration. Together they had re-created genuine English light opera. Their partnership was one of the most brilliant in the history of any art—a partnership in which the originality, wit, and invention of the author was perfectly matched by the composer. Gilbert was a master of fantastic plots and ludicrous situations and, while possessing a genuine poetic vein, he had great metrical skill. In the speed and humour

QUEEN VICTORIA OPENING THE GREAT EXHIBITION, 1 MAY 1851

On the dais are the Queen, the Prince Consort, the Prince of Wales (later Edward VII) in Highland dress,
Princess Victoria, the Duchess of Kent, and others. Detail from the painting by H. C. Selous

of his rhythms Sullivan showed a genius equal to Gilbert's own.

SUN YAT-SEN (1866–1925). The 'Father of the Chinese Republic' was the youngest son of a farmer in the province of Kwangtung, who claimed descent from an imperial general of the T'ang dynasty. The boy passed an ordinary, happy childhood attending the village festivals, obediently worshipping the idols in the temple, and burning incense before the gods of the village and before Kuan Ti, the god of war. It was later claimed that even as a child he threw down the village idols, but this is not very probable. When Sun Yat-sen was 13 he went to Honolulu, where his brother was already a moderately rich rice-merchant and farmer. Sun Yat-sen helped in the paddy-fields and went to school, where he won prizes. One prize was a Bible bound in pigskin, presented to him by King Kalakaua of Honolulu.

Sun Yat-sen declared that this Bible changed his whole life. He became deeply religious and turned his mind to how he could most help the people of China, where starvation and disease were commonplace. He decided to become a doctor. China at this time was in turmoil following her defeat in the Sino-Japanese War. Her government was corrupt and her Manchu rulers decadent (*see* CHINESE PEOPLES, Vol. I). Revolutionary groups sprang up everywhere, and Sun Yat-sen, outwardly a simple medical student in Canton and later in Hongkong, came to know the revolutionaries and soon became a revolutionary leader. The revolutionaries, realizing that first they must overthrow the Manchus, made constant efforts to send secret armies into China, sometimes led by Sun Yat-sen, more often organized by him from a distance. But all their attempts failed. In 1896 Sun Yat-sen, now 30, decided to go abroad to rouse interest and collect money for the revolution.

He went first to America and then to London. In London his old medical professor, Dr. Cantlie, warned him that the Chinese Ambassador meant to arrest him. Sun Yat-sen disregarded the warning, and shortly afterwards was seized in front of the Chinese Embassy and imprisoned in the Embassy while the Chinese officials decided what to do with him. Fortunately for him, they were apprehensive and delayed their decision long enough for him to smuggle a letter out to Dr. Cantlie, who, having guessed what had happened, had already appealed to Scotland Yard. Four days after the arrest the London newspapers published headlines reading CHINESE REVOLUTIONARY KIDNAPPED IN LONDON, and almost immediately a vast crowd surged round the Embassy, demanding Sun Yat-sen's release. The Chinese Embassy had no alternative but to release him.

For the next 14 years Sun Yat-sen lived in exile, studying for a while in the British Museum, living under an assumed name in Japan, and travelling round the world. More unsuccessful revolts were attempted, including a serious attack in 1911 on the government building in Canton.

About 6 months later a much more powerful attack was launched, which won for the revolutionaries the industrial city of Hankow and within a month most of south and much of north China. Sun Yat-sen, who was in America at the time, hurried back, and was acclaimed President of China. But China was not yet ready to accept a single ruler. The north and the south could not agree, and to avoid civil war Sun Yat-sen resigned the Presidency after a few weeks, saying he would put his efforts into creating a large and efficient railway system, which would do more to unite China than anything else. The new President was not a sincere republican, intending rather to establish his own dynasty as soon as he could. In 1916, he made himself Emperor; but within 6 months the people of China turned against him, and he died mysteriously, probably of poison.

There followed a period of anarchy, China being overrun by war-lords, military commanders who raised armies and taxed the people at their pleasure. Sun Yat-sen saw that he could establish his revolutionary principles only by becoming a war-lord too; but he was never very successful. His attempts to march north against Peking were beaten back, and he found treachery in his own ranks. Failing to get help from America, Britain, or France, he turned increasingly to Soviet Russia, and himself became more autocratic. The Kuomintang (or National party), with its headquarters in Canton, was modelled largely on the Russian Communist party; the Military Academy was staffed with Russian advisers; and the Russian-inspired left-wing party grew at the expense of the more moderate party. In his own writings, Sun Yat-sen's ideas of democracy were becoming strangely mixed with totalitarianism. But it was not Sun Yat-sen's ideas so much as his moral authority which impressed people; to the end he seemed to be the representative of the poor. Unlike the war-lords, he amassed no wealth and was simple in his manner. He seems to have realized quite early that he could not unite China.

In 1924 the ruler of large provinces in North China invited the Chinese leaders to meet in Peking in order to inaugurate a National Assembly. Sun Yat-sen, though he knew this might be a trap, accepted the invitation, and journeyed north by slow stages. But he developed pleurisy in the cold North China winter, and died in Peking.

See also Vol. I: CHINESE PEOPLES.
See also Vol. X: TOTALITARIANISM; REVOLUTION.

SUVÁROV, Alexander (1730–1800). Suvárov was one of the greatest of all Russian soldiers. Handicapped by a stumpy, misshapen body and a face so ugly that it was said that he loathed to see himself in a mirror, he won high command in the Russian army by outstanding military ability.

Being fired with a longing for military glory

MARSHAL SUVÁROV
From an engraving of 1800

even as a child, he enlisted in the army when he was 12. He distinguished himself by his impetuous bravery both in the Seven Years War and in the Russian-Polish War, and by the time he was 44 he was commanding the Russian army against the Turks.

Suvárov brought to Russian actions something of the fury of the TARTARS (q.v. Vol. I), and his name is associated with the storming of great fortified places. His terrible driving force, together with a grim indifference to losses, made a Russian army under his leadership a tremendous engine of war. His storming of Ismail (1790), in the Second Turkish War, was followed by a sack and butchery which had scarcely been seen in Europe since the horrors of the Thirty Years War. Two years later he laid waste the city of Warsaw with the same terrible ruthlessness.

When CATHERINE THE GREAT (q.v.), who had favoured Suvárov, died, her successor, the mad Tsar Paul, deprived him of his command; for a time even his life was in danger. But when Russia joined with other European States against France in 1798 (*see* NAPOLEONIC WARS, Vol. X), Suvárov was recalled and given command of the Russian troops which invaded Italy. With his old energy Suvárov swept through northern Italy, defeating the French in three battles. He was then directed to cross the Alps and link up with a second Russian army to drive the French from Switzerland. Suffering terrible hardship and heavy loss of men, Suvárov crossed the great mountains only to find that the French, under MASSÉNA (q.v.), had already defeated the second Russian army at Zürich. Suvárov was forced to retire, and was later recalled to Russia, where he died.

In the field Suvárov always lived with rough simplicity, sleeping on a pallet of straw and sharing the cruellest weather in the open with his troops. There was no luxury and little display of rank at his headquarters. If he drove his soldiers to the utmost, they knew that he shared their fatigue and something of their danger.

SWEDENBORG, Emanuel (1688–1772). This Swedish religious visionary, born at Stockholm, was in his early years interested chiefly in mathematics, military engineering, and astronomy. He worked at plans for a submarine, a quick-firing airgun, and a flying machine, efforts which his contemporaries thought mad. In 1711 he visited England, made contact with the leading astronomers, and also read widely among English poets.

In 1745, after an emotional experience which he called the opening of his spiritual sight, Swedenborg turned to religion. He believed he had converse with angels, and that the secrets of the universe were revealed to him. Both angels and demons, he said, were once men, their destinies being due to their use or misuse of life on earth. Swedenborg accepted the Christian doctrine that God became man in Jesus Christ. He also regarded the Bible as God's Word and therefore sacred, but he interpreted it in a spiritual and symbolic way. His numerous religious works contain much that is suggestive and beautiful; and after his death his followers founded a 'New Church' to preserve his teachings. He died in London and was buried in Stockholm.

SWIFT, Jonathan (1667–1745). The author of *Gulliver's Travels* was a bitter, disappointed man who, in spite of many friends and the success of his work, suffered much unhappiness, and towards the end of his life became mad, a fate he had long feared. Yet the tenderness of his letters to his friend Esther Johnson (*The Journal to Stella*), full of affectionate, charming, witty nonsense, makes it easy to understand why people loved him, and why ADDISON (q.v.) spoke of him as 'the most agreeable companion, the truest friend, and the greatest genius of his age'.

Swift was born in Dublin of English parents. His father having died before his birth, he was brought up by an uncle who sent him to Trinity College, Dublin, rather than to Oxford or Cambridge—a fact which Swift resented. On leaving the University he became secretary to an English kinsman, Sir William Temple, a position of dependence which he disliked, being both proud and sensitive. His duties included the education of the little girl, Esther Johnson, daughter of the housekeeper; and so began that strange friendship which lasted all Esther's life.

At 27, Swift became a clergyman, hoping through his influential friends to win promotion in the Church and become independent. When his hopes failed, he turned seriously to writing. His political and satirical writings soon won him the reputation of being the most brilliant wit in London, admired by his friends and feared by those he opposed. His passion for 'proper words in proper places', his hatred of trite common-

GULLIVER IN BROBDINGNAG

Engraving by I. S. Muller from *Travels into Several Remote Nations of the World by Lemuel Gulliver*. Vol. I of Swift's *Works*, 1755

places, and his vigorous, clear, ironical style made him a very successful writer of political and religious SATIRE (q.v. Vol. XII). Swift himself describes satire as 'a sort of glass, wherein beholders do generally discover everybody's face but their own'.

In 1704 *The Battle of the Books* and *The Tale of a Tub* were published. In the former, Swift makes fun of a contemporary controversy on the merits of ancient and modern writers by imagining a battle between the books in the King's library. In *The Tale of a Tub* he shows up contemporary abuses in the Church in the story of three brothers, Peter (the Roman Catholic), Martin (the Anglican), and Jack (the Dissenter), who all find authority in their father's will (the Bible) to justify their own wishes.

After this direct attack on organized religion, Swift did not get the English bishopric he hoped for; but in 1713 he was made Dean of St. Patrick's, Dublin. This meant exile from the pleasures of London political and social life. But in Ireland he had the companionship of Esther Johnson who, with her housekeeper Mrs. Dingley, came to live in Dublin. To Ireland also came Esther Vanhomrigh (the 'Vanessa' of Swift's poetry), 23 years younger than Swift and greatly in love with him. Swift soon became embroiled in Irish politics, and he savagely exposed, in letters and pamphlets, the miseries of the Irish poor, not so much for love of Ireland as from indignation at the oppressions of the English Government.

In 1726 he wrote *Gulliver's Travels*. It was not written as a children's book, and though the fascinating account of Gulliver shipwrecked among the tiny Lilliputians and the giant Brobdingnagians is witty and inventive, Swift's caustic irony is never far absent. The later stories in the book, which tell of Gulliver's adventures in the land of horses (called Houyhnhnms), are more savage in their humour and do not conceal his contempt for mankind.

Although Swift spent most of his life mocking the human race, its shams and hypocrisies, he showed great affection for many individual people. In a letter to Pope he says, 'But principally I hate and detest that animal called man, although I heartily love John, Peter, Thomas, and so forth.' And in verses written in 1731 on his own death, he says:

> Yet malice never was his aim
> He lash'd the vice, but spared the name.

See also Vol. XII: AUGUSTAN LITERATURE; SATIRE.

SWINBURNE, Algernon Charles (1837–1909). There has been no poet in the English language quite like Swinburne. He had an astonishing fluency and, combined with this, he had great metrical invention. The sound of Swinburne's verse is enchanting, which disguises the fact that the sense is often trite or obscure. He began his career in the circle of Rossetti and the PRE-RAPHAELITES (q.v. Vol. XII), but his development was individual. His atheistical beliefs shocked his contemporaries as did his love poetry; the real trouble with Swinburne is that almost all his beliefs were literary ones. But his unique command of language, evidenced in *Atalanta in Calydon*, *Tristram of Lyonesse*, and the two volumes of *Songs and Ballads*, give him a place as one of the most remarkable minor poets in the English language.

See also Vol. XII: VERSIFICATION.

ALGERNON CHARLES SWINBURNE
Caricature by 'Ape' in *Vanity Fair*

SYNGE, John Millington (1871–1909). The genius of the Irish dramatist, Synge, was first recognized by his friend W. B. YEATS (q.v.). On Yeats's advice Synge went to live among the Aran Islanders, from whom he learnt the magnificently poetic and flexible dialect he used in his plays. When his most famous play *The Playboy of the Western World* was first produced at the Abbey Theatre, Dublin, it caused a riot, since Synge showed Irishmen to themselves in a satirical and realistic way that they found hard to stomach. Now, however, Synge's plays are recognized as fine works of art.

Besides *The Playboy* Synge wrote *In the Shadow of the Glen*, *The Well of the Saints*, *Deirdre of the Sorrows*, and *Riders to the Sea*. The disadvantage of his plays is that it is difficult to perform them adequately without actors who can really speak the dialect in which he chose to write.

See also Vol. XII: DRAMA.

T

TACITUS (*c.* A.D. 55–120), *see* Vol. XII: HISTORIES; LATIN LITERATURE.

TAGORE, Sir Rabindranath (1861–1941). Tagore, the greatest of modern Indian writers, is best known for his poems and songs, but is also the author of a large number of plays (*The Sacrifice* and *The King of the Dark Chamber*), novels (*Gora, The Home and the World*), short stories (*Hungry Stones and Other Stories*), and essays. As a poet he is greatest in his lyrics, in which his poetic and musical gifts blend, and in his devotional and mystical poems, some of which are as beautiful as his pure lyrics. He was also the pioneer of modern Bengali prose writing.

Alexander Margulies

RABINDRANATH TAGORE
Bust by Jacob Epstein

Tagore's activities were mainly literary, but he took some part in politics and in social and religious reform, and founded a school—the Shantiniketan—and a university—the Viswabharati. As a native of Bengal he originally wrote in Bengali, but he also made for himself a place in the English-speaking world by translating some of his own works. The English *Gitanjali* (Song Offerings) and *The Gardener* contain some of his best religious and secular poems. Tagore was awarded the Nobel Prize for literature in 1913, and he enjoyed an international reputation. He travelled to most European countries, to America, China, and Japan, and all over India. His essential character and outlook were Indian, but he was European in form and technique, and his works are among the finest products of the meeting of East and West.

See also Vol. XII: INDIAN LITERATURE.

TALLEYRAND (1754–1838). Charles Maurice Talleyrand de Périgord was Foreign Minister to NAPOLEON (q.v.) for 8 years. Though a brilliant diplomat, he was often shamelessly corrupt.

A cripple from childhood, Talleyrand entered the Church as a young man, though much against his will, for he was sceptical in his religious views and loose in morals. Like most nobles who entered the Church, he soon became a bishop. As a member of the revolutionary party, he represented his diocese at the meeting of the States-General which led immediately to the outbreak of the FRENCH REVOLUTION (q.v. Vol. X). But he disliked the extreme revolutionaries, and after the execution of the King he took refuge in America. He returned to France in 1795, and 2 years later became Foreign Minister, which post he resumed under Napoleon. Talleyrand tried unsuccessfully to persuade Napoleon to follow a peaceful, moderate policy. When convinced that Napoleon's aggressive schemes would ruin both himself and France, Talleyrand resigned and made secret contact with Napoleon's enemies. In spite of this, Napoleon still consulted him until the collapse of France in 1814.

Talleyrand was largely responsible for obtaining a moderate peace for France and for restoring the Bourbon monarchy. At the Congress of Vienna his clever exploitation of differences among the Allies after the Battle of Waterloo succeeded in restoring to France much of her lost influence in Europe. At the age of 76

Talleyrand became French Ambassador in London. He retired in 1834 and died 4 years later.

See also Vol. X: NAPOLEONIC WARS.

TAMBURLAINE (1336–1405). The name Timur Lenk (Timur the Lame) has become in its Western form Tamburlaine—the version Marlowe used in his famous play *Tamburlaine the Great*—or Tamerlaine. This great Mongol conqueror, whose ambition was to rebuild the empire of his ancestor GENGHIS KHAN (q.v.) was born near Samarkand in that part of Turkestan now called UZBEKISTAN (q.v. Vol. III). He was well-educated, being particularly well-read in history, and he was brought up a Moslem (*see* ISLAM, Vol. I).

When he was about 25, Tamburlaine started

Bodleian Library

TAMBURLAINE SEATED UNDER A CANOPY, SURROUNDED BY
HIS COURT

Frontispiece from a Persian history of Tamburlaine, 1556

a career of military aggression, accompanied by treachery and hideous violence, which lasted till his death at 69. His first act was to supplant by cunning treachery his kinsman, Haji Barlas, as overlord of Kesh. Then he united with his brother-in-law, Mir Husein, to gain control of the lands directly north of the river Oxus; but, having achieved his end, he turned on his ally, drove him out of his kingdom, and was almost certainly responsible for his assassination.

The naturally warlike people of these regions followed Tamburlaine eagerly. He led his plundering hordes into Persia, southern Russia, and Mongolia. Then he attacked India, sacked Delhi with fearful brutality, and returned to Samarkand, with fabulous booty. He next marched westward, over-running Syria and Turkey. Finally he planned to conquer China and convert her to Islam, but he died of fever on his way.

The frightful brutalities of Genghis Khan may be somewhat excused because he was an ignorant barbarian, and because he left behind him a well-organized empire; Tamburlaine, an educated man, did nothing but destroy. He beautified his capital, Samarkand, and irrigated the surrounding country; but his ravaging armies turned every other land into a desert. A Turkish historian writes thus of him: 'The compulsion of his nature was to lay waste the world and torture the sons of Adam. . . . Wherever he dwelt, Doomsday dawned; whatever land he traversed, no land remained.'

See also GENGHIS KHAN.
See also Vol. I: SOVIET CENTRAL ASIAN PEOPLES.

TASMAN, Abel (*c.* 1603–59). The discoverer of New Zealand was a Dutch sailor serving the Dutch East India Company. He was sent by Van Diemen, the Governor of Java, to determine how far south the western coast of Australia extended, and to find 'the remaining unknown part of the terrestrial globe'. Sailing east in the latitude of the 'Roaring Forties' (the region south of 40° South) in 1642, he discovered the southern tip of Tasmania, which he called Van Diemen's Land. A month later he located the western coast of New Zealand, which was not visited again until Captain James COOK (q.v.) charted it more than 100 years later. The Maoris attacked his men, so he sailed off, and on his way home discovered Tonga and Fiji. The Dutch, not realizing the importance of Tasman's dis-

Roger Wood

SCENE FROM ACT III OF TCHAIKOVSKY'S 'SLEEPING BEAUTY' PERFORMED AT COVENT GARDEN, LONDON

coveries, made no use of them, and Tasman received no recognition

See also Vol. IV: EXPLORATION.

TASSO, Torquato (1544–95), Poet, *see* Vol. XII: ITALIAN LITERATURE.

TCHAIKOVSKY, Peter Ilyitch (1840–93). This Russian composer, born near the Ural Mountains, was the son of a well-to-do mining engineer. The family moved to St. Petersburg, then the Russian capital, where Tchaikovsky trained as a lawyer and eventually found a job in the Ministry of Justice. Even as a child he had shown considerable talent at the piano, and he soon decided he could not be content merely to compose music as a hobby. He became a student at the St. Petersburg Conservatoire (school of music), and afterwards became a music master.

At the school, students were taught to compose in the spirit of the German composers. But Tchaikovsky made friends with a group of young Russian composers—calling themselves 'The Five'—who were writing music that drew inspiration from Russian life and art, using Russian folk-tunes, and aiming at a truly national spirit. Balakirev, the leading spirit, helped Tchaikovsky

to compose with a true Russian 'accent'. His first symphony, performed soon after he left the Conservatoire, was well received. With Balakirev's encouragement he wrote the fantasy-overture *Romeo and Juliet*, an orchestral tone-poem which already showed Tchaikovsky's splendid sense of drama, the gift of writing tunes that were completely his own, and his gloriously rich harmony and orchestration.

In 1877 he made a disastrous marriage which lasted only a few weeks; but in the same year his music attracted the admiration of a rich widow, Madame van Meck, who wrote to him constantly and provided him with enough money to live on. During the 20 years of their friendship Tchaikovsky and Madame van Meck never met to talk, which was perhaps fortunate, for Tchaikovsky never got on well with women. Madame van Meck, to whom he could pour out his heart in letters, made a perfect friend, supplying the feminine sympathy which Tchaikovsky had known only from his mother whom he adored and who died when he was a boy. Tchaikovsky was an unhappy person, and this can be noticed in the Fourth, Fifth, and Sixth Symphonies, the opera *Eugene Onegin*, and many of his songs. But he could write gay, brilliant music, too, as in the Scherzo of the Fourth Symphony, in the three

Piano Concertos and the Violin Concerto in D, and in three ballets, *Swan Lake* (*Lac des Cygnes*), *The Sleeping Beauty*, and *Nutcracker* (*Cassenoisette*). These ballets, which contain some of Tchaikovsky's best music, are dramatic and fairly long, but they are composed in rather short 'numbers', not long extended movements. Tchaikovsky admitted that he found it difficult to write at length; he knew that the movements of his symphonies and other big works contained too much 'padding'—that is, unimportant pattern-making. These short ballet movements are full of the haunting dance-rhythms (waltzes, polonaises, mazurkas) and flowing tunes that Tchaikovsky could compose so well. He thought of himself as an opera composer above all, but only two of his operas are often performed outside Soviet Russia—*Eugene Onegin* and *Queen of Spades*; both contain splendid music. Tchaikovsky wrote beautifully for the voice. A few of his songs are often sung: 'At the Ball', 'None but the Lonely Heart', 'Don Juan's Serenade', as well as Tatiana's 'Letter' song from *Onegin* and Joan of Arc's farewell from *The Maid of Orleans*.

In his later years Tchaikovsky toured abroad conducting his own works. His music was warmly appreciated in both Britain and America, where he was the first Russian composer to become well known. In 1893 he returned to Russia to conduct the first performance of his 'Pathetic' Symphony, which was poorly received by the audience. A week later, as the result of drinking a glass of polluted water, he caught cholera, as his mother had 40 years before, and died in 4 days.

Tchaikovsky was a victim of his own emotions, and so an emotional rather than an intellectual composer. He felt rather than thought his music. He felt it so deeply, so tunefully, and so dramatically that he carries the listener away with his own feelings of misery or happiness.

See also Vol. XII: BALLET MUSIC.

TELFORD, Thomas (1757–1834). This civil engineer, a native of Dumfriesshire, made his reputation by constructing the Ellesmere Canal to connect the rivers Mersey, Dee, and Severn. He came to London in 1801, and was commissioned by the government to make a naval defence survey of Scottish ports and harbours. He produced plans which included the building of the Caledonian Canal from sea to sea through the Highlands. He was made engineer-in-charge of the work which began in 1804, and the first

vessel passed through it in 1822. It was not, however, as successful commercially as another of Telford's ship canals, the Swedish Göta Canal, between the Baltic and the North Sea, which he planned between 1808 and 1810. Telford also greatly improved many Scottish harbours, and he engaged in much road-making and bridge-building. He was an excellent road-maker, his most famous road being the Holyhead Road from Shrewsbury, through North Wales and Anglesey and over the MENAI SUSPENSION BRIDGE (q.v. Vol. IV), which was his most famous bridge.

See also Vol. IV: BRIDGES; ROADS, BRITISH; CANALS, BRITISH.

TELL, William (*c.* 14th century). According to legend this Swiss hero freed parts of Switzerland from the tyrannical rule of the Duke of Austria.

Tradition describes how the Austrians set up the Duke of Austria's hat on a pole in the market square of Altdorf, and declared that everyone must bow to the hat. Tell refused to bow, and was brought before the Austrian governor of the district. The governor commanded that Tell's eldest son should be bound to a tree with an apple placed on his head, and that Tell should try to split the apple with an arrow. Should he hit the boy or miss the apple, he would be killed; and should he refuse to make the attempt, both father and son would be executed.

Tell, who was a magnificent crossbowman, split the apple; but he then insulted the governor and was sentenced to life imprisonment. He was taken in a boat with an escort of Austrian soldiers across Lake Uri, but when a storm arose, Tell was released to navigate the boat for them. He drew the boat alongside some rocks, leapt ashore, and escaped, leaving the Austrians to fend for themselves. The governor, hearing of Tell's escape, led an expedition to capture him, but was ambushed and shot through the heart by Tell himself, who then led a rising of the Swiss to overthrow the Austrian rule and eventually to win independence for Switzerland.

This romantic story, which has inspired an opera by Rossini and a play by SCHILLER (q.v.), is now regarded as mostly myth. Although Tell probably did live in the 14th century, the events in the story are almost certainly based on earlier incidents between the Swiss and Austrians.

See also Vol. I: SWISS.

TEMPLE, William (1881–1944). This English Archbishop had great influence on public life at a time when the authority of the Church had been weakened by the advance of scientific knowledge and when the consciences of Englishmen were deeply concerned about the problem of mass unemployment and other social evils.

Temple was the son of a remarkable father, who had also been Archbishop of Canterbury. Frederick Temple distinguished himself at Oxford, then entered the ministry of the Church, won the admiration of the Prince Consort, and became Chaplain to Queen Victoria and headmaster of Rugby School before he was made a bishop. William, brought up in a family atmosphere favouring social reform, repeated his father's brilliant record at Oxford, became headmaster of Repton at 29, Bishop of Manchester at 40, and Archbishop of York at 48. He became head of the English Church as Archbishop of Canterbury at 61, but died 2 years later, leaving a serious gap in public life towards the end of the Second World War.

William Temple had a natural sense of religion, and also an independent conscience. When he was about to enter the ministry, he could not accept some points of the Creed as then interpreted; one bishop therefore refused to ordain him, and he was ordained later by another. He was deeply interested in social welfare and reform, and in the new principles of social justice which were being debated. In early life he was in close sympathy with the Labour party, and encouraged adult education through the Workers' Educational Association. Later, when heavily burdened by Church affairs, he still insisted in sermons and lectures that true religion should result in better laws and fairer social conditions, and that the New Testament principles of justice and consideration for the weak were more important than personal gain.

In Manchester and York Temple lived in areas which experienced prolonged and tragic UNEMPLOYMENT (q.v. Vol. X) in the depression of the 1930's, and his sympathy and humanity won him respect and popularity far beyond the borders of the Church. Young people in particular listened to him with an attention which men of his position have not always received.

Temple was largely responsible for the Life and Liberty Movement, out of which grew the Church Assembly, an elected body of clergy and laymen which now administers the affairs of the

Elliott & Fry

ARCHBISHOP TEMPLE

Church of England. He also worked for better understanding between the various Christian Churches. In addition he wrote many books in which he presented Christian teaching and also revealed his deeply devotional spirit.

See also Vol. I: CLERGY, Section 2.

TENNYSON, Alfred (Baron) (1809–92). The poet Tennyson was born in Somersby, a remote village in Lincolnshire, where his father, Dr. Tennyson, was vicar. The family of twelve children grew up with an intimate knowledge and love of the countryside. At 7, Alfred was sent as a boarder to the grammar school at Louth, but he hated the restriction, and after four years he was brought home to be taught by his father until he went to Cambridge. He began writing poetry when he was about eight: 'I covered two sides of a slate with Thomsonian blank verse in praise of flowers for my brother Charles', he wrote. By the time he was 12 he had read Milton and Shakespeare with deep appreciation, and in his maturity he became one of the few great masters of blank verse. Such was his passion for poetry that when Byron died he felt 'as if the world had been darkened', and rushed out into the woods and carved 'Byron is dead' on a sandstone rock.

At Cambridge his closest friend was Arthur

Birmingham Art Gallery

TENNYSON READING 'MAUD', 1855
Drawing by D. G. Rossetti

most perfect he ever wrote—which he added to later editions of the poem. It is indeed as a lyric poet, a supreme master of meticulous and felicitous verbal description, especially of the English countryside and the English character, rather than as a philosopher, that Tennyson is remembered. In his lifetime he was regarded as something of a sage and his work still reflects the doubts and perplexities of the intelligent Victorian faced with an expanding universe in which new scientific discoveries challenged every accepted belief. His philosophy is typical of his age, but the lyrical quality of his poetry is timeless and above changing fashion.

For 17 years, ever since Arthur Hallam's death, Tennyson had been working at his great poem *In Memoriam A.H.H.* It was published in 1850, and established Tennyson as the greatest poet of his age. In that year he became Poet Laureate. He married happily and bought a house called Farringford in the Isle of Wight. There he wrote *Maud*, perhaps his masterpiece, but a poem which roused violent feelings owing to the melancholy atmosphere pervading it. In 1859 the first four *Idylls of the King* were published and were immensely popular. The *Idylls*, like all Tennyson's long poems, is a loose association of separate poems, here based on his readings in Malory's *Morte d'Arthur*. His intention was not merely descriptive but moral and didactic also. King Arthur was to be interpreted as 'the Ideal of the Soul of Man coming in contact with the warring elements of the flesh' (*see* Vol. XII, ARTHURIAN LITERATURE).

All his life long Tennyson loved walking through the countryside, particularly with his children or with young people, talking or declaiming poetry as he strode along. Carlyle described him as 'One of the finest looking men in the world. A great shock of rough, dusky hair; bright, laughing, hazel eyes; massive, aquiline face—most massive yet most delicate; of a sallow brown complexion, almost Indian-looking; clothes cynically loose, free and easy; smokes infinite tobacco. His voice is musical, metallic, fit for loud laughter and piercing wail, and all that may lie between . . .'.

Till the end of his long life he continued to write poetry (*Crossing the Bar* was written when he was over 80); when he was 65 he began to write poetic plays as well, plays which were all more or less successful on the stage. Tennyson, for his day, restored poetic drama to its rightful

Hallam, a young man of brilliant promise who became engaged to his sister Emily. His first important volume of poems, published when he was 23 and containing *The Lady of Shalott* and *The Lotos-Eaters*, did not meet with a favourable reception from the critics. This set-back, which wounded Tennyson bitterly, was followed in the very next year by the tragedy of Arthur Hallam's sudden death. For 10 years Tennyson published nothing. Then came a two-volume collection which contained the *Morte d'Arthur*, *Locksley Hall*, *St. Agnes Eve*, *Ulysses*, *Break, break, break*, and many other fine poems. These made his reputation—but not his fortune. He chose this moment to invest all his money in a project for carving oak panelling and furniture by machinery—and lost it all. He became ill with worry; but through the good offices of friends he was granted a Civil List pension at the early age of 33, and so was freed of financial worries for the rest of his life. Five years later he published *The Princess*, a long rambling poem which is remembered chiefly for its lyrics—some of the

place in the theatre. It is typical of him that when he felt himself to be dying he called out, 'Where is my Shakespeare? I must have my Shakespeare!' and his hand was resting upon his copy when he died.

TERESA OF AVILA, St. (1515–82). Teresa de Ahumada, the visionary, religious reformer, and writer, was the daughter of an impoverished but aristocratic Spanish family of Avila in Old Castile. In her 20th year, although a lively, restless girl, she decided to join a community of Carmelite nuns in Avila. The Carmelite Order, originally a very austere religious body founded in Palestine in the 12th century, had lost its early austerity, and Teresa was shocked by the laxity of the nuns. During the first years she suffered unusually bad health, and later, when she was about 40, she began to have mystical experiences which alarmed her as she feared they were delusions or visitations of Satan. In order to help her to understand and master these ordeals, her confessor commanded her to write all she could recall of her life, in particular her experiences when she prayed. This autobiography, the first of her books, contains a remarkable scientific analysis of the processes of prayer.

Teresa lived in the age of the Protestant REFORMATION (q.v. Vol. I). She saw the need for Catholic reform but believed it should come from within, and by means of a return to the original principles of holiness and austerity; and so she resolved to reform the Carmelite Order. This resolution plunged her into conflict with her superiors, but in spite of this, she accomplished her task. She began with the small convent, San José, in Avila, where she reimposed upon herself and some chosen companions the original 12th-century Rule. The nuns, for example, slept on straw, wore rope sandals, and ate no meat.

When Teresa was 52 she met a young Carmelite monk, Juan de Yepes, the son of a poor washerwoman in Avila, who ardently sought an ascetic life as a way to perfection. She persuaded him and his friend to establish the first community of Reformed Carmelite monks. Teresa and this young monk, now known as John of the Cross, worked tirelessly together for the rest of their lives for religious reform, regardless of ill health or hardship; and during Teresa's lifetime seventeen convents and sixteen

Anderson

ST. TERESA OF AVILA

Statue by Bernini in Santa Maria della Vittoria, Rome

monasteries accepted the reformed Rule. Both Teresa and John became great writers. Teresa's *Letters* and *Book of Foundations* are witty, vivid writings in a style at once spontaneous and economical. Her other books are more profound, difficult books of Christian mysticism. St. John of the Cross, the greatest of Spanish mystical poets, wrote in prose and in passionate and intensely personal verse classics such as *The Ascent of Mount Carmel*, *The Dark Night of the Soul*, and *The Spiritual Canticle*.

See also Vol. XII: SPANISH LITERATURE.

THACKERAY, William Makepeace (1811–63). Thackeray, the author of *Vanity Fair* and other well-known novels, was an only child, born in Calcutta. When he was 4 his father died, and 2 years later he was sent with a little cousin to England. He remembered all his life 'a ghaut, or river-stair at Calcutta, and a day when, down those steps, to a boat which was in waiting, came two children whose mothers remained on the shore'. His childhood before his mother joined him again was not happy, and by the time he was 8 he had been at two schools and had been miserable at both. At 11 he went to

Charterhouse, which, like most public schools of the day, was rough and brutal. With its bullying headmaster, it served as a model for the schools in *Pendennis* and *The Newcomes*. Here, in a fight, he broke his nose; the mark may be seen in any portrait of Thackeray.

His father had left him a great deal of money, which led him to be so recklessly extravagant at Cambridge that his guardians took him away and sent him to Germany for a year. On his return to London he began to study law, but when he came of age, he went to Paris to study art. Although he meant to be an artist (later, he illustrated most of his own books), to make ready money he started to work as a journalist. In 1836 he married a young Irish girl whose family lived in Paris; by that time none of his inheritance was left, and he had to write to earn his living. After 4 happy years his wife went mad and never recovered. Thackeray sent his two little daughters to his mother and step-father in Paris, though later they joined him in London and became his inseparable companions. The *Memoirs* of his daughter Anne (later Lady Ritchie) give an attractive picture of their life together.

Between 1837 and 1847 Thackeray wrote travel accounts and satirical sketches of Victorian society, mostly in serial form in *Fraser's Magazine* and *Punch*, and these include *The Book of Snobs*, humorous studies of social types of the time. In 1847–8 his first great book appeared in monthly numbers—*Vanity Fair*, whose chief character, the ambitious and scheming Becky Sharp, starts in the world as a poor governess. This novel, which brought him immense literary success, was followed by *Pendennis*, a tale of a young man of good family, not unlike Thackeray himself.

In 1852 and 1855 he gave lectures in America which were later reprinted as *English Humourists* and *The Four Georges*—two books about Thackeray's best-loved period, the 18th century. His favourite among his own novels, *The History of Henry Esmond* (1852), had an 18th-century historical setting, and was the only novel not published in monthly instalments. 'Here is the very best I can do', he wrote. After this came *The Newcomes*, again a family history, but set in Thackeray's own time, *The Rose and the Ring*, a humorous fairy-tale delightfully written and illustrated for his own children, and *The Virginians*, the story of Esmond's descendants in

ILLUSTRATION BY THACKERAY FOR 'VANITY FAIR'
The scheming Becky Sharp tries to ensnare Mr. Jos. Sedley into marriage

America. In 1860 Thackeray became editor of a new magazine, *The Cornhill*.

Thackeray was a big man (6 ft. 3 in. tall); but between hard work, restless travelling, and a strenuous, sociable life, he was often ill, and he died at the age of 52, leaving an unfinished novel *Denis Duval*, an adventure story of 18th-century smugglers.

Thackeray, unlike DICKENS (q.v.), wrote much more effectively about professional and upper-class people than about the poor. His favourite characters were drawn from life. They are real; they are neither wholly bad nor wholly good—even his heroes are not perfect—and they are among the first in fiction to develop naturally as time passes in the story. His very individual style reflects his humour, good taste, and well-stored mind, as well as an intimate personal feeling towards his reader.

See also Vol. XII: NOVEL.

THEMISTOCLES (*c*. 523–*c*. 459 B.C.). Enterprising, witty, and imaginative, but also grasping and unprincipled, the statesman Themistocles had in excess the typical Athenian qualities. Having saved Greece from the Persian invader and laid the foundations of Athens' greatness as a sea power, he died in exile, a vassal of the Persian king.

In 493 B.C. he started fortifying the Piraeus, the port of Athens, and 10 years later he persuaded the Athenians to spend the wealth from a newly discovered silver mine on building a fleet instead of distributing it among themselves. These were the ships that saved Greece from XERXES (q.v.) and the Persians in 480 B.C.

When the invaders bore down on Athens, Themistocles organized its evacuation, and then induced the Greek admiral-in-chief to confront the enemy fleet at Salamis, just off the Athenian coast. The story is that the crafty Themistocles sent a slave to Xerxes warning him that unless he attacked at once the Greeks would escape. This lured the Persian fleet into the narrow strait where it was utterly defeated.

After the war the Spartans objected to the rebuilding of Athens' walls, but Themistocles baffled them with characteristic subtlety. About 471 B.C., however, when the friends of Sparta became powerful in Athens, Themistocles' anti-Spartan views led to his temporary banishment. The Spartans then tried to arrest him, but after an exciting chase through the north of Greece he escaped to Persia, where he was received with honour and remained for the rest of his life.

THEOCRITUS (3rd century B.C.), Greek poet, *see* Vol. XII: PASTORALS.

THEODORIC (A.D. 455–526), King of the Ostrogoths, *see* Vol. I: GOTHS.

THOMSON, Sir Joseph John (1856–1940). The physicist Thomson, who made the Cavendish Laboratory at Cambridge University the most famous physics laboratory in the world, was a graduate of Manchester University, who became professor at Cambridge when only 28.

Thomson as a theoretical physicist continued the work of Clerk MAXWELL and Lord KELVIN (qq.v.). In 1897 his brilliant experimental work led to the discovery of the electron, the basis of electricity and magnetism, and an essential part of modern atomic physics (*see* ATOM, Vol. III). He found about the same period that gases could be made conductors of electricity if waves and particles, which had been recently discovered, were passed through them. This

discovery paved the way for the THERMIONIC VALVE (q.v. Vol. VIII), and thus for wireless speech, television, and radar.

For more than 30 years a stream of original papers on physics and mathematics came from Thomson's laboratory, and more than seventy of the scientists trained under him became professors of physics. Several won NOBEL Prizes (q.v.), and one, Lord RUTHERFORD (q.v.), became greater than his master.

See also Vol. VIII: NUCLEAR ENERGY.

THUCYDIDES (*c.* 460–*c.* 399 B.C.). In the time of Thucydides, one of the greatest historians who have ever lived, Athens, his native city, rose to be the most important city in the Mediterranean. She finally lost her Empire, however, in the long war with Sparta (431–404 B.C.). The greatness of Athens and her decline in military and political power are the themes of Thucydides' history of the Peloponnesian War.

Thucydides probably belonged to a wealthy family, associated with what may be called the Conservative party in Athens, and therefore opposed to the great statesman PERICLES (q.v.). Thucydides himself was an ardent supporter of Pericles and his policy of democratic imperialism. He was convinced that had Athens followed Pericles' advice she would have won the war, and that, even though Athenian imperialism might interfere with the liberties of other States, Athens was the best fitted of all States to exercise power.

When war broke out with Sparta, Thucydides, believing that this was going to be the most important war that had ever taken place, began to write his history. In 430 B.C. the terrible disaster of the plague fell on Athens, causing enormous numbers of deaths both in Athens itself and in the armies overseas. Thucydides caught the disease, but recovered. His description of its effects shows that combination of realism and humanity which is so characteristic of him.

In the year 424 B.C. Thucydides, who was in command of a fleet in the northern Aegean, arrived too late with his ships to save the important town of Amphipolis from the brilliant Spartan commander Brasidas. Though his vigorous action prevented Brasidas from capturing another important place in the area, he was exiled for his failure, and he remained in exile for 20 years until the war was over.

His *History of the Peloponnesian War* is remarkable not only for its scrupulous accuracy, but because it is based on a general view of human nature and a keen understanding of what was involved in the struggle between the Athenian and Spartan ways of life. Some of the most impressive passages are in the form of speeches which Thucydides puts into the mouths of various statesmen and generals—a dramatic device for impressing the reader with the principles underlying the events of the war. Thucydides aimed at writing something of permanent value; he believed that history was likely to repeat itself, and that by giving an accurate record of events he could help men to deal with similar situations in the future. It is for this reason that many people, even today, would say that his history remains the best work on politics that has ever been written.

See also Vol. I: GREEK CIVILIZATION; SPARTANS.
See also Vol. XII: HISTORIES; GREEK LITERATURE.

TINTORETTO (1518–94). The painter Jacopo Robusti, the son of a Venetian dyer (the nickname Tintoretto means 'little dyer'), lived and

died at Venice and was a follower of TITIAN (q.v.). He is said to have aimed at combining in his art the colouring of Titian with the draughtsmanship of MICHELANGELO (q.v.), and to some extent he succeeded. His colours have an intensity which falls little short of the later works of Titian, and he frequently painted naked figures in poses demanding difficult foreshortening, as Michelangelo had done. His compositions are full of figures in violent movement, and the subjects are presented very dramatically. His ideas were always original, and though some of them appear a little farfetched, the result is nearly always exciting. As he grew older he seems to have painted with increasing speed and at times with almost frenzied haste, covering acres of canvas in churches and palaces at Venice with decorations, mainly religious. He was also a distinguished portraitist.

See also Vol. XII: VENETIAN PAINTING.

TITIAN (*c.* 1480–1576). Tiziano Vecelli, called Titian, was the greatest of Venetian painters. The date of his birth is derived from a letter

Anderson

THE LAST SUPPER
Painting by Tintoretto. San Giorgio Maggiore, Venice

Anderson

THE LAMENTATION OVER THE DEAD CHRIST
Painting by Titian. Accademia, Venice

of the Frari at Venice; among the figures in the painting is apparently a portrait of himself supporting the body of Christ.

Titian is chiefly famous for the beauty of the colours in his pictures. In those which he painted as a young man he used a great many delicate and beautiful shades. But as he grew older he changed his method; he would no longer place a bright red next to a bright blue, but would choose a few colours which were related to each other— such as purple or a warm brown with red, or green or a cool grey with blue. When pictures painted in this way are seen from a distance, the colours (which are usually not bright in themselves) tend to blend into a general tint or 'tone'. Titian was the first painter to perfect this method, which has since been widely used. At the same time as he was developing this system of colouring he also began to define the forms in his pictures less clearly, so that it is necessary to stand at some distance to see what they represent.

No painter had used colour before as Titian used it, but later VENETIAN PAINTING (q.v. Vol. XII) owed much to his example, and many painters, notably RUBENS, VAN DYCK, and VELAZQUEZ (qq.v.), were influenced by him.

written by Titian to King Philip II of Spain in 1571 in which he describes himself as 'an old man of 95'; but many people now believe that he was at least 10 years younger than he said.

Titian was born in the village of Cadore, in the Alps above Venice, and most of his long life was spent in Venice. He was a worldly man, fond of the good things of life, and he became extremely rich from the sale of his pictures. He also enjoyed the society of princes, and was on friendly terms not only with many Italian ruling families and with the Pope, but also with King Francis I of France, the Emperor Charles V, and King Philip II of Spain (*see* pp. 85 and 361). Charles V conferred a knighthood on Titian, at the time an unheard-of honour for a painter, and he also raised the artist's children to the rank of Nobles of the Empire.

This success, which Titian so much enjoyed, was only his due. He was equally at home in all fields of painting—portraits, religious pictures, allegories, and scenes from Greek and Roman legends. He painted almost ceaselessly for perhaps 70 years, and his last picture—one of his greatest—representing the lamentation over the Dead Christ, was unfinished when he fell victim to the plague. He intended this painting for his own tomb, which is in the church

TOLSTOY, Count Leo (1828–1910). When Tolstoy, the Russian novelist and social reformer, was born on his parents' estate of Yasnaya Polyana, not far from Moscow, the majority of the people of Russia still lived in a condition of serfdom, not unlike that of medieval England under the FEUDAL SYSTEM (q.v. Vol. X). The gentry, to which class Tolstoy belonged, owned the land, and the serfs worked for them under conditions often little better than those of animals, with no education and very little chance of bettering themselves.

Tolstoy and his brothers and sister were left orphans at an early age, and were brought up by elderly aunts who gave them the traditional education of the Russian aristocracy. When Tolstoy came into his inheritance, he settled on his large estate and set out to improve the condition of his serfs. His efforts were unsuccessful,

TOLSTOY IN HIS STUDY

and in disappointment he went to Moscow and St. Petersburg. After 2 years, however, he came home again and began to keep a remarkable diary which, with one long gap, covers the whole of his adult life.

When he was 23, he and his brother joined the army in the Caucasus to fight against the mountain tribesmen; and during the CRIMEAN WAR (q.v. Vol. X) he served throughout the siege of Sebastopol. His first works, *Childhood*, *Boyhood*, and *Youth*, were written at this period, and were followed by *Sebastopol Sketches*, a vivid picture of war as the soldier sees it. After the fall of Sebastopol Tolstoy was sent with dispatches to St. Petersburg, where he made the acquaintance of literary men such as TURGENEV (q.v.); but his association with them was not happy.

After leaving the army he travelled abroad; but the social order which he found in western Europe did not appeal to him, and was not, he felt convinced, the remedy for Russia's ills. He began now to concentrate more and more on the problem of the peasants, especially on the education of peasant children: he opened twelve schools and himself taught personally at Yasnaya Polyana. After the liberation of the serfs in 1861 (*see* ALEXANDER II), he sat on one of the commissions charged with settling boundary disputes between gentry and peasants; but he saw the problems so much from the point of view of the peasants that he drew to himself the attention of the police.

In 1862 he married and settled down to many years of happy family life, and to the writing of *War and Peace*, which many people think is not only the greatest of Tolstoy's works but the greatest of all novels. It re-creates the movement of Russian history in the period of the NAPOLEONIC WARS (q.v. Vol. X), depicting surpassingly well the principal episodes—the Battle of Austerlitz, the Treaty of Tilsit, and the campaign of 1812—as well as the leading participants such as Alexander I, Napoleon, and the Russian General Kutuzov. But, for Tolstoy, the semi-conscious movement of the mass of the people was more important than the 'great men'. He sees Napoleon's invasion of Russia as a tidal wave of men surging towards the European east, to be shattered by a similar but mightier wave moving westward. Kutuzov, who intuitively understands the hopes and desires of his people, appears as a great commander; while Napoleon, who imagines himself responsible for the cataclysm in which he is caught up, appears as a hollow braggart. But *War and Peace* is not a history book but a novel, full of characters who live and love and laugh and suffer. Pierre, the hero, Prince Andrew, and the charming Rostov family are some of the most life-like creations of any novelist.

In 1873 Tolstoy started work on *Anna Karenina*, intending merely to finish an incomplete short story by PUSHKIN (q.v.); but the story grew until he soon saw that he had embarked upon a major work, which took him 4 years to finish. *Anna Karenina* is a tragedy of contemporary life. The story in itself is commonplace: a newspaper report of a divorce-court case served his need, for plot was never his chief concern. It is his understanding of Anna which makes the novel a masterpiece. He himself appears among his characters as Levin, and the other characters in the book—Karenin, Vronsky, Kitty, the feckless Stiva Oblonsky, and his unhappy wife Dolly, are as convincing as the characters of *War and Peace*, and are portrayed with Tolstoy's wise humanity.

At this time Tolstoy began to experience the spiritual crisis which was to convert him into a moral reformer and which gave everything he wrote a moral purpose. He became a prophet of a new kind of Christianity and his teaching, with its stress on the obligations of work and of non-resistance to evil, came close to the doctrine of GANDHI (q.v.). He made over his wealth to his wife, and tried to live like the peasants, wearing peasant dress and working in the fields, but continuing to write. In books such as *The Kreutzer Sonata, Resurrection, Hadji Murat*, and others he describes the ideal life as he sees it.

Tolstoy's moral doctrine made converts in many countries, and Yasnaya Polyana became a place of international pilgrimage. But as his wife and family did not sympathize with his social and religious views, his relations with them became painfully strained. Finally, when he was 82, he fled from home, accompanied only by his youngest daughter. In the course of their journey to the Caucasus he caught pneumonia and died at the station of Astapovo (now renamed 'Lyev Tolstoy'). His funeral was the occasion of a national demonstration.

See also Vol. I: RUSSIANS.
See also Vol. XII: NOVEL; RUSSIAN LITERATURE.

TOUSSAINT L'OUVERTURE (1743–1803).
This Negro ex-slave was one of the liberators of Santo Domingo (now the Dominican Republic) in the West Indies, and was the island's first governor. The name *L'Ouverture* ('Opening') was given him because of his bravery in breaking open the enemy's ranks in battle.

Part of Santo Domingo was under French rule and part under Spanish rule. In 1791 the French Government passed a law in their part of the country giving mulattoes (half-castes) and Negroes equal rights with white citizens. But the whites protested, and when the law was revoked the Negroes revolted. For years the country was in turmoil; the rebels quarrelled amongst themselves and with the mulattoes, and the country was further divided by a declaration of war between France and Spain.

Toussaint, who had received a good education and had become superintendent of the slaves on his master's plantation, joined the rebel forces against France and served as a physician. But when France again freed the slaves, he served with France against the Spaniards and mulattoes. He was given command of a large Negro army, and rescued the last French garrison holding out against the mulattoes. Within 2 years the French had made him commander-in-chief of a powerful and highly trained force, and by 1800 the whole of the French part of the island was under his control; the following year he seized the part remaining to Spain.

Toussaint's power was so great (he called himself 'Bonaparte') that he was, in fact, independent of France, though he always tried to act under French authority, and had refused a British offer to make him king of the island. He drafted a constitution, with himself as governor for life, and submitted it to NAPOLEON's Government for approval (q.v.). Toussaint restored order to the island; he gave it a sound economy, and agriculture prospered. But his remarkable personal qualities aroused the hatred of Napoleon, who disliked the emancipation of Negroes, and he declared the re-establishment of slavery on the island. Toussaint refused to obey, and Napoleon sent an army of 25,000 men against him.

The general commanding this army at first agreed to Toussaint's terms, but later arrested him, and renounced all the promises he had made. (Napoleon later described this act of treachery, which he had himself planned, as his greatest act of folly.) Rebellion soon broke out again, and with the arrival of a British fleet, the French abandoned the island in 1803. The same year Toussaint died in the French dungeon in which he was held prisoner. Wordsworth commemorated his great struggle for liberty in his sonnet *To Toussaint L'Ouverture*.

See also Vol. I: WEST INDIANS.

TRAJAN (A.D. 53–117). After a successful military career, Trajan became Roman Emperor when he was 45. He did everything possible to win favour. He entered his capital on foot—a gesture of modesty which won him immediate popularity. He consulted the Senate frequently and was on friendly terms with its members, disarming opposition by trust. He gave lavish gifts to the people. He was the first Emperor to receive the title Optimus ('the best'). For all his tact he was a firm ruler, keeping a close watch on the affairs of his Empire: in his letters to Pliny he gives sensible advice about the treatment of Christians and about a host of quite trivial problems. He built many roads and also

Vasari
TRAJAN
Statue in the Villa Albani Museum, Rome

a great forum in Rome, in which stands TRAJAN'S COLUMN (q.v. Vol. XII).

Trajan followed a policy of conquest and expansion in the East. After hard fighting, he created the province of Dacia (now Roumania). He annexed Armenia and, sweeping through Mesopotamia, reached the shores of the Persian Gulf. He wished, like ALEXANDER (q.v.), to invade India; but his lines of communication were threatened, and he had to hurry back to deal with trouble in other parts of the Empire. In Asia Minor he had a stroke and died.

Trajan did much to strengthen the Empire, within and without, but it was left to his successor HADRIAN (q.v.) to consolidate his work.

See also Vol. I: ROMAN CIVILIZATION.

TROLLOPE, Anthony (1815–82). The father of this Victorian novelist was a barrister and Oxford don and his mother, Frances Trollope, was in her day a well-known novelist. When Trollope was 19, he became an inspector in the postal service. Apart from official work and authorship, he lived the life of a country gentleman, being particularly fond of riding to hounds. His *Autobiography* (edited by his son, and published after his death) shocked some people because in it he showed that the business of writing was not just an affair of genius and inspiration but also involved hard work and regular hours.

In all, Trollope wrote sixty novels. The most successful, and those which made his reputation, were those about clerical life in and around the cathedral town of Barchester. In Barset he added a county to England as surely as Anthony Hope later put Ruritania on the map of Europe. To create such a personal world, true in essence though in fact imaginary, is one of the signs of a great writer. His novels are full of humour, with effectively restrained use of satire and caricature. His Barsetshire novels began with *The Warden* (1855) and continued to *The Last Chronicle of Barset* (1867), the children in the earlier books often appearing as grown-up people in the later ones. He wrote also a series of political novels, of which *Phineas Finn* is typical.

TROTSKY (1877–1940). Lev Davidovich Bronstein is the real name of the Russian revolutionary, Trotsky. He was the son of a well-to-do Jewish landowner in southern Russia, and received a conventional middle-class education at Odessa. He was expelled from the university for political activities, and rapidly became a leading figure among the Russian followers of Karl MARX (q.v.) because of his gifts as writer and orator. As a political offender he was banished to Siberia, but he escaped from there and went abroad. He returned to Russia at the time of the short-lived 1905 Revolution, in which he was the dominant personality as leader of the Workers' Council (Soviet) of St. Petersburg (now Leningrad). After the failure of the Revolution he was again exiled to Siberia, from which he once more escaped. He lived abroad until the Revolution of 1917, winning a reputation as a political journalist and taking an active part in the international Socialist movement. He held aloof to some degree from the struggles between LENIN (q.v.) and his opponents among the Russian Marxists (see Vol. X, COMMUNISM).

Trotsky returned to Russia in 1917 during the First World War, when the old Imperial Government collapsed and was replaced by a provisional Liberal Government. In the autumn came the critical stage of the RUSSIAN REVOLUTION (q.v. Vol. X). Trotsky, President of the Workers' Council of St. Petersburg, was a principal organizer of the final triumph of the extreme revolutionaries in November, of which his *History of the Russian Revolution* gives a celebrated account. He became Commissar (Minister) for Foreign Affairs in the new Bolshevik Government, and at once appealed to the peoples of the fighting nations over the heads of their governments, urging them to make peace; and he published certain secret treaties of the Allies in an effort to discredit their cause. After making peace with Germany in March 1918, the Russian leaders soon realized that the Bolshevik Revolution had failed to spread to Germany, and Trotsky was transferred to the more crucial post of Commissar for War. He was mainly responsible for the Bolshevik victory in the bitter Civil War of 1918–20, and was thus the real founder of the modern Red Army.

Trotsky soon came into conflict with other leaders, especially STALIN (q.v.), who set about undermining his position. Trotsky held that the revolution in Russia could not be self-sufficient, and that the success of a new Socialist society depended on the Revolution spreading to more advanced countries. Stalin opposed these views, and after Lenin's death, he manœuvred Trotsky out of power, finally driving him to resign his post in 1925. Trotsky was expelled from the Bolshevik party in 1927, and from Russia itself in 1929.

From exile he denounced the degeneration of the Soviet State under Stalin into a TOTALITARIAN State governed by a BUREAUCRACY (qq.v. Vol. X). In the 1936 'treason trials' held in Russia, Trotsky, in his absence, was charged with plotting against the Russian State with her enemies; and in 1940 he was murdered in Mexico, almost certainly by an agent of the Soviet secret police.

TURGENEV, Ivan Sergeivich (1818–83). It was as a writer of short stories that Turgenev became the first Russian writer with a European reputation. He belonged to an aristocratic family, and as a young man he quarrelled with his mother for her harsh treatment not only of her own family but also of the serfs on the estate. He left home and lived on his wits till her death made him rich. His early *Sportsman's Sketches* revealed a brilliant writer with a sympathetic knowledge of peasant life and thought.

Turgenev wrote supernatural stories, love-stories, novels, essays, and plays. The love-stories derived from his lasting passion for the famous singer Pauline Viardot Garcia. He lived for some 24 years in Paris, where he became the friend of Flaubert and Zola. He quarrelled with most other Russian writers, though when he returned to Russia he was reconciled with DOSTOEVSKY (q.v.).

Turgenev's political ideas were liberal, but not revolutionary. His work gives an unrivalled picture of Russian life in the middle years of the 19th century, and among his finest work are his novels *Fathers and Sons*, *Smoke*, and *Virgin Soil*.

TURNER, Joseph Mallord William (1775–1851). When this English landscape artist, in some ways a solitary and eccentric figure, died at the age of 76, he had raised himself by his industry and genius to a supreme position in English art. (*See* Vol. XII, LANDSCAPE PAINTING.)

Born in Covent Garden, London, the son of a barber, he studied from the age of 14 at the Royal Academy Schools, where he won distinction as an architectural and topographical draughtsman. His water-colours were exhibited at the Royal Academy from the time he was 15. His professional success was rapid; already in his early 20's he was complaining that he had more

Tate Gallery

THE FIGHTING 'TEMERAIRE' BEING TOWED TO HER LAST BERTH
Painting by J. M. W. Turner

sketches which, on his return, he worked up as oil-paintings and water-colours. Compared with CONSTABLE (q.v.), Turner's approach to nature was less humble; what he saw was often moulded by his own imagination and by literary associations. For many years he worked on a long poem called *Fallacies of Hope*, and he often took quotations from this poem or from poems by established poets to go with his pictures when they were exhibited. Although he was a shrewd and genial companion, he was not a good speaker, and his lectures at the Royal Academy were chiefly redeemed by the excellence of the drawings he had prepared to illustrate his often inaudible words.

From 1829 onwards Turner's literary and romantic characteristics were superseded by more visionary ones. He became more and more absorbed in problems of light and atmosphere, just as, later, the French IMPRESSIONIST painters (q.v. Vol. XII) were. In this Turner was far in advance of his time and the pictures he painted in this new atmospheric manner, in which all solid forms are dissolved in sunlight or mist or both, aroused much contemporary criticism and ridicule in the newspapers and journals. It was these ignorant attacks which led to RUSKIN's (q.v.) glowing championship of Turner's art in *Modern Painters* in 1843.

About this time Turner bought a cottage on the banks of the Thames at Chelsea, where, from an especially constructed balcony on the roof, he loved to watch the clouds and river transformed by the daily passage of the sun, and it was here that he died. By the terms of his will most of his pictures and drawings were bequeathed to the nation and are now divided between the National and Tate Galleries and the British Museum.

commissions than he could carry out. At 24 he was made an associate of the Royal Academy and at 27 a full Academician. He took an active interest in the affairs of the Academy and long held the position of Professor of Perspective there.

Turner's first oil-paintings were in the classical manner; but soon a life-long enthusiasm for the 17th-century French master, CLAUDE 'Lorraine' (q.v.), was aroused when he saw two of Claude's paintings that had recently been brought to England. They appealed most strongly to his own latent romanticism and love of natural scenery. One of them he declared to be 'beyond the power of imitation'. Nevertheless he deliberately tried to rival Claude in several of his large romantic oil-paintings, such as 'Dido Building Carthage' (in the National Gallery); and Claude must have been in his mind when in 1807 he began to work on his 'Liber Studiorum', a large series of mezzotints which partly occupied him for many years but which was finally abandoned.

He made many sketching tours in England and Wales, including an extensive tour of the north of England, where he drew ruined abbeys and castles in Yorkshire and elsewhere, for engraving. In 1802 he had an opportunity of visiting Paris and of travelling from there to Switzerland. His first visit to Italy was made in 1819, when he was away for 6 months making

TUTANKHAMEN (*c.* 1358–1340 B.C.), King of Egypt, *see* AKHNATEN. *See also* Vol. XII: TUTANKHAMEN'S TOMB.

MARK TWAIN
From Alvin Langdon Coburn, *Men of Mark*
(Duckworth & Co.)

TWAIN, Mark (1835–1910). The real name of this American writer and humorist was Samuel Langhorne Clemens. Brought up on the banks of the Missouri, he worked as printer, Mississippi river pilot, and gold-miner before he took to journalism. His pen name, 'Mark Twain', was a cry Mississippi pilots used when they were taking soundings.

Innocents Abroad, an account of a Mediterranean tour written for a San Francisco paper, was published in 1869, and immediately made his name as a humorist. His later books became internationally famous, particularly his superb stories of pioneering life, such as *Roughing It* and *Life on the Mississippi*. *The Adventures of Tom Sawyer* appeared in 1873, and *The Adventures of Huckleberry Finn* followed in 1884. *Huckleberry Finn* is one of the most triumphant accounts ever written of a boy's campaign to stop his elders improving him when he doesn't want to be

improved. Tom's and Huckleberry's adventures really are adventurous—but they are never incredible, and both books give a wonderful picture of life on and around the Mississippi during an exciting era, described with the greatest honesty and precision as boys would see it.

TYLER, Wat (died 1381). Little is known of Tyler except that he led the Kentish rebels in the Peasants' Revolt of 1381, and that the rebels from other districts seem to have looked to him for guidance. The revolt occurred chiefly in south-east England and was not confined to peasants but supported also by craftsmen, priests, and small squires. The old FEUDAL SYSTEM (q.v. Vol. X) was breaking down; the Black Death of 1348 caused a shortage of labour and a demand for higher wages; and the Statute of Labourers in 1351 had attempted to force wages back to the old level. The country was ill-governed and the French War was going badly for the English. In 1381 the government tried to raise money by levying a Poll Tax (payment per head), and outbreaks of rebellion immediately followed.

Wat Tyler and the Kentish rebels seized Canterbury and marched towards London. On the way they freed from prison John Ball, an ex-priest and popular roadside orator; he urged the rebels to attack the wealthy, saying,

> When Adam delved and Eve span,
> Who was then a gentleman?

In London the rebels were joined by the mob; palaces were burnt and the King's chief Minister, the Archbishop of Canterbury, was murdered. King Richard II, then only 14, boldly rode out to meet the rebels and spoke with Wat Tyler. He granted all Tyler's demands —in particular the abolition of serfdom and wage restrictions. At a second meeting, however, he gave evasive answers to more sweeping demands, and Tyler became threatening; the Lord Mayor of London struck him down and he was killed by one of the King's squires. His death marked the collapse of the revolt. An armed force dispersed the rebels; several ringleaders, including John Ball, were executed; and the promises which the King had made to Tyler were withdrawn.

V

VANBRUGH, Sir John (1664–1726). This dramatist and architect was the son of a well-to-do London tradesman of German descent. He first went to France, where he studied the arts; he then became a soldier, and while in France was arrested as a suspected spy. During his imprisonment in the Bastille in Paris he began to write plays, and when he returned to London he produced several comedies, of which *The Relapse* and *The Provok'd Wife* are the best known. They are typical of their age: gay, witty, and coarse, the dialogue being more interesting than the plots (*see* RESTORATION DRAMA, Vol. XII). He also became interested in opera, and later built an opera-house in the Haymarket, and lost much money over the productions. Vanbrugh's good looks, wit, and charm made him acceptable in aristocratic society, and he became a member of the Kit-Kat Club. Through these connexions he obtained his first architectural commission in 1699 to build Castle Howard in Yorkshire for the Earl of Carlisle. Vanbrugh apparently had had no architectural training, but this enormous house proves that he had an artist's imagination, and also that he had studied French buildings to some good purpose. Instead of building a large single block, then the normal form of house construction in England, he built a series of blocks of different heights with a dome forming the centre of the design. For the inside, too, he had original ideas. The hall, grandly designed in stone, is more like a Baroque Continental church than, for instance, WREN's (q.v.) panelled or painted interiors. Although much of the detail is clumsy, the plan shows an advance towards comfort; for example, the rooms for the first time open into corridors instead of opening one from another. Vanbrugh seems to have made up for his lack of experience by taking Nicholas Hawksmoor, Wren's chief

assistant, into a kind of partnership, to help him carry out the work.

In 1702 Vanbrugh's position as an architect was assured by his appointment as Comptroller of the Surveyor's Office under Wren. With Hawksmoor, he completed the work on Greenwich Royal Hospital for seamen, which had been begun by Wren. In 1705 he received the important commission to build Blenheim Palace, the house to be presented by the nation to the Duke of MARLBOROUGH (q.v.) after the Battle of Blenheim. Vanbrugh conceived a heroic design to match the occasion—a massive house on a grand scale. Though classical forms are used, Blenheim also suggests the strength of a medieval castle, a style of architecture that Vanbrugh is known to have admired. It has been criticized as being too heavy, but it certainly achieves the architect's aim of expressing military power.

Vanbrugh's later houses, such as King's Weston, near Bristol, Seaton Delaval, Northumberland, and the entrance side of Grimsthorpe, Lincolnshire, are more compact. He also built a house for himself at Blackheath, now known as Vanbrugh Castle, in which the medieval element is very marked. At Seaton Delaval, perhaps his most successful work, he combines medieval and

Country Life

SEATON DELAVAL, DESIGNED BY VANBRUGH

classical motifs in an imaginative and highly individual way. He was more interested in mass than in elegance, though his interiors show that he appreciated the contrast between heavy stone-work and fine iron-work. His style reflects his robust temperament and zest for life.

The strength of his art lies in the daring and often unorthodox originality of his designs, especially his large-scale designs such as Blenheim, and in his use of dramatic emphasis; but he never reaches the serenity and perfection of Wren's best work, nor the scholarly grandeur of some of the independent work of Nicholas Hawksmoor.

VAN DYCK, Sir Anthony (1599–1641). This Flemish painter was born at Antwerp, the son of a wool merchant. When he was still a boy he began to work in RUBENS's studio (q.v.), and he formed his style on that of Rubens. Finding that Antwerp was too small to hold both of them, Van Dyck came to England and entered the service of James I in 1620. The works he painted at that time are not known. In the next year he returned to Antwerp, and then visited Italy from 1622 until 1627, where he painted some of his greatest works in Genoa and Rome. In 1632 he returned to England as official painter to Charles I, whom he immortalized in his portraits, together with the Queen and those families nearest to the Court (*see* picture, p. 83). He was received with great favour, loaded with honours, and knighted. No artist had ever received such favours in England before. The portraits he painted, even if they are flattering, are undoubtedly of great perception, variety, and truth, and they had an immense and lasting influence on European portrait painting. He married the granddaughter of a Scottish earl, and died in London when he was only 42. Van Dyck also painted some religious pictures, such as the 'Ecstasy of St. Augustine' for the Augustinian monastery in Antwerp; but most of his pictures were portraits.

See also Vol. XII: FLEMISH ART; PORTRAITS.

VAUGHAN WILLIAMS, Ralph (1872–1958). The English composer Vaughan Williams was born in Down Ampney, Gloucestershire, a village since made famous because he named after it one of his most beautiful hymn tunes. He went to school at Charterhouse and afterwards studied at the Royal College of Music and at Cambridge. Later he studied with the German composer Max Bruch and with the Frenchman Maurice Ravel. Nevertheless, his musical style always remained unmistakably English.

The principal reason for this was the strong influence of ENGLISH FOLK-SONG (q.v. Vol. XII) on his music. He himself collected many songs from country singers, and works such as his *English Folk-Song Suite* are based directly on folk-tunes; he also quoted folk-songs in other works, especially in the operas *Hugh the Drover* (in which an English boxing match is the chief centre of action) and *Sir John in Love* (based on Shakespeare's story of Falstaff). But often—as in his most popular song, *On Linden Lea*—a folk-song basis is suspected when the music is in fact completely original.

Another source of inspiration was the English music of the 16th century, as can be seen in the lovely *Fantasia on a Theme of Tallis* and in the *Mass in G minor*.

Vaughan Williams wrote many extended works, including no less than nine symphonies. Several have titles which give a clue to their character. The first, the *Sea Symphony*, uses a chorus which sings words by Walt Whitman. In the second, *A London Symphony*, you can hear the chimes of Big Ben and other common London sounds which he loved. His third, the *Pastoral Symphony*, shows his abiding love for the English country-side. The mood of the symphonies varies greatly from one to another: the *Pastoral Symphony* was followed by the harsh and violent No. 4 in F minor, and this in turn by the contemplative, peaceful No. 5 in D. Symphony No. 6 sounds a stern note; written after the Second World War it is a strikingly original and thoughtful product of our own troubled times. New possibilities interested him: Symphony No. 8 includes a vibraphone obligato! He also wrote a *Romance* for harmonica, and he was enthusiastic in writing music for films, producing memorable scores for *49th Parallel* and *Scott of the Antarctic*. The latter served as a basis for the 7th Symphony, *Sinfonia Antartica*.

Music, to Vaughan Williams, was something you do (even if you can't do it very well!) rather than something you talk about. He gave endless encouragement to young professional musicians as well as to amateurs. There was no pretence or insincerity in his character. He accepted few honours, one of the exceptions being the rarely awarded Order of Merit.

Anderson

THE MAIDS OF HONOUR: PAINTING BY VELAZQUEZ

This shows Velazquez working on a portrait of the King and Queen, who are reflected in the mirror on the far wall. In the foreground is their daughter, the Infanta Margarita, with her maids of honour, tutors, and dwarfs. Prado, Madrid

VELAZQUEZ, Diego (1599–1660). The greatest Spanish painter, Diego Rodríguez de Silva y Velazquez, was born in Seville. At the age of 14 he was apprenticed for 4 years to an artist of little talent, from whom he can have learned

only the elements of drawing and painting. At first he painted subjects taken from the street life of Seville, with strongly modelled figures and exaggerated contrasts of light and shade, and conscientiously realistic still-lifes (the most famous example, 'The Water-Carrier', is in the Wellington Museum, London). In 1622 Velazquez went to Madrid, but he was unsuccessful there and soon returned home. The next year he was recalled to Madrid by King Philip IV's Minister, and on this occasion his success was immediate and great. Almost at once he was commissioned to paint the King, and was soon appointed a court painter with the promise that he alone should paint the King. From this time onward he remained attached to the Court, engaged principally in making portraits of the royal family and their circle.

In the royal collection at Madrid Velazquez was able to study properly for the first time the works of the great masters of Italian art. The effect of these studies, particularly of TITIAN (q.v.), was to change the cold colour, black shadows, and literal realism of his early years to a more flowing technique, warmer and richer colour, and lighter tone. He visited Italy from 1629–31, seeing Rome, Venice, and Naples, and the further knowledge he gained there of the Venetian painters completed the transformation of his style. Striking evidence of this is the full-length portrait of Philip IV, now in the National Gallery in London, painted on his return to Spain, and 'The Surrender of Breda' ('The Lances') now in Madrid.

Velazquez visited Italy again from 1649–51 to acquire paintings and sculpture for the decoration of the Spanish palaces. Once more the full impact of the Venetian painters continued the development of his style and his technique, and prepared the way for the great artistic triumphs of his last years. In Rome he painted his most celebrated portrait, that of Pope Innocent X, and the 'Rokeby Venus' (now in the National Gallery) was probably also painted at about this time.

Velazquez had always been a slow worker, and now his duties as Marshal of the Palace, which included the organizing of royal functions, took up more and more of his time, so that he produced fewer works in these last years than at any other period. Yet among them are his greatest achievements, including 'The Tapestry Weavers' and 'The Maids of Honour', two of the greatest expressions of visual realism in European art.

He remained largely unknown outside Spain until the 19th century, when his work began to arouse attention, especially among French

VERDI
Caricature by 'T' from *Vanity Fair*, 1879

artists. The study of his painting and that of GOYA (q.v.) led to the development of the French School of IMPRESSIONIST PAINTING (q.v. Vol. XII).

See also RUBENS.
See also Vol. XII: SPANISH ART.

VERDI, Giuseppe (1813–1901). Verdi, the great Italian opera composer, was the son of a village shopkeeper in northern Italy. By good luck his musical gifts interested a wealthy merchant who paid for his teaching, but this could not get him admitted to the academy of music at Milan. Verdi stayed in Milan and studied privately. In 1836, he married his benefactor's daughter, and they lived in Milan, where his first opera was produced. During the next 3 years his wife and both his children died, and Verdi, overcome with grief, vowed he would never write music again. After an interval, however, he began work on an opera, *Nebuchadnezzar*—called, for short, *Nabuco* (from the Italian). This was enthusiastically received, mainly because part of Italy at that time was held by Austrian troops, and the Italians were stirred to excitement by a drama about freedom and tyranny. Verdi became popular, and produced several more operas. His fame began to spread abroad, and in 1846 he was invited to Paris, and in the following year to London. But Verdi's music was too vigorous for French and English audiences, who preferred the operas of Bellini and Donizetti, with their flowery melodies and lack of dramatic interest.

Verdi had written fifteen operas by the time he was 38; in the next 3 years he wrote his three best-known operas—*Rigoletto*, *Il Trovatore*, and *La Traviata*—as well as some less successful ones. In 1868 he was invited by the ruler of Egypt to compose an opera for the opening of the Suez Canal; the result was *Aïda*, a spectacular and dramatic but more dignified opera than its predecessors. His Requiem Mass, completed in 1874 to commemorate Manzoni, the Italian poet and novelist, is a masterpiece of 19th-century sacred music, and is dramatic, indeed operatic, in character.

Verdi had remarried, and now, over 60 and with twenty-five operas to his credit, he determined to seek the peace and quiet of his country home. Many people thought that he would compose no more, but when he was 74, he startled the world with *Otello*—the finest opera he had yet written. Even this was not the end, for when he was 80 he once more astonished the world by his comic opera, *Falstaff*, which is brimming over with a vitality and humour amazing in a man of any age.

The vigour of Verdi's early operas remained characteristic of his work all his life; but in middle age he learned also to create characters of real vividness and subtlety. His musical language became more elaborate; he was not content with tune-and-simple-accompaniment numbers (though he never lost his marvellous gift for melody), but gave the orchestra an important role to play in creating atmosphere and in setting scenes. He began to compose each scene as an unbroken dramatic whole instead of bringing the music to a halt after each song or chorus, as previous composers had done. Verdi's greatness was in his genius for creating dramatic forms and characters, while the music lost none of its beauty or excitement.

See also Vol. XII: Opera, History of.

VERMEER, Jan (1632–75). This Dutch painter was born and died in Delft, the small town near Rotterdam with which his name is linked. He is the greatest of the Dutch masters born about a generation later than Rembrandt (q.v.), and his paintings, lucid as a pool of clear sunlit water, reflect the calm conditions of middle-class life in Holland after the prolonged struggle for independence had been won (*see* Dutch, Vol. I).

Vermeer's earliest paintings are religious or mythological, but most of his mature pictures are of domestic interiors in which one or two people are performing a simple task. In a room almost always lighted by a window on the left, a girl reads a letter or a servant pours milk from a jug. The psychological atmosphere may be suggested with great subtlety, but the most important problem to Vermeer was the rendering of form and light. He seems to have painted very slowly, for only about forty pictures are known today. After his death they ceased to be valued, until in the mid-19th century a French critic recognized their extraordinary merits.

Rijksmuseum, Amsterdam

THE COOK
Painting by Vermeer

By gracious permission of H.M. the Queen

QUEEN VICTORIA AT OSBORNE, 1865
Her gillie, John Brown, holds her horse. Painting by Landseer

Now they are among the most prized paintings in the world.

See also Vol. IX: picture opposite p. 304.
See also Vol. XII: DUTCH ART.

VESALIUS, Andreas (1514–64). This cele-brated anatomist, whose work is a landmark in the history of medicine, came of a medical family, his father being Flemish and his mother English. When he was only 23 Vesalius became Professor of Anatomy at Padua, in Italy, then one of the finest centres of medical study in Europe.

In 1543, the year in which COPERNICUS (q.v.) published his great book on the universe, Vesalius published an equally important work on the structure of the human body. His book was based on actual dissection and examination of human bodies, and it confounded many traditional views which had been handed down unquestioned from the ancients. Vesalius advised doctors, instead of learning medicine from printed books, to go to 'the great book of nature' and study the body itself. His methods aroused great hostility among the supporters of the ancient writers, and Vesalius gave up his teaching and spent the rest of his life as physician to the Emperor Charles V. When he was 49 he died as the result of a shipwreck.

See also Vol. XI: MEDICINE, HISTORY OF; ANATOMY.

VICTORIA (1819–1901). Great Britain reached the summit of her power and prosperity during the 63 years of Queen Victoria's reign—the longest in British history. Victoria came to the throne when she was 18, after her uncles, George IV and William IV, had died without heirs. She had been brought up in stifling seclusion (not even having a room to herself until she was Queen) by her widowed mother, the Duchess of Kent, who was on bad terms with the rest of the royal family.

Victoria heard of her accession from the Archbishop of Canterbury and the Lord Cham-berlain early in the morning of 20 June 1837, and the young Queen began her reign on the flood tide of popular enthusiasm. She at once showed unsuspected qualities of determination, even of obstinacy. She quietly pushed her mother into the background, and entrusted herself entirely to her Prime Minister, Lord Melbourne, who spent several hours a day with her, tactfully teaching her the duties of monarchy. She gave to him personally a warm affection; but the partisanship which she showed to his party, the Whigs, dampened her early popularity. In 1839 the Tory leader, Sir Robert Peel, refused to take office because the Queen would not dismiss some of her Whig ladies-in-waiting as a gesture of confidence in the Tories, an incident which was magnified into the 'Bedchamber Plot'. Political feeling against her ran high, and the Crown became dangerously entangled in party politics.

At this time Victoria was gay, eager, and inexperienced, short of stature, not beautiful, but with a good speaking voice and an astonishing dignity. She was pleasure-loving and energetic, liking to dance into the dawn and to ride 20 miles in a day. A change came over her after her marriage, in 1840, to her cousin, Prince ALBERT of Saxe-Coburg-Gotha (q.v.). She became more serious, more conscious of her responsibilities, more businesslike. She had, in addition, the cares of bringing up the first of her nine children. The idea of duty, rather solemnly performed, came to the forefront of her life; the age of Victorian respectability had begun. She depended more and more on the Prince, and under his guidance she became impartial in politics.

Albert's death, in 1861, was a shock from which Victoria never recovered; she wore mourning for the rest of her life. 'It is', she wrote, 'my firm resolve, my irrevocable decision . . . that his wishes—his plans—about everything are to be my law. And no human power will make me swerve from what he decided and wished.' For a time, she withdrew entirely from public life, and consequently became rather unpopular, for many people felt that the institution of monarchy must suffer if the Sovereign were never seen; indeed, there was even a brief republican movement. The Queen was a tragically lonely figure, the loss of the Prince having removed her closest adviser; and she began to slip back towards the political partisanship of her youth. She never understood or liked GLADSTONE (q.v.), and was cold, mistrusting,

and often unfair both to him and to his party, the Liberals. She intrigued against him and criticized him unceasingly, often wildly and indiscreetly. Gladstone showed impeccable loyalty, though 'the Queen', he once said to a friend, 'is enough to kill a man'.

Victoria's relations with Gladstone's rival, DISRAELI (q.v.), were very different. Gladstone, it was said, treated her like a public meeting; Disraeli treated her very much as a woman, coaxing and flattering her unblushingly, and using her friendship for the benefit of his party. She found new life in his society, and 'Dear Lord Beaconsfield' filled the place in the 1870's which had been filled by 'Dear Lord Melbourne' in the 1830's. She felt his death, in 1881, as a personal bereavement.

Queen Victoria took a very considerable share in politics, though she never understood such changes as the widening of the franchise (see ELECTION, Vol. X) and the tighter organization of POLITICAL PARTIES (q.v. Vol. X), with the gradual shift of power from the Crown to the Cabinet. She continued, to the end of her life, to act as Albert had taught her to do, though the circumstances were different. Although her Ministers usually had their own way in conflicts with her, the task of persuading or satisfying the Queen added to the friction of government. She occasionally rebuked Ministers, and sometimes refused to approve appointments. She intervened in matters concerning the Army and Navy and the Church, and also in foreign affairs —she was related to most of the Sovereigns of Europe. She was never slow to point out to Ministers acts which, she thought, decreased the power and prestige of Britain. She was delighted when Disraeli gained for her the title of Empress of India.

From Disraeli's time onwards, she came more and more out of retirement. The old lady, in her widow's weeds, became a national figure. As she grew older, her contemporaries died away, leaving her lonelier than ever, but increasing her prestige. By the end of her reign her experience overtopped that of all her Ministers. She had lived through changes greater than those seen by any other European ruler, many of which she either disliked or misunderstood. She thought that increases in the electorate would lead to revolution, and that women who pressed for equal rights for their sex were guilty of 'mad, wicked folly . . . forgetting every sense of womanly feeling and propriety'. She had come to the throne at a time when the Sovereign was required to intervene directly in politics; when she died, the Crown was, rather, the link between the parts of an Imperial Commonwealth moving towards self-government.

Her first Jubilee, in 1887, was greeted with warmth; her second, in 1897, was made the occasion for the greatest demonstration of public loyalty and imperial splendour which England had ever seen. Her subjects venerated her and admired her courage (shown in her bearing during six attempts on her life, in the course of her reign) and her dignity. She became a symbolic figure, silhouetted in lonely majesty against the greatest Empire which the world had ever known. Her death was rightly felt to be the end of an epoch.

VILLON, François (born 1431). The real name of this remarkable 15th-century French poet is uncertain. His father, a Parisian, died when he was small, and François found a kindly protector in a priest, Guillaume de Villon, whose name he later adopted. He went to Paris University, where he became master of arts.

France, in the last stages of the HUNDRED YEARS WAR (q.v. Vol. X), was in a state of lawlessness, the University, in particular, being a centre of trouble. Villon apparently fell in with some very doubtful companions; in 1455 he killed a man in a brawl, and later was involved in a highly profitable robbery. These and other offences kept him in and out of prison; he was twice condemned to death—though his sentences were reduced to banishment. After the second occasion, in 1464, he left Paris, and nothing more is known of him.

Villon's poetry is intensely personal and he shifts from mood to mood with great rapidity—from repentant horror at the thought of death on the gallows (as in the *Ballade des pendus*) to a flippant bravado as in a poem in which he thanks the court for letting him off the death sentence: yet his sincerity in each mood is convincing. His two longish works, the *Petit Testament* and the *Grand Testament*, consist of a series of ironical bequests to his friends and enemies interspersed with some of the finest and most moving 'ballades' in the French language, of which the *Ballade des dames du temps jadis* is the best known.

See also Vol. XII: FRENCH LITERATURE.

VIRGIL (70–19 B.C.). Publius Vergilius Maro was a great Roman poet whose poems, especially the *Georgics* and the *Aeneid*, are known to almost everyone who has read Latin. Virgil, the son of successful farming people, was born near Mantua in the valley of the river Po. He was tall, countrified in manner, shy, and often ill. He had a saintly character, a powerful intellect, a great love of the country, an intense patriotism, and a beautiful voice for speaking poetry. He was given the best education, his parents intending him for the legal profession, and perhaps politics. But when he went to Rome he found he could not bear the life, and, after making one speech in a law court, decided, probably when he was about 25, to join a kind of private university kept by the Greek Epicurean philosopher Siro at Naples (*see* EPICURUS).

Before he left home Virgil had gained some reputation for his poetry, and both then, and afterwards in Rome, he won the favour of rich patrons, including Octavian, later AUGUSTUS CAESAR (q.v.), the first Roman Emperor. This enabled him to live quietly, free to write. He read and remembered an enormous number of books, both prose and poetry, old and new, and this knowledge helped him in forming his own poetry. He used to compose very many lines in the morning, and then, as he said himself, would 'lick them into shape'. He revised with such care, and discarded so much of what he wrote,

Bardo Museum, Tunis
VIRGIL WITH THE MUSES OF HISTORY AND TRAGEDY
2nd-century floor mosaic from a Roman villa at Uthica, Africa. Virgil was held in great veneration at this time

that his output of satisfactory lines would often average only one a day.

Some poetry has been doubtfully attributed to Virgil, but he left three works, all written in hexameters (*see* VERSIFICATION, Vol. XII) which are certainly his: the *Bucolics* or *Eclogues*, the *Georgics*, and the *Aeneid*. The *Eclogues* (probably written between 43 B.C. and 39 B.C.) are ten short pieces which follow the convention of 'pastoral' poetry (*see* PASTORALS, Vol. XII). The four books of the *Georgics*, composed between about 37 B.C. and 29 B.C., deal poetically with life and work on the farm. The *Aeneid*, a long epic poem in twelve books, tells the story of the legendary hero Aeneas, who fled from Troy, and after many adventures, was shipwrecked at Carthage. There he fell in love with Queen Dido, but cruelly abandoned her when the gods commanded him to sail for Italy. In Italy he was to found the Julian family and the Roman nation. The *Aeneid* also imparts to careful readers profound truths about Roman civilization, and about human life. In 19 B.C. Virgil started for Greece, intending to spend 3 years revising the *Aeneid*; but he became very ill and had to return. He died at Brundisium. He was so dissatisfied with the *Aeneid* as it was that he wanted to burn it; but Augustus had it published after his death.

After the publication of the *Eclogues* Virgil acquired almost legendary fame and popularity. There were many stories and rumours about him: he later came to be celebrated as a magician, and tales of his supposed miracles were current all over Europe. It was also believed that he had prophesied the coming of Christianity. Virgil's special qualities as a poet are the expressive, musical perfection and majesty of his verse, and its great wealth of wisdom often concentrated in phrases of two or three words.

See also Vol. XII: LATIN LITERATURE; EPIC POETRY.

VOLTAIRE (1694–1778). Few writers have so influenced the course of history as François Marie Arouet—known by his assumed name, Voltaire. He was born in Paris in the great age of LOUIS XIV (q.v.), when France had become the most powerful country in Europe with an art and literature admired by cultivated people everywhere. But by the time he had begun to write, the despotic power of the French kings was decaying. Voltaire was the most brilliant of a group of writers known as 'the Philosophers' who, in challenging the religious and social traditions of the old order, prepared the way for the FRENCH REVOLUTION (q.v. Vol. X).

Voltaire was a remarkable looking man, with a tall and extraordinarily thin body, and a face which in his old age reminded people of a skull. He took little exercise and drank endless cups of coffee, yet, in spite of poor health, his astonishing vitality showed itself in his keen, sparkling eyes and gesticulating hands. His character was a curious mixture of contradictions: he was vain, jealous, greedy for money (he became very wealthy), and quite unscrupulous in attacking his enemies; but he was also a devoted friend, a generous benefactor to causes he approved, and an indefatigable champion of people he thought had been unjustly treated.

Voltaire first made his name as a poet and author of rather dull verse tragedies, and he did not discover his true bent until, when he was 30, a quarrel forced him to leave France for England. During his 3 years' stay there he learned to appreciate not only such English institutions as parliamentary government but also English writers such as Shakespeare, who at that time were almost unknown in France. What chiefly impressed him was the contrast between England's prosperity and tolerance and the poverty and lack of freedom in his own country. On his return, he published his first important book, *Lettres philosophiques sur les Anglais*, which described his impressions of English life. There

J. E. Bulloz

VOLTAIRE IN HIS STUDY

Porcelain figure, about 1773. Musée Carnavalet, Paris

was nothing revolutionary in it, but the government, thinking praise of the English implied criticism of the French, had it burned by the public executioner, and Voltaire was forced to leave Paris once again. For the next 15 years he lived on a country estate in Lorraine, where he studied science, began a history of the reign of Louis XIV, and wrote plays and satirical novels which make witty attacks on prejudice and superstition. These writings made him even more unpopular with the authorities, and after spending 3 years in Prussia with FREDERICK THE GREAT (q.v.), followed by a period of wandering, he finally settled down at Ferney, conveniently situated on the frontier of France and Switzerland so that he could escape into Switzerland in case of trouble.

ENGRAVING OF THE CHÂTEAU DE FERNEY, WHERE VOLTAIRE LIVED FROM 1758
By Queverdo, after Signy. Bédier et Hazard, *Littérature française* (Larousse)

Voltaire was now 60, and the most famous writer in Europe. But his prodigious energy made these last 20 years of his life even more productive and influential. He kept open house for statesmen, aristocrats, philosophers, and writers; he wrote, or dictated, some twenty letters a day (10,000 of them have been published) to people in every class of society, whether monarchs such as Catherine of Russia or quite unknown people who sought his advice. He took a keen interest in the affairs of his estate, and established saw-mills and a watch-making industry. He built a private theatre and performed in his own plays. And he poured out a constant stream of essays, pamphlets, plays, historical works, dialogues, and novels, all brilliantly written and usually attacking what he considered to be the abuses and injustices of the time. His method was to apply reason and common sense to the ancient and accepted beliefs and traditions on which rested the established order under the French monarchy. Voltaire condemned with characteristic wit and eloquence the cruelty and inefficiency of the legal system, the privileged position of the nobles, the fanaticism of the Church, and the hindrances to trade. He preached continuously the need for toleration and liberty of speech. 'I disagree with what you say', he wrote once to a contemporary, 'but I will defend to the death your right to say it.'

At Ferney he wrote his masterpiece, the novel *Candide*. This is an amusing satire on the philosophy of LEIBNIZ (q.v.), who is caricatured in Candide's friend and tutor, Dr. Pangloss. This optimistic philosopher, despite suffering appalling indignities and disasters, holds to his belief that all is for the best in the best of all possible worlds. Candide, however, is brought to recognize that man can only be happy if he works and 'cultivates his garden'.

Voltaire was a propagandist who aimed at interesting people in his ideas by entertaining them. He perfected a clear, simple, and witty style—a style still characteristic of the best French writing. There was, however, nothing poetic in his temperament, and he was blind to certain aspects of art and religion. His mind was dry, sceptical, ironic, and consequently his best work was in prose.

At the end of his life, when he was 84, Voltaire went back to Paris once again, and there received the most spectacular welcome ever given to a writer. When his play *Irène* was performed, his bust was crowned with laurel on the stage and the whole audience stood to cheer him in his box. The excitement, however, was too much for him, and he died soon afterwards—11 years before the French Revolution swept away the old régime which he had attacked with such untiring energy.

W

WAGNER, Richard (1813–83). The German composer, Wagner, was the contemporary of the other great 'romantics', BERLIOZ, MENDELSSOHN, CHOPIN, SCHUMANN, LISZT, VERDI, and BRAHMS, and was the immediate successor of BEETHOVEN (qq.v.) and Weber, whose works had a considerable influence on him. He lived in an age of new materialistic philosophies and great technical advances, and his lifetime saw the rise of Germany to power in Europe (*see* BISMARCK). All these things affected his life and music.

He is important chiefly as the creator of a new kind of opera, or 'music-drama' as he preferred to call it. He conceived his work as a whole, without the old distinction between recitative (dialogue) and aria (song); all the arts were united to contribute to the total effect of the drama. For this idea Wagner went back to an earlier reformer of opera, the composer GLUCK (q.v.). Wagner always wrote the libretti, or words, for his operas himself, often long before composing the music; he was in any case a slow composer. In his later works he achieved musical unity by his characteristic use of *leitmotiv*, that is, the use of various recurrent musical themes, each representing a character or an idea. These later operas resemble gigantic symphonies accompanied by stage action, rather than plays with music.

Of his chief works, *Tannhäuser* and *Lohengrin* are based on medieval German stories, and THE RING OF THE NIBELUNGS (a cycle of operas, *Rhine-gold*, *The Valkyrie*, *Siegfried*, and *The Twilight of the Gods*) on Nordic legend (q.v. Vol. XII). *Tristan and Isolde*, from the Arthurian legend, is the most passionate expression of human love in the whole of music; *The Mastersingers of Nuremberg* is a comic opera set in the 16th century; *Parsifal* is a mystical religious drama, the story of the search for the Grail (the cup used by Christ at the Last Supper).

Wagner was born in Leipzig during the Napoleonic Wars. His own life was eventful and stormy, and would appear even more so if his numerous love-affairs were described. One of these inspired *Tristan and Isolde*, which, with *The Mastersingers* (also partly autobiographical), is probably his most attractive work.

After a childhood spent mostly in Leipzig and Dresden, he went as a young man to Paris, where his first opera, *Rienzi*, was finished in a debtor's prison. In the meantime he had married Minna Planer, an actress who determined to make him a successful conductor and a respectable citizen; but she did not understand his mind or his aims and only succeeded in making his life a burden. He continued to love her dearly; one of his few kindly actions was the affection and sympathy he showed to Minna, even when it became clear that they could no longer live happily together.

Wagner returned to Dresden, where *The Flying Dutchman* and *Tannhäuser* were produced, but was exiled for openly siding with the revolutionary party which held the city for 2 days in 1848. He spent much of his exile in Switzerland, during which time Liszt produced *Lohengrin* at Weimar with great success. When Wagner was

Radio Times Hulton Lib.

RICHARD WAGNER

42 he made a very successful visit to London, and in 1864 he went to Munich under the generous patronage of King Ludwig II of Bavaria, but he soon had to leave because he quarrelled with the court officials. Some of his greatest works, *The Mastersingers*, *Rhine-gold*, and *The Valkyrie*, were first performed in Munich.

Wagner now married Liszt's daughter, Cosima, after she had broken her marriage with a friend of Wagner's. She proved an understanding wife, determined to foster Wagner's greatness. Together they planned their own festival theatre at Bayreuth in Bavaria, and there, in 1876, 28 years after its first conception, *The Ring* was given its first complete performance, before two emperors and a king. In 1882 *Parsifal* was finished and produced at Bayreuth; and in the following year, at the age of 70, Wagner died in Venice.

Wagner's family have continued to organize yearly festivals at Bayreuth, to which people from all over the world go to see *Parsifal*, *The Ring*, and a selection of Wagner's other music dramas given under the best possible conditions. At first Cosima organized them, then Wagner's son Siegfried, and now his two grandsons manage and produce the festival.

Wagner's dramatic skill developed very early —probably encouraged by his stepfather, who was an actor—and at 15 he wrote a long Shakespearian drama. Wishing to set it to music, he took lessons in composition; but he quarrelled impatiently with his teacher, and abandoned music until he was inspired again by hearing the Seventh and Ninth Symphonies of Beethoven. It was not until he was well over 30 that Wagner the musician caught up with Wagner the dramatist. As a person Wagner never seems to have grown up at all; a sensitive and wilful child, he became a completely self-centred and unscrupulous man, uncontrolled yet hypocritical, impatient of criticism and with a mania for self-justification.

His prose writings setting forth his theories, together with his somewhat unreliable autobiography, *My Life*, fill more volumes than do his musical compositions. His revolutionary ardour was only the outward sign of his own frustration. His anti-Semitism, later exploited by the Nazis under Hitler, reflects the hatred felt by Wagner himself—poor, undersized, and unsuccessful—for the rich, tall, gentlemanly, and immensely popular Jewish composer, Meyerbeer, who had befriended him, and from whom Wagner learned much about dramatic and orchestral effect. Wagner's undoubted charm, especially for women, and his plausibility enabled him to live on his friends for a great part of his life; but he treated them all abominably. His life was filled with broken friendships and bad debts of every kind. The only qualities that can perhaps be admired in the man, as distinct from the artist, are his almost incredible self-confidence and utter determination to succeed at all costs.

See also Vol. XII: OPERA, HISTORY OF.

WAKEFIELD, Edward Gibbon (1796–1862).

Wakefield had a considerable influence on colonial development in the 19th century, and himself worked with enthusiasm to colonize parts of Australia and New Zealand. As a young man Wakefield was unscrupulous and unpredictable. When he was 20 he eloped with a rich heiress, a ward in Chancery, but he overcame the opposition of the court and married her. After his wife had died, 10 years later, he ran away with another heiress, a schoolgirl. But this time he was sentenced to 3 years' imprisonment for abduction.

In Newgate prison Wakefield devoted his time to studying colonial problems. He saw the danger of colonizing new lands with convicts only (*see* TRANSPORTATION, Vol. X), and wanted, instead, to set up a respected, non-convict community which should eventually become self-governing. He urged the government not to give land to emigrants but to sell it at a price which the poorer emigrants could pay after they had worked for a period as labourers and had saved money. The money derived from such sales, he pointed out, could be devoted to assisting the emigration of further selected emigrants and their families; and this would ensure enough labour to work the new lands. In South Australia a colony of free settlers, founded at Adelaide in accordance with Wakefield's main principles, proved very successful.

In 1838 Lord Durham invited Wakefield to accompany him when he went to be Governor-General of Canada. He had some influence on Durham's famous *Report* on Canada, in which he urged for more self-government in the colonies. Wakefield then turned his attention to colonizing parts of New Zealand. From the time of the founding of the New Zealand Colonization

Company in 1838, the importance of his work in forwarding emigration and settlement cannot be over-estimated. He was responsible for the Canterbury settlements, and those which founded Wellington, Nelson, and New Plymouth. In 1853 he went to New Zealand himself as a colonist, and died 10 years later at Wellington.

See also Vol. I: AUSTRALIANS.
See also Vol. X: BRITISH COMMONWEALTH.

WALLACE, Alfred Russell (1823–1913). This English naturalist and traveller was trained as an architect and surveyor. He joined a friend on a journey of exploration up the river Amazon, but lost all his collections and notes during his return to England. He set out to gather a similar collection of plants and insects from the Malay archipelago, and his observations during his 8 years' stay led him to the same conclusions on evolution and natural selection as were held by DARWIN (q.v.). Wallace sent home notes of his views to Darwin, and in 1858 Darwin published a preliminary paper on EVOLUTION (q.v. Vol. II) under both their names. Wallace later became well known as a writer and lecturer on scientific subjects.

Wallace's most important scientific work was on the geographical distribution of animals. The imaginary line through the Malay archipelago which separates Oriental from Australian fauna is still called the 'Wallace line'.

See also Vol. II: ANIMAL AND PLANT DISTRIBUTION.

WALLACE, Sir William (c. 1274–1305). Little is known about this Scottish patriot before 1297, when he raised an army of men resolved to free their country from the English, and won the great victory of Stirling Bridge.

When the King of Scotland, Alexander III, was killed in an accident in 1286, a long period of peaceful and well-governed prosperity in Scotland came to an end. Alexander's granddaughter, the little Queen Margaret, the 'Maid of Norway,' died on her way from Norway, and there was then no obvious successor to the Crown. The two principal claimants were Robert Bruce, who was very old, and John Baliol, who was justly nicknamed the 'Empty Jacket'. To avoid civil war, the Scots called upon Edward I of England to arbitrate; and he, regardless of his recent treaty of alliance, and knowing Scotland to be leaderless and unprepared for defence, broke his trust, annexed Scotland, and proclaimed Baliol king as his vassal. The Scots were divided in allegiance between Baliol and Bruce, and Edward was able to garrison all Scotland with ease.

The next year risings occurred throughout the country, and when the young Wallace, son of an old Scottish family and a born soldier and leader, led the Scots to victory at Stirling Bridge, new hope was stirred. Wallace was made regent for Baliol, who was Edward's prisoner. The next year he met a further English invasion at Falkirk where, though his foot-soldiers defeated the English heavy cavalry, they were themselves destroyed by the new English weapon, the long bow (see LAND WARFARE, Vol. X). In face of this disaster the Bruce and Baliol parties united under the leadership of Bruce's young son, Robert BRUCE (q.v.) and Baliol's nephew, John Comyn. The Scottish lords were jealous of Wallace and drove him from the regency; but he continued to fight steadfastly for another 6 years, undismayed by failure, loss of power, and the constant quarrels among the Scottish lords. Wallace put his hopes in young Bruce, who was later crowned by the Bishops of St. Andrews and Glasgow, and who learnt to resemble Wallace rather than his father. In 1304, however, Scottish resistance collapsed, and soon afterwards Wallace was captured by treachery, taken to London, and in 1305 was put to a cruel and disgusting death. Although Wallace's life appeared to end in complete failure, the spirit he had aroused in his own country was not killed, and he left behind his pupil Bruce to bring his struggle to a victorious end.

WALLENSTEIN, Albrecht von (1583–1634). Wallenstein was the most famous general of the Thirty Years War (1618–48), a long succession of religious wars between the Catholic and Protestant rulers of the various independent States of the HOLY ROMAN EMPIRE (q.v. Vol. I) which ravaged central Europe. The champion of the Protestants was Frederick, the ruler of the Palatinate, who held the princely rank of Elector since he was one of those entitled to elect the Emperor. The champion of the Catholics was Ferdinand of Austria, who had already been elected Emperor. The throne of Bohemia fell vacant, and although the Emperor was the natural heir, Frederick was elected King of Bohemia instead.

Wallenstein was born in Bohemia of Protes-

THE MURDER OF WALLENSTEIN AT EGER IN 1634
Contemporary German print

tant parents. He was later converted to Catholicism, but in fact he had little religious faith, and directed his life by what his astrologers told him the stars foretold. When the war broke out, Wallenstein took the side of the Emperor, and after the rout of the Protestants in an early battle, he enriched himself from their confiscated estates, making himself the most powerful person in Bohemia. Later he raised a large army for the Emperor, defeated the Protestants at Dessau, in north Germany, and carried the war into Denmark, a land which supported the Protestant princes; there he conquered the Jutland peninsula. By 1629 the Emperor, triumphant all over Germany, made Wallenstein Duke of Mecklenburg and one of the Princes of the Empire.

Differences, however, now arose between Wallenstein and the Emperor, especially over the policy of making conquered Germany Catholic by force. Wallenstein wanted peace, with both Catholics and Protestants living together with equal rights. The German princes, both Catholic and Protestant, feared the enormous power of Wallenstein and his influence over the Emperor, and demanded his dismissal. The Emperor weakly yielded.

Wallenstein retired, but almost immediately the victorious advance into Germany of King GUSTAVUS ADOLPHUS of Sweden (q.v.) compelled the Emperor to appeal to him for help. Wallenstein agreed but on his own terms, and, attracted by his fame and the hope of rich spoils, soldiers of all nations and creeds entered his army, and by their ruthless plundering devastated the countryside. Wallenstein met Gustavus Adolphus at the Battle of Lützen where the Swedish King, although victorious, was killed.

After this battle, Wallenstein ceased to conduct the war with any resolution. He wanted peace in which to secure his own political power, and he began secretly negotiating with the enemy. But he became so involved in his own intrigues and changes of policy that all parties came to distrust him, even his own army. His enemies persuaded the Emperor to dismiss him and later to declare him a traitor. Wallenstein then withdrew with his remaining troops to a Bohemian fortress, meaning to join the Swedes, and there he was murdered by traitors among his soldiers.

Wallenstein was tall and muscular, with a thin beard and cold glittering eyes. He was proud and domineering, a stern disciplinarian,

SIR ROBERT WALPOLE SPEAKING IN THE HOUSE OF COMMONS
He is standing beside the Speaker. Contemporary engraving

a remarkable military organizer and general, and a far-seeing politician. His career inspired SCHILLER's dramatic trilogy *Wallenstein* (q.v.).

He was a soldier to be admired but neither loved nor trusted. And, in spite of his great ambition and greed, he was sometimes curiously irresolute.

WALPOLE, Sir Robert (1676–1745). Walpole has often been called the first English Prime Minister, though that office was not recognized until the end of the 18th century (*see* MINISTERS OF THE CROWN, Vol. X). In Walpole's day it was still thought that the King himself should lead his Ministers, and so Walpole had not only to win authority and use it, but also to conceal that he did so.

Walpole first made a reputation as a financier, and when the confidence of the country was shaken by the speculation of the SOUTH SEA BUBBLE (q.v. Vol. VII), Walpole was called upon to restore order in public affairs. He became Chancellor of the Exchequer, and so skilfully handled both George I and George II and the House of Commons that he retained the chief power in his hands for 20 years. He gave his friends profitable positions in the government, and met his enemies with soft answers and rough good humour. Though a man of great subtlety and guile, he liked to appear as a simple Norfolk squire who wished to let other country gentlemen live in peace, and who thought that politics should not interfere with something important like fox-hunting.

Under Walpole the country recovered from the exhausting wars of Queen Anne's reign (*see* MARLBOROUGH), the results of the REVOLUTION OF 1688 (q.v. Vol. X) were permanently established, and considerable prosperity was attained. Walpole's faults lay in his cynical belief that every man had his price, and his habit of elbowing able rivals out of power so that they were driven into opposition against him.

Despite his peace-at-any-price foreign policy, war eventually broke out with France and Spain. Walpole was forced from office in 1742. He was created Earl of Orford, and retired to the splendid mansion at Houghton, Norfolk, which he had filled with the finest private collection of pictures in the country.

See also Vol. X: POLITICAL PARTIES; MINISTERS OF THE CROWN.

WALTON, Izaak (1593–1683). Walton is remembered for a single masterpiece, *The Compleat Angler*, written when the author was 60. He came from Staffordshire and, though he lived in London for years and had his own ironmongery shop in Fleet Street, he remained a countryman at heart. He became friendly with John DONNE (q.v.) and through him met other distinguished men. When Donne's *Sermons* were published in 1640, Walton prefaced them with a short biography, the first of his series of *Lives*, which JOHNSON (q.v.) took as his model. The *Lives*—mainly of 17th-century ecclesiastics—reflect Walton's strong Anglican and Royalist convictions.

The Compleat Angler, published in 1653, is mostly in the form of a dialogue between a hunter and a fisherman (the author) who expounds the art of freshwater fishing as they fish together along the banks of the river Lea, near London. The book is a perfect mirror of Walton's gentle, contemplative nature and of the countryside and the watermeadows he loved.

See also Vol. IX: ANGLING, FRESHWATER.

WASHINGTON, Booker (*c.* 1859–1915). This leader of Negro education and emancipation in the United States was himself a Negro, born in slavery. His mother was a slave on a plantation in Virginia; his father was believed to be white.

The boy's childhood both in slavery and in freedom was harsh. Even after SLAVERY (q.v. Vol. X) had been brought to an end, the lot of Negroes was hard, and education for them was almost unknown. Young Booker Washington, however, had sufficient ability to win free schooling at a school for coloured children, but he had to serve as school porter to pay for his keep. Later, he himself began to teach in coloured schools, and when he was 25 he became principal of the new Tuskegee Institute for Negroes in Alabama. It consisted then of little more than a mission hall; but by the time of his death, 34 years later, it had grown into more than 100 buildings.

Washington was a striking and popular speaker, and it was a speech in 1893 which made him the leader of the American Negroes. He urged them to seek education, learn skilled crafts and professions, and understand the dignity of efficient labour rather than claim political rights before they were ready for them. Though many Negro leaders were impatient with this view, his teaching met with great success. He was admired by President Theodore Roosevelt and dined with him at the White House. He wrote several works, including the story of his life, *Up From Slavery*, which was translated into at least eighteen languages.

See also Vol. I: AMERICAN NEGROES.
See also Vol. X: COLOUR PROBLEM; SLAVERY.

WASHINGTON, George (1732–99). After commanding the army of the American Colonists against Britain in the AMERICAN WAR OF INDEPENDENCE (q.v. Vol. X), Washington became the first President of the United States. After his death he became a legend, and he is now venerated as the most famous figure in American history and as 'the father of his country'.

Washington was descended from a prosperous English family which had left Northamptonshire for Virginia in the middle of the 17th century. When he was 20 he inherited his family's tobacco estates in Virginia and settled to the life of a planter. He was already a man of wealth, with the tastes of an English country squire.

At this time bitter rivalry between Britain and France for territory in North America led to outbreaks of fighting between the two countries. Washington served with distinction in the British forces and, at 23, having already commanded an expedition against the French, he joined another expedition under General Braddock, whose ideas of warfare were thoroughly conventional. Washington pleaded for more imaginative tactics: for example, the use of Red Indian scouts and tree-to-tree fighting. He also wanted the troops to wear the loose dress of the Red Indians. Braddock, however, was impatient and shocked at such suggestions. In the attack that followed, the British and Colonial troops, the former conspicuous in glittering scarlet uniforms, were caught in a murderous crossfire from a handful of hidden French as they stormed a hill in close formation; and they suffered defeat with a great sacrifice of men. Washington's own escape was amazing. Two horses were shot from under him, and four bullets passed through his coat.

When peace came, Washington, then widely known and respected, returned to his estates in Virginia, where he married a wealthy widow and developed his estates so efficiently that he became one of the wealthiest men in Virginia. He was a man of wisdom and judgement rather than of intellectual brilliance, with no outstanding talents, but with solid gifts of character which made men trust him. These qualities, and his experience as a soldier, made the Colonists choose him as commander-in-chief when their quarrel with the British Government flared into open war in 1775.

During the 6 years of fighting, Washington held his army together with great tenacity, in the face of all manner of difficulties. It was hard to raise recruits; even harder to persuade the thirteen Colonies to combine together to support an army. But, though he often expressed bitter thoughts about his thankless task, Washington's courage never flagged. With a small nondescript force of farmers and mechanics, undisciplined, poorly supplied, ill-clad, and often hungry, he could scarcely hope to drive the British out of America. Instead, he settled down to the grim task of wearing the enemy out. In the first year of the war Washington compelled the large, well-trained British army to withdraw from Boston, but soon after he was crushingly defeated, and his army almost annihilated. Washington built up a new army, with which he fought further costly, but indecisive, battles; and then for 3 years, with his army crumbling to pieces, he waited for a British move that never came.

At last in 1781 the British General Cornwallis moved into Virginia and established his headquarters at Yorktown. Washington, supported by Britain's European enemy France, moved rapidly southward and encircled Cornwallis's army. The British fleet, defeated at sea, was unable to bring any support, and Cornwallis surrendered. This was the real end of the war; though it was 2 years before the British recognized American independence at the Peace of Versailles.

Washington returned once more to Virginia; but his greatest work was still ahead of him. The thirteen former colonies, linked by loose Articles of Confederation, had held together during the war only after many disputes and differences. But now it seemed obvious that the new States needed a stronger central government if independence was not to lead to anarchy. In 1787, at the instigation of James Madison and Alexander HAMILTON (q.v.), a Convention met at Philadelphia to attempt 'to form a more perfect Union'. Washington was chosen to preside over the meetings, and his dignity and quiet firmness did much to smooth over growing animosities. In 1789, after the new AMERICAN CONSTITUTION (q.v. Vol. X) had been accepted, he was elected the first President of the United States.

The task before him was of terrifying complexity. The new Federal Government had as yet scarcely any institutions or forms of organization, and no traditions or clear purpose. Its

Parker Gallery

WASHINGTON GIVING LAST ORDERS FOR THE ATTACK ON YORKTOWN IN 1781

The Americans were reinforced on this occasion by 6,000 French troops, and the French general, Rochambeau, is seen standing beside Washington. Coloured print by E. Massard after Coudert

powers over the States, most of which were nearly bankrupt, were still uncertain, and already quarrels were developing between the States and between the new leaders. Some feared that a strong Federal Government would become tyrannical; others that, without a strong power at the centre, disorder would reign and property be endangered.

In the two terms (each of 4 years) of his Presidency, Washington led his country resolutely through these difficulties. Almost everything which he did established a precedent, thus building up an interpretation of some part of the Constitution. He lent great dignity to his office by surrounding the Presidency with ceremony, driving to Congress in a cream-coloured coach drawn by white horses, and with liveried servants, and holding receptions which were more formal than those of European royalty. His example has created a tradition highly honoured by the American people. His government, as it grew stable, built up national credit, settled many land problems, and preserved peace by insisting on American neutrality in the NAPOLEONIC WARS (q.v. Vol. X). Later, Washington made a treaty with Britain, unpopular because the United States seemed to have conceded far more than she had gained. This treaty, however, settled many problems still outstanding between the two countries, and provided a basis on which friendship could be built in the future.

In the turmoil of these years, two political parties began to appear in America. The Federalists (later the Republican party), led by Alexander Hamilton, Secretary of the Treasury, favoured a strong central government and American neutrality; the Republicans (later the Democrat party) led by Thomas JEFFERSON (q.v.), Secretary of State, favoured less central authority and greater powers for the States.

Washington himself at first tried to hold an even balance between the rival groups. But eventually the Democrats attacked him in a venomous political campaign, and Washington gave his full support to the Federalists.

Washington had been unwilling to accept a second term of office; by refusing to accept a third he created a tradition which lasted until President ROOSEVELT (q.v.) was elected to a third term in 1940. (A constitutional amendment now forbids a president to take a third term of office.) In 1797, with party violence increasing on both sides, Washington was happy to return to a private life on his country estates. In a great farewell address he forecast the difficulties lying ahead of the new nation. He warned the country against any attempts to break up the Union, dwelt on the importance of a strong government, and spoke of 'the baneful effects of the spirit of party'. In foreign affairs, he said, 'America should steer clear of permanent alliances with any portion of the foreign world . . .'. It was not until 1949 that the United States formed a permanent alliance with a European country.

Washington's great fame grew slowly during the next generation until, the bitterness of party strife forgotten, Americans thought of him as 'first in war, first in peace, and first in the hearts of his countrymen'.

WATT, James (1736–1819). In partnership with Matthew Boulton (1728–1809), James Watt gave to the world the first efficient steam-engine on which modern industry has been built. Watt did not himself invent the STEAM-ENGINE (q.v. Vol. VIII), for crude engines had been in use since 1712; but he did transform it from a cumbersome monster into an efficient machine. Watt provided the inventive talent in the partnership, Boulton the organizing power and the capital.

Watt was born at Greenock on the Clyde, the son of a master carpenter and merchant. As a boy he spent much time in his father's shop, and he became so good a craftsman that the workmen used to say 'Jamie has gotten a fortune at his fingers' ends'. At 18 he decided to become an instrument-maker. Finding no opportunities in Glasgow, he went to London, where he served a year's irregular apprenticeship. Low pay and poor working conditions had a bad effect on his naturally poor health, and he suffered greatly from sick headaches and depression which dogged much of the rest of his life.

When he was 20 he set up for himself as an instrument-maker in Glasgow, and soon made friends with scientists of the University. In 1763 he was asked by the University to repair a model of an 'atmospheric' engine—a type of steam-engine invented many years earlier by Thomas Newcomen for pumping water out of mines. The engine, though it achieved its purpose, was very inefficient and extravagant in fuel. Watt was led to think about the causes of this inefficiency; he made many experiments and reflected on current discoveries about heat. But for 2 years he could think of no means of improvement, until suddenly a solution flashed into his mind while he was taking a Sunday afternoon walk on Glasgow Green. His discovery was the separate condenser (*see* ENGINES, HISTORY OF, Vol. VIII)—the greatest single advance in the whole history of steam.

It took but a few days to make a model which showed that his ideas were essentially correct. But now his difficulties began: he could find no workmen in Glasgow skilled enough to turn his brilliant idea into a working machine; he was always short of money for pursuing his experiments; and his poor health was a continual hindrance. Watt's invention might have been thwarted had he not been able to join forces with Boulton in Birmingham.

Boulton, the son of a 'toymaker'—what we should call a maker of trinkets—had set up the famous Soho Manufactory on Handsworth Heath, near Birmingham, in 1762. Here he introduced many revolutionary principles in the toymaker's industry. Instead of selling his wares through a middleman, Boulton sold direct to the vast export market by establishing agents in every great town of Europe, and instead of working in a small workshop in his dwelling-house, Boulton, with the sales assured by his commercial organization, set up a large factory, employing up to 1,000 workers with ample floor-space and plenty of water-power. He gathered at the Soho factory an assembly of skilled workmen, unusual at that time, and so raised the quality of all his products. It was this great reserve of skill, together with the engineering resources of the Black Country and Shropshire iron industries, that enabled Watt to make a success of his invention.

In 1769 Watt was introduced to Boulton.

WATT'S WORKSHOP IN A GARRET AT HEATHFIELD, NEAR BIRMINGHAM

The two farther busts are of Watt, and the two large machines are for copying sculpture. From an exhibit in the Science Museum, South Kensington

Boulton saw the great advantages to be won from an efficient steam-engine, and offered to co-operate with Watt in producing his engine. In 1774, his other schemes for financing his experiments having failed, Watt left Glasgow and entered into partnership with Boulton. Within less than 2 years the first two engines were delivered to customers.

Watt's engine was still suitable only for pumping, or for blowing in blast furnaces. But, encouraged by Boulton, Watt went on to invent his 'rotative' engine for turning machinery, patented in 1781, and then to add many further improvements.

Boulton, for his part, having seen the steam-engine successfully started on its career, turned to a new field—the improvement of coinage. His improved coining presses of 1790 were so advanced that machines on these lines installed at the Royal Mint in 1805–10 were not superseded till 1881–2.

See also STEPHENSON.
See also Vol. VIII: STEAM-ENGINE.

WATTEAU, Antoine (1684–1721). This painter's work reflects the taste for elegance, frivolity, and delicate colours of the 18th-century French nobility. This fashion, which Watteau himself helped to mould, was known as ROCOCO (q.v. Vol. XII). In his *fêtes galantes* beautiful ladies and gentlemen picnic or listen to music in an enchanted landscape; other pictures show scenes from popular Italian comedy.

Watteau was born at Valenciennes, which had formerly been a Flemish city, and his interest in naturalism and detail was probably Flemish. His drawings, often in red chalk, as well as the paintings, show a most careful study of nature.

THE CHAMPS ÉLYSÉES: PAINTING BY WATTEAU
Society ladies and gentlemen are picnicking in a rustic setting

He worked mostly in Paris, at first preparing decorations for the opera and then working for a decorator and engraver. He had studied the works of the Venetians and of RUBENS (q.v.), a more robust painter than himself, whose colours he transformed to subtle and silvery tones. He was always poor but was helped by wealthy admirers. He suffered from consumption and perhaps his illness was responsible for the melancholy which seems to lie behind the outward gaiety of his figures.

See also Vol. XII: FRENCH ART; ROCOCO ART.

WEBB, Sidney (1859–1947) and **Beatrice** (1858–1943.) Sidney, a brilliant civil servant, and Beatrice his wealthy and remarkable wife, were both writers on social reform, whose work did much to change the social outlook in Britain between the last 10 years of Queen Victoria's reign and the Second World War. They were prominent members of the Fabian Society, a reforming political body founded in 1884, to which G. B. SHAW and H. G. WELLS (qq.v.) also belonged, and which did much to spread SOCIALISM (q.v. Vol. X). Its principle was 'the inevitability of gradualness', and its title was taken from Quintus Fabius Maximus, a Roman general famous for his delaying tactics.

Sidney Webb was sent to school in Germany and Switzerland, and after that largely educated himself, principally at London University evening classes. At 19 he entered the Civil Service, and soon passed very high up into its senior or administrative grade. His ability and intelligence soon showed. He was a marvellously quick reader, and could master the essentials of a piece of writing in a very short time.

Beatrice Potter was the serious-minded daughter of a wealthy family living in the Cotswolds. After reading deeply in philosophy, economics, and politics, she went to London when she was 28 to help her cousin, Charles

Booth, to collect material in the slums for his famous social survey, *Life and Labour of the People in London*. She joined the Fabians, and in 1889 brought out a volume of Fabian Essays and also published *The Co-operative Movement in Great Britain*. This led to her first meeting with Sidney Webb, and they married in 1892. Beatrice was better at devising plans than executing them; but Sidney possessed the executive power and driving force which she lacked. Beatrice's money made it possible for Sidney to give up his work as a civil servant.

In 1892 Sidney was elected to the London County Council, where he took a leading part in the development of technical education. Two years later the Webbs published their first joint work, *A History of Trade Unionism*. Then Sidney, using a legacy of £10,000 left him for this purpose, and with the help of others, founded the London School of Economics (*see* LONDON UNIVERSITY, Vol. X). In 1895 they published their second joint book, *Industrial Democracy*. In the same year Beatrice was appointed a member of the Royal Commission on the POOR LAW (q.v. Vol. X): she and her husband were jointly responsible for a famous Minority Report of the Commission. Just before the outbreak of the First World War they founded the political weekly paper, the *New Statesman*.

The Webbs played a growing part in the politics of the Labour Party. In 1922 Sidney was elected M.P. for Seaham Harbour; and later he was a Minister in two governments. After their visit to Russia, they published in 1935 their last important work: *Soviet Communism: A New Civilization?* Meanwhile Sidney had been made a peer, and had taken the title of Lord Passfield.

The Webbs gave drawing-room receptions on true Victorian and Edwardian lines, to which resorted all the progressive politicians, writers, and thinkers of the day. Both were models of courtesy and kindness to all, irrespective of their rank. Beatrice described her youth in *My Apprenticeship* and their joint life in *Our Partnership*, which was published after Sidney's death. Their ashes lie together in Westminster Abbey.

See also Vol. X: SOCIALISM.

WEBSTER, John (*c*. 1580–*c*. 1634). We know very little of the life of this outstanding Elizabethan and Jacobean writer of tragic drama.

His fame rests upon his two great plays, *The White Devil* and *The Duchess of Malfi*, each of which is a drama of revenge, set in Renaissance Italy. Despite much that is melodramatic, and despite the crude horror of his plots, Webster managed to express the tragic emotions of pity and terror in magnificent dramatic poetry. One of the most famous lines of the Jacobean stage is Ferdinand of Calabria's 'Cover her face, mine eyes dazzle: she died young', as he looks down at the face of his sister, the Duchess of Malfi, who has been murdered at his command. After a long period of neglect, Webster, like many other Elizabethan dramatists, was rediscovered by Charles LAMB (q.v.) in his *Specimens of English Dramatic Poets*; and again by Rupert Brooke in this century.

See also Vol. XII: DRAMA.

WEDGWOOD, Josiah (1730–95). Born at Burslem in Staffordshire, Wedgwood came of an old family of Staffordshire potters, the youngest of thirteen children. He himself was set to make pots when he was 9. The next year he caught smallpox, and this left him with an injured leg. He was lame all his life and could not work the potter's wheel.

Wedgwood lived at the beginning of the INDUSTRIAL REVOLUTION (q.v. Vol. VII), when factories were replacing the hand-made products of small groups of craftsmen. He soon developed into a business man who realized that true business success was founded on good workmanship. He was a Radical in politics and a religious Dissenter, with high moral standards, and was not only concerned in making money. He opened his own works in 1759 and soon showed great gifts of organization. He developed the use of moulds from which an infinite number of pieces can be cast, though most of the vases were still thrown on the wheel (*see* POTTERY, Vol. VII); and he employed first-class artists, such as John Flaxman, to design his models. The style of his designs, based on the classic models which were being discovered at the time in Italy and Greece, suited the architecture and furniture of the time, especially that of the ADAM BROTHERS (q.v.).

In 1768 he built near Hanley new works which he called Etruria, after the Etruscan (pre-Roman) civilization. He took Thomas Bentley into partnership, and together they revolutionized the manufacture of pottery. Till then

Josiah Wedgwood & Son

WEDGWOOD WARE

Black Basalt vases (left); Queen's Ware plate from the service made for Empress Catherine in 1774; and Jasper vases

the pottery used by ordinary people was coarse and dark in colour; only the rich could afford PORCELAIN. Wedgwood produced a fine cream-coloured EARTHENWARE (qq.v. Vol. VII) which was very successful and was called 'Queen's Ware' by command of Queen Charlotte. This was used for 'useful wares', such as cups and saucers. Wedgwood also produced 'ornamental wares', such as vases and medallions, which were made of a very thin, hard, stone-like pottery. About 1764 he began using a ware called Black Basalt for 'Etruscan' vases, some of which were painted in red and white in imitation of ancient Greek pottery; and about the same time he used an ornamental ware called Jasper, on which white figures in relief stand out against a coloured ground, usually pale blue. Wedgwood's pottery was in such demand that he opened showrooms in London, and people from all over Europe visited it. The Empress Catherine of Russia ordered a dinner service for 50 people, and Wedgwood made a magnificent service of 952 pieces in Queen's Ware decorated with views of England painted in purplish-black.

Wedgwood did a great deal to improve the Staffordshire Potteries, especially its roads and canals, and he made it one of the richest districts in England. After his death his family carried on the business, then extremely wealthy, and Jasper Ware and Queen's Ware are still made at Etruria.

See also Vol. VII: POTTERY.

WELLINGTON, Duke of (1769–1852). Sir Arthur Wellesley, first Duke of Wellington, was born in the same year as his great opponent, NAPOLEON (q.v.). He is the only British general since Cromwell to have held also the highest political office. In 5 years of bitter struggle against the French in the Peninsular War, he proved himself a tactician and strategist of genius. At the great Battle of Waterloo he was the conqueror of NAPOLEON (q.v.) and the saviour of Europe. He was afterwards Prime Minister, and when he died there was at his funeral a demonstration of national mourning without parallel in the 19th century.

Arthur Wellesley divided his early years between soldiering and politics. At 21 he was a member of the Irish Parliament, and 4 years later, soon after the outbreak of the NAPOLEONIC WARS (q.v. Vol. X), he saw active service as colonel of his regiment in Holland. There, as he watched the enemy charging in dense columns, Wellesley decided that the French could be beaten by resolute troops fighting in line; some 13 years later he was to employ those very tactics with resounding success (*see* TACTICS AND STRATEGY, Vol. X).

There followed a period of brilliant service in India at a time when India was torn by outbreaks of rebellion and threatened by Napoleon's presence in Egypt. Wellesley was promoted to command, as major-general, a mixed British and Indian army of 10,000 men, and with this he routed a hostile army nearly 50,000 strong, thus removing any threat to the British Empire there.

In 1808 Napoleon poured troops into Spain and Portugal in an attempt to close the remaining European ports to British trade. The Spaniards flared into revolt, and the British Government sent an army under Wellesley to their help. He defeated the French in an early battle, but was prevented by a senior officer (who had just arrived from England) from following up his victory, and the French were able to withdraw. Wellesley was recalled to England, but after the death of Sir John MOORE (q.v.), to whom the command had passed, he returned to the Peninsula as commander-in-chief.

Wellesley had a small but efficient and rigorously disciplined British army, aided by Portuguese troops, whom he raised and trained on British lines, and large numbers of Spanish guerrillas. The French at one time had in the Peninsula 300,000 of the finest troops in Europe, but they were scattered about a hostile country, and were never able to concentrate in superior numbers for a long campaign. So long as they remained separated Wellesley was reasonably safe; if they should decide to mass, the Spanish guerrillas would attack the French lines of communication and so force them apart. With the sea and the Royal Navy at his back, Wellesley was certain of receiving supplies and whatever reinforcements the British Government could send him. Drawing on his experience in India, he supplied his forward troops in the rough country they occupied by a primitive but extraordinarily effective system of bullock carts. But he had to face constant difficulties with the Spaniards who were troublesome allies, and he was under nagging criticism from the Opposition at home, who often charged him with excessive caution. Wellesley knew that he was commanding Britain's only army against some of the finest generals in the world, and feared that defeat might cause Britain to give up the struggle against Napoleon.

After immediate successes in which he drove the French from Portugal, Wellesley advanced into Spain and beat the French at Talavera. But the Spanish armies were everywhere defeated, and in the following year a French army under Marshal MASSÉNA (q.v.) made a determined effort to drive the British into the sea. Wellesley retired into the impregnable Lines of Torres Vedras, which he had secretly built round Lisbon. These tremendous fortifications linked hills and ravines by artificial mounds and ditches. Thousands of olive trees had been flung

The Earl Bathurst

THE DUKE OF WELLINGTON ON HIS HORSE, 'COPENHAGEN', 1815

Painting by Sir Thomas Lawrence

into ravines, to make them impassable; trees had been cut down to give a clear field of fire; artificial mounds had been built to take artillery; and the whole country outside had been swept bare of supplies. Masséna was eventually forced to retreat to avoid starvation, and Wellesley cautiously pressed him out of Portugal, and then advanced once more into Spain, and prepared to capture the great fortress of Badajoz which barred his way to Madrid.

But despite these limited successes, by the end of 1811 large areas of Spain were still in French hands, and their forces were vastly superior in number. Moreover, Napoleon threatened to take the field in person. But in 1812 war broke out between France and Russia, and Napoleon was forced to withdraw many of his troops. Wellesley turned to the offensive, and confounded his critics by his boldness. He stormed the fortresses of Badajoz and Ciudad Rodrigo, and at Salamanca defeated the enemy in a brilliantly improvised battle—'beating 40,000

WELLINGTON'S FUNERAL HEARSE

This bronze hearse, designed by the sculptor, Alfred Stevens, is now in the crypt of St. Paul's Cathedral, where Wellington is buried

Frenchmen in 40 minutes'. As a result the French had to call in all their troops from outlying provinces to oppose him, and although Wellesley retired into Portugal at the end of the year, he had freed huge tracts of the Peninsula. In the following year he advanced again, and this time there was no turning back. He won another great offensive victory at Vittoria, drove the French over the Pyrenees and out of Spain, and in the following year invaded the south of France. His advance was halted by the news that Napoleon had abdicated. Wellesley was made Field Marshal, and in 1814 he was created first Duke of Wellington. He also received several high Spanish and Portuguese honours and titles.

In the following year Napoleon escaped from imprisonment at Elba, and Wellington was appointed to command the Allied army which had gathered in Belgium to oppose him. Napoleon advanced from Paris and threw himself against the Prussians under Blücher, sending another army against Wellington at Quatre-Bras. Blücher was defeated, but retreating in good order he hastened to join Wellington, who had fallen back to the little village of Waterloo.

After a night of heavy rain the Battle of Waterloo opened with a furious cannonade at about 11.30 a.m. The French were in excellent spirits and were all experienced campaigners. Many of the Allies, on the other hand, were half-trained recruits, and for hours it seemed that the battle might go against them. In the early afternoon a critical situation was saved by a gallant charge of the Household Cavalry; at 4 p.m. the French hurled four great cavalry attacks against the British centre, but despite heavy losses the British squares stood firm; at 7.30 p.m. Napoleon ordered his Imperial Guards to advance in a last attempt to crush the British. Once more the British line held firm, and the Imperial Guards, their columns shattered, were flung back in disorder. Blücher's Prussians had already joined the battle, and the French fell back on all fronts. The retreat turned into a rout beyond recovery and Napoleon himself fled for his life from the advancing Prussians. Wellington's crowning victory was won.

Wellington was now one of the most influential men in Europe. On his return to England in 1818 he entered the Cabinet, and for the next 37 years remained a powerful force in British politics. By temperament and conviction he was a Tory, averse from change. But his political motto was 'the King's service must be carried on', and he regarded himself as the first servant of the Crown rather than a party man. From 1828 to 1830 he was Prime Minister, an office in which he was not altogether a success. Able to command, he could not always persuade; and his political beliefs were often too rigid for day-to-day political manœuvre. He was bitterly criticized from both sides: by reformers because he objected to Catholic emancipation and parliamentary reform, and by extreme Tories because in the end he helped to carry both these measures. But as a detached adviser to all governments, and the confidential adviser to the Crown, he was a stabilizing element in government, and constantly used his influence to help forward measures which had wide popular support.

Wellington was slightly built, of medium height. In habits he was frugal, in speech abrupt. He ruled his army with severity and a complete absence of sentiment. He believed that the British soldier was recruited from the dregs of the population, and could be disciplined only by the lash: 'they have all enlisted for drink', he once remarked. His troops never loved him, but they gave him their respect and confidence. At the end of his life, a bent, deaf old man, with a hooked nose and a piercing eye, he was a national figure, whom Tennyson, the Poet Laureate, honoured in his *Ode on the Death of the Duke of Wellington*.

See also NAPOLEON; MASSÉNA.
See also Vol. X: NAPOLEONIC WARS.

WELLS, Herbert George (1866–1946). In the second half of Queen Victoria's reign science and engineering were changing the face of the world. There was a sense of excitement, a hope that great new possibilities were opening in the lives of everyone. H. G. Wells above all others caught this sense of excitement and expressed it in writing. He wrote of wonderful inventions: of a machine which could travel forward into the future, and of a drug which could make a man invisible. He wrote, too, of fantastic adventures: of the first men in the moon, and of the invasion of the earth by the inhabitants of Mars. These strange stories are curiously convincing because the adventures happen to characters who seem truly alive and real, the sort of people we might meet any day in the street. For Wells was not only passionately interested in science, but also in people, especially in ordinary people; and he really knew how ordinary people lived.

Wells himself came from quite a poor family. His father was a professional cricketer in the days when professional cricketers earned very little money, and Wells had a hard struggle before he was able to make a real start in life. After a sketchy education, he was apprenticed first to a draper and then to a chemist; he then worked as a pupil-teacher until he won a scholarship to study science in London. Then, having first made his name with his science stories, he began to write novels, such as *Kipps* and *Mr. Polly*, based on his early experiences as apprentice and student. These catch most wonderfully the spirit of the age and of the place in which they are set—the promenade at Folkestone at the beginning of this century, the little haberdasher's shop in a small country town, or the science class at a London college at a time when many people still thought biology rather shocking. As well as their humour and high spirits, these novels have behind them a deep concern for the problems and privations which Wells saw in the England of his day. He and Bernard SHAW (q.v.) had an enormous influence, especially on young people. His revolt against convention, his bias against religion and any form of mysticism, and his belief in scientific planning widely affected contemporary political and social thinking.

Later, Wells gave almost his whole attention to such problems as poverty, ignorance, and war. In the 1920's he helped to lead a campaign for world peace. He believed that if everyone were properly educated to understand the nature of social problems and the danger of war, then those problems and that danger would largely disappear. Accordingly, he planned a series of popular educational works—a *History of the World* and an introduction to the study of biology, called *The Science of Life*. These books, which sold by the million, helped to make him well known all over the world. They helped, too, to change public opinion on many topics. His optimism, however, failed when faced with the Second World War, and as an old man he predicted a disastrous end to the human race.

Wells's private life had its difficulties. He was a sufferer from diabetes and for some years depended on daily injections of insulin. He was unconventional in his attitude towards marriage both in his novels and also in his own life; and his touchy, easily roused temper resulted in many quarrels with his contemporaries. His character and point of view are revealed with remarkable frankness in his *Experiment in Autobiography* (1934).

WESLEY, John (1703–91). This great religious reformer, creator of the METHODIST Church (q.v. Vol. I), was the fifteenth of Samuel and Susannah Wesley's nineteen children. His grandfathers were Puritan ministers who had given up their livings in 1662 rather than conform to the Prayer Book. His father, however, entered the Established Church and was rector of Epworth, a rough country parish in Lincolnshire, where John was born. John went to Charterhouse School and then to Oxford, where he was ordained deacon in 1725, and became a Fellow of Lincoln College. Before being ordained priest he helped his father at Epworth for a time, and then returned to Oxford. There his younger brother Charles had started the Holy Club, a group of earnest young men who were nicknamed 'methodists' because they lived by rule, studying the New Testament and going with strict regularity to Holy Communion.

In 1735 John and Charles Wesley went out as missionaries to the American colony of Georgia, where they had hoped to preach to the Indians; though this proved impossible. Charles returned home, but John remained as pastor of the small colony. An unfortunate love-affair, however, and his extremely intolerant high church views led him into difficulties; and in 1738 he decided to return to England, sick at heart because of his failure.

Wesley had earlier been influenced by the Moravian movement, and now in London he met Peter Böhler, a minister of the MORAVIAN CHURCH (q.v. Vol. I), who told him that he was still not converted because he had no faith. This faith came to Wesley one night at a gospel meeting in Aldersgate Street when, listening to a preface written by LUTHER (q.v.) to the *Epistle to the Romans*, he felt his heart 'strangely warmed'. Henceforth his way was clear, and he embarked on a career which has strongly influenced English religious life. For the rest of his life, more than 50 years, he preached his faith all over England, in churches while they

National Portrait Gallery

JOHN WESLEY PREACHING
Portrait by Nathaniel Hone

were open to him, and in the open air when they were not, travelling on horseback at least 4,000 miles a year, and preaching over 40,000 sermons. He had no desire to break from the Church of England, but many of the clergy disliked his revivalist methods. Neither this nor attacks by hostile mobs in the streets quenched his spirit or sapped his physical strength. He married, but not happily: indeed Wesley was by nature such an autocrat that he could not have been an easy husband.

Wherever Wesley went he left a band of believers, small but organized and disciplined, with lay-preachers to help in the evangelistic work. He was much helped by his brother Charles, especially in hymn writing. For Holy Communion the Methodists were bidden to attend their parish churches, but they were not always welcome there. Towards the end of his life Wesley realized that some means must be found of giving Methodist leaders power to administer the sacrament of Communion. He, therefore, because he could see no alternative, assumed the power of a bishop and ordained a number of ministers, some of whom went to

America to lead the Methodist movement there. The Church of England would not recognize Wesley's ministers, so that Wesley reluctantly saw his movement grow into a completely separate church. It was not until after his death that lay-preachers began in special circumstances to administer Communion, an action which he would not have approved.

Wesley's teaching was based on the belief that God loved all men and that Christ died for all, however great their sin. This was very different from CALVINIST teaching (q.v. Vol. I), which held that Christ died only for the elect.

See also Vol. I: METHODIST.

WHISTLER, James Abbott McNeill (1834–1903). Born at Lowell, Massachusetts, U.S.A., this American painter and engraver was the son of an engineer of Irish descent and an American mother. After training as a soldier and then as a draughtsman in the Coast Survey Department, he left America in 1857 to study art in Paris, where he came under the influence of some of the leading French painters, such as Degas. In 1866 he settled in London, living at Chelsea overlooking the Thames. He made a large series of etchings as well as many paintings of the river. His portraits include the famous portrait of his mother and a portrait of Thomas Carlyle (*see* p. 71). In landscape, as in portraiture, he insisted that a painting must pre-eminently be a work of art, that is, a 'harmony' or 'symphony' of exquisite shapes and colours giving pleasure independently of the subject-matter—hence his battle-cry 'Art for Art's Sake'. His paintings were misunderstood by the older critics, notably John RUSKIN (q.v.), whom Whistler sued in 1878 for libel. Partly as a result of this famous lawsuit in which he was awarded a farthing damages, Whistler went bankrupt and retreated to Venice. He later became president of the Society of British Artists, received many foreign honours, and published a brilliantly witty book called *The Gentle Art of Making Enemies*.

WHITE, Gilbert (1720–93), Naturalist, *see* Vol. XII: NATURE WRITING.

WHITMAN, Walt (1819–92). Whitman, the contemporary of Tennyson, is regarded as one of the greatest American poets, and as an embodiment of what DEMOCRACY (q.v. Vol. X) stands for. He was a big, handsome man, slow of speech and movement, and a first-rate carpenter. He came of mixed English and Dutch ancestry and was born on Long Island where his father was a farmer. All his life he never left America. He had various jobs: he began as a lawyer's errand boy, then worked in a printing office, then as a schoolteacher. He edited two newspapers; he built and sold wooden houses. As he worked he made notes for a series of poems which he had long been pondering. They were to be new, under no influence from the past. 'Poet,' he wrote once, 'beware lest your poems are made in the Spirit that comes from the study of pictures of things—and not from the spirit that comes from the contact of real things themselves.'

Whitman himself never lost contact with real things. His poems, written in free unrhyming lines, express the whole spirit of 19th-century America. His subjects—the comradeship of men, the pride of craftsmanship, sex—portray the whole fabric of poor working men's lives. The impression his work leaves is one of abounding vitality and love and compassion for humanity.

Leaves of Grass (1855), once it had been publicly praised by EMERSON (q.v.), made him famous. During the AMERICAN CIVIL WAR (q.v. Vol. X) he worked as a volunteer nurse, and some of his finest poems (*Drum-taps*, 1862) come from his experiences of that struggle. Whitman was a simple, emotional man who identified himself with the poor not only in his work but in his whole way of life. He is the first really American poet, as opposed to those Americans who wrote in the English tradition and idiom.

See also Vol. XII: AMERICAN LITERATURE.

WHITTINGTON, Richard (died 1423). This famous Lord Mayor of London was a Gloucestershire gentleman who acquired great wealth as a London merchant. He was Lord Mayor four times, and mayor of the Staple in London and Calais (*see* MERCHANTS OF THE STAPLE, Vol. VII).

According to tradition Dick Whittington came to London as a poor orphan of 13, and was employed as a scullion in the kitchen of a rich London merchant, Sir Hugh Fitzwarren. Whenever one of Fitzwarren's ships sailed abroad, the servants were allowed to send something to be traded, and Whittington sent his cat. The animal fetched a great price from a foreign ruler who was pestered with rats and mice, and Whittington's fortune was made. But before the ships had arrived with his prize, Whittington had run away from the house because the cook ill-treated him. As he ran, he heard Bow Bells pealing out

Turn again Whittington
Lord Mayor of London,

and so he turned back. He became a wealthy merchant, married his master's daughter, Alice, and later was made Lord Mayor.

This legend, first recorded in 1605, grew up probably as the result of Whittington's great popularity in London. He spent his great fortune generously, rebuilding Newgate prison, restoring St. Bartholomew's Hospital and the Guildhall, and founding a college and alms-house in the City. This almshouse, later re-moved to Highgate, at the very spot where Whittington is reputed to have turned back, is still maintained today by the Mercers' Company.

See also Vol. X: CITY OF LONDON CORPORATION.

WHYMPER, Edward (1840–1911). Edward Whymper, the pioneer mountaineer, was the second son of a London wood-engraver, to whom he was apprenticed when he was 14. As a boy he read of the exploits of many polar explorers, and decided that he wanted to explore.

Whymper's chance of adventure came in 1860 when he was commissioned by Longmans the publishers to make some drawings of the Dauphiné Alps to illustrate *Peaks, Passes and Glaciers*, a record of adventure by members of the Alpine Club. On this trip Whymper visited several districts of the Alps, crossed some easy passes, met English climbers at Zermatt, and had his first view of the Matterhorn. He also appreciated the chances of scientific observation offered by the glacier region of the Alps. The next year he went to climb mountains as well as draw them and made his first reconnaisance of the Matterhorn, then considered impregnable. In 1862 and 1863 he made several attempts from the Italian side, either alone or in the company of a guide called J. A. Carrel. In 1864 and 1865 Whymper did a splendid series of first ascents in the Dauphiné and Mont Blanc regions, and these were crowned, when he was only 25 years old, by his final triumph on the Matterhorn on 14 July 1865.

Whymper had hoped to secure Carrel for the climb, but, finding him already engaged, he crossed to Zermatt, where he engaged two local

WHYMPER PITCHING CAMP IN A BLIZZARD DURING THE ASCENT OF MOUNT COTOCACHI

Illustration by Whymper from his book, *Travels amongst the Great Andes*

guides, the Taugwalders. He then joined forces with Charles Hudson, one of the best climbers of his day, Michael Croz, an experienced Cha-monix guide, and two younger men, Douglas and Hadow. They found the Swiss side of the mountain easier than they had expected, and reached the top triumphantly. On the way down, however, disaster befell them. Hadow slipped, dragging Hudson, Douglas, and Croz with him; the rope broke, and the four hurtled to death. Whymper and the Taugwalders got down safely. Whymper never got over this terrible experience, which for a time aroused public opposition to mountain-climbing. The tragedy and the triumph of this climb are described in his magnificent *Scrambles among the Alps* (1871), illustrated with his own drawings— a book which shows Whymper to be first-class as a climber, writer, and illustrator of moun-tains (*see* Vol. IX: pp. 332 and 333).

After this accident Whymper did no more serious climbing in the Alps, though he re-visited them nearly ever summer. He made two expeditions to Greenland and, accompanied by his old guide and rival Carrel, he made a most successful expedition to the Andes of Ecuador. They climbed Chimborazo, Cotopaxi, and Cayambe, and proved that men can not only climb but sleep at heights of 20,000 feet. In his later years Whymper lectured on the Alps and Andes, visited the Canadian Rockies, and advised the Canadian Pacific Railway on hotels and mountaineering. He wrote two excellent guide-books to Zermatt and Chamonix, as well as his *Travels among the Great Andes*. He died at Chamonix in 1911.

Whymper was a difficult man, not readily liked; and in his old age he grew more crotchety. He had reached his life's ambition at 25 and had seen it turn to tragedy; and the strain may have been too great for him to bear.

See also Vol. III: ALPS; ECUADOR; ROCKY MOUNTAINS.
See also Vol. IX: MOUNTAINEERING.

National Portrait Gallery
WILLIAM WILBERFORCE, 1828
Portrait by Sir Thomas Lawrence

WILBERFORCE, William (1759–1833). The man who was mainly responsible for the abolition of slavery was the eldest son of a wealthy Yorkshire merchant engaged in the Baltic trade. At Cambridge University Wilberforce led a gay and hospitable life; there was always a 'great Yorkshire pie' in his rooms, to which all friends were welcome. At Cambridge he first met William PITT (q.v.), the future Prime Minister, with whom he later became great friends. After Cambridge he went to London intending to take up politics, and in September 1780 was elected M.P. for Hull, his old home. He continued his gay and hospitable life and was a very popular person, belonging to several clubs and gambling a good deal. He was an excellent singer and a great mimic, and took life rather light-heartedly. On one occasion however, he won £600 from friends who could ill afford to lose, and this so disturbed him that he gave up gambling.

When he was 23 he went on a Continental tour with his old Hull headmaster, Isaac Milner, by then Dean of Carlisle and a deeply religious person; and they read and talked a great deal about religious matters. The result of this tour was the complete conversion of Wilberforce to energetic and practical Christianity. He became impressed by the low standard of conduct and morals in the world in general, and in Britain in particular. The continuance of the SLAVE TRADE (q.v. Vol. VII), to which Liver-

pool owed much of her wealth, struck him as particularly odious. When still at school he had written a letter of protest against the slave trade to a York newspaper. He learned more about this terrible trade from another Cambridge man, Thomas Clarkson, who for years had been carrying on an anti-slavery campaign based on the facts he learned about the treatment of slaves from captains of slave ships and others. Clarkson and others of his movement, mostly Quakers or followers of John WESLEY (q.v.), cagerly accepted Wilberforce as their spokesman, and in 1787 Wilberforce began to demand a law to abolish the slave trade. Pitt, by that time Prime Minister, backed him whole-heartedly, but by 1793 Britain was at war with France, and Pitt had to put most of his energies into running the war.

Wilberforce was the ideal leader for such an agitation. He had large private means, high principles, and a singular charm of manner which made him popular even with his opponents. Almost immediately, however, he had a dangerous illness, and for the rest of his life he had to take care of his health. During this illness Pitt made himself responsible for legislation against the slave trade, and got an Act through both Houses imposing some restrictions. When he was recovered Wilberforce returned to the struggle, being further encouraged by a dying message from John Wesley. But although many attempts were made to get legislation through Parliament, the Bills passed by the Commons were invariably rejected by the House of Lords.

In 1798 Wilberforce married Barbara Anne Spooner, and went to live at Clapham Common, near London. Here he and others formed the 'Clapham Sect' of Evangelicals. He was lavish in his charities, always prepared to give help to anybody who asked for it—sometimes, indeed, helping those who were thoroughly undeserving of it. He founded the Church Missionary Society and the Bible Society.

In 1806, Pitt, Wilberforce's lifelong friend and supporter, died, having been unable to help his friend to final victory. But his successor Charles James Fox (q.v.), one of the original supporters of Clarkson's anti-slavery campaign, took up the fight with energy. At last, in 1807, Parliament passed a law abolishing the British slave trade, the shipping and sale of slaves. But the emancipation and freedom of the slaves themselves had still to come. Wilberforce feared the effects on Negro slaves of a sudden freedom for which they had not been carefully prepared. He therefore turned his attention for a time to other matters, including Catholic emancipation. Later he formed the Anti-Slavery Society, and in 1833 slavery itself was abolished by Parliament, and all slaves in British colonies were freed. In the same year Wilberforce died and was buried in Westminster Abbey. He was a man whose personal character was as fine as his public deeds.

See also Vol. VII: SLAVE TRADE.
See also Vol. X: SLAVERY.

WILKES, John (1727–97). Wilkes, famous for his action in safeguarding men's personal liberties against the illegal power of the State, was a politician and witty writer. He entered Parliament when he was 30, and 5 years later founded a political magazine called the *North Briton*, in which he published a violent attack on the King's speech made at the opening of Parliament in 1763. George III treated the attack as a personal insult, and had a general warrant issued for the arrest of Wilkes and forty-eight others. Wilkes was released a week later, and immediately protested against his arrest. In the legal actions which followed Wilkes established a principle of the utmost importance to British justice. The Crown declared that it had acted 'of State necessity' in arresting Wilkes; but the judge ruled that 'public policy was not an argument in a court of law'. Thereafter general warrants of arrest were declared illegal. The

ENGLISH LIBERTY established, or a MIRROUR for POSTERITY. JOHN WILKES, Esq.ʳ the undaunted ASSERTOR of the LIBERTY of the PRESS, and the RIGHTS of ENGLISHMEN.

Warmed with the love of freedom & his Country. He hears their threats unmov'd And with superior greatness smiles.

Englishmen freed from the Fear of General Warrants, and the Seizure of Papers, by the Magnanimity of ONE MAN.

And the People delight to honour him

To the Gentlemen, Clergy, and Freeholders of the County of Middlesex, and the Liverymen of the City of London, who voted for Mr. WILKES, and to all the Sons of Liberty, this Plate is inscrib'd.

Meade Collection

HEADING OF A MANIFESTO PUBLISHED BY WILKES IN 1768

North Briton article, however, was declared a seditious LIBEL (q.v. Vol. X); Wilkes fled to Paris, and in his absence was sentenced to imprisonment and expelled from Parliament.

Four years later Wilkes returned, and was elected as Parliamentary candidate for Middlesex amid scenes of wild enthusiasm. But he was then imprisoned for his old offence. There followed months of stormy political agitation as Wilkes was repeatedly re-elected to Parliament, only to be expelled by the government. 'Wilkes and Liberty!' became a battle-cry in the streets. Wilkes began reporting Parliamentary debates, reports which the government tried to suppress. The London mob, however, so strongly supported Wilkes that the government gave in. Wilkes took his seat at Westminster, and began campaigning for Parliamentary reform. His actions had revealed the unrepresentative nature of the Parliament of his day. Wilkes later became Lord Mayor of London.

See also GEORGE III.

WILLIAM I (1027–87). William the Conqueror,

the first of the Norman Kings of England, was the illegitimate son of the Duke of Normandy and a tanner's daughter. When he was 8 his father died and the chief noblemen chose him as ruler. But he had to fight to hold his power against rebellious lords. When the English King, Edward the Confessor, died, William claimed the English throne, which he said Edward had promised him. But the English chose Harold; and William invaded England in 1066. On 14 October he defeated and killed King Harold at HASTINGS (q.v. Vol. X) in one of the decisive battles of the world. After his victory William marched to London, and at Berkhamsted he received the submission of a representative group of English leaders. On Christmas Day he was crowned in Westminster Abbey. For the next few years he had to face a series of rebellions—a great rising of the north, for example, in which the English enlisted help from Denmark, and the gallant stand of Hereward the Wake and his band of Englishmen in the marshy fens of Ely. These and other risings were all fiercely suppressed. William established his control of England by the creation of strong earldoms on its borders, by the building of stone castles, such as the castles of Durham and Carlisle, Chester and Ludlow, and the Tower of London, and by a series of bargains with his

Victoria & Albert Museum

WILLIAM THE CONQUEROR WITH HIS HALF-BROTHERS, BISHOP ODO AND COUNT ROBERT OF MORTAIGNE

Detail from the Bayeux Tapestry

principal followers whereby they contracted to supply him with armed knights in return for their lands (*see* FEUDAL SYSTEM, Vol. X). Towards the end of his reign he ordered the compilation of the great DOMESDAY BOOK (q.v. Vol. X), which provided him with a detailed picture of the whole country, 'how it was peopled and with what sort of men'.

William I was a conqueror but not a tyrant. Believing himself to be the true heir of the old English royal house, he sought to preserve the rights and customs of Englishmen and to trust them so far as was possible. The Norman Conquest probably meant no great change in the way of life of the common man. The English language was only temporarily submerged; such old English institutions as shire and borough remained (*see* LOCAL GOVERNMENT, HISTORY OF, Vol. X); the English Church was reformed but not destroyed. The English chronicler groans at William's heavy taxes and the severity of the Forest Laws which he devised for the protection of the tall deer which 'he loved as if he were their father'; but he admits that he was wise, splendid, and powerful, that he was mild to the good men who loved God, and that he kept the land in peace.

WILLIAM THE SILENT (1533–84).

The hero of the Dutch struggle for independence was the son of the Count of Nassau, a Rhineland province. He inherited the French principality of Orange as well as his large family estates in the Netherlands, and so became one of the wealthiest noblemen of Europe. At this time Holland was part of the Netherlands (Low Countries), a collection of provinces, including much of what we now know as Belgium and Flanders, and ruled by a regent for the Emperor CHARLES V (q.v.), who was also King of Spain.

William, as was then the custom for the most important young noblemen, was sent away from home to be brought up at the Court of Charles V. Though his parents were Protestants, he grew up a Catholic—a charming young man and a favourite of Charles, who recommended him to his son PHILIP II (q.v.). When he was only 22 Philip II made him 'Stadholder' (chief ruler) of Holland, Zeeland, and Utrecht. But William, though a Catholic and loyal to Philip, found himself opposed to Philip's oppressive policy in the Netherlands, in particular his cruel suppression of Protestantism. With prudence and patience William tried to control the more violent of the Protestant nobles, but finally in 1567 he resigned his post.

The Netherlands, at this time the most advanced trading and manufacturing centre in Europe, felt more and more that their interests were different from those of Spain. This, together with the growth of Protestantism (*see* CALVINIST, Vol. I), made them ready to rebel against the oppressive Spanish rule. The arrival of the fanatical and cruel Duke of Alva to subdue rebellion and crush Protestantism with his 'Council of Blood' forced William to become the leader of the Netherlands' fight for liberty, and to adopt the Protestant faith. William, however, was always more concerned with fighting for liberty, religious or political, than in supporting the Protestant cause against Catholicism. When Alva outlawed him, he retreated to Germany; but the next year, with the aid of German Protestants, he invaded the Netherlands. Alva crushed the invasion, and all seemed lost.

William had a great capacity for fighting a seemingly hopeless battle. 'With God's help', he wrote, 'I shall go on.' He allied himself to the famous 'Sea Beggars', semi-piratical Dutch patriots who continued to attack by sea, with surreptitious help from England. In 1572 they were strong enough to make a successful invasion, and after some heroic fighting succeeded in freeing and uniting the northern provinces. The liberating forces were heartened by the example of the heroic city of Leyden which, besieged and nearly starved, opened the dikes to let in the sea rather than yield to the enemy. Outbreaks of mutiny among the Spanish forces also eased their task. In spite of some setbacks whereby the Spanish regained control of the southern provinces, the northern provinces in 1579 signed the Union of Utrecht proclaiming independence from Spain, and shortly afterwards they elected William as the first hereditary Stadholder. Three years later he was shot at Delft by a Catholic fanatic acting for Philip II.

Although William's task of uniting a liberated Netherlands was not completed, two of his sons, Maurice and Frederick Henry, carried on his work. In the historian Motley's famous words, 'As long as he lived he was the guiding star of a

Gemälde-Galerie, Kassel

WILLIAM THE SILENT, AGED 22
Portrait by Anthonis Mor

whole brave nation, and when he died the little children cried in the streets.' He earned the name 'Silent' because of his statesmanlike ability to keep his counsel—in particular in 1560 when Henry II of France unwisely confided in him a Catholic plan for crushing heresy in France and the Netherlands.

See also PHILIP II.

See also Vol. I: DUTCH; INQUISITION; CALVINIST.

WILSON, Thomas Woodrow (1856–1924).

This President of the United States during the period of the FIRST WORLD WAR (q.v. Vol. X) is remembered chiefly for his progressive ideas of International Co-operation and for the part he played in framing the Covenant of the League of Nations after the war.

The son of a Presbyterian minister, Wilson was born in Virginia. He studied law, and then taught history, economics, and law at various colleges. In 1902 he became President of Princeton University, where he introduced the 'preceptorial' type of instruction, based on the tutorial system of Oxford and Cambridge Universities, which he much admired.

In 1910 Wilson became Governor of the State of New Jersey. He stood as Democratic candidate for the Presidency, and was elected in 1912. Wilson had great admiration for British Parliamentary institutions, which he thought had some advantages over the American system where the functions of the legislative and the executive are sharply separated (see AMERICAN CONSTITUTION, Vol. X). Wilson tried, therefore, as President, to give something of the leadership of a Prime Minister in Congress as well as out of it, and he pushed through Congress a great mass of reform legislation. Although he was rather aloof from his colleagues, his direct appeals to the people enabled him to carry everything before him.

In 1914 American opinion was deeply divided about the part the U.S.A. should take in the war. Wilson, therefore, kept his country neutral until Germany's submarine attacks on American shipping had united public opinion in favour of intervention. In 1917 he was responsible for the great mobilizing of American resources for waging war. He also began a campaign for educating Americans to the point of view that unrestricted nationalism of States was one of the principal causes of war, and could be controlled only by an effective international organization, such as the League of Nations, which he worked to establish. He caught the ear of the world by his 'Fourteen Points', which included open discussion in place of secret treaty-making, freedom of the seas, reduction of armaments, rights for native colonial peoples, and above all an association of nations to guarantee the rights of all. He declared that 'the world must be made safe for democracy'. To secure these conditions of future peace and to ensure a just but generous peace settlement, he attended the peace negotiations at Versailles —being the first President to leave America during his term of office.

Wilson secured peace settlements more merciful than they would have been without him, and he launched the League of Nations; but his ideals were ahead of his time, and he could not remove the fear, suspicion, and hatred which soon directed European policies. In America opinion turned against him. During the harsh and prolonged struggle for American ratification of the peace treaty, Wilson suffered a complete nervous breakdown, and after a few years as a broken-hearted invalid he died.

See also Vol. X: INTERNATIONAL CO-OPERATION; FIRST WORLD WAR.

WOLFE, James (1727–59). This brilliant soldier, a major-general at the age of 32, won Canada for Britain by his great victory over the French at Quebec during the Seven Years War (1756–63.)

Wolfe entered the army when only a boy, and at 16 was already adjutant of his regiment. He saw service at the Battle of Dettingen, in the war of the Austrian Succession, and 2 years later fought at Falkirk and Culloden against the 'Young Pretender' (see STUART). At 23 he was a lieutenant-colonel, and proved himself one of the ablest regimental officers in the British army.

On the outbreak of the Seven Years War Wolfe's outstanding qualities attracted the attention of William Pitt (see CHATHAM), who sent him to North America to assist in the capture of the great French fortress of Louisbourg. Wolfe's skill and courage in this enterprise decided Pitt, a year later, to select him to command the expedition to drive the French from Canada by an attack on Quebec.

Quebec, on the towering cliffs over the St. Lawrence, known as the Heights of Abraham, was a formidable fortress, and Wolfe's first,

Parker Gallery

THE TAKING OF QUEBEC

The British troops are storming the Heights of Abraham. Coloured line engraving, 1797

orthodox attempts at direct attack failed. He then decided on an assault of tremendous daring. He embarked half his army in a fleet of small boats and landed them secretly by night up the higher reaches of the river. The troops then had to scale the great cliffs by a narrow path. It was a route so perilous that, as the French commander afterwards declared, 'a hundred men would stop a whole army'. But it was not well guarded, and by the morning Wolfe had placed over 4,000 men on the Heights. In the pitched battle that followed, the French were decisively defeated. Wolfe himself, after being twice wounded, was mortally hit in the chest. He asked repeatedly for news of the battle, and when, in the moment of victory news was brought that the French everywhere gave ground, he exclaimed: 'Then I die contented.'

Wolfe was tall and slight, with reddish hair. He was delicate, even sickly, in health. His profile was long and sharp, 'like the flap of an envelope'. His self-confidence sometimes showed itself in arrogance, and some thought him eccen-

tric. This view was not shared by George II, who is said to have exclaimed, 'Mad, is he? Then I hope he will bite some of my other generals.' Wolfe was scholarly in his tastes, and before his last battle, as his boats moved up the St. Lawrence, he is said to have recited Gray's *Elegy*, and to have remarked, 'I would rather be the author of that piece than take Quebec'.

See also Vol. I: CANADIANS.

WOLSEY, Thomas (*c.* 1472–1530). Cardinal Wolsey, Lord Chancellor of England, leading statesman, and head of the English Church, was the brilliant and ambitious adviser to King HENRY VIII (q.v.). The concentration of such immense authority—legal, political, and spiritual—in the hands of one man foreshadowed the despotism of King Henry himself.

The son of a butcher and innkeeper of Ipswich, Wolsey went to Magdalen College, Oxford, and obtained his degree at the early age of 15. He spent 19 years at Oxford, becoming a Fellow of Magdalen. He took Holy Orders and, anxious for promotion, he sought influential patrons. With their help he became chaplain to Henry VII, who employed him on diplomatic business. When Henry VIII became King, Wolsey contrived to enter his service. By 1511 he was a Privy Councillor and as he grew in favour he became the special mouthpiece of the King.

Wolsey took promotion in the Church whenever he could get it, holding more than one post at the same time. He was Dean of Hereford in 1509, Dean of York in 1513, Bishop of Lincoln and Archbishop of York a year later. Realizing that the Archbishopric of Canterbury was unlikely to become vacant, he made himself supreme in the English Church by persuading the Pope to make him a Cardinal in 1515. He took complete control of the English Church, filling important offices with his own creatures and seizing several for himself.

Wolsey also took complete charge of the country's legal system, and had himself made Lord Chancellor. Although English law generally was administered in the courts of Common Law there remained a reserve of justice in the Crown itself, which had the power on occasions to override the law-courts in the interests of justice. This prerogative of the Crown was exercised partly by the Privy Council, acting through the Court of the STAR CHAMBER (q.v. Vol. X), and partly by the Lord Chancellor, as 'Keeper of the King's Conscience'. Wolsey, as both Lord Chancellor and a member of the Privy Council, was able to control and use this prerogative as he wished.

Wolsey was not only Cardinal and Chancellor but also what is now called Prime Minister: he directed the country's domestic and foreign policy. He kept good order at home, but his financial system was bad and resulted in heavy and continued demands to Parliament for money. Though he founded Cardinal College (now Christ Church) at Oxford, and appeared genuinely anxious to promote learning, his dissolution of more than thirty monasteries, though carried through with the Pope's approval, was a dangerous example to the King.

Abroad he plunged into an ambitious policy of alliances, partly to exploit for England's benefit the rivalry between the Emperor CHARLES V (q.v.) and Francis, King of France, and partly in the vain hope that Charles would make him Pope.

When Henry sought to break his marriage

CARDINAL WOLSEY IN 1526

The building in the background is Christ Church, Oxford. Portrait by Sampson Strong. By permission of the Governing Body of Christ Church

with Catherine of Aragon, Wolsey was in a dilemma. If he failed to persuade the Pope to annul the marriage, Henry would be furious; if he succeeded, he would install as Queen, Anne Boleyn, niece of the Duke of Norfolk, the most powerful of his enemies. With a representative of the Pope Wolsey sat in judgement on the case, but arrived at no solution. At the same unlucky moment an alliance between Charles V and Francis, England's two chief rivals, discredited Wolsey's foreign policy. Wolsey was ruined. Henry allowed him to be attacked for a breach of the Statutes of *Praemunire* (a law forbidding the Pope to encroach on the power of the Crown), though Wolsey had plainly sought the Pope's aid for Henry's benefit. He was condemned, but allowed to keep some of his wealth and retire to his see of York. However, when he began again to plunge into politics, the King ordered his arrest for high treason. He died at Leicester Abbey on the way to face his trial in London, and was buried there.

See also HENRY VII; HENRY VIII.

WORDSWORTH, William (1770–1850).

Wordsworth, who defined a poet as 'a man

Mrs. E. F. Rawnsley

WILLIAM WORDSWORTH, 1805
Pencil drawing by Henry Edridge

speaking to men' and the object of poetry as 'truth . . . carried alive into the heart with passion', was himself the greatest poet of the English ROMANTIC MOVEMENT (q.v. Vol. XII).

He was born and grew up in Cumberland, the English Lake District, where the beauty and grandeur of the scenery and the independence of the people profoundly influenced his development. On his mother's death, when he was 8, he went to Hawkshead Grammar School, where the teaching was good and the boys outside school-hours were left free to fish and boat on the lake, to go birds-nesting or setting snares on the hills. While Wordsworth was still at school his father died, leaving his children in the care of guardians with whom they were never happy. At Cambridge University, Wordsworth read widely and wrote some of his early poems. During one summer vacation he went for a walking tour on the Continent with a friend. France, then in the early stages of the Revolution, was 'mad with joy', and Wordsworth became an enthusiastic republican. On leaving Cambridge he went back to France for a year. There he fell in love with Annette Vallon, a girl of royalist family, who bore him a daughter. But soon after, England declared war on France, and Wordsworth was unable to return to France until 1802, when he saw Annette for the last time and wrote the sonnet 'It is a beauteous evening' for his daughter. Through her he still has French descendants.

In 1795 a friend left him a small legacy—enough to make him independent. Wordsworth, now resolved to be a poet, first settled with his sister Dorothy at Racedown in Dorset, and then moved to Alfoxden to be nearer COLERIDGE (q.v.). The next 3 years are momentous in the history of English poetry. Together with Dorothy, a woman of great gifts, acutely observant and sensitive as her *Journals* show, Wordsworth and Coleridge talked continuously of poetry as they walked over the Quantock hills. 'We are three people', wrote Coleridge, 'but only one soul.' Together they worked out their poetic beliefs which found expression in their *Lyrical Ballads* (1798). The book, published anonymously, claimed to be no more than an experiment. Wordsworth in the Prefaces written to successive editions had much to say on the nature of poetry, 'the spontaneous overflow of natural feeling', and explained his intention to use everyday language and to make ordinary events the material of his poetry. It was a bold challenge by two young and unknown poets to the artificial conventions of 18th-century poetry. There had been other rebels—BLAKE and BURNS (qq.v.), for instance; but Blake was unknown, and Burns, writing in the Scottish dialect, was outside the tradition of English poetry. *Lyrical Ballads* met with ridicule; indeed the poets were not wholly successful in their intention. One of the greatest poems in the book, however, is Wordsworth's *Lines written a few miles above Tintern Abbey*, which defines his early philosophy and already uses his distinctive blank verse, powerful in rhythm and magnificent in sound.

As a boy, Wordsworth says,

> The sounding cataract
> Haunted me like a passion. . . .

and

> Nature then
> To me was all in all.

As a young man he was a 'worshipper of Nature'; as he grew older, he heard more often 'the still, sad music of humanity'. Wordsworth's love of Nature was his lifelong inspiration. But he knew that, beside feeling, deep thought and long reflection ('emotion recollected in tranquillity') were equally essential to his poetry.

While still at Alfoxden, Wordsworth discussed with Coleridge the idea of writing a long philosophical poem, to be the history of a poet's mind. The original poem was never written (fragments of it were published as *The Excursion* in 1814); but what was to have been merely an introduction developed into the world's greatest poetic autobiography covering the whole period of Wordsworth's life up till the time he settled at Racedown. The intensity and excitement of the descriptions of boyhood lead up to the account of his self-dedication to poetry when he was on holiday in Hawkshead at the end of his first year at Cambridge. After a night spent in dancing, Wordsworth was surprised by a magnificent sunrise as he was returning home. The beauty and solemnity of the scene made such an impression on him that from that hour he felt himself a 'dedicated spirit', one whose whole duty was to be a poet. The poem, finished in 1805, was constantly revised, and was published posthumously in 1850, when it was first called *The Prelude* by Mrs. Wordsworth.

In 1799 William and Dorothy moved to Dove Cottage, Grasmere, and in the following year Coleridge joined Southey not far off at Keswick. Later, Wordsworth and Coleridge quarrelled, and though they were reconciled, they never again became close friends. In 1802 Wordsworth married Mary Hutchinson, whom he had known since childhood, and by her had three daughters, two of whom died as children, and two sons who survived him. Dorothy continued to live with them until 1826 when she had a nervous breakdown from which she never recovered, though she outlived her brother.

In 1807 Wordsworth published a collection of poems—among them his finest sonnets, *To Milton, To Sleep, On Westminster Bridge*, and also the odes *To Duty*, and the *Intimations of Immortality*. Yet the book was attacked and ridiculed by contemporary critics: indeed, it was not until after 1820 that Wordsworth was at last recognized as an important poet. In 1813 Wordsworth moved to Rydal Mount and obtained the office of Distributor of Stamps for Westmorland, which post he held till 1842 when he was granted a government pension; in the following year he succeeded his friend Southey as Poet Laureate. He died at the age of 80.

The range of Wordsworth's genius is immense, yet everything he wrote bears the mark of his individuality, from the simplicity of the early 'Lucy' poems, the vitality and power of the *Prelude*, the romantic and personal charm of lyrics like *The Highland Reaper* and *The Glowworm*, to the sonnets and the great *Immortality Ode*.

See also Vol. XII: ROMANTIC MOVEMENT.

WREN, Sir Christopher (1632–1723). This great architect, who was also an astronomer and mathematician, was born at East Knoyle in Wiltshire. Both his father and uncle held high positions in the Church and at Court, and Wren was brought up among the leading scholars of the day. He was educated at Westminster School and Oxford University. As a boy he was keenly interested in mathematics, astronomy, and anatomy. His genius for invention ranged from glass eyes to navigational instruments, and among other things he later made a model of the moon.

The scientific meetings held by Wren and his friends, first at Oxford, and later at Gresham College, London (where Wren was appointed Professor of Astronomy), led to the foundation of the Royal Society in 1660. The next year Wren became Professor of Astronomy at Oxford, and about this time his interest in architecture began. Throughout his life he kept in touch with scientists, meeting them for long discussions in the coffee-houses which had become popular.

A few years after the Restoration of Charles II, Wren was given his first official architectural appointment, and for more than 50 years was the most productive and influential architect in England. His first buildings were Pembroke College Chapel, Cambridge, and the Sheldonian Theatre, Oxford, in which he solved triumphantly the problem of roofing a wide span without supporting pillars (*see* Vol. X, p. 307).

In 1665, at the time of the Great Plague, Wren paid his only visit to the Continent, studying French buildings and meeting leading French architects and the great Italian BERNINI (q.v.), who showed him his designs for the Palace of the Louvre. Soon after his return, the Fire of London in 1666 gave him his great opportunity. As a Commissioner for the rebuilding of the City, he produced an ideal and lucid plan: but this was not adopted owing largely to the cost of buying out owners of sites. Nevertheless, as architect of ST. PAUL'S CATHEDRAL (q.v. Vol. XII), of fifty-one parish churches (mostly in the City), of Temple

THE TOWER OF ST. MARY-LE-BOW, CHEAPSIDE, LONDON

One of the churches built by Wren after the Great Fire
and badly damaged in 1940. By permission of the Controller, H.M.S.O.

Bar, and of the Monument, Wren still played a
large part in the rebuilding of London.

Most of the churches were built between 1670
and 1685. Wren's ingenious solutions for dealing
with awkward and cramped sites reflect his
mathematical and scientific training: one of his
churches had a ten-sided plan and another is
octagonal inside. Since not all the burnt
churches were to be rebuilt, each church had
to house larger congregations, and Wren set
himself so to arrange his interiors that everyone
could see and hear the preacher, making much
use of galleries. The towers, with their lanterns,
cupolas, and spires—built in the white Portland
stone Wren loved to use—are wonderfully varied
in design. The interior cones which he used to
support the structure saved the steeples when
many of the churches were burnt out during air
raids in the Second World War. The churches
are mainly in a simple, classical style, with the
enrichment concentrated in the woodwork and
plasterwork of the interior, and on doorways and
towers.

All this time Wren was constantly occupied
with plans for St. Paul's, from the making of the
first model in 1672 to the completion of the
building in 1711. He also carried out a vast
amount of other work. In 1669 he was made
Surveyor to the Crown, and was knighted. In
1676 he built the Library of Trinity College,
Cambridge. This, like all his early work, has
links with 16th-century Italian architecture and
with the style of Inigo JONES (q.v.). With
Chelsea Hospital, however, and a palace begun
but never finished for Charles II at Winchester,
his style became more BAROQUE (q.v. Vol. XII);
he began to think in larger masses, to design
giant porticos, and to place cupolas as accents
on important points in his designs. He also used
the contrast between brick and stone to em-
phasize these accents.

The same characteristics of dramatic emphasis
appear at Greenwich where he converted the
royal palace into a hospital for seamen. Long
colonnades and two small domes link the buildings on each side of the great court with the
Queen's House beyond them, making one grand
design of the whole group of buildings. His
later work is moderate and serene rather than
richly dramatic, and the need for economy often
compelled him to use brick, reserving stone for
important parts such as windows, as may be
seen at Hampton Court Palace.

He was consulted about many buildings, both public and private, but did not himself design any important private houses. He died when he was 91, and was buried in St. Paul's.

See also Vol. XII: BRITISH ART.

WYCLIFFE, John (*c.* 1320–84). Little is known of the early life of this important religious reformer and translator of the Bible. He studied at Oxford, where he won a great reputation as a lecturer and theologian. It was not till about 12 years before his death that he came into public notice. In 1374 Edward III sent him with others to Bruges to discuss a dispute between the Pope and the King.

About this time Wycliffe began to publish pamphlets attacking not only the Popes but all the richer clergy for setting worldly wealth above true religion. He also wrote treatises on divine and civil lordship in which he pictured God as a feudal sovereign who entrusts all dominion, in Church or in State, to men who have the right to hold it only so long as they are worthy of their trust. Those who hold Church positions only for the sake of riches should lose their positions. This doctrine was welcomed by many of the nobles, including John of Gaunt, Edward III's fourth son, because they hoped it would lead to the confiscation of rich Church lands and that they would share in the spoils. The bishops, however, were angry; they summoned Wycliffe to London to St. Paul's Cathedral to answer for his attacks, and the Pope tried to silence him. But Wycliffe with John of Gaunt's support came to no harm.

In 1378 a quarrel over the choice of Pope arose in Rome, two rival candidates being elected. Each tried to rule the Church and to defeat the other. This so angered Wycliffe that he began to attack not only individual Popes but the institution of the Papacy itself. He also challenged the doctrine of the Church called transubstantiation, which asserts that the bread and wine become the Body and Blood of Christ after consecration in the Mass. Wycliffe did not deny the presence of Christ's Body in the Mass, but explained it in a different way, which the Church authorities feared might lessen the power of the clergy. This doctrine separated him from

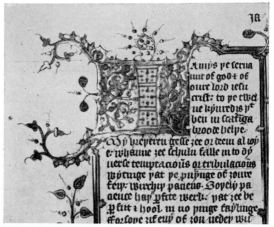

British Museum

THE WYCLIFFE BIBLE

The beginning of St. James's Epistle (*Egerton MS.* 618)

many of his supporters, and he was forbidden to preach at Oxford. So he retired to Lutterworth, Leicestershire, of which he was rector.

There he gathered a band of followers, known as his 'poor priests', who went round the villages preaching. To help them in their teaching he began his greatest work, the first translation of the whole Bible into English. Wycliffe believed that the Bible was the surest foundation for Christian doctrine, and that the common man should be able to read it for himself so that he could test the truth of the teaching he was given. Several others helped in Wycliffe's translation, but he himself is believed to have translated the New Testament. Copies of the new Bible were rapidly circulated.

Wycliffe was highly esteemed by ordinary people, whose difficulties and problems he understood and with whose troubles he sympathized. His enemies said that he and his 'poor priests' were responsible for the unrest which led to the Peasants' Revolt, led by Wat TYLER (q.v.) and John Ball in 1381; but he certainly did not preach revolutionary teaching of this sort. His popularity, however, was such that in spite of many threats he was never arrested, but was allowed to die in peace in his own home.

See also Vol. I: REFORMATION.
See also Vol. XII: TRANSLATIONS.

X

XAVIER, St. Francis (1506–52), *see* LAS CASAS; LOYOLA.

XENOPHON (*c.* 430–355 B.C.), Greek historian, *see* Vol. XII: HISTORIES.

XERXES (died 465 B.C.). Xerxes succeeded Darius as Emperor of Persia in 485 B.C. After first subduing a revolt in Egypt, he decided to carry out Darius's plans against Greece. He made enormous preparations, including the cutting of a canal 1½ miles long through the peninsula of Mount Athos. In 480 B.C. he carried his huge forces across the Hellespont (Dardanelles) on a bridge of boats a mile long. They then marched along the coast of Thrace, the defenceless Greek cities capitulating as they went. They met no resistance until at the narrow pass of Thermopylae a force of 300 SPARTANS (q.v. Vol. I) under King Leonidas checked them. A traitor betrayed a by-path over the hills, and the Persians took the defenders in the rear and annihilated them. Xerxes then marched on to Athens, which had been evacuated, and sacked the city. Shortly afterwards, however, the Persian fleet was defeated at the Battle of Salamis, the battle being watched by Xerxes from the cliffs. Afraid of being cut off, he withdrew hastily, and his army the following year was defeated at Plataea. The expedition is described by Herodotus with much picturesque detail and some exaggeration of the Persian forces and the glorious part played by Athens. The Battle of Salamis is also described by AESCHYLUS in his drama *The Persians* (q.v.).

Xerxes had none of the wise moderation and humanity of his predecessors, CYRUS and DARIUS (qq.v.). To the Greeks he was a typical cruel oriental despot. He met his death by assassination.

See also Vol. I: PERSIAN ANCIENT CIVILIZATION.

Oriental Institute, Chicago

EAST PORTAL OF THE GATEWAY TO THE PALACE BUILT BY XERXES AT PERSEPOLIS

Y

YEATS, William Butler (1865–1939). In his lifetime Yeats was recognized as an important poet, and at his death many critics hailed him as the greatest poet of 'the last hundred years'— a period which includes Tennyson, Browning, and Hardy. Yeats was an Irishman, and his long life was spent in manifold endeavours to influence the culture of his country. As a young man he collected and preserved much folk-lore and mythology, and his early poetry is full of allusions to such Irish legendary figures as Deirdre and Cuchulain. At the same time he worked with Lady Gregory to found the Abbey Theatre in Dublin and did much to encourage the great Irish playwright J. M. SYNGE (q.v.). What is called the Celtic Revival owes much to Yeats's energy, for besides his experiments in various forms of mysticism and the supernatural he was a shrewd man of affairs. Though not active in politics he was a member of the Irish Republican Brotherhood, and the Easter Rising of 1916, in which many of his friends were killed, brought him face to face with violent reality. He saw Ireland's past greatness revived and her legendary figures personified in that bitter struggle.

Yeats spent the rest of his life interpreting that tragic vision. Few poets have had such a long poetical life—his first book was published in 1887, his last just after his death in 1939—and perhaps no poet has ever written with such steadily increasing power and wisdom. It is for the work of his middle and old age—*The Tower* (1928), *The Winding Stair* (1933), and *Last Poems* (1939)—that he will be best remembered.

Yeats came of a remarkable family; his brother, Jack, who died in 1957 at the age of 90, was an outstanding and original painter.

YOUNG, Arthur (1741–1820). This agricultural writer and exponent of scientific farming

Glasgow Art Gallery and Museum
WILLIAM BUTLER YEATS
Portrait by Augustus John

came from a landed family, his father being rector of Bradfield in Suffolk. At 20 he went to London, but failing to earn a living by writing, he came home 2 years later to manage one of his mother's farms. Young was not a successful practical farmer, being much more interested in the scientific and economic aspects of farming, and in 1767 he set out on a series of expeditions to study farming in other parts of the British Isles. He began seriously to write on agricultural matters. In 1784 he embarked on the publication of *Annals of Agriculture*, which ran into forty-five volumes, and to which GEORGE III (q.v.), 'Farmer George', himself contributed.

Young stimulated an intense national interest in scientific farming, and he and others succeeded in persuading the government to set up a Board of Agriculture (not a Government Department but a National Society), of which Arthur Young became the first Secretary.

Z

ZENO (*c.* 336–264 B.C.). The founder of the Stoic school of philosophy was born in Cyprus. He came to Athens as a young man, and after many years of study under famous teachers he opened his own school in a colonnade decorated with splendid frescoes, called the Painted Porch, or *stoa*: and those who met there became known as Stoics. Zeno taught that God, the soul of the world, penetrated all things. Virtue was the only good, vice the only evil; and therefore Stoics did good not for its own sake but in order to be virtuous. Worldly things, such as wealth, fame, and pleasure, were matters of indifference, and consequently the Stoics tended to repress feeling, good and bad, and to be hard and indifferent—hence our word 'stoical'. They taught prudence, temperance, courage, justice, and the value of equality, virtues gladly acknowledged by the early Christians. A famous Stoic, Epictetus, following Zeno's teaching said, 'See, I have nothing; no shelter but the earth, the sky, and one poor cloak. Yet what do I lack?' Stoicism was the greatest moral force in the Graeco-Roman world when CHRISTIANITY (q.v. Vol. I) arose. Zeno himself in his extreme old age committed suicide.

See also Vol. I: ASCETICISM.

ZWINGLI, Ulrich (1484–1531). Zwingli was born in Switzerland within a few weeks of the German reformer LUTHER (q.v.). He was ordained priest, and when about 35 he came to Zürich. In that independent city he began to put into practice his ideas of Church reform. Influenced by ERASMUS (q.v.), the humanist,

ZWINGLI
Engraving from Beza, *Icones*, 1580

Zwingli wanted to take the Church back to the simple beliefs and practices of the New Testament. He preached on the Sermon on the Mount and on the Acts and St. Paul's Epistles to show what the early Church was like. As a result priests began to marry, fasts were disregarded, and images, relics, and organs were destroyed. Zwingli regarded the body of citizens as the real Church; and in Zürich he would not allow either bishop or Pope to interfere. Some of the Swiss cantons followed Zwingli, others remained faithful to Rome, and religious war broke out. Zwingli took part, and was killed in battle.

Zwingli had a coldly rational temperament, quite the opposite of Luther's, and the two could not understand each other. Luther thought Zwingli un-Christian, while Zwingli thought Luther was worse than the Romanists. In consequence, Zwingli's Reformed Church remained quite distinct from the Lutherans.